AF779887

Ibbotson® SBBI®
2008 Classic Yearbook

Market Results for
Stocks, Bonds, Bills, and Inflation
1926–2007

SBBI

MORNINGSTAR®

2008 Ibbotson® Stocks, Bonds, Bills, and Inflation® Classic Yearbook

Stocks, Bonds, Bills, and Inflation® and SBBI® are registered trademarks of Morningstar, Inc. Ibbotson® and Ibbotson Associates® are registered trademarks of Ibbotson Associates, a wholly owned subsidiary of Morningstar, Inc., and are used with permission.

The information presented in this publication has been obtained with the greatest of care from sources believed to be reliable, but is not guaranteed to be complete, accurate or timely. Morningstar and its affiliated companies expressly disclaim any liability, including incidental or consequential damages, arising from the use of this publication or any errors or omissions that may be contained in it.

© 2008 Morningstar. All rights reserved. No part of this publication may be reproduced or used in any other form or by any other means—graphic, electronic, or mechanical, including photocopying, recording, taping, or information storage and retrieval systems—without Morningstar's prior, written permission. To obtain permission, please call Product Sales or write to the address below. Your request should specify the data or other information you wish to use and the manner in which you wish to use it. In addition, you will need to include copies of any charts, tables, and/or figures that you have created based on that information. There is a $1500 processing fee per request. There may be additional fees depending on your proposed usage.

Published by:
Morningstar, Inc.
225 West Wacker Dr.
Chicago, Illinois 60606

Main (312) 696-6000
Product Sales (888) 298-3647
Fax (312) 696-6010
global.morningstar.com/SBBIYearbooks

ISBN 978-0-9792402-2-5
ISSN 1047-2436

The data in the *2008 Ibbotson® SBBI® Classic Yearbook* is also available within many of Morningstar's software products. Statistics and graphs can be quickly accessed over any subperiod. For more information about Morningstar's software and data products for individuals, advisors, and institutions, see "Investment Tools and Resources" at the back of this book, or call (800) 735-0700.

Ibbotson Associates® is a leading authority on asset allocation with expertise in capital market expectations and portfolio implementation. Approaching portfolio construction from the top-down through a research-based investment process, its experienced consultants and portfolio managers serve mutual fund firms, banks, broker-dealers, and insurance companies worldwide. Ibbotson Associates' methodologies and services address all investment phases, from accumulation to retirement and the transition between the two. Visit Ibbotson.com for contact information, published research, product fact sheets and other information.

Additional copies of the *2008 Ibbotson® SBBI® Classic Yearbook* may be obtained for $150 per book, plus shipping and handling. Archived editions (2007 and prior) are available in limited quantities for $175 per book, plus shipping and handling. For purchasing or other information related to volume discounts or companion publications, please call (888) 298-3647, or write to the address above.

Table of Contents

Most Commonly Used References

Graph/Table/Equation

List of Tables
(Text)

List of Graphs
(Text)

List of Graphs

(Image)

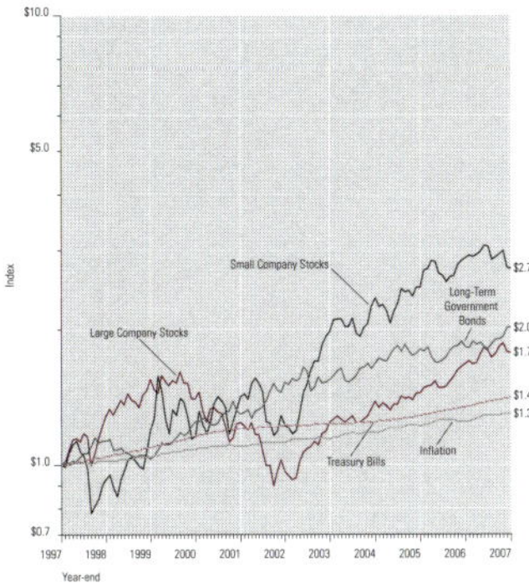

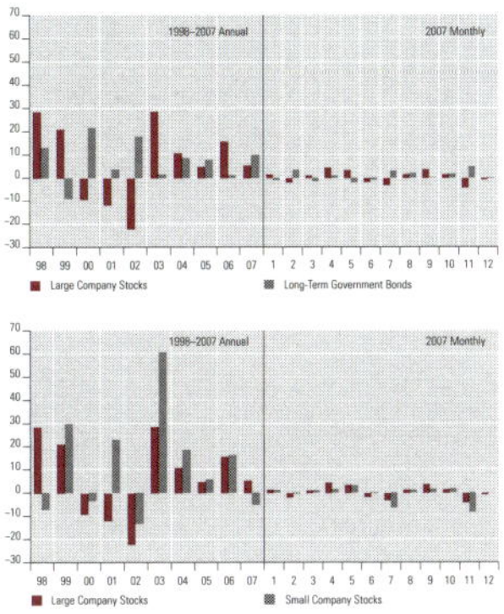

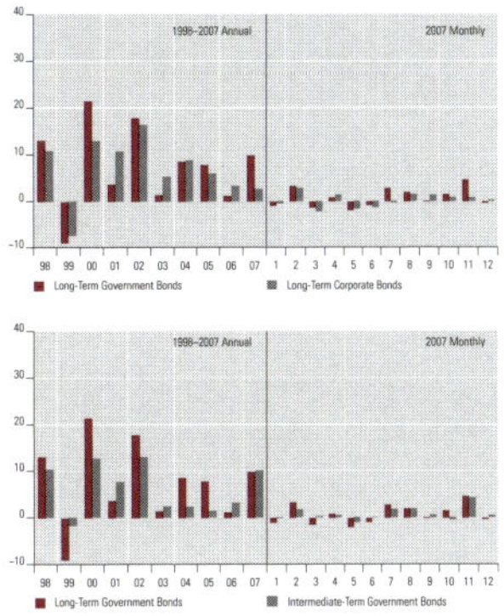

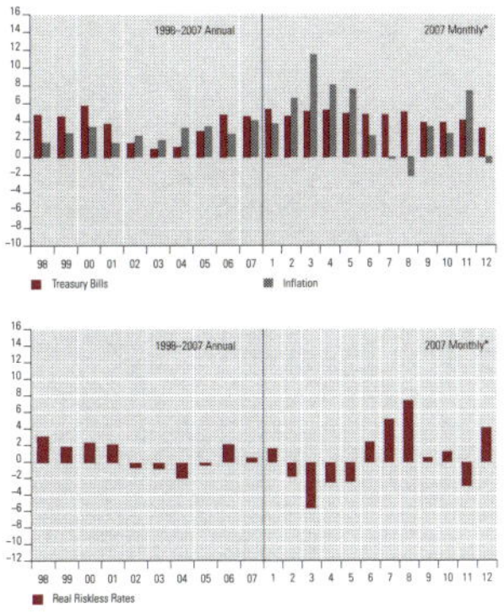

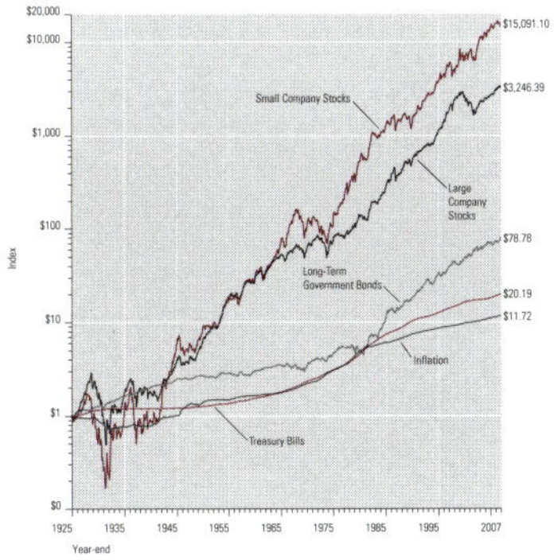

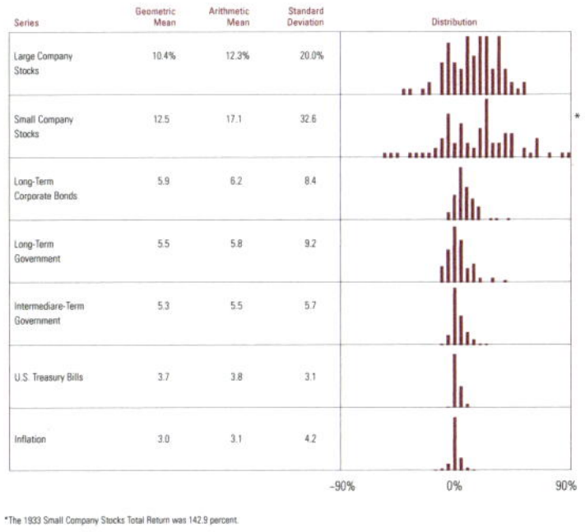

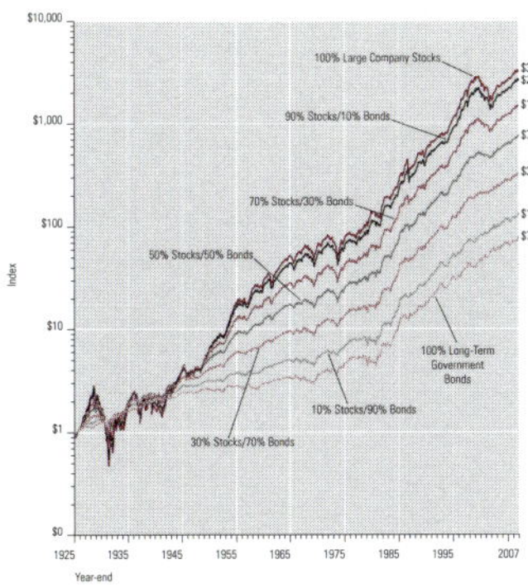

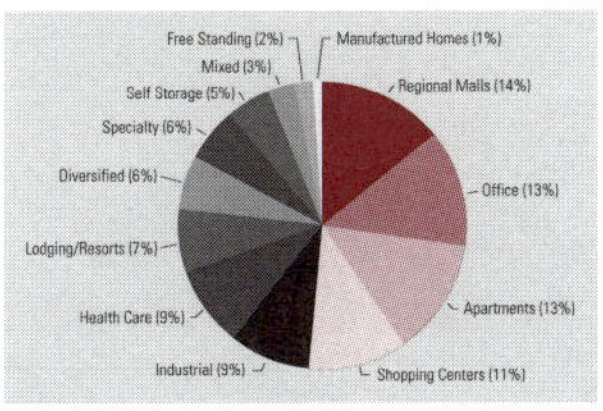

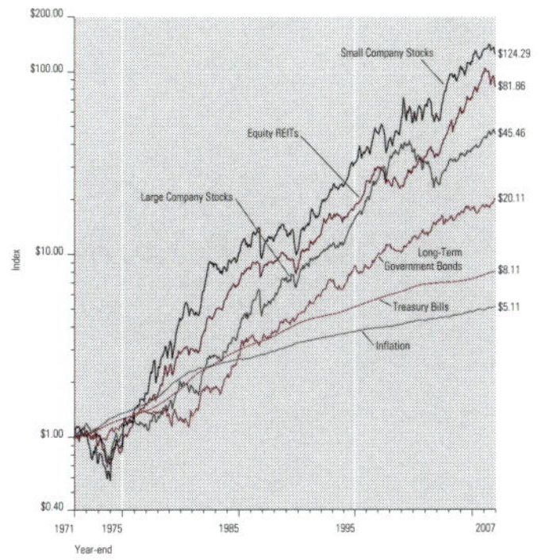

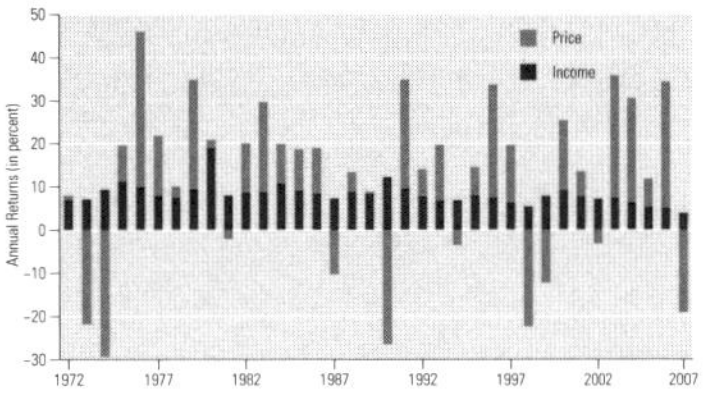

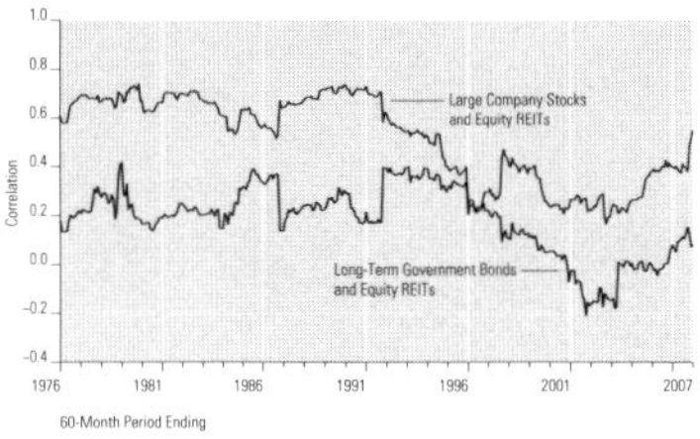

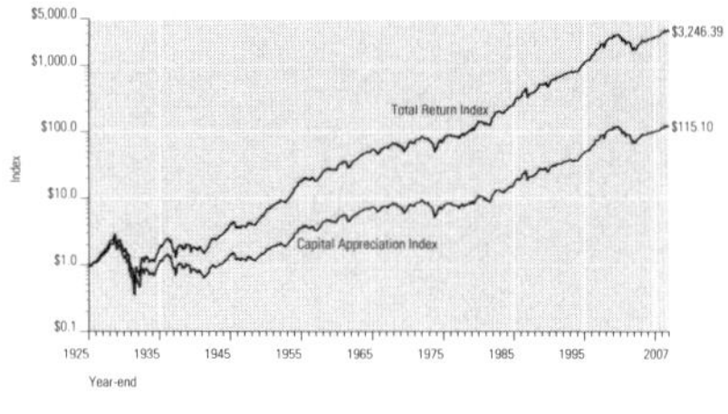

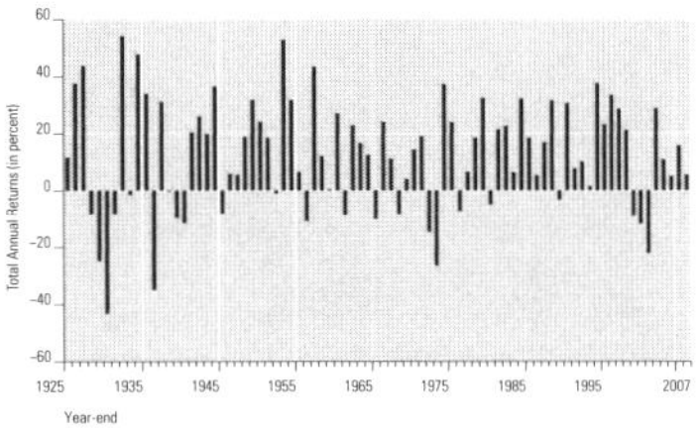

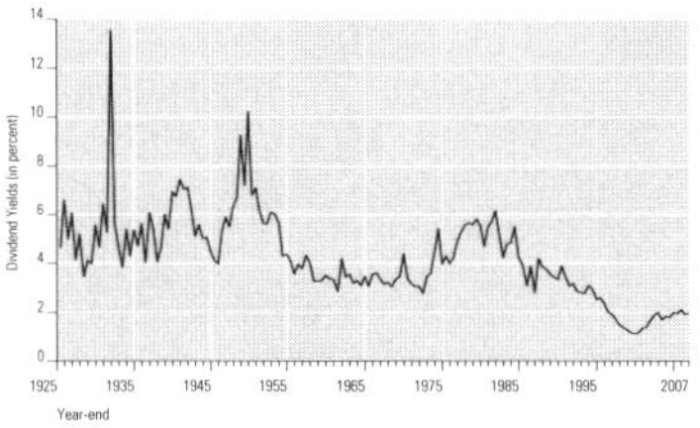

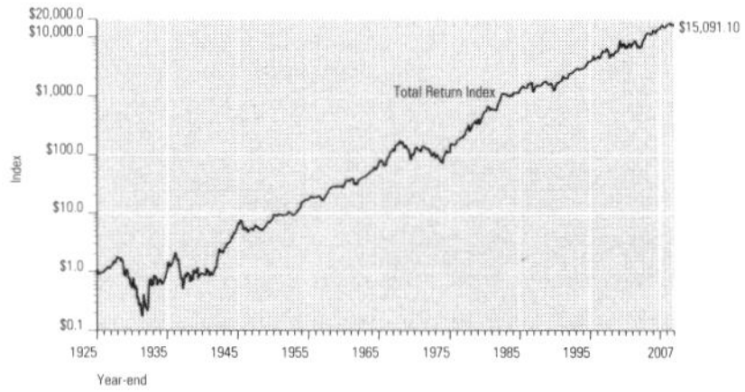

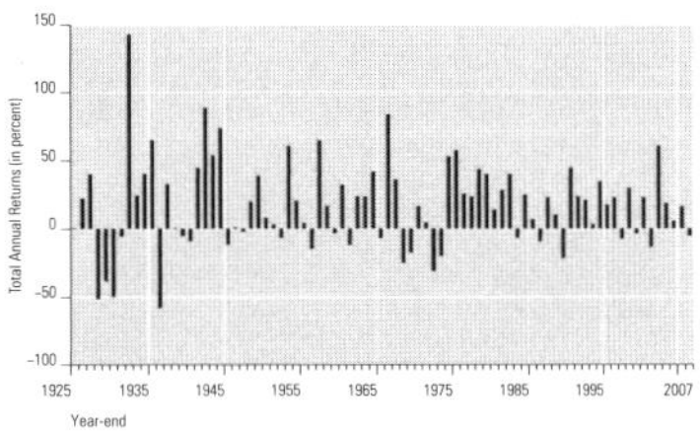

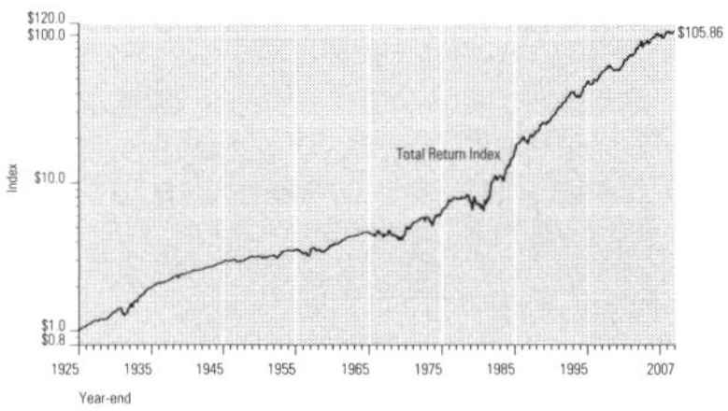

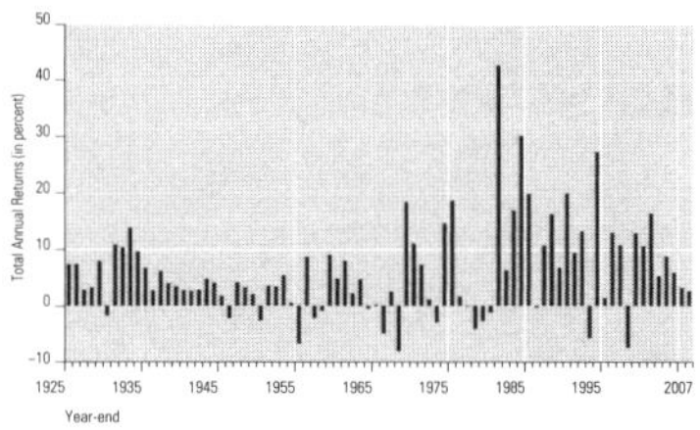

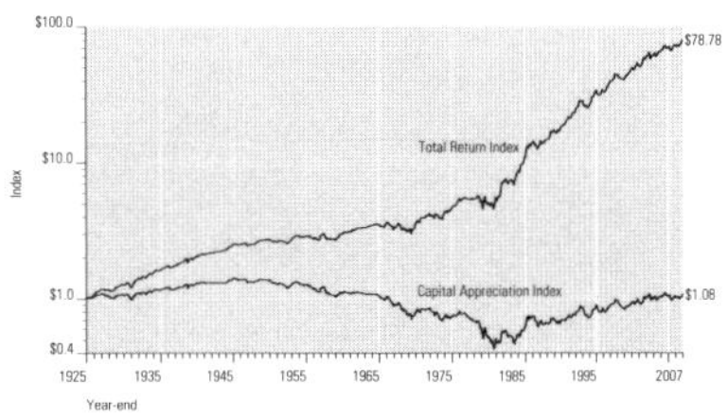

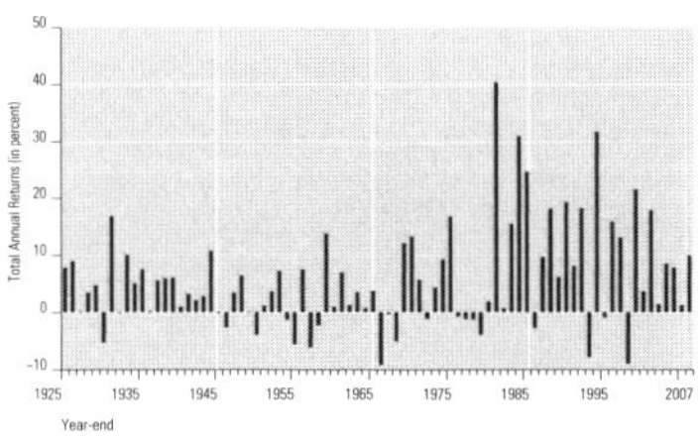

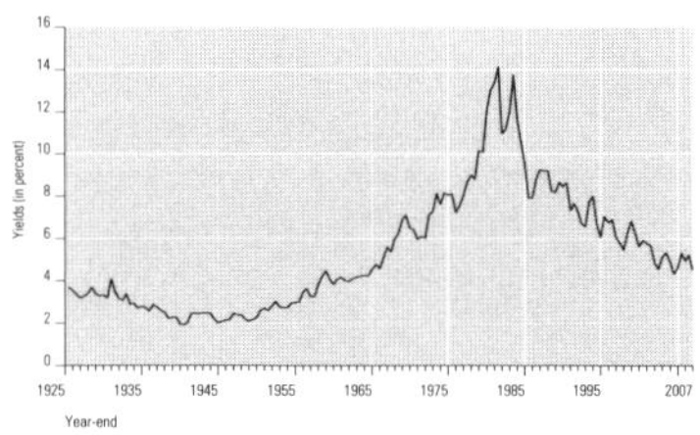

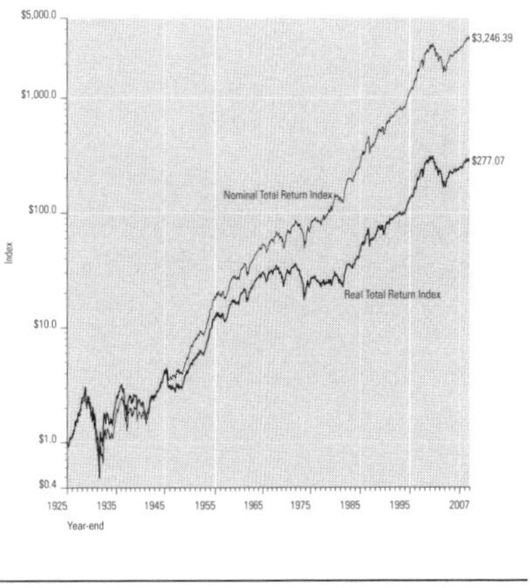

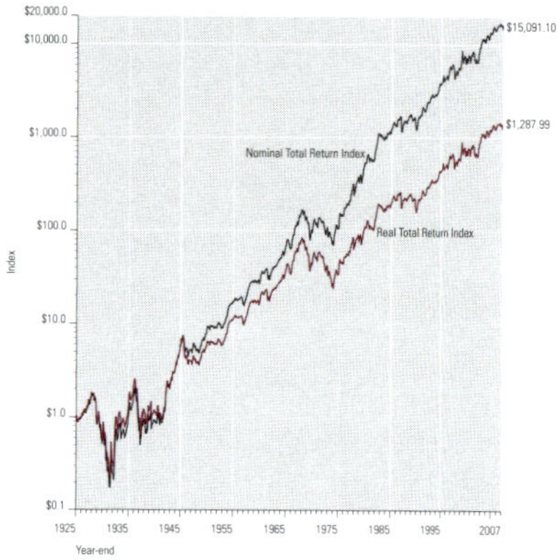
Nominal Total Return Index
Real Total Return Index
Index
Year-end

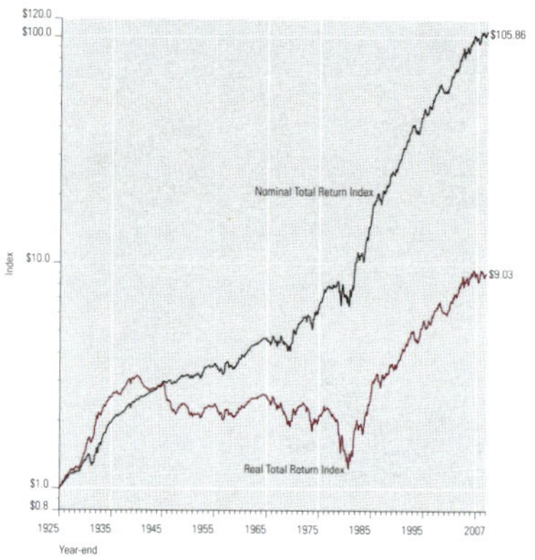
Nominal Total Return Index
Real Total Return Index
Index
Year-end

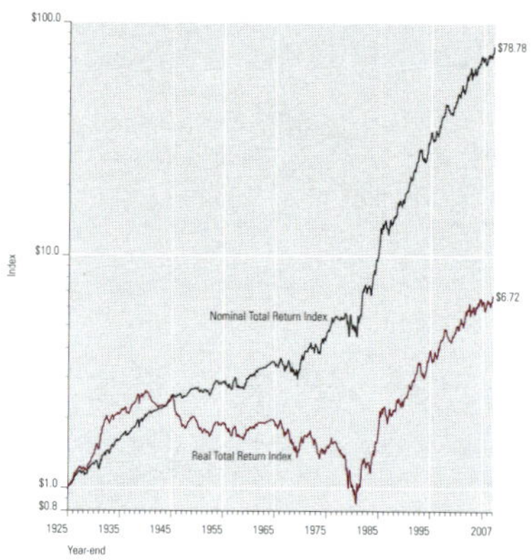
Nominal Total Return Index
Real Total Return Index
Index
Year-end

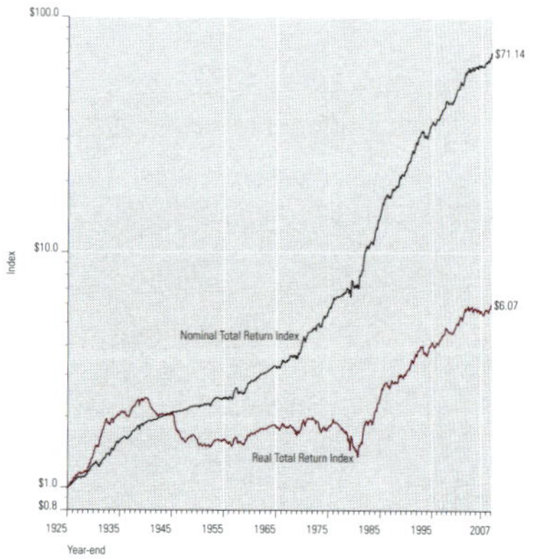
Nominal Total Return Index
Real Total Return Index
Index
Year-end

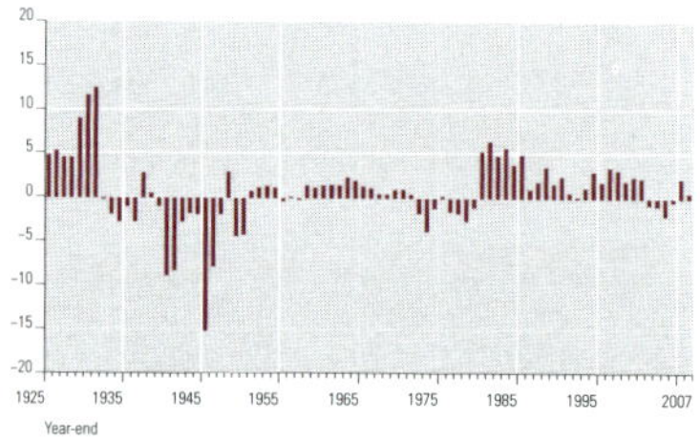
Year-end

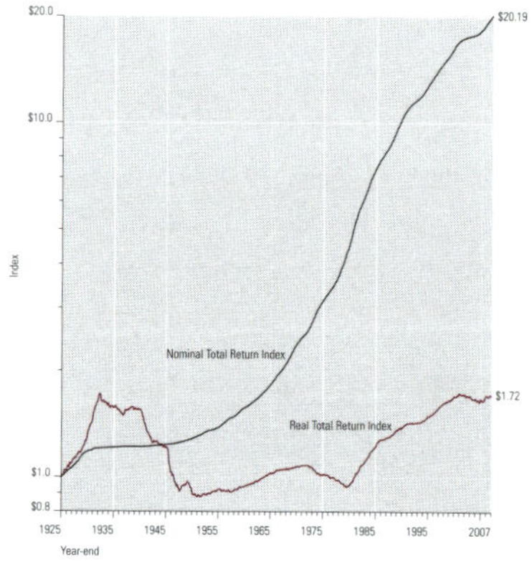
Nominal Total Return Index
Real Total Return Index
Index
Year-end

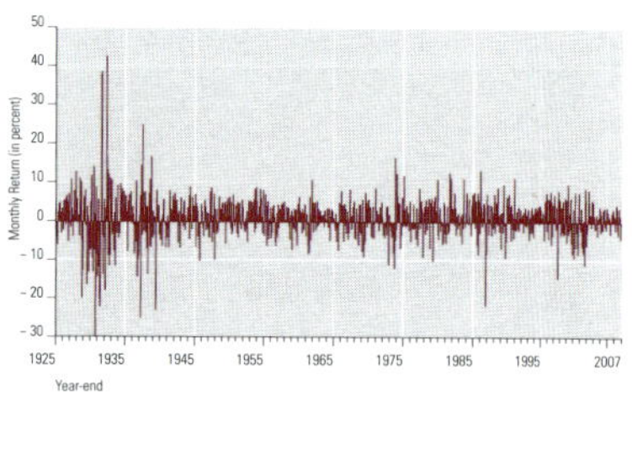
Monthly Return (in percent)
Year-end

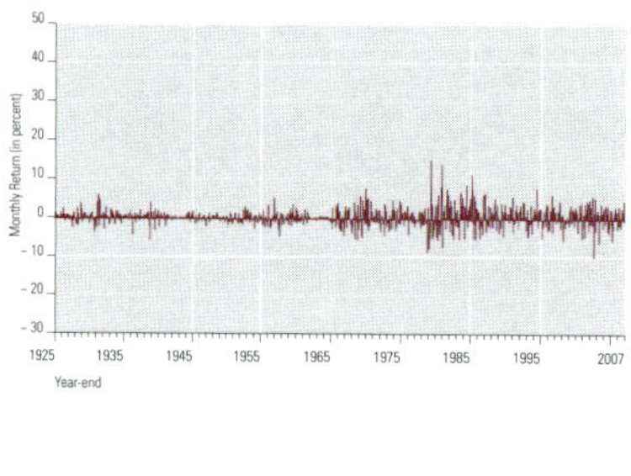
Monthly Return (in percent)
Year-end

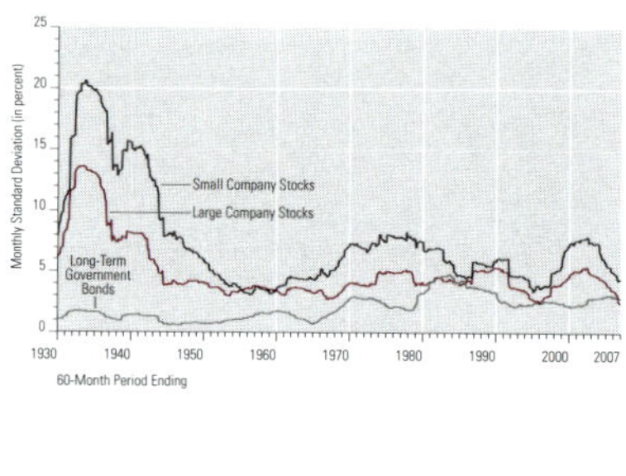
Small Company Stocks
Large Company Stocks
Long-Term Government Bonds
Monthly Standard Deviation (in percent)
60-Month Period Ending

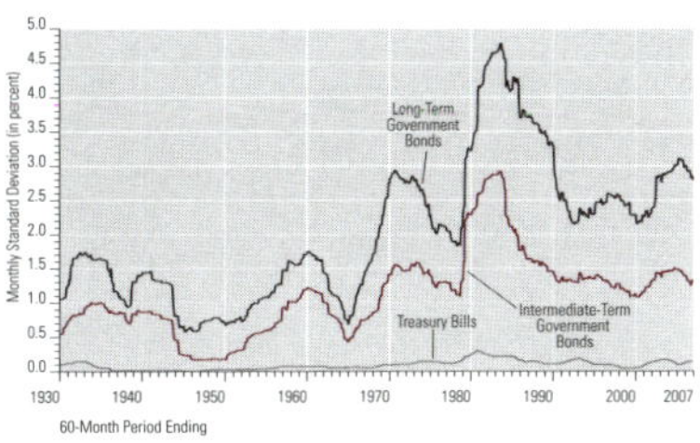
Long-Term Government Bonds
Intermediate-Term Government Bonds
Treasury Bills
60-Month Period Ending

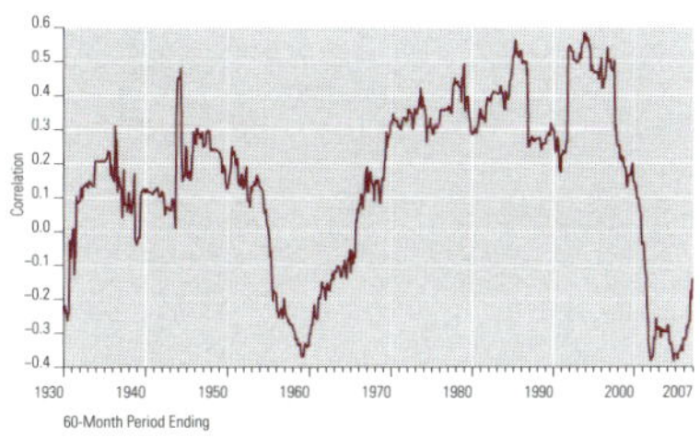
Correlation
60-Month Period Ending

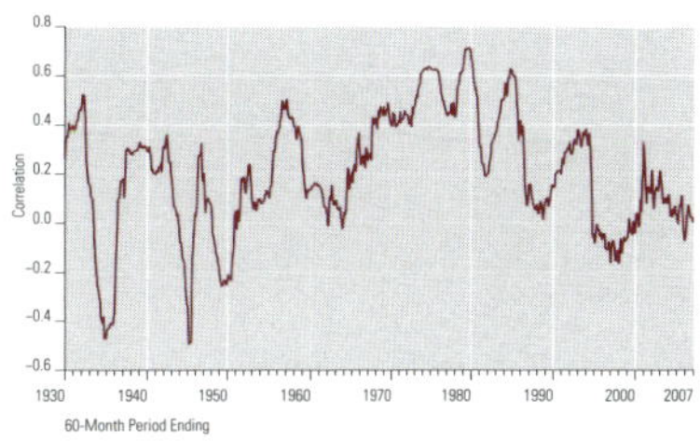
Correlation
60-Month Period Ending

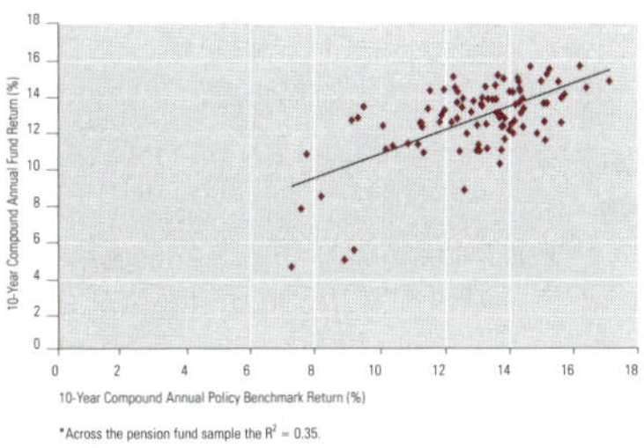

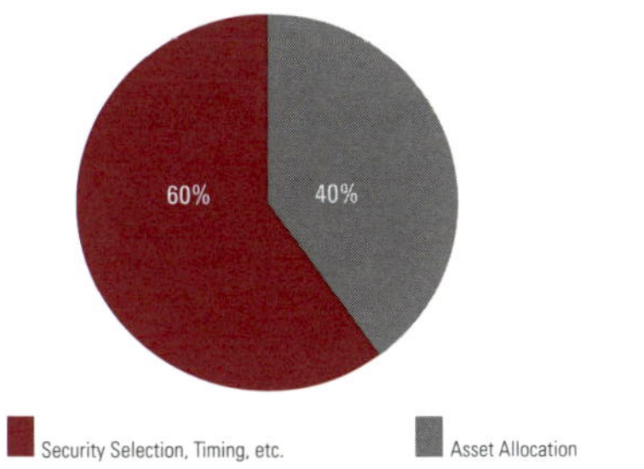
60%
40%
Security Selection, Timing, etc.
Asset Allocation

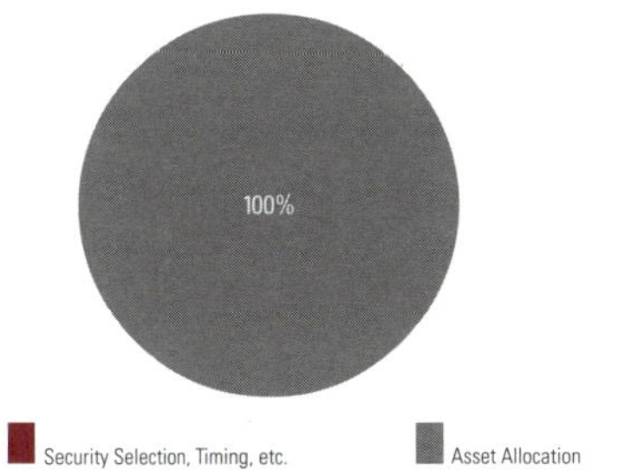
100%
Security Selection, Timing, etc.
Asset Allocation

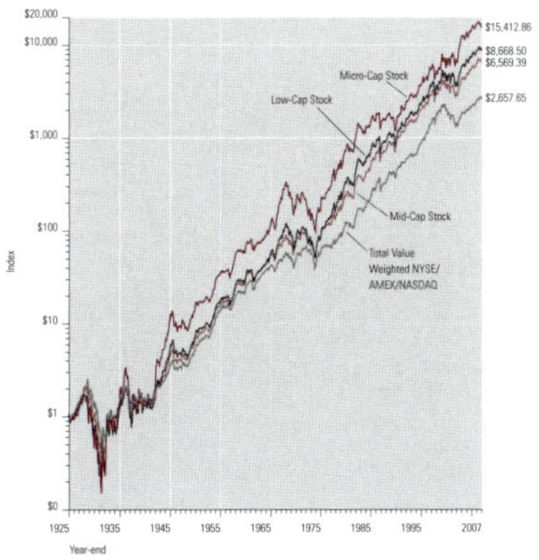
Micro-Cap Stock
Low-Cap Stock
Mid-Cap Stock
Total Value Weighted NYSE/AMEX/NASDAQ
Year-end

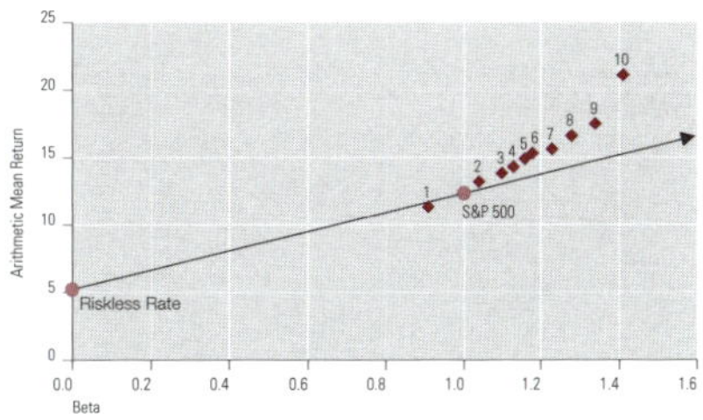
Arithmetic Mean Return
S&P 500
Riskless Rate
Beta

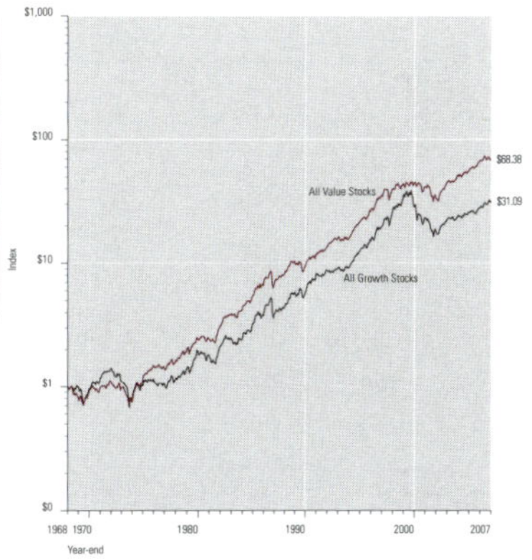
All Value Stocks
All Growth Stocks
Year-end

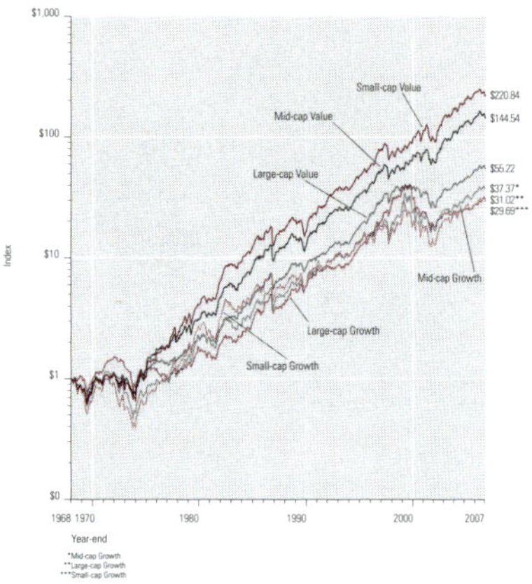
Small-cap Value
Mid-cap Value
Large-cap Value
Mid-cap Growth
Large-cap Growth
Small-cap Growth
Year-end

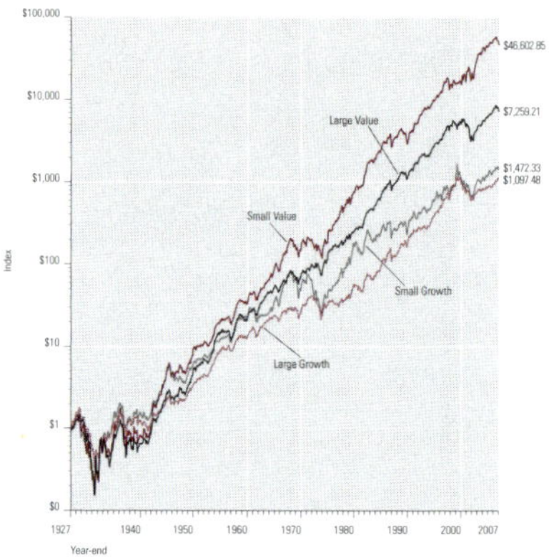
Large Value
Small Value
Small Growth
Large Growth
Year-end

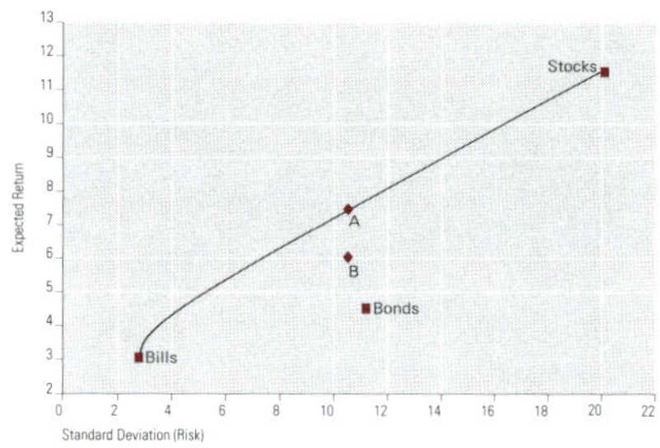
Stocks
A
B
Bonds
Bills
Standard Deviation (Risk)

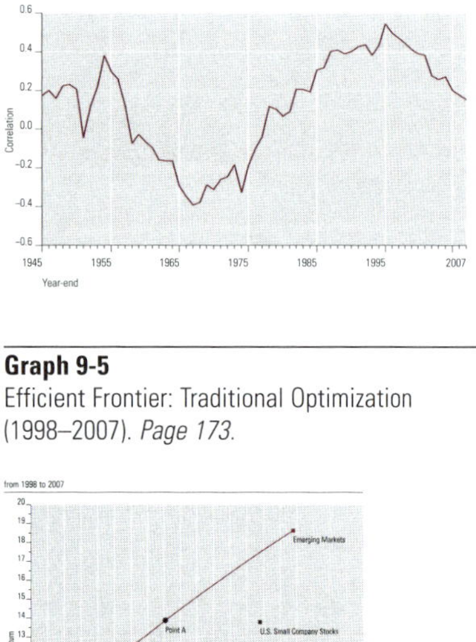
Correlation
Year-end

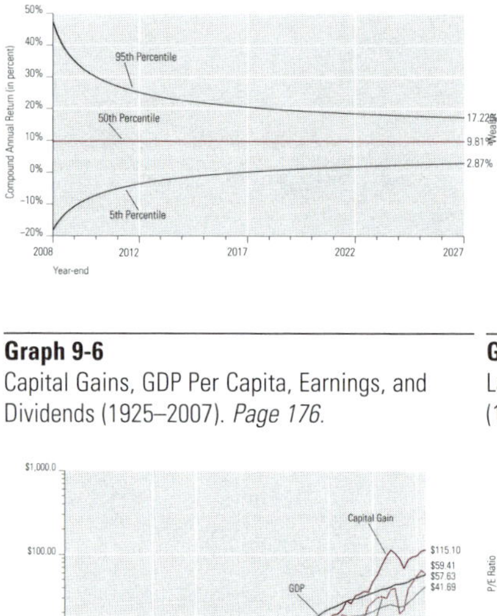
95th Percentile
50th Percentile
5th Percentile
Compound Annual Return (in percent)
Year-end

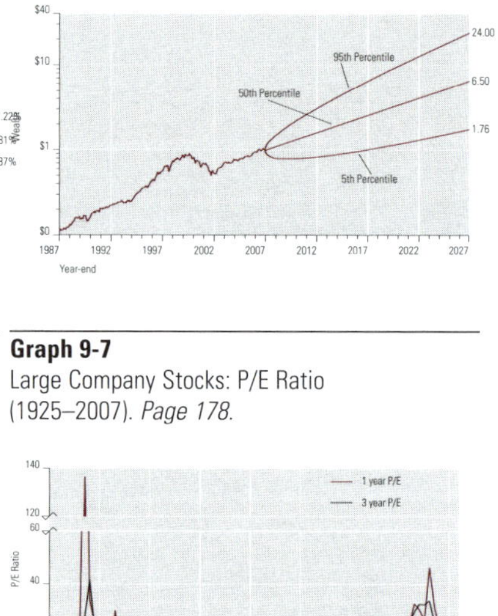
95th Percentile
50th Percentile
5th Percentile
24.00
6.50
1.76
Year-end

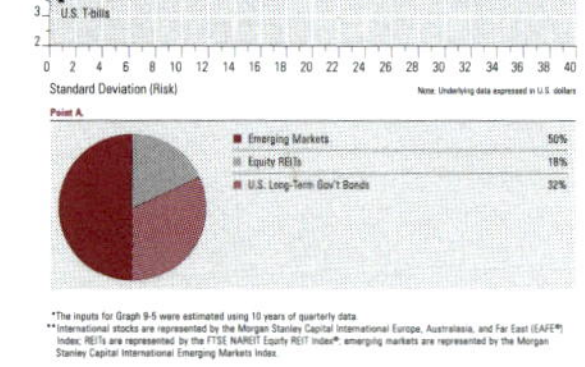
Emerging Markets
Point A
U.S. Small Company Stocks
Equity REITS
International Stocks
U.S. Long-Term Gov't Bonds
U.S. Large Company Stocks
U.S. Long-Term Corp. Bonds
U.S. Intermediate-Term Gov't Bonds
U.S. T-bills
Standard Deviation (Risk)

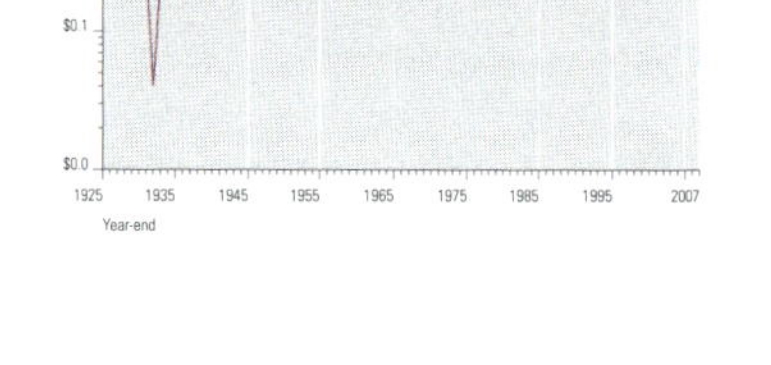
Capital Gain
GDP
Earnings
Dividends
$115.10
$59.41
$57.63
$41.69
Year-end

1 year P/E
3 year P/E
P/E Ratio
Year-end

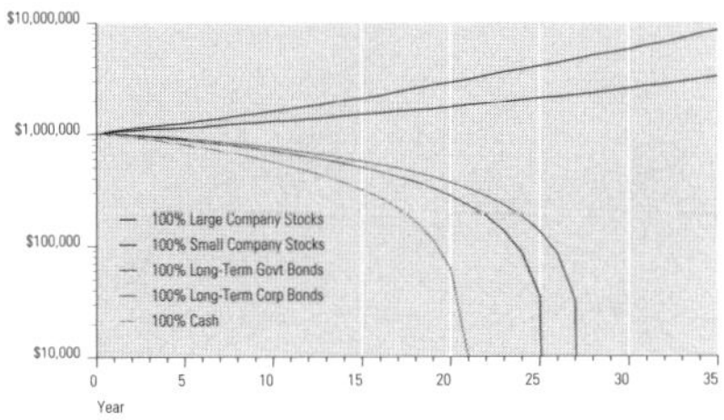
$10,000,000
$1,000,000
$100,000
$10,000
100% Large Company Stocks
100% Small Company Stocks
100% Long-Term Govt Bonds
100% Long-Term Corp Bonds
100% Cash
0 5 10 15 20 25 30 35
Year

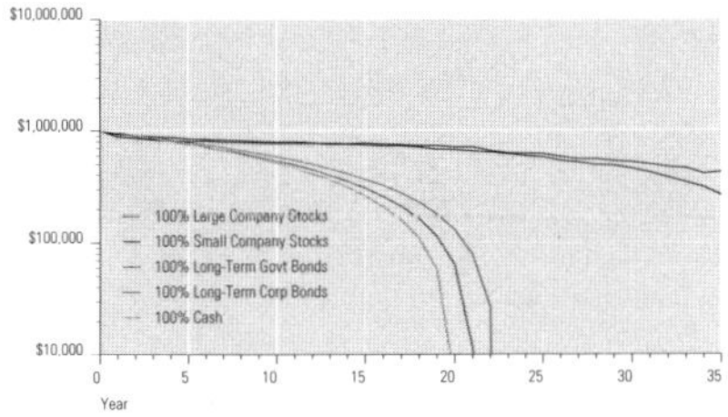
$10,000,000
$1,000,000
$100,000
$10,000
100% Large Company Stocks
100% Small Company Stocks
100% Long-Term Govt Bonds
100% Long-Term Corp Bonds
100% Cash
0 5 10 15 20 25 30 35
Year

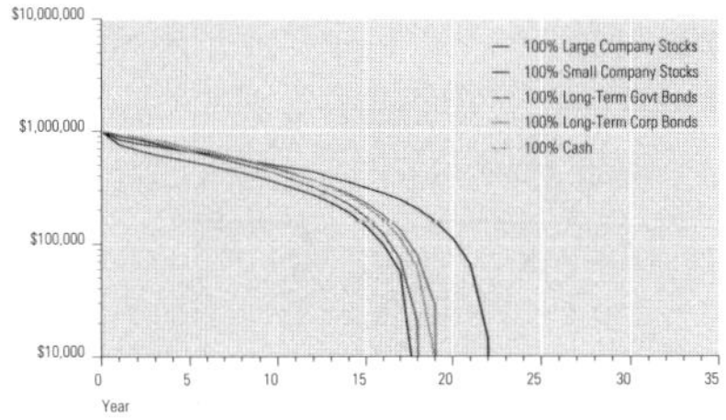
$10,000,000
$1,000,000
$100,000
$10,000
100% Large Company Stocks
100% Small Company Stocks
100% Long-Term Govt Bonds
100% Long-Term Corp Bonds
100% Cash
0 5 10 15 20 25 30 35
Year

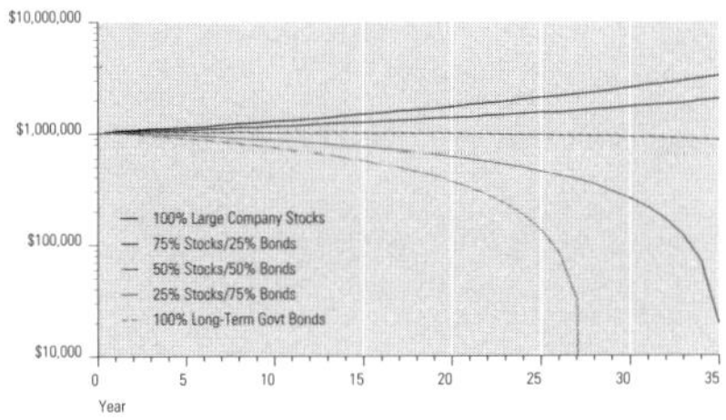
$10,000,000
$1,000,000
$100,000
$10,000
100% Large Company Stocks
75% Stocks/25% Bonds
50% Stocks/50% Bonds
25% Stocks/75% Bonds
100% Long-Term Govt Bonds
0 5 10 15 20 25 30 35
Year

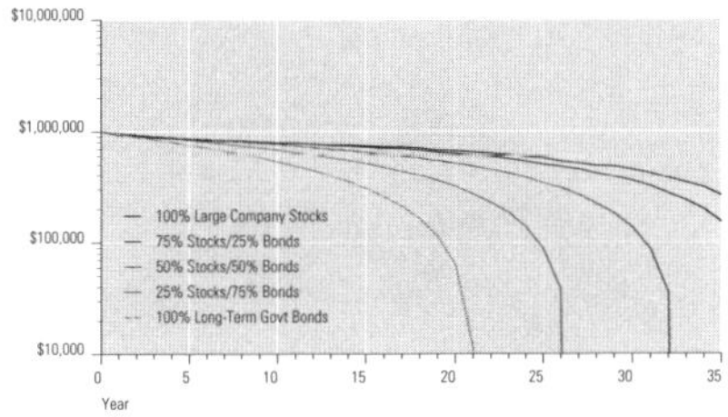
$10,000,000
$1,000,000
$100,000
$10,000
100% Large Company Stocks
75% Stocks/25% Bonds
50% Stocks/50% Bonds
25% Stocks/75% Bonds
100% Long-Term Govt Bonds
0 5 10 15 20 25 30 35
Year

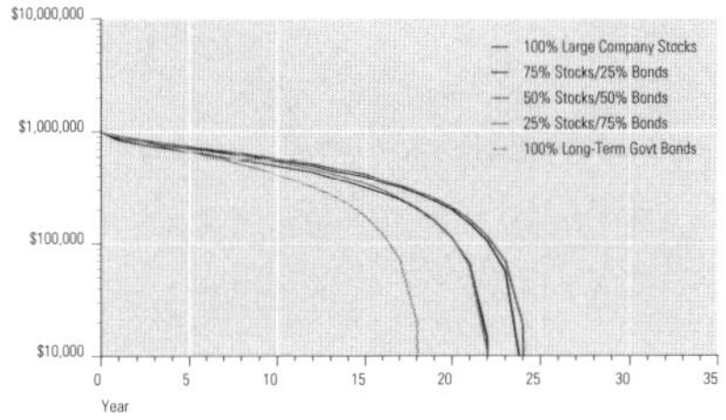
$10,000,000
$1,000,000
$100,000
$10,000
100% Large Company Stocks
75% Stocks/25% Bonds
50% Stocks/50% Bonds
25% Stocks/75% Bonds
100% Long-Term Govt Bonds
0 5 10 15 20 25 30 35
Year

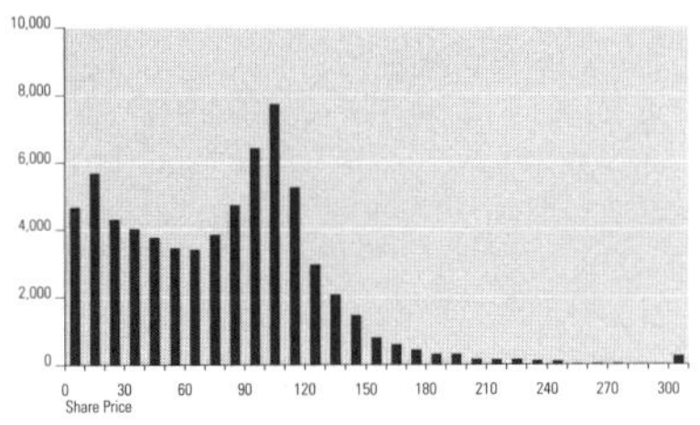
10,000
8,000
6,000
4,000
2,000
0
0 30 60 90 120 150 180 210 240 270 300
Share Price

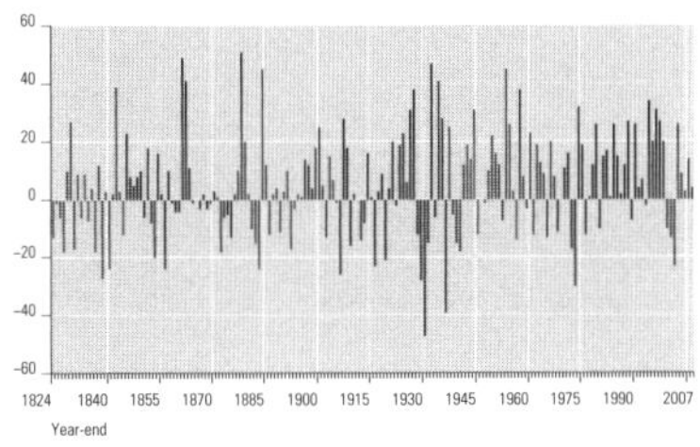
60
40
20
0
-20
-40
-60
1824 1840 1855 1870 1885 1900 1915 1930 1945 1960 1975 1990 2007
Year-end

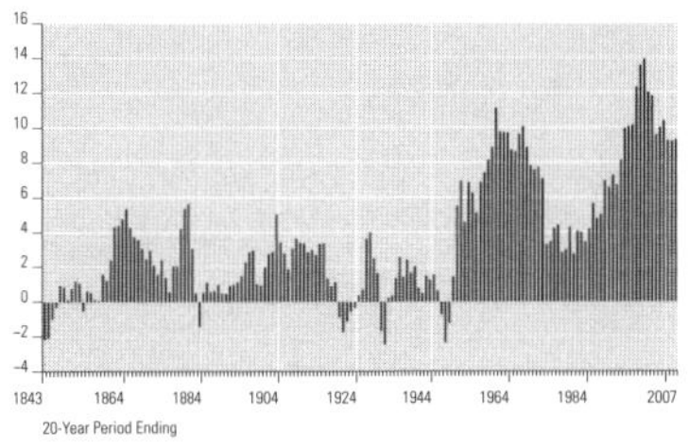
16
14
12
10
8
6
4
2
0
-2
-4
1843 1864 1884 1904 1924 1944 1964 1984 2007
20-Year Period Ending

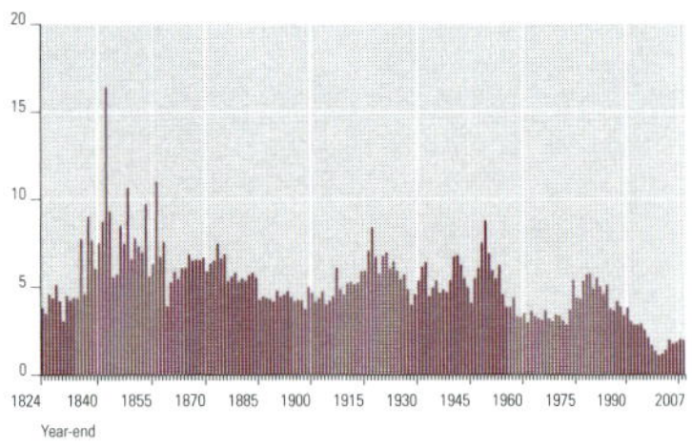

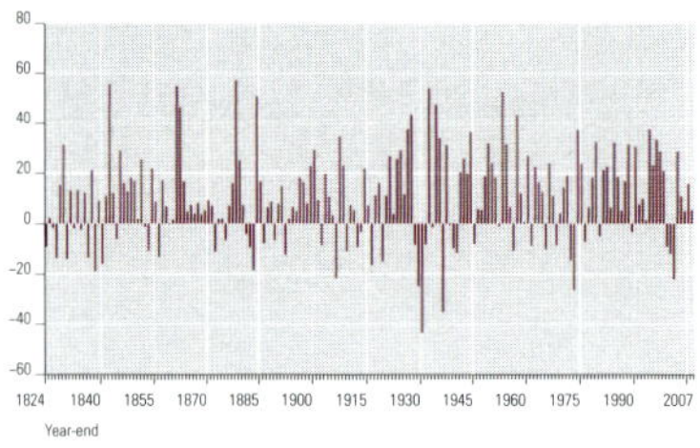

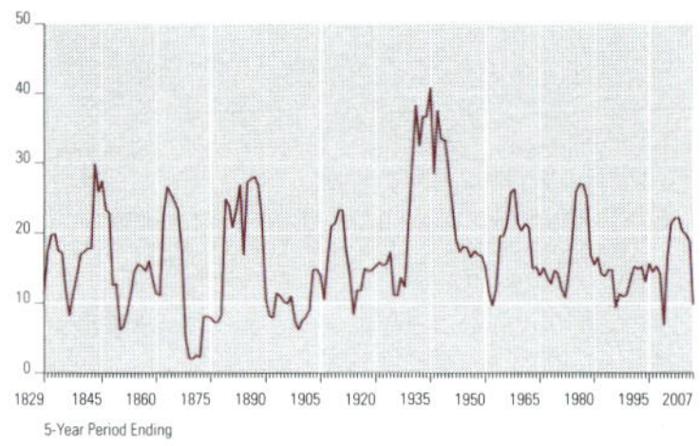

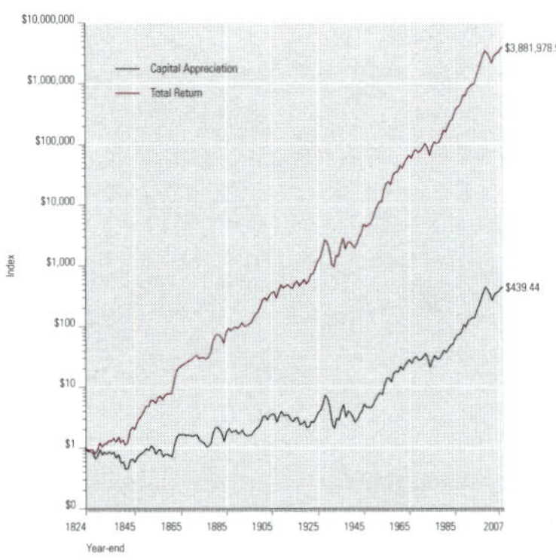

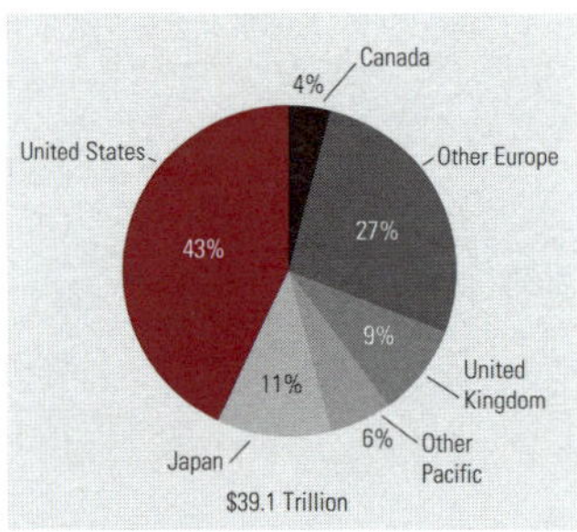

Note: Underlying data expressed in U.S. dollars

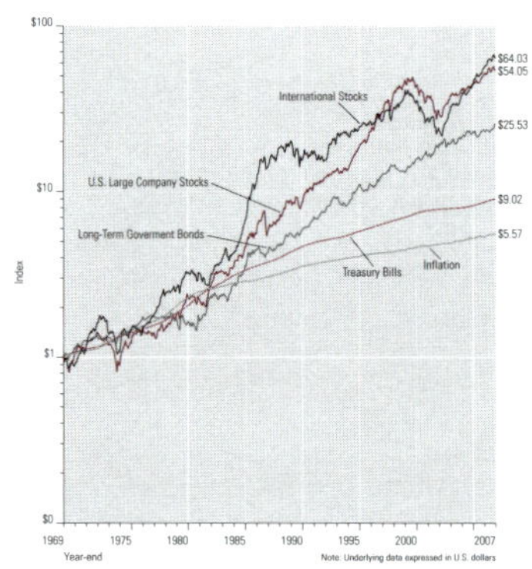

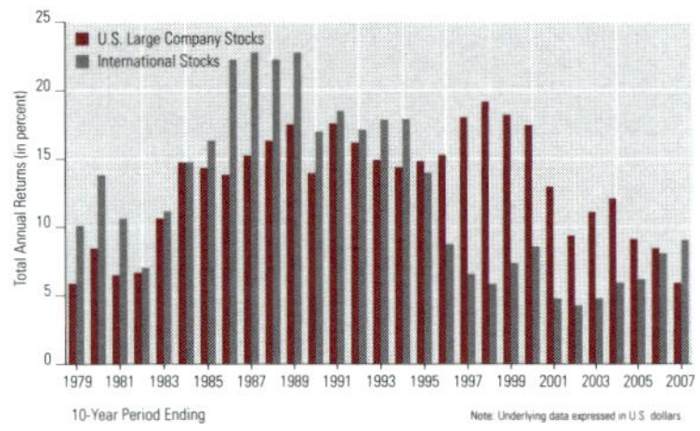

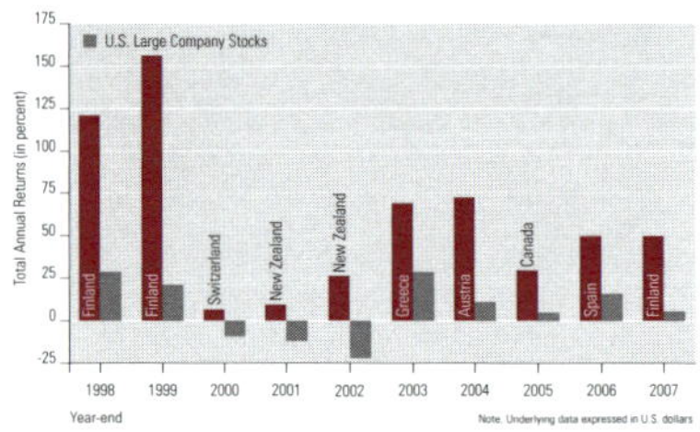

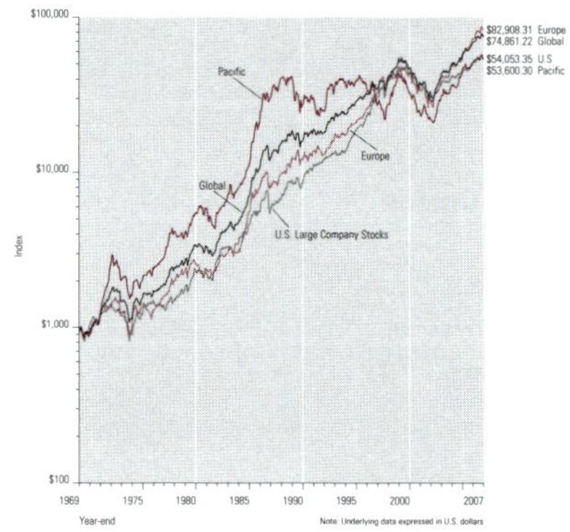

Acknowledgements

We thank, foremost, Roger G. Ibbotson, professor in the practice of finance at the Yale School of Management and founder of Ibbotson Associates®, for his contributions to this book. Professor Ibbotson and Rex A. Sinquefield, a director of Dimensional Fund Advisors (Santa Monica, CA), wrote the two journal articles and four books upon which the Ibbotson® Stocks, Bonds, Bills, and Inflation® Classic Yearbook is based and formulated much of the philosophy and methodology. Dimensional Fund Advisors also provides the small stock returns, as it has since 1982.

We thank others who contributed to this book. Rolf W. Banz provided the small stock returns for 1926–1981. Thomas S. Coleman (Greenwich, CT), Professor Lawrence Fisher of Rutgers University, and Roger Ibbotson constructed the model used to generate the intermediate-term government bond series for 1926–1933. The pioneering work of Professors Fisher and James H. Lorie of the University of Chicago inspired the original monograph. We also wish to acknowledge the valuable role of Dr. Stan V. Smith, President of Smith Economics Group, Ltd. and former managing director of Ibbotson Associates, who originated the idea of the Yearbook. The Center for Research in Security Prices at the University of Chicago contributed the data and methodology for the returns on the NYSE by capitalization decile used in Chapter 7, Firm Size and Return. Ken French, of Dartmouth College, and Eugene Fama, of the University of Chicago, contributed the data and methodology for the returns on the growth and value portfolios. William N. Goetzmann and Liang Peng, both at the Yale School of Management, helped with the assembly of the New York Stock Exchange database for the period prior to 1926, while James Licato converted the research into Chapter 11, Stock Market Returns from 1815–1925. James Licato, formerly of Ibbotson Associates and now research manager in the financial communications group at Morningstar, also converted work originally authored by Peng Chen, president of Ibbotson Associates, into Chapter 10, Wealth Forecasting with Monte Carlo Simulation, created Chapter 12, International Equity Investing, and contributed to other chapters. Paul Kaplan, while at Ibbotson Associates, was the main contributor to Chapter 9, Using Historical Data in Forecasting and Optimization. Paul, now vice president of quantitative research at Morningstar, Peng Chen, president of Ibbotson Associates, and Thomas Idzorek, vice president and director of research at Ibbotson Associates, all continue to provide valuable insights and analysis for the SBBI yearbook series.

We also thank Laurence B. Siegel, former managing director of Ibbotson Associates and presently director of research at the Ford Foundation, and Michael Barad, formerly of Ibbotson Associates and now vice president of the financial communications group at Morningstar, for their many contributions to the Yearbook.

Senior Editor
James P. Harrington

Contributing Editors
Susan Dziubinski
Hasan Haq
Kolleen Jennings
Aki Kudo
Warren Miller
Catherine Morris

Director of Design
David Williams

Designers
Christopher Cantore
Lisa Lindsay
Brian MacKenzie

Copy Editor
Janice Frankel

President, Individual Investor Business & Securities Research
Catherine Odelbo

Chairman and CEO
Joe Mansueto

Introduction

Who Should Read This Book

The *Ibbotson® Stocks, Bonds, Bills, and Inflation® Classic Yearbook* is a history of the returns on the capital markets in the United States from 1926 to the present. It is useful to a wide variety of readers. Foremost, anyone serious about investments or investing needs an appreciation of capital market history. Such an appreciation, which can be gained from this book, is equally valuable to the individual and institutional investor. For students at both the graduate and undergraduate levels, this book is both a source of ideas and a reference. Other intended readers include teachers of these students; practitioners and scholars in finance, economics, and business; portfolio strategists; and security analysts.

Chief financial officers and, in some cases, chief executive officers of corporations will find this book useful. More generally, persons concerned with history may find it valuable to study the detail of economic history as revealed in more than eight decades of capital market returns.

To these diverse readers, we provide two resources. One is the data. The other is a thinking person's guide to using historical data to understand the financial markets and make decisions. This historical record raises many questions. This book represents our way of appreciating the past—only one of the many possible ways—but one grounded in real theory. We provide a means for the reader to think about the past and the future of financial markets.

How to Read This Book

Intended Reader	Most Important Chapters	Other Related Chapters, Graphs, Tables, and Appendices
Persons Concerned with Data	Chapters 1, 2, 3, 11, and 12	Chapters 4, 7, and 8; Graphs 2-1, 11-7, and 12-2; Tables 2-1, 11-1, 11-2, 12-2, and 12-6; and Appendices A, B, and C
Financial Planners, Asset Allocators, and Investment Consultants	Chapters 1, 2, 8, 9, 10, 11, and 12	Chapter 6; Graphs 2-1, 9-1, 9-5, 11-7, and 12-2; and Tables 2-7, 6-6, and 11-1
Individual Investors	Chapters 1, 2, and 10	Graph 2-1; and Tables 2-1, 10-9, 10-10, and 10-11
Institutional Investors, Portfolio Managers, and Security Analysts	Chapters 1 through 12	Graphs 2-1, 11-7, and 12-2; Tables 2-7, 6-6, 7-1, 11-1, 11-2, 12-2, and 12-6
Students, Faculty, and Economists	Chapters 2, 5, 6, 7, 8, 9, 10, 11, and 12	Graphs 2-1, 11-7, and 12-2; Tables 6-6, 11-1, 11-2, 12-2, and 12-6
Brokers and Security Sales Representatives	Chapters 1, 2, and 10	Graph 2-1; and Tables 2-1, 2-5, 10-9, 10-10, and 10-11
Investment Bankers and Security Sales Representatives	Chapters 2, 7, 8, and 12	Table 2-1
Executives, Corporate Planners, Chief Financial Officers, Chief Executive Officers, and Treasurers	Chapters 1 and 2	Graph 2-1; and Table 2-1
Pension Plan Sponsors	Chapters 1, 2, 6, 9, and 10	Graph 2-1; and Tables 2-1 and 2-4

The Journal of Business published Roger G. Ibbotson and Rex A. Sinquefield's two companion papers on security returns in January 1976 and July 1976. In the first paper, the authors collected historical data on the returns from stocks, government and corporate bonds, U.S. Treasury bills, and consumer goods (inflation). To uncover the risk/return and the real/nominal relationship in the historical data, they presented a framework in which the return on an asset class is the sum of two or more elemental parts. These elements, such as real returns (returns in excess of inflation) and risk premia (for example, the net return from investing in large company stocks rather than bills), are referred to throughout the book as derived series.

In the second paper, the authors analyzed the time series behavior of the derived series and the information contained in the U.S. government bond yield curve to obtain inputs for a simulation model of future security price behavior. Using the methods developed in the two papers, they forecast security returns through the year 2000.

The response to these works showed that historical data are fascinating in their own right. Both total and component historical returns have a wide range of applications in investment management, corporate finance, academic research, and industry regulation. Subsequent work—the 1977, 1979, and 1982 Institute of Chartered Financial Analysts (ICFA) monographs; the 1989 Dow Jones-Irwin book; and the Ibbotson 1983 through 2008 *Stocks, Bonds, Bills, and Inflation Classic Yearbooks*—updated and further developed the historical data and forecasts. (All references to previous works used in the development of Stocks, Bonds, Bills, and Inflation [SBBI] data appear at the end of this introduction in the References section.)

In 1981, Ibbotson and Sinquefield began tracking a new asset class: small company stocks. This class consists of issues listed on the New York Stock Exchange (NYSE) that rank in the ninth and tenth (lowest) deciles when sorted by capitalization (price times number of shares outstanding), plus non-NYSE issues of comparable capitalization. This asset class has been of interest to researchers and investors because of its high long-term returns. Intermediate-term (five years to maturity) government bonds were added in 1988. Monthly and annual total returns, income returns, capital appreciation returns, and yields are presented.

The 2008 Ibbotson® Stocks, Bonds, Bills, and Inflation® Classic Yearbook

In the present volume the historical data are updated. The motivations are: 1) to document this history of security market returns; 2) to uncover the relationships between the various asset class returns as revealed by the derived series: inflation, real interest rates, risk premia, and other premia; 3) to encourage deeper understanding of the underlying economic history through the graphic presentation of data; and 4) to answer questions most frequently asked by subscribers. In keeping with the spirit of the previous work, the asset classes contained in this edition highlight the differences between targeted segments of the financial markets in the United States. Our intent is to show historical trade-offs between risk and return. International data was introduced in the 2002 edition.

In this book, the equity markets are segmented between large and small company stocks. Fixed income markets are segmented on two dimensions. Riskless U.S. government securities are differentiated by maturity or investment horizon. U.S. Treasury bills with approximately 30 days to maturity are used to describe the short end of the horizon; U.S. Treasury securities with approximately five years to maturity are used to describe the middle horizon segment;

and U.S. Treasury securities with approximately 20 years to maturity are used to describe the long maturity end of the market. A corporate bond series with a long maturity is used to describe fixed income securities that contain risk of default.

Some indices of the stock and bond markets are broad, capturing most or all of the capitalization of the market. Our indices are intentionally narrow. The large company stock series captures the largest issues (those in the Standard & Poor's 500 Composite Index), while the small company stock series is composed of the smallest issues. By studying these polar cases, we identify the small stock premium (small minus large stock returns) and the premium of large stocks over bonds and bills. Neither series is intended to be representative of the entire stock market. Likewise, our long-term government bond and U.S. Treasury bill indices show the returns for the longest and shortest ends of the yield curve, rather than the return for the entire Treasury float. Readers and investors should understand that our bond indices do not, and are not intended to, describe the experience of the typical bond investor who is diversified across maturities; rather, we present returns on carefully focused segments of the market for U.S. Treasury securities.

Recent Changes and Additions

In 2007 we added expanded commentary on the evolution and construction of indices in Chapter 5, "Annual Returns and Indices," and a new table summarizing the major capitalization and style indices of the U.S. equity market. (Page 106).

The *2008 Ibbotson® SBBI® Classic Yearbook* features new research by a team led by Professor Roger Ibbotson that creates retirement savings guidelines for individuals based on age, current income level, and current savings. Please see Chapter 10, "Wealth Forecasting with Monte Carlo Simulation," for a full description of this exciting new research.

In 2008 we also added an overview of enhancements to standard mean-variance optimization (MVO) to Chapter 9, "Using Historical Data in Forecasting and Optimization." Thomas Idzorek, vice president and director of research at Ibbotson Associates, describes how efficient frontiers based on historical data can lead to highly concentrated asset allocations, and discusses some of the creative, cutting edge solutions that are available to address this problem.

Another significant development is the continuing redesign of the Yearbook itself. As you have probably noticed, the award-winning Morningstar design department has given the Yearbook a fresh new look with a well-deserved nod to past designs.

Morningstar, which acquired Ibbotson Associates in early 2006, will continue to publish this valuable and widely used resource with the same accurate data and analysis.

Your comments are important to us, and are the source of many of our ideas for keeping Morningstar products the best in the business. We welcome your questions, comments, and ideas.

James Harrington
Senior Editor
Ibbotson® SBBI® Classic Yearbook

The Ibbotson® SBBI® Data Series

The series presented here are total returns, and where applicable or available, capital appreciation returns and income returns for:

SBBI Data Series	Series Construction	Index Components	Approximate
1. **Large Company Stocks**	S&P 500 Composite with dividends reinvested. (S&P 500, 1957–Present; S&P 90, 1926–1956)	Total Return Income Return Capital Appreciation Return	N/A
2. **Small Company Stocks**	Fifth capitalization quintile of stocks on the NYSE for 1926–1981. Performance of the DFA U.S. 9-10 Small Company Portfolio January 1982–March 2001. Performance of the DFA U.S. Micro Cap Portfolio April 2001–Present.	Total Return	N/A
3. **Long-Term Corporate Bonds**	Citigroup Long-Term High Grade Corporate Bond Index	Total Return	20 Years
4. **Long-Term Government Bonds**	A One-Bond Portfolio	Total Return Income Return Capital Appreciation Return Yield	20 Years
5. **Intermediate-Term Government Bonds**	A One-Bond Portfolio	Total Return Income Return Capital Appreciation Return Yield	5 Years
6. **U.S. Treasury Bills**	A One-Bill Portfolio	Total Return	30 Days
7. **Consumer Price Index**	CPI—All Urban Consumers, not seasonally adjusted	Inflation Rate	N/A

References

1. **Stocks, Bonds, Bills, and Inflation® Yearbook, annual.**
1983, 1984, 1985, 1986, 1987, 1988, 1989, 1990, 1991, 1992, 1993, 1994, 1995, 1996, 1997, 1998, 1999, 2000, 2001, 2002, 2003, 2004, 2005, 2006, 2007.

Ibbotson Associates, Chicago.

2. **Banz, Rolf W.**
"The Relationship Between Return and Market Value of Common Stocks,"

Journal of Financial Economics 9:3–18, 1981.

3. **Brinson, Gary P., L. Randolph Hood, and Gilbert P. Beebower**
"Determinants of Portfolio Performance,"

Financial Analysts Journal, July/August 1986.

4. **Brinson, Gary P., Brian D. Singer, and Gilbert P. Beebower**
"Determinants of Portfolio Performance II,"

Financial Analysts Journal, May/June 1991.

5. **Coleman, Thomas S., Lawrence Fisher, and Roger G. Ibbotson**
Historical U.S. Treasury Yield Curves 1926–1992 with 1994 update,

Ibbotson Associates, Chicago, 1994.

6. **Coleman, Thomas S., Lawrence Fisher, and Roger G. Ibbotson**
U.S. Treasury Yield Curves 1926–1988,

Moody's Investment Service, New York, 1990.

7. **Cottle, Sidney, Roger F. Murray, and Frank E. Block**
"Graham and Dodd's Security Analysis,"

Fifth Edition, McGraw-Hill, 1988.

8. **Cowles, Alfred**
Common Stock Indices,

Principia Press, Bloomington, 1939.

9. **Goetzmann, William N., Roger G. Ibbotson, and Liang Peng**
"A New Historical Database for the NYSE 1815 to 1925: Performance and Predictability,"

Journal of Financial Markets, December 2000.

10. **Ibbotson, Roger G., and Rex A. Sinquefield**
Speech to the Center for Research in Security Prices, May 1974.

11. **Ibbotson, Roger G., and Paul D. Kaplan**
"Does Asset Allocation Policy Explain 40, 90, or 100 Percent of Performance?,"

Financial Analysts Journal, January/February 2000.

12. **Ibbotson, Roger G., and Peng Chen**
"Long-Run Stock Returns: Participating in the Real Economy."

Financial Analysts Journal, January/February 2003.

13. **Ibbotson, Roger G., and Rex A. Sinquefield (foreword by Jack L. Treynor)**
Stocks, Bonds, Bills, and Inflation: The Past (1926–1976) and the Future (1977–2000), 1977 ed.,

Institute of Chartered Financial Analysts, Charlottesville, VA, 1977.

14. **Ibbotson, Roger G., and Rex A. Sinquefield, (foreword by Laurence B. Siegel)**
Stocks, Bonds, Bills, and Inflation: The Past and the Future, 1982 ed.,

Institute of Chartered Financial Analysts, Charlottesville, VA, 1982.

15. **Ibbotson, Roger G., and Rex A. Sinquefield**
Stocks, Bonds, Bills, and Inflation: Historical Returns (1926–1987), 1989 ed.,

Dow-Jones Irwin, Homewood, IL, 1989.

16. **Ibbotson, Roger G., and Rex A. Sinquefield**
Stocks, Bonds, Bills, and Inflation: Historical Returns (1926–1978),

Institute of Chartered Financial Analysts, Charlottesville, VA, 1979.

17. **Ibbotson, Roger G., and Rex A. Sinquefield**
"Stocks, Bonds, Bills, and Inflation: Year-By-Year Historical Returns (1926–1974),"

The Journal of Business 49, No. 1 (January 1976), pp. 11–47.

18. **Ibbotson, Roger G., and Rex A. Sinquefield**
"Stocks, Bonds, Bills, and Inflation: Simulations of the Future (1976–2000),"

The Journal of Business 49, No. 3 (July 1976), pp. 313–338.

19. **Ibbotson, Roger G., James Xiong, Robert P. Kreitler, Charles F. Kreitler, and Peng Chen**
"National Savings Rate Guidelines for Individuals,"

Journal of Financial Planning, April 2007, pp. 50–61.

20. **Levy, Haim, and Deborah Gunthorpe**
"Optimal Investment Proportions in Senior Securities and Equities Under Alternative Holding Periods,"

Journal of Portfolio Management, Summer 1993, page 33.

21. **Lewis, Alan L., Sheen T. Kassouf, R. Dennis Brehm, and Jack Johnston**
"The Ibbotson-Sinquefield Simulation Made Easy,"

The Journal of Business 53, No. 2 (1980), pp. 205–214.

22. **Markowitz, Harry M.**
Portfolio Selection: Efficient Diversification of Investments,

John Wiley & Sons, New York, 1959.

23. **Nuttall, Jennifer A., and John Nuttall**
"Asset Allocation Claims—Truth or Fiction?," (unpublished), 1998.

24. **Sharpe, William F.**
"The Arithmetic of Active Management,"

Financial Analysts Journal, January/February 1991.

25. **Stevens, Dale H., Ronald J. Surz, and Mark E. Wimer**
"The Importance of Investment Policy,"

The Journal of Investing, Winter 1999.

Chapters

Chapter 1

Highlights of the 2007 Markets and the Past Decade

Events of 2007

The stock market in the year 2007 produced positive returns for large company stocks and negative returns for small company stocks. Large company stocks finished the year ahead of small company stocks for the first time since 1998.

Long-term government bonds and intermediate-term government bonds posted returns nearly twice their historical long-term averages in 2007; long-term corporate bonds, while producing positive returns, performed less than half as well in 2007 as their long-term average return. Both long- and intermediate-term government bonds outperformed long-term corporate bonds in 2007. Yields decreased on long-term government bonds and on their intermediate-term counterparts. The Consumer Price Index (a measure of inflation) rose more in 2007 than in any year since 1990.

GDP and Corporate Profits Estimate

Real Gross Domestic Product (GDP), a measure of the market value of all goods and services produced within the U.S., grew at an estimated rate of 2.2 percent in 2007, compared to 2.9 percent in 2006. Most of the growth was in quarters two and three, which experienced 3.8 percent and 4.9 percent (annualized) growth, respectively. Quarters one and four experienced significantly lesser growth at an estimated 0.6 percent each.

According to the U.S. Bureau of Economic Analysis, the major contributors to the increase in real GDP in 2007 were "consumer spending on services, exports, and investment in business structures," while the "continued drag from housing and a drawdown in inventories accounted for a significant share of the slowdown in growth compared to 2006."

Federal Reserve

After raising the federal funds target rate seventeen times from June 30, 2004, to June 29, 2006, the Federal Reserve Open Market Committee (FOMC) reversed itself in the second half of 2007 and began lowering rates in an effort to mitigate a banking credit crunch brought about by problems in the subprime housing market. Subprime loans are loans made to borrowers who, because of less-than-perfect credit ratings, do not qualify for loans at the best rates.

Under the chairmanship of Ben Bernanke (confirmed January 31, 2006), the FOMC lowered the federal funds target rate from 5.25 percent to 4.25 percent in 2007. Beginning with a 50 basis points reduction on September 18, the committee followed up with two additional reductions of 25 basis points each on October 31 and December 11.

The yield curve, a graph that shows the relationship between yield and maturity, was relatively flat and, by some measures, inverted, in the first half of 2007, but it returned to a relatively normal shape by the end of the year.

Oil/Gas/Gold/Currencies

The price of oil closed at $95.98 per barrel on the New York Mercantile Exchange at the end of 2007, marking a year in which rising tensions in the Middle East and global economic uncertainty pushed prices up over 57 percent. (Oil finished out 2006 at $61.05 per barrel.) The price of U.S. retail gasoline rose sharply in the first half of the year, decreased slightly through the summer, and increased again in the fourth quarter to $3.05 per gallon, compared with $2.34 at the end of 2006. Gold was also up for the year, closing at $838 per ounce at the end of 2007, up from $638 at the end of 2006.

The U.S. dollar declined against most major currencies in 2007. One euro bought nearly $1.47 by the end of December 2007; at the end of 2006, a single euro purchased $1.32. One U.S. dollar purchased 112 Japanese yen at the end of 2007, while at the end of 2006, one U.S. dollar purchased 119 Japanese yen. The U.S. dollar lost nearly 20 percent versus the Canadian dollar, and one Canadian dollar purchased slightly more than one U.S. dollar near the end of 2007.

Housing Market

New home sales in November 2007 were a seasonally adjusted annual 647,000 units, compared with 987,000 units (revised) for the year-ago period, representing an estimated year-over-year drop of more than 34 percent. According to the U.S. Department of Housing and Urban Development, the median sales price of new houses sold in November 2007 was $239,100, down from $251,700 in November 2006, representing a 5 percent year-over-year decrease.

Building permits for housing units declined 25.3 percent in 2007 from an estimated 1,838,900 in 2006 to an estimated 1,376,100 in 2007. Housing starts declined 24.8 percent in 2007 from an estimated 1,800,900 in 2006 to an estimated 1,353,700 in 2007. Housing completions declined 24.2 percent in 2007 from an estimated 1,979,400 in 2006 to an estimated 1,500,200 in 2007.

On December 6, President Bush proposed a plan that included working with lenders to delay adjusting adjustable-rate mortgages for those borrowers who match certain criteria. To qualify, borrowers must be facing a reset between Jan. 1, 2008, and July 31, 2010, be up to date on their current payments, and be able to prove that a reset would be unaffordable. The Senate also moved to assist homeowners as they introduced, and passed, two bills. One will give certain tax breaks for those who have their mortgage forgiven. In the past, forgiven debt was considered ordinary taxable income. This is no longer the case, so borrowers that can work out an agreement with their lenders will not be taxed on any debt that was forgiven last year, this year, or next year. The other law extended the mortgage insurance deduction that was started in 2007.

Retail Sales

According to the U.S. Census Bureau, "advance" estimates of December 2007 U.S. retail and food services sales showed a muted increase of 0.7 percent over December 2006. Overall retail sales for 2007 were up an estimated 4.2 percent compared with 2006.

Iraq

As the Iraqi conflict continued, 2007 marked the deadliest year in Iraq for United States troops, with 899 deaths. An estimated 18,000 civilian deaths occurred, according to the Iraqi Ministry of the Interior. A dramatic decrease in violence in the second half of the year was attributed to the surge in American forces implemented by President Bush, the growing number and quality of Iraqi police officers, and a marked increase in Iraqi cooperation against the insurgents. A cautiously optimistic General David Petraeus, the senior U.S. commander in Iraq, warned that these signs of progress were "reversible."

In what many consider a pivotal moment, General Petraeus testified to Congress on September 10 and 11 about the status of the war in Iraq. He emphasized that the military surge is meeting many of its objectives, and although a withdrawal of nearly 30,000 troops by next summer may be possible, the situation was considered too fragile to withdraw troops at that time. Throughout 2007, multiple attempts by congressional Democrats to insert language requiring timetables for troop withdrawal into war-funding legislation either failed or were blocked by the White House.

Iran

Worries over Iran's nuclear ambitions continued throughout 2007. On March 23rd, Iran captured fifteen British sailors, accusing them of operating in Iranian waters. The sailors were released a few weeks later. In a unanimous vote on March 24, the U.N. Security Council voted to impose a ban on Iranian arms sales and freeze some Iranian assets in response to Iran's refusal to halt its nuclear program. Iran's foreign minister said that the vote was "unlawful, unnecessary and unjustifiable" and "pressure and intimidation" would not force Iran to give up its nuclear program, which it claims is for peaceful energy-production purposes only.

In November, a CIA National Intelligence Estimate was released which stated, "We judge with high confidence that in fall 2003, Tehran halted its nuclear weapons program." Although some cast doubts on the reports credibility, the report had the effect of taking U.S. military intervention in Iran off the table, and muddled any progress the administration had made in lobbying the international community to isolate the Iranian regime.

Unrest in Pakistan

On October 4, 2007, Pakistan's President Pervez Musharraf permitted former two-time prime minister Benazir Bhutto to return to the country in a move viewed optimistically by those hoping for a larger role for alternative voices in the nation. Upon Bhutto's arrival in Karachi on October 18 two large explosions went off near her party, killing over 100 people. President Musharraf imposed a state of emergency on November 3, purportedly in an effort to ward off attacks from Islamic extremists in the time leading up to elections scheduled for January 8, but lifted the state of emergency on December 15th in the face of mounting internal and international pressure. More turmoil soon followed, however, when Bhutto was assassinated at a political rally on December 27, 2007, and the year ended in a veil of uncertainty.

Chinese Product Safety Concerns Continue

Concerns regarding the safety of a variety of goods produced in China erupted onto the scene in 2007. Contaminated toothpaste, pet food, seafood, and children's toys sounded the alarms and resulted in various product recalls. In one example, the Food and Drug Administration (FDA) blocked the import of several types of fish from China because of possible contamination with unsafe drugs. China is currently the world's largest producer of seafood.

Beijing subsequently released a number of safety initiatives and agreed to strengthen product standards. China's trade surplus finished the year at $262.2 billion, up nearly 50% over 2006.

Subprime Lending Losses

Citigroup announced a $5.9 billion write down of that firm's souring investments in subprime mortgages in October and later announced an additional write down of $8 to $11 billion. Chairman and chief executive Charles O. Prince subsequently resigned Nov. 5, 2007. Merrill Lynch CEO Stan O'Neal was also forced to retire after Merrill announced nearly $8 billion in subprime losses, and Morgan Stanley and Bear Stearns also reported losses, writing down approximately $9.4 billion and $1.9 billion, respectively.

By year's end, an increasing number of large U.S. financial institutions were turning toward the Middle East and Asia for quick infusions of cash in an effort to shore up their ailing balance sheets.

Stock Markets Experience Mixed Results

After closing at an all-time high of 14,164.53 on October 9, the Dow Jones Industrial Average settled back to close out 2007 at 13,264.82, compared with 12,463.15 at year-end 2006. The S&P 500 closed the year out at 1,468.36, compared with 1,418.30 at the end of 2006. The Nasdaq finished 2007 at 2652.28, compared with 2415.29 at the end of 2006.

Washington D.C.

2007 marked surprising turnovers in prominent Washington positions. Following alleged nepotism regarding his girlfriend's position at the Bank, Paul Wolfowitz was replaced by Robert Zoellick as the president of the World Bank. Former Attorney General Alberto Gonzales resigned in August after a long battle over his role in the firing of several United States attorneys; Gonzales was replaced by former federal judge Michael Mukasey. Deputy Chief of Staff and political advisor to the President, Karl Rove, also stepped down in August of 2007. President Bush commuted Scooter Libby's jail sentence after the former top aid to Vice President Dick Cheney was convicted of lying to a jury and obstructing justice during an investigation into whether the White House had intentionally leaked the name of CIA employee Valerie Plame.

Mergers and Acquisitions

Despite a tightening in the credit market toward the end of the year, 2007 reached a record high in mergers: a volume of $1.57 trillion was reached in the United States, while mergers soared to $4.38 trillion globally. This global value shows an uptick of 21 percent over 2006. Mergers in Europe outpaced those in the United States for the first time in five years, as Europe's mergers reached $1.78 trillion. The largest domestic merger was the buyout of TXU Corp., the power company for $44.4 billion by private equity firms. First Data Corp., the largest processor of credit card data, was also bought out in 2007. The private equity firm Kolberg Kravis and Roberts made the purchase for $27.0 billion. The wireless phone company Alltel was purchased by a group of private equity firms, including the Texas Pacific Group and the private equity division of Goldman Sachs, for $27.5 billion. BHP Billiton, the world's largest mining company, offered a bid to purchase Rio Tinto for $140 billion, but Rio Tinto, currently the third largest producer of iron ore globally, rejected the offer as being too low. Demand for iron ore is growing, especially from China. CVS, the country's largest retail pharmacy chain, acquired Caremark, the second-largest pharmacy service provider for $26.5 billion, creating a $75 billion firm better positioned for competing for customers and negotiations with drug makers. In a major media merger, Rupert Murdoch's News Corp. purchased Dow Jones, the owner of the Wall Street Journal, Barron's, the industry website Marketwatch.com and the Dow Jones newswires. Though some members of the Bancroft family, long the owners of a controlling stake in the esteemed publication, were reluctant, a deal was reached for $5.6 billion. News Corp assured those worried about possible interference with the editorial process at the newspaper that a special committee would be formed to assure the independence of the publication.

In a move seen by many to be a direct threat to Microsoft, which had also been bidding for the online advertising company, Google acquired DoubleClick for $3.1 billion in cash in April. The purchase allows Google access to DoubleClick's advertising software as well as a relationship network with advertisers.

On April 21, Bank of America agreed to purchase the Chicago-based, US retail banking arm of ABN AMRO, LaSalle Bank, for $21 billion. The deal increased Bank of America's presence in the Midwest, namely in LaSalle's territory in Illinois, Indiana and Michigan. It also brought about an opportunity to increase their business through acquisitions without crossing regulatory influence lines. The deal caused a stir as shareholder groups filed a lawsuit with the Dutch government to prevent the deal from closing under the complaint that shareholders were not consulted about the move, which they claim, hindered the potential for a bid to buy the entirety of ABN AMRO, including LaSalle. It was argued that the sale of ABN AMRO to a trio of European banks would be a more financially sound deal than the sale of LaSalle Bank and the rest of ABN AMRO separately. In return, Bank of America sued ABN AMRO for not following through with their contract to sell LaSalle. On July 13th, the Dutch Supreme Court agreed that ABN AMRO was not obligated to gain approval from shareholders in their decision to sell the bank, which allowed for the completion of the sale. On October 1st, the sale was finalized and Bank of America took over operations of LaSalle Bank.

On the same day that ABN AMRO announced B of A's bid for LaSalle, they also announced Barclay's $91.2 billion bid for the purchase of ABN AMRO minus the LaSalle division of the behemoth, Amsterdam-based bank. Four days later, on April 25, the Royal Bank of Scotland, Banco Santander and Fortis announced their $95.6 billion offer for the ABN AMRO with the stipulation that LaSalle Bank be included in the sale. This set off a firestorm and multiple lawsuits were filed in attempts to block, and to proceed with, the initial plan to sell LaSalle Bank. A July 13th decision by the Dutch Supreme Court cleared the way for the initial agreement to be honored. On October 10th, the trio's offer of $110 billion was accepted after Barcley's dropped its bid of $63 billion. The three banks that won the bid were expected to break up the company with Fortis taking over operations of the banking entities in the Netherlands, Santander taking the Italian and Brazilian assets and the Royal Bank of Scotland accepting the remaining pieces.

On July 9, Chicago Board of Trade shareholders agreed to allow the purchase of the firm by Chicago Mercantile Exchange Holdings for $11.9 billion. This appeared to bring mixed reactions. Many touted the merger as a rival that could outpace the top worldwide exchanges. A few lamented the loss of independence by the 150 year-old Chicago financial institution and the possibility that the merger could create an exchange that would overwhelm the markets due to its size.

Graph 1-1

The Decade: Wealth Indices of Investments in U.S. Stocks, Bonds, Bills, and Inflation

Year-End 1997 = $1.00

from 1997 to 2007

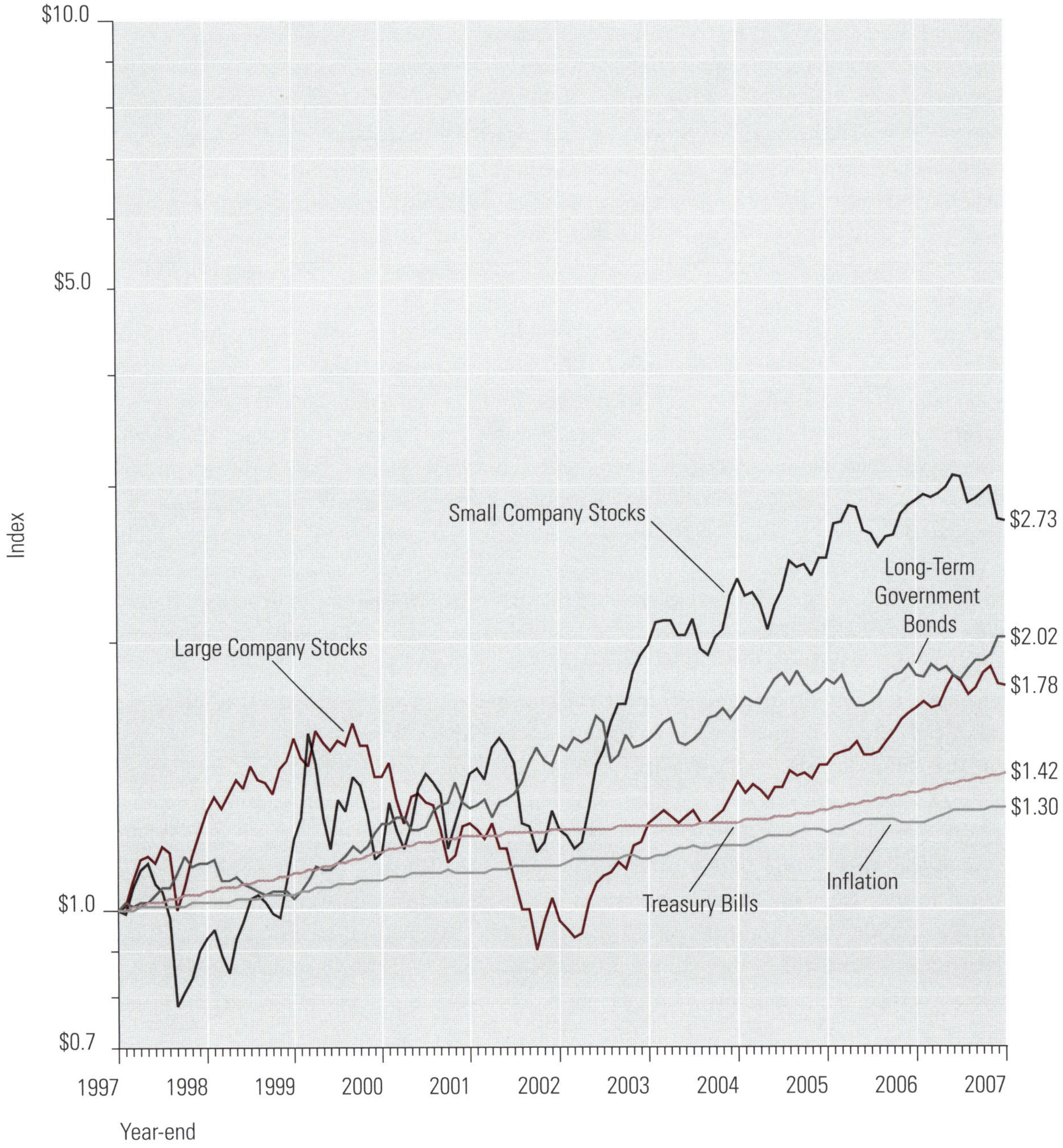

IPO Market

Despite the turmoil in the financial industry during 2007, four of the five largest initial public offerings during the year hail from that sector. The largest IPO of the year, Blackstone (BX), garnered $4.1 billion during the summer at the height of the private-equity boom. After an initial spike in the private-equity asset manager's shares, the stock decline to close the year at $22.13, down nearly 29% from the $31 offer price. The other three large financial offerings turned in mixed performances. Shares of asset manager Och-Ziff (OZM) closed 2007 at $26.28, down 18% from the $32 offer price. On the other hand, electronic market maker Interactive Brokers (IBKR) and derivatives broker MF Global (MF) skated modestly ahead to year end closes of $32.32 and $31.47. Both firm offered shares at $30 each. Rounding out the top five, MetroPCS took advantage of favorable telecom valuations earlier in the year to raise $1.15 billion, but the shares sagged 15% to end the year at $19.45 from the $23 offer price on worries that larger rivals will pressure growth at the wireless carrier.

Results of 2007 Capital Markets

Large Company Stocks

The market for U.S. large company stocks is represented here by the total return on the S&P 500 (the total return includes reinvestment of dividends). Large company stocks for the year produced a total return of 5.49 percent, below the long-term average return (1926 to 2007) of 10.36 percent. Seven of the twelve months between January and December 2007 produced positive returns. The month of April produced the highest return at 4.43 percent. The year 2007 marked the fifth year in a row large company stocks provided a positive total return after a three-year stretch (from 2000 to 2002) in which large company stocks produced negative returns, and the twenty-third year (out of twenty-eight) that large company stocks have provided a positive return since 1980.

An index of large company stock total returns, initialized at $1.00 on December 31, 1925, closed up from the previous year. The index increased to $3,246.39 by the end of 2007, compared with $3,077.33 a year earlier.

Small Company Stocks

After outperforming large company stocks for eight years (1999–2006), small company stocks underperformed larger companies in 2007, with a total return of –5.22 percent. The 2007 return was significantly below the long-term average return (1926 to 2007) of 12.45 percent. Seven of the twelve months of 2007 produced positive returns. The month of May produced the highest return at 3.15 percent, while the month of November produced the lowest return at –8.42 percent. The small stock premium, or geometric difference of small over large stocks, was –10.16 percent (versus 0.32 percent in 2006).

The cumulative wealth index, initialized at $1.00 at the end of 1925, closed down, falling to $15,091.10 at the end of 2007, compared with $ 15,922.43 at the end of 2006.

Long-Term Government Bonds

Long-term government bonds (with maturity near 20 years) returned 9.88 percent in 2007. This return was significantly higher than both the 1.19 percent return seen in 2006 and the long-term average return (1926–2007) of 5.47 percent. The 2007 year-end yield on long-term government bonds was 4.50 percent compared with 4.91 percent at year-end 2006.

A wealth index of long-term government bonds, initialized at $1.00 at year-end 1925, grew to $78.78 by December 2007. The capital appreciation index of long-term government bond returns closed at $1.08 at year's end, up from $1.03 in 2006. This index reached its all-time high of $1.43 in early 1946.

Intermediate-Term Government Bonds

The total return on intermediate-term government bonds (with maturity near 5 years) in 2007 was 10.05 percent. This return was considerably higher than both the 3.14 percent return seen in 2006 and the long-term average return (1926–2007) of 5.34 percent. The yield on intermediate-term government bonds was 3.28 percent as 2007 closed out, compared with 4.65 percent at year-end 2006. The drop in 2007 intermediate-term yields broke a four-year trend of rising yields (year-end to year-end).

The wealth index of intermediate-term government bonds, initialized at $1.00 at year-end 1925, rose to $71.14 at the end of 2007, up from $64.64 at year-end 2006.

Long-Term Corporate Bonds

Long-term corporate bonds (with maturity near 20 years), posted a total return of 2.60 percent in 2007. Total returns were positive in seven of the twelve months during the year, with the highest being 2.87 percent, achieved in February, and the lowest, −2.31, in March.

The bond default premium, or net return from investing in long-term corporate bonds rather than long-term government bonds of equal maturity, was −6.63 percent in 2007, compared with 2.03 percent in 2006. The long-term (1926 to 2007) average is 0.36 percent. A dollar invested in long-term corporate bonds at year-end 1925 rose to $ 105.86 by the end of 2007, compared with $ 103.18 at the end of 2006.

Treasury Bills

An investment in bills with approximately 30 days to maturity had a year-end total return of 4.66 percent, above the long-term average (1926 to 2007) of 3.73 percent. The cumulative index of Treasury bill total returns ended the year at $ 20.19, compared with $19.29 a year earlier. Because monthly Treasury bill returns are nearly always positive, each monthly index value typically sets a new all-time high.

Inflation

Consumer prices rose 4.08 percent in 2007, which is higher than the long-term historical average (1926–2007) of 3.05 percent. Inflation has remained below 5 percent for twenty-five of the last twenty-six years. (The exception was the 6.11 percent rate seen in 1990.)

A cumulative inflation index, initialized at $1.00 at year-end 1925, finished 2007 at $11.72, up from $11.26 at year-end 2006. That is, a "basket" of consumer goods and services that cost $1.00 in 1925 would cost $11.72 today. The two baskets are not identical, but are intended to be comparable.

A Graphic View of the Decade

Over the past decade, 1998 to 2007, large company stocks returned an average 5.91 percent and small company stocks returned and average of 10.58 percent. Large company stocks performed extremely well in 1998 and 1999, only to post negative returns in 2000, 2001, and 2002, but have posted positive returns in each of the years from 2003 to present. Small company stocks had negative returns in 1998, 2000, 2002, and 2007, but returned 60.70 percent in 2003, marking the highest return since 1967's 83.57 percent gain, and the 7th highest from 1926 to 2007.

Graph 1-1 shows the market results for the past decade—illustrating the growth of $1.00 invested on December 31, 1997 in stocks, bonds, and bills, along with an index of inflation. A review of the major themes of the past decade, as revealed in the capital markets, appears later in this chapter.

The Decade in Perspective

The great stock and bond market rise of the 1980s and 1990s was one of the most unusual in the history of the capital markets. In terms of the magnitude of the rise, these decades most closely resembled the 1920s and 1950s. These four decades accounted for a majority of the market's cumulative total return over the past 82 years. While the importance of a long-term view of investing is noted consistently in this book and elsewhere, the counterpart of this observation is: To achieve high returns on your investments, you only need to participate in the few periods of truly outstanding return. The bull markets of 1922 to mid-1929, 1949–1961 (roughly speaking, the Fifties), mid-1982 to mid-1987, and 1991–1999 were such periods. As noted, the 2000s got off to a poor start for large company stocks—producing negative returns in 2000, 2001, and 2002. However, the 2003 total return for large company stocks was 28.70 percent, followed by positive returns the next four years. Small company stocks posted negative returns in 2000, 2002, and 2007 and positive returns in 2001, 2003, 2004, 2005 and 2006. The bond market has been strong through much of the 2000s.

Table 1-1
Compound Annual Rates of Return by Decade (in percent)

	1920s*	1930s	1940s	1950s	1960s	1970s	1980s	1990s	2000s**	1998-07
Large Company	19.2	–0.1	9.2	19.4	7.8	5.9	17.5	18.2	1.7	5.9
Small Company	–4.5	1.4	20.7	16.9	15.5	11.5	15.8	15.1	10.8	10.6
Long-Term Corporate	5.2	6.9	2.7	1.0	1.7	6.2	13.0	8.4	8.1	6.7
Long-Term Government	5.0	4.9	3.2	–0.1	1.4	5.5	12.6	8.8	8.8	7.3
Intermediate-Term Government	4.2	4.6	1.8	1.3	3.5	7.0	11.9	7.2	6.4	6.0
Treasury Bills	3.7	0.6	0.4	1.9	3.9	6.3	8.9	4.9	3.2	3.5
Inflation	–1.1	–2.0	5.4	2.2	2.5	7.4	5.1	2.9	2.8	2.7

*Based on the period 1926–1929.

**Based on the period 2000–2007.

Table 1-1 compares the returns by decade on all of the basic asset classes covered in this book. It is notable that either large company stocks or small company stocks were the best performing asset class in every full decade save one (the 1930s). In this table, the Twenties cover the period 1926–1929 and the 2000s cover the period 2000–2007.

It is interesting to place the decades of superior performance in historical context. The Twenties were preceded by mediocre returns and high inflation and were followed by the most devastating stock market crash and economic depression in American history. This sequence of events mitigated the impact of the Twenties bull market on investor wealth. Nevertheless, the stock market became a liquid secondary market in the Twenties, rendering that period important for reasons other than return. In contrast, the Fifties were preceded and followed by decades with roughly average equity returns. The Eighties were preceded by a decade of "stagflation" where modest stock price gains were seriously eroded by inflation and were followed by a period of stability in the Nineties.

The bond market performance of the Eighties and Nineties has no precedent. Bond yields, which had risen consistently since the 1940s, reached unprecedented levels in 1980–1981. (Other countries experiencing massive inflation have had correspondingly high interest rates.) Never before having had so far to fall, bond yields dropped further and faster than at any other time, producing what is indisputably the greatest bond bull market in history. Unfortunately, the boom came to an end in 1994. After falling to 21-year lows one year earlier, bond yields rose in 1994 to their highest level in over three years. Both long-term and intermediate-term government bond yields have generally fallen in the 2000s.

The historical themes of the past decade, as they relate to the capital markets, can be summarized in three observations. First, the 17½ year period starting in mid-1982 and ending in 1999 comprised a rare span of time in which investors quickly accumulated wealth.

Second, the postwar aberration of ever-higher inflation rates ended with a dramatic disinflation in the early Eighties. In the Nineties, inflation was a relatively low 2.9 percent compound annual rate compared to the long term compound annual rate as of the end of that decade (1926–1999), which was 3.1 percent. The trend of relatively low inflation has continued thus far in the 2000s, with the compound annual rate of 2.8 percent coming in below the long term average (1926–2007) compound annual rate of 3.0 percent. It should be noted, however, that the annual rate of inflation in 2007 of 4.1 percent was the highest rate since the 6.1 percent recorded in 1990.

Finally, participation in the returns of the capital markets reached levels not even approached in the Twenties, the Fifties, or the atypical boom period of 1967–1972. The vast size and importance of pension funds and 401(k)s, as well as the rapidly increasing popularity of stock and bond mutual funds as a basic savings vehicle have enabled more individuals to experience the returns of the capital markets than ever before.

Graphic Depiction of Returns in the Decade

Graphs 1-2, 1-3, and 1-4 contain bar graphs of 1998–2007 annual and 2007 monthly total returns on the assets discussed above. The top part of Graph 1-2 compares large company stocks to long-term government bonds (approximately 20-year maturity). Long-term bonds have outperformed large company stocks in five of the last ten years. In overall return, long-term bonds bested large company stocks over the 1998–2007 period, returning 7.26 percent and 5.91 percent, respectively. The bottom half of Graph 1-2 compares large company stocks to small company stocks. Small company stocks have outperformed large company stocks in eight years of the past ten (1998 and 2007 were the exceptions). In overall return, small company stocks bested large company stocks over the 1998–2007 period, returning 10.58 percent and 5.91 percent, respectively.

The top part of Graph 1-3 compares corporate and government bonds of like maturity (approximately 20 years). Long-term government bonds have outperformed long-term corporate bonds in five of the last ten years. In overall return, long-term government bonds bested long-term corporate bonds over the 1998–2007 period, returning 7.26 percent and 6.69 percent, respectively. Historically though, long-term government bonds have tended to underperform long-term corporate bonds, returning an average of 5.47 percent and 5.85 percent, respectively, over the time period 1926–2007. The bottom part of Graph 1-3 compares long-term and intermediate-term government bonds. Intermediate-term bonds are less volatile and tend to return less than long-term bonds. In overall return, long-term government bonds bested intermediate-term government bonds over the 1998–2007 period, returning 7.26 percent and 5.96 percent, respectively.

Graph 1-4 displays bar graphs of the 1998–2007 annual and 2007 monthly Treasury bill returns, inflation rates, and real riskless rates of return. The top part of Graph 1-4 compares Treasury bills and inflation. The bottom part of Graph 1-4 shows month-by-month real riskless rates of return, defined as Treasury bill returns in excess of inflation.

Tables of Market Results for 1998–2007

The 1998–2007 annual and 2007 quarterly and monthly total returns on the seven basic asset classes studied in this book are presented in Table 1-2. Table 1-3 displays cumulative indices of the returns shown in Table 1-2, based on a starting value of $1.00 on December 31, 1925.

For the past decade, both large and small company stocks have performed quite well, with the exception of a few years. Bonds produced returns that were above their long-term historical averages, while inflation rates fell below their 82-year average for most of the decade.

Graph 1-2

1998–2007 Annual and 2007 Monthly Total Returns

A Comparison of Large Company Stocks with Long-Term Government Bonds, and Large Company Stocks with Small Company Stocks (in percent)

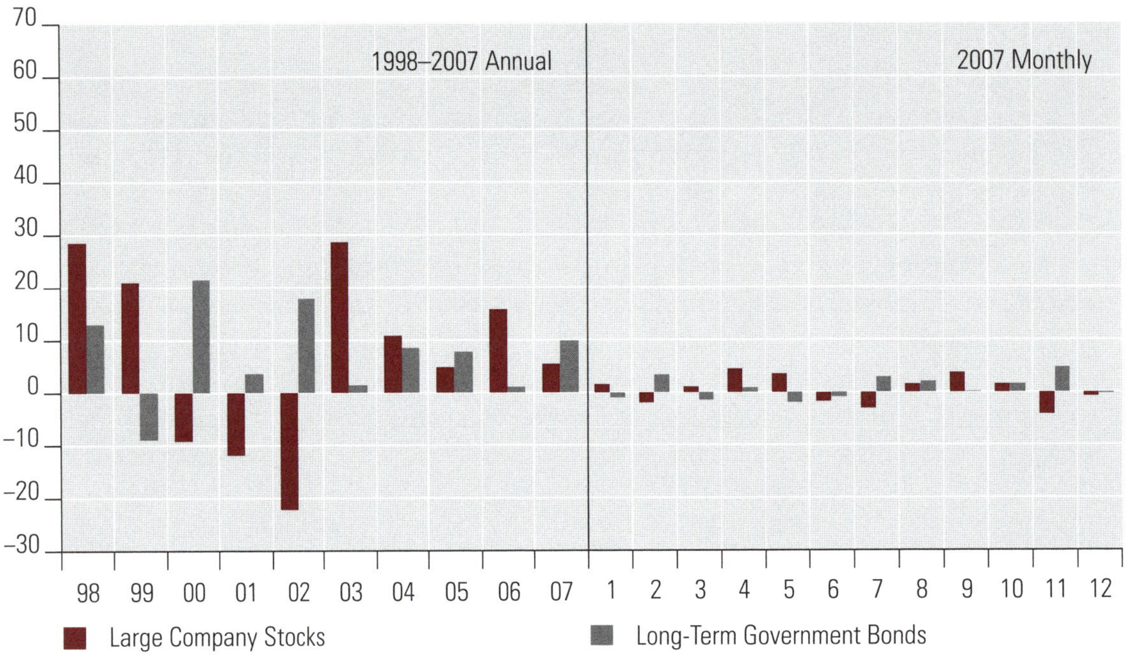

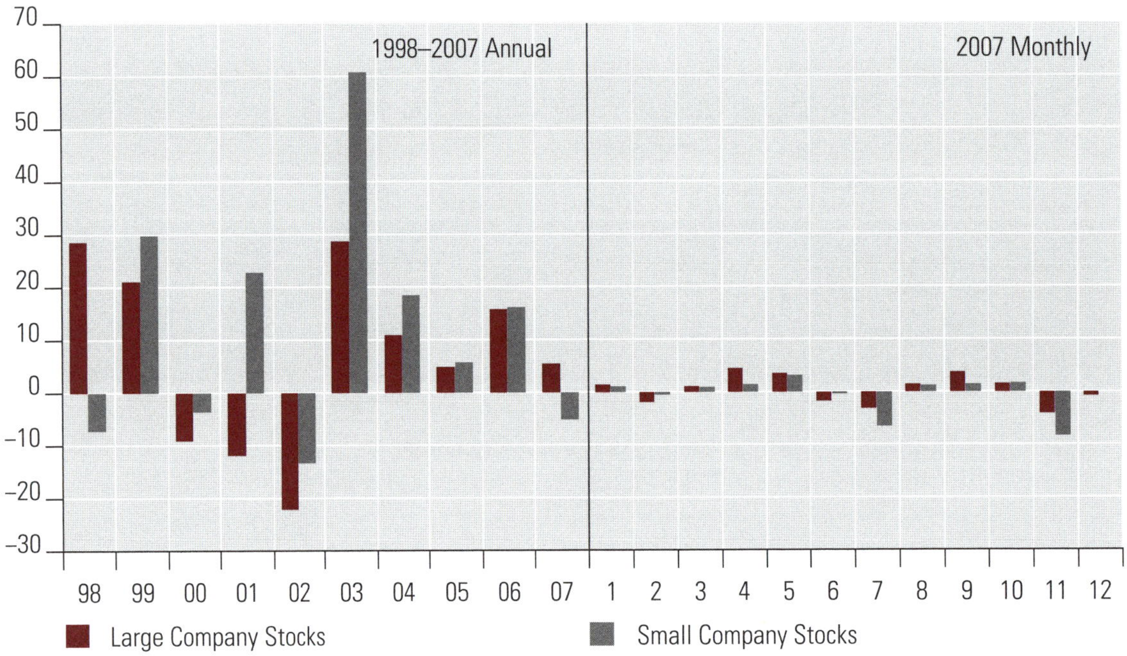

Graph 1-3

1998–2007 Annual and 2007 Monthly Total Returns

A Comparison of Long-Term Government Bonds with Long-Term Corporate Bonds, and Long-Term Government Bonds with Intermediate-Term Government Bonds (in percent)

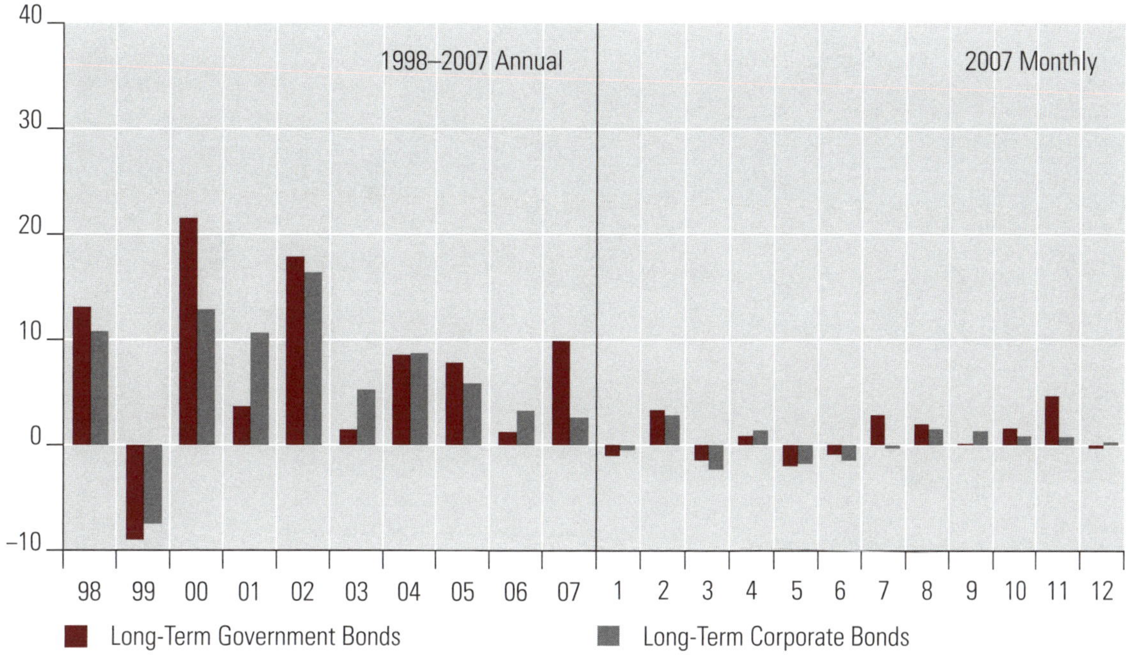

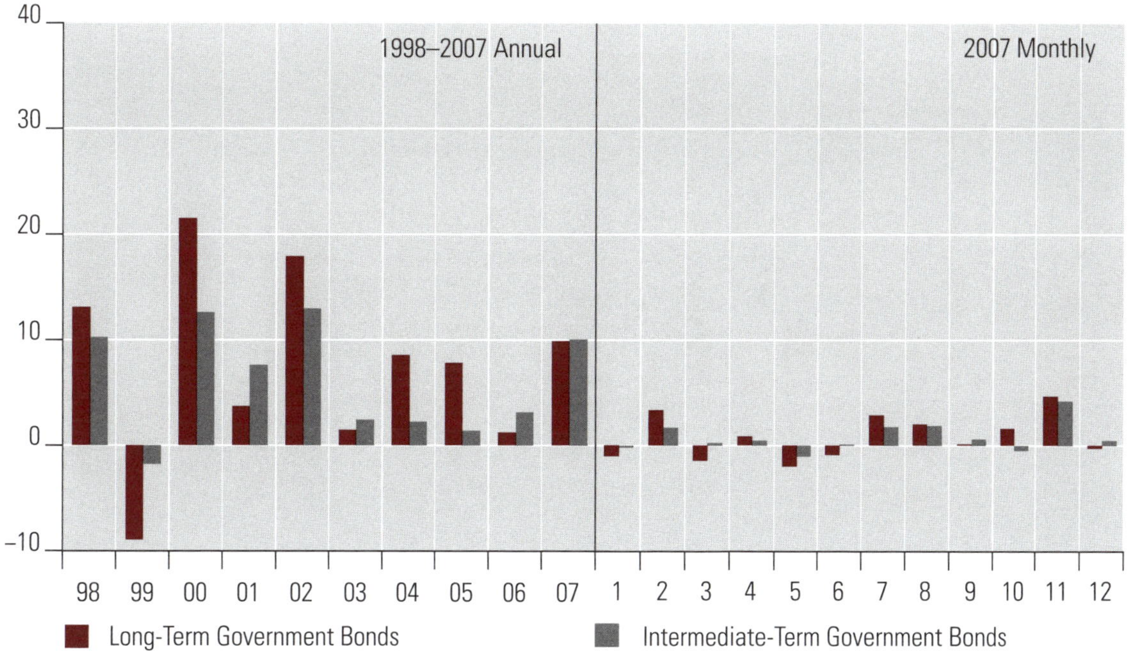

Graph 1-4

1998–2007 Annual and 2007 Monthly Total Returns

Treasury Bills, Inflation and Real Riskless Rates of Return (in percent)

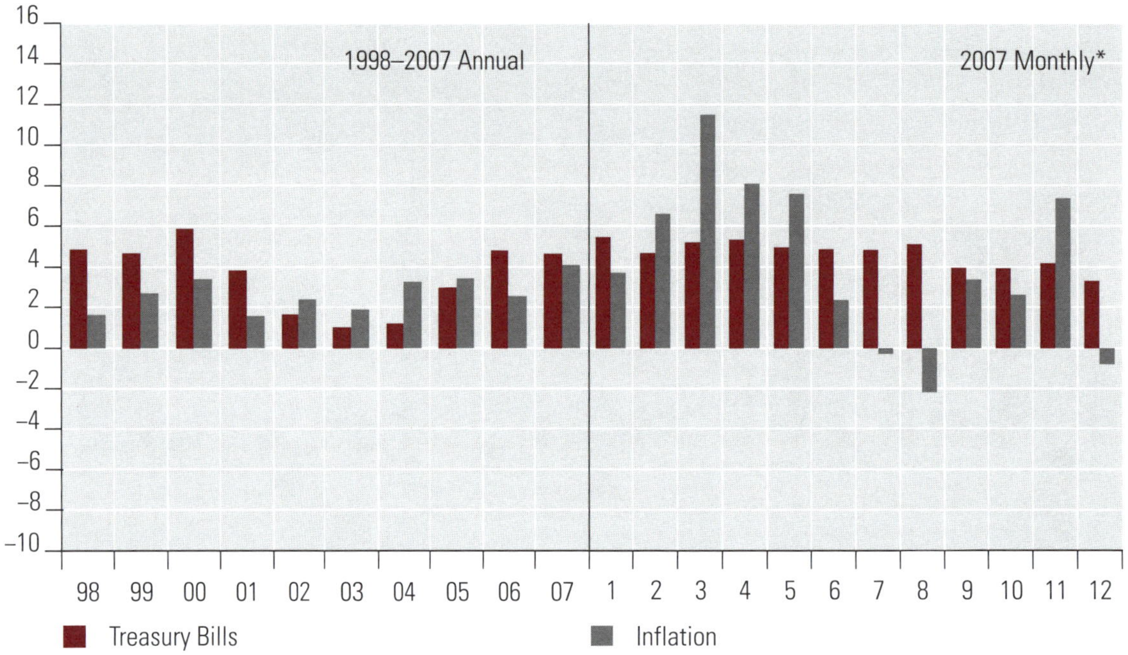

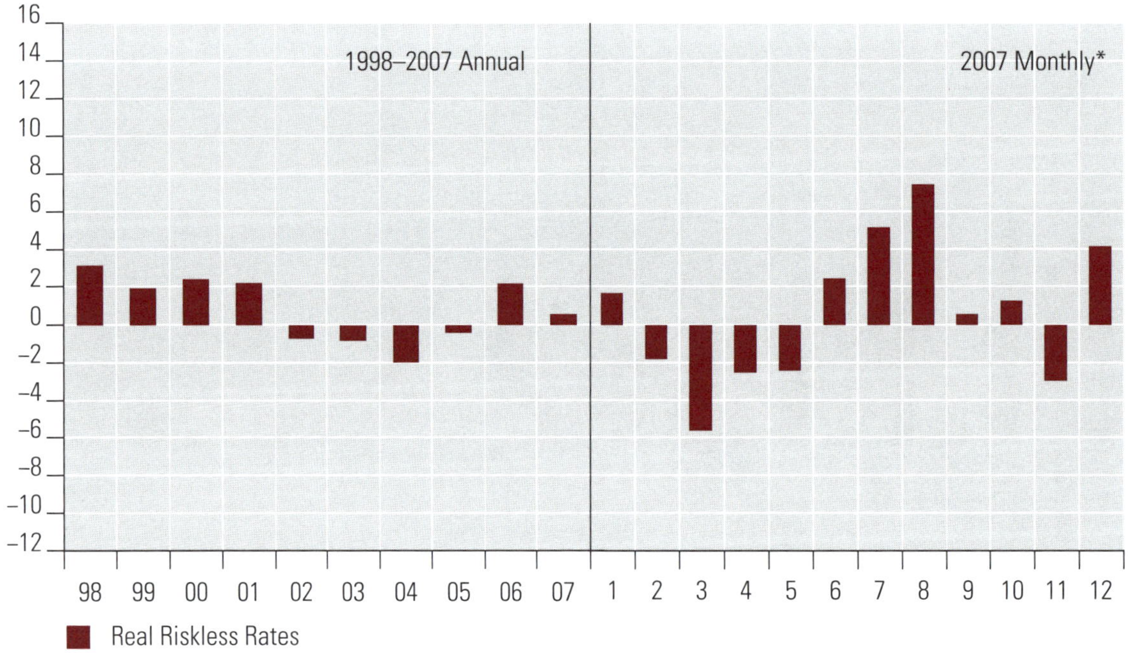

*2007 Monthly Shown As Annual Rates

Table 1-2

1998–2007 Annual and 2007 Quarterly and Monthly Market Results

Returns on Stocks, Bonds, Bills, and Inflation (in percent)

Year	Large Company Stocks	Small Company Stocks	Long-Term Corporate Bonds	Long-Term Government Bonds	Intermediate Government Bonds	U.S. Treasury Bills	Inflation
1998–2007 Annual Returns							
1998	28.58	–7.31	10.76	13.06	10.21	4.86	1.61
1999	21.04	29.79	–7.45	–8.96	–1.77	4.68	2.68
2000	–9.11	–3.59	12.87	21.48	12.59	5.89	3.39
2001	–11.88	22.77	10.65	3.70	7.62	3.83	1.55
2002	–22.10	–13.28	16.33	17.84	12.93	1.65	2.38
2003	28.70	60.70	5.27	1.45	2.40	1.02	1.88
2004	10.87	18.39	8.72	8.51	2.25	1.20	3.26
2005	4.91	5.69	5.87	7.81	1.36	2.98	3.42
2006	15.80	16.17	3.24	1.19	3.14	4.80	2.54
2007	5.49	–5.22	2.60	9.88	10.05	4.66	4.08
2007 Quarterly Returns							
I-07	0.64	1.67	–0.01	0.81	1.75	1.26	1.76
II-07	6.28	4.35	–1.88	–2.06	–0.45	1.25	1.46
III-07	2.03	–4.03	2.56	5.00	4.22	1.14	0.07
IV-07	–3.33	–6.92	1.96	5.99	4.25	0.94	0.74
2007 Monthly Returns							
12-06	1.40	1.61	–2.32	–2.36	–0.67	0.40	0.15
01-07	1.51	1.15	–0.51	–1.02	–0.20	0.44	0.31
02-07	–1.96	–0.50	2.87	3.35	1.70	0.38	0.54
03-07	1.12	1.02	–2.31	–1.45	0.24	0.43	0.91
04-07	4.43	1.50	1.40	0.85	0.47	0.44	0.65
05-07	3.49	3.15	–1.78	–2.00	–1.02	0.41	0.61
06-07	–1.66	–0.33	–1.48	–0.91	0.11	0.40	0.19
07-07	–3.10	–6.51	–0.32	2.84	1.75	0.40	–0.03
08-07	1.50	1.16	1.52	1.99	1.85	0.42	–0.18
09-07	3.74	1.48	1.35	0.12	0.57	0.32	0.28
10-07	1.59	1.70	0.88	1.55	–0.48	0.32	0.21
11-07	–4.18	–8.42	0.79	4.68	4.25	0.34	0.59
12-07	–0.69	–0.06	0.28	–0.29	0.48	0.27	–0.07

Table 1-3

1998–2007 Annual and 2007 Monthly Market Results

Indices of Returns on Stocks, Bonds, Bills, and Inflation

Year-End 1925 = $1.00

Year	Large Company Stocks	Small Company Stocks	Long-Term Corporate Bonds	Long-Term Government Bonds	Intermediate Government Bonds	U.S. Treasury Bills	Inflation
1998–2007 Annual Indices							
Dec-98	2350.892	5116.648	61.339	44.178	43.933	14.942	9.143
Dec-99	2845.629	6640.788	56.772	40.218	43.155	15.641	9.389
Dec-00	2586.524	6402.228	64.077	48.856	48.589	16.563	9.707
Dec-01	2279.127	7860.048	70.900	50.662	52.291	17.197	9.857
Dec-02	1775.341	6816.409	82.480	59.699	59.054	17.480	10.091
Dec-03	2284.785	10953.944	86.824	60.564	60.469	17.659	10.281
Dec-04	2533.204	12968.476	94.396	65.717	61.832	17.871	10.616
Dec-05	2657.559	13706.149	99.937	70.852	62.674	18.403	10.978
Dec-06	3077.329	15922.429	103.178	71.694	64.643	19.287	11.257
Dec-07	3246.391	15091.095	105.858	78.779	71.142	20.186	11.717
2007 Monthly Indices							
12-06	3077.329	15922.429	103.178	71.694	64.643	19.287	11.257
01-07	3123.868	16105.537	102.652	70.961	64.515	19.372	11.292
02-07	3062.769	16025.009	105.602	73.335	65.615	19.447	11.352
03-07	3097.026	16188.464	103.167	72.272	65.775	19.529	11.456
04-07	3234.210	16431.291	104.616	72.887	66.084	19.615	11.530
05-07	3347.068	16948.877	102.756	71.428	65.407	19.694	11.600
06-07	3291.462	16892.945	101.231	70.782	65.477	19.773	11.623
07-07	3189.411	15793.215	100.905	72.790	66.620	19.851	11.620
08-07	3237.220	15976.416	102.437	74.235	67.852	19.934	11.599
09-07	3358.292	16212.867	103.825	74.323	68.241	19.998	11.631
10-07	3411.722	16488.486	104.735	75.476	67.911	20.063	11.655
11-07	3269.078	15100.155	105.559	79.009	70.799	20.131	11.725
12-07	3246.391	15091.095	105.858	78.779	71.142	20.186	11.717

Chapter 2

The Long Run Perspective

Motivation

A long view of capital market history, exemplified by the 82-year period (1926–2007) examined here, uncovers the basic relationships between risk and return among the different asset classes and between nominal and real (inflation-adjusted) returns. The goal of this study of asset returns is to provide a period long enough to include most or all of the major types of events that investors have experienced and may experience in the future. Such events include war and peace, growth and decline, bull and bear markets, inflation and deflation, and other less dramatic events that affect asset returns.

By studying the past, one can make inferences about the future. While the actual events that occurred during 1926–2007 will not be repeated, the event-types (not specific events) of that period can be expected to recur. It is sometimes said that only a few periods are unusual, such as the crash of 1929–1932 and World War II. This logic is suspicious because all periods are unusual. Some of the most unusual events of the century—the stock market crash of 1987, the equally remarkable inflation of the 1970s and early 1980s, and the more recent events of September 11, 2001—took place over the last three decades. From the perspective that historical event-types tend to repeat themselves, an 82-year examination of past capital market returns reveals a great deal about what may be expected in the future. [See Chapter 9.]

Historical Returns on Stocks, Bonds, Bills, and Inflation

Graph 2-1 graphically depicts the growth of $1.00 invested in large company stocks, small company stocks, long-term government bonds, Treasury bills, and a hypothetical asset returning the inflation rate over the period from the end of 1925 to the end of 2007. All results assume reinvestment of dividends on stocks or coupons on bonds and no taxes. Transaction costs are not included, except in the small stock index starting in 1982.

Each of the cumulative index values is initialized at $1.00 at year-end 1925. The graph vividly illustrates that large company stocks and small company stocks were the big winners over the entire 82-year period: investments of $1.00 in these assets would have grown to $3,246.39 and $15,091.10 respectively, by year-end 2007. This phenomenal growth was earned by taking substantial risk. In contrast, long-term government bonds (with an approximate 20-year maturity), which exposed the holder to much less risk, grew to only $78.78.

The lowest-risk strategy over the past 82 years (for those with short-term time horizons) was to buy U.S. Treasury bills. Since Treasury bills tended to track inflation, the resulting real (inflation-adjusted) returns were just above zero for the entire 1926–2007 period.

Graph 2-1
Wealth Indices of Investments in the U.S. Capital Markets
Year-End 1925 = $1.00

from 1925 to 2007

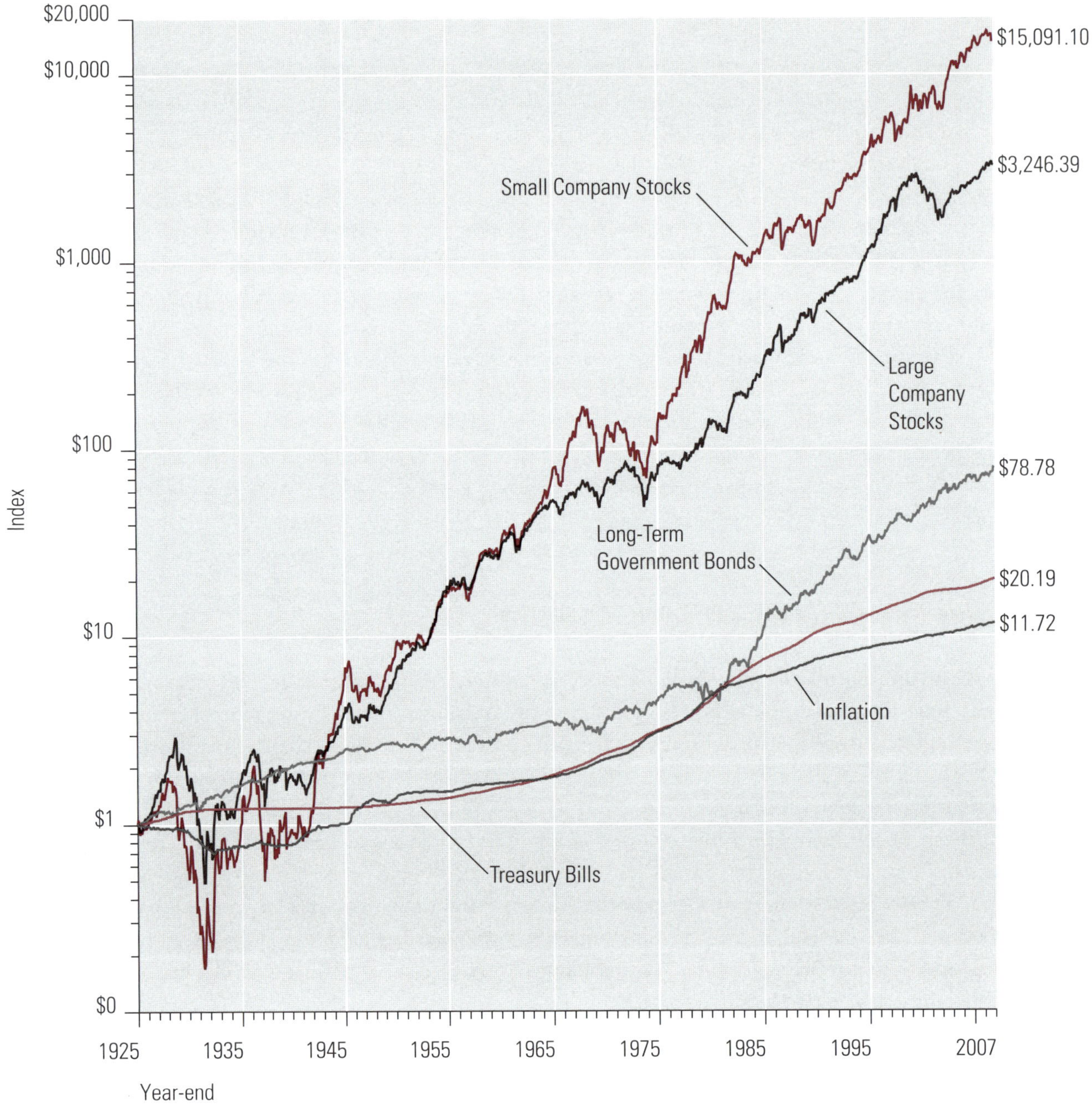

Logarithmic Scale on the Index Graphs

A logarithmic scale is used on the vertical axis of our index graphs. The date appears on the horizontal axis.

A logarithmic scale allows for the direct comparison of the series' behavior at different points in time. Specifically, the use of a logarithmic scale allows the following interpretation of the data: the same vertical distance, no matter where it is measured on the graph, represents the same percentage change in the series. On the log scale shown below, a 50 percent gain from $10 to $15 occupies the same vertical distance as a 50 percent gain from $100 to $150. On the linear scale, the same percentage gains look different.

Linear Scale

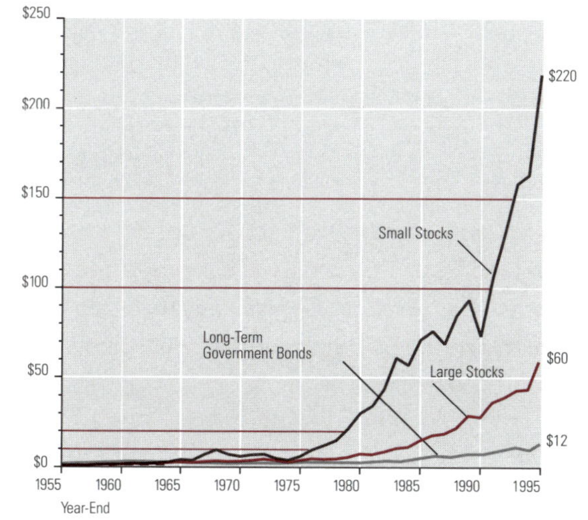

Logarithmic Scale

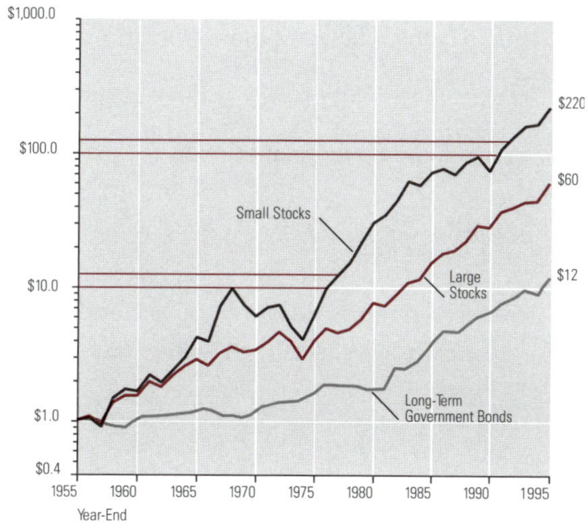

A logarithmic scale allows the viewer to compare investment performance across different time periods; thus the viewer can concentrate on rates of return, without worrying about the number of dollars invested at any given time. An additional benefit of the logarithmic scale is the way the scale spreads the action out over time. This allows the viewer to more carefully examine the fluctuations of the individual time series in different periods.

Large Company Stocks

As noted above, an index of S&P 500 total returns, initialized on December 31, 1925, at $1.00, closed 2007 at $3,246.39, a compound annual growth rate of 10.4 percent. The inflation-adjusted S&P 500 total return index closed 2007 at a level of $277.07.

Small Company Stocks

Over the long run, small stock returns surpassed the S&P 500, with the small stock total return index ending 2007 at a level of $15,091.10. This represents a compound annual growth rate of 12.5 percent, the highest rate among the asset classes studied here.

Long-Term Government Bonds

The long-term government bond total return index, constructed with an approximate 20-year maturity, closed 2007 at a level of $78.78 (based on year-end 1925 equaling $1.00). Based on the capital appreciation component alone, the $1.00 index closed at $1.08, an 8 percent capital gain over the period 1926–2007. This indicates that more than all of the positive historical returns on long-term government bonds were due to income returns. The compound annual total return for long-term government bonds was 5.5 percent.

Intermediate-Term Government Bonds

One dollar invested in intermediate-term bonds at the end of 1925, with coupons reinvested, grew to $71.14 by year-end 2007, compared to $64.64 at year-end 2006. The compound annual total return for intermediate-term government bonds was 5.3 percent. Capital appreciation caused $1.00 to increase to $1.45 over the 82-year period, representing a compound annual growth rate of 0.5 percent.

Long-Term Corporate Bonds

Long-term corporate bonds outperformed both categories of government bonds over the 1926–2007 period with a compound annual total return of 5.9 percent. One dollar invested in the long-term corporate bond index at year-end 1925 was worth $105.86 by the end of 2007. This higher return reflected the risk premium that investors require for investing in corporate bonds, which are subject to the risk of default.

Treasury Bills

One dollar invested in Treasury bills at the end of 1925 was worth $20.19 by year-end 2007, with a compound annual growth rate of 3.7 percent. Treasury bill returns followed distinct patterns, described on the next page. Moreover, Treasury bills tended to track inflation; therefore, the average inflation-adjusted return on Treasury bills (or real riskless rate of return) was only 0.7 percent over the 82-year period. This real return also followed distinct patterns.

Patterns in Treasury Bill Returns

During the late 1920s and early 1930s, Treasury bill returns were just above zero. (These returns were observed during a largely deflationary period.) Beginning in late 1941, the yields on Treasury bills were pegged by the government at low rates while high inflation was experienced.

Treasury bills closely tracked inflation after March 1951, when Treasury bill yields were deregulated in the U.S. Treasury-Federal Reserve Accord. (Treasury bill returns after that date reflect free market rates.) This tracking relationship has weakened since 1973. From about 1974 to 1980, Treasury bill returns were consistently lower than inflation rates. Since 1981, real returns on Treasury bills have still been positive, with the exception of 2002–2005. Since 2006, real returns on Treasury bills have been positive.

Federal Reserve Operating Procedure Changes

The disparity between performance and volatility for the periods prior to and after October 1979 can be attributed to the Federal Reserve's new operating procedures. Prior to this date, the Fed used the federal funds rate as an operating target. Subsequently, the Fed de-emphasized this rate as an operating target and, instead, began to focus on the manipulation of the money supply (through nonborrowed reserves). As a result, the federal funds rate underwent much greater volatility, thereby bringing about greater volatility in Treasury returns.

In the fall of 1982, however, the Federal Reserve again changed the policy procedures regarding its monetary policy. The Fed abandoned its new monetary controls and returned to a strategy of preventing excessive volatility in interest rates. Volatility in Treasury bill returns from the fall of 1979 through the fall of 1982 was significantly greater than that which has occurred since.

Inflation

The compound annual inflation rate over 1926–2007 was 3.0 percent. The inflation index, initiated at $1.00 at year-end 1925, grew to $11.72 by year-end 2007. The entire increase occurred during the postwar period. The years 1926–1933 were marked by deflation; inflation then raised consumer prices to their 1926 levels by the middle of 1945. After a brief postwar spurt of inflation, prices rose slowly over most of the 1950s and 1960s. Then, in the 1970s, inflation reached a pace unprecedented in peacetime, peaking at 13.3 percent in 1979. (On a month-by-month basis, the peak inflation rate was a breathtaking 24.0 percent, stated in annualized terms, in August 1973.) The 1980s saw a reversion to more moderate, though still substantial, inflation rates averaging about 5 percent. Inflation rates continued to decline in the 1990s with a compound annual rate of 2.9 percent.

Summary Statistics of Total Returns

Table 2-1 presents summary statistics of the annual total returns on each asset class over the entire 82-year period of 1926–2007. The data presented in these exhibits are described in detail in Chapters 3 and 6.

Note that in Table 2-1, the arithmetic mean returns are always higher than the geometric mean returns. The difference between these two means is related to the standard deviation, or variability, of the series. [See Chapter 6.]

The "skylines" or histograms to the right in Table 2-1 show the frequency distribution of returns on each asset class. The height of the common stock skyline in the range between +10 and +20 percent, for example, shows the number of years in 1926–2007 that large company stocks had a return in that range. The histograms are shown in 5 percent increments to fully display the spectrum of returns as seen over the last 82 years, especially in stocks.

Riskier assets, such as large company stocks and small company stocks, have low, spread-out skylines, reflecting the broad distribution of returns from very poor to very good. Less risky assets, such as bonds, have narrow skylines that resemble a single tall building, indicating the tightness of the distribution around the mean of the series. The histogram for Treasury bills is one-sided, lying almost entirely to the right of the vertical line representing a zero return; that is, Treasury bills rarely experienced negative returns on a yearly basis over the 1926–2007 period. The inflation skyline shows both positive and negative annual rates. Although a few deflationary months and quarters have occurred recently, the last negative annual inflation rate occurred in 1954.

The histograms in Tables 2-2 through 2-4 show the total return distributions on the basic series over the past 82 years. These histograms are useful in determining the years with similar returns. The stock histograms are shown in 10 percent increments while the bond, bill, and inflation histograms are in 2 percent increments. The increments are smaller for the assets with less widely distributed returns. Treasury bills are the most tightly clustered of any of the asset classes, confirming that this asset bears little risk; the annual return usually fell near zero.

Table 2-1
Basic Series: Summary Statistics of Annual Total Returns

from 1926 to 2007

Series	Geometric Mean	Arithmetic Mean	Standard Deviation	Distribution
Large Company Stocks	10.4%	12.3%	20.0%	
Small Company Stocks	12.5	17.1	32.6	*
Long-Term Corporate Bonds	5.9	6.2	8.4	
Long-Term Government	5.5	5.8	9.2	
Intermediare-Term Government	5.3	5.5	5.7	
U.S. Treasury Bills	3.7	3.8	3.1	
Inflation	3.0	3.1	4.2	

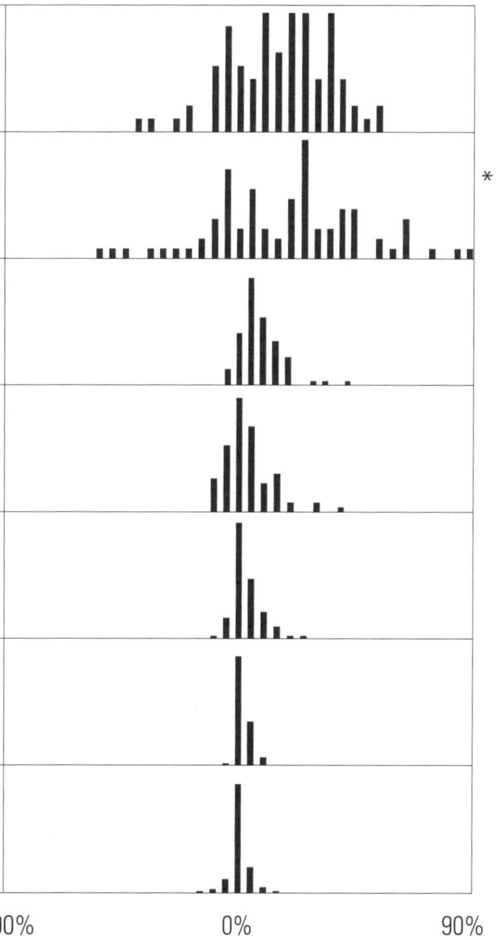

*The 1933 Small Company Stocks Total Return was 142.9 percent.

Table 2-2
Histogram
Large Company Stock and Small Company Stock Total Returns (in percent)

from 1926 to 2007

Large Company Stocks

Percent	Years
–50 to –40	1931
–40 to –30	1937
–30 to –20	2002, 1974, 1930
–20 to –10	2001, 1973, 1966, 1957, 1941
–10 to 0	2000, 1990, 1981, 1977, 1969, 1962, 1953, 1946, 1940, 1939, 1934, 1932, 1929
0 to 10	2007, 2005, 1994, 1993, 1992, 1987, 1984, 1978, 1970, 1960, 1956, 1948, 1947
10 to 20	2006, 2004, 1988, 1986, 1979, 1972, 1971, 1968, 1965, 1964, 1959, 1952, 1949, 1944, 1926
20 to 30	2003, 1999, 1998, 1996, 1983, 1982, 1976, 1967, 1963, 1961, 1951, 1943, 1942
30 to 40	1997, 1995, 1991, 1989, 1985, 1980, 1975, 1955, 1950, 1945, 1938, 1936, 1927
40 to 50	1958, 1935, 1928
50 to 60	1954, 1933

–80 –70 –60 –50 –40 –30 –20 –10 0 10 20 30 40 50 60 70 80 90
Percent

Small Company Stocks

Percent	Years
–60 to –50	1937, 1929
–50 to –40	1931
–40 to –30	1973, 1930
–30 to –20	1990, 1969
–20 to –10	2002, 1974, 1970, 1962, 1957, 1946
–10 to 0	2007, 2000, 1998, 1987, 1984, 1966, 1960, 1953, 1948, 1941, 1940, 1932
0 to 10	2005, 1994, 1986, 1972, 1956, 1952, 1951, 1947, 1939, 1926
10 to 20	2006, 2004, 1996, 1989, 1981, 1971, 1959, 1949
20 to 30	2001, 1999, 1997, 1993, 1992, 1988, 1985, 1982, 1978, 1977, 1964, 1963, 1955, 1934, 1927
30 to 40	1995, 1983, 1980, 1968, 1961, 1950, 1938, 1928
40 to 50	1991, 1979, 1965, 1942, 1935
50 to 60	1976, 1975, 1944
60 to 70	2003, 1958, 1954, 1936
70 to 80	1945
80 to 90	1967, 1943
140 to 150	1933

–80 –70 –60 –50 –40 –30 –20 –10 0 10 20 30 40 50 60 70 80 90 140 150
Percent

Table 2-3

Histogram

Long-Term Government Bond and Intermediate-Term Government Bond Total Returns (in percent)

from 1926 to 2007

Long-Term Government Bonds

Percent	Years
−10 to −8	1999, 1967
−8 to −6	1994, 1958
−6 to −4	1969, 1956, 1931
−4 to −2	1987, 1980, 1959, 1951, 1947
−2 to 0	1996, 1979, 1978, 1977, 1973, 1968, 1955, 1946, 1933
0 to 2	2006, 2003, 1983, 1981, 1965, 1963, 1961, 1952, 1950, 1941, 1937, 1928
2 to 4	2001, 1966, 1964, 1953, 1948, 1944, 1943, 1942, 1929
4 to 6	1974, 1972, 1939, 1938, 1935, 1930
6 to 8	2005, 1990, 1962, 1957, 1954, 1949, 1940, 1936, 1926
8 to 10	2007, 2004, 1992, 1988, 1975, 1927
10 to 12	1945, 1934
12 to 14	1998, 1971, 1970, 1960
14 to 16	1997, 1984
16 to 18	2002, 1976, 1932
18 to 20	1993, 1991, 1989
20 to 24	2000
24 to 26	1986
26 to 30	
30 to 32	1995, 1985
32 to 40	
40 to 42	1982

Intermediate-Term Government Bonds

Percent	Years
−10 to −8	
−8 to −6	
−6 to −4	1994
−4 to −2	1931
−2 to 0	1999, 1969, 1959, 1958, 1956, 1955
0 to 2	2005, 1977, 1967, 1965, 1963, 1961, 1952, 1951, 1950, 1948, 1947, 1946, 1944, 1942, 1941, 1937, 1933, 1928
2 to 4	2006, 2004, 2003, 1996, 1987, 1980, 1978, 1954, 1953, 1949, 1945, 1943, 1940, 1936
4 to 6	1979, 1974, 1973, 1972, 1968, 1966, 1964, 1962, 1939, 1927, 1926
6 to 8	2001, 1992, 1988, 1983, 1975, 1957, 1938, 1935, 1930, 1929
8 to 10	1997, 1990, 1981, 1971, 1934, 1932
10 to 12	2007, 1998, 1993, 1960
12 to 14	2002, 2000, 1989, 1976
14 to 16	1991, 1986, 1984
16 to 18	1995, 1970
18 to 20	
20 to 22	1985
22 to 24	
24 to 26	
26 to 28	
28 to 30	1982
30 to 32	

Table 2-4
Histogram
U.S. Treasury Bill Total Returns and Inflation (in percent)

from 1926 to 2007

U.S. Treasury Bills

Percent	Years
−2 to 0	1938
0 to 2	2004 2003 2002 1958 1955 1954 1953 1952 1951 1950 1949 1948 1947 1946 1945 1944 1943 1942 1941 1940 1939 1937 1936 1935 1934 1933 1932 1931
2 to 4	2005 2001 1994 1993 1992 1972 1965 1964 1963 1962 1961 1960 1959 1957 1956 1930 1928 1927 1926
4 to 6	2007 2006 2000 1999 1998 1997 1996 1995 1991 1987 1977 1976 1975 1971 1968 1967 1966 1929
6 to 8	1990 1988 1986 1985 1978 1973 1970 1969
8 to 10	1989 1984 1983 1974
10 to 12	1982 1980 1979
14 to 16	1981

−18 −16 −14 −12 −10 −8 −6 −4 −2 0 2 4 6 8 10 12 14 16 18 20 22 24
Percent

Inflation

Percent	Years
−12 to −10	1932
−10 to −8	1931
−8 to −6	1930
−4 to −2	1939 1938 1929 1928 1927
−2 to 0	1954 1949 1926
0 to 2	2003 2001 1998 1997 1986 1965 1964 1963 1962 1961 1960 1959 1958 1955 1953 1952 1944 1940 1936 1933
2 to 4	2006 2005 2004 2002 2000 1999 1996 1995 1994 1993 1992 1991 1985 1984 1983 1982 1972 1971 1967 1966 1957 1956 1948 1945 1943 1937 1935 1934
4 to 6	2007 1989 1988 1987 1976 1970 1968 1951 1950
6 to 8	1990 1977 1975 1969
8 to 10	1981 1978 1973 1947 1942 1941
12 to 14	1980 1979 1974
18 to 20	1946

−18 −16 −14 −12 −10 −8 −6 −4 −2 0 2 4 6 8 10 12 14 16 18 20 22 24
Percent

Annual Total Returns

Table 2-5 shows annual total returns for the seven basic asset classes for the full 82-year time period. This table can be used to compare the performance of each asset class for the same annual period. Monthly total returns for large company stocks, small company stocks, long-term corporate bonds, long-term government bonds, intermediate-term government bonds, Treasury bills, and inflation rates are presented in Appendix A: Tables A-1, A-4, A-5, A-6, A-10, A-14, and A-15, respectively.

Capital Appreciation, Income, and Reinvestment Returns

Table 2-6 provides further detail on the returns of large company stocks, and long- and intermediate-term government bonds. Total annual returns are shown as the sum of three components: capital appreciation returns, income returns, and reinvestment returns. The capital appreciation and income components are explained in Chapter 3. The third component, reinvestment return, reflects monthly income reinvested in the total return index in subsequent months in the year. Thus, for a single month the reinvestment return is zero, but over a longer period of time it is non-zero. Since the returns in Table 2-6 are annual, reinvestment return is relevant.

The annual total return formed by compounding the monthly total returns does not equal the sum of the annual capital appreciation and income components; the difference is reinvestment return. A simple example illustrates this point. In 1995, an "up" year on a total return basis, the total annual return on large company stocks was 37.4 percent. The annual capital appreciation was 34.1 percent and the annual income return was 2.9 percent. These two components sum to 37.0 percent; the remaining 0.4 percent of the total 1995 return came from the reinvestment of dividends in the market. For more information on calculating annual total and income returns, see Chapter 5.

Monthly income and capital appreciation returns for large company stocks are presented in Appendix A: Tables A-2 and A-3, respectively. Monthly income and capital appreciation returns are presented for long-term government bonds in Appendix A: Tables A-7 and A-8; and for intermediate-term government bonds in Tables A-11 and A-12.

Table 2-5
Basic Series
Annual Total Returns (in percent)

from 1926 to 1970

Year	Large Company Stocks	Small Company Stocks	Long-Term Corporate Bonds	Long-Term Government Bonds	Intermediate-Term Government Bonds	U.S. Treasury Bills	Inflation
1926	11.62	0.28	7.37	7.77	5.38	3.27	−1.49
1927	37.49	22.10	7.44	8.93	4.52	3.12	−2.08
1928	43.61	39.69	2.84	0.10	0.92	3.56	−0.97
1929	−8.42	−51.36	3.27	3.42	6.01	4.75	0.20
1930	−24.90	−38.15	7.98	4.66	6.72	2.41	−6.03
1931	−43.34	−49.75	−1.85	−5.31	−2.32	1.07	−9.52
1932	−8.19	−5.39	10.82	16.84	8.81	0.96	−10.30
1933	53.99	142.87	10.38	−0.07	1.83	0.30	0.51
1934	−1.44	24.22	13.84	10.03	9.00	0.16	2.03
1935	47.67	40.19	9.61	4.98	7.01	0.17	2.99
1936	33.92	64.80	6.74	7.52	3.06	0.18	1.21
1937	−35.03	−58.01	2.75	0.23	1.56	0.31	3.10
1938	31.12	32.80	6.13	5.53	6.23	−0.02	−2.78
1939	−0.41	0.35	3.97	5.94	4.52	0.02	−0.48
1940	−9.78	−5.16	3.39	6.09	2.96	0.00	0.96
1941	−11.59	−9.00	2.73	0.93	0.50	0.06	9.72
1942	20.34	44.51	2.60	3.22	1.94	0.27	9.29
1943	25.90	88.37	2.83	2.08	2.81	0.35	3.16
1944	19.75	53.72	4.73	2.81	1.80	0.33	2.11
1945	36.44	73.61	4.08	10.73	2.22	0.33	2.25
1946	−8.07	−11.63	1.72	−0.10	1.00	0.35	18.16
1947	5.71	0.92	−2.34	−2.62	0.91	0.50	9.01
1948	5.50	−2.11	4.14	3.40	1.85	0.81	2.71
1949	18.79	19.75	3.31	6.45	2.32	1.10	−1.80
1950	31.71	38.75	2.12	0.06	0.70	1.20	5.79
1951	24.02	7.80	−2.69	−3.93	0.36	1.49	5.87
1952	18.37	3.03	3.52	1.16	1.63	1.66	0.88
1953	−0.99	−6.49	3.41	3.64	3.23	1.82	0.62
1954	52.62	60.58	5.39	7.19	2.68	0.86	−0.50
1955	31.56	20.44	0.48	−1.29	−0.65	1.57	0.37
1956	6.56	4.28	−6.81	−5.59	−0.42	2.46	2.86
1957	−10.78	−14.57	8.71	7.46	7.84	3.14	3.02
1958	43.36	64.89	−2.22	−6.09	−1.29	1.54	1.76
1959	11.96	16.40	−0.97	−2.26	−0.39	2.95	1.50
1960	0.47	−3.29	9.07	13.78	11.76	2.66	1.48
1961	26.89	32.09	4.82	0.97	1.85	2.13	0.67
1962	−8.73	−11.90	7.95	6.89	5.56	2.73	1.22
1963	22.80	23.57	2.19	1.21	1.64	3.12	1.65
1964	16.48	23.52	4.77	3.51	4.04	3.54	1.19
1965	12.45	41.75	−0.46	0.71	1.02	3.93	1.92
1966	−10.06	−7.01	0.20	3.65	4.69	4.76	3.35
1967	23.98	83.57	−4.95	−9.18	1.01	4.21	3.04
1968	11.06	35.97	2.57	−0.26	4.54	5.21	4.72
1969	−8.50	−25.05	−8.09	−5.07	−0.74	6.58	6.11
1970	4.01	−17.43	18.37	12.11	16.86	6.52	5.49

Table 2-5 (continued)

Basic Series

Annual Total Returns (in percent)

from 1971 to 2007

Year	Large Company Stocks	Small Company Stocks	Long-Term Corporate Bonds	Long-Term Government Bonds	Intermediate-Term Government Bonds	U.S. Treasury Bills	Inflation
1971	14.31	16.50	11.01	13.23	8.72	4.39	3.36
1972	18.98	4.43	7.26	5.69	5.16	3.84	3.41
1973	–14.66	–30.90	1.14	–1.11	4.61	6.93	8.80
1974	–26.47	–19.95	–3.06	4.35	5.69	8.00	12.20
1975	37.20	52.82	14.64	9.20	7.83	5.80	7.01
1976	23.84	57.38	18.65	16.75	12.87	5.08	4.81
1977	–7.18	25.38	1.71	–0.69	1.41	5.12	6.77
1978	6.56	23.46	–0.07	–1.18	3.49	7.18	9.03
1979	18.44	43.46	–4.18	–1.23	4.09	10.38	13.31
1980	32.42	39.88	–2.76	–3.95	3.91	11.24	12.40
1981	–4.91	13.88	–1.24	1.86	9.45	14.71	8.94
1982	21.41	28.01	42.56	40.36	29.10	10.54	3.87
1983	22.51	39.67	6.26	0.65	7.41	8.80	3.80
1984	6.27	–6.67	16.86	15.48	14.02	9.85	3.95
1985	32.16	24.66	30.09	30.97	20.33	7.72	3.77
1986	18.47	6.85	19.85	24.53	15.14	6.16	1.13
1987	5.23	–9.30	–0.27	–2.71	2.90	5.47	4.41
1988	16.81	22.87	10.70	9.67	6.10	6.35	4.42
1989	31.49	10.18	16.23	18.11	13.29	8.37	4.65
1990	–3.17	–21.56	6.78	6.18	9.73	7.81	6.11
1991	30.55	44.63	19.89	19.30	15.46	5.60	3.06
1992	7.67	23.35	9.39	8.05	7.19	3.51	2.90
1993	9.99	20.98	13.19	18.24	11.24	2.90	2.75
1994	1.31	3.11	–5.76	–7.77	–5.14	3.90	2.67
1995	37.43	34.46	27.20	31.67	16.80	5.60	2.54
1996	23.07	17.62	1.40	–0.93	2.10	5.21	3.32
1997	33.36	22.78	12.95	15.85	8.38	5.26	1.70
1998	28.58	–7.31	10.76	13.06	10.21	4.86	1.61
1999	21.04	29.79	–7.45	–8.96	–1.77	4.68	2.68
2000	–9.11	–3.59	12.87	21.48	12.59	5.89	3.39
2001	–11.88	22.77	10.65	3.70	7.62	3.83	1.55
2002	–22.10	–13.28	16.33	17.84	12.93	1.65	2.38
2003	28.70	60.70	5.27	1.45	2.40	1.02	1.88
2004	10.87	18.39	8.72	8.51	2.25	1.20	3.26
2005	4.91	5.69	5.87	7.81	1.36	2.98	3.42
2006	15.80	16.17	3.24	1.19	3.14	4.80	2.54
2007	5.49	–5.22	2.60	9.88	10.05	4.66	4.08

Table 2-6

Large Company Stocks, Long-Term Government Bonds, and Intermediate-Term Government Bonds

Annual Total, Income, Capital Appreciation, and Reinvestment Returns (in percent)

from 1926 to 1970

	Large Company Stocks				Long-Term Government Bonds					Intermediate-Term Government Bonds				
Year	Capital Apprec. Return	Income Return	Reinvest-ment Return	Total Return	Capital Apprec. Return	Income Return	Reinvest-ment Return	Total Return	Year-end Yield	Capital Apprec. Return	Income Return	Reinvest-ment Return	Total Return	Year-end Yield
1926	5.72	5.41	0.50	11.62	3.91	3.73	0.13	7.77	3.54	1.51	3.78	0.10	5.38	3.61
1927	30.91	5.71	0.87	37.49	5.40	3.41	0.12	8.93	3.16	0.96	3.49	0.07	4.52	3.40
1928	37.88	4.81	0.91	43.61	−3.12	3.22	0.01	0.10	3.40	−2.73	3.64	0.01	0.92	4.01
1929	−11.91	3.98	−0.49	−8.42	−0.20	3.47	0.15	3.42	3.40	1.77	4.07	0.18	6.01	3.62
1930	−28.48	4.57	−0.98	−24.90	1.28	3.32	0.05	4.66	3.30	3.30	3.30	0.11	6.72	2.91
1931	−47.07	5.35	−1.62	−43.34	−8.46	3.33	−0.17	−5.31	4.07	−5.40	3.16	−0.08	−2.32	4.12
1932	−15.15	6.16	0.80	−8.19	12.94	3.69	0.22	16.84	3.15	5.02	3.63	0.16	8.81	3.04
1933	46.59	6.39	1.01	53.99	−3.14	3.12	−0.05	−0.07	3.36	−0.99	2.83	−0.02	1.83	3.25
1934	−5.94	4.46	0.04	−1.44	6.76	3.18	0.09	10.03	2.93	5.97	2.93	0.09	9.00	2.49
1935	41.37	4.95	1.35	47.67	2.14	2.81	0.03	4.98	2.76	4.94	2.02	0.05	7.01	1.63
1936	27.92	5.36	0.64	33.92	4.64	2.77	0.10	7.52	2.55	1.60	1.44	0.02	3.06	1.29
1937	−38.59	4.66	−1.09	−35.03	−2.48	2.66	0.05	0.23	2.73	0.05	1.48	0.03	1.56	1.14
1938	25.21	4.83	1.07	31.12	2.83	2.64	0.06	5.53	2.52	4.37	1.82	0.04	6.23	1.52
1939	−5.45	4.69	0.35	−0.41	3.48	2.40	0.06	5.94	2.26	3.18	1.31	0.03	4.52	0.98
1940	−15.29	5.36	0.14	−9.78	3.77	2.23	0.09	6.09	1.94	2.04	0.90	0.02	2.96	0.57
1941	−17.86	6.71	−0.44	−11.59	−1.01	1.94	0.00	0.93	2.04	−0.17	0.67	0.00	0.50	0.82
1942	12.43	6.79	1.12	20.34	0.74	2.46	0.02	3.22	2.46	1.17	0.76	0.00	1.94	0.72
1943	19.45	6.24	0.21	25.90	−0.37	2.44	0.02	2.08	2.48	1.23	1.56	0.02	2.81	1.45
1944	13.80	5.48	0.47	19.75	0.32	2.46	0.03	2.81	2.46	0.35	1.44	0.01	1.80	1.40
1945	30.72	4.97	0.74	36.44	8.27	2.34	0.12	10.73	1.99	1.02	1.19	0.01	2.22	1.03
1946	−11.87	4.09	−0.29	−8.07	−2.15	2.04	0.01	−0.10	2.12	−0.08	1.08	0.00	1.00	1.12
1947	0.00	5.49	0.22	5.71	−4.70	2.13	−0.06	−2.62	2.43	−0.30	1.21	0.00	0.91	1.34
1948	−0.65	6.08	0.08	5.50	0.96	2.40	0.04	3.40	2.37	0.27	1.56	0.01	1.85	1.51
1949	10.26	7.50	1.03	18.79	4.15	2.25	0.06	6.45	2.09	0.95	1.36	0.01	2.32	1.23
1950	21.78	8.77	1.16	31.71	−2.06	2.12	0.00	0.06	2.24	−0.69	1.39	0.00	0.70	1.62
1951	16.46	6.91	0.65	24.02	−6.27	2.38	−0.04	−3.93	2.69	−1.63	1.98	0.01	0.36	2.17
1952	11.78	5.93	0.66	18.37	−1.48	2.66	−0.02	1.16	2.79	−0.57	2.19	0.01	1.63	2.35
1953	−6.62	5.46	0.18	−0.99	0.67	2.84	0.12	3.64	2.74	0.61	2.55	0.07	3.23	2.18
1954	45.02	6.21	1.39	52.62	4.35	2.79	0.05	7.19	2.72	1.08	1.60	0.01	2.68	1.72
1955	26.40	4.56	0.60	31.56	−4.07	2.75	0.03	−1.29	2.95	−3.10	2.45	0.00	−0.65	2.80
1956	2.62	3.83	0.11	6.56	−8.46	2.99	−0.12	−5.59	3.45	−3.45	3.05	−0.02	−0.42	3.63
1957	−14.31	3.84	−0.30	−10.78	3.82	3.44	0.20	7.46	3.23	4.05	3.59	0.20	7.84	2.84
1958	38.06	4.38	0.93	43.36	−9.23	3.27	−0.14	−6.09	3.82	−4.17	2.93	−0.05	−1.29	3.81
1959	8.48	3.31	0.16	11.96	−6.20	4.01	−0.07	−2.26	4.47	−4.56	4.18	−0.01	−0.39	4.98
1960	−2.97	3.26	0.19	0.47	9.29	4.26	0.23	13.78	3.80	7.42	4.15	0.19	11.76	3.31
1961	23.13	3.48	0.28	26.89	−2.86	3.83	0.00	0.97	4.15	−1.72	3.54	0.03	1.85	3.84
1962	−11.81	2.98	0.10	−8.73	2.78	4.00	0.11	6.89	3.95	1.73	3.73	0.10	5.56	3.50
1963	18.89	3.61	0.30	22.80	−2.70	3.89	0.02	1.21	4.17	−2.10	3.71	0.03	1.64	4.04
1964	12.97	3.33	0.18	16.48	−0.72	4.15	0.07	3.51	4.23	−0.03	4.00	0.07	4.04	4.03
1965	9.06	3.21	0.18	12.45	−3.45	4.19	−0.04	0.71	4.50	−3.10	4.15	−0.03	1.02	4.90
1966	−13.09	3.11	−0.08	−10.06	−1.06	4.49	0.22	3.65	4.55	−0.41	4.93	0.17	4.69	4.79
1967	20.09	3.64	0.25	23.98	−13.55	4.59	−0.23	−9.18	5.56	−3.85	4.88	−0.02	1.01	5.77
1968	7.66	3.18	0.22	11.06	−5.51	5.50	−0.25	−0.26	5.98	−0.99	5.49	0.03	4.54	5.96
1969	−11.42	3.04	−0.13	−8.50	−10.83	5.95	−0.19	−5.07	6.87	−7.27	6.65	−0.11	−0.74	8.29
1970	0.16	3.41	0.43	4.01	4.84	6.74	0.52	12.11	6.48	8.71	7.49	0.66	16.86	5.90

Table 2-6 (continued)

Large Company Stocks, Long-Term Government Bonds, and Intermediate-Term Government Bonds

Annual Total, Income, Capital Appreciation, and Reinvestment Returns (in percent)

from 1971 to 2007

	Large Company Stocks				Long-Term Government Bonds					Intermediate-Term Government Bonds				
Year	Capital Apprec. Return	Income Return	Reinvest-ment Return	Total Return	Capital Apprec. Return	Income Return	Reinvest-ment Return	Total Return	Year-end Yield	Capital Apprec. Return	Income Return	Reinvest-ment Return	Total Return	Year-end Yield
1971	10.79	3.33	0.19	14.31	6.61	6.32	0.31	13.23	5.97	2.72	5.75	0.25	8.72	5.25
1972	15.63	3.09	0.26	18.98	−0.35	5.87	0.17	5.69	5.99	−0.75	5.75	0.16	5.16	5.85
1973	−17.37	2.86	−0.16	−14.66	−7.70	6.51	0.08	−1.11	7.26	−2.19	6.58	0.22	4.61	6.79
1974	−29.72	3.69	−0.44	−26.47	−3.45	7.27	0.54	4.35	7.60	−1.99	7.24	0.44	5.69	7.12
1975	31.55	5.37	0.29	37.20	0.73	7.99	0.47	9.20	8.05	0.12	7.35	0.36	7.83	7.19
1976	19.15	4.38	0.31	23.84	8.07	7.89	0.80	16.75	7.21	5.25	7.10	0.51	12.87	6.00
1977	−11.50	4.31	0.01	−7.18	−7.86	7.14	0.04	−0.69	8.03	−5.15	6.49	0.06	1.41	7.51
1978	1.06	5.33	0.17	6.56	−9.05	7.90	−0.03	−1.18	8.98	−4.49	7.83	0.14	3.49	8.83
1979	12.31	5.71	0.42	18.44	−9.84	8.86	−0.25	−1.23	10.12	−5.07	9.04	0.12	4.09	10.33
1980	25.77	5.73	0.92	32.42	−14.00	9.97	0.08	−3.95	11.99	−6.81	10.55	0.17	3.91	12.45
1981	−9.72	4.89	−0.08	−4.91	−10.33	11.55	0.64	1.86	13.34	−4.55	12.97	1.03	9.45	13.96
1982	14.76	5.50	1.15	21.41	23.95	13.50	2.91	40.36	10.95	14.23	12.81	2.06	29.10	9.90
1983	17.27	5.00	0.24	22.51	−9.82	10.38	0.09	0.65	11.97	−3.30	10.35	0.35	7.41	11.41
1984	1.39	4.56	0.31	6.27	2.32	11.74	1.42	15.48	11.70	1.22	11.68	1.12	14.02	11.04
1985	26.34	5.10	0.72	32.16	17.84	11.25	1.88	30.97	9.56	9.01	10.29	1.04	20.33	8.55
1986	14.63	3.74	0.10	18.47	14.99	8.98	0.56	24.53	7.89	6.99	7.72	0.43	15.14	6.85
1987	2.03	3.64	−0.44	5.23	−10.69	7.92	0.06	−2.71	9.20	−4.75	7.47	0.19	2.90	8.32
1988	12.41	4.17	0.24	16.81	0.36	8.97	0.34	9.67	9.18	−2.26	8.24	0.13	6.10	9.17
1989	27.26	3.85	0.38	31.49	8.62	8.81	0.68	18.11	8.16	4.34	8.46	0.49	13.29	7.94
1990	−6.56	3.36	0.03	−3.17	−2.61	8.19	0.61	6.18	8.44	1.02	8.15	0.56	9.73	7.70
1991	26.31	3.82	0.42	30.55	10.10	8.22	0.98	19.30	7.30	7.36	7.43	0.67	15.46	5.97
1992	4.46	3.03	0.18	7.67	0.34	7.26	0.45	8.05	7.26	0.64	6.27	0.28	7.19	6.11
1993	7.06	2.83	0.11	9.99	10.71	7.17	0.35	18.24	6.54	5.56	5.53	0.15	11.24	5.22
1994	−1.54	2.82	0.03	1.31	−14.29	6.59	−0.08	−7.77	7.99	−11.14	6.07	−0.08	−5.14	7.80
1995	34.11	2.91	0.41	37.43	23.04	7.60	1.03	31.67	6.03	9.66	6.69	0.45	16.80	5.38
1996	20.26	2.54	0.27	23.07	−7.37	6.18	0.26	−0.93	6.73	−3.90	5.82	0.18	2.10	6.16
1997	31.01	2.11	0.25	33.36	8.51	6.64	0.71	15.85	6.02	1.95	6.14	0.30	8.38	5.73
1998	26.67	1.68	0.24	28.58	6.89	5.83	0.34	13.06	5.42	4.66	5.29	0.25	10.21	4.68
1999	19.53	1.36	0.15	21.04	−14.35	5.57	−0.19	−8.96	6.82	−7.06	5.30	−0.01	−1.77	6.45
2000	−10.14	1.10	−0.07	−9.11	14.36	6.50	0.62	21.48	5.58	5.94	6.19	0.46	12.59	5.07
2001	−13.04	1.18	−0.03	−11.88	−1.89	5.53	0.06	3.70	5.75	3.23	4.27	0.12	7.62	4.42
2002	−23.37	1.39	−0.13	−22.10	11.69	5.59	0.56	17.84	4.84	8.65	3.98	0.30	12.93	2.61
2003	26.38	2.00	0.31	28.70	−3.36	4.80	0.01	1.45	5.11	−0.48	2.85	0.03	2.40	2.97
2004	8.99	1.75	0.13	10.87	3.26	5.02	0.23	8.51	4.84	−1.07	3.28	0.04	2.25	3.47
2005	3.00	1.84	0.07	4.91	3.02	4.69	0.10	7.81	4.61	−2.58	3.92	0.03	1.36	4.34
2006	13.62	2.01	0.17	15.80	−3.64	4.68	0.15	1.19	4.91	−1.51	4.54	0.11	3.14	4.65
2007	3.53	1.96	0.00	5.49	4.69	4.86	0.33	9.88	4.50	5.33	4.44	0.28	10.05	3.28

Rolling Period Returns

The highest and lowest returns on the basic series, expressed as annual rates, are shown for 1-, 5-, 10-, and 20-year holding periods in Table 2-7. This exhibit also shows the number of times that an asset had a positive return, and the number of times that an asset's return was the highest among all those studied. The number of times positive (or times highest) is compared to the total number of observations—that is, 82 annual, 78 overlapping 5-year, 73 overlapping 10-year, and 63 overlapping 20-year holding periods.

Tables 2-8, 2-9, and 2-10 show the compound annual total returns for 5-, 10-, and 20-year holding periods. Often, these calculations are referred to as rolling period returns as they are obtained by rolling a data window of fixed length along each time series. They are useful for examining the behavior of returns for holding periods similar to those actually experienced by investors and show the effects of time diversification. Holding assets for long periods of time has the effect of lowering the risk of experiencing a loss in asset value.

Table 2-7
Basic Series
Maximum and Minimum Values of Returns for 1-, 5-, 10-, and 20-Year Holding Periods
(compound annual rates of return in percent)

Series

Annual Returns	Maximum Value Return and Year(s)		Minimum Value Return and Year(s)		Times Positive (out of 82 years)	Times Highest Returning Asset
Large Company Stocks	53.99	1933	–43.34	1931	59	16
Small Company Stocks	142.87	1933	–58.01	1937	57	36
Long-Term Corporate Bonds	42.56	1982	–8.09	1969	65	6
Long-Term Government Bonds	40.36	1982	–9.18	1967	61	9
Intermediate-Term Govt. Bonds	29.10	1982	–5.14	1994	74	3
U.S. Treasury Bills	14.71	1981	–0.02	1938	81	6
Inflation	18.16	1946	–10.30	1932	72	6

5-Year Rolling Period Returns	Maximum Value Return and Year(s)		Minimum Value Return and Year(s)		(out of 78 overlapping 5-year periods)	Times Highest Returning Asset
Large Company Stocks	28.55	1995–99	–12.47	1932	68	23
Small Company Stocks	45.90	1941–45	–27.54	1932	69	43
Long-Term Corporate Bonds	22.51	1982–86	–2.22	1969	75	7
Long-Term Government Bonds	21.62	1982–86	–2.14	1969	72	2
Intermediate-Term Govt. Bonds	16.98	1982–86	0.96	1959	78	2
U.S. Treasury Bills	11.12	1979–83	0.07	1942	78	0
Inflation	10.06	1977–81	–5.42	1932	71	1

10-Year Rolling Period Returns	Maximum Value Return and Year(s)		Minimum Value Return and Year(s)		(out of 73 overlapping 10-year periods)	Times Highest Returning Asset
Large Company Stocks	20.06	1949–58	–0.89	1938	71	20
Small Company Stocks	30.38	1975–84	–5.70	1938	71	43
Long-Term Corporate Bonds	16.32	1982–91	0.98	1956	73	6
Long-Term Government Bonds	15.56	1982–91	–0.07	1959	72	0
Intermediate-Term Govt. Bonds	13.13	1982–91	1.25	1956	73	2
U.S. Treasury Bills	9.17	1978–87	0.15	1942	73	1
Inflation	8.67	1973–82	–2.57	1935	67	1

20-Year Rolling Period Returns	Maximum Value Return and Year(s)		Minimum Value Return and Year(s)		(out of 63 overlapping 20-year periods)	Times Highest Returning Asset
Large Company Stocks	17.87	1980–99	3.11	1948	63	9
Small Company Stocks	21.13	1942–61	5.74	1948	63	54
Long-Term Corporate Bonds	12.13	1982–01	1.34	1969	63	0
Long-Term Government Bonds	12.09	1982–01	0.69	1969	63	0
Intermediate-Term Govt. Bonds	9.97	1981–00	1.58	1959	63	0
U.S. Treasury Bills	7.72	1972–91	0.42	1950	63	0
Inflation	6.36	1966–85	0.07	1945	63	0

Table 2-8
Basic Series
Compound Annual Returns for 5-Year Holding Periods (percent per annum)

from 1926 to 1970

Period	Large Company Stocks	Small Company Stocks	Long-Term Corporate Bonds	Long-Term Government Bonds	Intermediate Government Bonds	U.S. Treasury Bills	Inflation
1926–1930	8.68	–12.44	5.76	4.93	4.69	3.42	–2.10
1927–1931	–5.10	–23.74	3.87	2.25	3.11	2.98	–3.75
1928–1932	–12.47	–27.54	4.52	3.69	3.95	2.54	–5.42
1929–1933	–11.24	–19.06	6.01	3.66	4.13	1.89	–5.14
1930–1934	–9.93	–2.37	8.09	4.95	4.71	0.98	–4.80
1931–1935	3.12	14.99	8.42	5.01	4.77	0.53	–3.04
1932–1936	22.47	45.83	10.26	7.71	5.90	0.35	–0.84
1933–1937	14.29	23.96	8.60	4.46	4.45	0.22	1.96
1934–1938	10.67	9.86	7.75	5.61	5.33	0.16	1.29
1935–1939	10.91	5.27	5.81	4.81	4.46	0.13	0.78
1936–1940	0.50	–2.64	4.59	5.03	3.65	0.10	0.38
1937–1941	–7.51	–13.55	3.79	3.71	3.13	0.08	2.02
1938–1942	4.62	10.70	3.76	4.32	3.21	0.07	3.21
1939–1943	3.77	18.71	3.10	3.63	2.54	0.14	4.44
1940–1944	7.67	29.28	3.25	3.01	2.00	0.20	4.98
1941–1945	16.96	45.90	3.39	3.90	1.85	0.27	5.25
1942–1946	17.87	45.05	3.19	3.69	1.95	0.33	6.82
1943–1947	14.86	35.00	2.17	2.49	1.75	0.37	6.77
1944–1948	10.87	18.43	2.43	2.75	1.55	0.47	6.67
1945–1949	10.69	12.66	2.15	3.46	1.66	0.62	5.84
1946–1950	9.91	7.72	1.76	1.39	1.36	0.79	6.57
1947–1951	16.70	12.09	0.87	0.60	1.23	1.02	4.25
1948–1952	19.37	12.55	2.05	1.37	1.37	1.25	2.65
1949–1953	17.86	11.53	1.91	1.41	1.64	1.45	2.23
1950–1954	23.92	18.27	2.31	1.55	1.72	1.41	2.50
1951–1955	23.89	14.97	1.98	1.28	1.44	1.48	1.43
1952–1956	20.18	14.21	1.10	0.93	1.28	1.67	0.84
1953–1957	13.58	10.01	2.10	2.15	2.49	1.97	1.27
1954–1958	22.31	23.22	0.96	0.16	1.58	1.91	1.49
1955–1959	14.96	15.54	–0.29	–1.67	0.96	2.33	1.90
1956–1960	8.92	10.58	1.36	1.16	3.37	2.55	2.12
1957–1961	12.79	15.93	3.77	2.53	3.83	2.48	1.68
1958–1962	13.31	16.65	3.63	2.42	3.39	2.40	1.33
1959–1963	9.85	10.11	4.55	3.97	4.00	2.72	1.30
1960–1964	10.73	11.43	5.73	5.17	4.91	2.83	1.24
1961–1965	13.25	20.28	3.82	2.63	2.81	3.09	1.33
1962–1966	5.72	12.13	2.88	3.17	3.38	3.61	1.86
1963–1967	12.39	29.86	0.30	–0.14	2.47	3.91	2.23
1964–1968	10.16	32.37	0.37	–0.43	3.04	4.33	2.84
1965–1969	4.96	19.78	–2.22	–2.14	2.08	4.93	3.82
1966–1970	3.34	7.51	1.23	–0.02	5.10	5.45	4.54
1967–1971	8.42	12.47	3.32	1.77	5.90	5.38	4.54
1968–1972	7.53	0.47	5.85	4.90	6.75	5.30	4.61
1969–1973	2.01	–12.25	5.55	4.72	6.77	5.65	5.41
1970–1974	–2.36	–11.09	6.68	6.72	8.11	5.93	6.60

Table 2-8 (continued)

Basic Series

Compound Annual Returns for 5-Year Holding Periods (percent per annum)

from 1971 to 2007

Period	Large Company Stocks	Small Company Stocks	Long-Term Corporate Bonds	Long-Term Government Bonds	Intermediate Government Bonds	U.S. Treasury Bills	Inflation
1971–1975	3.21	0.56	6.00	6.16	6.39	5.78	6.90
1972–1976	4.87	6.80	7.42	6.82	7.19	5.92	7.20
1973–1977	–0.21	10.77	6.29	5.50	6.41	6.18	7.89
1974–1978	4.32	24.41	6.03	5.48	6.18	6.23	7.94
1975–1979	14.76	39.80	5.78	4.33	5.86	6.69	8.15
1976–1980	13.95	37.35	2.36	1.68	5.08	7.77	9.21
1977–1981	8.08	28.75	–1.33	–1.05	4.44	9.67	10.06
1978–1982	14.05	29.28	5.57	6.03	9.60	10.78	9.46
1979–1983	17.27	32.51	6.87	6.42	10.42	11.12	8.39
1980–1984	14.76	21.59	11.20	9.80	12.45	11.01	6.53
1981–1985	14.71	18.82	17.86	16.83	15.80	10.30	4.85
1982–1986	19.87	17.32	22.51	21.62	16.98	8.60	3.30
1983–1987	16.49	9.51	14.06	13.02	11.79	7.59	3.41
1984–1988	15.38	6.74	15.00	14.98	11.52	7.10	3.53
1985–1989	20.40	10.34	14.88	15.50	11.38	6.81	3.67
1986–1990	13.14	0.58	10.43	10.75	9.34	6.83	4.13
1987–1991	15.36	6.86	10.44	9.81	9.40	6.71	4.52
1988–1992	15.89	13.63	12.50	12.14	10.30	6.31	4.22
1989–1993	14.50	13.28	13.00	13.84	11.35	5.61	3.89
1990–1994	8.69	11.79	8.36	8.34	7.46	4.73	3.49
1991–1995	16.57	24.51	12.22	13.10	8.81	4.29	2.79
1992–1996	15.20	19.47	8.52	8.98	6.17	4.22	2.84
1993–1997	20.24	19.35	9.22	10.51	6.40	4.57	2.60
1994–1998	24.06	13.16	8.74	9.52	6.20	4.96	2.37
1995–1999	28.55	18.49	8.35	9.24	6.95	5.12	2.37
1996–2000	18.35	10.87	5.79	7.49	6.17	5.18	2.54
1997–2001	10.70	11.82	7.66	8.48	7.29	4.90	2.18
1998–2002	–0.59	4.31	8.29	8.85	8.18	4.17	2.32
1999–2003	–0.57	16.44	7.20	6.51	6.60	3.40	2.37
2000–2004	–2.30	14.32	10.70	10.32	7.46	2.70	2.49
2001–2005	0.54	16.44	9.30	7.72	5.22	2.13	2.49
2002–2006	6.19	15.16	7.79	7.19	4.33	2.32	2.69
2003–2007	12.83	17.23	5.12	5.70	3.79	2.92	3.03

Table 2-9
Basic Series
Compound Annual Returns for 10-Year Holding Periods (percent per annum)

from 1926 to 1970

Period	Large Company Stocks	Small Company Stocks	Long-Term Corporate Bonds	Long-Term Government Bonds	Intermediate Government Bonds	U.S. Treasury Bills	Inflation
1926–1935	5.86	0.34	7.08	4.97	4.73	1.97	–2.57
1927–1936	7.81	5.45	7.02	4.95	4.50	1.66	–2.30
1928–1937	0.02	–5.22	6.54	4.08	4.20	1.37	–1.80
1929–1938	–0.89	–5.70	6.88	4.63	4.73	1.02	–1.98
1930–1939	–0.05	1.38	6.95	4.88	4.58	0.55	–2.05
1931–1940	1.80	5.81	6.49	5.02	4.21	0.32	–1.34
1932–1941	6.43	12.28	6.97	5.69	4.51	0.21	0.58
1933–1942	9.35	17.14	6.15	4.39	3.83	0.15	2.59
1934–1943	7.17	14.20	5.40	4.62	3.93	0.15	2.85
1935–1944	9.28	16.66	4.53	3.91	3.22	0.17	2.86
1936–1945	8.42	19.18	3.99	4.46	2.75	0.18	2.79
1937–1946	4.41	11.98	3.49	3.70	2.54	0.20	4.39
1938–1947	9.62	22.24	2.96	3.40	2.48	0.22	4.97
1939–1948	7.26	18.57	2.77	3.19	2.04	0.30	5.55
1940–1949	9.17	20.69	2.70	3.24	1.83	0.41	5.41
1941–1950	13.38	25.37	2.57	2.64	1.60	0.53	5.91
1942–1951	17.28	27.51	2.02	2.13	1.59	0.67	5.53
1943–1952	17.09	23.27	2.11	1.93	1.56	0.81	4.69
1944–1953	14.31	14.93	2.17	2.08	1.60	0.96	4.43
1945–1954	17.12	15.43	2.23	2.51	1.69	1.01	4.16
1946–1955	16.69	11.29	1.87	1.33	1.40	1.14	3.96
1947–1956	18.43	13.14	0.98	0.76	1.25	1.35	2.53
1948–1957	16.44	11.27	2.07	1.76	1.93	1.61	1.96
1949–1958	20.06	17.23	1.43	0.79	1.61	1.68	1.86
1950–1959	19.35	16.90	1.00	–0.07	1.34	1.87	2.20
1951–1960	16.16	12.75	1.67	1.22	2.40	2.01	1.77
1952–1961	16.43	15.07	2.43	1.73	2.55	2.08	1.26
1953–1962	13.44	13.28	2.86	2.29	2.94	2.19	1.30
1954–1963	15.91	16.48	2.74	2.05	2.78	2.31	1.40
1955–1964	12.82	13.47	2.68	1.69	2.92	2.58	1.57
1956–1965	11.06	15.33	2.58	1.89	3.09	2.82	1.73
1957–1966	9.20	14.02	3.33	2.85	3.60	3.05	1.77
1958–1967	12.85	23.08	1.95	1.13	2.93	3.15	1.78
1959–1968	10.00	20.73	2.44	1.75	3.52	3.52	2.07
1960–1969	7.81	15.53	1.68	1.45	3.48	3.88	2.52
1961–1970	8.18	13.72	2.51	1.30	3.95	4.26	2.92
1962–1971	7.06	12.30	3.10	2.47	4.63	4.49	3.19
1963–1972	9.93	14.22	3.04	2.35	4.59	4.60	3.41
1964–1973	6.00	7.77	2.93	2.11	4.89	4.98	4.12
1965–1974	1.24	3.20	2.13	2.20	5.05	5.43	5.20
1966–1975	3.27	3.98	3.59	3.03	5.74	5.62	5.71
1967–1976	6.63	9.60	5.35	4.26	6.54	5.65	5.86
1968–1977	3.59	5.50	6.07	5.20	6.58	5.74	6.24
1969–1978	3.16	4.48	5.79	5.10	6.47	5.94	6.67
1970–1979	5.86	11.49	6.23	5.52	6.98	6.31	7.37

Table 2-9 (continued)
Basic Series
Compound Annual Returns for 10-Year Holding Periods (percent per annum)

from 1971 to 2007

Period	Large Company Stocks	Small Company Stocks	Long-Term Corporate Bonds	Long-Term Government Bonds	Intermediate Government Bonds	U.S. Treasury Bills	Inflation
1971–1980	8.44	17.53	4.16	3.90	5.73	6.77	8.05
1972–1981	6.47	17.26	2.95	2.81	5.80	7.78	8.62
1973–1982	6.68	19.67	5.93	5.76	8.00	8.46	8.67
1974–1983	10.61	28.40	6.45	5.95	8.28	8.65	8.16
1975–1984	14.76	30.38	8.46	7.03	9.11	8.83	7.34
1976–1985	14.33	27.75	9.84	8.99	10.31	9.03	7.01
1977–1986	13.82	22.90	9.95	9.70	10.53	9.14	6.63
1978–1987	15.26	18.99	9.73	9.47	10.69	9.17	6.39
1979–1988	16.33	18.93	10.86	10.62	10.97	9.09	5.93
1980–1989	17.55	15.83	13.02	12.62	11.91	8.89	5.09
1981–1990	13.93	9.32	14.09	13.75	12.52	8.55	4.49
1982–1991	17.59	11.97	16.32	15.56	13.13	7.65	3.91
1983–1992	16.19	11.55	13.28	12.58	11.04	6.95	3.81
1984–1993	14.94	9.96	14.00	14.41	11.43	6.35	3.71
1985–1994	14.40	11.06	11.57	11.86	9.40	5.76	3.58
1986–1995	14.84	11.90	11.32	11.92	9.08	5.55	3.46
1987–1996	15.28	12.98	9.48	9.39	7.77	5.46	3.68
1988–1997	18.05	16.46	10.85	11.32	8.33	5.44	3.41
1989–1998	19.19	13.22	10.85	11.66	8.74	5.29	3.12
1990–1999	18.20	15.09	8.36	8.79	7.20	4.92	2.93
1991–2000	17.46	17.49	8.96	10.26	7.48	4.74	2.66
1992–2001	12.93	15.58	8.09	8.73	6.73	4.56	2.51
1993–2002	9.33	11.58	8.75	9.67	7.29	4.37	2.46
1994–2003	11.06	14.79	7.97	8.01	6.40	4.18	2.37
1995–2004	12.07	16.39	9.52	9.78	7.20	3.90	2.43
1996–2005	9.08	13.62	7.53	7.60	5.69	3.64	2.52
1997–2006	8.42	13.48	7.72	7.83	5.80	3.60	2.44
1998–2007	5.91	10.58	6.69	7.26	5.96	3.54	2.68

Table 2-10
Basic Series
Compound Annual Returns for 20-Year Holding Periods (percent per annum)

from 1926 to 1970

Period	Large Company Stocks	Small Company Stocks	Long-Term Corporate Bonds	Long-Term Government Bonds	Intermediate Government Bonds	U.S. Treasury Bills	Inflation
1926–1945	7.13	9.36	5.52	4.72	3.73	1.07	0.07
1927–1946	6.10	8.67	5.24	4.32	3.51	0.93	0.99
1928–1947	4.71	7.64	4.74	3.74	3.33	0.80	1.53
1929–1948	3.11	5.74	4.80	3.91	3.38	0.66	1.72
1930–1949	4.46	10.61	4.80	4.06	3.20	0.48	1.61
1931–1950	7.43	15.17	4.51	3.82	2.90	0.42	2.22
1932–1951	11.72	19.65	4.47	3.90	3.04	0.44	3.02
1933–1952	13.15	20.16	4.11	3.15	2.69	0.48	3.63
1934–1953	10.68	14.56	3.77	3.34	2.76	0.55	3.64
1935–1954	13.13	16.04	3.37	3.20	2.45	0.59	3.51
1936–1955	12.48	15.17	2.92	2.89	2.07	0.66	3.37
1937–1956	11.20	12.56	2.23	2.22	1.90	0.77	3.46
1938–1957	12.98	16.63	2.52	2.58	2.20	0.91	3.45
1939–1958	13.48	17.90	2.10	1.98	1.83	0.99	3.69
1940–1959	14.15	18.78	1.85	1.57	1.58	1.14	3.79
1941–1960	14.76	18.89	2.12	1.93	2.00	1.27	3.82
1942–1961	16.86	21.13	2.22	1.93	2.07	1.37	3.37
1943–1962	15.25	18.17	2.48	2.11	2.25	1.50	2.98
1944–1963	15.11	15.70	2.45	2.06	2.19	1.63	2.90
1945–1964	14.95	14.44	2.45	2.10	2.30	1.79	2.86
1946–1965	13.84	13.29	2.23	1.61	2.24	1.97	2.84
1947–1966	13.72	13.58	2.15	1.80	2.42	2.19	2.15
1948–1967	14.63	17.03	2.01	1.45	2.43	2.38	1.87
1949–1968	14.92	18.97	1.93	1.26	2.56	2.60	1.96
1950–1969	13.43	16.21	1.34	0.69	2.41	2.87	2.36
1951–1970	12.10	13.23	2.09	1.26	3.17	3.13	2.35
1952–1971	11.65	13.67	2.77	2.10	3.58	3.28	2.22
1953–1972	11.67	13.75	2.95	2.32	3.76	3.39	2.35
1954–1973	10.85	12.04	2.83	2.08	3.83	3.64	2.75
1955–1974	6.87	8.21	2.41	1.94	3.98	4.00	3.37
1956–1975	7.10	9.51	3.08	2.46	4.41	4.21	3.70
1957–1976	7.91	11.78	4.34	3.55	5.06	4.34	3.80
1958–1977	8.12	13.95	3.99	3.15	4.74	4.44	3.98
1959–1978	6.53	12.31	4.10	3.41	4.99	4.72	4.34
1960–1979	6.83	13.49	3.93	3.46	5.22	5.09	4.92
1961–1980	8.31	15.61	3.34	2.59	4.84	5.51	5.46
1962–1981	6.76	14.75	3.03	2.64	5.21	6.12	5.87
1963–1982	8.30	16.92	4.47	4.04	6.28	6.51	6.01
1964–1983	8.28	17.63	4.68	4.01	6.57	6.80	6.12
1965–1984	7.79	16.00	5.25	4.58	7.06	7.12	6.26
1966–1985	8.66	15.25	6.67	5.97	8.00	7.31	6.36
1967–1986	10.17	16.06	7.63	6.94	8.52	7.38	6.24
1968–1987	9.27	12.04	7.88	7.31	8.62	7.44	6.31
1969–1988	9.54	11.47	8.30	7.82	8.70	7.50	6.30
1970–1989	11.55	13.64	9.58	9.01	9.42	7.59	6.22

Table 2-10 (continued)
Basic Series
Compound Annual Returns for 20-Year Holding Periods (percent per annum)

from 1971 to 2007

Period	Large Company Stocks	Small Company Stocks	Long-Term Corporate Bonds	Long-Term Government Bonds	Intermediate Government Bonds	U.S. Treasury Bills	Inflation
1971–1990	11.15	13.35	9.01	8.71	9.08	7.66	6.26
1972–1991	11.89	14.58	9.43	9.00	9.40	7.72	6.24
1973–1992	11.33	15.54	9.54	9.12	9.51	7.70	6.21
1974–1993	12.76	18.82	10.16	10.10	9.85	7.49	5.91
1975–1994	14.58	20.33	10.00	9.42	9.25	7.29	5.44
1976–1995	14.59	19.57	10.58	10.45	9.69	7.28	5.22
1977–1996	14.55	17.84	9.71	9.54	9.14	7.28	5.14
1978–1997	16.65	17.71	10.29	10.39	9.51	7.29	4.89
1979–1998	17.75	16.04	10.86	11.14	9.85	7.17	4.52
1980–1999	17.87	15.46	10.66	10.69	9.53	6.89	4.00
1981–2000	15.68	13.33	11.49	11.99	9.97	6.62	3.57
1982–2001	15.24	13.76	12.13	12.09	9.88	6.09	3.21
1983–2002	12.71	11.57	10.99	11.12	9.15	5.65	3.13
1984–2003	12.99	12.35	10.94	11.16	8.89	5.26	3.04
1985–2004	13.23	13.69	10.54	10.82	8.30	4.83	3.00
1986–2005	11.93	12.76	9.41	9.74	7.37	4.59	2.98
1987–2006	11.80	13.23	8.60	8.61	6.78	4.53	3.06
1988–2007	11.81	13.48	8.75	9.27	7.14	4.49	3.04

Portfolio Performance

A portfolio is a group of assets, such as stocks and bonds, that are held by an investor. Because stocks, bonds, and cash generally do not react identically to the same economic or market stimulus, combining these assets can often produce a more appealing risk-and-return tradeoff.

By looking at Table 2-5, one notices that there are plenty of years in which stock returns were up at times when bond returns were down, and vice versa. These offsetting movements can assist in reducing portfolio volatility. Some recent examples include the years 2000 through 2002. Large company stocks posted negative returns of −9.11, −11.88, and −22.10 percent, while long-term government bonds posted positive returns of 21.48, 3.70, and 17.84 percent. This illustrates the low correlation of stocks and bonds; that is, they tend to move independently of each other. (See Chapter 6 for a more detailed discussion on correlation).

While bond prices tend to fluctuate less than stock prices, they are still subject to price movement. By investing in a mix of asset classes such as stocks, bonds, and Treasury bills (cash), an investor may protect their portfolio from major downswings in a single asset class. One of the main advantages of diversification is that it makes investors less dependent on the performance of any single asset class.

Rolling Period Portfolio Returns

While Table 2-7 displays the performance of single asset classes over various rolling periods, Table 2-11 shows the performance of different portfolio allocations over various rolling periods. Once again, the table outlines the number of times that each portfolio has a positive return, and the number of times that each portfolio's return was the highest among all those studied. Maximum and minimum returns are also shown. The portfolios presented throughout the analysis are rebalanced so that the allocations remain the same. The data assumes reinvestment of all income and does not account for taxes or transaction costs. The exception to this is Table 2-13, which contains portfolios that never rebalance for comparison purposes.

The 1-year holding period results make it clear that 1933 was a great year for large company stocks, while long-term government bonds shined in 1982. The 30% stock and 70% bond portfolio was the only portfolio that posted positive returns during all 5-year holding periods, while the 10% stock and 90% bond portfolio was never the highest returning portfolio. The 10-year holding period analysis shows that the 100% stock and bond portfolios were the only portfolios that posted a negative 10-year holding period return. For the 20-year period, there were no negative holding period returns. The effects of time diversification are clearly evident. When portfolios, as well as individual asset classes, are held for longer periods of time, the possibility of losing portfolio value is lowered.

Summary Statistics of Portfolio Total Returns

Table 2-12 presents summary statistics of the annual total returns on each portfolio over the entire 82-year period of 1926 to 2007. The summary statistics presented are geometric mean, arithmetic mean, and standard deviation. As more fixed-income is added to the portfolio, the returns as well as the standard deviations decrease. Moving from a 100% stock portfolio to a 70% stock and 30% bond portfolio decreases the geometric mean by 1.1 percent but also decreases the standard deviation by 5.5 percent. This corresponds to the risk-return tradeoff. Large company stocks have a higher level of risk than long-term government bonds and are rewarded accordingly. One exception to the risk-return tradeoff is the return and standard deviation of the 100% bond portfolio compared to that of the 10% stock and 90% bond portfolio. This obviously defies the risk-return tradeoff and serves as an extreme case highlighting the benefits of diversification.

The portfolio's asset mix originally created by an investor inevitably changes as a result of differing returns among the various asset classes. As a result, the percentage allocated to the different asset classes will change. This change may have a dramatic effect on the risk of the portfolio. Table 2-13 presents summary statistics of the annual total returns on portfolios that neglect rebalancing. It also presents the new allocations that result. Since stocks have outperformed bonds over the long run, it only makes sense that the proportion allocated to stocks will inevitably grow over time as well. The 50% stock and 50% bond portfolio, after 82 years, turned into a 97.6% stock and 2.4% bond portfolio. The geometric mean increased from 8.4 percent to 9.5 percent; however, the standard deviation as a result also increased from 11.4 percent to 15.2 percent. Large company stocks are much more volatile than long-term government bonds.

Table 2-14 shows the compound returns by decade for the various portfolios. The 100% stock portfolio was the highest returning portfolio in every full decade except the 1930s and the 1970s, while the 100% bond portfolio has been the top performer thus far for the 2000s. Graph 2-2 graphically depicts the growth of $1.00 invested in the various portfolio allocations over the period from the end of 1925 to the end of 2007. The 100% stock portfolio is clearly the winner, but this growth was earned by taking substantial risk. The 50% stock and 50% bond portfolio falls right in the middle. Table 2-15 presents year-by-year total returns from 1926 to 2007 of the different portfolios.

Table 2-11
Portfolios
Maximum and Minimum Values of Returns for 1-, 5-, 10-, and 20-Year Holding Periods
(compound annual rates of return in percent)

Portfolio

Annual Returns	Maximum Value Return and Year(s)		Minimum Value Return and Year(s)		Times Positive (out of 82 years)	Times Highest Returning Portfolio
100% Large Company Stocks	53.99	1933	–43.34	1931	59	50
90% Stocks/10% Bonds	49.03	1933	–39.73	1931	60	0
70% Stocks/30% Bonds	38.68	1933	–32.31	1931	62	0
50% Stocks/50% Bonds	34.64	1995	–24.70	1931	64	0
30% Stocks/70% Bonds	34.68	1982	–16.96	1931	66	0
10% Stocks/90% Bonds	38.47	1982	–9.19	1931	64	0
100% Long-Term Govt. Bonds	40.36	1982	–9.18	1967	61	32

5-Year Rolling Period Returns	Maximum Value Return and Year(s)		Minimum Value Return and Year(s)		(out of 78 overlapping 5-year periods)	Times Highest Returning Portfolio
100% Large Company Stocks	28.55	1995–99	–12.47	1928–32	68	54
90% Stocks/10% Bonds	26.62	1995–99	–10.31	1928–32	71	1
70% Stocks/30% Bonds	22.74	1995–99	–6.31	1928–32	73	1
50% Stocks/50% Bonds	21.00	1982–86	–2.77	1928–32	73	2
30% Stocks/70% Bonds	21.31	1982–86	0.12	1965–69	78	2
10% Stocks/90% Bonds	21.54	1982–86	–1.38	1965–69	75	0
100% Long-Term Govt. Bonds	21.62	1982–86	–2.14	1965–69	72	18

10-Year Rolling Period Returns	Maximum Value Return and Year(s)		Minimum Value Return and Year(s)		(out of 73 overlapping 10-year periods)	Times Highest Returning Portfolio
100% Large Company Stocks	20.06	1949–58	–0.89	1929–38	71	52
90% Stocks/10% Bonds	18.50	1989–98	0.27	1929–38	73	3
70% Stocks/30% Bonds	17.31	1982–91	1.75	1965–74	73	6
50% Stocks/50% Bonds	16.96	1982–91	1.99	1965–74	73	4
30% Stocks/70% Bonds	16.49	1982–91	2.14	1965–74	73	1
10% Stocks/90% Bonds	15.90	1982–91	1.81	1950–59	73	5
100% Long-Term Govt. Bonds	15.56	1982–91	–0.07	1950–59	72	2

20-Year Rolling Period Returns	Maximum Value Return and Year(s)		Minimum Value Return and Year(s)		(out of 63 overlapping 20-year periods)	Times Highest Returning Portfolio
100% Large Company Stocks	17.87	1980–99	3.11	1929–48	63	58
90% Stocks/10% Bonds	17.27	1980–99	3.58	1929–48	63	0
70% Stocks/30% Bonds	16.03	1979–98	4.27	1929–48	63	3
50% Stocks/50% Bonds	14.75	1979–98	4.60	1929–48	63	2
30% Stocks/70% Bonds	13.37	1979–98	3.63	1955–74	63	0
10% Stocks/90% Bonds	12.53	1982–01	1.98	1950–69	63	0
100% Long-Term Govt. Bonds	12.09	1982–01	0.69	1950–69	63	0

Table 2-12
Summary Statistics of Annual Returns (in percent)
from 1926 to 2007

Portfolio (Always Rebalance)	Geometric Mean	Arithmetic Mean	Standard Deviation
100% Large Company Stocks	10.4	12.3	20.0
90% Stocks/10% Bonds	10.1	11.6	18.0
70% Stocks/30% Bonds	9.3	10.3	14.5
50% Stocks/50% Bonds	8.4	9.0	11.4
30% Stocks/70% Bonds	7.3	7.7	9.3
10% Stocks/90% Bonds	6.1	6.5	8.7
100% Long-Term Gov't Bonds	5.5	5.8	9.2

Table 2-13
Summary Statistics of Annual Returns (in percent)
from 1926 to 2007

Beginning Portfolio	Ending Portfolio (Never Rebalance)	Geometric Mean	Arithmetic Mean	Standard Deviation
100% Large Company Stocks	100% Large Company Stocks	10.4	12.3	20.0
90% Stocks/10% Bonds	99.7% Stocks/0.3% Bonds	10.2	11.9	18.9
70% Stocks/30% Bonds	99.0% Stocks/1.0% Bonds	9.9	11.3	17.0
50% Stocks/50% Bonds	97.6% Stocks/2.4% Bonds	9.5	10.6	15.2
30% Stocks/70% Bonds	94.7% Stocks/5.3% Bonds	8.8	9.7	13.4
10% Stocks/90% Bonds	82.1% Stocks/17.9% Bonds	7.6	8.1	10.7
100% Long-Term Gov't Bonds	100% Long-Term Gov't Bonds	5.5	5.8	9.2

Table 2-14
Compound Annual Rates of Return by Decade (in percent)

	1920s*	1930s	1940s	1950s	1960s	1970s	1980s	1990s	2000s**	1998-07
100% Large Company Stocks	19.2	−0.1	9.2	19.4	7.8	5.9	17.5	18.2	1.7	5.9
90% Stocks/10% Bonds	18.0	1.0	8.7	17.4	7.2	5.9	17.2	17.3	2.5	6.2
70% Stocks/30% Bonds	15.3	2.8	7.6	13.4	6.1	6.0	16.5	15.5	4.1	6.7
50% Stocks/50% Bonds	12.5	4.1	6.5	9.5	4.8	6.0	15.5	13.6	5.6	7.1
30% Stocks/70% Bonds	9.6	4.8	5.2	5.6	3.5	5.9	14.5	11.7	7.0	7.3
10% Stocks/90% Bonds	6.6	5.0	3.9	1.8	2.1	5.7	13.3	9.8	8.2	7.3
100% Long-Term Govt. Bonds	5.0	4.9	3.2	−0.1	1.4	5.5	12.6	8.8	8.8	7.3

*Based on the period 1926–1929.

**Based on the period 2000–2007.

Graph 2-2
Wealth Indices of Investments in Various Portfolio Allocations
Year-End 1925 = $1.00

from 1925 to 2007

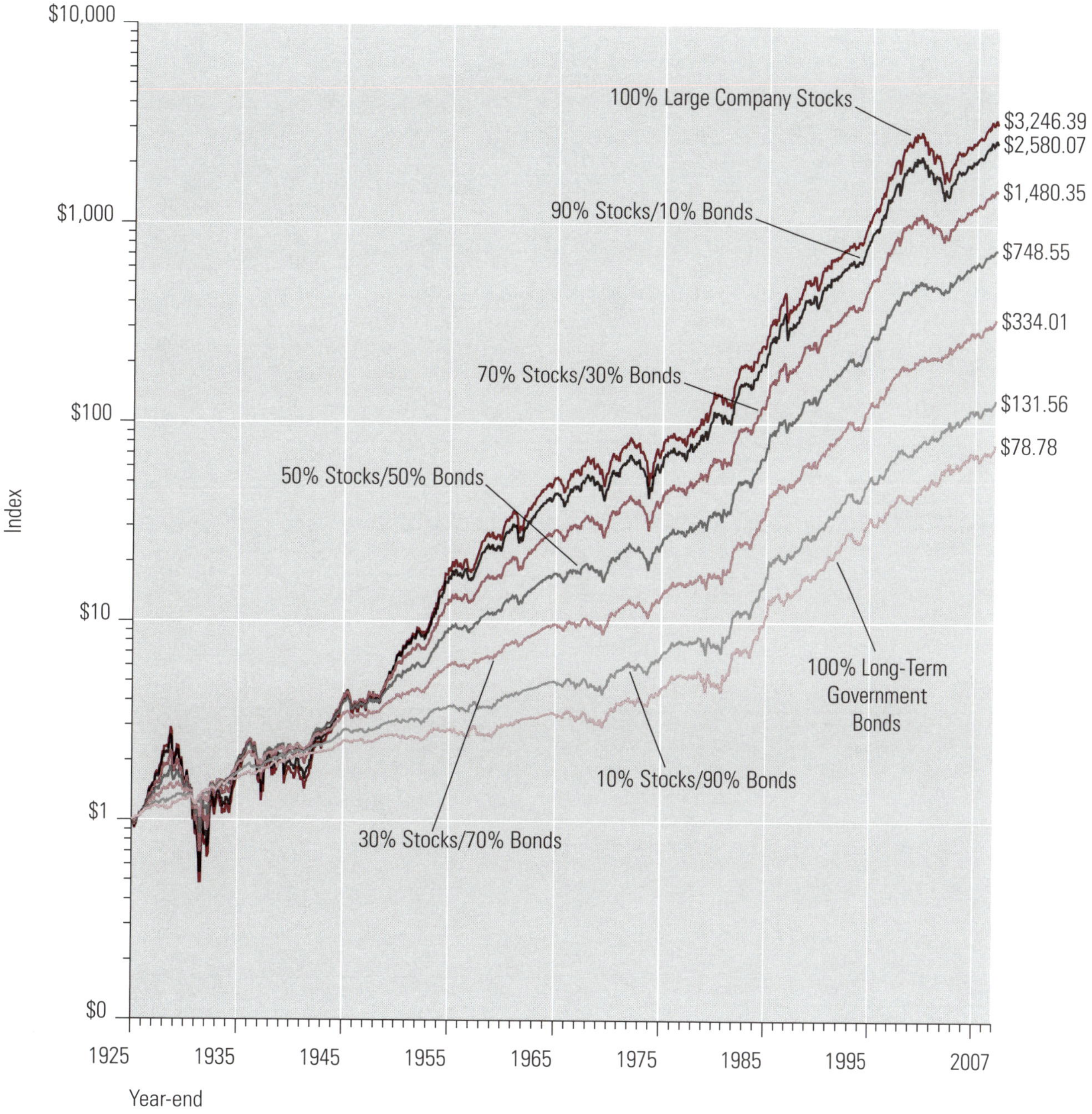

Table 2-15
Portfolios
Annual Total Returns (in percent)

from 1926 to 1970

Year	100% Large Company Stocks	90% Stocks/ 10% Bonds	70% Stocks/ 30% Bonds	50% Stocks/ 50% Bonds	30% Stocks/ 70% Bonds	10%Stocks/ 90% Bonds	100% Long-Term Govt. Bonds
1926	11.62	11.30	10.61	9.87	9.07	8.22	7.77
1927	37.49	34.45	28.49	22.69	17.06	11.60	8.93
1928	43.61	38.74	29.35	20.44	11.98	3.95	0.10
1929	–8.42	–6.76	–3.77	–1.19	0.97	2.71	3.42
1930	–24.90	–22.08	–16.33	–10.46	–4.48	1.59	4.66
1931	–43.34	–39.73	–32.31	–24.70	–16.96	–9.19	–5.31
1932	–8.19	–4.45	2.43	8.28	12.85	15.93	16.84
1933	53.99	49.03	38.68	27.89	16.80	5.56	–0.07
1934	–1.44	–0.13	2.38	4.76	6.99	9.05	10.03
1935	47.67	42.94	33.80	25.06	16.73	8.80	4.98
1936	33.92	31.15	25.69	20.35	15.12	10.02	7.52
1937	–35.03	–31.93	–25.44	–18.58	–11.34	–3.72	0.23
1938	31.12	29.24	24.93	19.99	14.51	8.61	5.53
1939	–0.41	0.65	2.51	4.00	5.09	5.77	5.94
1940	–9.78	–8.04	–4.65	–1.40	1.70	4.66	6.09
1941	–11.59	–10.33	–7.81	–5.30	–2.80	–0.31	0.93
1942	20.34	18.62	15.18	11.75	8.32	4.91	3.22
1943	25.90	23.43	18.54	13.73	9.00	4.37	2.08
1944	19.75	17.98	14.49	11.06	7.71	4.43	2.81
1945	36.44	33.72	28.39	23.18	18.11	13.16	10.73
1946	–8.07	–7.17	–5.42	–3.78	–2.23	–0.78	–0.10
1947	5.71	4.89	3.24	1.58	–0.10	–1.78	–2.62
1948	5.50	5.46	5.26	4.91	4.41	3.77	3.40
1949	18.79	17.55	15.07	12.60	10.13	7.68	6.45
1950	31.71	28.24	21.50	15.04	8.85	2.93	0.06
1951	24.02	20.97	15.05	9.36	3.88	–1.38	–3.93
1952	18.37	16.60	13.10	9.64	6.22	2.83	1.16
1953	–0.99	–0.50	0.47	1.41	2.32	3.21	3.64
1954	52.62	47.50	37.65	28.33	19.51	11.18	7.19
1955	31.56	27.98	21.02	14.32	7.89	1.70	–1.29
1956	6.56	5.42	3.08	0.68	–1.79	–4.31	–5.59
1957	–10.78	–8.99	–5.39	–1.75	1.92	5.61	7.46
1958	43.36	37.57	26.60	16.38	6.89	–1.93	–6.09
1959	11.96	10.49	7.59	4.72	1.90	–0.88	–2.26
1960	0.47	1.83	4.53	7.21	9.86	12.48	13.78
1961	26.89	24.10	18.65	13.38	8.29	3.37	0.97
1962	–8.73	–7.11	–3.90	–0.74	2.37	5.40	6.89
1963	22.80	20.52	16.03	11.66	7.40	3.25	1.21
1964	16.48	15.13	12.46	9.84	7.27	4.75	3.51
1965	12.45	11.26	8.89	6.53	4.19	1.86	0.71
1966	–10.06	–8.72	–6.02	–3.29	–0.53	2.25	3.65
1967	23.98	20.28	13.14	6.36	–0.10	–6.23	–9.18
1968	11.06	9.98	7.79	5.54	3.25	0.92	–0.26
1969	–8.50	–8.08	–7.28	–6.56	–5.91	–5.33	–5.07
1970	4.01	4.92	6.68	8.35	9.92	11.40	12.11

Table 2-15 (continued)
Portfolios
Annual Total Returns (in percent)

from 1971 to 2007

Year	100% Large Company Stocks	90% Stocks/ 10% Bonds	70% Stocks/ 30% Bonds	50% Stocks/ 50% Bonds	30% Stocks/ 70% Bonds	10%Stocks/ 90% Bonds	100% Long-Term Govt. Bonds
1971	14.31	14.30	14.22	14.05	13.79	13.44	13.23
1972	18.98	17.60	14.89	12.21	9.57	6.97	5.69
1973	−14.66	−13.29	−10.56	−7.84	−5.13	−2.44	−1.11
1974	−26.47	−23.67	−17.87	−11.83	−5.54	1.00	4.35
1975	37.20	34.28	28.50	22.84	17.29	11.86	9.20
1976	23.84	23.20	21.86	20.47	19.03	17.53	16.75
1977	−7.18	−6.53	−5.22	−3.92	−2.62	−1.33	−0.69
1978	6.56	5.85	4.39	2.87	1.29	−0.34	−1.18
1979	18.44	16.36	12.28	8.29	4.41	0.62	−1.23
1980	32.42	28.64	21.15	13.79	6.56	−0.49	−3.95
1981	−4.91	−4.15	−2.69	−1.30	0.02	1.27	1.86
1982	21.41	23.30	27.09	30.88	34.68	38.47	40.36
1983	22.51	20.20	15.65	11.22	6.91	2.71	0.65
1984	6.27	7.25	9.18	11.06	12.87	14.63	15.48
1985	32.16	32.10	31.95	31.74	31.48	31.15	30.97
1986	18.47	19.17	20.51	21.77	22.94	24.02	24.53
1987	5.23	5.05	4.22	2.82	0.92	−1.41	−2.71
1988	16.81	16.10	14.68	13.26	11.83	10.39	9.67
1989	31.49	30.19	27.56	24.90	22.21	19.48	18.11
1990	−3.17	−2.21	−0.31	1.57	3.44	5.27	6.18
1991	30.55	29.48	27.30	25.07	22.80	20.47	19.30
1992	7.67	7.73	7.84	7.93	8.00	8.04	8.05
1993	9.99	10.82	12.47	14.12	15.77	17.42	18.24
1994	1.31	0.39	−1.43	−3.25	−5.07	−6.87	−7.77
1995	37.43	36.89	35.78	34.64	33.47	32.28	31.67
1996	23.07	20.51	15.48	10.61	5.88	1.30	−0.93
1997	33.36	31.59	28.06	24.55	21.05	17.58	15.85
1998	28.58	27.33	24.60	21.59	18.33	14.86	13.06
1999	21.04	17.75	11.36	5.23	−0.63	−6.25	−8.96
2000	−9.11	−6.31	−0.53	5.46	11.69	18.16	21.48
2001	−11.88	−10.18	−6.85	−3.64	−0.58	2.32	3.70
2002	−22.10	−18.46	−10.91	−3.04	5.12	13.54	17.84
2003	28.70	25.87	20.28	14.77	9.37	4.06	1.45
2004	10.87	10.69	10.29	9.84	9.34	8.80	8.51
2005	4.91	5.28	5.96	6.58	7.12	7.60	7.81
2006	15.80	14.30	11.34	8.40	5.49	2.61	1.19
2007	5.49	6.03	7.03	7.95	8.79	9.54	9.88

Real Estate Investment Trusts

Real estate investment trusts, commonly referred to as REITs, are companies that own and operate, as well as finance, income-generating real estate. To qualify as a REIT, a company is obligated to pay out at least 90 percent of its taxable profit to shareholders on an annual basis. This distribution comes in the form of dividends. By achieving REIT status, the real estate company avoids paying income taxes since it distributes almost all of its taxable income to shareholders. Taxes are paid by the shareholders. REITs were created by the United States Congress in 1960 to allow any investor, big or small, the opportunity to invest in large institutional-grade commercial real estate—pieces of property that may have been unaffordable any other way.

Types of REITs

REITs can be categorized into three different types: equity, mortgage, and hybrid. Equity REITs are companies that own and operate income-generating real estate, while mortgage REITs invest in mortgages (loans secured by real estate). Hybrid REITs take both direct ownership in real estate and invest in mortgages. As of December 31, 2007 there are 152 publicly-traded REITs in the United States (118 equity, 29 mortgage, 5 hybrid). In most cases these companies are traded on major stock market exchanges. Investors can buy shares through a stock broker or by purchasing shares in a mutual fund, which is managed by a portfolio manager skilled in the real estate industry.

Graph 2-3
U.S. REIT Industry by Property Type*
Year-End 2007

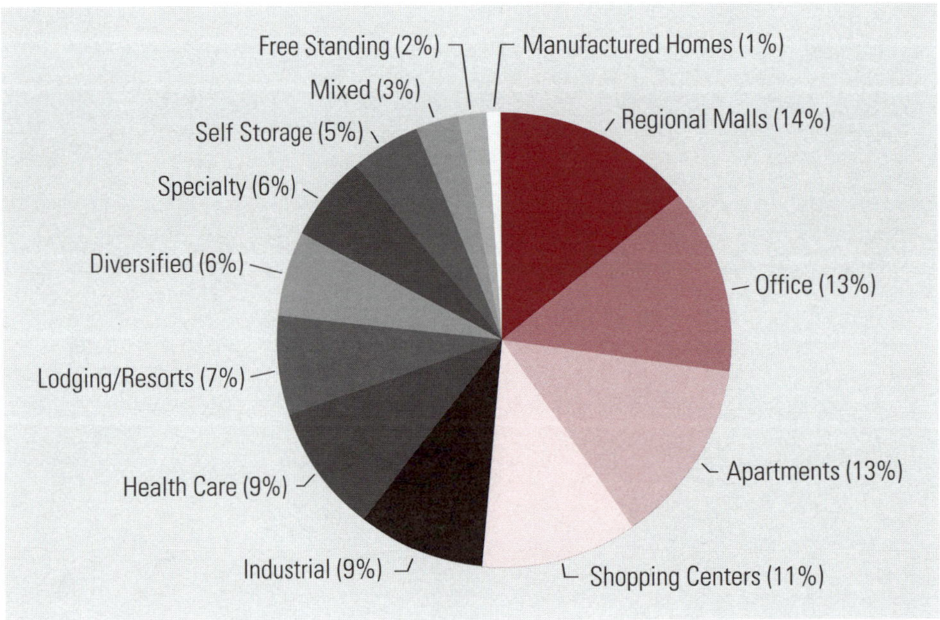

Source: National Association of Real Estate Investment Trusts®

*Numbers do not total to 100% due to rounding.

Equity REITs invest in all major property types and in most geographic regions. Graph 2-3 illustrates the breakdown of the total assets of the U.S. REIT industry by property type. A rather large percentage of the real estate held by REIT companies is invested in office buildings, residential properties, and malls and shopping centers. Other investments can be found in industrial facilities, resorts, etc.

In 2001, Standard & Poor's added REITs to the most widely followed investment performance benchmark for the U.S. equity markets—the Standard & Poor's 500 index. The addition to this famed index recognizes the significance of real estate in the overall economy.

Equity REIT Index Construction Methodology

As discussed earlier, most REITs fall into the equity REIT category. The source of the data presented throughout this section, in commentary, graphs, and tables, is that of the National Association of Real Estate Investment Trusts® (NAREIT) Equity Index.

NAREIT Equity Index

NAREIT Equity Index data is based upon the last closing price of the month for all tax-qualified REITs listed on the New York Stock Exchange (NYSE), the American Stock Exchange (AMEX), and the NASDAQ National Market System. The data is market-value-weighted. Prior to 1987, REITs were added to the index the January following their listing. Since 1987, newly formed or listed REITs are added to the index in the month in which they become public. Newly issued shares by existing REITs are added to the total shares outstanding figure in the month that the shares are issued. Only common shares issued by the REIT are included in the index. The total return calculation is based upon the weighting at the beginning of the period. Only those REITs listed for the entire period are used in the total return calculation. Dividends are included in the month based upon their payment date. There is no smoothing of income. Liquidating dividends, whether full or partial, are treated as income.

Historical Returns on Equity REITs

Graph 2-4 depicts the growth of $1.00 invested in equity REITs as well as U.S. small and large company stocks, long-term government bonds, Treasury bills, and a hypothetical asset returning the inflation rate over the period from the end of 1971 to the end of 2007. Of the asset classes shown, small company stocks accumulated the highest ending wealth. An investment of $1.00 in small company stocks at year-end 1971 would have grown to $124.29 by the end of December 2007, a compound return of 14.3 percent. Notice, however, that the same investment in equity REITs would have returned $81.86, a compound return of 13.0 percent. Equity REITs outperformed large company stocks, long-term government bonds, Treasury bills, and inflation during the time period.

Graph 2-4
Wealth Indices of Investments in Equity REITs and Basic Series
Year-End 1971 = $1.00

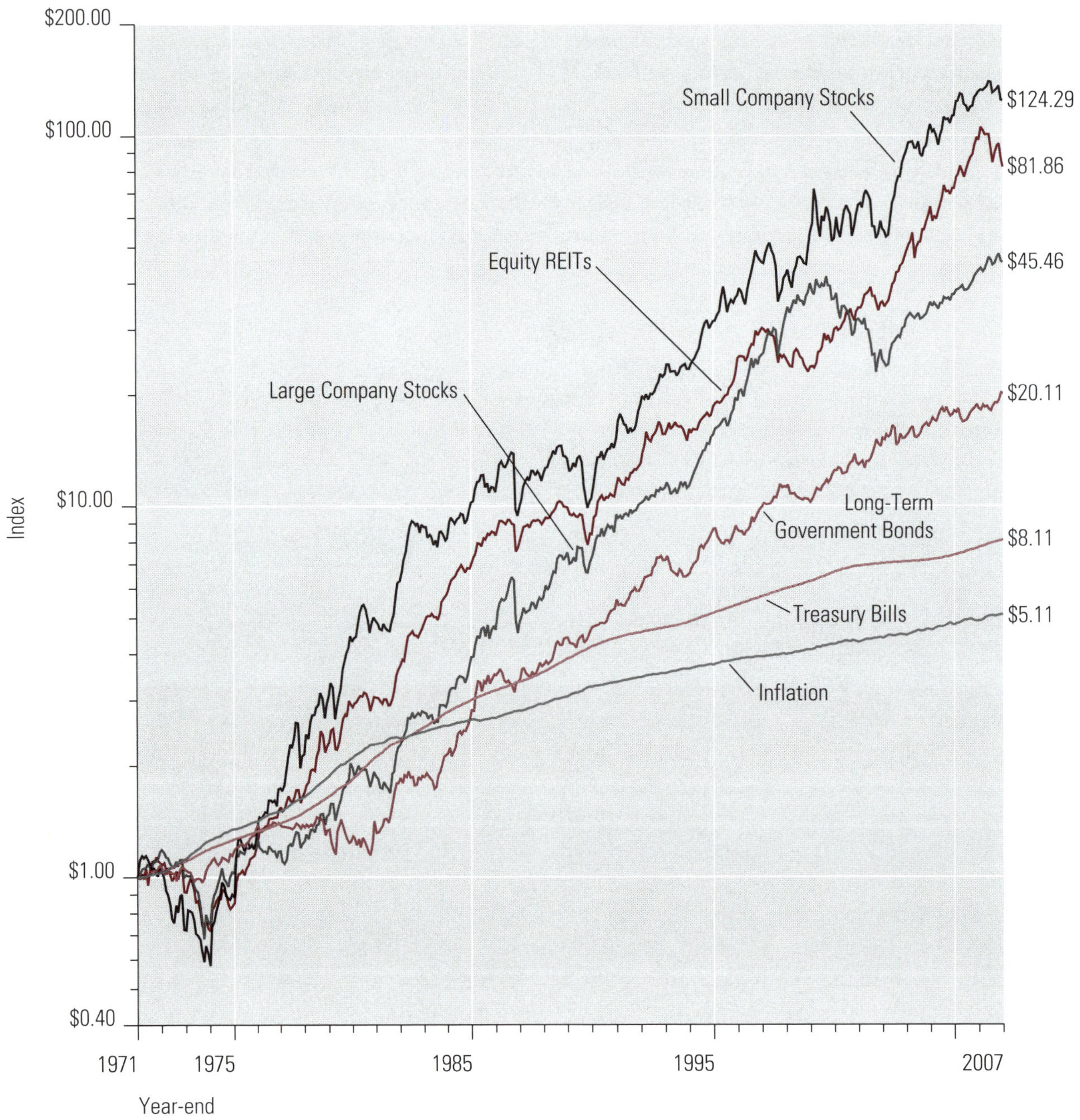

Income Returns

REITs are obligated to pay out at least 90 percent of their taxable profit to shareholders on an annual basis. As a result, the income generated from REITs has proven to be steady and reasonably predictable.

Graph 2-5 shows both the income return and capital appreciation return of REITs on an annual basis from 1972 to 2007. REITs, similar to equity asset classes, can be quite volatile but do offer the potential for good price appreciation. However, price appreciation is by no means guaranteed (note 2007's return of –19.1 percent). On the other hand, the income produced by REITs has been relatively stable since 1972. Equity REITs posted an average annual income return during that period of 8.1 percent. The highest annual income return was 18.8 percent in 1980, while the lowest was 3.8 percent in 2007.

Graph 2-5
Annual Returns on Equity REITs
from 1972 to 2007

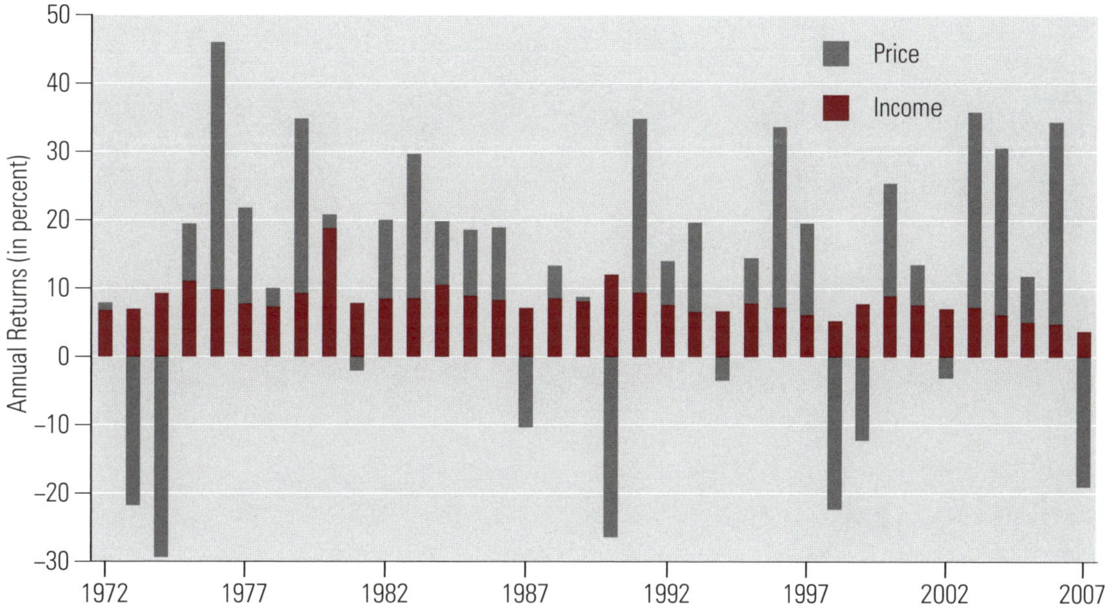

Diversification

Along with the relatively predictable revenue stream provided by equity REITs, they can also offer another important advantage to investors—diversification. As the REIT industry has grown over time, REITs have exhibited characteristics similar to both bonds and stocks. REITs typically provide a consistent stream of dividend payments similar to bonds, and hold the potential for long-term capital appreciation, similar to stocks.

In addition, REIT returns have had a low and declining correlation to both stocks and bonds. The cross-correlation between two asset classes measures the extent to which they are linearly related. The correlation coefficient measures the sensitivity of returns on one asset class to the returns of another. A value of +1 indicates a perfectly positive relationship, –1 indicates a perfectly inverse relationship, and 0 indicates no relationship between the two asset classes. Correlation is discussed in greater detail in Chapter 6, Statistical Analysis of Returns.

Graph 2-6 shows the cross-correlations between large company stocks and equity REITs and between long-term government bonds and equity REITs for 60-month rolling periods. The first rolling period covered is January 1972 to December 1976. The graph illustrates that cross correlation between large company stocks and equity REITS and the correlation between long-term government bonds and equity REITS has generally fallen since the early 1990s. The cross-correlation between equity REITs and long-term government bonds has been negative for much of the 2000s.

Graph 2-6
Rolling 60-Month Correlations of Equity REITs
from January 1972—December 1976 to January 2003—December 2007

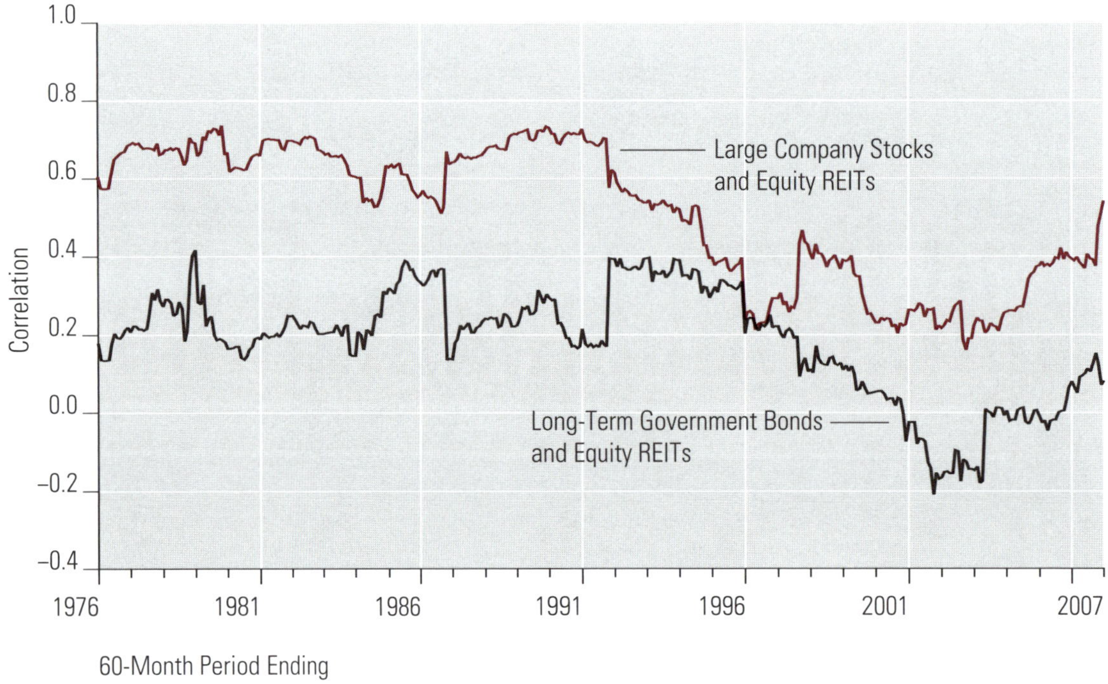

Summary Statistics for Equity REITs and Basic Series

Table 2-16 shows summary statistics of annual total returns for equity REITs and the basic series over the period 1972 to 2007. The summary statistics presented are geometric mean, arithmetic mean, and standard deviation.

While small company stocks posted the highest geometric mean over the time period analyzed, it was accompanied by the highest amount of risk. When comparing equity REITs to large company stocks, equity REITs produced a higher return with only slightly higher risk.

Table 2-16
Summary Statistics of Annual Returns (in percent)
From 1972 to 2007

	Geometric Mean	Arithmetic Mean	Standard Deviation
Equity REITs	13.0	14.4	17.4
Large Company	11.2	12.5	17.0
Small Company	14.3	16.5	22.5
Long-Term Corp	8.6	9.1	10.7
Long-Term Govt	8.7	9.3	11.5
Inter-Term Govt	8.0	8.1	6.6
Treasury Bills	6.0	6.0	2.9
Inflation	4.6	4.7	3.2

Table 2-17 presents annual cross-correlations and serial correlations from 1972 to 2007 for equity REITs and the six basic series and inflation. Mentioned earlier, equity REITs, when compared to large company stocks and bonds, provide a low cross-correlation. The cross-correlation between equity REITs and U.S. Treasury Bills is negative. The serial correlation, or the extent to which the return in one period is related to the return in the next period (discussed in greater detail in Chapter 6), of equity REITs suggests no pattern, and the return from period to period can best be interpreted as random or unpredictable.

Table 2-17
Serial and Cross-Correlations of Historical Annual Returns
From 1972 to 2007

	Equity Reits	Large Company Stocks	Small Company Stocks	Long-Term Corp Bonds	Long-Term Govt Bonds	Intermediate Govt Bonds	Treasury Bills	Inflation
Equity REITS	1.00							
Large Company Stocks	0.46	1.00						
Small Company Stocks	0.75	0.67	1.00					
Long-Term Corp Bonds	0.28	0.35	0.18	1.00				
Long-Term Govt Bonds	0.17	0.27	0.05	0.95	1.00			
Inter-Term Govt Bonds	0.11	0.22	0.04	0.90	0.92	1.00		
Treasury Bills	−0.05	0.05	−0.01	0.02	0.04	0.31	1.00	
Inflation	−0.14	−0.22	−0.01	−0.43	−0.37	−0.19	0.62	1.00
Serial Correlation	0.09	0.03	0.00	−0.06	−0.25	−0.02	0.82	0.74

In summary, equity REITs have historically offered an attractive risk/return trade-off for investors. They have provided a current income stream along with the potential for long-term capital appreciation. Due to the declining correlation of REIT returns with other investments, diversification benefits have also been increasing.

Chapter 3

Description of the Basic Series

This chapter presents the returns for the seven basic asset classes and describes the construction of these returns. More detail on the construction of some series can be found in the January 1976 *Journal of Business* article, referenced at the end of the Introduction. Annual total returns and capital appreciation returns for each asset class are formed by compounding the monthly returns that appear in Appendix A. Annual income returns are formed by summing the monthly income payments and dividing this sum by the beginning-of-year price. Returns are formed assuming no taxes or transaction costs, except for returns on small company stocks that show the performance of an actual, tax-exempt investment fund including transaction and management costs, starting in 1982.

Large Company Stocks

Overview

One dollar invested in large company stocks at year-end 1925, with dividends reinvested, grew to $3,246.39 by year-end 2007; this represents a compound annual growth rate of 10.4 percent. [See Graph 3-1.] Capital appreciation alone caused $1.00 to grow to $115.10 over the 82-year period, a compound annual growth rate of 6.0 percent. Annual total returns ranged from a high of 54.0 percent in 1933 to a low of –43.3 percent in 1931. The 82-year average annual dividend yield was 4.2 percent.

Total Returns

From September 1997 to the present, the large company stock total return is provided by Standard and Poor's, which calculates the total return based on the daily reinvestment of dividends on the ex-dividend date. Standard and Poor's uses closing pricing (usually from the New York Stock Exchange) in their calculation. From 1977 to August 1997, the total return was provided by the American National Bank and Trust Company of Chicago, which modified monthly income numbers provided by Wilshire Associates, Santa Monica, California. Dividends (measured as of the ex-dividend date) are accumulated over the month and invested on the last trading day of the month in the S&P 500 index at the day's closing level. Wilshire uses the last trading price of the day for the stocks, usually from the Pacific Stock Exchange. Prior to 1977, the total return for a given month was calculated by summing the capital appreciation return and the income return as described on the following pages.

The large company stock total return index is based upon the S&P Composite Index. This index is a readily available, carefully constructed, market-value-weighted benchmark of large company stock performance. Market-value-weighted means that the weight of each stock in the index, for a given month, is proportionate to its market capitalization (price times the number of shares outstanding) at the beginning of that month. Currently, the S&P Composite includes 500 of the largest stocks (in terms of stock market value) in the United States; prior to March 1957 it consisted of 90 of the largest stocks.

Graph 3-1
Large Company Stocks
Return Indices, Returns, and Dividend Yields

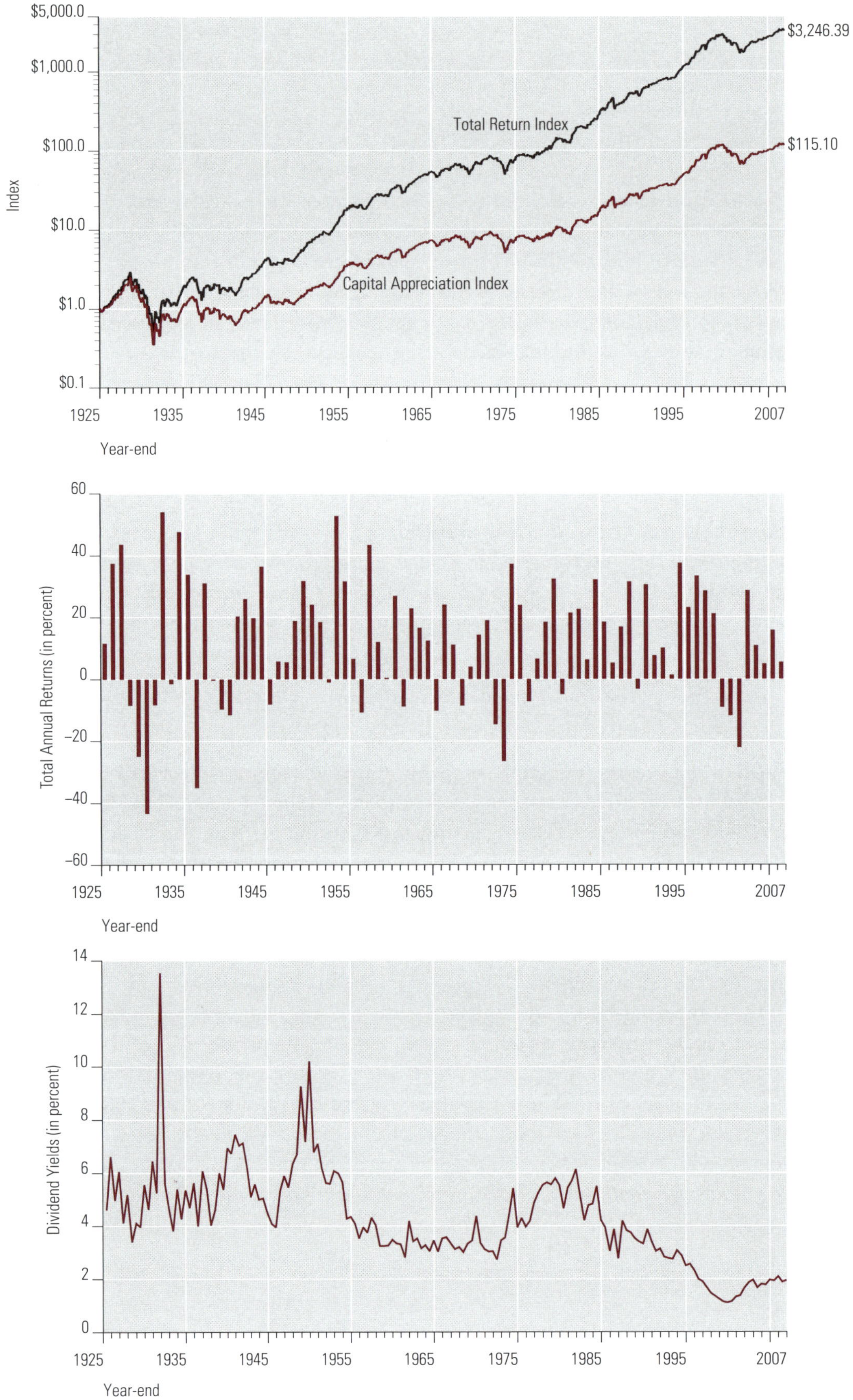

Capital Appreciation Return

The capital appreciation component of the large company stock total return is the change in the S&P 500-stock index (or 90-stock index) as reported in *The Wall Street Journal* for the period 1977–2007, and in Standard & Poor's *Trade and Securities Statistics* from 1926–1976.

Income Return

For 1977–2007, the income return was calculated as the difference between the total return and the capital appreciation return. For 1926–1976, quarterly dividends were extracted from rolling yearly dividends reported quarterly in S&P's *Trade and Securities Statistics*, then allocated to months within each quarter using proportions taken from the 1974 actual distribution of monthly dividends within quarters.

The dividend yields depicted in the bottom graph of Graph 3-1 were derived by annualizing the semiannual income return.

Small Company Stocks

Overview

One dollar invested in small company stocks at year-end 1925 grew to $15,091.10 by year-end 2007. [See Graph 3-2.] This represents a compound annual growth rate of 12.5 percent over the past 82 years. Total annual returns ranged from a high of 142.9 percent in 1933 to a low of –58.0 percent in 1937.

DFA U.S. Micro Cap Portfolio (April 2001–December 2007)

For April 2001 to December 2007, the small company stock return series is the total return achieved by the DFA U.S. Micro Cap Portfolio net of fees and expenses. In April 2001, Dimensional Fund Advisors renamed the DFA U.S. 9 -10 Small Company Portfolio (see below) the DFA U.S. Micro Cap Portfolio and changed some of the criteria. The fund is designed to capture the returns and diversification benefits of a broad cross-section of U.S. small companies on a market-cap weighted basis. The fund's target buy range includes those companies whose market capitalization falls in the lowest 4 percent of the market universe, defined as the aggregate of the New York Stock Exchange, American Stock Exchange, and NASDAQ National Market System. As of year-end 2007, companies with a market capitalization of approximately $880 million or less were eligible for purchase.

The market universe is examined on a dynamic basis to determine which issues are eligible for purchase or sale based on market capitalization. To minimize turnover, a hold or buffer range is created for issues that migrate above the buy range. The upper bound of the hold range is the 5th percentile of the market universe. Issues that migrate above the hold range are eligible for sale and proceeds are reinvested into the portfolio.

At year-end 2007, the DFA U.S. Micro Cap Portfolio contained 2,421 stocks, with a weighted average market capitalization of $507 million. The unweighted average market capitalization was $270 million, while the median was $164 million.

Graph 3-2
Small Company Stocks
Return Index and Returns

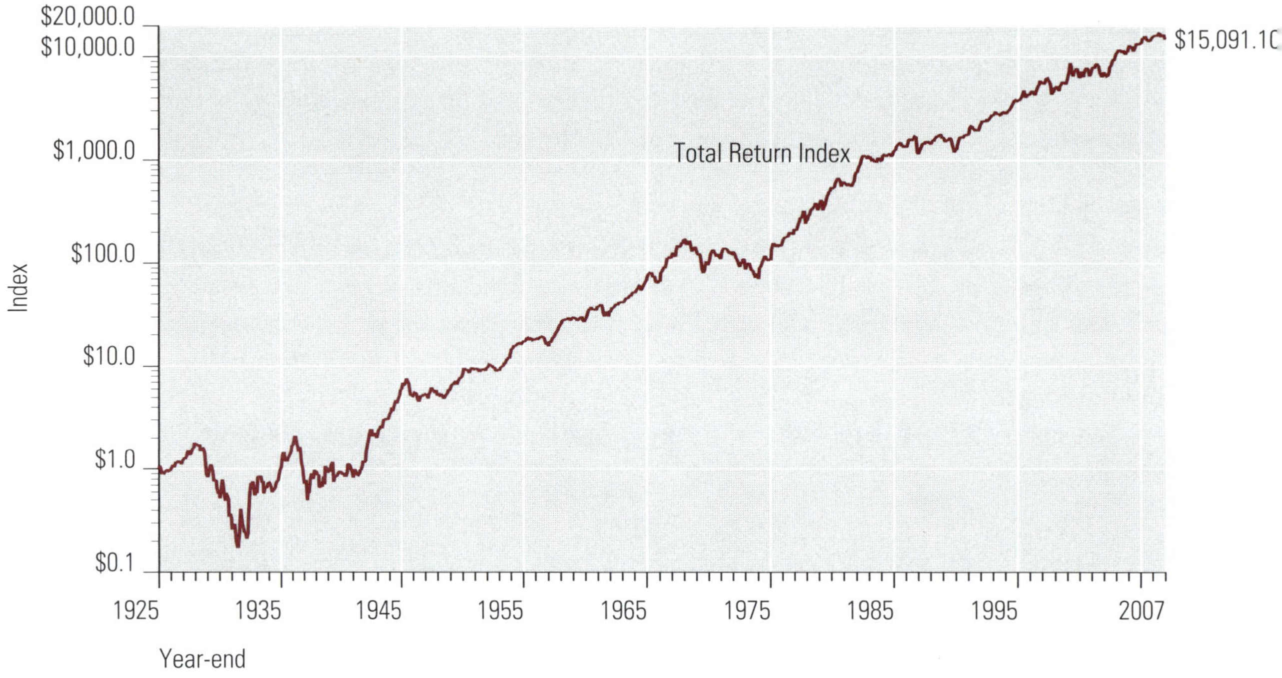

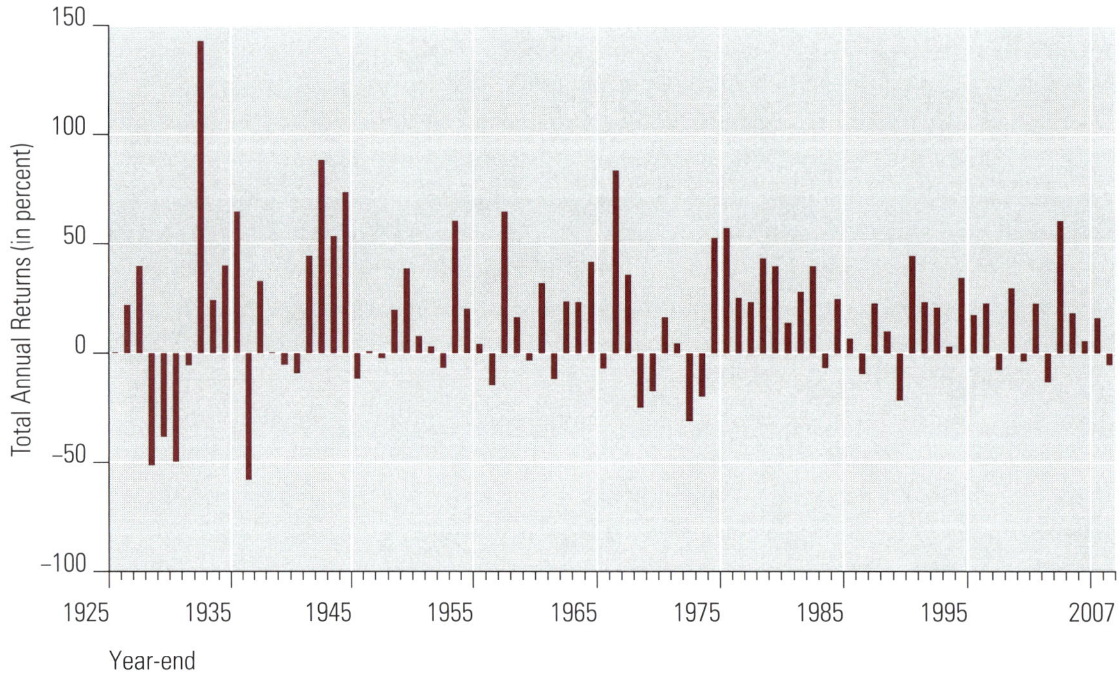

DFA U.S. 9–10 Small Company Portfolio (January 1982–March 2001)

For January 1982–March 2001, the small company stock return series was the total return achieved by the DFA U.S. Small Company 9–10 (for ninth and tenth deciles) Portfolio. The fund's target buy range was a market-value-weighted universe of the ninth and tenth deciles of the New York Stock Exchange (NYSE), plus stocks listed on the American Stock Exchange (AMEX) and NASDAQ National Market (NMS) with the same or less capitalization as the upper bound of the NYSE ninth decile. Since the lower bound of the tenth decile is near zero, stocks were not purchased if they were smaller than $10 million in market capitalization (although they were held if they fell below that level).

Stocks remained in the portfolio if they rose into the eighth NYSE decile, but they were sold when they rose into the seventh NYSE decile or higher. The returns for the DFA U.S. 9–10 Small Company Portfolio are net of transaction costs, fees and expenses, while the returns for the other asset classes and for pre-1982 small company stocks are before-transaction-cost returns and are not diminished by fees and expenses.

NYSE Fifth Quintile Returns (1926–1981)

The equities of smaller companies from 1926 to 1980 are represented by the historical series developed by Professor Rolf W. Banz (see reference section). This is composed of stocks making up the fifth quintile (i.e., the ninth and tenth deciles) of the New York Stock Exchange (NYSE); the stocks on the NYSE are ranked by capitalization (price times number of shares outstanding), and each decile contains an equal number of stocks at the beginning of each formation period. The ninth and tenth decile portfolio was first ranked and formed as of December 31, 1925. This portfolio was "held" for five years, with value-weighted portfolio returns computed monthly. Every five years the portfolio was rebalanced (i.e., all of the stocks on the NYSE were re-ranked, and a new portfolio of those falling in the ninth and tenth deciles was formed) as of December 31, 1930 and every five years thereafter through December 31, 1980. This method avoided survivorship bias by including the return after the delisting or failure of a stock in constructing the portfolio returns. (Survivorship bias is caused by studying only stocks that have survived events such as bankruptcy and acquisition.)

For 1981, Dimensional Fund Advisors, Inc. updated the returns using Professor Banz' methods. The data for 1981 are significant to only three decimal places (in decimal form) or one decimal place when returns are expressed in percent.

Long-Term Corporate Bonds

Overview

One dollar invested in long-term high-grade corporate bonds at the end of 1925 was worth $105.86 by year-end 2007. [See Graph 3-3.] The compound annual growth rate over the 82-year period was 5.9 percent. Total annual returns ranged from a high of 42.6 percent in 1982 to a low of –8.1 percent in 1969.

Total Returns

For 1969–2007, corporate bond total returns are represented by the Citigroup Long-Term High-Grade Corporate Bond Index (formerly Salomon Brothers). Since most large corporate bond transactions take place over the counter, a major dealer is the natural source of these data. The index includes nearly all Aaa- and Aa-rated bonds. If a bond is downgraded during a particular month, its return for the month is included in the index before removing the bond from future portfolios.

Over 1926–1968 total returns were calculated by summing the capital appreciation returns and the income returns. For the period 1946–1968, Ibbotson and Sinquefield backdated the Salomon Brothers' index, using Salomon Brothers' monthly yield data with a methodology similar to that used by Salomon for 1969–2007. Capital appreciation returns were calculated from yields assuming (at the beginning of each monthly holding period) a 20-year maturity, a bond price equal to par, and a coupon equal to the beginning-of-period yield.

For the period 1926–1945, Standard & Poor's monthly High-Grade Corporate Composite yield data were used, assuming a 4 percent coupon and a 20-year maturity. The conventional present-value formula for bond price was used for the beginning and end-of-month prices. (This formula is presented in Ross, Stephen A., and Randolph W. Westerfield, *Corporate Finance*, Times Mirror/Mosby, St. Louis, 1990, p. 97 ["Level-Coupon Bonds"]). The monthly income return was assumed to be one-twelfth the coupon.

Long-Term Government Bonds

Overview

One dollar invested in long-term government bonds at year-end 1925, with coupons reinvested, grew to $78.78 by year-end 2007; this represents a compound annual growth rate of 5.5 percent. [See Graph 3-4.] Returns from the capital appreciation component alone caused $1.00 to grow to $1.08 over the 82-year period, representing a compound annual growth rate of 0.09 percent. Total annual returns ranged from a high of 40.4 percent in 1982 to a low of –9.2 percent in 1967.

Total Returns

The total returns on long-term government bonds from 1977 to 2007 are constructed with data from The Wall Street Journal. The bond used in 2007 is the 6.375 percent issue that matures on August 15, 2027. The data from 1926–1976 are obtained from the Government Bond File at the Center for Research in Security Prices (CRSP) at the University of Chicago Graduate School of Business. The bonds used to construct the index are shown in Table 3-1. To the greatest extent possible, a one-bond portfolio with a term of approximately 20 years and a reasonably current coupon—whose returns did not reflect potential tax benefits, impaired negotiability, or special redemption or call privileges—was used each year. Where "flower" bonds (tenderable to the Treasury at par in payment of estate taxes) had to be used, we chose the bond with the smallest potential tax benefit. Where callable bonds had to be used, the term of the bond was assumed to be a simple average of the maturity and first call dates minus the current date. The bond was "held" for the calendar year and returns were computed.

Graph 3-3
Long-Term Corporate Bonds
Return Index and Returns

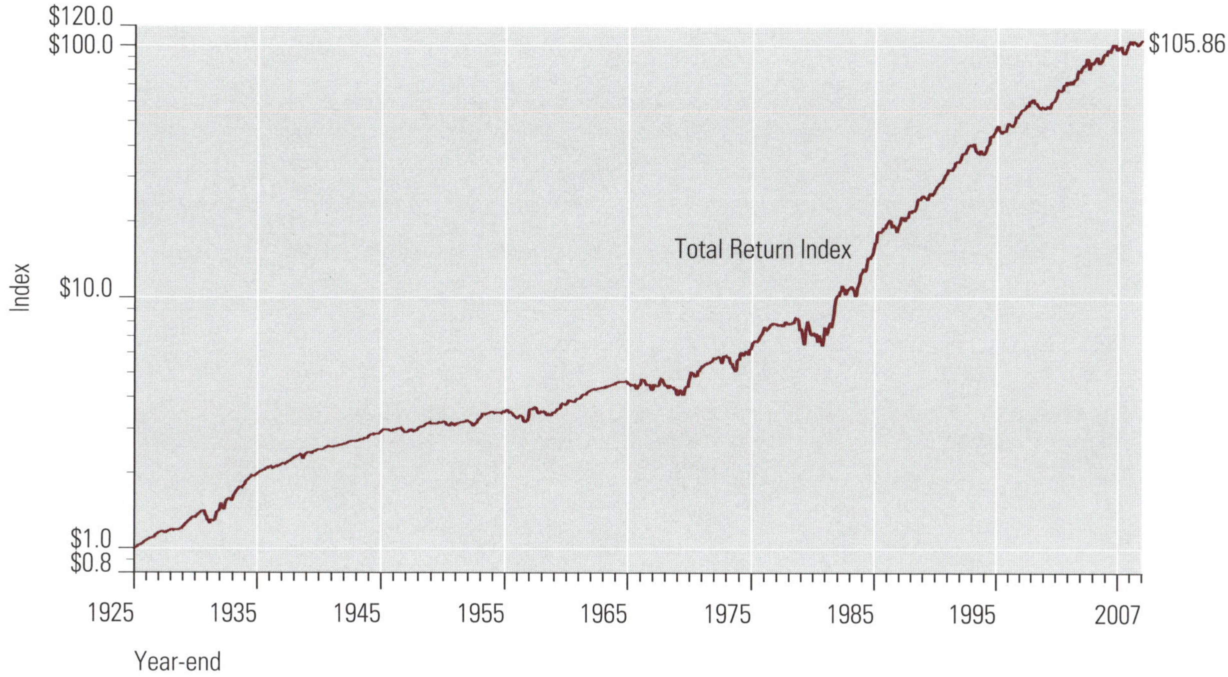

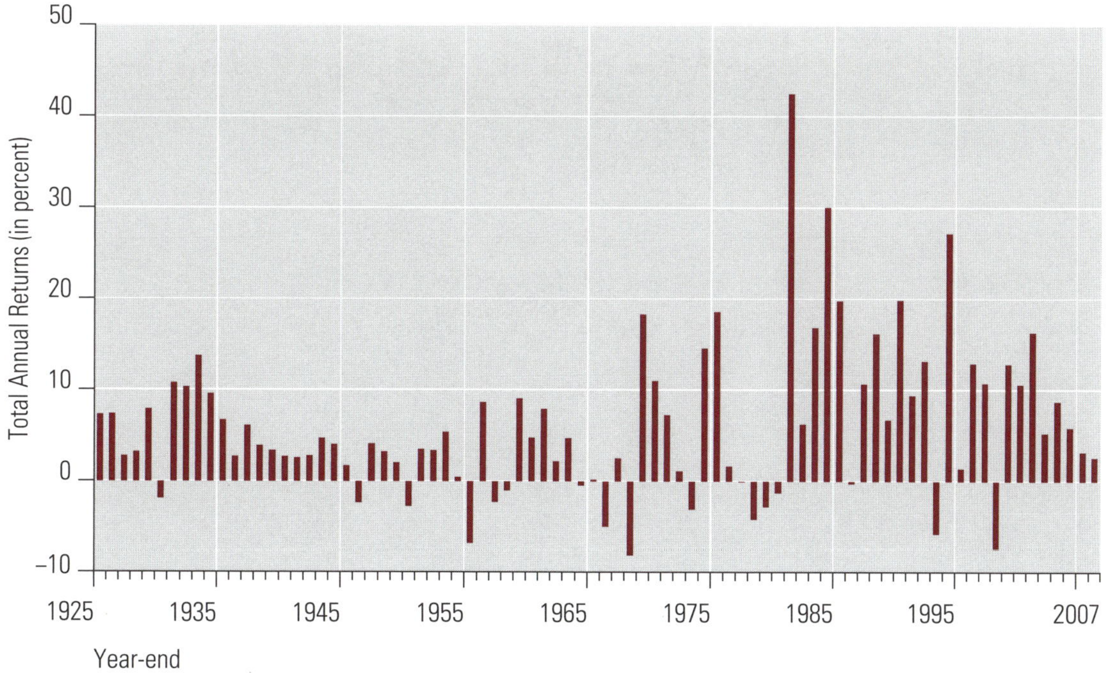

Graph 3-4
Long-Term Government Bonds
Return Indices, Returns, and Yields

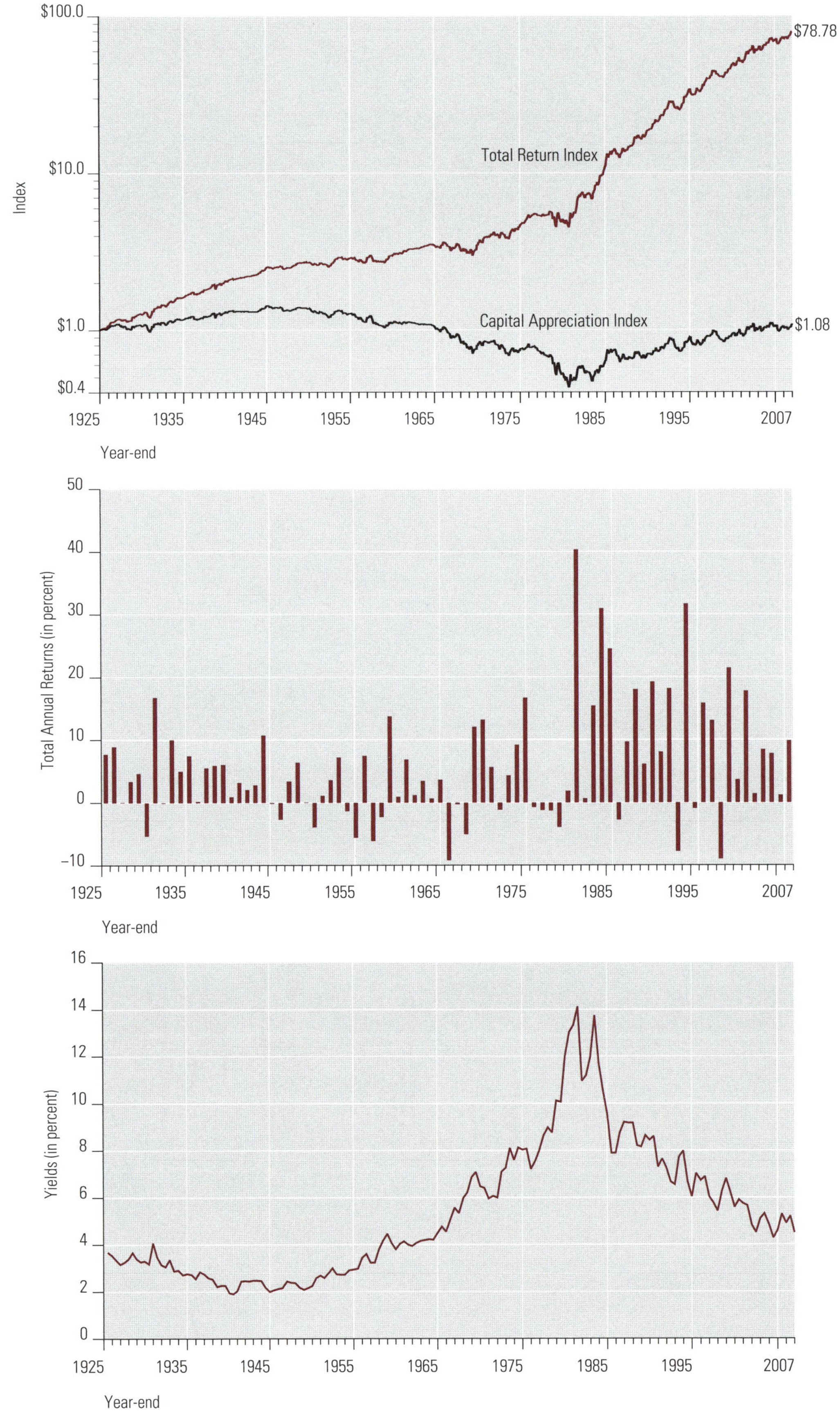

Total returns for 1977–2007 are calculated as the change in the flat or and-interest price.[1] The flat price is the average of the bond's bid and ask prices, plus the accrued coupon.[2] The accrued coupon is equal to zero on the day a coupon is paid, and increases over time until the next coupon payment according to this formula:

$$A = fC \qquad (1)$$

where,

A = accrued coupon;

C = semiannual coupon rate; and

$$f = \frac{\text{number of days since last coupon payment}}{\text{number of days from last coupon payment to next coupon payment}}$$

Income Return

For 1977–2007, the income return is calculated as the change in flat price plus any coupon actually paid from one period to the next, holding the yield constant over the period. As in the total return series, the exact number of days comprising the period is used. For 1926–1976, the income return for a given month is calculated as the total return minus the capital appreciation return.

Capital Appreciation or Return in Excess of Yield

For 1977–2007, capital appreciation is taken as the total return minus the income return for each month. For 1926–1976, the capital appreciation return (also known as the return in excess of yield) is obtained from the CRSP Government Bond File.

A bond's capital appreciation is defined as the total return minus the income return; that is, the return in excess of yield. This definition omits the capital gain or loss that comes from the movement of a bond's price toward par (in the absence of interest rate change) as it matures. Capital appreciation, as defined here, captures changes in bond prices caused by changes in the interest rate.

Yields

The yield on the long-term government bond series is defined as the internal rate of return that equates the bond's price (the average of bid and ask, plus the accrued coupon) with the stream of cash flows (coupons and principal) promised to the bondholder. The yields reported for 1977–2007 were calculated from *The Wall Street Journal* prices for the bonds listed in Table 3-1. For noncallable bonds, the maturity date is shown. For callable bonds, the first call date and the maturity dates are shown as in the following example: 10/15/47–52 refers to a bond that is first callable on 10/15/1947 and matures on 10/15/1952. Dates from 47–99 refer to 1947–1999; 00–16 refers to 2000–2016. For callable bonds trading below par, the yield to maturity is used; above par, the yield to call is used. The yields for 1926–1976 were obtained from the CRSP Government Bond File.

1 "Flat price" is used here to mean the unmodified economic value of the bond, i.e., the and-interest price, or quoted price plus accrued interest. In contrast, some sources use flat price to mean the quoted price.

2 For the purpose of calculating the return in months when a coupon payment is made, the change in the flat price includes the coupon.

Graph 3-5
Intermediate-Term Government Bonds
Return Indices, Returns, and Yields

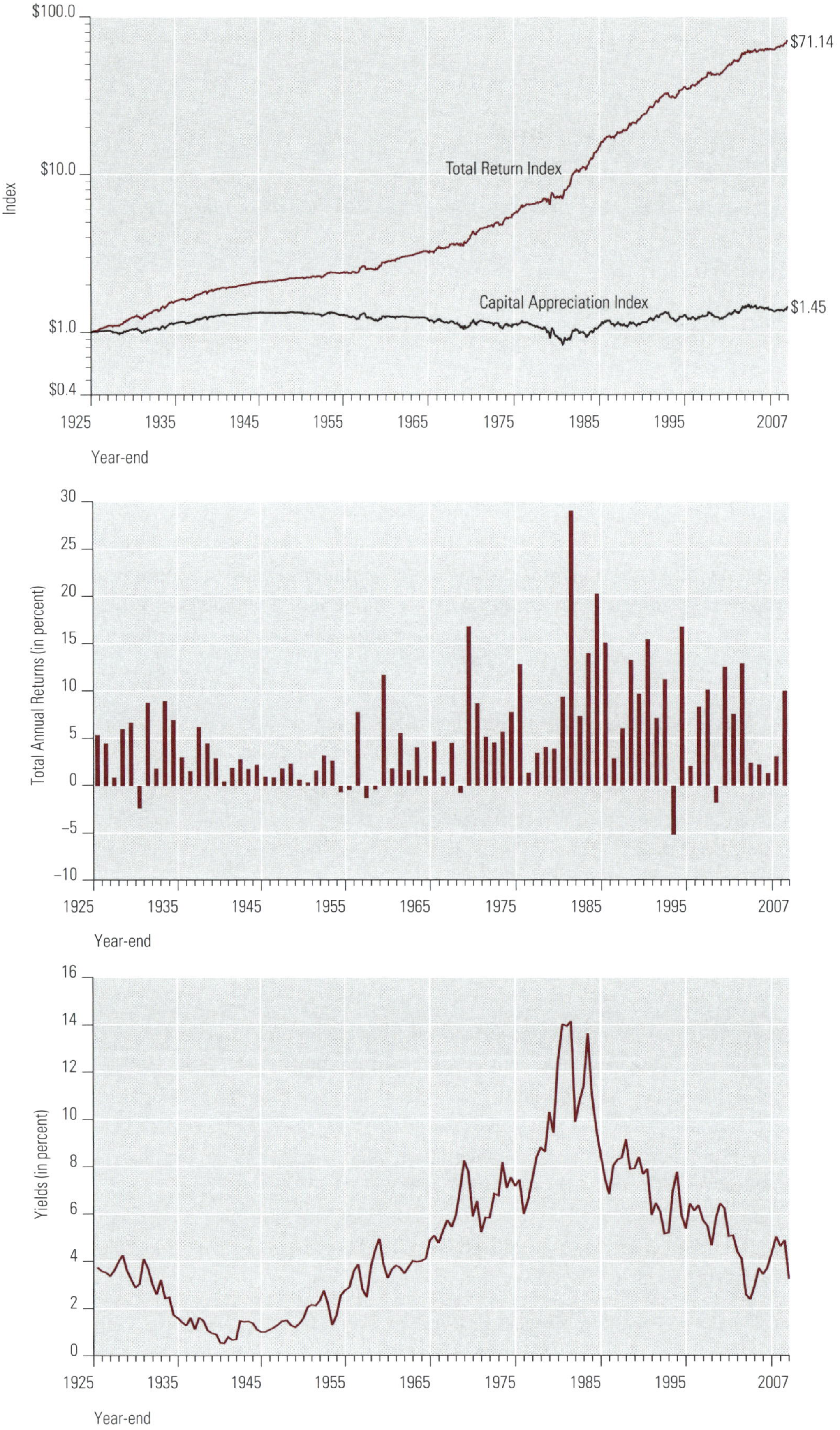

Intermediate-Term Government Bonds

Overview

One dollar invested in intermediate-term government bonds at year-end 1925, with coupons reinvested, grew to $71.14 by year-end 2007. [See Graph 3-5.] This represents an 82-year compound annual growth rate of 5.3 percent. Total annual returns ranged from a high of 29.1 percent in 1982 to a low of −5.1 percent in 1994.

Capital appreciation caused $1.00 to increase to $1.45 over the 82-year period, representing a compound annual growth rate of 0.5 percent. This increase was unexpected: Since yields rose on average over the period, capital appreciation on a hypothetical intermediate-term government bond portfolio with a constant five-year maturity should have been negative. An explanation of the positive average return is given at the end of this chapter.

Total Returns

Total returns of the intermediate-term government bonds for 1987–2007 are calculated from *The Wall Street Journal* prices, using the coupon accrual method described above for long-term government bonds. [See Equation (1).] The bond used in 2007 is the 4.875 percent issue maturing on February 15, 2012. Returns over 1934–1986 are obtained from the CRSP Government Bond File. The bonds used to construct the index over 1934–2007 are shown in Table 3-1.

As with long-term government bonds, one-bond portfolios are used to construct the intermediate-term government bond index. The bond chosen each year is the shortest noncallable bond with a maturity not less than five years, and it is "held" for the calendar year. Monthly returns are computed. (Bonds with impaired negotiability or special redemption privileges are omitted, as are partially or fully tax-exempt bonds starting with 1943.)

Over 1934–1942, almost all bonds with maturities near five years were partially or fully tax-exempt and selected using the rules described above. Personal tax rates were generally low in that period, so that yields on tax-exempt bonds were similar to yields on taxable bonds.

Over 1926–1933, there are few bonds suitable for construction of a series with a five-year maturity. For this period, five-year bond yield estimates are used. These estimates are obtained from Thomas S. Coleman, Lawrence Fisher, and Roger G. Ibbotson, *Historical U.S. Treasury Yield Curves: 1926–1992* with 1995 update (Ibbotson Associates, Chicago, 1995). The estimates reflect what a "pure play" five-year Treasury bond, selling at par and with no special redemption or call provisions, would have yielded had one existed. Estimates are for partially tax-exempt bonds for 1926–1932 and for fully tax-exempt bonds for 1933. Monthly yields are converted to monthly total returns by calculating the beginning and end-of-month flat prices for the hypothetical bonds. The bond is "bought" at the beginning of the month at par (i.e., the coupon equals the previous month-end yield), assuming a maturity of five years. It is "sold" at the end of the month, with the flat price calculated by discounting the coupons and principal at the end-of-month yield, assuming a maturity of 4 years and 11 months. The flat price is the price of the bond including coupon accruals, so that the change in flat price represents total return. Monthly income returns are assumed to be equal to the previous end-of-month yield, stated in monthly terms. Monthly capital appreciation returns are formed as total returns minus income returns.

Table 3-1
Long-Term and Intermediate-Term Government Bond Issues

Long-Term Government Bonds

Period Bond is Held in Index	Coupon (%)	Call/Maturity Date
1926–1931	4.25	10/15/47–52
1932–1935	3.00	9/15/51–55
1936–1941	2.875	3/15/55–60
1942–1953	2.50	9/15/67–72
1954–1958	3.25	6/15/78–83
1959–1960	4.00	2/15/80
1961–1965	4.25	5/15/75–85
1966–1972	4.25	8/15/87–92
1973–1974	6.75	2/15/93
1975–1976	8.50	5/15/94–99
1977–1980	7.875	2/15/95–00
1981	8.00	8/15/96–01
1982	13.375	8/15/01
1983	10.75	2/15/03
1984	11.875	11/15/03
1985	11.75	2/15/05–10
1986–1989	10.00	5/15/05–10
1990–1992	10.375	11/15/07–12
1993–1996	7.25	5/15/16
1997–1998	8.125	8/15/19
1999–2001	8.125	8/15/21
2002	6.250	8/15/23
2003–2004	7.500	11/15/24
2005	6.875	8/15/25
2006	6.750	8/15/26
2007	6.375	8/15/27

Intermediate-Term Government Bonds

Period Bond is Held in Index	Coupon (%)	Call/Maturity Date
1934–1936	3.25	8/01/41
1937	3.375	3/15/43
1938–1940	2.50	12/15/45
1941	3.00	1/01/46
1942	3.00	1/01/47
1943	1.75	6/15/48
1944–1945	2.00	3/15/50
1946	2.00	6/15/51
1947	2.00	3/15/52
1948	2.00	9/15/53
1949	2.50	3/15/54
1950	2.25	6/15/55
1951–1952	2.50	3/15/58
1953	2.375	6/15/58
1954	2.375	3/15/59
1955	2.125	11/15/60
1956	2.75	9/15/61
1957–1958	2.50	8/15/63
1959	3.00	2/15/64

Intermediate-Term Government Bonds (continued)

Period Bond is Held in Index	Coupon (%)	Call/Maturity Date
1960	2.625	2/15/65
1961	3.75	5/15/66
1962	3.625	11/15/67
1963	3.875	5/15/68
1964	4.00	2/15/69
1965	4.00	8/15/70
1966	4.00	8/15/71
1967	4.00	2/15/72
1968	4.00	8/15/73
1969	5.625	8/15/74
1970	5.75	2/15/75
1971	6.25	2/15/76
1972	1.50	10/01/76
1973	6.25	2/15/78
1974	6.25	8/15/79
1975	6.875	5/15/80
1976	7.00	2/15/81
1977	6.375	2/15/82
1978	8.00	2/15/83
1979	7.25	2/15/84
1980	8.00	2/15/85
1981	13.50	2/15/86
1982	9.00	2/15/87
1983	12.375	1/01/88
1984	14.625	1/15/89
1985	10.50	1/15/90
1986	11.75	1/15/91
1987	11.625	1/15/92
1988	8.75	1/15/93
1989	9.00	2/15/94
1990	8.625	10/15/95
1991–1992	7.875	7/15/96
1993	6.375	1/15/99
1994	5.50	4/15/00
1995	8.50	2/15/00
1996	7.75	2/15/01
1997	6.375	8/15/02
1998	5.75	8/15/03
1999	7.25	8/15/04
2000	6.50	8/15/05
2001	6.50	10/15/06
2002	6.125	8/15/07
2003	5.625	5/15/08
2004	5.50	5/15/09
2005	5.75	8/15/10
2006	5.00	8/15/11
2007	4.875	2/15/12

Income Return and Capital Appreciation

For the period 1987–2007, the income return is calculated according to the methodology stated under "Long-Term Government Bonds." Monthly capital appreciation (return in excess of yield) over this same period is the difference between total return and income return.

For 1934–1986, capital appreciation (return in excess of yield) is taken directly from the CRSP Government Bond File. The income return is calculated as the total return minus the capital appreciation return. Prior to 1934, the income and capital appreciation components of total return are generated from yield estimates as described earlier under Total Returns.

Yields

The yield on an intermediate-term government bond is the internal rate of return that equates the bond's price with the stream of cash flows (coupons and principal) promised to the bondholder. The yields reported for 1987–2007 are calculated from *The Wall Street Journal* bond prices listed in Table 3-1. For 1934–1986, yields were obtained from the CRSP Government Bond File. Yields for 1926–1933 are estimates from Coleman, Fisher, and Ibbotson, *Historical U.S. Treasury Yield Curves: 1926–1992* with 1995 update.

U.S. Treasury Bills

Overview

One dollar invested in U.S. Treasury bills at year-end 1925 grew to $20.19 by year-end 2007; this represents a compound annual growth rate of 3.7 percent. [See Graph 3-6.] Total annual returns ranged from a high of 14.7 percent in 1981 to a low of 0.0 percent for the period 1938 to 1940.

Total Returns

For the U.S. Treasury bill index, data from *The Wall Street Journal* are used for 1977–2007; the CRSP U.S. Government Bond File is the source until 1976. Each month a one-bill portfolio containing the shortest-term bill having not less than one month to maturity is constructed. (The bill's original term to maturity is not relevant.) To measure holding period returns for the one-bill portfolio, the bill is priced as of the last trading day of the previous month-end and as of the last trading day of the current month.

Graph 3-6
U.S. Treasury Bills
Return Index and Returns

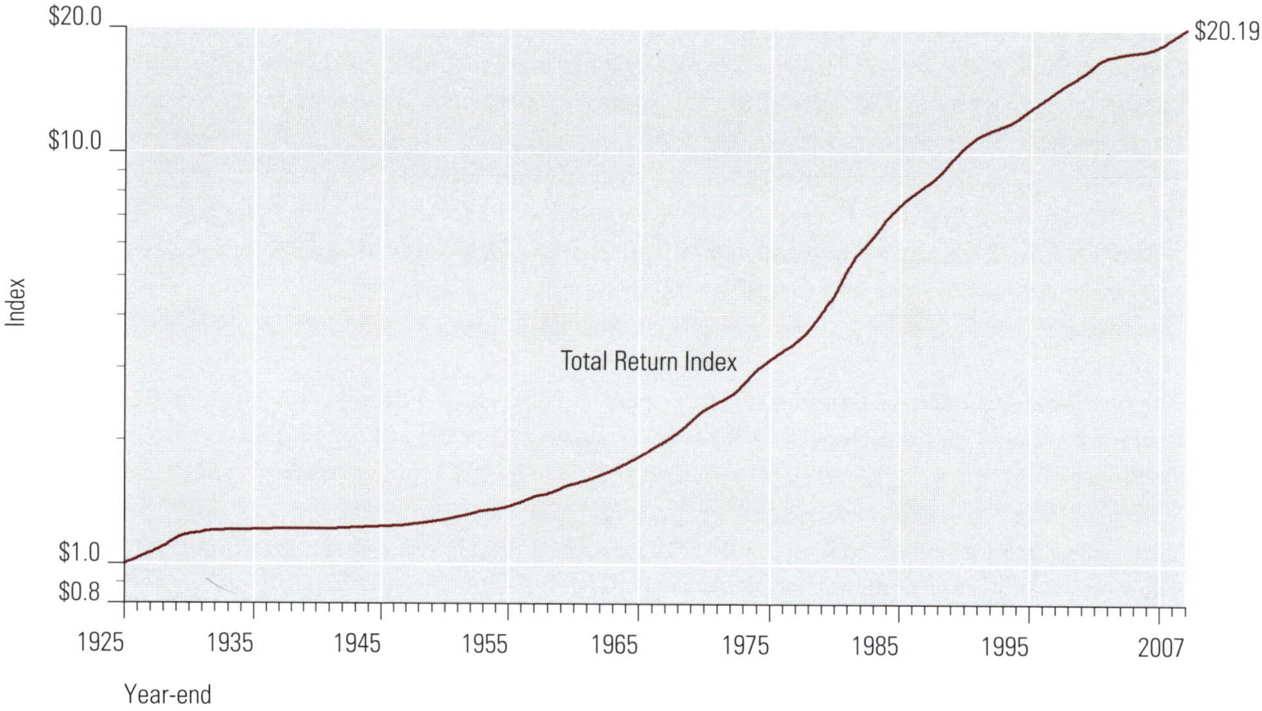

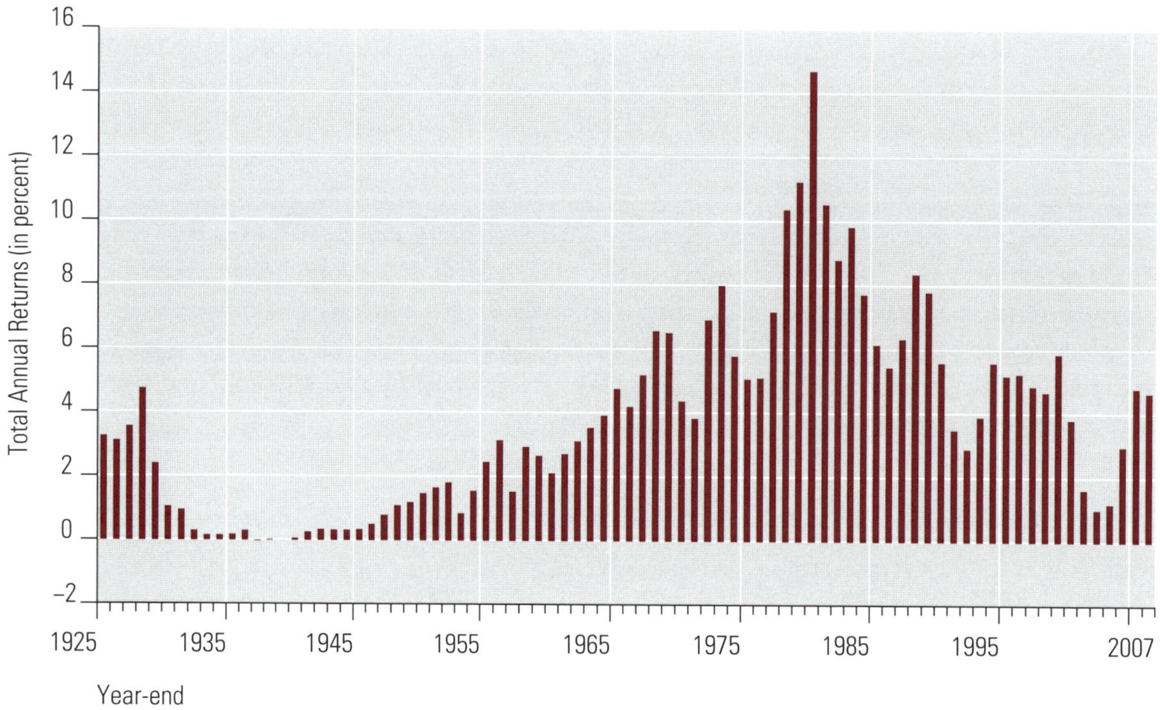

The price of the bill **(P)** at each time **(t)** is given as:

$$P_t = \left[1 - \frac{rd}{360}\right] \quad (2)$$

where,

r = decimal yield (the average of bid and ask quotes) on the bill at time **t**; and,

d = number of days to maturity as of time **t**.

The total return on the bill is the month-end price divided by the previous month-end price, minus one.

Negative Returns on Treasury Bills

Monthly Treasury bill returns (as reported in Appendix A-14) were negative in February 1933, and in 12 months during the 1938–1941 period. Also, the annual Treasury bill return was negative for 1938. Since negative Treasury bill returns contradict logic, an explanation is in order.

Negative yields observed in the data do not imply that investors purchased Treasury bills with a guaranteed negative return. Rather, Treasury bills of that era were exempt from personal property taxes in some states, while cash was not. Further, for a bank to hold U.S. government deposits, Treasury securities were required as collateral. These circumstances created excessive demand for the security, and thus bills were sold at a premium. Given the low interest rates during the period, owners of the bills experienced negative returns.

Inflation

Overview

A basket of consumer goods purchased for $1.00 at year-end 1925 would cost $11.72 by year-end 2007. [See Graph 3-7.] Of course, the exact contents of the basket changed over time. This increase represents a compound annual rate of inflation of 3.0 percent over the past 82 years. Inflation rates ranged from a high of 18.2 percent in 1946 to a low of –10.3 percent in 1932.

Inflation

The Consumer Price Index for All Urban Consumers (CPI-U), not seasonally adjusted, is used to measure inflation, which is the rate of change of consumer goods prices. Unfortunately, the CPI is not measured over the same period as the other asset returns. All of the security returns are measured from one month-end to the next month-end. CPI commodity prices are collected during the month. Thus, measured inflation rates lag the other series by about one-half month. Prior to January 1978, the CPI (as compared with CPI-U) was used. For the period 1978 through 1987, the index uses the year 1967 in determining the items comprising the basket of goods. Following 1987, a three-year period, 1982 through 1984, was used to determine the items making up the basket of goods. All inflation measures are constructed by the U.S. Department of Labor, Bureau of Labor Statistics, Washington.

Graph 3-7
Inflation
Cumulative Index and Rates of Change

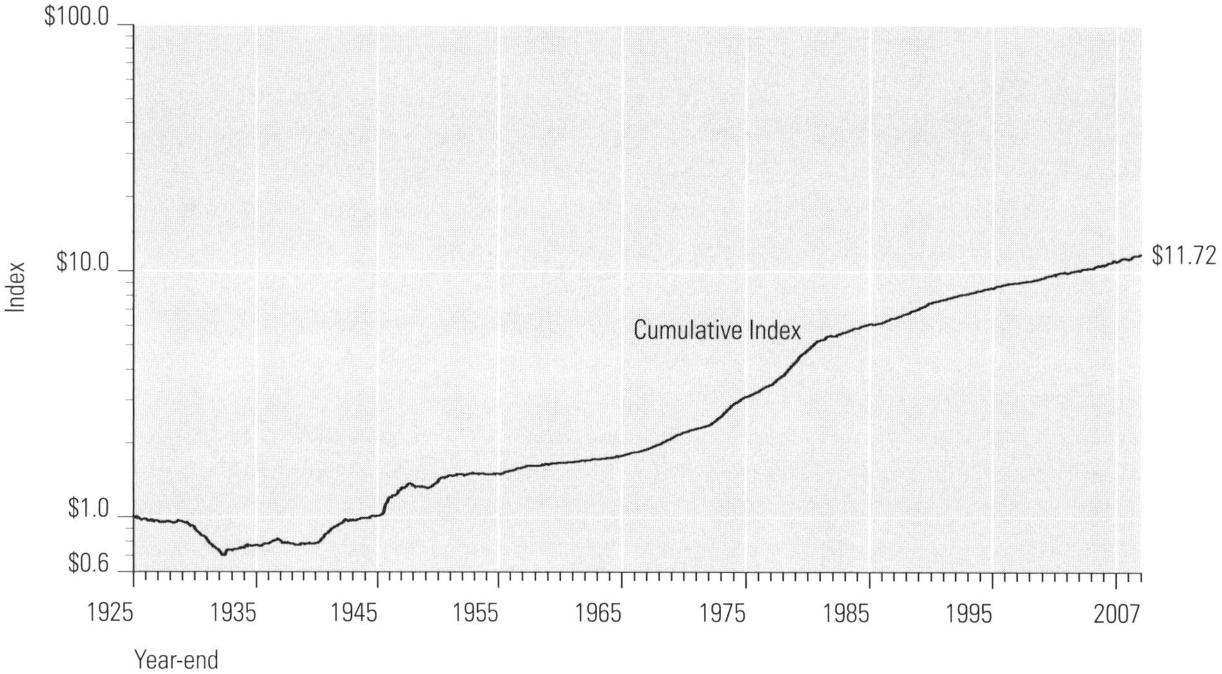

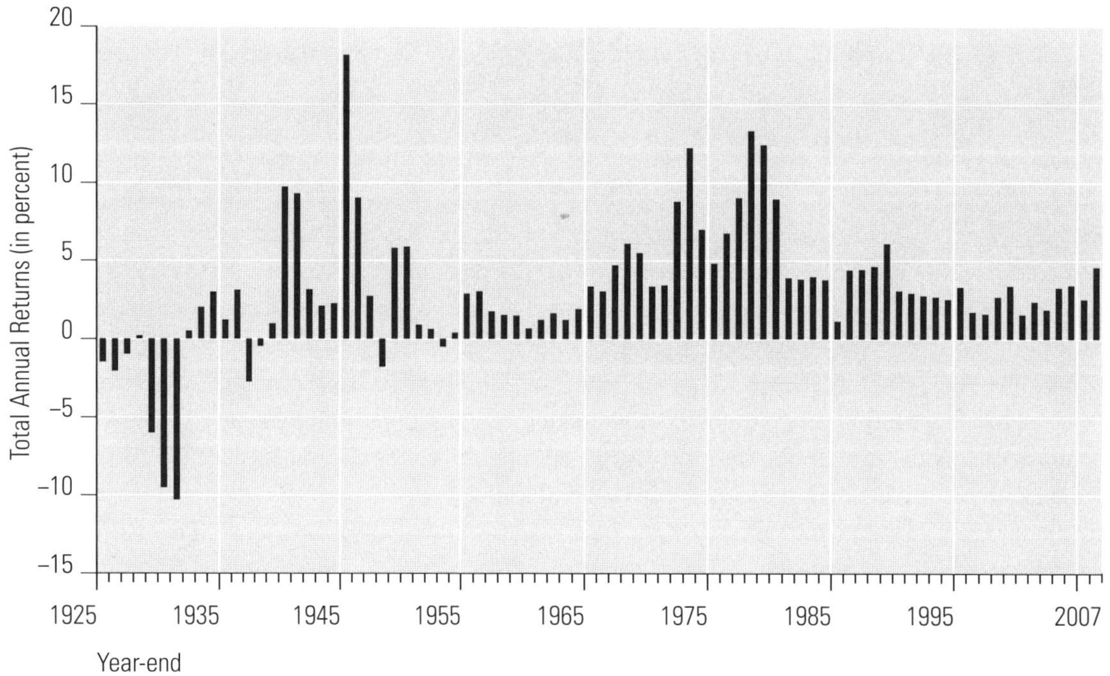

Positive Capital Appreciation on Intermediate-Term Government Bonds

The capital appreciation component of intermediate-term government bond returns caused $1.00 invested at year-end 1925 to grow to $1.45 by the end of 2007, representing a compound annual rate of 0.5 percent. This is surprising because yields, on average, rose over the period.

An investor in a hypothetical five-year constant maturity portfolio, with continuous rebalancing, suffered a capital loss (that is, excluding coupon income) over 1926–2007. An investor who rebalanced yearly, choosing bonds according to the method set forth above, fared better. This investor would have earned the 0.5 percent per year capital gain recorded here.

This performance relates to the construction of the intermediate-term bond series. For 1926–1933, the one-bond portfolio was rebalanced monthly to maintain a constant maturity of five years. For the period 1934–2007, one bond (the shortest bond not less than five years to maturity) was chosen at the beginning of each year and priced monthly. New bonds were not picked each month to maintain a constant five years to maturity intrayear.

There are several possible reasons for the positive capital appreciation return. Chief among these reasons are convexity of the bond portfolio and the substitution of one bond for another at each year-end.

Convexity

Each year, we "bought" a bond with approximately five years to maturity and held it for one year. During this period, the market yield on the bond fluctuates. Because the duration of the bond shortens (the bond becomes less interest-rate sensitive) as yields rise and the duration lengthens as yields fall, more is gained from a fall in yield than is lost from a rise in yield. This characteristic of a bond is known as convexity.

For example, suppose an 8 percent coupon bond is bought at par at the beginning of a year; the yield fluctuates (but the portfolio is not rebalanced) during the year; and the bond is sold at par at the end of the year. The price of the bond at both the beginning and end of the year is $100; the change in bond price is zero. However, the fluctuations will have caused the gains during periods of falling yields to exceed the losses during periods of rising yields. Thus the total return for the year exceeds 8 percent. Since our measure of capital appreciation is the return in excess of yield, rather than the change in bond price, capital appreciation for this bond (as measured) will be greater than zero.

In 1992, the yield for intermediate-term government bonds started the year at 5.97 percent, rose, fell, and finally rose again to end at 6.11 percent, slightly higher than the starting point. In the absence of convexity, the capital appreciation return for 1992 would be negative. Because of the fluctuation of yields during the year, however, the capital appreciation return on the intermediate-term government bond index was positive 0.64 percent.

It should be noted that the return in excess of yield, or capital gain, from convexity is caused by holding, over the year, a bond whose yield at purchase is different than the current market yield. If the portfolio were rebalanced each time the data were sampled (in this case, monthly), by selling the old bond and buying a new five-year bond selling at par, the portfolio would have no convexity. That is, over a period where yields ended where they started, the measured capital appreciation would be zero. However, this is neither a practical way to construct an index of actual bonds nor to manage a bond portfolio.

Bond Substitution

Another reason why the intermediate-term government bond series displays positive capital appreciation even though yields rose is the way in which bonds were removed from the portfolio and replaced with other bonds. In general, it was not possible to replace a bond "sold" by buying one with exactly the same yield. This produces a spurious change in the yield of the series—one that should not be associated with a capital gain or loss.

For example: Suppose a five-year bond yielding 8 percent is bought at par at the beginning of the year; at that time, four-year bonds yield 7 percent. Over the year, the yield curve rises in parallel by one percentage point so that when it comes time to sell the bond at year-end, it yields 8 percent and has four years to maturity. Therefore, at both the beginning and end of the year, the price of the bond is $100.

The proceeds from the sale are used to buy a new five-year bond yielding 9 percent. While the bond price change was zero over the year, the yield of the series has risen from 8 percent to 9 percent. Thus it is possible, because of the process of substituting one bond for another, for the yield series to contain a spurious rise that is not, and should not be expected to be, associated with a decline in the price of any particular bond. This phenomenon is likely to be the source of some of the positive capital appreciation in our intermediate-term government bond series.

Other Issues

While convexity and bond substitution may explain the anomaly of positive capital appreciation in a bond series with rising yields, there are other incomplete-market problems that may also help explain the capital gain. For example, intermediate-term government bonds were scarce in the 1930s and 1940s. As a result, the bonds chosen for this series occasionally had maturities longer than five years, ranging as high as eight years when bought. The 1930s and the first half of the 1940s were bullish for the bond market. Longer bonds included in this series had higher yields and substantially higher capital gain returns than bonds with exactly five years to maturity might have had if any existed. This upward bias is particularly noticeable in 1934, 1937, and 1938.

In addition, callable and fully or partially tax-exempt bonds were used when necessary to obtain a bond for some years. The conversion of the Treasury bond market from tax-exempt to taxable status produced a one-time upward jump in stated yields, but not a capital loss on any given bond. Therefore, part of the increase in stated yields over 1926–2007 was a tax effect that did not cause a capital loss on the intermediate-term bond index. Further, the callable bonds used in the early part of the period may have commanded a return premium for taking this extra risk.

Chapter 4

Description of the Derived Series

Historical data suggests that investors are rewarded for taking risks and that returns are related to inflation rates. The risk/return and the real/nominal relationships in the historical data are revealed by looking at the risk premium and inflation-adjusted series derived from the basic asset series. Annual total returns for the four risk premia and six inflation-adjusted series are presented in Table 4-1 of this chapter.

Geometric Differences Used to Calculate Derived Series

Derived series are calculated as the geometric differences between two basic asset classes. Returns on basic series **A** and **B** and derived series **C** are related as follows:

$$(1+C)=\left[\frac{1+A}{1+B}\right] \qquad (3)$$

where the series **A**, **B**, and **C** are in decimal form (i.e., 5 percent is indicated by 0.05). Thus **C** is given by:

$$C=\left[\frac{1+A}{1+B}\right]-1\approx A-B \qquad (4)$$

As an example, suppose return **A** equals 15%, or 0.15; and return **B** is 5%, or 0.05. Then **C** equals (1.15 / 1.05) − 1 = 0.0952, or 9.52 percent. This result, while slightly different from the simple arithmetic difference of 10 percent, is conceptually the same.

Definitions of the Derived Series

From the seven basic asset classes—large company stocks, small company stocks, long-term corporate bonds, long-term government bonds, intermediate-term government bonds, U.S. Treasury bills, and consumer goods (inflation)—10 additional series are derived representing the component or elemental parts of the asset returns.

Two Categories of Derived Series

The 10 derived series are categorized as risk premia, or payoffs for taking various types of risk; and as inflation-adjusted asset returns. The risk premia series are the bond horizon premium, the bond default premium, the equity risk premium, and the small stock premium. The inflation-adjusted asset return series are constructed by geometrically subtracting inflation from each of the six asset total return series.

These 10 derived series are:

Series	Derivation
Risk Premia	
Equity Risk Premium	$\frac{(1 + \text{Large Stock TR})}{(1 + \text{Treasury Bill TR})} - 1$
Small Stock Premium	$\frac{(1 + \text{Small Stock TR})}{(1 + \text{Large Stock TR})} - 1$
Bond Default Premium	$\frac{(1 + \text{LT Corp Bond TR})}{(1 + \text{LT Govt Bond TR})} - 1$
Bond Horizon Premium	$\frac{(1 + \text{LT Govt Bond TR})}{(1 + \text{Treasury Bill TR})} - 1$
Inflation-Adjusted	
Large Company Stock Returns	$\frac{(1 + \text{Large Stock TR})}{(1 + \text{Inflation})} - 1$
Small Company Stock Returns	$\frac{(1 + \text{Small Stock TR})}{(1 + \text{Inflation})} - 1$
Corporate Bond Returns	$\frac{(1 + \text{Corp Bond TR})}{(1 + \text{Inflation})} - 1$
Long-Term Government Bond Returns	$\frac{(1 + \text{LT Govt Bond TR})}{(1 + \text{Inflation})} - 1$
Intermediate-Term Government Bond Returns	$\frac{(1 + \text{IT Govt Bond TR})}{(1 + \text{Inflation})} - 1$
Treasury Bill Returns (Real Riskless Rate of Returns)	$\frac{(1 + \text{Treasury Bill TR})}{(1 + \text{Inflation})} - 1$

TR = Total Return

Equity Risk Premium

Large company stock returns are composed of inflation, the real riskless rate, and the equity risk premium. The equity risk premium is the geometric difference between large company stock total returns and U.S. Treasury bill total returns.

Because large company stocks are not strictly comparable with bonds, horizon and default premia are not used to analyze the components of equity returns. (Large company stocks have characteristics that are analogous to horizon and default risk, but they are not equivalent.)
The monthly equity risk premium is given by:

$$\frac{(1+\text{Large Stock TR})}{(1+\text{Treasury Bill TR})}-1 \qquad (5)$$

Graph 4-1 shows equity risk premium volatility over the last 82 years.

Graph 4-1
Equity Risk Premium Annual Returns (in percent)

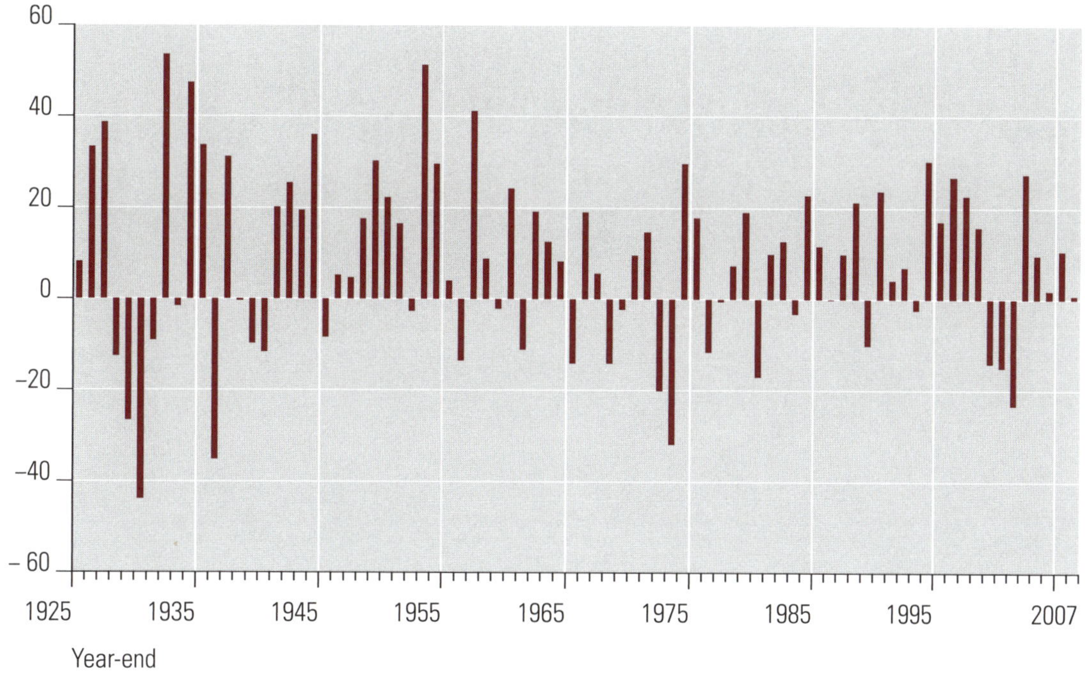

Small Stock Premium

The small stock premium is the geometric difference between small company stock total returns and large company stock total returns. The monthly small stock premium is given by:

$$\frac{(1 + \text{Small Stock TR})}{(1 + \text{Large Stock TR})} - 1 \qquad (6)$$

Graph 4-2 shows small stock premium volatility over the last 82 years.

Graph 4-2
Small Stock Premium Annual Returns (in percent)

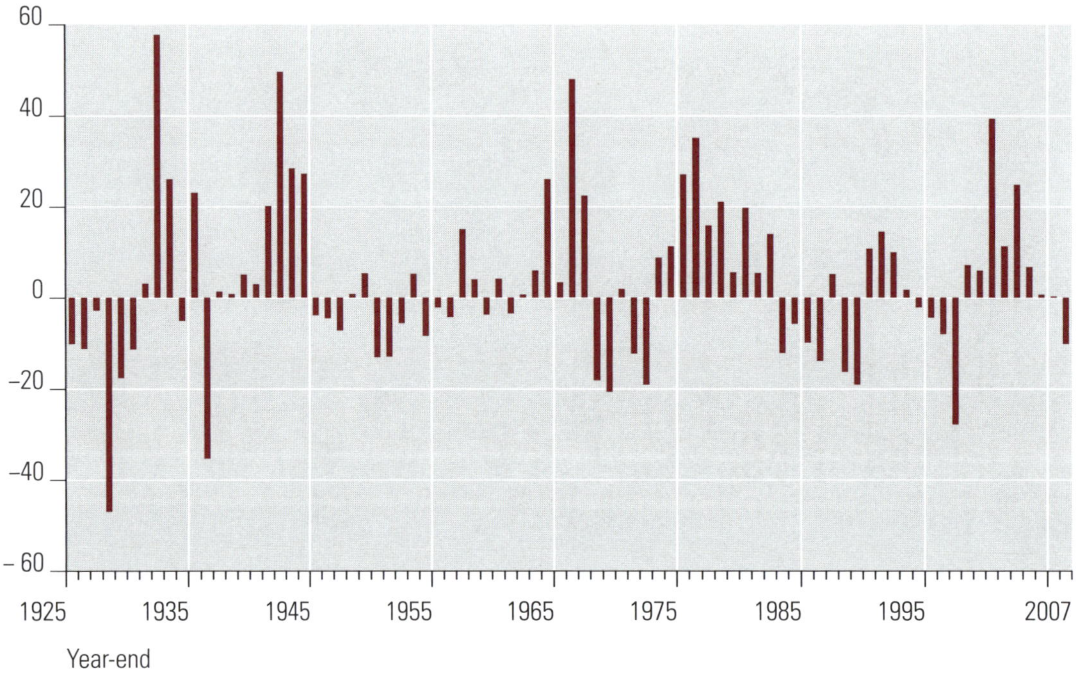

Bond Default Premium

The bond default premium is defined as the net return from investing in long-term corporate bonds rather than long-term government bonds of equal maturity. Since there is a possibility of default on a corporate bond, bondholders receive a premium that reflects this possibility, in addition to inflation, the real riskless rate, and the horizon premium.

The monthly bond default premium is given by:

$$\frac{(1 + \text{LT Corp Bond TR})}{(1 + \text{LT Govt Bond TR})} - 1 \qquad (7)$$

Components of the Default Premium

Bonds susceptible to default have higher returns (when they do not default) than riskless bonds. Default on a bond may be a small loss, such as a late or skipped interest payment; it may be a larger loss, such as the loss of any or all principal as well as interest. In any case, part of the default premium on a portfolio of bonds is consumed by the losses on those bonds that do default.

The remainder of the default premium—over and above the portion consumed by defaults—is a pure risk premium, which the investor demands and, over the long run, receives for taking the risk of default. The expected return on a corporate bond, or portfolio of corporate bonds, is less than the bond's yield. The portion of the yield that is expected to be consumed by defaults must be subtracted. The expected return on a corporate bond is equal to the expected return on a government bond of like maturity, plus the pure risk premium portion of the bond default premium.

Callability Risk is Captured in the Default Premium

Callability risk is the risk that a bond will be redeemed (at or near par) by its issuer before maturity, at a time when market interest rates are lower than the bond's coupon rate. The possibility of redemption is risky because it would prevent the bondholder of the redeemed issue from reinvesting the proceeds at the original (higher) interest rate. The bond default premium, as measured here, also inadvertently captures any premium investors may demand or receive for this risk.

Graph 4-3 shows bond default premium volatility over the last 82 years.

Graph 4-3
Bond Default Premium Annual Returns (in percent)

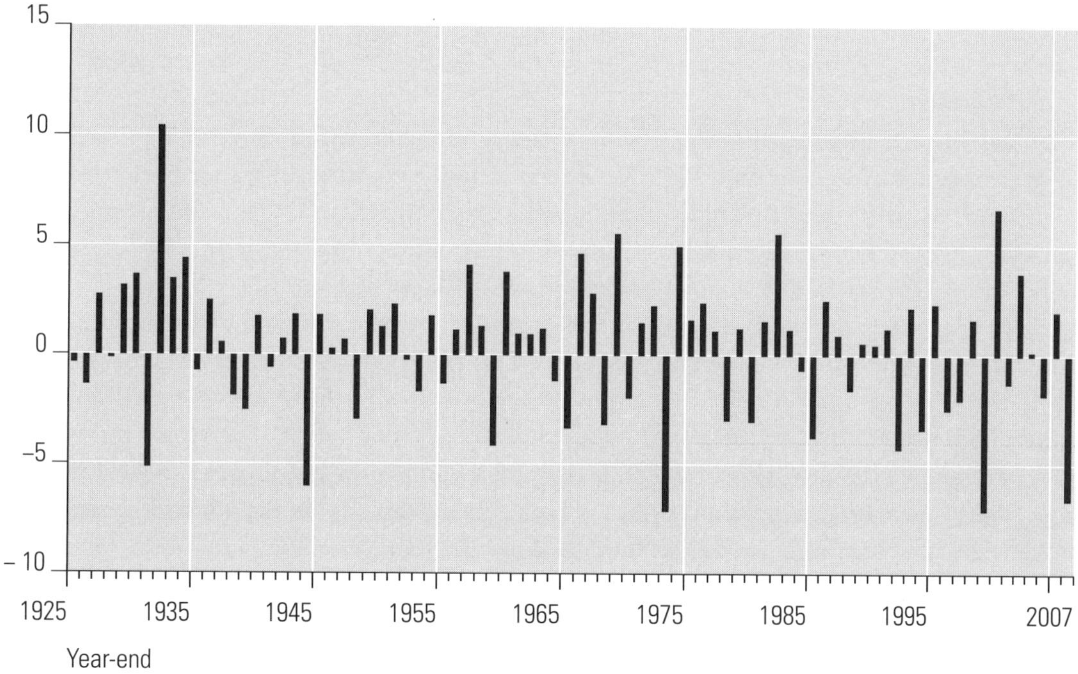

Bond Horizon Premium

Long-term government bonds behave differently than short-term bills in that their prices (and hence returns) are more sensitive to interest rate fluctuations. The bond horizon premium is the premium investors demand for holding long-term bonds instead of U.S. Treasury bills.

The monthly bond horizon premium is given by:

$$\frac{(1+\text{LT Govt Bond TR})}{(1+\text{Treasury Bill TR})}-1 \qquad (8)$$

Long-term rather than intermediate-term government bonds are used to derive the bond horizon premium so as to capture a "full unit" of price fluctuation risk. Intermediate-term government bonds may display a partial horizon premium, which is smaller than the difference between long-term bonds and short-term bills.

Does Maturity or Duration Determine the Bond Premium?

Duration is the present-value-weighted average time to receipt of cash flows (coupons and principal) from holding a bond, and can be calculated from the bond's yield, coupon rate, and term to maturity. The duration of a given bond determines the amount of return premium arising from differences in bond life. The bond horizon premium is also referred to as the "maturity premium," based on the observation that bonds with longer maturities command a return premium over shorter-maturity bonds. Duration, not term to maturity, however, is the bond characteristic that determines this return premium.

Why a "Horizon" Premium?

Investors often strive to match the duration of their bond holdings (cash inflows) with the estimated duration of their obligations or cash outflows. Consequently, investors with short time horizons regard long-duration bonds as risky (due to price fluctuation risk), and short-term bills as riskless. Conversely, investors with long time horizons regard short-term bills as risky (due to the uncertainty about the yield at which bills can be reinvested), and long-duration bonds as riskless or less risky.

Empirically, long-duration bonds bear higher yields and greater returns than short-term bills; that is, the yield curve slopes upward on average over time. This observation indicates that investors are more averse to the price fluctuation risk of long-duration bonds than to the reinvestment risk of bills.

Bond-duration risk is thus in the eye of the beholder, or bondholder. Therefore, rather than identifying the premium as a payoff for long-bond risk (which implies a judgment that short-horizon investors are "right" in their risk perceptions), it is better to go directly to the source of the return differential (the differing time horizons of investors) and use the label "horizon premium."

Graph 4-4 shows the bond horizon premium over the last 82 years.

Graph 4-4

Bond Horizon Premium Annual Returns (in percent)

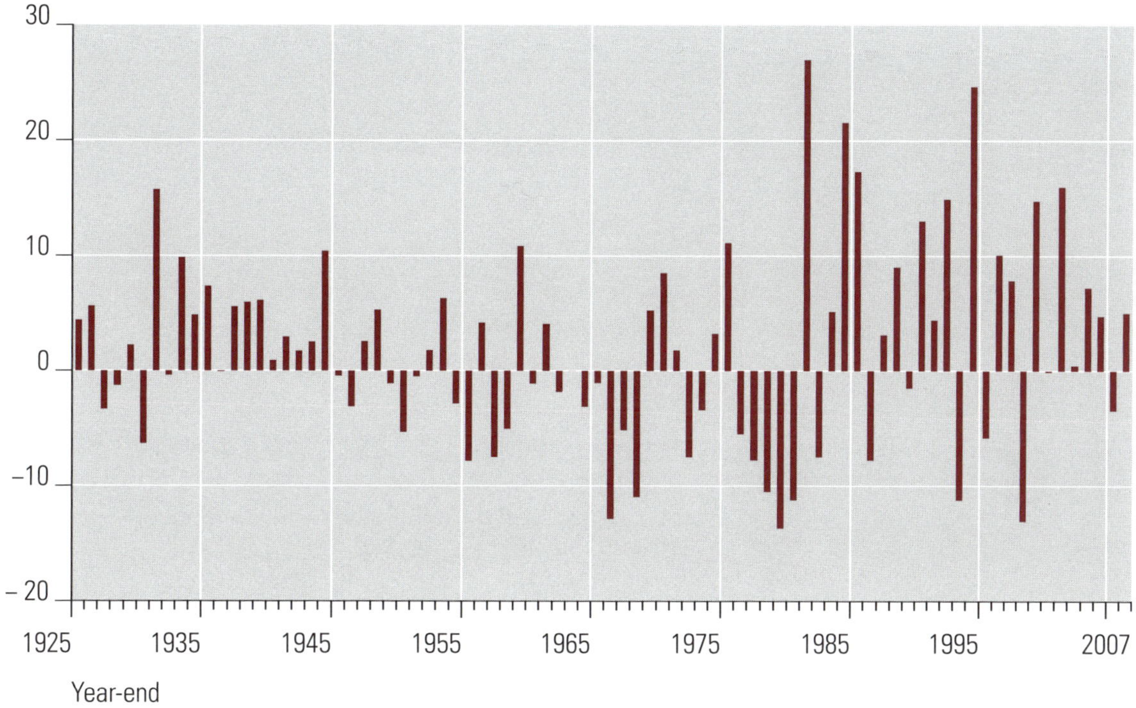

Inflation-Adjusted Large Company Stock Returns

Overview

Large company stock total returns were 10.4 percent compounded annually over the period 1926–2007 in nominal terms. [See Graph 4-5.] In real (inflation-adjusted) terms, stocks provided a 7.1 percent compound annual return. Thus, a large company stock investor would have experienced a substantial increase in real wealth, or purchasing power, over the 82-year period.

Construction

The inflation-adjusted return is a geometric difference and is approximately equal to the arithmetic difference between the large company stock total return and the inflation rate. The monthly inflation-adjusted large company stock return is given by:

$$\frac{(1 + \text{Large Stock TR})}{(1 + \text{Inflation})} - 1 \qquad (9)$$

Graph 4-5
Large Company Stocks
Real and Nominal Return Indices
Year-End 1925 = $1.00

from 1925 to 2007

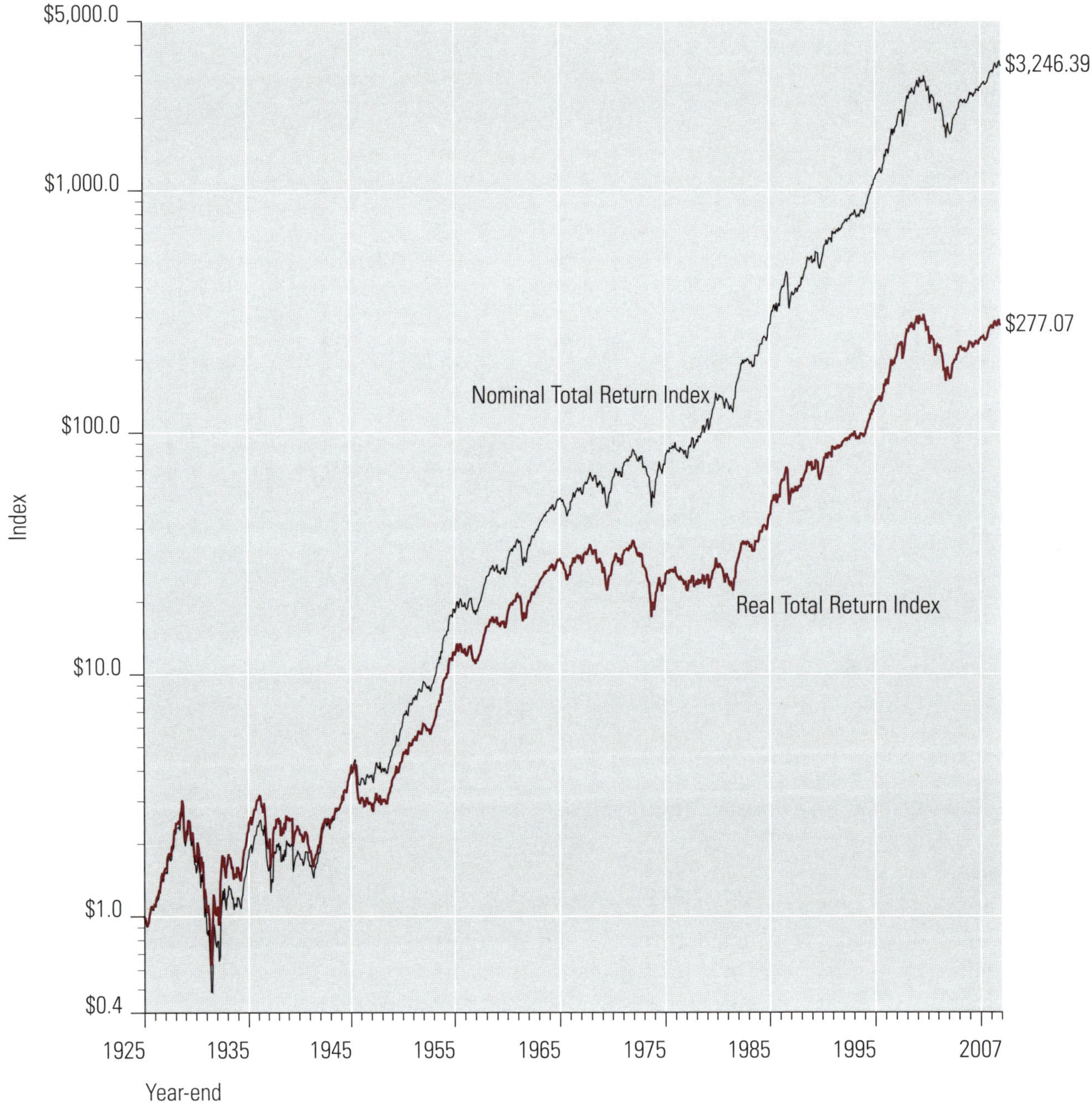

The inflation-adjusted large company stock return may also be expressed as the geometric sum of the real riskless rate and the equity risk premium:

$$[(1+\text{Real Riskless Rate})\times(1+\text{Equity Risk Premium})]-1 \qquad (10)$$

Inflation-Adjusted Small Company Stock Returns

Overview

Small company stock total returns were 12.5 percent compounded annually over the period 1926–2007 in nominal terms. [See Graph 4-6.] In real terms, small company stocks provided a 9.1 percent compound annual return. Thus, long-term a small company stock investor would have experienced a substantial increase in real wealth, or purchasing power, over the 82-year period.

Construction

The inflation-adjusted return is a geometric difference and is approximately equal to the arithmetic difference between the small company stock total return and the inflation rate. The monthly inflation-adjusted small company stock return is given by:

$$\frac{(1+\text{Small Stock TR})}{(1+\text{Inflation})}-1 \qquad (11)$$

Inflation-Adjusted Long-Term Corporate Bond Returns

Overview

Corporate bonds returned 5.9 percent compounded annually over the period 1926–2007 in nominal terms, and a 2.7 percent compound annual return in real (inflation-adjusted) terms. [See Graph 4-7.] Thus, corporate bonds have outpaced inflation over the past 82 years.

Construction

The inflation-adjusted return is a geometric difference and is approximately equal to the arithmetic difference between the long-term corporate bond total return and the inflation rate. The monthly inflation-adjusted corporate bond total return is given by:

$$\frac{(1+\text{Corp Bond TR})}{(1+\text{Inflation})}-1 \qquad (12)$$

Graph 4-6
Small Company Stocks
Real and Nominal Return Indices
Year-End 1925 = $1.00

from 1925 to 2007

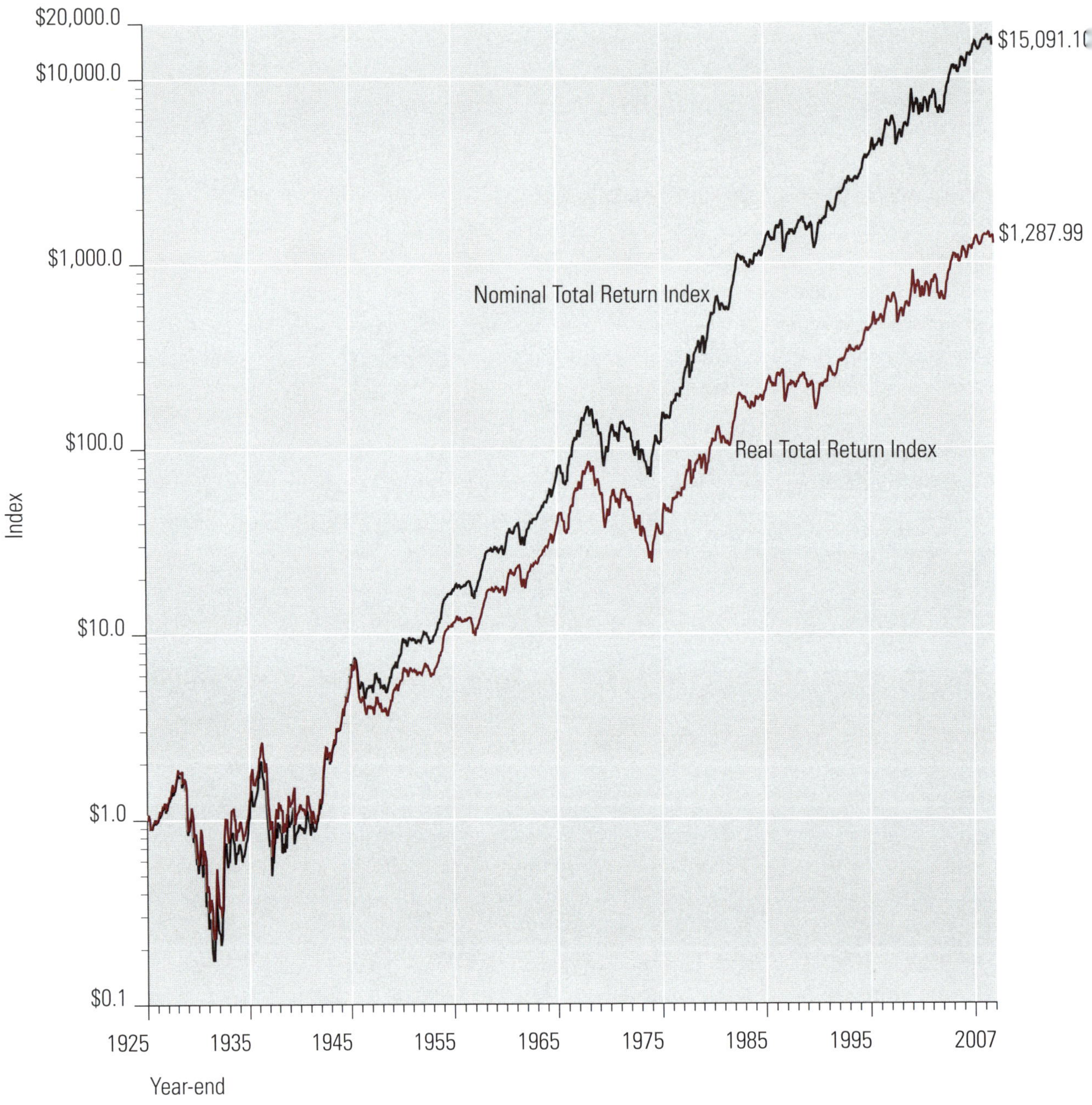

Graph 4-7
Long-Term Corporate Bonds
Real and Nominal Return Indices
Year-End 1925 = $1.00

from 1925 to 2007

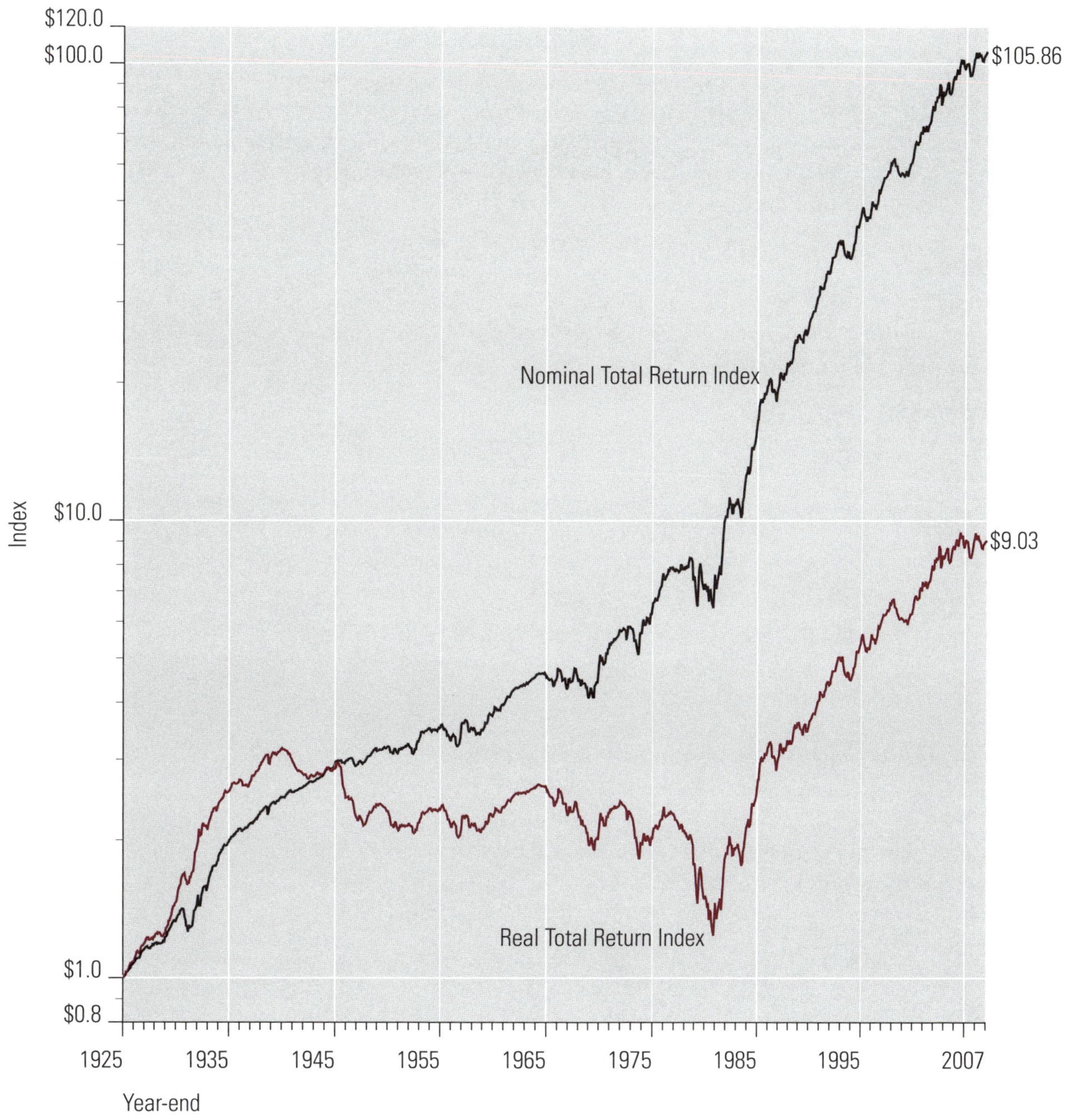

Inflation-Adjusted Long-Term Government Bond Returns

Overview

Long-term government bonds returned 5.5 percent compounded annually over the period 1926–2007 in nominal terms, and a 2.4 percent compound annual return in real (inflation-adjusted) terms. [See Graph 4-8.] Thus, long-term government bonds have outpaced inflation over the past 82 years despite falling bond prices over most of the period.

Construction

The inflation-adjusted return is a geometric difference and is approximately equal to the arithmetic difference between the long-term government bond total return and the inflation rate. The monthly inflation-adjusted long-term government bond total return is given by:

$$\frac{(1+\text{LT Govt Bond TR})}{(1+\text{Inflation})}-1 \qquad (13)$$

Since government bond returns are composed of inflation, the real riskless rate, and the horizon premium, the inflation-adjusted government bond returns may also be expressed as:

$$[(1+\text{Real Riskless Rate})\times(1+\text{Horizon Premium})]-1 \qquad (14)$$

Inflation-Adjusted Intermediate-Term Government Bond Returns

Overview

Intermediate-term government bonds returned 5.3 percent compounded annually in nominal terms, and 2.2 percent in real (inflation-adjusted) terms. [See Graph 4-9.]

Construction

The inflation-adjusted return is a geometric difference and is approximately equal to the arithmetic difference between the intermediate-term government bond total return and the inflation rate. The monthly inflation-adjusted intermediate-term government bond return is given by:

$$\frac{(1+\text{IT Govt Bond TR})}{(1+\text{Inflation})}-1 \qquad (15)$$

Graph 4-8
Long-Term Government Bonds
Real and Nominal Return Indices
Year-End 1925 = $1.00

from 1925 to 2007

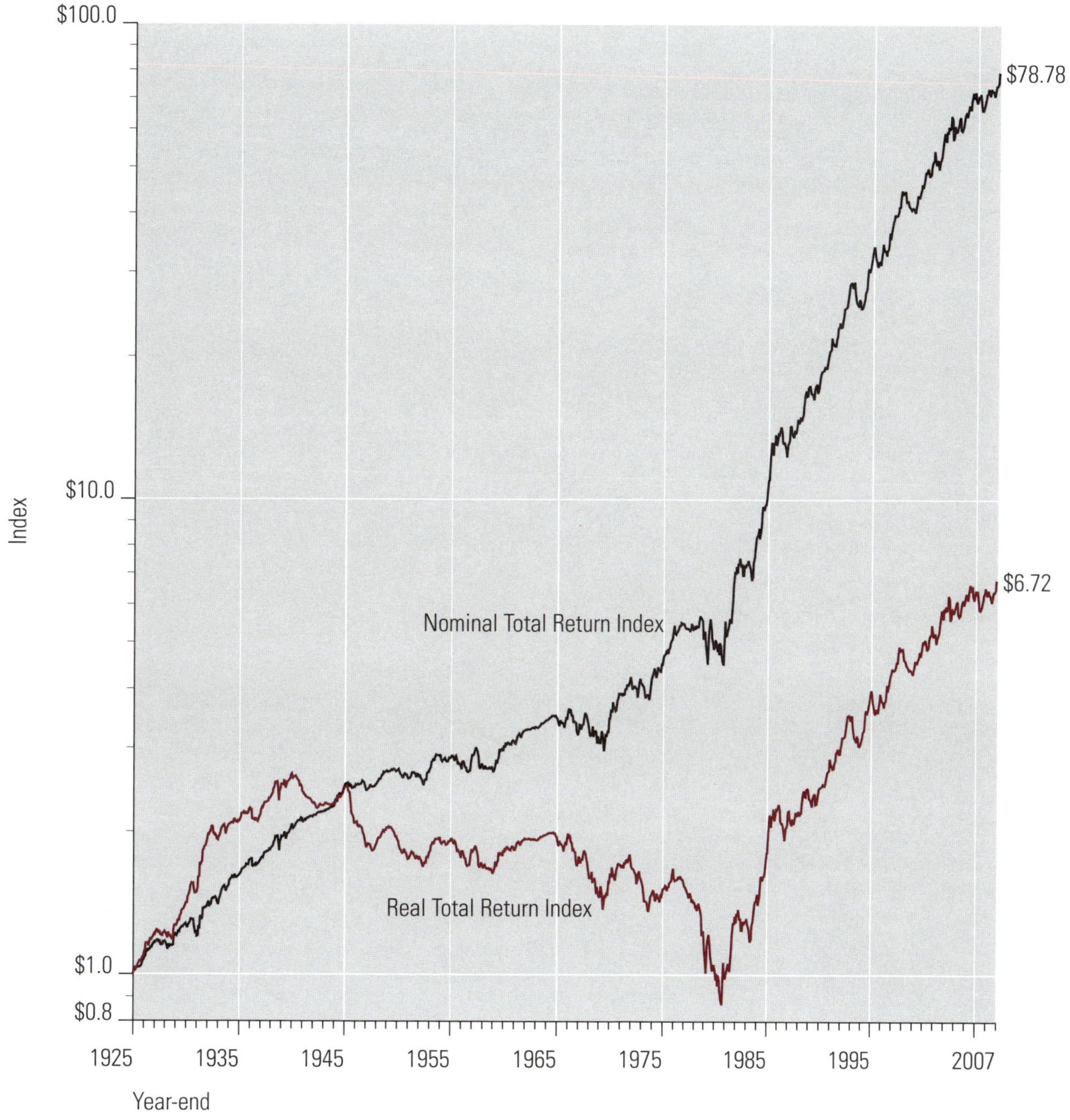

Graph 4-9
Intermediate-Term Government Bonds
Real and Nominal Return Indices
Year-End 1925 = $1.00

from 1925 to 2007

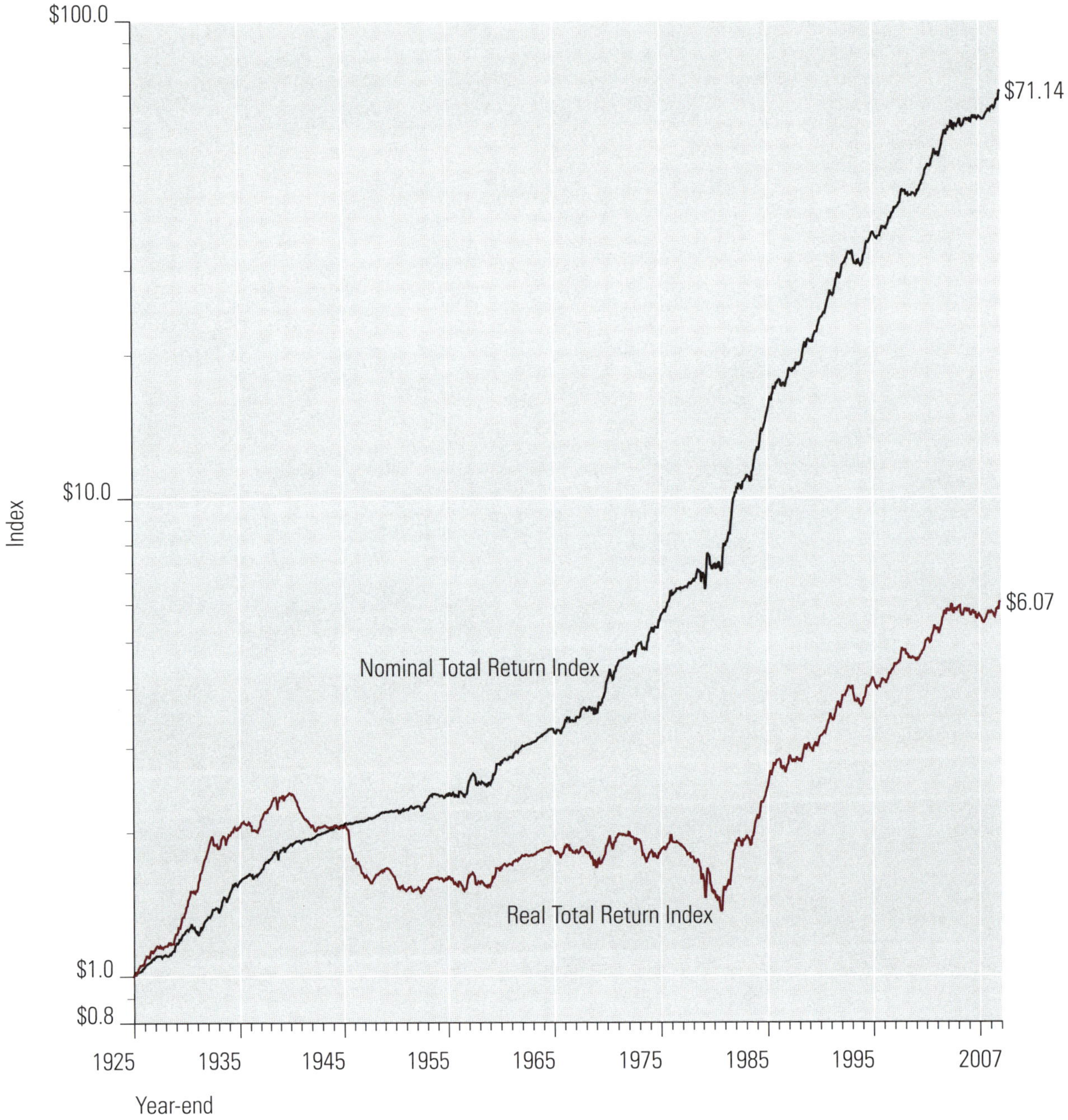

Inflation-Adjusted U.S. Treasury Bill Returns (Real Riskless Rates of Return)

Overview

Treasury bills returned 3.7 percent compounded annually over 1926–2007, in nominal terms, but only a 0.7 percent compound annual return in real (inflation-adjusted) terms. [See Graph 4-11.] Thus, an investor in Treasury bills would have barely beaten inflation over the 82-year period.

Construction

The real riskless rate of return is the difference in returns between riskless U.S. Treasury bills and inflation. This is given by:

$$\frac{(1+\text{Treasury Bill TR})}{(1+\text{Inflation})}-1 \qquad (16)$$

Graph 4-10 shows the levels, volatility, and patterns of real interest rates over the last 82 years.

Graph 4-10

Annual Real Riskless Rates of Return (in percent)

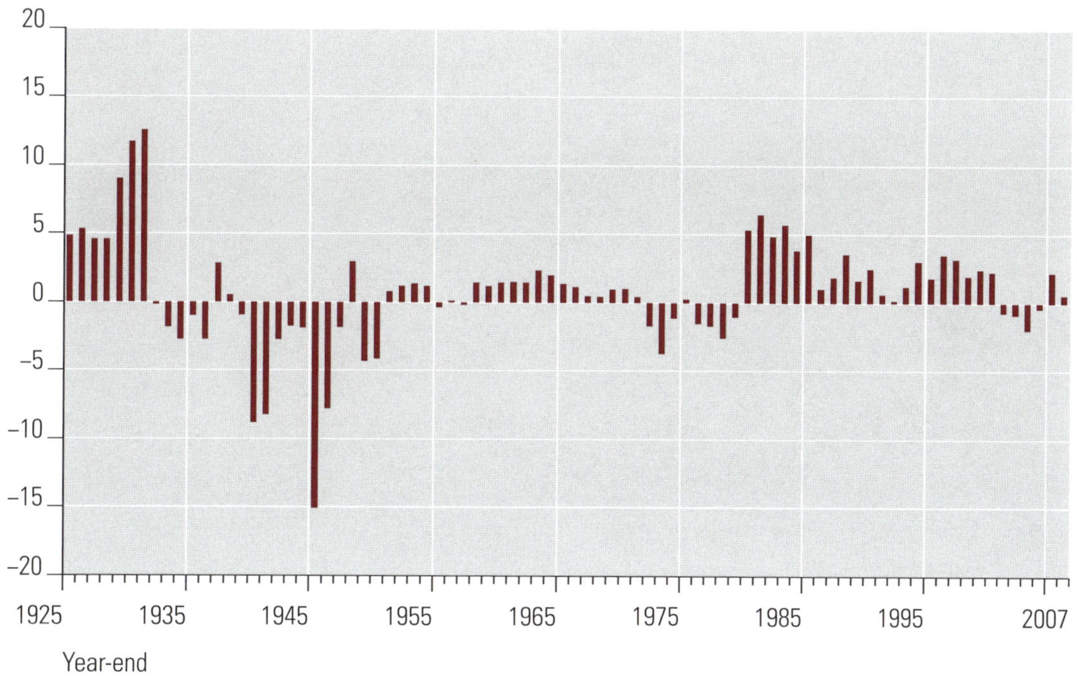

Returns on the Derived Series

Annual returns for the 10 derived series are calculated from monthly returns in the same manner as the annual basic series. Table 4-1 presents annual returns for each of the 10 derived series. Four of the derived series are risk premia and six are inflation-adjusted total returns on asset classes.

Graph 4-11
U.S. Treasury Bills
Real and Nominal Return Indices
Year-End 1925 = $1.00

from 1925 to 2007

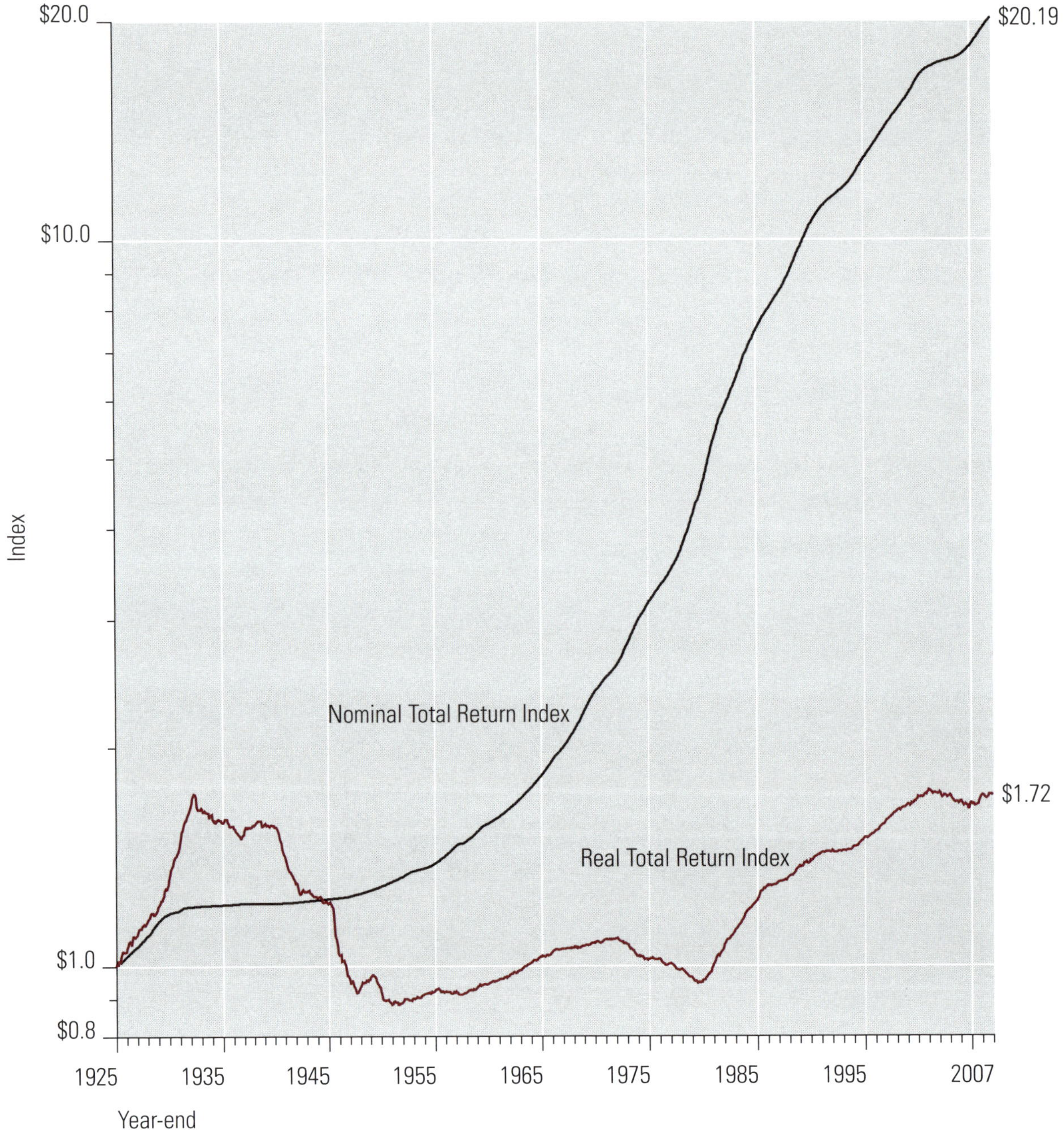

Table 4-1
Derived Series
Annual Returns (in percent)

from 1926 to 1970

					Inflation-Adjusted					
Year	Equity Risk Premia	Small Stock Premia	Default Premia	Horizon Premia	Large Company Stocks	Small Company Stocks	Long-Term Corp. Bonds	Long-Term Govt. Bonds	Intermed. Govt. Bonds	U.S. Treasury Bills
1926	8.09	–10.17	–0.37	4.36	13.31	1.79	9.00	9.40	6.97	4.83
1927	33.32	–11.19	–1.36	5.63	40.41	24.69	9.73	11.24	6.74	5.31
1928	38.67	–2.73	2.73	–3.34	45.01	41.06	3.84	1.08	1.90	4.57
1929	–12.57	–46.89	–0.14	–1.27	–8.59	–51.45	3.07	3.22	5.81	4.54
1930	–26.66	–17.64	3.17	2.20	–20.08	–34.18	14.90	11.38	13.56	8.98
1931	–43.94	–11.33	3.65	–6.31	–37.37	–44.46	8.48	4.66	7.96	11.71
1932	–9.07	3.05	–5.15	15.73	2.35	5.47	23.54	30.26	21.30	12.55
1933	53.53	57.72	10.46	–0.37	53.21	141.63	9.82	–0.58	1.31	–0.21
1934	–1.60	26.04	3.47	9.85	–3.40	21.75	11.58	7.84	6.83	–1.83
1935	47.42	–5.06	4.41	4.81	43.39	36.13	6.44	1.94	3.91	–2.73
1936	33.68	23.06	–0.72	7.32	32.32	62.83	5.47	6.23	1.83	–1.02
1937	–35.23	–35.37	2.51	–0.08	–36.98	–59.27	–0.35	–2.78	–1.50	–2.71
1938	31.14	1.28	0.57	5.55	34.87	36.59	9.16	8.55	9.27	2.84
1939	–0.43	0.76	–1.86	5.92	0.07	0.83	4.46	6.45	5.02	0.50
1940	–9.79	5.13	–2.54	6.08	–10.64	–6.05	2.41	5.08	1.99	–0.94
1941	–11.64	2.93	1.78	0.87	–19.42	–17.06	–6.37	–8.01	–8.40	–8.80
1942	20.02	20.08	–0.60	2.94	10.11	32.23	–6.12	–5.55	–6.73	–8.25
1943	25.46	49.62	0.73	1.73	22.04	82.60	–0.32	–1.04	–0.34	–2.73
1944	19.36	28.37	1.87	2.48	17.28	50.55	2.57	0.69	–0.31	–1.74
1945	35.99	27.25	–6.01	10.37	33.43	69.79	1.78	8.30	–0.03	–1.88
1946	–8.39	–3.87	1.83	–0.45	–22.20	–25.21	–13.91	–15.46	–14.52	–15.07
1947	5.18	–4.53	0.29	–3.11	–3.03	–7.42	–10.41	–10.67	–7.43	–7.80
1948	4.65	–7.22	0.71	2.57	2.72	–4.69	1.39	0.67	–0.84	–1.85
1949	17.50	0.80	–2.95	5.29	20.97	21.95	5.21	8.40	4.20	2.96
1950	30.16	5.34	2.05	–1.12	24.50	31.15	–3.47	–5.42	–4.81	–4.34
1951	22.19	–13.07	1.29	–5.34	17.14	1.82	–8.09	–9.26	–5.21	–4.14
1952	16.44	–12.96	2.33	–0.49	17.33	2.13	2.62	0.27	0.74	0.77
1953	–2.76	–5.55	–0.22	1.78	–1.60	–7.07	2.77	2.99	2.59	1.19
1954	51.32	5.21	–1.68	6.27	53.39	61.38	5.91	7.72	3.20	1.37
1955	29.52	–8.45	1.80	–2.82	31.07	19.99	0.10	–1.66	–1.02	1.19
1956	4.00	–2.13	–1.30	–7.85	3.59	1.38	–9.41	–8.21	–3.19	–0.39
1957	–13.50	–4.25	1.17	4.19	–13.40	–17.08	5.52	4.31	4.67	0.11
1958	41.19	15.01	4.13	–7.52	40.88	62.03	–3.91	–7.72	–3.00	–0.22
1959	8.75	3.97	1.32	–5.06	10.30	14.68	–2.43	–3.70	–1.86	1.43
1960	–2.14	–3.74	–4.14	10.83	–0.99	–4.70	7.48	12.12	10.13	1.17
1961	24.25	4.10	3.81	–1.13	26.04	31.21	4.12	0.30	1.17	1.44
1962	–11.16	–3.48	0.99	4.04	–9.83	–12.97	6.64	5.59	4.29	1.49
1963	19.09	0.62	0.97	–1.85	20.81	21.56	0.54	–0.43	–0.01	1.44
1964	12.50	6.04	1.22	–0.03	15.11	22.07	3.54	2.29	2.82	2.32
1965	8.20	26.06	–1.16	–3.10	10.33	39.08	–2.33	–1.19	–0.89	1.97
1966	–14.15	3.39	–3.33	–1.06	–12.98	–10.03	–3.06	0.29	1.29	1.36
1967	18.97	48.07	4.66	–12.85	20.32	78.15	–7.76	–11.86	–1.97	1.13
1968	5.57	22.43	2.84	–5.20	6.05	29.84	–2.05	–4.76	–0.18	0.46
1969	–14.16	–18.09	–3.18	–10.94	–13.77	–29.37	–13.38	–10.54	–6.45	0.45
1970	–2.36	–20.61	5.59	5.24	–1.41	–21.73	12.21	6.27	10.78	0.98

Table 4-1 (continued)

Derived Series

Annual Returns (in percent)

from 1971 to 2007

					Inflation-Adjusted					
Year	Equity Risk Premia	Small Stock Premia	Default Premia	Horizon Premia	Large Company Stocks	Small Company Stocks	Long-Term Corp. Bonds	Long-Term Govt. Bonds	Intermed. Govt. Bonds	U.S. Treasury Bills
1971	9.51	1.91	–1.96	8.47	10.60	12.71	7.41	9.55	5.19	0.99
1972	14.58	–12.22	1.49	1.78	15.05	0.99	3.72	2.20	1.69	0.41
1973	–20.19	–19.03	2.27	–7.52	–21.56	–36.49	–7.04	–9.10	–3.85	–1.72
1974	–31.92	8.87	–7.11	–3.38	–34.46	–28.65	–13.60	–6.99	–5.80	–3.74
1975	29.68	11.38	4.99	3.21	28.21	42.80	7.13	2.04	0.76	–1.13
1976	17.85	27.08	1.62	11.11	18.16	50.15	13.20	11.40	7.69	0.26
1977	–11.70	35.08	2.41	–5.53	–13.07	17.43	–4.74	–6.99	–5.02	–1.55
1978	–0.58	15.86	1.12	–7.80	–2.26	13.24	–8.34	–9.36	–5.08	–1.69
1979	7.31	21.13	–2.98	–10.52	4.53	26.62	–15.43	–12.83	–8.13	–2.59
1980	19.04	5.63	1.24	–13.65	17.81	24.45	–13.48	–14.54	–7.55	–1.03
1981	–17.10	19.76	–3.04	–11.20	–12.71	4.53	–9.34	–6.50	0.47	5.30
1982	9.83	5.43	1.57	26.97	16.88	23.23	37.25	35.13	24.28	6.42
1983	12.61	14.00	5.57	–7.49	18.03	34.56	2.37	–3.03	3.48	4.82
1984	–3.26	–12.17	1.20	5.12	2.22	–10.22	12.42	11.08	9.68	5.67
1985	22.68	–5.67	–0.67	21.58	27.36	20.13	25.36	26.21	15.96	3.81
1986	11.59	–9.81	–3.76	17.30	17.15	5.66	18.51	23.14	13.85	4.98
1987	–0.22	–13.81	2.51	–7.76	0.79	–13.13	–4.48	–6.82	–1.44	1.01
1988	9.84	5.19	0.94	3.13	11.87	17.67	6.02	5.03	1.61	1.85
1989	21.33	–16.21	–1.59	8.99	25.65	5.29	11.07	12.87	8.26	3.56
1990	–10.19	–18.99	0.57	–1.51	–8.74	–26.08	0.64	0.07	3.42	1.61
1991	23.63	10.79	0.49	12.98	26.67	40.33	16.32	15.75	12.03	2.46
1992	4.02	14.56	1.24	4.39	4.64	19.87	6.31	5.01	4.17	0.59
1993	6.89	9.99	–4.28	14.91	7.05	17.74	10.16	15.08	8.26	0.14
1994	–2.50	1.78	2.18	–11.24	–1.33	0.42	–8.22	–10.17	–7.62	1.20
1995	30.15	–2.16	–3.39	24.69	34.03	31.13	24.06	28.41	13.91	2.98
1996	16.98	–4.43	2.35	–5.83	19.12	13.84	–1.86	–4.12	–1.18	1.82
1997	26.70	–7.94	–2.51	10.07	31.13	20.72	11.06	13.91	6.57	3.49
1998	22.63	–27.91	–2.04	7.83	26.54	–8.78	9.00	11.27	8.46	3.19
1999	15.63	7.22	1.67	–13.04	17.88	26.39	–9.87	–11.34	–4.34	1.95
2000	–14.16	6.07	–7.09	14.72	–12.08	–6.75	9.17	17.50	8.90	2.42
2001	–15.13	39.33	6.70	–0.13	–13.23	20.89	8.96	2.11	5.97	2.24
2002	–23.37	11.33	–1.28	15.93	–23.91	–15.29	13.63	15.10	10.31	–0.71
2003	27.39	24.87	3.76	0.42	26.32	57.73	3.32	–0.42	0.51	–0.84
2004	9.56	6.78	0.19	7.22	7.38	14.66	5.29	5.09	–0.97	–1.99
2005	1.87	0.74	–1.80	4.69	1.44	2.20	2.37	4.25	–1.99	–0.42
2006	10.49	0.32	2.03	–3.45	12.93	13.29	0.69	–1.32	0.59	2.20
2007	0.79	–10.16	–6.63	4.99	1.36	–8.94	–1.43	5.57	5.74	0.56

Chapter 5

Annual Returns and Indices

Returns and indices are used to measure the rewards investors earn for holding an asset class. Indices represent levels of wealth or prices, while returns represent changes in levels of wealth. Total returns for specific asset classes consist of component returns that are defined by the nature of the rewards being measured. For example: The total return on a security can be divided into income and capital appreciation components. The income return measures the cash income stream earned by holding the security, such as coupon interest or dividend payments. In contrast, the capital appreciation return results from a change in the price of the security. The method for computing a return varies with the nature of the payment (income or capital appreciation) and the time period of measure (monthly or annual frequency). Indices are computed by establishing a base period and base value and increasing that value by the successive returns. Indices are used to illustrate the cumulative growth of wealth from holding an asset class. This chapter describes the computation of the annual returns and indices.

The first generation of stock indices was created to assess the market's general direction. One of the oldest and most recognizable market indices is the Dow Jones Industrial Average (DJIA), first published on May 26, 1896. When Charles Dow initially calculated the DJIA, which originally consisted of only twelve stocks[1], the process was simple: Add up the share prices of the stocks in the index and then divide this result by the number of stocks in the index. In this type of index, which is known as a price-weighted index, higher-priced stocks have a greater influence than lower-priced stocks.

Most modern indices, however, are market weighted. With market-weighted indices, companies with greater overall market capitalization (share price times number of shares outstanding) have a larger influence than companies with lesser market capitalization. Market weighting has a strong theoretical motivation because the capital asset pricing model (CAPM) implies that every investor should hold every security in proportion to its market capitalization. In contrast, price weighting lacks any theoretical motivation so it is rarely used outside of the Dow Jones Averages (Dow Jones uses market weighting for all of its other indexes). Market weighting is widely considered to be the central organizing principle of good index construction. Its practical advantage is that the weights adjust automatically as share prices fluctuate, eliminating the need for the frequent and expensive rebalancing that can occur with other weighting schemes.

Market weighting is usually implemented with a "float" adjustment that subtracts the number of closely-held and illiquid shares from the number of shares outstanding. A float-adjusted market-cap weighted portfolio is macroconsistent, meaning that if all investors held such a portfolio, all available shares of its constituent stocks would be held, with none left over. With all other weighting schemes, it is mathematically impossible for all investors to hold the index portfolio.

While there is wide agreement on the general principles of equity index construction, index providers differ in their methodologies in the process by which stocks are selected for inclusion, the number of stocks to include, and other details. Table 5-3 summaries the construction methodologies of the major broad indexes of the U.S. equity market.

1 Of the original twelve companies listed in the DJIA, General Electric is the only company that remains a component of the average. The total number of companies listed in the DJIA has not changed since 1928 when the number of companies in the index was increased to thirty. For more information on the historical make up of the DJIA, please visit the Dow Jones website at http://www.dowjones.com.

Annual and Monthly Returns

Returns on the Basic Asset Classes

Annual total returns on each of the seven basic asset classes are presented in Table 2-5 in Chapter 2. The monthly total returns on the asset classes appear in Appendix A: Tables A-1, A-4, A-5, A-6, A-10, A-14, and A-15.

Calculating Annual Returns

Annual returns are formed by compounding the 12 monthly returns. Compounding, or linking, monthly returns is multiplying together the return relatives, or one plus the return, then subtracting one from the result. The equation is denoted as the geometric sum as follows:

$$r_{year} = [(1 + r_{Jan})(1 + r_{Feb}) \ldots (1 + r_{Dec})] - 1 \qquad (17)$$

where,

r_{year} = the compound total return for the year; and,

$r_{Jan}, r_{Feb}, \ldots, r_{Dec}$ = the returns for the 12 months of the year.

The compound return reflects the growth of funds invested in an asset. The following example illustrates the compounding method for a hypothetical year:

Month	Return (Percent)	Return (Decimal)	Return Relative
January	1%	0.01	1.01
February	6	0.06	1.06
March	2	0.02	1.02
April	1	0.01	1.01
May	–3	–0.03	0.97
June	2	0.02	1.02
July	–4	–0.04	0.96
August	–2	–0.02	0.98
September	3	0.03	1.03
October	–3	–0.03	0.97
November	2	0.02	1.02
December	1	0.01	1.01

The return for this hypothetical year is the geometric sum:

$$(1.01 \times 1.06 \times 1.02 \times 1.01 \times 0.97 \times 1.02 \times 0.96 \times 0.98 \times 1.03 \times 0.97 \times 1.02 \times 1.01) - 1 = 1.0567 - 1 = 0.0567$$

or a gain of 5.67 percent. Note that this is different than the simple addition result, (1 + 6 + 2 + 1 – 3 + 2– 4 – 2 + 3 – 3 + 2 + 1) = 6 percent. One dollar invested in this hypothetical asset at the beginning of the year would have grown to slightly less than $1.06.

Calculation of Returns from Index Values

Equivalently, annual returns, r_t, can be formed by dividing index values according to:

$$r_t = \left[\frac{V_t}{V_{t-1}}\right] - 1 \qquad (18)$$

where,
r_t = the annual return in period **t**;
V_t = the index value as of year-end **t**; and,
V_{t-1} = the index value as of the previous year-end, **t − 1**.
The construction of index values is discussed later in this chapter.

Calculation of Annual Income Returns

The conversion of monthly income returns to annual income returns is calculated by adding all the cash flows (income payments) for the period, then dividing the sum by the beginning period price:

$$r_I = \frac{(I_{Jan} + I_{Feb} \ldots + I_{Dec})}{P_0} \qquad (19)$$

where,
r_I = the income return for the year;
$I_{Jan}, I_{Feb}, \ldots, I_{Dec}$ = the income payments for the 12 months of the year; and,
P_0 = the price of the security at the beginning of the year.

The following example illustrates the method for a hypothetical year:

Month	Beginning of Month Price	Income Return (Decimal)	Income Payment
January	$100	0.006	$0.60
February	102	0.004	0.41
March	105	0.002	0.21
April	101	0.001	0.10
May	99	0.005	0.50
June	103	0.004	0.41
July	105	0.003	0.32
August	103	0.002	0.21
September	105	0.003	0.32
October	103	0.004	0.41
November	106	0.001	0.11
December	105	0.002	0.21

Sum the income payments (not the returns), and divide by the price at the beginning of the year:

$$(0.60 + 0.41 + 0.21 + 0.10 + 0.50 + 0.41 + 0.32 + 0.21 + 0.32 + 0.41 + 0.11 + 0.21) / 100 = 0.0381$$

or an annual income return of 3.81 percent.

Annual income and capital appreciation returns do not sum to the annual total return. The difference may be viewed as a reinvestment return, which is the return from investing income from a given month into the same asset class in subsequent months within the year.

Index Values

Index values, or indices, represent the cumulative effect of returns on a dollar invested. For example: One dollar invested in large company stocks (with dividends reinvested) as of December 31, 1925 grew to $1.12 by December 1926, reflecting the 11.6 percent total return in 1926. [See Table 5-1.] Over the year 1927, the $1.12 grew to $1.53 by December, reflecting the 37.5 percent total return for that year. By the end of 2007, the $1.00 invested at year-end 1925 grew to $3,246.39. Such growth reveals the power of compounding (reinvesting) one's investment returns.

Year-end indices of total returns for all seven basic asset classes are displayed in Table 5-1. This table also shows indices of capital appreciation for large company stocks as well as long- and intermediate-term government bonds. Indices of the inflation-adjusted return series are presented in Table 5-2. Monthly indices of total returns and, where applicable, capital appreciation returns on the basic asset classes are presented in Appendix B: Tables B-1 through B-10.

Graphs of index values, such as Graph 2-1 "Wealth Indices of Investments in the U.S. Capital Markets," depict the growth of wealth. The vertical scale is logarithmic so that equal distances represent equal percentage changes anywhere along the axis.

The inflation-adjusted indices in Table 5-2 are notable in that they show the growth of each asset class in constant dollars, or (synonymously) in real terms. Thus an investor in large company stocks, with dividends reinvested, would have multiplied his or her wealth in real terms, or purchasing power, by a factor of 277.1 between the end of 1925 and the end of 2007.

Calculation of Index Values

It is possible to mathematically describe the nature of the indices in Tables 5-1 and 5-2 precisely. At the end of each month, a cumulative wealth index (V_n) for each of the monthly return series (basic and derived) is formed. This index is initialized as of December 1925 at $1.00 (represented by $V_0 = 1.00$). This index is formed for month n by taking the product of one plus the returns each period, as in the following manner:

$$V_n = V_0 \left[\prod_{t=1}^{n} (1 + r_t) \right] \tag{20}$$

where,
V_n = the index value at end of period **n**;
V_0 = the initial index value at time **0**; and,
r_t = the return in period **t**.

Using Index Values for Performance Measurement

Index values can be used to determine whether an investment portfolio accumulated more wealth for the investor over a period of time than another portfolio, or whether the investment performed as well as an industry benchmark. In the following example, which produced more wealth—the "investor portfolio" or a hypothetical S&P 500 index fund returning exactly the S&P total return? Each index measures total return and assumes monthly reinvestment of dividends.

	Investor Portfolio	S&P 500
January 1990	–5.35%	–6.71%
February 1990	0.65	1.29
March 1990	0.23	2.63
Accumulated wealth of $1	$0.955	$0.970

Taking December 1989 as the base period, and using the computation method described above, the S&P 500 outperformed the investor portfolio.

Computing Returns for Non-Calendar Periods

Index values are also useful for computing returns for non-calendar time periods. To compute the capital appreciation return for long-term government bonds from the end of June 1987 through the end of June 1988, divide the index value in June 1988, 0.661, by the index value in June 1987, 0.683, and subtract 1. [Refer to Table B-6 in Appendix B.]

This yields: $(0.661/\,0.683) - 1 = -0.0322$, or -3.22 percent.

Table 5-1
Basic Series
Indices of Year-End Cumulative Wealth
Year-End 1925 = $1.00

from 1925 to 1970

	Large Stocks		Small Stocks	Long-Term Corp Bonds	Long-Term Government Bonds		Intermediate-Term Government Bonds		U.S. T-Bills	
Year	Total Returns	Capital Apprec	Total Returns	Total Returns	Total Returns	Capital Apprec	Total Returns	Capital Apprec	Total Returns	Inflation
1925	1.000	1.000	1.000	1.000	1.000	1.000	1.000	1.000	1.000	1.000
1926	1.116	1.057	1.003	1.074	1.078	1.039	1.054	1.015	1.033	0.985
1927	1.535	1.384	1.224	1.154	1.174	1.095	1.101	1.025	1.065	0.965
1928	2.204	1.908	1.710	1.186	1.175	1.061	1.112	0.997	1.103	0.955
1929	2.018	1.681	0.832	1.225	1.215	1.059	1.178	1.014	1.155	0.957
1930	1.516	1.202	0.515	1.323	1.272	1.072	1.258	1.048	1.183	0.899
1931	0.859	0.636	0.259	1.299	1.204	0.982	1.228	0.991	1.196	0.814
1932	0.789	0.540	0.245	1.439	1.407	1.109	1.337	1.041	1.207	0.730
1933	1.214	0.792	0.594	1.588	1.406	1.074	1.361	1.031	1.211	0.734
1934	1.197	0.745	0.738	1.808	1.547	1.146	1.483	1.092	1.213	0.749
1935	1.767	1.053	1.035	1.982	1.624	1.171	1.587	1.146	1.215	0.771
1936	2.367	1.346	1.705	2.116	1.746	1.225	1.636	1.165	1.217	0.780
1937	1.538	0.827	0.716	2.174	1.750	1.195	1.661	1.165	1.221	0.804
1938	2.016	1.035	0.951	2.307	1.847	1.229	1.765	1.216	1.221	0.782
1939	2.008	0.979	0.954	2.399	1.957	1.272	1.845	1.255	1.221	0.778
1940	1.812	0.829	0.905	2.480	2.076	1.319	1.899	1.280	1.221	0.786
1941	1.602	0.681	0.823	2.548	2.096	1.306	1.909	1.278	1.222	0.862
1942	1.927	0.766	1.190	2.614	2.163	1.316	1.946	1.293	1.225	0.942
1943	2.427	0.915	2.242	2.688	2.208	1.311	2.000	1.309	1.229	0.972
1944	2.906	1.041	3.446	2.815	2.270	1.315	2.036	1.314	1.233	0.993
1945	3.965	1.361	5.983	2.930	2.514	1.424	2.082	1.327	1.237	1.015
1946	3.645	1.199	5.287	2.980	2.511	1.393	2.102	1.326	1.242	1.199
1947	3.853	1.199	5.335	2.911	2.445	1.328	2.122	1.322	1.248	1.307
1948	4.065	1.191	5.223	3.031	2.529	1.341	2.161	1.326	1.258	1.343
1949	4.829	1.313	6.254	3.132	2.692	1.396	2.211	1.338	1.272	1.318
1950	6.360	1.600	8.677	3.198	2.693	1.367	2.227	1.329	1.287	1.395
1951	7.888	1.863	9.355	3.112	2.587	1.282	2.235	1.307	1.306	1.477
1952	9.336	2.082	9.638	3.221	2.617	1.263	2.271	1.300	1.328	1.490
1953	9.244	1.944	9.013	3.331	2.713	1.271	2.345	1.308	1.352	1.499
1954	14.108	2.820	14.473	3.511	2.907	1.326	2.407	1.322	1.364	1.492
1955	18.561	3.564	17.431	3.527	2.870	1.272	2.392	1.281	1.385	1.497
1956	19.778	3.658	18.177	3.287	2.710	1.165	2.382	1.237	1.419	1.540
1957	17.646	3.134	15.529	3.573	2.912	1.209	2.568	1.287	1.464	1.587
1958	25.298	4.327	25.605	3.494	2.734	1.098	2.535	1.233	1.486	1.615
1959	28.322	4.694	29.804	3.460	2.673	1.030	2.525	1.177	1.530	1.639
1960	28.455	4.554	28.823	3.774	3.041	1.125	2.822	1.264	1.571	1.663
1961	36.106	5.607	38.072	3.956	3.070	1.093	2.874	1.243	1.604	1.674
1962	32.954	4.945	33.540	4.270	3.282	1.124	3.034	1.264	1.648	1.695
1963	40.469	5.879	41.444	4.364	3.322	1.093	3.084	1.237	1.700	1.723
1964	47.139	6.642	51.193	4.572	3.438	1.085	3.209	1.237	1.760	1.743
1965	53.008	7.244	72.567	4.552	3.462	1.048	3.242	1.199	1.829	1.777
1966	47.674	6.295	67.479	4.560	3.589	1.037	3.394	1.194	1.916	1.836
1967	59.104	7.560	123.870	4.335	3.259	0.896	3.428	1.148	1.997	1.892
1968	65.642	8.139	168.429	4.446	3.251	0.847	3.583	1.136	2.101	1.981
1969	60.059	7.210	126.233	4.086	3.086	0.755	3.557	1.054	2.239	2.102
1970	62.465	7.222	104.226	4.837	3.460	0.792	4.156	1.145	2.385	2.218

Table 5-1 (continued)

Basic Series

Indices of Year-End Cumulative Wealth

Year-End 1925 = $1.00

from 1971 to 2007

	Large Stocks		Small Stocks	Long-Term Corp Bonds	Long-Term Government Bonds		Intermediate-Term Government Bonds		U.S. T-Bills	
Year	**Total Returns**	**Capital Apprec**	**Total Returns**	**Total Returns**	**Total Returns**	**Capital Apprec**	**Total Returns**	**Capital Apprec**	**Total Returns**	**Inflation**
1971	71.406	8.001	121.423	5.370	3.917	0.844	4.519	1.177	2.490	2.292
1972	84.956	9.252	126.807	5.760	4.140	0.841	4.752	1.168	2.585	2.371
1973	72.500	7.645	87.618	5.825	4.094	0.777	4.971	1.142	2.764	2.579
1974	53.311	5.373	70.142	5.647	4.272	0.750	5.254	1.120	2.986	2.894
1975	73.144	7.068	107.189	6.474	4.665	0.755	5.665	1.121	3.159	3.097
1976	90.584	8.422	168.691	7.681	5.447	0.816	6.394	1.180	3.319	3.246
1977	84.077	7.453	211.500	7.813	5.410	0.752	6.484	1.119	3.489	3.466
1978	89.592	7.532	261.120	7.807	5.346	0.684	6.710	1.069	3.740	3.778
1979	106.113	8.459	374.614	7.481	5.280	0.617	6.985	1.015	4.128	4.281
1980	140.514	10.639	523.992	7.274	5.071	0.530	7.258	0.946	4.592	4.812
1981	133.616	9.605	596.717	7.185	5.166	0.476	7.944	0.903	5.267	5.242
1982	162.223	11.023	763.829	10.242	7.251	0.589	10.256	1.031	5.822	5.445
1983	198.745	12.926	1066.828	10.883	7.298	0.532	11.015	0.997	6.335	5.652
1984	211.199	13.106	995.680	12.718	8.427	0.544	12.560	1.009	6.959	5.875
1985	279.117	16.559	1241.234	16.546	11.037	0.641	15.113	1.100	7.496	6.097
1986	330.671	18.981	1326.275	19.829	13.745	0.737	17.401	1.177	7.958	6.166
1987	347.967	19.366	1202.966	19.776	13.372	0.658	17.906	1.121	8.393	6.438
1988	406.458	21.769	1478.135	21.893	14.665	0.661	18.999	1.096	8.926	6.722
1989	534.455	27.703	1628.590	25.447	17.322	0.718	21.524	1.143	9.673	7.034
1990	517.499	25.886	1277.449	27.173	18.392	0.699	23.618	1.155	10.429	7.464
1991	675.592	32.695	1847.629	32.577	21.942	0.769	27.270	1.240	11.012	7.693
1992	727.412	34.155	2279.039	35.637	23.709	0.772	29.230	1.248	11.398	7.916
1993	800.078	36.565	2757.147	40.336	28.034	0.855	32.516	1.317	11.728	8.133
1994	810.538	36.002	2842.773	38.012	25.856	0.733	30.843	1.170	12.186	8.351
1995	1113.918	48.282	3822.398	48.353	34.044	0.901	36.025	1.283	12.868	8.563
1996	1370.946	58.066	4495.993	49.031	33.727	0.835	36.782	1.233	13.538	8.847
1997	1828.326	76.071	5519.969	55.380	39.074	0.906	39.864	1.257	14.250	8.998
1998	2350.892	96.359	5116.648	61.339	44.178	0.968	43.933	1.316	14.942	9.143
1999	2845.629	115.174	6640.788	56.772	40.218	0.829	43.155	1.223	15.641	9.389
2000	2586.524	103.496	6402.228	64.077	48.856	0.949	48.589	1.296	16.563	9.707
2001	2279.127	89.997	7860.048	70.900	50.662	0.931	52.291	1.338	17.197	9.857
2002	1775.341	68.969	6816.409	82.480	59.699	1.039	59.054	1.453	17.480	10.091
2003	2284.785	87.163	10953.944	86.824	60.564	1.004	60.469	1.446	17.659	10.281
2004	2533.204	95.002	12968.476	94.396	65.717	1.037	61.832	1.431	17.871	10.616
2005	2657.559	97.853	13706.149	99.937	70.852	1.069	62.674	1.394	18.403	10.978
2006	3077.329	111.180	15922.429	103.178	71.694	1.030	64.643	1.373	19.287	11.257
2007	3246.391	115.104	15091.095	105.858	78.779	1.078	71.142	1.446	20.186	11.717

Table 5-2
Inflation-Adjusted Series
Indices of Year-End Cumulative Wealth
Year-End 1925 = $1.00

from 1925 to 1970

	Inflation-Adjusted					
	Large Company Stocks	Small Company Stocks	Long-Term Corporate Bonds	Long-Term Government Bonds	Intermediate Government Bonds	U.S. Treasury Bills
1925	1.000	1.000	1.000	1.000	1.000	1.000
1926	1.133	1.018	1.090	1.094	1.070	1.048
1927	1.591	1.269	1.196	1.217	1.142	1.104
1928	2.307	1.790	1.242	1.230	1.164	1.154
1929	2.109	0.869	1.280	1.270	1.231	1.207
1930	1.685	0.572	1.471	1.414	1.398	1.315
1931	1.056	0.318	1.596	1.480	1.509	1.469
1932	1.080	0.335	1.971	1.928	1.831	1.654
1933	1.655	0.810	2.165	1.917	1.855	1.650
1934	1.599	0.986	2.415	2.067	1.982	1.620
1935	2.292	1.342	2.571	2.107	2.059	1.576
1936	3.033	2.185	2.712	2.238	2.097	1.560
1937	1.912	0.890	2.702	2.176	2.065	1.517
1938	2.578	1.216	2.950	2.362	2.257	1.561
1939	2.580	1.226	3.082	2.514	2.370	1.568
1940	2.305	1.152	3.156	2.642	2.417	1.554
1941	1.858	0.955	2.955	2.430	2.214	1.417
1942	2.046	1.263	2.774	2.295	2.065	1.300
1943	2.496	2.306	2.765	2.271	2.058	1.264
1944	2.928	3.472	2.836	2.287	2.052	1.242
1945	3.907	5.895	2.887	2.477	2.051	1.219
1946	3.039	4.409	2.485	2.094	1.753	1.035
1947	2.947	4.081	2.227	1.871	1.623	0.955
1948	3.027	3.890	2.258	1.883	1.609	0.937
1949	3.662	4.744	2.375	2.042	1.677	0.965
1950	4.560	6.221	2.293	1.931	1.596	0.923
1951	5.341	6.335	2.107	1.752	1.513	0.885
1952	6.267	6.469	2.162	1.757	1.524	0.891
1953	6.166	6.012	2.222	1.809	1.564	0.902
1954	9.458	9.703	2.354	1.949	1.614	0.914
1955	12.397	11.642	2.356	1.917	1.597	0.925
1956	12.843	11.803	2.134	1.759	1.547	0.922
1957	11.122	9.788	2.252	1.835	1.619	0.923
1958	15.669	15.859	2.164	1.694	1.570	0.921
1959	17.283	18.187	2.112	1.631	1.541	0.934
1960	17.111	17.333	2.270	1.829	1.697	0.945
1961	21.567	22.741	2.363	1.834	1.717	0.958
1962	19.447	19.792	2.520	1.937	1.791	0.973
1963	23.494	24.060	2.534	1.928	1.790	0.987
1964	27.044	29.370	2.623	1.972	1.841	1.010
1965	29.838	40.848	2.562	1.949	1.825	1.029
1966	25.964	36.751	2.484	1.955	1.848	1.043
1967	31.239	65.471	2.291	1.723	1.812	1.055
1968	33.129	85.005	2.244	1.641	1.808	1.060
1969	28.567	60.042	1.944	1.468	1.692	1.065
1970	28.164	46.993	2.181	1.560	1.874	1.075

Table 5-2 (continued)

Inflation-Adjusted Series

Indices of Year-End Cumulative Wealth

Year-End 1925 = $1.00

from 1971 to 2007

	Inflation-Adjusted					
	Large Company Stocks	Small Company Stocks	Long-Term Corporate Bonds	Long-Term Government Bonds	Intermediate Government Bonds	U.S. Treasury Bills
1971	31.149	52.968	2.343	1.709	1.971	1.086
1972	35.837	53.492	2.430	1.746	2.005	1.091
1973	28.110	33.971	2.259	1.587	1.927	1.072
1974	18.422	24.238	1.951	1.476	1.815	1.032
1975	23.619	34.612	2.091	1.506	1.829	1.020
1976	27.908	51.971	2.366	1.678	1.970	1.023
1977	24.260	61.029	2.254	1.561	1.871	1.007
1978	23.712	69.108	2.066	1.415	1.776	0.990
1979	24.786	87.502	1.747	1.233	1.632	0.964
1980	29.201	108.894	1.512	1.054	1.508	0.954
1981	25.489	113.831	1.371	0.985	1.515	1.005
1982	29.792	140.278	1.881	1.332	1.884	1.069
1983	35.165	188.759	1.926	1.291	1.949	1.121
1984	35.947	169.470	2.165	1.434	2.138	1.184
1985	45.781	203.588	2.714	1.810	2.479	1.230
1986	53.631	215.106	3.216	2.229	2.822	1.291
1987	54.053	186.867	3.072	2.077	2.782	1.304
1988	60.466	219.893	3.257	2.182	2.826	1.328
1989	75.977	231.516	3.617	2.462	3.060	1.375
1990	69.333	171.148	3.641	2.464	3.164	1.397
1991	87.822	240.179	4.235	2.852	3.545	1.431
1992	91.893	287.908	4.502	2.995	3.693	1.440
1993	98.369	338.990	4.959	3.447	3.998	1.442
1994	97.059	340.412	4.552	3.096	3.693	1.459
1995	130.085	446.387	5.647	3.976	4.207	1.503
1996	154.953	508.167	5.542	3.812	4.157	1.530
1997	203.190	613.460	6.155	4.342	4.430	1.584
1998	257.121	559.616	6.709	4.832	4.805	1.634
1999	303.094	707.326	6.047	4.284	4.597	1.666
2000	266.472	659.577	6.601	5.033	5.006	1.706
2001	231.215	797.393	7.193	5.140	5.305	1.745
2002	175.925	675.462	8.173	5.916	5.852	1.732
2003	222.231	1065.440	8.445	5.891	5.882	1.718
2004	238.625	1221.614	8.892	6.191	5.824	1.683
2005	242.070	1248.459	9.103	6.454	5.709	1.676
2006	273.361	1414.399	9.165	6.369	5.742	1.713
2007	277.071	1287.985	9.035	6.724	6.072	1.723

Table 5-3
The Major Capitalization and Style Indexes of the U.S. Equity Market*

	Index Family				
	Morningstar	**DJ/Wilshire**	**MSCI**	**Russell**	**S&P/Citigroup**
Broad Market Index	Morningstar US Market Index	Dow Jones Wilshire 5000 Composite	MSCI Investable Market	Russell 3000	S&P Composite 1500**
Percent U.S. Market Cap Coverage for Broad Market Index	97%	>99%	98%	99%	85%
Total Number of Stocks	2000+	5000	2500	3000	1500
Transparent, Rule-based Methodology	Yes	Yes	Yes	Yes	No
Eligibility	Stocks of companies domiciled in U.S. listed on the NYSE, AMEX, or Nasdaq	Stocks of U.S. domiciled companies for which prices are available and listed on a U.S. exchange	Stocks of companies domiciled in U.S. listed on the NYSE, AMEX, or Nasdaq	Stocks of the largest 3,000 companies domiciled in the U.S. listed on a U.S. exchange or the Nasdaq	Stocks of U.S. domiciled companies listed on the NYSE, AMEX, or Nasdaq chosen for market size, liquidity, and industry group representation by the S&P Index Committee
Exclusion Criteria	ADRs Limited Partnerships Investment Trusts (except REITs) Tracking Stocks Holding Companies	ADRs Over the Counter Issues	ADRs Limited Partnerships Investment Trusts (except REITs) Mutual Funds Equity Derivatives Royalty Trusts and LLCs	ADRs Limited Partnerships Closed-end mutual funds Price < $1 Royalty Trusts and LLCs	ADRs Limited Partnerships Investment Trusts (except REITs) Tracking Stocks Holding Companies Royalty Trusts and LLCs
Market Cap Cut-off Method	Market Cap Percent	Fixed Number of Stocks	Fixed Number of Stocks	Fixed Number of Stocks	Fixed Number of Stocks
Unique Cap Classification	Yes	No, stocks may be included in more than one cap index	Yes	Yes	Yes
Unique Style Classification	Yes	Yes	No, stocks may be included in more than one style index	No, stocks may be included in more than one style index	No, stocks may be included in more than one style index
Core Style Index	Yes	No	No	No	No
Reconstitution Frequency	Semi-Annual	Semi-Annual	Semi-Annual	Annual	Ad hoc

*The broad market indices shown in Table 5-3 can be disaggregated into capitalization and style indices. For example, the S&P Composite 1500 can be disaggregated into the S&P 500 (large-cap stocks), S&P 400 (mid-cap stocks), and the S&P 600 (small-cap stocks).

**The market for U.S. large company stocks is represented by the S&P 500 throughout the Ibbotson® SBBI® Yearbook series.

Chapter 6

Statistical Analysis of Returns

Statistical analysis of historical asset returns can reveal the growth rate of wealth invested in an asset or portfolio, the riskiness or volatility of asset classes, the comovement of assets, and the random or cyclical behavior of asset returns. This chapter focuses on arithmetic and geometric mean returns, standard deviations, and serial and cross-correlation coefficients, and discusses the use of each statistic to characterize the various asset classes by growth rate, variability, and safety.

Calculating Arithmetic Mean Returns

The arithmetic mean of a series is the simple average of the elements in the series. The arithmetic mean return equation is:

$$r_A = \frac{1}{n}\sum_{t=1}^{n} r_t \qquad (21)$$

where,

r_A = the arithmetic mean return;

r_t = the series return in period **t**, that is, from time **t – 1** to time **t**; and,

n = the inclusive number of periods.

Calculating Geometric Mean Returns

The geometric mean of a return series over a period is the compound rate of return over the period. The geometric mean return equation is:

$$r_G = \left[\prod_{t=1}^{n}(1 + r_t)\right]^{\frac{1}{n}} - 1 \qquad (22)$$

where,

r_G = the geometric mean return;

r_t = the series return in period **t**; and,

n = the inclusive number of periods.

The geometric mean return can be restated using beginning and ending period index values. The equation is:

$$r_G = \left[\frac{V_n}{V_0}\right]^{\frac{1}{n}} - 1 \qquad (23)$$

where,

r_G = the geometric mean return;

V_n = the ending period index value at time **n**;

V_0 = the initial index value at time **0**; and,

n = the inclusive number of periods.

The annualized geometric mean return over any period of months can also be computed by expressing n as a fraction. For example: starting at the beginning of 1996 to the end of May 1996 is equivalent to five-twelfths of a year, or 0.4167. V_n would be the index value at the end of May 1996, V_0 would be the index value at the beginning of 1996, and n would be 0.4167.

Geometric Mean Versus Arithmetic Mean

A simple example illustrates the difference between geometric and arithmetic means. Suppose $1.00 was invested in a large company stock portfolio that experiences successive annual returns of +50 percent and –50 percent. At the end of the first year, the portfolio is worth $1.50. At the end of the second year, the portfolio is worth $0.75. The annual arithmetic mean is 0.0 percent, whereas the annual geometric mean is –13.4 percent. Both are calculated as follows:

$$r_A = \frac{1}{2}(0.50 - 0.50) = 0.0, \text{ and}$$

$$r_G = \left[\frac{0.75}{1.00}\right]^{\frac{1}{n}} - 1 = -0.134$$

The geometric mean is backward-looking, measuring the change in wealth over more than one period. On the other hand, the arithmetic mean better represents a typical performance over single periods.

In general, the geometric mean for any time period is less than or equal to the arithmetic mean. The two means are equal only for a return series that is constant (i.e., the same return in every period). For a non-constant series, the difference between the two is positively related to the variability or standard deviation of the returns. For example, in Table 6-7, the difference between the arithmetic and geometric mean is much larger for risky large company stocks than it is for nearly riskless Treasury bills.

Calculating Standard Deviations

The standard deviation of a series is a measure of the extent to which observations in the series differ from the arithmetic mean of the series. For a series of asset returns, the standard deviation is a measure of the volatility, or risk, of the asset. The standard deviation is a measure of the variation around an average or mean.

In a normally distributed series, about two-thirds of the observations lie within one standard deviation of the arithmetic mean; about 95 percent of the observations lie within two standard deviations; and more than 99 percent lie within three standard deviations.

For example, the standard deviation for large company stocks over the period 1926–2007 was 20.0 percent with an annual arithmetic mean of 12.3 percent. Therefore, roughly two-thirds of the observations have annual returns between –7.7 percent and 32.3 percent (12.3 ± 20.0); approximately 95 percent of the observations are between –27.7 percent and 52.3 percent (12.3 ± 40.0).

The equation for the standard deviation of a series of returns (σ_r) is:

$$\sigma_r = \sqrt{\frac{1}{n-1}\sum_{t=1}^{n}(r_t - r_A)^2} \qquad (24)$$

where,
r_t = the return in period **t**;
r_A = the arithmetic mean of the return series **r**; and,
n = the number of periods.

The scaling of the standard deviation depends on the frequency of the data; therefore, a series of monthly returns produces a monthly standard deviation. For example, using the monthly returns for the hypothetical year on page 98, a monthly standard deviation of 2.94 percent is calculated following equation (24):

$$\left[\tfrac{1}{12-1}((0.01 - 0.005)^2 + (0.06 - 0.005)^2 + (0.02 - 0.005)^2 + (0.01 - 0.005)^2 + (-0.03 - 0.005)^2 + (0.02 - 0.005)^2 + (-0.04 - 0.005)^2 + (-0.02 - 0.005)^2 + (0.03 - 0.005)^2 + (-0.03 - 0.005)^2 + (0.02 - 0.005)^2 + (0.01 - 0.005)^2)\right]^{\frac{1}{2}} = 0.0294$$

It is sometimes useful to express the standard deviation of the series in another time scale. To calculate the annualized monthly standard deviations (σ_n), one uses equation (25).[1]

$$\sigma_n = \sqrt{\left[\sigma_1^2 + (1+\mu_1)^2\right]^n - (1+\mu_1)^{2n}} \qquad (25)$$

where,
n = the number of periods per year, e.g. 12 for monthly, 4 for quarterly, etc.;
σ_1 = the monthly standard deviation; and,
μ_1 = the monthly arithmetic mean.

Applying this formula to the prior monthly standard deviation of 2.94 percent results in an annualized monthly standard deviation of 10.78 percent. The annualized monthly standard deviation is calculated with equation (25) as follows:

$$\sqrt{\left[0.0294^2 + (1+0.005)^2\right]^{12} - (1+0.005)^{2(12)}} = 0.1078$$

This equation is the exact form of the common approximation:

$$\sigma_n \approx \sqrt{n}\,\sigma_1$$

1 The equation appears in Haim Levy and Deborah Gunthorpe, "Optimal Investment Proportions in Senior Securities and Equities Under Alternative Holding Periods," *Journal of Portfolio Management*, Summer 1993, page 33.

The approximation treats an annual return as if it were the sum of 12 independent monthly returns, whereas equation (25) treats an annual return as the compound return of 12 independent monthly returns. [See Equation (17)]. While the approximation can be used for "back of the envelope" calculations, the exact formula should be used in applications of quantitative analysis. Forming inputs for mean-variance optimization is one such example. Note that both the exact formula and the approximation assume that there is no monthly autocorrelation.

Volatility of the Markets

The volatility of stocks and long-term government bonds is shown by the bar graphs of monthly returns in Graph 6-1. The stock market was tremendously volatile in the first few years studied; this period was marked by the 1920s boom, the crash of 1929–1932, and the Great Depression years. The market settled after World War II and provided more stable returns in the postwar period. In the 1970s and 1980s, stock market volatility increased, but not to the extreme levels of the 1920s and 1930s, with the exception of October 1987. In the 1990s and 2000s, volatility was relatively moderate.

Bonds present a mirror image. Long-term government bonds were extremely stable in the 1920s and remained so through the crisis years of the 1930s, providing shelter from the storms of the stock markets. Starting in the late 1960s and early 1970s, however, bond volatility soared; in the 1973–1974 stock market decline, bonds did not provide the shelter they once did. Bond pessimism (i.e., high yields) peaked in 1981 and subsequent returns were sharply positive. While the astronomical interest rates of the 1979–1981 period have passed, the volatility of the bond market remains higher.

Graph 6-1
Month-by-Month Returns on Stocks and Bonds
Large Company Stocks and Long-Term Government Bonds

from 1926 to 2007

Large Company Stocks

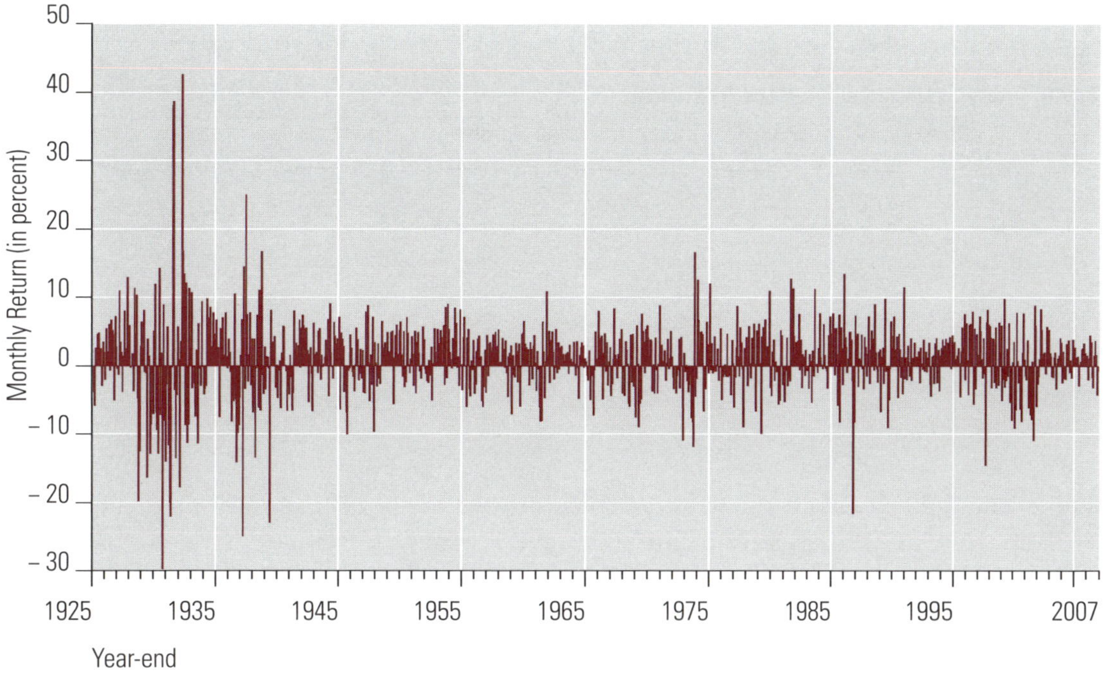

Long-Term Government Bonds

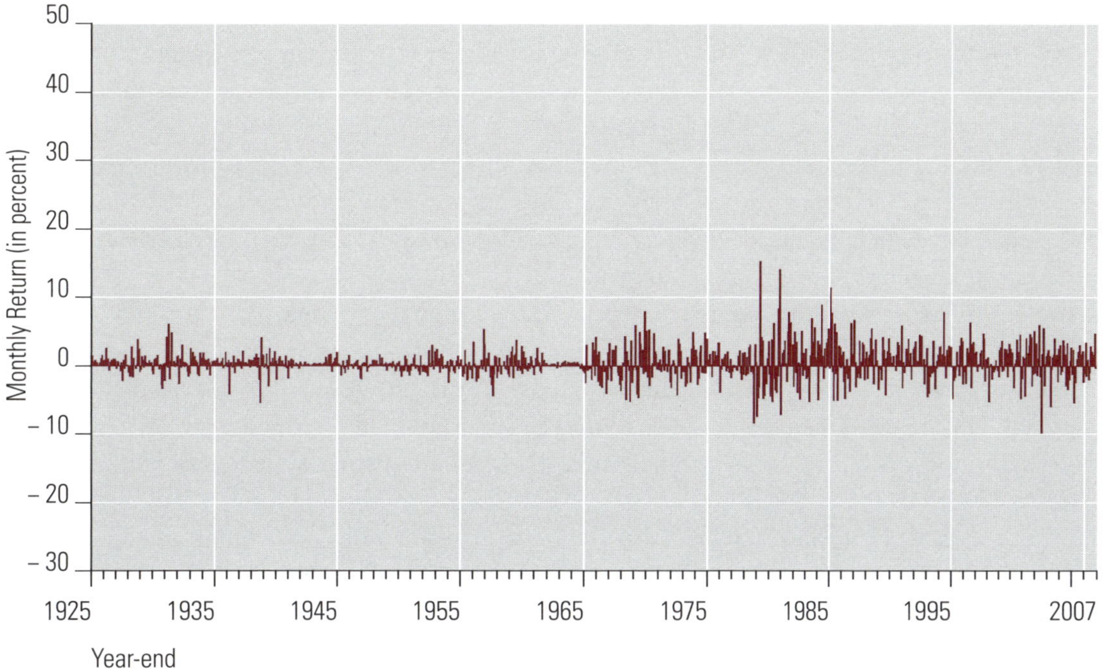

Changes in the Risk of Assets Over Time

Table 6-1
Annualized Monthly Standard Deviations by Decade

	1920s*	1930s	1940s	1950s	1960s	1970s	1980s	1990s	2000s**	1998–2007
Large Company	23.9%	41.6%	17.5%	14.1%	13.1%	17.1%	19.4%	15.8%	14.2%	15.7%
Small Company	24.7	78.6	34.5	14.4	21.5	30.8	22.5	20.2	24.4	24.7
Long-Term Corp	1.8	5.3	1.8	4.4	4.9	8.7	14.1	6.9	8.6	8.1
Long-Term Govt	4.1	5.3	2.8	4.6	6.0	8.7	16.0	8.9	10.2	9.6
Inter-Term Govt	1.7	3.3	1.2	2.9	3.3	5.2	8.8	4.6	4.9	4.8
Treasury Bills	0.3	0.2	0.1	0.2	0.4	0.6	0.9	0.4	0.5	0.5
Inflation	2.0	2.5	3.1	1.2	0.7	1.2	1.3	0.7	1.3	1.2

*Based on the period 1926–1929.

**Based on the period 2000–2007.

Another time series property of great interest is change in volatility or riskiness over time. Such change is indicated by the standard deviation of the series over different subperiods. Table 6-1 shows the annualized monthly standard deviations of the basic data series by decade beginning in 1926 and illustrates differences and changes in return volatility. In this table, the '20s cover the period 1926–1929 and the 2000s cover the period 2000–2007. Equity returns have been the most volatile of the basic series, with volatility peaking in the 1930s due to the instability of the market following the 1929 market crash. The significant bond yield fluctuations of the '80s caused the fixed income series' volatility to soar compared to prior decades.

The standard deviation of a series for a particular year is the standard deviation of the 12 monthly returns for that year around that year's arithmetic mean. This monthly estimate is then annualized according to equation (25). Table 6-2 displays the annualized standard deviation of the monthly returns on each of the basic and derived series from 1926 to 2007. The estimates in this table and in Table 6-1 are not strictly comparable to Table 2-1 and Table 6-7 and 6-8, where the 82-year period standard deviation of annual returns around the 82-year annual arithmetic mean is reported. The arithmetic mean drifts for a series that does not follow a random pattern. A series with a drifting mean will have much higher deviations around its long-term mean than it has around the mean during a particular calendar year.

As shown in Table 6-2, large company stocks and equity risk premia have virtually the same annualized monthly standard deviations because there is very little deviation in the U.S. Treasury bill series. These two series also have much higher variability in the pre-World War II period than in the postwar period. On the other hand, the various bond series (long- and intermediate-term government bonds, long-term corporate bonds, horizon premia, and default premia) were less volatile in the pre-World War II period.

The series with drifting means (U.S. Treasury bills, inflation rates, and inflation-adjusted U.S. Treasury bills) all tend to have very low annualized monthly standard deviations, since these series are quite predictable from month to month. As seen in Tables 6-7 and 6-8, however, there is much less predictability for these series over the long term. Since it is difficult to forecast the direction and magnitude of the drift in the long-term mean, these series have higher standard deviations over the long term in comparison to their annualized monthly standard deviations.

Correlation Coefficients: Serial and Cross-Correlations

The behavior of an asset return series over time reveals its predictability. For example, a series may be random or unpredictable; or it may be subject to trends, cycles, or other patterns, making the series predictable to some degree. The serial correlation coefficient of a series determines its predictability given knowledge of the last observation. The cross-correlation coefficient (often shortened to "correlation") between two series determines the predictability of one series, conditional on knowledge of the other.

Serial Correlations

The serial correlation of a return series, also known as the first-order autocorrelation, describes the extent to which the return in one period is related to the return in the next period. A return series with a high (near one) serial correlation is very predictable from one period to the next, while one with a low (near zero) serial correlation is random and unpredictable.

The serial correlation of a series is closely approximated by the equation for the cross-correlation between two series, which is given in equation (26). The data, however, are the series and its "lagged" self. For example, the lagged series is the series of one-period-old returns:

Year	Return Series (X)	Lagged Return Series (Y)
1	0.10	undefined
2	–0.10	0.10
3	0.15	–0.10
4	0.00	0.15

Table 6-2
Basic and Derived Series
Annualized Monthly Standard Deviations (in percent)

from 1926 to 1970

	Basic Series							Derived Series				
Year	Large Company Stocks	Small Company Stocks	Long-Term Corporate Bonds	Long-Term Govt Bonds	Intermediate-Term Govt Bonds	U.S. Treasury Bills	Inflation	Equity Risk Premia	Small Stock Premia	Bond Default Premia	Bond Horizon Premia	Inflation-Adjusted T-Bills
1926	13.10	16.89	0.96	1.88	1.02	0.32	2.03	12.73	9.74	1.63	1.68	2.06
1927	17.90	21.19	1.49	2.88	1.05	0.11	2.78	17.35	11.13	2.90	2.76	3.03
1928	24.62	28.68	1.87	3.21	1.27	0.32	1.72	23.65	14.48	2.74	3.06	1.84
1929	30.55	18.35	2.42	6.56	2.82	0.21	1.62	29.16	7.76	6.79	6.20	1.62
1930	21.19	25.55	2.38	2.34	2.43	0.30	2.03	20.65	11.68	2.45	2.12	2.31
1931	30.04	45.35	5.91	5.24	3.72	0.16	1.35	29.72	27.44	5.25	5.18	1.75
1932	83.36	147.23	7.71	9.50	2.94	0.29	1.74	82.72	41.92	12.69	9.35	2.40
1933	99.82	286.56	11.74	5.11	3.70	0.10	4.24	99.27	72.06	7.67	5.06	4.15
1934	22.64	73.85	3.10	4.50	4.07	0.04	2.03	22.59	42.03	2.52	4.46	1.94
1935	23.73	36.09	2.53	2.88	2.78	0.01	2.18	23.69	15.08	1.36	2.88	2.05
1936	19.06	66.23	1.18	2.25	1.27	0.02	1.55	19.02	37.72	1.78	2.25	1.51
1937	16.33	21.81	1.99	5.04	2.44	0.05	1.74	16.28	16.46	3.93	5.01	1.63
1938	58.87	114.31	2.38	2.35	2.48	0.07	1.78	58.85	30.94	1.89	2.31	1.89
1939	31.09	95.06	5.36	8.59	5.06	0.02	2.26	31.07	43.55	8.40	8.59	2.24
1940	25.56	46.88	2.02	5.20	3.25	0.02	1.09	25.55	25.68	3.92	5.19	1.07
1941	12.95	29.10	1.67	3.71	1.50	0.03	2.30	12.92	20.75	3.59	3.70	1.90
1942	17.67	37.55	0.73	1.42	0.79	0.03	1.39	17.60	25.78	1.16	1.42	1.17
1943	19.59	71.56	0.90	0.65	0.51	0.01	2.35	19.53	33.94	0.58	0.65	2.21
1944	9.30	28.75	1.34	0.37	0.29	0.01	0.97	9.27	15.14	1.11	0.37	0.94
1945	17.64	37.50	1.42	2.97	0.50	0.01	1.32	17.59	16.92	1.92	2.96	1.26
1946	17.72	27.25	2.15	2.73	0.94	0.00	6.65	17.65	12.20	1.74	2.72	4.66
1947	10.15	18.24	2.13	2.86	0.52	0.07	3.34	10.09	10.58	3.26	2.90	2.79
1948	21.49	24.11	2.20	1.95	0.59	0.07	2.90	21.30	6.44	1.92	1.96	2.73
1949	12.02	18.75	2.17	1.83	0.47	0.02	1.63	11.89	6.72	2.44	1.80	1.71
1950	13.99	20.58	1.07	1.45	0.34	0.03	1.81	13.83	8.82	1.35	1.44	1.62
1951	15.04	16.02	3.92	3.03	1.91	0.05	1.79	14.80	6.12	2.67	2.95	1.63
1952	13.32	9.66	2.85	3.24	1.32	0.08	1.15	13.11	3.78	3.82	3.23	1.14
1953	9.32	10.90	5.53	5.16	3.26	0.11	1.01	9.21	8.74	3.50	5.07	0.95
1954	19.27	20.02	2.35	3.47	1.93	0.06	0.74	19.08	10.08	2.33	3.42	0.77
1955	16.11	7.70	2.17	3.60	1.65	0.14	0.67	15.91	8.83	2.36	3.47	0.71
1956	15.86	8.39	3.00	4.28	2.64	0.10	1.08	15.50	7.87	2.60	4.15	1.00
1957	11.48	10.42	9.40	8.26	5.57	0.07	0.66	11.13	9.98	5.48	8.00	0.65
1958	8.74	15.44	4.56	6.29	4.50	0.27	0.90	8.47	7.99	3.73	6.16	0.88
1959	8.91	10.34	3.91	3.25	2.72	0.18	0.65	8.67	7.31	3.35	3.18	0.59
1960	13.63	13.37	3.93	6.45	4.99	0.27	0.71	13.36	7.07	3.85	6.22	0.80
1961	11.16	19.02	3.63	3.55	1.57	0.07	0.51	10.94	7.72	3.93	3.51	0.50
1962	18.97	21.58	2.27	3.70	2.15	0.08	0.67	18.46	8.38	2.17	3.63	0.70
1963	11.91	13.47	1.25	0.72	0.60	0.08	0.55	11.54	7.26	1.28	0.72	0.55
1964	4.63	7.05	1.46	0.91	0.78	0.06	0.41	4.47	3.78	1.84	0.87	0.38
1965	9.56	20.55	1.96	1.51	1.83	0.08	0.67	9.26	11.19	1.09	1.47	0.64
1966	9.96	17.80	4.80	8.08	4.13	0.11	0.71	9.50	13.76	5.39	7.66	0.73
1967	14.89	36.96	7.33	6.58	3.81	0.16	0.44	14.24	17.30	5.14	6.27	0.54
1968	14.49	28.29	7.39	7.93	3.50	0.09	0.42	13.76	16.40	3.57	7.52	0.40
1969	12.10	18.71	6.93	9.95	5.54	0.22	0.62	11.35	9.73	7.39	9.34	0.63
1970	21.60	27.68	11.28	15.07	7.05	0.22	0.44	20.33	13.19	9.22	14.11	0.47

Table 6-2 (continued)

Basic and Derived Series

Annualized Monthly Standard Deviations (in percent)

from 1971 to 2007

	Basic Series							Derived Series				
Year	Large Company Stocks	Small Company Stocks	Long-Term Corporate Bonds	Long-Term Govt Bonds	Intermediate-Term Govt Bonds	U.S. Treasury Bills	Inflation	Equity Risk Premia	Small Stock Premia	Bond Default Premia	Bond Horizon Premia	Inflation-Adjusted T-Bills
1971	15.64	29.73	11.12	10.67	6.98	0.19	0.57	14.97	14.61	6.12	10.15	0.63
1972	7.80	16.60	3.21	5.85	1.97	0.17	0.41	7.51	11.39	3.97	5.61	0.42
1973	12.15	21.94	7.57	8.38	4.99	0.37	1.53	11.27	14.21	5.12	7.71	1.34
1974	18.74	20.15	11.45	8.64	5.73	0.36	0.91	17.52	22.03	5.76	8.05	0.89
1975	24.38	46.28	11.49	9.13	5.68	0.21	0.78	23.00	19.98	4.43	8.55	0.77
1976	16.89	50.83	5.21	5.43	4.24	0.13	0.48	16.00	27.53	1.55	5.15	0.45
1977	8.97	17.05	4.57	5.69	2.73	0.19	0.77	8.49	13.33	1.56	5.41	0.85
1978	17.92	42.56	4.45	4.45	2.07	0.36	0.67	16.75	26.56	1.66	4.21	0.78
1979	15.79	34.71	10.43	10.81	7.31	0.29	0.53	14.28	15.64	2.16	9.77	0.60
1980	24.19	39.80	20.12	21.16	16.77	0.98	1.45	22.26	14.54	4.57	18.60	1.18
1981	12.44	21.37	20.21	23.25	11.84	0.51	1.15	10.85	16.03	5.23	20.23	1.00
1982	23.38	21.97	17.80	14.40	8.91	0.78	1.64	21.57	7.84	5.37	13.37	1.42
1983	12.02	21.83	10.86	11.43	5.72	0.18	0.73	11.13	14.33	3.98	10.52	0.67
1984	15.00	14.57	12.97	13.34	7.17	0.34	0.61	13.63	4.37	1.92	11.97	0.61
1985	15.85	18.10	13.28	15.78	6.69	0.18	0.33	14.66	6.42	2.56	14.56	0.35
1986	21.39	15.49	9.71	21.58	6.53	0.20	1.03	20.12	6.61	9.54	20.26	1.17
1987	34.04	34.45	9.67	10.09	4.93	0.23	0.68	32.38	11.21	3.03	9.49	0.64
1988	11.69	16.08	9.10	11.03	5.00	0.36	0.57	11.07	11.14	2.45	10.45	0.64
1989	16.03	11.65	7.13	9.53	6.07	0.23	0.63	14.80	6.87	2.36	8.73	0.67
1990	18.25	16.85	7.55	9.89	4.75	0.18	1.16	16.93	6.83	2.67	9.18	1.16
1991	20.49	22.50	5.08	7.33	3.49	0.17	0.54	19.40	9.75	2.13	6.99	0.51
1992	7.91	21.58	5.77	7.62	5.83	0.14	0.54	7.68	19.95	2.32	7.38	0.53
1993	6.69	11.43	5.53	8.38	4.44	0.05	0.57	6.52	8.37	2.38	8.15	0.57
1994	10.74	10.38	6.70	8.12	4.50	0.24	0.47	10.31	6.35	2.27	7.77	0.62
1995	6.95	12.65	7.37	9.70	3.94	0.13	0.60	6.63	8.39	1.88	9.11	0.64
1996	13.29	21.06	7.62	9.33	3.89	0.09	0.61	12.67	15.16	2.14	8.87	0.62
1997	21.08	22.13	8.00	10.44	4.10	0.13	0.53	19.99	16.40	2.30	9.91	0.60
1998	27.90	25.76	5.91	7.70	4.63	0.16	0.30	26.69	6.81	4.35	7.24	0.31
1999	15.78	26.31	4.57	5.25	3.45	0.10	0.77	15.02	19.21	1.90	5.00	0.77
2000	16.02	40.42	5.88	6.92	3.43	0.17	1.00	15.14	44.92	4.10	6.58	1.07
2001	18.15	34.55	8.17	9.69	5.00	0.39	1.25	17.52	21.21	6.02	9.31	0.99
2002	16.90	20.14	8.82	12.36	6.77	0.04	0.83	16.64	18.02	4.50	12.15	0.79
2003	14.48	25.04	13.47	14.82	6.22	0.04	1.21	14.33	10.89	2.77	14.66	1.17
2004	8.06	18.81	9.13	9.73	4.88	0.12	1.14	7.90	10.57	1.03	9.61	1.17
2005	8.31	16.11	8.56	9.66	3.76	0.19	1.96	8.03	8.78	1.38	9.39	1.97
2006	6.46	16.09	8.23	8.82	2.46	0.11	1.55	6.18	9.96	2.19	8.38	1.61
2007	10.20	11.57	5.49	7.95	5.33	0.19	1.19	9.71	6.03	4.81	7.64	1.11

Cross-Correlations

The cross-correlation between two series measures the extent to which they are linearly related.[2] The correlation coefficient measures the sensitivity of returns on one asset class or portfolio to the returns of another. The correlation equation between return series **X** and **Y** is:

$$\rho_{X,Y} = \left[\frac{Cov(X,Y)}{\sigma_X \sigma_Y}\right]$$

where,

$Cov(X,Y)$ = the covariance of **X** and **Y**, defined below;

σ_X = the standard deviation of **X**; and,

σ_Y = the standard deviation of **Y**.

The covariance equation is:

$$Cov(X,Y) = \frac{1}{n-1}\sum_{t=1}^{n}(r_{X,t} - r_{X,A})(r_{Y,t} - r_{Y,A})$$

where,

$r_{X,t}$ = the return for series **X** in period **t**;

$r_{Y,t}$ = the return for series **Y** in period **t**;

$r_{X,A}$ = the arithmetic mean of series **X**;

$r_{Y,A}$ = the arithmetic mean of series **Y**; and,

n = the number of periods.

Correlations of the Basic Series

Table 6-3 presents the annual cross-correlations and serial correlations for the seven basic series. Long-term government and long-term corporate bond returns are highly correlated with each other but negatively correlated with inflation. Since the inflation was largely unanticipated, it had a negative effect on fixed income securities. In addition, U.S. Treasury bills and inflation are reasonably highly correlated, a result of the post-1951 "tracking" described in Chapter 2. Lastly, both the U.S. Treasury bills and inflation series display high serial correlations.

2 Two series can be related in a non-linear way and have a correlation coefficient of zero. An example is the function $y = x^2$, for which $\rho_{x,y} = 0$.

Table 6-3
Basic Series
Serial and Cross Correlations of Historical Annual Returns from 1926 to 2007

Series	Large Company Stocks	Small Company Stocks	Long-Term Corp Bonds	Long-Term Govt Bonds	Intermediate Govt Bonds	U.S. Treasury Bills	Inflation
Large Company Stocks	1.00						
Small Company Stocks	0.79	1.00					
Long-Term Corporate Bonds	0.19	0.08	1.00				
Long-Term Govt Bonds	0.12	−0.02	0.93	1.00			
Intermediate-Term Govt Bonds	0.04	−0.07	0.89	0.90	1.00		
U.S. Treasury Bills	−0.02	−0.10	0.20	0.23	0.48	1.00	
Inflation	−0.02	0.04	−0.15	−0.14	0.01	0.40	1.00
Serial Correlations	0.03	0.06	0.08	−0.08	0.15	0.91	0.65

Correlations of the Derived Series

The annual cross-correlations and serial correlations for the four risk premium series and inflation are presented in Table 6-4. Notice that inflation is negatively correlated with the horizon premium. Increasing inflation causes long-term bond yields to rise and prices to fall; therefore, a negative horizon premium is observed in times of rising inflation.

Table 6-4
Risk Premia and Inflation
Serial and Cross Correlations of Historical Annual Returns from 1926 to 2007

Series	Equity Risk Premia	Small Stock Premia	Default Premia	Horizon Premia	Inflation
Equity Risk Premia	1.00				
Small Stock Premia	0.29	1.00			
Default Premia	0.18	0.21	1.00		
Horizon Premia	0.13	−0.07	−0.36	1.00	
Inflation	−0.08	0.11	−0.02	−0.28	1.00
Serial Correlations	0.03	0.37	−0.35	−0.13	0.65

Table 6-5 presents annual cross-correlations and serial correlations for the inflation-adjusted asset return series. It is interesting to observe how the relationship between the asset returns are substantially different when these returns are expressed in inflation-adjusted terms (as compared with nominal terms). In general, the cross-correlations between asset classes are higher when one accounts for inflation (i.e., subtracts inflation from the nominal returns).

Table 6-5
Inflation-Adjusted Series
Serial and Cross Correlations of Historical Annual Returns from 1926 to 2007

	Inflation-Adjusted						
Series	**Large Company Stocks**	**Small Company Stocks**	**Long-Term Corp Bonds**	**Long-Term Govt Bonds**	**Inter-mediate Govt Bonds**	**T-Bills (Real Interest Rates)**	**Inflation**
Inflation-Adjusted Large Company Stocks	1.00						
Inflation-Adjusted Small Company Stocks	0.79	1.00					
Inflation-Adjusted Long-Term Corporate Bonds	0.26	0.11	1.00				
Inflation-Adjusted Long-Term Govt Bonds	0.20	0.02	0.95	1.00			
Inflation-Adjusted Intermd-Term Govt Bonds	0.14	–0.03	0.93	0.93	1.00		
Inflation-Adjusted T-Bills (Real Interest Rates)	0.11	–0.06	0.57	0.56	0.72	1.00	
Inflation	–0.22	–0.08	–0.56	–0.52	–0.60	–0.74	1.00
Serial Correlations	0.02	0.03	0.19	0.02	0.23	0.67	0.65

Serial Correlation in the Derived Series: Trends or Random Behavior?

The risk/return relationships in the historical data are represented in the equity risk premia, the small stock premia, the bond horizon premia, and the bond default premia. The real/nominal historical relationships are represented in the inflation rates and the real interest rates. The objective is to uncover whether each series is random or is subject to any trends, cycles, or other patterns.

The one-year serial correlation coefficients measure the degree of correlation between returns from each year and the previous year for the same series. Highly positive (near 1) serial correlations indicate trends, while highly negative (near –1) serial correlations indicate cycles. There is strong evidence that both inflation rates and real riskless rates follow trends. Serial correlations near zero suggest no patterns (i.e., random behavior); equity risk premia and bond horizon premia are random variables. Small stock premia and bond default premia fall into a middle range where it cannot be determined that they either follow a trend or behave randomly, although the serial correlation of annual small stock premia is high enough to suggest a trend.

Each of the component series' serial correlations can be interpreted as following a random pattern, trend or uncertain path, as given in Table 6-6.

Table 6-6
Interpretation of the Annual Serial Correlations from 1926 to 2007

Series	Serial Correlation	Interpretation
Equity Risk Premia	0.03	Random
Small Stock Premia	0.37	Likely Trend
Bond Default Premia	–0.35	Possible Cycle
Bond Horizon Premia	–0.13	Random
Inflation Rates	0.65	Trend
Real Interest Rates	0.67	Trend

Summary Statistics for Basic and Inflation-Adjusted Series

Table 6-7 presents summary statistics of annual total returns, and where applicable, income and capital appreciation, for each asset class. The summary statistics presented here are arithmetic mean, geometric mean, standard deviation, and serial correlation. Table 6-8 presents summary statistics for the six inflation-adjusted total return series.

Table 6-7
Total Returns, Income Returns, and Capital Appreciation of the Basic Asset Classes
Summary Statistics of Annual Returns from 1926 to 2007

Series	Geometric Mean	Arithmetic Mean	Standard Deviation	Serial Correlation
Large Company Stocks				
Total Returns	10.4	12.3	20.0	0.03
Income	4.2	4.2	1.6	0.89
Capital Appreciation	6.0	7.8	19.3	0.03
Small Company Stocks (Total Returns)	12.5	17.1	32.6	0.06
Long-Term Corporate Bonds (Total Returns)	5.9	6.2	8.4	0.08
Long-Term Government Bonds				
Total Returns	5.5	5.8	9.2	−0.08
Income	5.2	5.2	2.7	0.96
Capital Appreciation	0.1	0.4	8.0	−0.23
Intermediate-Term Government Bonds				
Total Returns	5.3	5.5	5.7	0.15
Income	4.7	4.7	2.9	0.96
Capital Appreciation	0.5	0.5	4.4	−0.19
Treasury Bills (Total Returns)	3.7	3.8	3.1	0.91
Inflation	3.0	3.1	4.2	0.65

Total return is equal to the sum of three component returns; income return, capital appreciation return, and reinvestment return. Annual reinvestment returns for select asset classes are provided in Table 2-6.

Highlights of the Summary Statistics

Table 6-7 shows that over 1926–2007 small company stocks were the riskiest asset class with a standard deviation of 32.6 percent, but provide the greatest rewards to long-term investors, with an arithmetic mean annual return of 17.1 percent. The geometric mean of the small stock series is 12.5 percent. Large company stocks, long-term government bonds, long-term corporate bonds, and intermediate-term government bonds are progressively less risky, and have correspondingly lower average returns. Treasury bills were nearly riskless and had the lowest return. In general, risk is rewarded by a higher return over the long term.

Inflation-adjusted basic series summary statistics are presented in Table 6-8. Note that the real rate of interest is close to zero (0.7 percent) on average. For the 82-year period, the geometric and arithmetic means are lower by the amount of inflation than those of the nominal series.

The standard deviations of large company stock and small company stock returns remain approximately the same after adjusting for inflation, while inflation-adjusted bonds and bills are more volatile (i.e., have higher standard deviations).

Table 6-8
Inflation-Adjusted Series
Summary Statistics of Annual Returns from 1926 to 2007

Series	Geometric Mean	Arithmetic Mean	Standard Deviation	Serial Correlation
Inflation-Adjusted Large Company Stocks	7.1%	9.0%	20.1%	0.02
Inflation-Adjusted Small Company Stocks	9.1	13.6	32.0	0.03
Inflation-Adjusted Long-Term Corporate Bonds	2.7	3.2	9.6	0.19
Inflation-Adjusted Long-Term Government Bonds	2.4	2.8	10.3	0.02
Inflation-Adjusted Intermediate-Term Government Bonds	2.2	2.4	6.8	0.23
Inflation-Adjusted U.S. T-Bills (Real Riskless Rates of Returns)	0.7	0.7	3.9	0.67

Rolling Period Standard Deviations

Rolling period standard deviations are obtained by rolling a view window of fixed length along each time series and computing the standard deviation for the asset class for each window of time. They are useful for examining the volatility or riskiness of returns for holding periods similar to those actually experienced by investors. Graph 6-2 graphically depicts the volatility. Monthly data are used to maximize the number of data points included in the standard deviation computation.

The upper graph places the 60-month rolling standard deviation for large company stocks, small company stocks, and long-term government bonds on the same scale. It is interesting to see the relatively high standard deviation for small company stocks and large company stocks in the 1930s, with an apparent lessening of volatility for 60-month holding periods during the 1980s. Note also how the standard deviation for long-term government bonds reaches the level of both common stock asset classes during part of the 1980s.

The lower graph places the 60-month rolling standard deviation for long- and intermediate-term government bonds, and Treasury bills on the same scale.

Graph 6-2
Rolling 60-Month Standard Deviation
Small Company Stocks, Large Company Stocks, Long-Term Government Bonds, Intermediate Bonds, and Treasury Bills

from January 1926–December 1930 to January 2003–December 2007

Small Company Stocks, Large Company Stocks, Long-Term Government Bonds

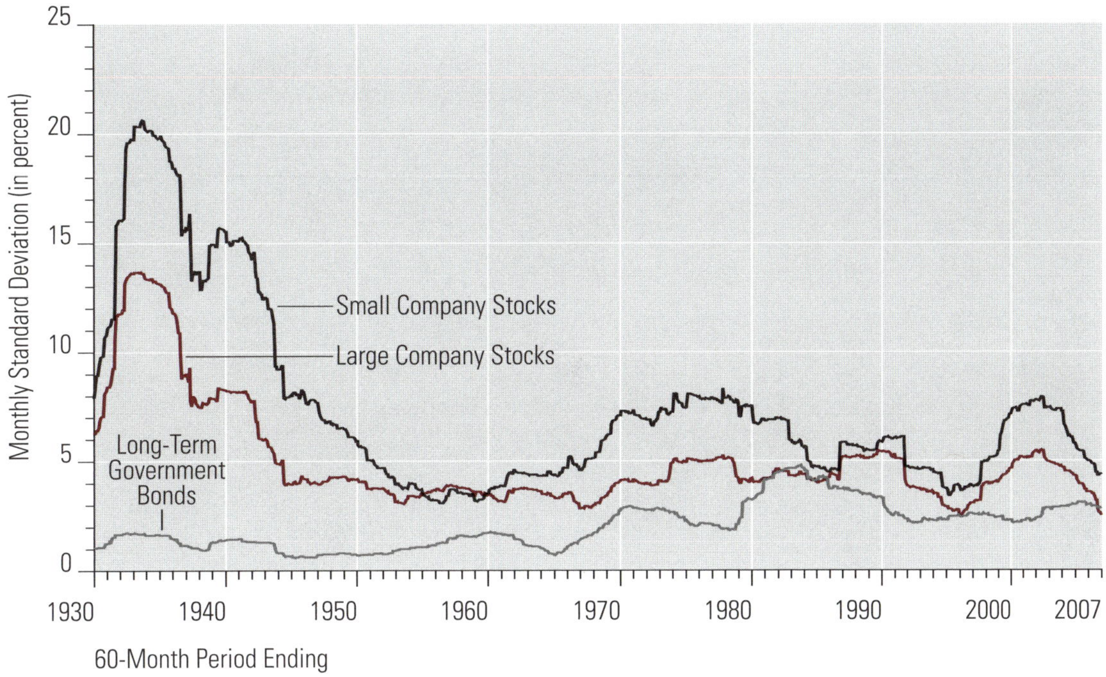

Long-Term Government Bonds, Intermediate-Term Government Bonds, Treasury Bills

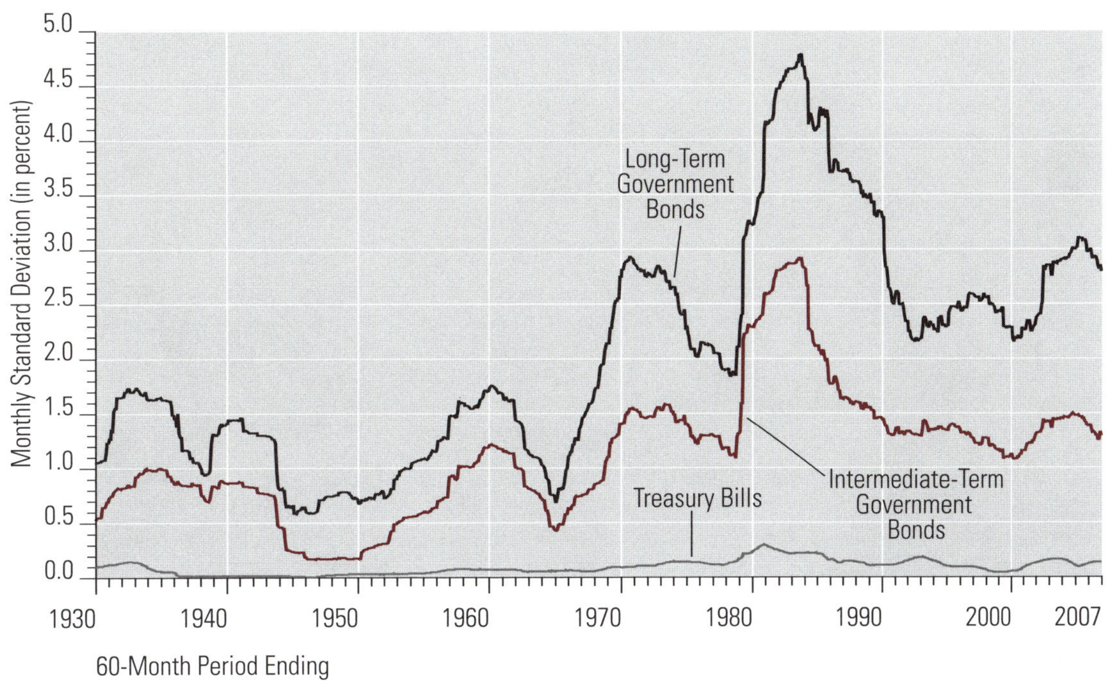

Graph 6-3
Rolling 60-Month Correlations
Large Company Stocks, Long-Term Government Bonds, Treasury Bills, and Inflation

from January 1926–December 1930 to January 2003–December 2007

Large Company Stocks and Long-Term Government Bonds

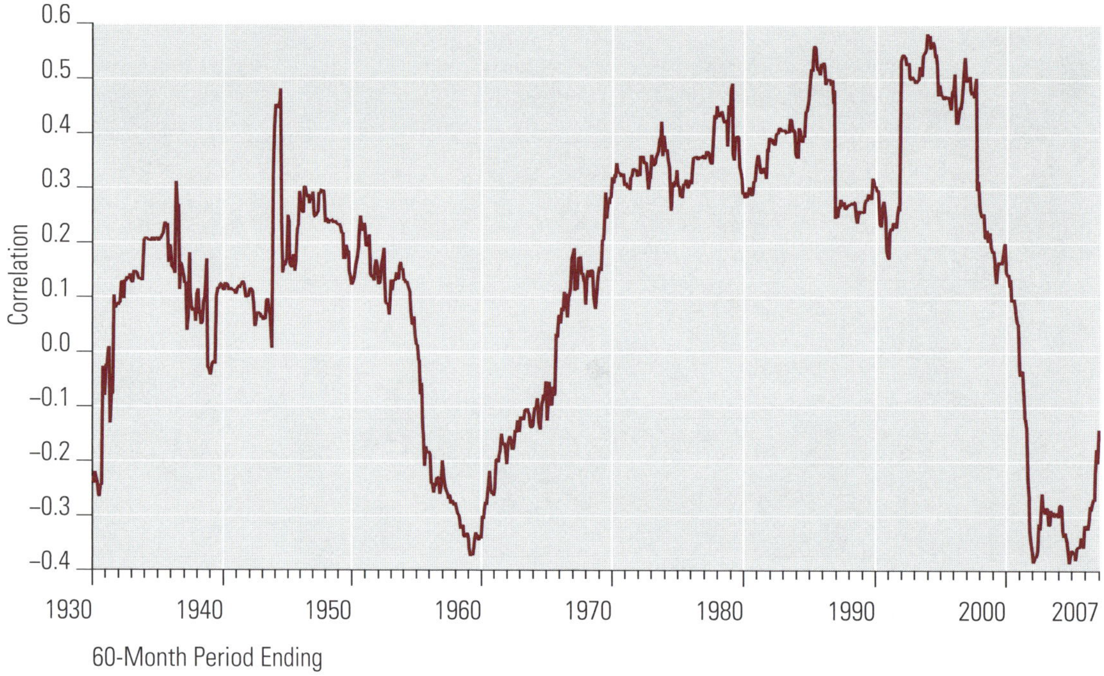

Treasury Bills and Inflation

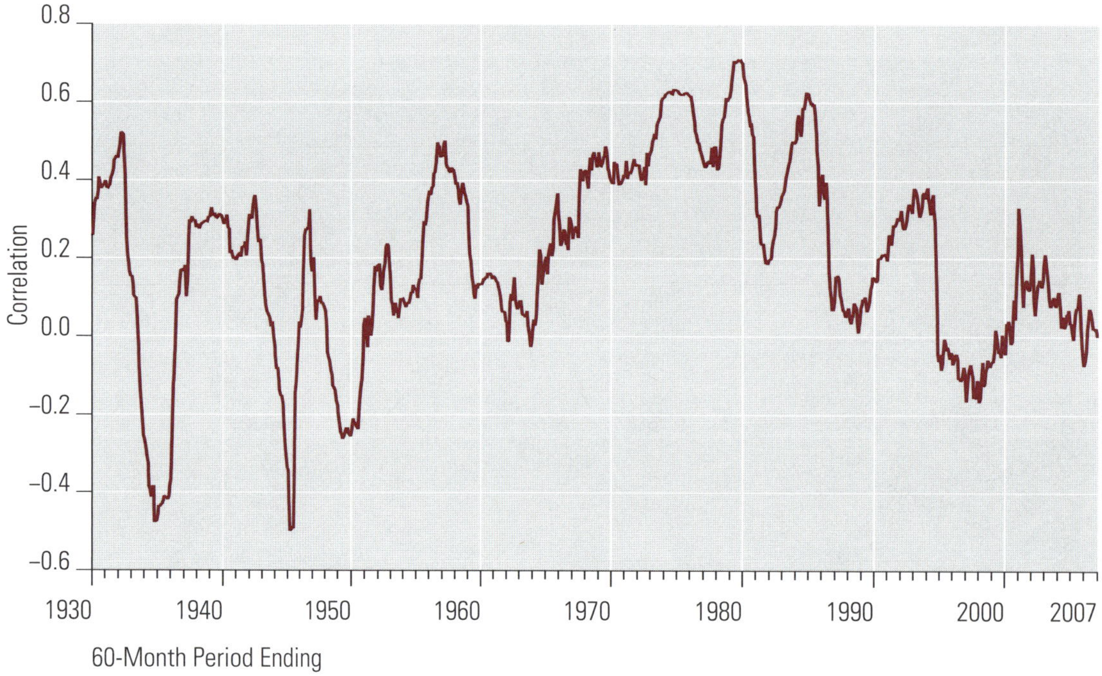

Rolling Period Correlations

Rolling period correlations are obtained by moving a view window of fixed length along time series for two asset classes and computing the cross-correlation between the two asset classes for each window of time. They are useful for examining how asset class returns vary together for holding periods similar to those actually experienced by investors. Monthly data are used to maximize the number of data points included in the correlation computation.

Graph 6-3 shows cross correlations between two asset classes for five year (60 months of monthly data) holding periods. The first rolling period covered is January 1926–December 1930 so the graphs begin at December 1930. The top graph shows the volatility of the correlations between large company stocks and long-term government bonds. There are wide fluctuations between strong positive and strong negative correlations over the past 82 years.

The lower graph shows the correlation between Treasury bills and inflation. These asset classes also show wide fluctuations in correlation over the past 82 years.

The True Impact of Asset Allocation on Returns

Universal Misunderstanding

How important is asset allocation policy and what type of impact does it have on fund returns? This is a frequently asked question throughout the financial world, with the answer depending on how you ask the question and what you are trying to explain. Financial professionals generally assert that asset allocation is the most important determinant of returns, accounting for more than 90 percent of fund performance. This assertion stems from the well-known studies by Brinson, Hood, and Beebower[3] which state, "...investment policy dominates investment strategy (market timing and security selection), explaining on average 93.6 percent of the variation in total plan return." Specific claims to the above statement vary, but if you are trying to explain the variability of returns over time, asset allocation is of prime importance.

However, a great deal of confusion in both the academic and financial community has arisen, and the results of the Brinson studies are attributed to questions that the studies never intended to answer. A survey by Nuttall & Nuttall[4] reveals that out of fifty writers who quoted Brinson et al., only one quoted them correctly. Thirty-seven writers misinterpreted Brinson's work as an answer to the question, "What percent of total return is explained by asset allocation policy?" while five writers misconstrued the Brinson conclusion as an answer to the question, "What is the impact of choosing one asset allocation over another?"

3 "Determinants of Portfolio Performance," Gary P. Brinson, L. Randolph Hood, and Gilbert P. Beebower, *Financial Analysts Journal*, July/August 1986.

"Determinants of Portfolio Performance II," Gary P. Brinson, Brian D. Singer, and Gilbert P. Beebower, *Financial Analysts Journal*, May/June 1991.

4 "Asset Allocation Claims—Truth or Fiction?," Jennifer A. Nuttall and John Nuttall (unpublished), 1998.

This section is based upon the work by Roger G. Ibbotson and Paul D. Kaplan.[5] The goal of the study is to clear up this universal misinterpretation and explain the link between asset allocation and investment returns.

The Brinson Studies

According to the well-known studies by Brinson, Hood, and Beebower, more than 90 percent of the variability of a portfolio's performance over time is due to asset allocation. In other words, Brinson is measuring the relationship between the movement of a portfolio and the movement of the overall stock market. They find that more than 90 percent of a portfolio's movement from quarter to quarter is due to market movement of the asset classes in which the portfolio is invested.

Thus, while the Brinson studies state that more than 90 percent of the variability of a portfolio's performance over time is due to asset allocation, they are frequently misinterpreted and the results are attributed to questions that the studies never intended to answer. Two prime examples being:

- "When choosing between two different asset allocations, how much of a difference does it really make if I choose one over the other?"
- "What portion of my total return is due to asset allocation?"

Data Analysis Framework

To answer the above questions, as well as to confirm the Brinson result, ten years of monthly returns on 94 balanced mutual funds and five years of quarterly returns on 58 pension funds were analyzed. The 94 funds represent all of the balanced funds in the Morningstar universe that had at least ten years of data ending March 31, 1998. The data collected consist of the total return for each fund for each period of time—either monthly or quarterly.

For the mutual funds, the policy weights were determined by using returns-based style analysis over the entire 120-month period.

Dale Stevens[6] provided the same type of analysis on quarterly returns of 58 pension funds over a five-year period 1993–1997. However, rather than using estimated policy weights and the same asset class benchmarks for all funds, the actual policy weights and asset class benchmarks of the pension funds were used. In each quarter, the policy weights are known in advance of the realized returns.

5 "Does Asset Allocation Policy Explain 40, 90, or 100 Percent of Performance?," Roger G. Ibbotson and Paul D. Kaplan, *Financial Analysts Journal*, January/February 2000.

6 "The Importance of Investment Policy," Dale H. Stevens, Ronald J. Surz, and Mark E. Wimer, *The Journal of Investing*, Winter 1999.

Questions and Answers

"How much of the movement in a fund's returns over time is explained by its asset allocation policy?"

The Brinson studies from 1986 and 1991 answer the above question. To confirm the results of the Brinson study, each fund's total returns is regressed against its policy returns with the R-squared value being reported for each fund.

Our results confirm the Brinson result that approximately 90 percent of the variability of a fund's return across time is explained by asset allocation. However, almost any stock market performance index would explain a high percentage of the time series variation. As Table 6-9 shows, even the S&P 500 index explains about 80 percent of the average fund's performance, almost as high as the fund's specific asset allocation policy benchmark. This is because all benchmarks and funds rise in a bull market and fall in a bear market.

Table 6-9
Asset Allocation Policy or Market Participation?
Time-Series R^2s Compared to:

	Benchmark	
	S&P 500	**Fund Policy**
Mean	75.2%	81.4%
Median	81.9%	87.6%

"When choosing between two different asset allocations, how much of a difference does it really make if I choose one over the other?"

To answer the above question, each fund's return must be compared to the other in order to determine how much of the return variation across funds is explained by the funds' asset allocation variations. A cross-sectional regression of entire-period compound annual total returns on entire period compound annual policy returns was performed. The R-squared statistic gives us the percentage of the variation explained.

For the mutual fund sample, 40 percent of the return difference from one fund to another was explained by asset allocation, while for pension funds the result was 35 percent. Graph 6-4 shows the plot of the 10-year compound annual total returns against the 10-year compound annual policy returns for the mutual fund sample. For example, if one portfolio returns 5 percent more than the other, then on average, about 2 percent of the difference (40 percent of 5 percent) is attributable to the different asset allocations. The remaining 3 percent difference (60 percent of 5 percent) is explained by other factors such as asset class timing, security selection, and fees.

Graph 6-4
10-Year Compound Annual Return Across Mutual Funds*

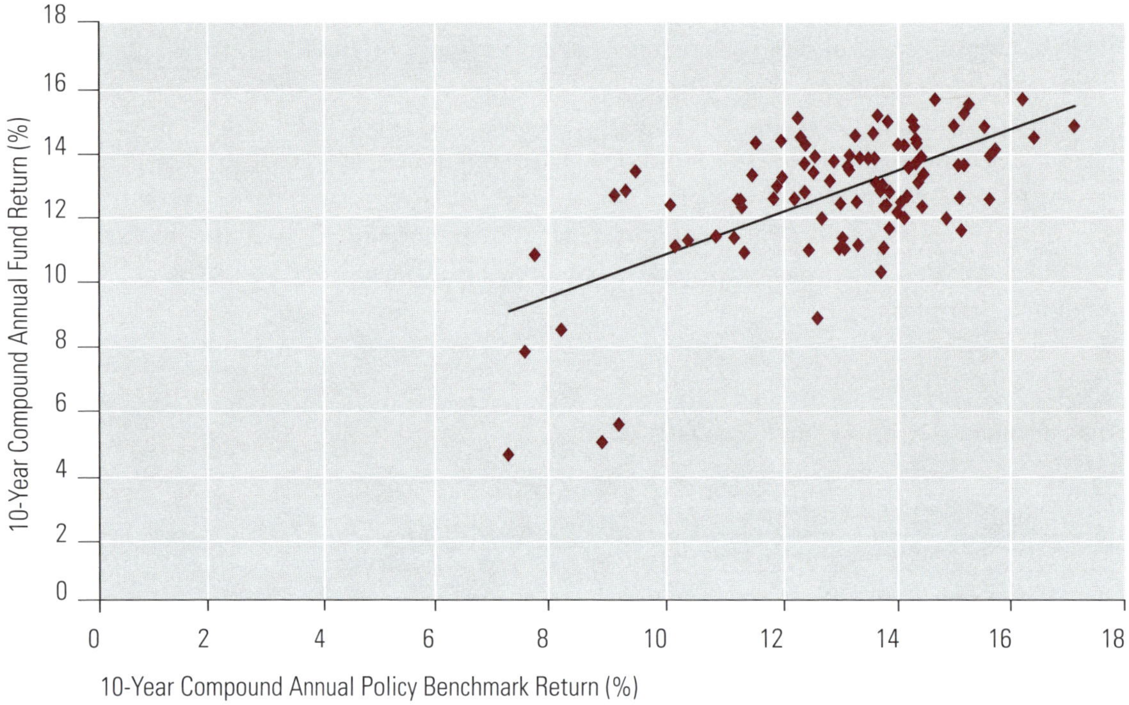

*Across the pension fund sample the $R^2 = 0.35$.

"What portion of my total return is due to asset allocation?"

To answer the above question, the percent of fund return explained by asset allocation was calculated for each fund as the ratio of compound annual policy return divided by the compound annual total return. In other words, we create a portfolio of benchmark asset classes that matches a balanced fund's asset allocation policy and then divide the return of the benchmark portfolio by the fund's return. This ratio of compound returns serves as a performance measure. A fund that has stayed exactly at its asset allocation mix and has invested passively will have a ratio of 1.0 or 100 percent. A fund that has outperformed its asset allocation will have a ratio of less than one, while a fund that has underperformed its asset allocation policy will have a ratio of greater than one.

$$\text{\% of Return due to Policy} = \frac{\text{Policy Return}}{\text{Total Return}}$$

We find that, on average, the policy benchmarks perform as well as the actual portfolios producing a ratio of 1.0, or 100 percent. It is safe to say that, on average, the pension funds and balanced mutual funds are not adding value above their asset allocation policy due to their combination of timing, security selection, management fees, and expenses. Thus, about 100 percent of the total return is explained by asset allocation policy.

Graph 6-5

Variation of Returns Across Funds Explained by Asset Allocation

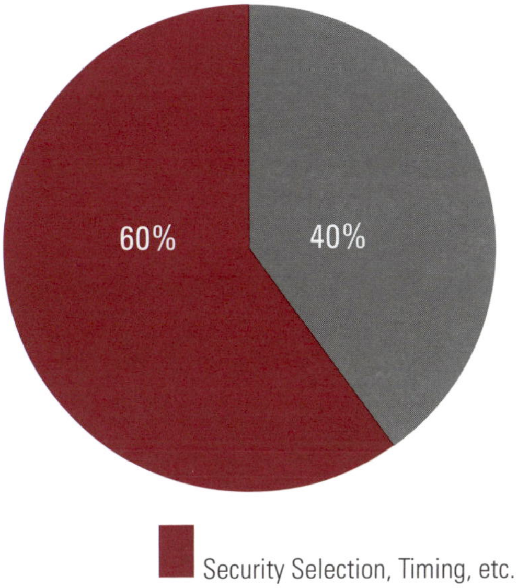

Percentage of a Fund's Total Return Explained by Asset Allocation

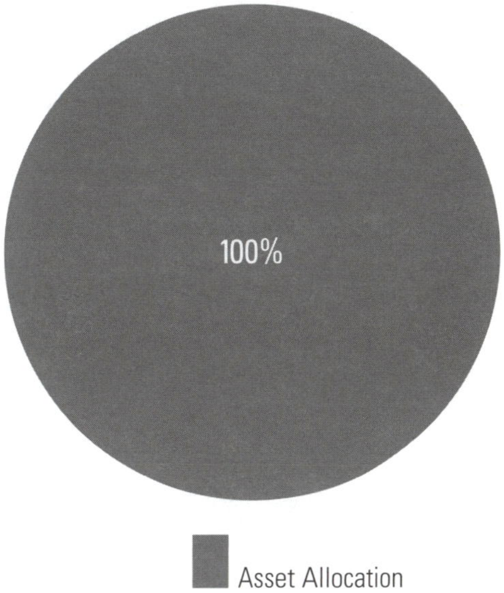

The above results were anticipated by William Sharpe.[7] Sharpe pointed out that since the aggregation of all investors is the market, the average performance before costs of all investors must equal the performance of the market. This implies that, on average, nearly 100 percent of the level of a fund's total return should be expected from asset allocation. Our results confirm such a prediction.

In summary, much of the recent controversy over the importance of asset allocation is due to the misinterpretation of the Brinson studies. These studies successfully provided an answer to one question, but never intended to address the two questions discussed in the above study. While the Brinson studies show that more than 90 percent of the variability of a portfolio's performance over time is due to asset allocation, through careful analysis, we have also come to the conclusion that asset allocation explains about 40 percent of the variation of returns across funds and about 100 percent of a fund's total return.

7 "The Arithmetic of Active Management," William F. Sharpe, *Financial Analysts Journal*, January/February 1991.

Chapter 7

Firm Size and Return

The Firm Size Phenomenon

One of the most remarkable discoveries of modern finance is the finding of a relationship between firm size and return.[1] On average, small companies have higher returns than large ones. Earlier chapters document this phenomenon for the smallest stocks on the New York Stock Exchange (NYSE). The relationship between firm size and return cuts across the entire size spectrum; it is not restricted to the smallest stocks. In this chapter, the returns across the entire range of firm size are examined.

Construction of the Decile Portfolios

The portfolios used in this chapter are those created by the Center for Research in Security Prices (CRSP) at the University of Chicago's Graduate School of Business. CRSP has refined the methodology of creating size-based portfolios and has applied this methodology to the entire universe of NYSE/AMEX/NASDAQ-listed securities going back to 1926.

In 1993, CRSP changed the method used to construct these portfolios, thereby causing the return and index values in Table 7-2 and 7-3 to be significantly different from those reported in previous editions of the Yearbook. Previously, some eligible companies had been excluded or delayed from inclusion when the portfolios were reformed at the end of each calendar quarter. Also, while in prior editions of the Yearbook we used NYSE-listed securities only in the composition of size decile portfolios, starting with the 2001 edition we use the entire population of NYSE, AMEX, and NASDAQ-listed securities for use in the firm size chapter.

The New York Stock Exchange universe excludes closed-end mutual funds, preferred stocks, real estate investment trusts, foreign stocks, American Depository Receipts, unit investment trusts, and Americus Trusts. All companies on the NYSE are ranked by the combined market capitalization of all their eligible equity securities. The companies are then split into 10 equally populated groups or deciles. Eligible companies traded on the American Stock Exchange (AMEX) and the Nasdaq National Market (NASDAQ) are then assigned to the appropriate deciles according to their capitalization in relation to the NYSE breakpoints. The portfolios are rebalanced using closing prices for the last trading day of March, June, September, and December. Securities added during the quarter are assigned to the appropriate portfolio when two consecutive month-end prices are available. If the final NYSE price of a security that becomes delisted is a month-end price, then that month's return is included in the quarterly return of the portfolio. When a month-end NYSE price is missing, the month-end value is derived from merger terms, quotations on regional exchanges, and other sources. If a month-end value is not available, the last available daily price is used.

Base security returns are monthly holding period returns. All distributions are added to the month-end prices. Appropriate adjustments are made to prices to account for stock splits and dividends. The return on a portfolio for one month is calculated as the weighted average of the returns for the individual stocks in the portfolio. Annual portfolio returns are calculated by compounding the monthly portfolio returns.

1 Rolf W. Banz was the first to document this phenomenon. See Banz, Rolf W., "The Relationship Between Returns and Market Value of Common Stocks," *Journal of Financial Economics*, Volume 9 (1981), pp. 3–18.

Aspects of the Firm Size Effect

The firm size phenomenon is remarkable in several ways. First, the greater risk of small stocks does not, in the context of the Capital Asset Pricing Model, fully account for their higher returns over the long term. In the CAPM, only systematic, or beta risk, is rewarded. Small company stocks have had returns in excess of those implied by the betas of small stocks. Secondly, the calendar annual return differences between small and large companies are serially correlated. This suggests that past annual returns may be of some value in predicting future annual returns. Such serial correlation, or autocorrelation, is practically unknown in the market for large stocks and in most other capital markets.

In addition, the firm size effect is seasonal. For example, small company stocks outperformed large company stocks in the month of January in a large majority of the years. Again, such predictability is surprising and suspicious in the light of modern capital market theory. These three aspects of the firm size effect (long-term returns in excess of risk, serial correlation and seasonality) will be analyzed after the data are presented.

Table 7-1
Size-Decile Portfolios of the NYSE/AMEX/NASDAQ
Summary Statistics of Annual Returns
from 1926 to 2007

Decile	Geometric Mean	Arithmetic Mean	Standard Deviation	Serial Correlation
1-Largest	9.6	11.3	18.91	0.08
2	10.9	13.2	21.62	0.04
3	11.3	13.7	23.31	–0.03
4	11.1	14.1	25.68	–0.01
5	11.7	14.8	26.49	–0.02
6	11.7	15.1	27.10	0.03
7	11.6	15.5	29.47	0.01
8	11.8	16.6	34.18	0.05
9	11.9	17.3	36.45	0.04
10-Smallest	13.6	21.0	44.58	0.16
Mid Cap	11.3	14.0	24.42	–0.02
Low Cap	11.7	15.5	29.03	0.03
Micro	12.5	18.5	38.84	0.08
NYSE/AMEX/NASDAQ Total Value Weighted Index	10.1	12.0	19.94	0.03

Source: ©200801 CRSP®, Center for Research in Security Prices. Graduate School of Business, The University of Chicago used with permission. All rights reserved. www.crsp.chicagogsb.edu

Results are for quarterly re-ranking for the deciles. The small company stock summary statistics presented in earlier chapters comprise a re-ranking of the portfolios every five years prior to 1982.

Presentation of the Decile Data

Summary statistics of annual returns of the 10 deciles from 1926–2007 are presented in Table 7-1. Note from this exhibit that the average return tends to increase as one moves from the largest decile to the smallest. (Because securities are ranked quarterly, returns on the ninth and tenth deciles are different than those suggested by the small company stock index presented in earlier chapters. A detailed methodology for the small company stock index is included in Chapter 3.) The total risk, or standard deviation of annual returns, also increases with decreasing firm size. The serial correlations of returns are near zero for all but the smallest decile.

Table 7-2 is a year-by-year history of the returns for the different size categories. Table 7-3 shows the growth of $1.00 invested in each of the categories as of year-end 1925.

The sheer magnitude of the size effect in some years is noteworthy. While the largest stocks actually declined in 2001, the smallest stocks rose more than 30 percent. A more extreme case occurred in the depression-recovery year of 1933, when the difference between the first and tenth decile returns was far more substantial. The divergence in the performance of small and large company stocks is a common occurrence.

In Table 7-4, the decile returns and index values of the NYSE/AMEX/NASDAQ population are broken down into mid-cap, low-cap, and micro-cap stocks. Mid-cap stocks are defined here as the aggregate of deciles 3–5. Based on the most recent data, as shown in the bottom section of Table 7-5, companies within this mid-cap range have market capitalizations at or below $9,206,713,000, but greater than $2,411,794,000. Low-cap stocks include deciles 6–8, and currently include all companies in the NYSE/AMEX/NASDAQ with market capitalizations at or below $2,411,794,000 but greater than $723,258,000. Micro-cap stocks include deciles 9–10, and include companies with market capitalizations at or below $723,258,000. The returns and index values of the entire NYSE/AMEX/NASDAQ population are also included. All returns presented are value-weighted based on the market capitalizations of the deciles contained in each sub-group. Graph 7-1 graphically depicts the growth of $1.00 invested in each of these capitalization groups.

Table 7-2
Size-Decile Portfolios of the NYSE/AMEX/NASDAQ
Year-by-Year Returns

from 1926 to 1970

	Decile 1	Decile 2	Decile 3	Decile 4	Decile 5	Decile 6	Decile 7	Decile 8	Decile 9	Decile 10
1926	0.1359	0.0598	0.0248	0.0226	−0.0236	0.0522	−0.0143	−0.1085	−0.0815	−0.0567
1927	0.3407	0.3051	0.3150	0.3890	0.3434	0.2558	0.3468	0.2833	0.2567	0.2619
1928	0.3920	0.3764	0.3843	0.3471	0.5520	0.2718	0.3520	0.3174	0.3983	0.6895
1929	−0.1080	−0.0793	−0.2184	−0.3431	−0.2510	−0.4096	−0.3725	−0.4019	−0.4973	−0.5266
1930	−0.2452	−0.3743	−0.3527	−0.3488	−0.3578	−0.3643	−0.3624	−0.4931	−0.4463	−0.4807
1931	−0.4141	−0.5115	−0.4628	−0.4609	−0.4696	−0.5174	−0.4881	−0.4928	−0.5029	−0.4942
1932	−0.1094	0.0252	−0.0374	−0.1264	−0.1378	0.0726	−0.1440	0.0246	−0.0093	0.3981
1933	0.4601	0.7625	1.0089	1.1243	0.9510	1.0247	1.1046	1.7322	1.7477	2.1844
1934	0.0208	0.0583	0.0864	0.1845	0.0929	0.1951	0.1434	0.3076	0.2156	0.3489
1935	0.4170	0.5630	0.3705	0.3751	0.6525	0.5091	0.6671	0.6459	0.5849	0.8226
1936	0.2990	0.3437	0.2736	0.4170	0.4952	0.4927	0.5413	0.5036	0.8772	0.8523
1937	−0.3188	−0.3699	−0.3812	−0.4371	−0.4852	−0.4664	−0.4984	−0.5300	−0.5230	−0.5643
1938	0.2494	0.3401	0.3423	0.3512	0.5040	0.4189	0.3574	0.4344	0.3388	0.0540
1939	0.0480	−0.0388	−0.0279	0.0042	0.0173	0.0603	0.0482	−0.0425	−0.0526	0.1737
1940	−0.0702	−0.0884	−0.0844	−0.0405	−0.0079	−0.0580	−0.0574	−0.0632	−0.0491	−0.3114
1941	−0.1069	−0.0778	−0.0590	−0.0984	−0.1197	−0.0990	−0.0890	−0.0893	−0.1253	−0.1798
1942	0.1337	0.2365	0.2026	0.2031	0.2097	0.2463	0.2915	0.2971	0.4429	0.8021
1943	0.2344	0.3526	0.3343	0.4049	0.4949	0.4129	0.7226	0.7146	0.8725	1.3764
1944	0.1719	0.2539	0.2299	0.3309	0.4004	0.4405	0.3841	0.4888	0.5649	0.7055
1945	0.2950	0.4764	0.5448	0.6366	0.5341	0.6117	0.6509	0.6896	0.7690	0.9559
1946	−0.0446	−0.0439	−0.0794	−0.1267	−0.0896	−0.0615	-0.1484	−0.1533	−0.0972	−0.1833
1947	0.0578	0.0079	−0.0013	0.0207	0.0341	−0.0335	−0.0217	−0.0323	−0.0356	−0.0053
1948	0.0371	0.0016	0.0253	−0.0206	−0.0252	−0.0344	−0.0329	−0.0659	−0.0741	−0.0520
1949	0.1846	0.2518	0.2595	0.1953	0.1861	0.2329	0.2177	0.1652	0.1979	0.2489
1950	0.2879	0.2892	0.2672	0.3137	0.3703	0.3387	0.3786	0.3995	0.4132	0.5514
1951	0.2141	0.2286	0.2116	0.1663	0.1439	0.1372	0.1812	0.1511	0.1125	0.0685
1952	0.1428	0.1294	0.1213	0.1190	0.1107	0.1012	0.1039	0.0767	0.0852	0.0230
1953	0.0115	0.0169	0.0033	−0.0136	−0.0293	−0.0095	−0.0241	−0.0772	−0.0464	−0.0818
1954	0.4850	0.4815	0.5892	0.5083	0.5673	0.5956	0.5738	0.5287	0.6366	0.6863
1955	0.2846	0.1877	0.1834	0.1933	0.1770	0.2267	0.1843	0.2024	0.2055	0.2556
1956	0.0795	0.1108	0.0741	0.0902	0.0806	0.0594	0.0830	0.0523	0.0590	−0.0072
1957	−0.0931	−0.0869	−0.1285	−0.1079	−0.1384	−0.1821	−0.1677	−0.1855	−0.1423	−0.1685
1958	0.4073	0.4969	0.5407	0.5965	0.5583	0.5629	0.6817	0.6527	0.7145	0.6975
1959	0.1236	0.0967	0.1363	0.1523	0.1994	0.1517	0.1988	0.1799	0.2011	0.1542
1960	0.0037	0.0548	0.0482	0.0128	−0.0165	−0.0087	−0.0586	−0.0507	−0.0378	−0.0690
1961	0.2627	0.2710	0.2893	0.2934	0.2856	0.2699	0.3042	0.3378	0.3021	0.3201
1962	−0.0878	−0.0959	−0.1194	−0.1296	−0.1634	−0.1793	−0.1641	−0.1474	−0.1701	−0.1456
1963	0.2249	0.2141	0.1647	0.1712	0.1273	0.1853	0.1782	0.1997	0.1280	0.1117
1964	0.1599	0.1428	0.1997	0.1625	0.1623	0.1666	0.1597	0.1714	0.1532	0.2094
1965	0.0893	0.1925	0.2483	0.2425	0.3217	0.3776	0.3373	0.3190	0.3194	0.4315
1966	−0.1027	−0.0574	−0.0507	−0.0623	−0.0721	−0.0452	−0.0955	−0.0864	−0.0589	−0.1008
1967	0.2197	0.2079	0.3169	0.4564	0.5145	0.5343	0.6472	0.8133	0.9064	1.1416
1968	0.0753	0.1654	0.1979	0.1829	0.2759	0.3047	0.2673	0.4047	0.3711	0.6136
1969	−0.0584	−0.1295	−0.1172	−0.1662	−0.1808	−0.1871	−0.2445	−0.2471	−0.3158	−0.3290
1970	0.0231	0.0182	0.0330	−0.0699	−0.0601	−0.0593	−0.0973	−0.1614	−0.1526	−0.1785

Table 7-2 (continued)
Size-Decile Portfolios of the NYSE/AMEX/NASDAQ
Year-by-Year Returns

from 1971 to 2007

	Decile 1	Decile 2	Decile 3	Decile 4	Decile 5	Decile 6	Decile 7	Decile 8	Decile 9	Decile 10
1971	0.1484	0.1328	0.2011	0.2472	0.1890	0.2244	0.2018	0.1735	0.1647	0.1853
1972	0.2212	0.1278	0.0938	0.0881	0.0863	0.0695	0.0632	0.0205	−0.0229	−0.0057
1973	−0.1274	−0.2266	−0.2278	−0.2680	−0.3217	−0.3191	−0.3702	−0.3534	−0.3897	−0.4203
1974	−0.2803	−0.2441	−0.2458	−0.2834	−0.2167	−0.2694	−0.2558	−0.2423	−0.2635	−0.2715
1975	0.3169	0.4573	0.5363	0.6168	0.5966	0.5675	0.6326	0.6579	0.6649	0.7579
1976	0.2073	0.3045	0.3811	0.4008	0.4363	0.4808	0.5018	0.5690	0.5101	0.5516
1977	−0.0884	−0.0367	0.0109	0.0376	0.1126	0.1408	0.1754	0.2261	0.2022	0.2310
1978	0.0637	0.0229	0.1084	0.0974	0.1207	0.1637	0.1705	0.1632	0.1605	0.2815
1979	0.1519	0.2871	0.3061	0.3516	0.3557	0.4888	0.4206	0.4638	0.4594	0.4158
1980	0.3275	0.3442	0.3186	0.3043	0.3193	0.3141	0.3623	0.3233	0.3823	0.3071
1981	−0.0833	0.0059	0.0372	0.0403	0.0484	0.0677	−0.0040	0.0055	0.0802	0.0856
1982	0.1964	0.1749	0.2081	0.2566	0.3076	0.2940	0.2919	0.2955	0.2608	0.2855
1983	0.2057	0.1686	0.2662	0.2633	0.2626	0.2589	0.2727	0.3721	0.3130	0.3690
1984	0.0840	0.0770	0.0253	−0.0458	−0.0269	0.0248	−0.0426	−0.0745	−0.0896	−0.1951
1985	0.3137	0.3770	0.2910	0.3390	0.3115	0.3097	0.3255	0.3651	0.3077	0.2582
1986	0.1801	0.1810	0.1636	0.1732	0.1512	0.0871	0.1250	0.0387	0.0572	0.0040
1987	0.0504	0.0036	0.0393	0.0167	−0.0402	−0.0509	−0.0843	−0.0804	−0.1269	−0.1488
1988	0.1486	0.1982	0.2126	0.2237	0.2138	0.2336	0.2394	0.2854	0.2285	0.2105
1989	0.3295	0.3008	0.2629	0.2308	0.2423	0.2107	0.1785	0.1788	0.1058	0.0550
1990	−0.0088	−0.0853	−0.1015	−0.0875	−0.1409	−0.1849	−0.1532	−0.1979	−0.2460	−0.3128
1991	0.3039	0.3463	0.4140	0.3883	0.4811	0.5326	0.4421	0.4707	0.5066	0.4807
1992	0.0474	0.1577	0.1387	0.1249	0.2613	0.1878	0.1920	0.1287	0.2495	0.3398
1993	0.0732	0.1319	0.1614	0.1562	0.1694	0.1726	0.1900	0.1853	0.1658	0.2558
1994	0.0174	−0.0174	−0.0423	−0.0098	−0.0166	0.0034	−0.0252	−0.0308	−0.0309	−0.0298
1995	0.3940	0.3526	0.3533	0.3275	0.3324	0.2692	0.3264	0.2935	0.3500	0.3047
1996	0.2375	0.1962	0.1714	0.1883	0.1366	0.1737	0.1965	0.1720	0.2064	0.1722
1997	0.3486	0.3012	0.2512	0.2611	0.1565	0.2864	0.3003	0.2538	0.2554	0.2204
1998	0.3515	0.1272	0.0758	0.0724	0.0054	0.0116	−0.0090	0.0098	−0.0503	−0.1155
1999	0.2450	0.1976	0.3433	0.3006	0.2595	0.3492	0.2570	0.3886	0.3430	0.2809
2000	−0.1362	−0.0030	−0.0620	−0.0997	−0.0710	−0.1028	−0.1068	−0.1300	−0.1336	−0.1295
2001	−0.1529	−0.0882	−0.0411	−0.0095	−0.0214	0.0952	0.1226	0.2111	0.3168	0.3672
2002	−0.2246	−0.1736	−0.1934	−0.1771	−0.1778	−0.2122	−0.2298	−0.1997	−0.1870	−0.0550
2003	0.2568	0.3738	0.4029	0.4438	0.4090	0.4877	0.5079	0.5775	0.6825	0.9232
2004	0.0794	0.2013	0.1796	0.1874	0.1734	0.2205	0.1888	0.2189	0.1518	0.1857
2005	0.0371	0.1215	0.1237	0.1059	0.1011	0.0306	0.1057	0.0751	0.0211	0.0591
2006	0.1561	0.1559	0.1453	0.1164	0.1557	0.1504	0.1627	0.1773	0.1723	0.1947
2007	0.0715	0.0745	0.0362	0.0436	0.0798	0.0502	−0.0181	−0.0574	−0.0655	−0.0988

Source: ©200801 CRSP®, Center for Research in Security Prices. Graduate School of Business, The University of Chicago used with permission. All rights reserved. www.crsp.chicagogsb.edu

Table 7-3
Size-Decile Portfolios of the NYSE/AMEX/NASDAQ
Year-End Index Values

from 1925 to 1970

	Decile 1	Decile 2	Decile 3	Decile 4	Decile 5	Decile 6	Decile 7	Decile 8	Decile 9	Decile 10
1925	1.000	1.000	1.000	1.000	1.000	1.000	1.000	1.000	1.000	1.000
1926	1.136	1.060	1.025	1.023	0.976	1.052	0.986	0.892	0.918	0.943
1927	1.523	1.383	1.348	1.420	1.312	1.321	1.328	1.144	1.154	1.190
1928	2.120	1.904	1.865	1.913	2.036	1.681	1.795	1.507	1.614	2.011
1929	1.891	1.753	1.458	1.257	1.525	0.992	1.126	0.902	0.811	0.952
1930	1.427	1.097	0.944	0.818	0.979	0.631	0.718	0.457	0.449	0.494
1931	0.836	0.536	0.507	0.441	0.519	0.304	0.368	0.232	0.223	0.250
1932	0.745	0.549	0.488	0.385	0.448	0.327	0.315	0.237	0.221	0.350
1933	1.087	0.968	0.980	0.819	0.874	0.661	0.662	0.649	0.608	1.113
1934	1.110	1.025	1.065	0.970	0.955	0.790	0.757	0.848	0.739	1.502
1935	1.573	1.602	1.460	1.334	1.578	1.192	1.263	1.396	1.171	2.737
1936	2.043	2.152	1.859	1.890	2.359	1.780	1.946	2.099	2.198	5.070
1937	1.392	1.356	1.150	1.064	1.215	0.950	0.976	0.987	1.049	2.209
1938	1.739	1.817	1.544	1.437	1.827	1.347	1.325	1.415	1.404	2.328
1939	1.822	1.747	1.501	1.443	1.858	1.429	1.389	1.355	1.330	2.732
1940	1.694	1.592	1.374	1.385	1.844	1.346	1.309	1.270	1.265	1.882
1941	1.513	1.468	1.293	1.248	1.623	1.212	1.193	1.156	1.106	1.543
1942	1.716	1.816	1.555	1.502	1.963	1.511	1.540	1.500	1.596	2.781
1943	2.118	2.456	2.075	2.110	2.935	2.135	2.653	2.571	2.989	6.609
1944	2.482	3.079	2.552	2.808	4.110	3.076	3.672	3.828	4.678	11.272
1945	3.214	4.546	3.942	4.596	6.305	4.957	6.062	6.468	8.275	22.046
1946	3.071	4.347	3.629	4.014	5.741	4.652	5.163	5.476	7.471	18.004
1947	3.248	4.381	3.625	4.097	5.936	4.496	5.050	5.299	7.205	17.909
1948	3.369	4.388	3.717	4.012	5.787	4.341	4.884	4.950	6.671	16.978
1949	3.991	5.493	4.681	4.796	6.864	5.353	5.948	5.768	7.992	21.203
1950	5.140	7.081	5.932	6.301	9.405	7.166	8.199	8.072	11.294	32.894
1951	6.240	8.699	7.187	7.349	10.759	8.149	9.685	9.292	12.565	35.147
1952	7.131	9.825	8.059	8.223	11.950	8.973	10.691	10.005	13.636	35.956
1953	7.213	9.991	8.085	8.111	11.600	8.888	10.433	9.232	13.004	33.013
1954	10.711	14.802	12.848	12.235	18.181	14.182	16.420	14.114	21.282	55.670
1955	13.760	17.580	15.205	14.599	21.400	17.397	19.446	16.970	25.656	69.900
1956	14.853	19.529	16.332	15.916	23.124	18.431	21.060	17.857	27.168	69.396
1957	13.470	17.832	14.233	14.198	19.924	15.076	17.529	14.546	23.303	57.705
1958	18.957	26.693	21.928	22.668	31.048	23.561	29.478	24.040	39.955	97.953
1959	21.300	29.275	24.918	26.121	37.239	27.135	35.337	28.365	47.990	113.061
1960	21.379	30.880	26.119	26.456	36.625	26.898	33.268	26.927	46.177	105.255
1961	26.996	39.248	33.676	34.217	47.083	34.158	43.387	36.023	60.125	138.951
1962	24.626	35.485	29.654	29.784	39.388	28.035	36.268	30.713	49.895	118.721
1963	30.163	43.082	34.539	34.883	44.402	33.230	42.730	36.845	56.280	131.978
1964	34.985	49.234	41.437	40.552	51.610	38.767	49.555	43.159	64.902	159.611
1965	38.108	58.713	51.723	50.386	68.213	53.405	66.272	56.926	85.635	228.480
1966	34.193	55.341	49.099	47.249	63.298	50.991	59.940	52.010	80.588	205.453
1967	41.705	66.847	64.658	68.813	95.866	78.234	98.734	94.311	153.636	439.993
1968	44.846	77.906	77.451	81.396	122.311	102.069	125.130	132.475	210.656	709.971
1969	42.226	67.817	68.375	67.872	100.202	82.976	94.532	99.739	144.137	476.376
1970	43.202	69.048	70.634	63.128	94.184	78.055	85.334	83.643	122.140	391.361

Table 7-3 (continued)

Size-Decile Portfolios of the NYSE/AMEX/NASDAQ

Year-End Index Values

from 1971 to 2007

	Decile 1	Decile 2	Decile 3	Decile 4	Decile 5	Decile 6	Decile 7	Decile 8	Decile 9	Decile 10
1971	49.614	78.220	84.840	78.733	111.986	95.574	102.555	98.152	142.251	463.897
1972	60.588	88.219	92.800	85.668	121.649	102.214	109.038	100.166	138.989	461.252
1973	52.872	68.225	71.661	62.705	82.511	69.595	68.675	64.766	84.822	267.379
1974	38.051	51.573	54.045	44.933	64.629	50.848	51.110	49.073	62.475	194.777
1975	50.107	75.156	83.029	72.648	103.187	79.706	83.441	81.356	104.015	342.394
1976	60.496	98.043	114.670	101.766	148.210	118.026	125.313	127.645	157.075	531.273
1977	55.150	94.447	115.917	105.594	164.897	134.645	147.294	156.511	188.836	654.010
1978	58.662	96.612	128.487	115.880	184.803	156.680	172.407	182.054	219.145	838.103
1979	67.573	124.353	167.818	156.623	250.536	233.273	244.923	266.484	319.830	1186.563
1980	89.701	167.152	221.286	204.280	330.543	306.533	333.657	352.628	442.096	1550.986
1981	82.225	168.142	229.516	212.522	346.545	327.292	332.330	354.563	477.533	1683.724
1982	98.373	197.556	277.278	267.058	453.151	423.504	429.345	459.342	602.061	2164.350
1983	118.613	230.863	351.083	337.382	572.155	533.157	546.428	630.267	790.532	2963.089
1984	128.580	248.647	359.950	321.924	556.787	546.386	523.167	583.294	719.739	2384.988
1985	168.909	342.377	464.695	431.051	730.235	715.608	693.473	796.261	941.193	3000.828
1986	199.333	404.336	540.738	505.722	840.656	777.940	780.160	827.051	995.039	3012.819
1987	209.373	405.791	561.967	514.158	806.865	738.379	714.401	760.568	868.719	2564.450
1988	240.479	486.219	681.430	629.189	979.398	910.856	885.452	977.657	1067.212	3104.231
1989	319.725	632.465	860.592	774.400	1216.701	1102.788	1043.520	1152.434	1180.144	3274.927
1990	316.902	578.507	773.211	706.642	1045.257	898.832	883.703	924.312	889.850	2250.599
1991	413.209	778.817	1093.351	980.996	1548.178	1377.587	1274.347	1359.413	1340.606	3332.408
1992	432.810	901.670	1245.020	1103.529	1952.780	1636.354	1519.061	1534.323	1675.153	4464.900
1993	464.503	1020.578	1445.962	1275.847	2283.644	1918.725	1807.736	1818.700	1952.842	5607.215
1994	472.589	1002.854	1384.863	1263.350	2245.744	1925.233	1762.129	1762.683	1892.418	5440.254
1995	658.780	1356.430	1874.151	1677.087	2992.225	2443.565	2337.375	2280.026	2554.811	7098.134
1996	815.253	1622.506	2195.427	1992.894	3400.933	2867.934	2796.556	2672.270	3082.007	8320.741
1997	1099.445	2111.187	2746.916	2513.238	3933.328	3689.300	3636.387	3350.379	3869.224	10154.708
1998	1485.915	2379.687	2955.039	2695.278	3954.470	3732.147	3603.656	3383.105	3674.528	8981.398
1999	1850.027	2850.031	3969.458	3505.544	4980.576	5035.437	4529.801	4697.756	4935.046	11504.455
2000	1598.084	2841.614	3723.175	3156.152	4626.887	4517.945	4046.134	4086.935	4275.709	10015.142
2001	1353.736	2591.047	3570.016	3126.178	4527.747	4948.263	4542.144	4949.628	5630.180	13692.776
2002	1049.719	2141.232	2879.527	2572.540	3722.803	3898.416	3498.349	3961.428	4577.542	12939.410
2003	1319.261	2941.558	4039.559	3714.332	5245.404	5799.749	5275.096	6249.216	7701.702	24885.064
2004	1424.057	3533.716	4764.974	4410.421	6154.827	7078.579	6270.782	7617.377	8870.497	29505.904
2005	1476.960	3963.004	5354.417	4877.438	6776.904	7295.351	6933.901	8189.383	9057.341	31248.240
2006	1707.561	4581.010	6132.574	5445.162	7832.365	8392.825	8062.291	9641.490	10617.624	37331.379
2007	1829.633	4922.512	6354.580	5682.401	8457.442	8814.025	7916.521	9087.966	9922.573	33643.819

Source: ©200801 CRSP®, Center for Research in Security Prices. Graduate School of Business, The University of Chicago used with permission. All rights reserved. www.crsp.chicagogsb.edu

Table 7-4
Size-Decile Portfolios of the NYSE/AMEX/NASDAQ
Mid-, Low-, Micro-, and Total Capitalization Returns and Index Values

from 1926 to 1965

	Total Return				Index Value			
Year	Mid-Cap Stocks	Low-Cap Stocks	Micro-Cap Stocks	Total Value Weighted NYSE/ AMEX/ NASDAQ	Mid-Cap Stocks	Low-Cap Stocks	Micro-Cap Stocks	Total Value Weighted NYSE/ AMEX/ NASDAQ
1925					1.000	1.000	1.000	1.000
1926	0.0150	−0.0042	−0.0732	0.0918	1.015	0.996	0.927	1.092
1927	0.3421	0.2914	0.2579	0.3326	1.362	1.286	1.166	1.455
1928	0.4041	0.3073	0.4685	0.3877	1.913	1.681	1.712	2.019
1929	−0.2617	−0.3953	−0.5042	−0.1447	1.412	1.017	0.849	1.727
1930	−0.3521	−0.3900	−0.4548	−0.2850	0.915	0.620	0.463	1.235
1931	−0.4632	−0.5040	−0.5028	−0.4356	0.491	0.308	0.230	0.697
1932	−0.0794	−0.0076	0.0890	−0.0868	0.452	0.305	0.251	0.636
1933	1.0296	1.1752	1.8694	0.5711	0.918	0.664	0.719	1.000
1934	0.1165	0.1990	0.2509	0.0429	1.025	0.796	0.899	1.043
1935	0.4181	0.5857	0.6484	0.4432	1.453	1.262	1.483	1.505
1936	0.3594	0.5103	0.8743	0.3226	1.975	1.906	2.779	1.991
1937	−0.4202	−0.4897	−0.5339	−0.3470	1.145	0.973	1.295	1.300
1938	0.3756	0.4029	0.2627	0.2804	1.575	1.365	1.635	1.664
1939	−0.0092	0.0360	0.0021	0.0286	1.561	1.414	1.639	1.712
1940	−0.0557	−0.0588	−0.1236	−0.0708	1.474	1.331	1.436	1.591
1941	−0.0835	−0.0935	−0.1373	−0.1004	1.351	1.206	1.239	1.431
1942	0.2042	0.2706	0.5247	0.1604	1.627	1.533	1.889	1.661
1943	0.3868	0.5728	1.0007	0.2834	2.256	2.411	3.779	2.131
1944	0.2953	0.4324	0.6051	0.2131	2.922	3.453	6.067	2.585
1945	0.5704	0.6423	0.8266	0.3808	4.589	5.671	11.081	3.570
1946	−0.0964	−0.1125	−0.1260	−0.0582	4.146	5.033	9.685	3.362
1947	0.0132	−0.0296	−0.0254	0.0373	4.201	4.884	9.438	3.488
1948	0.0000	−0.0412	−0.0660	0.0211	4.201	4.683	8.815	3.561
1949	0.2243	0.2127	0.2149	0.2014	5.143	5.679	10.709	4.278
1950	0.3027	0.3655	0.4591	0.2960	6.700	7.755	15.626	5.545
1951	0.1830	0.1546	0.0977	0.2068	7.926	8.954	17.153	6.691
1952	0.1184	0.0967	0.0647	0.1342	8.865	9.820	18.263	7.589
1953	−0.0084	−0.0290	−0.0578	0.0067	8.790	9.535	17.207	7.640
1954	0.5605	0.5747	0.6518	0.5008	13.717	15.016	28.423	11.466
1955	0.1850	0.2080	0.2213	0.2522	16.254	18.139	34.713	14.358
1956	0.0803	0.0654	0.0377	0.0827	17.559	19.324	36.021	15.546
1957	−0.1242	−0.1783	−0.1506	−0.1005	15.379	15.879	30.595	13.984
1958	0.5612	0.6188	0.7093	0.4502	24.009	25.705	52.296	20.279
1959	0.1536	0.1726	0.1868	0.1267	27.697	30.143	62.066	22.848
1960	0.0243	−0.0338	−0.0468	0.0116	28.372	29.125	59.162	23.114
1961	0.2897	0.2951	0.3077	0.2694	36.591	37.720	77.364	29.341
1962	−0.1314	−0.1683	−0.1648	−0.1017	31.784	31.373	64.612	26.356
1963	0.1593	0.1867	0.1193	0.2098	36.849	37.228	72.322	31.885
1964	0.1813	0.1652	0.1834	0.1613	43.531	43.380	85.589	37.027
1965	0.2608	0.3499	0.3798	0.1446	54.883	58.560	118.099	42.382

Table 7-4 (continued)

Size-Decile Portfolios of the NYSE/AMEX/NASDAQ

Mid-, Low-, Micro-, and Total Capitalization Returns and Index Values

from 1966 to 2007

	Total Return				Index Value			
Year	**Mid-Cap Stocks**	**Low-Cap Stocks**	**Micro-Cap Stocks**	**Total Value Weighted NYSE/ AMEX/ NASDAQ**	**Mid-Cap Stocks**	**Low-Cap Stocks**	**Micro-Cap Stocks**	**Total Value Weighted NYSE/ AMEX/ NASDAQ**
1966	−0.0586	−0.0710	−0.0825	−0.0874	51.667	54.402	108.350	38.678
1967	0.3994	0.6387	1.0344	0.2874	72.301	89.152	220.425	49.793
1968	0.2108	0.3182	0.5015	0.1414	87.541	117.516	330.968	56.835
1969	−0.1469	−0.2216	−0.3236	−0.1091	74.684	91.473	223.855	50.632
1970	−0.0201	−0.0987	−0.1681	0.0000	73.181	82.447	186.219	50.633
1971	0.2123	0.2032	0.1767	0.1615	88.720	99.201	219.119	58.808
1972	0.0906	0.0558	−0.0138	0.1684	96.760	104.740	216.094	68.710
1973	−0.2594	−0.3435	−0.4078	−0.1806	71.661	68.764	127.965	56.298
1974	−0.2513	−0.2587	−0.2676	−0.2704	53.654	50.977	93.719	41.076
1975	0.5709	0.6092	0.7150	0.3875	84.285	82.032	160.725	56.995
1976	0.3979	0.5074	0.5335	0.2676	117.824	123.659	246.479	72.247
1977	0.0385	0.1708	0.2177	−0.0426	122.364	144.775	300.133	69.170
1978	0.1075	0.1663	0.2245	0.0749	135.514	168.846	367.501	74.348
1979	0.3298	0.4626	0.4369	0.2262	180.207	246.954	528.062	91.169
1980	0.3144	0.3310	0.3464	0.3281	236.862	328.684	710.997	121.085
1981	0.0409	0.0305	0.0818	−0.0365	246.549	338.709	769.132	116.668
1982	0.2443	0.2939	0.2723	0.2100	306.780	438.251	978.589	141.169
1983	0.2644	0.2882	0.3410	0.2198	387.885	564.555	1312.296	172.191
1984	−0.0103	−0.0224	−0.1403	0.0451	383.886	551.933	1128.144	179.959
1985	0.3115	0.3283	0.2833	0.3217	503.449	733.158	1447.702	237.848
1986	0.1640	0.0876	0.0321	0.1619	586.028	797.391	1494.152	276.353
1987	0.0124	−0.0682	−0.1383	0.0166	593.295	742.983	1287.501	280.948
1988	0.2167	0.2474	0.2192	0.1803	721.864	926.810	1569.715	331.592
1989	0.2479	0.1923	0.0815	0.2886	900.803	1105.014	1697.698	427.301
1990	−0.1053	−0.1779	−0.2744	−0.0596	805.915	908.474	1231.790	401.841
1991	0.4191	0.4865	0.5005	0.3467	1143.665	1350.402	1848.285	541.148
1992	0.1612	0.1738	0.2814	0.0980	1327.972	1585.155	2368.310	594.169
1993	0.1627	0.1824	0.2010	0.1114	1543.968	1874.236	2844.304	660.341
1994	−0.0262	−0.0152	−0.0314	−0.0006	1503.455	1845.671	2755.122	659.943
1995	0.3404	0.2947	0.3320	0.3679	2015.193	2389.607	3669.698	902.746
1996	0.1685	0.1804	0.1926	0.2135	2354.833	2820.608	4376.369	1095.495
1997	0.2329	0.2804	0.2402	0.3140	2903.227	3611.590	5427.553	1439.479
1998	0.0591	0.0051	−0.0817	0.2429	3074.679	3630.005	4983.978	1789.136
1999	0.3135	0.3290	0.3165	0.2525	4038.478	4824.171	6561.244	2240.972
2000	−0.0755	−0.1100	−0.1307	−0.1144	3733.482	4293.368	5704.010	1984.685
2001	−0.0280	0.1324	0.3398	−0.1115	3628.977	4861.826	7642.314	1763.484
2002	−0.1850	−0.2159	−0.1386	−0.2115	2957.622	3812.278	6583.040	1390.564
2003	0.4161	0.5178	0.7806	0.3162	4188.202	5786.399	11722.090	1830.258
2004	0.1807	0.2103	0.1670	0.1196	4944.849	7002.991	13679.145	2049.203
2005	0.1136	0.0676	0.0362	0.0615	5506.364	7476.441	14174.565	2175.292
2006	0.1387	0.1620	0.1815	0.1547	6270.320	8687.837	16746.776	2511.871
2007	0.0477	−0.0022	−0.0797	0.0580	6569.388	8668.496	15412.865	2657.653

Source: ©200801 CRSP®, Center for Research in Security Prices. Graduate School of Business, The University of Chicago used with permission. All rights reserved. www.crsp.chicagogsb.edu

Graph 7-1

Size-Decile Portfolios of the NYSE/AMEX/NASDAQ: Wealth Indices of Investments in Mid-, Low-, Micro-, and Total Capitalization Stocks

Year-End 1925 = $1.00

from 1925 to 2007

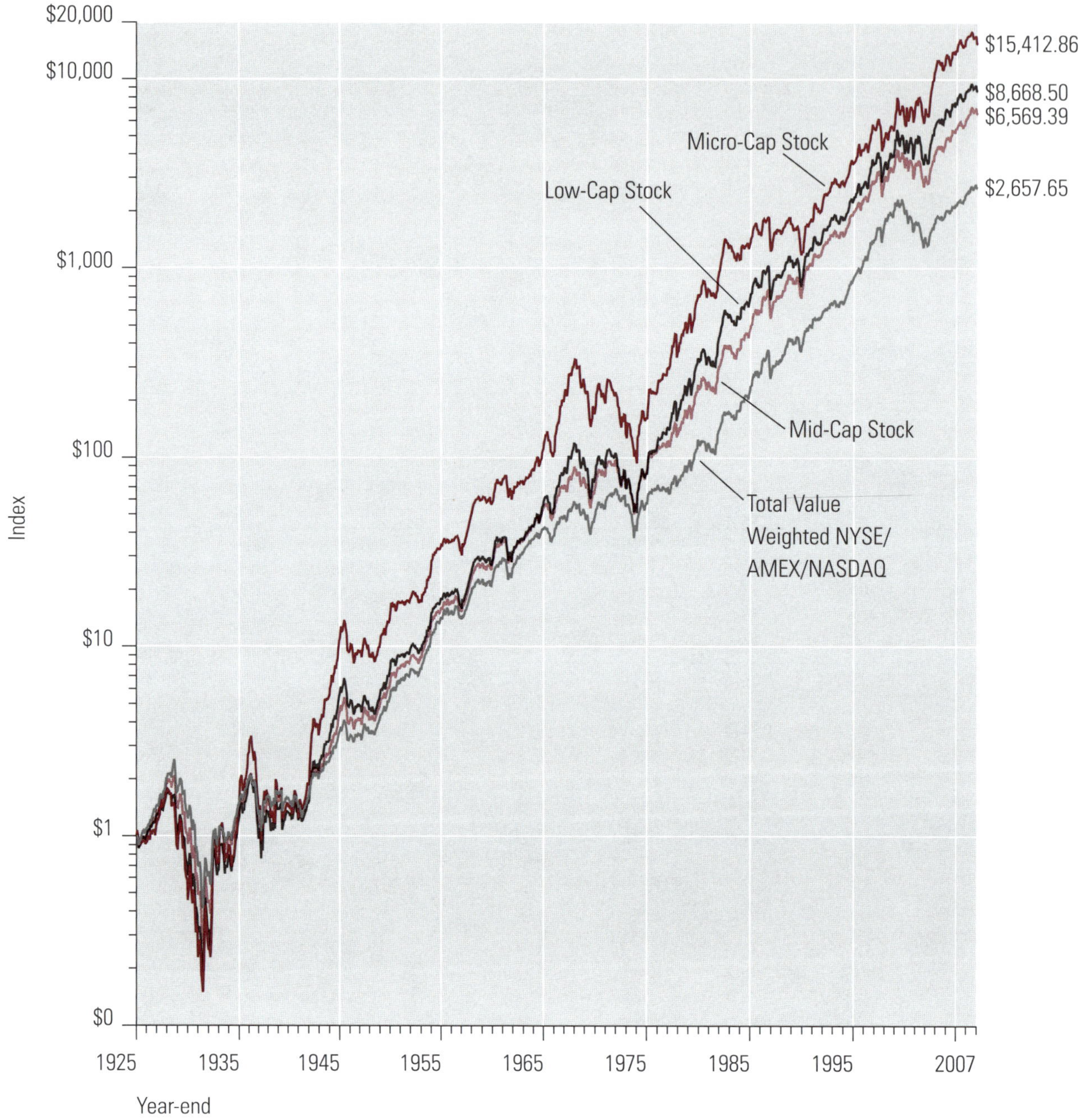

Source: ©200801 CRSP®, Center for Research in Security Prices. Graduate School of Business, The University of Chicago used with permission. All rights reserved. www.crsp.chicagogsb.edu

Size of the Deciles

Table 7-5 reveals that most of the market value of the stocks listed on the NYSE/AMEX/NASDAQ is represented by the top three deciles. Approximately two-thirds of the value is represented by the first decile, which currently consists of 167 stocks. The smallest decile represents just over one percent of the market value of the NYSE/AMEX/NASDAQ. The data in the second column of Table 7-5 are averages across all 82 years. Of course, the proportions represented by the various deciles vary from year to year.

In columns three and four are the number of companies and market capitalization. These present a snapshot of the structure of the deciles near the end of 2007.

The lower portion of Table 7-5 shows the largest firm in each decile and its market capitalization.

Table 7-5
Size-Decile Portfolios of the NYSE/AMEX/NASDAQ:
Bounds, Size, and Composition
from 1926 to 2007

Decile	Historical Average Percentage of Total Capitalization	Recent Number of Companies	Recent Decile Market Capitalization (in thousands)	Recent Percentage of Total Capitalization
1-Largest	63.22%	167	$10,357,817,750	62.34%
2	13.97%	174	2,327,351,920	14.01%
3	7.56%	192	1,111,672,200	6.69%
4	4.73%	184	709,696,610	4.27%
5	3.24%	203	541,399,790	3.26%
6	2.38%	251	411,039,680	2.47%
7	1.75%	275	379,465,160	2.28%
8	1.30%	380	291,182,590	1.75%
9	1.02%	641	284,538,240	1.71%
10-Smallest	0.83%	1775	201,705,150	1.21%
Mid-Cap 3–5	15.53%	579	2,362,768,280	14.22%
Low-Cap 6–8	5.43%	906	1,081,687,170	6.51%
Micro-Cap 9–10	1.85%	2,416	486,243,740	2.93%

Source: ©200801 CRSP®, Center for Research in Security Prices. Graduate School of Business, The University of Chicago used with permission. All rights reserved. www.crsp.chicagogsb.edu

Historical average percentage of total capitalization shows the average, over the last 82 years, of the decile market values as a percentage of the total NYSE/AMEX/NASDAQ calculated each month. Number of companies in deciles, recent market capitalization of deciles and recent percentage of total capitalization are as of September 30, 2007.

Decile	Recent Market Capitalization (in thousands)	Company Name
1-Largest	$472,518,672	Exxon Mobil Corp.
2	20,234,526	General Mills Inc.
3	9,206,713	Reliant Energy Inc.
4	5,012,577	Manitowoc Co Inc.
5	3,422,743	FMC Corp
6	2,411,794	Webster Financial Corp.
7	1,633,320	Simpson Manufacturing Co. Inc.
8	1,128,765	Metal Management Inc.
9	723,258	Citadel Broadcasting Corp.
10-Smallest	363,479	Emergency Medical Services Corp.

Source: ©200801 CRSP®, Center for Research in Security Prices. Graduate School of Business, The University of Chicago used with permission. All rights reserved. www.crsp.chicagogsb.edu

Market capitalization and name of largest company in each decile as of September 30, 2007.

Long-Term Returns in Excess of Risk

The Capital Asset Pricing Model (CAPM) does not fully account for the higher returns of small company stocks. Table 7-6 shows the returns in excess of risk over the past 82 years for each decile of the NYSE/AMEX/NASDAQ.

The CAPM can be expressed as follows:

$$k_s = r_f + (\beta_s \times ERP) \qquad (28)$$

where,

k_s = the expected return for company **s**;

r_f = the expected return of the riskless asset;

β_s = the beta of the stock of company **s**; and,

ERP = the expected equity risk premium, or the amount by which investors expect the future return on equities to exceed that on the riskless asset.

The amount of an asset's systematic risk is measured by its beta. A beta greater than 1 indicates that the security is riskier than the market, and according to the CAPM equation, investors are compensated for taking on this additional risk. However, based on historical return data on the NYSE/AMEX/NASDAQ decile portfolios, the smaller deciles have had returns that are not fully explainable by the CAPM. This return in excess of CAPM grows larger as one moves from the largest companies in decile 1 to the smallest in decile 10. The excess return is especially pronounced for micro-cap stocks (deciles 9–10). This size related phenomenon has prompted a revision to the CAPM that includes the addition of a size premium.

The CAPM is used here to calculate the CAPM return in excess of the riskless rate and to compare this estimate to historical performance. According to the CAPM, the return on a security should consist of the riskless rate plus an additional return to compensate for the systematic risk of the security. Table 7-6 uses the 82-year arithmetic mean income return component of 20-year government bonds as the historical riskless rate. (However, it is appropriate to match the maturity, or duration, of the riskless asset with the investment horizon.) This CAPM return in excess of the riskless rate is β (beta) multiplied by the realized equity risk premium. The realized equity risk premium is the return that compensates investors for taking on risk equal to the risk of the market as a whole (estimated by the 82-year arithmetic mean return on large company stocks, 12.26 percent, less the historical riskless rate, 5.21 percent). The difference between the excess return predicted by the CAPM and the realized excess return is the size premium, or return in excess of CAPM.

This phenomenon can also be viewed graphically, as depicted in the Graph 7-2. The security market line is based on the pure CAPM without adjusting for the size premium. Based on the risk (or beta) of a security, the expected return should fluctuate along the security market line. However, the expected returns for the smaller deciles of the NYSE/AMEX/NASDAQ lie above the line, indicating that these deciles have had returns in excess of their risk.

Table 7-6
Size-Decile Portfolios of the NYSE/AMEX/NASDAQ:
Long-Term Returns in Excess of CAPM
from 1926 to 2007

Decile	Beta*	Arithmetic Mean Return	Actual Return in Excess of Riskless Rate**	CAPM Return in Excess of Riskless Rate†	Size Premium (Return in Excess of CAPM)
1-Largest	0.91	11.31%	6.10%	6.45%	–0.34%
2	1.03	13.16%	7.95%	7.27%	0.68%
3	1.10	13.72%	8.51%	7.75%	0.76%
4	1.12	14.07%	8.86%	7.93%	0.93%
5	1.16	14.85%	9.64%	8.17%	1.47%
6	1.18	15.14%	9.93%	8.33%	1.60%
7	1.24	15.46%	10.26%	8.76%	1.50%
8	1.30	16.58%	11.38%	9.18%	2.20%
9	1.35	17.28%	12.07%	9.51%	2.56%
10-Smallest	1.41	20.98%	15.77%	9.95%	5.82%
Mid-Cap, 3–5	1.12	14.01%	8.81%	7.88%	0.92%
Low-Cap, 6–8	1.22	15.49%	10.29%	8.64%	1.65%
Micro-Cap, 9–10	1.36	18.46%	13.25%	9.59%	3.65%

*Betas are estimated from monthly returns in excess of the 30-day U.S. Treasury bill total return, January 1926–December 2007.

**Historical riskless rate measured by the 82-year arithmetic mean income return component of 20-year government bonds (5.21).

†Calculated in the context of the CAPM by multiplying the equity risk premium by beta. The equity risk premium is estimated by the arithmetic mean total return of the S&P 500 (12.26 percent) minus the arithmetic mean income return component of 20-year government bonds (5.21 percent) from 1926–2007.

Graph 7-2
Security Market Line Versus Size-Decile Portfolios of the NYSE/AMEX/NASDAQ:
from 1926 to 2007

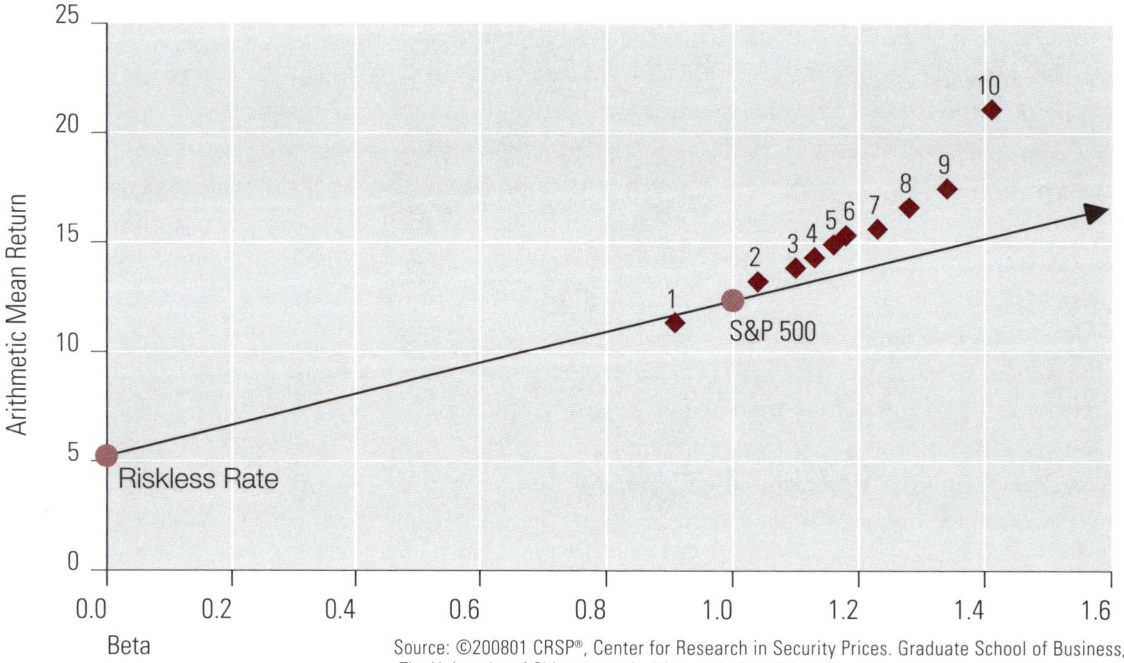

Source: ©200801 CRSP®, Center for Research in Security Prices. Graduate School of Business, The University of Chicago used with permission. All rights reserved. www.crsp.chicagogsb.edu

Serial Correlation in Small Company Stock Returns

The serial correlation, or first-order autocorrelation, of returns on large capitalization stocks is near zero. [See Table 7-1.] If stock returns are serially correlated, then one can gain some information about future performance based on past returns. For the smallest stocks, the serial correlation is near or above 0.1. This observation bears further examination.

Table 7-7
Size-Decile Portfolios of the NYSE/AMEX/NASDAQ:
Serial Correlations of Annual Returns in Excess of Decile 1 Returns
1926–2007

Decile	Serial Correlations of Annual Returns in Excess of Decile 1 Return
Decile 2	0.26
Decile 3	0.29
Decile 4	0.25
Decile 5	0.26
Decile 6	0.34
Decile 7	0.28
Decile 8	0.34
Decile 9	0.30
Decile 10	0.41

Source: ©200801 CRSP®, Center for Research in Security Prices. Graduate School of Business, The University of Chicago used with permission. All rights reserved. www.crsp.chicagogsb.edu

To remove the randomizing effect of the market as a whole, the returns for decile 1 are geometrically subtracted from the returns for deciles 2 through 10. The result illustrates that these series differences exhibit greater serial correlation than the decile series themselves. Table 7-7 above presents the serial correlations of the excess returns for deciles 2 through 10. These serial correlations suggest some predictability of smaller company excess returns. However, caution is necessary. The serial correlation of small company excess returns for non-calendar years (February through January, etc.) do not always confirm the results shown here for calendar (January through December) years. The results for the non-calendar years (not shown in this book) suggest that predicting small company excess returns may not be easy.

Seasonality

Unlike the returns on large company stocks, the returns on small company stocks appear to be seasonal. In January, small company stocks often outperform larger stocks by amounts far greater than in any other month.

Table 7-8 shows the returns of capitalization deciles 2 through 10 in excess of the return on decile 1. This table segregates excess returns into months. For each decile and for each month, the exhibit shows both the average excess return as well as the number of times the excess return is positive. These two statistics measure the seasonality of the excess return in different ways. The average excess return illustrates the size of the effect, while the number of positive excess returns shows the reliability of the effect.

Virtually all of the small stock effect occurs in January. The excess outcomes of the other months are on net, mostly negative for small company stocks. Excess returns in January relate to size in a precisely rank-ordered fashion. This "January effect" seems to pervade all size groups.

Table 7-8
Size-Decile Portfolios of the NYSE/AMEX/NASDAQ:
Returns in Excess of Decile 1 (in percent)
from 1926 to 2007

First row: average excess return in percent
Second row: number of times excess return was positive (in 82 years)

Decile	Jan	Feb	Mar	Apr	May	Jun	Jul	Aug	Sep	Oct	Nov	Dec	Total (Jan–Dec)
2	0.85%	0.51%	–0.01%	–0.32%	0.07%	–0.09%	–0.07%	0.18%	0.06%	–0.25%	0.15%	0.34%	1.47%
	62	54	39	29	41	41	36	43	43	39	47	44	
3	1.14%	0.33%	0.07%	–0.12%	–0.15%	–0.13%	–0.08%	0.34%	–0.06%	–0.29%	0.53%	0.27%	1.89%
	60	51	39	29	36	36	41	48	39	35	47	46	
4	1.34%	0.60%	–0.05%	–0.34%	0.05%	–0.07%	–0.12%	0.28%	0.09%	–0.74%	0.37%	0.44%	1.96%
	59	52	39	32	39	40	36	47	42	30	44	46	
5	2.20%	0.62%	–0.05%	–0.30%	–0.15%	0.01%	–0.11%	0.28%	0.05%	–0.72%	0.35%	0.30%	2.60%
	60	50	38	34	37	39	40	46	41	33	47	44	
6	2.57%	0.46%	–0.11%	–0.18%	0.28%	–0.06%	–0.24%	0.52%	0.17%	–1.17%	0.29%	0.19%	2.86%
	62	51	43	33	39	38	40	47	44	35	44	43	
7	3.20%	0.66%	–0.14%	–0.21%	0.11%	–0.27%	–0.14%	0.22%	0.22%	–0.99%	0.22%	–0.04%	2.87%
	63	53	41	35	35	34	36	39	44	31	44	39	
8	4.34%	0.69%	–0.32%	–0.46%	0.37%	–0.40%	0.00%	0.19%	0.00%	–0.98%	0.21%	–0.31%	3.69%
	61	47	36	32	33	37	38	38	42	34	38	36	
9	5.67%	0.95%	–0.15%	–0.30%	0.21%	–0.39%	–0.10%	0.12%	–0.09%	–1.14%	0.11%	–0.99%	4.20%
	63	45	41	32	34	33	35	42	38	33	36	33	
10	9.03%	0.95%	–0.76%	–0.19%	0.53%	–0.61%	0.50%	–0.17%	0.55%	–1.31%	–0.40%	–1.64%	7.27%
	75	41	34	34	35	34	38	30	40	29	31	29	

Source: ©200801 CRSP®, Center for Research in Security Prices. Graduate School of Business, The University of Chicago used with permission. All rights reserved. www.crsp.chicagogsb.edu

Chapter 8

Growth and Value Investing

Discussion of Style Investing

The concept of equity investment style has come into being over the past thirty years or so. Investment style can broadly be defined as common types of characteristics that groups of stocks or portfolios share. Probably the first discussion and consideration of style related to large company versus small company investing, and even this distinction was not too prominent until the 1960s. Now, styles of investing are broken down into more detail and used for performance measurement, asset allocation, and other purposes. Mutual funds and other investment portfolios are often measured against broad growth or value benchmarks. In some cases, investment manager-specific style benchmarks are constructed to separate pure stock selection ability from style effects.

Most investors agree on the broad definitions of growth and value, but when it comes to specific definitions, there are many ways of defining a growth stock and a value stock. In general, growth stocks have high relative growth rates of earnings, sales, or return on equity. Growth stocks usually have relatively high price-to-earnings and price-to-book ratios. Value stocks will generally have lower price-to-earnings and price-to-book values, and often have higher dividend yields. Value stocks are often turn-around opportunities, companies that have had disappointing news, or companies with low growth prospects. Value investors generally believe that a value stock has been unfairly beaten down by the market, making the stock sell below its "intrinsic" value. Therefore, they buy the stock with the hope that the market will realize its full value and bid the price up to its fair value.

Different Ways of Measuring Growth and Value

In order to objectively measure the performance of value and growth stocks, several different data providers have constructed value and growth indices. Each index provider uses a different methodology to draw the line between growth and value, but all of the methodologies rely on some combination of accounting data, analyst growth estimates, and market capitalization. Three of the more prominent growth/value index providers are S&P/Citigroup, Russell, and Wilshire.

S&P/Citigroup has two sets of style indices. They start by assigning stocks standardized growth and value scores based on three growth and four value factors. The Style Index series divides the complete market capitalization of each parent index into approximately equal growth and value indices. This series uses a market capitalization weighting scheme. Stocks that do not fall into pure style baskets have their market capitalization distributed between value and growth indices. The Pure Style Index series includes only pure growth and value stocks. There are no overlapping stocks, and these indices do not have the size bias induced by market capitalization weighting, since stocks are weighted in proportion to their relative style attractiveness. Style scores are recalculated and indices rebalanced each December. All indices are available from July 1995.

Russell also has large-, mid-, and small-cap style indices. To determine growth or value, each company is first ranked by a composite score of price-to-book and Institutional Brokers' Estimate System (IBES) forecast long-term growth mean. Using this score and a proprietary algorithm, 70 percent of companies are classified as all value or all growth, and 30 percent are weighted proportionately to both value and growth. Russell style indices are available starting in January 1979.

Wilshire defines growth and value by looking at two factors: price-to-book and projected price-to-earnings ratio. Wilshire style indices are available starting in January 1978.

It is evident that the prominent index providers use different measures to determine value and growth, and use different techniques for constructing portfolios. None of these three providers have growth and value indices going back before 1978. Growth and value stocks were certainly around before then, but much of the accounting data is not readily available today. However, Eugene Fama and Ken French constructed growth and value data from both Compustat and hand-collected data for the early years of the series. The Fama-French series use book-to-market to define value and growth. In addition to the Fama-French series, Ibbotson Associates, with the help of the Center for Research in Security Prices at the University of Chicago (CRSP), developed a set of growth and value indices dating back to 1969. This chapter places a heavy emphasis on the Ibbotson data but will also present the Fama-French data to some degree.

Growth and Value Index Construction Methodology

As discussed earlier, most growth and value indices go only as far back as the late-1970s. However, both the Fama-French indices as well as the Ibbotson series date back even further.

Fama-French Methodology

Fama-French use all stocks traded on the New York Stock Exchange (NYSE) to set both growth/value and small/large breakpoints. They then apply these breakpoints to all stocks traded on NYSE, AMEX, and NASDAQ to construct each index.

The market capitalization breakpoint between small and large stocks is set as the median market capitalization of NYSE stocks. This breakpoint is then applied to all stocks traded on NYSE, AMEX, and NASDAQ.

To define value and growth, Fama-French use the book value of equity (BE) divided by market capitalization (ME), which is the inverse of how much investors are willing to pay for a dollar of book value. Value companies will have a high book-to-market ratio, while growth companies will have a low book-to-market ratio. Fama-French used Compustat as their data source to calculate book value from 1963 forward, and hand-collected data for 1928 to 1962.

Book value was calculated as follows:

$$BV = SE + DT + ITC - PS \qquad (29)$$

where,

BV = Fama-French book value;

SE = book value of stockholders' equity;

DT = balance sheet deferred taxes;

ITC = investment tax credit (if available); and,

PS = book value of preferred stock. Depending on availability, either redemption, liquidation, or par value (in that order) is used to estimate book value of preferred stock.

Stocks are put into three groups based on book-to-market: low, medium, or high. The definition of low, medium, and high is based on the breakpoints for the bottom 30 percent, middle 40 percent, and top 30 percent of the value of book-to-market for NYSE stocks. These breakpoints are then applied to all NYSE, AMEX, and NASDAQ stocks. For the growth/value analysis shown in this chapter, only the low and high portfolios are used. The medium portfolios, which are blends of growth and value, are not shown.

Firms with negative book values are not used when calculating the book-to-market breakpoints or when calculating size-specific book-to-market breakpoints. Also, only firms with ordinary common equity (as classified by CRSP) are included in the portfolios. This excludes ADRs, REITs, and unit trusts.

The four size-specific style indices used in this chapter are small value, small growth, large value, and large growth. These portfolios are defined as the intersections of the two size groups and the low and high book-to-market groups.

Ibbotson Associates Methodology

Ibbotson Associates developed the methodology to construct the style indices, and then contracted CRSP to fill in the back history of asset class returns. Please note that CRSP recently has made major revisions to the underlying data in our growth/value study. These changes dramatically improve the quality of the data and the corresponding results. Starting with the 2004 Yearbook, all data presented includes the revisions that CRSP has made.

The screening process starts each period by trimming the CRSP database of NYSE, AMEX, and NASDAQ securities to eliminate American Depository Receipts (ADRs), Unit Investment Trusts, Closed-End Funds, Real Estate Investment Trusts, American Trusts, and foreign-incorporated securities. Four portfolios were then formed based on size at the end of June of each year by sorting the NYSE universe by June-end market capitalization into large-cap, mid-cap, small-cap, and micro-cap size groupings. These size portfolios were defined by selecting the top 20 percent (deciles 1-2) by number of companies for large-cap, the next 30 percent (deciles 3-5) for mid-cap, the next 30 percent (deciles 6-8) for small-cap, and the smallest 20 percent (deciles 9-10) for micro-cap. Once the breakpoints were established, similar-sized AMEX and NASDAQ companies were assigned to the corresponding portfolios.

The next step involved calculating the book-to-price ratios for each eligible company. For book-to-price ratios, Ibbotson Associates used the S&P Compustat measure of common equity for the last fiscal year ended by December 31 of the previous year and divided that by market capitalization at the end of December of the previous year. All companies that had valid book-to-price ratios were assigned to size portfolios based on their June-end market capitalization and the breakpoints described earlier.

With a comprehensive set of size portfolios constructed, the next step was to divide them into style classifications. The companies in each of the four size portfolios were ranked by book-to-price, and created a growth (low B/P) and value (high B/P) portfolio within each size grouping where the total market capitalization of the growth and value indices are equal within each portfolio.

Once the large-, mid-, small-, and micro-cap growth and value portfolios were constructed, the last step was to create asset class returns. Portfolios were formed at June-end of each year, and value-weighted monthly returns were calculated from July to the following June. Lagged market values were used so that the returns for each month are weighted by the market values of the previous month-end.

Using the resulting data sets, it was determined that 1969 was the most appropriate starting date for asset class analysis. The Ibbotson style indices were actually created going back further, but 1969 was the year in which the series covered at least 70 percent of the available market. Although the 2003 Yearbook contained the micro-cap series, it has been determined that the series will not be presented going forward. The quality of the micro-cap data may not be as good as that of the small-, mid-, and large-cap series. The percentage of market coverage for the micro-cap series is quite low at times and falls significantly during the 1980s and 1990s.

In addition to the size-based portfolios, an all-capitalization index called "IA all value" was created using the lagged market capitalization-weighted returns of the large-, mid-, and small-cap value series. The same procedure was used to create an "IA all growth" series from the three growth asset classes.

Ibbotson (IA) Growth and (IA) Value Series

The following commentary and corresponding data make use of the Ibbotson growth and value data series.

Historical Returns on Growth and Value

Graph 8-1 depicts the growth of $1.00 invested in IA all growth and IA all value stocks from the end of 1968 to the end of December 2007. The chart shows that over the long term value stocks have well outperformed growth stocks. An investment of $1.00 in value stocks at year-end 1968 would have returned $68.38 by the end of December 2007, a compound return of 11.4 percent. The same investment in growth stocks would have returned $31.09 to an investor, a compound return of 9.2 percent.

Graph 8-2 depicts the growth of $1.00 invested in IA large-cap value, large-cap growth, mid-cap value, mid-cap growth, small-cap value, and small-cap growth from the end of 1968 to the end of December 2007. The top three performers during this time period were small-cap value, mid-cap value, and large-cap value. Mid-cap growth was the best-performing growth series, followed in order of performance by small-cap growth and large-cap growth. Over time, a consistent pattern of value outperforming growth emerges within each of the size groupings.

Graph 8-1

IA All Growth Stocks vs. IA All Value Stocks

Year-End 1968 = $1.00

from 1968 to 2007

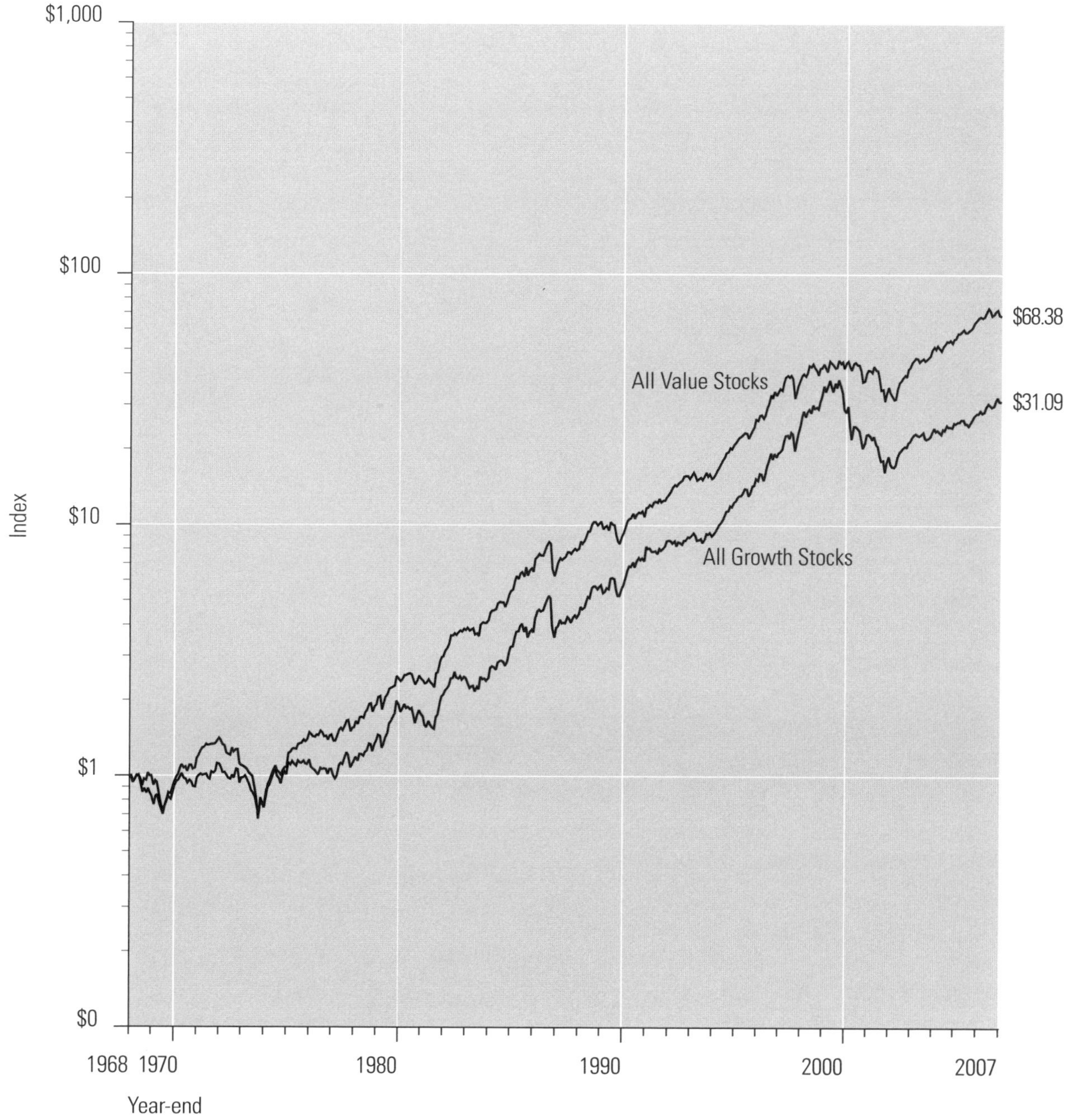

Graph 8-2

IA Large-cap Growth Stocks, IA Large-cap Value Stocks, IA Mid-cap Growth Stocks, IA Mid-cap Value Stocks, IA Small-cap Growth Stocks, IA Small-cap Value Stocks

Year-End 1968 = $1.00

from 1968 to 2007

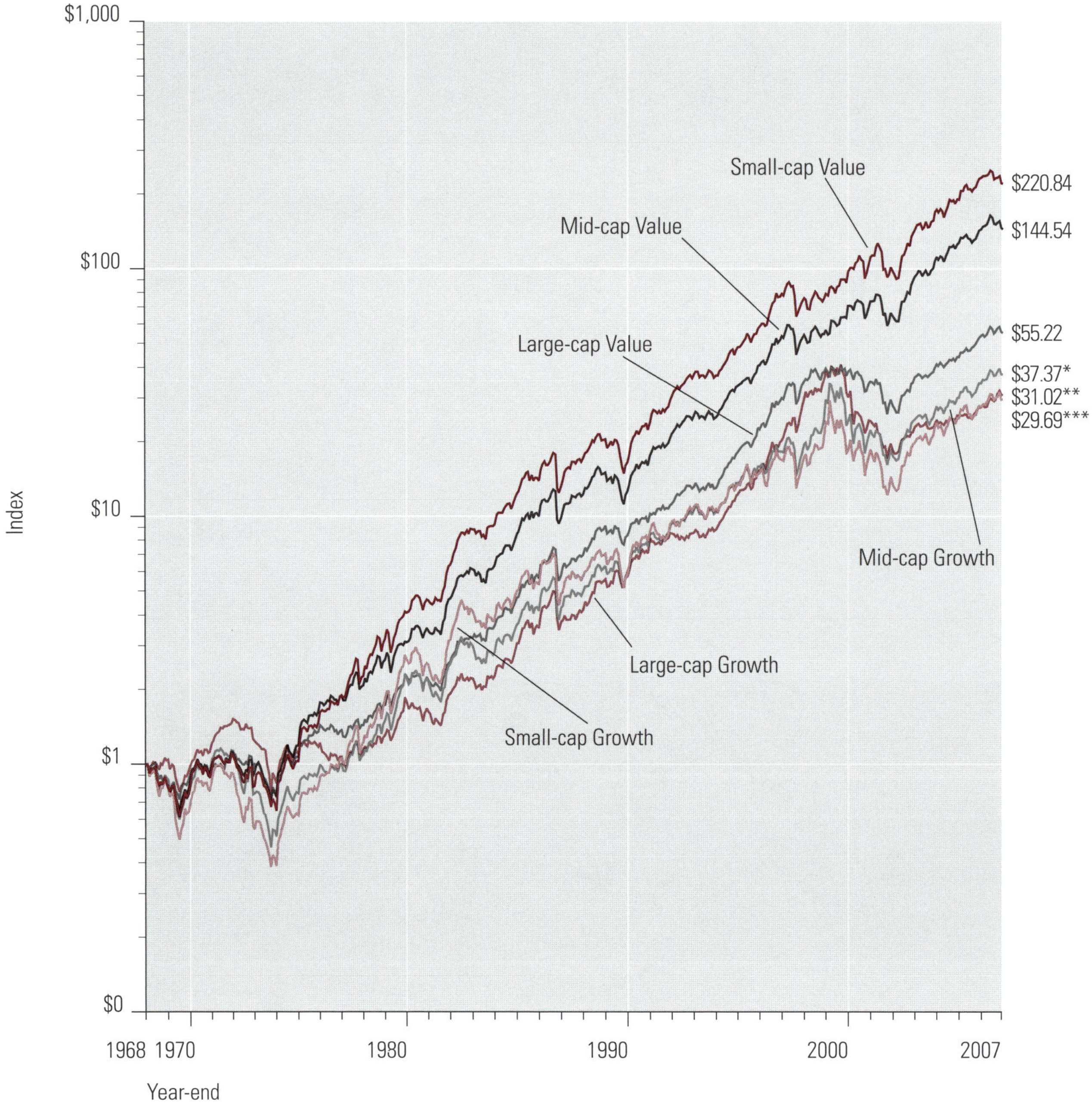

*Mid-cap Growth
**Large-cap Growth
***Small-cap Growth

Summary Statistics for Growth and Value Series

Table 8-1 shows summary statistics of annual total returns for all of the Ibbotson growth and value series. The summary statistics presented are geometric mean, arithmetic mean, and standard deviation.

Value significantly outperformed growth across the market capitalization spectrum. In addition to outperforming their growth counterparts, value series did so with lower volatility. The traditional risk-return tradeoff does not seem to hold with regard to the split between growth and value. The value series are offering more return and less risk.

Table 8-1
Total Returns and Standard Deviation of Value and Growth
Summary Statistics of Annual Returns
from 1969 to 2007

Series	Geometric Mean (%)	Arithmetic Mean (%)	Standard Deviation (%)
IA Large-Cap Growth Stocks	9.2	11.0	19.5
IA Large-Cap Value Stocks	10.8	12.0	16.3
IA Mid-Cap Growth Stocks	9.7	11.8	21.1
IA Mid-Cap Value Stocks	13.6	15.1	18.8
IA Small-Cap Growth Stocks	9.1	11.8	24.1
IA Small-Cap Value Stocks	14.8	16.8	21.2
IA All Growth Stocks	9.2	10.9	19.2
IA All Value Stocks	11.4	12.7	16.4

Returns by Decade

Table 8-2 shows the compound returns by decade for the growth and value series. Value stocks outperformed growth stocks during the 1970s and 1980s. The 1990s proved to be a little different with large-cap growth and mid-cap growth performing better than their value counterparts. However, small-cap value continued to outperform its growth counterpart. Value stocks have outperformed growth stocks during the last ten years, from 1998 to 2007.

Table 8-2
Compound Annual Rates of Return by Decade (in percent)

	1970s	1980s	1990s	2000s*	1998-07
IA Large-Cap Growth TR	2.4	15.6	21.4	−2.8	4.3
IA Large-Cap Value TR	7.7	18.1	15.8	4.2	6.3
IA Mid-Cap Growth TR	5.7	15.4	16.7	3.0	7.4
IA Mid-Cap Value TR	12.5	19.0	14.2	12.4	10.4
IA Small-Cap Growth TR	8.6	14.4	13.1	2.6	5.8
IA Small-Cap Value TR	14.9	20.3	14.5	13.6	10.8
IA All Growth TR	3.3	15.4	20.0	−1.8	4.7
IA All Value TR	8.8	18.4	15.6	5.7	6.9

*Based on the period 2000–2007

Monthly Standard Deviations

Table 8-3 shows the annualized monthly standard deviations of the growth and value data series by decade beginning in the 1970s and illustrates the differences and changes in return volatility. In this table, the 2000s cover the period 2000 to 2007. Value stocks across the various size groupings were less risky investments versus growth stocks in the 1970s, 1980s and 1990s based on standard deviation. Value stocks were also less risky in the 2000s and the last ten years.

Table 8-3
Annualized Monthly Standard Deviations by Decade (in percent)

	1970s	1980s	1990s	2000s*	1998-07
IA Large-Cap Growth TR	19.1	20.8	17.9	16.4	18.5
IA Large-Cap Value TR	16.5	18.3	15.3	14.3	15.7
IA Mid-Cap Growth TR	23.7	23.7	20.8	22.6	24.9
IA Mid-Cap Value TR	22.7	19.6	16.0	17.0	17.5
IA Small-Cap Growth TR	28.3	26.6	23.6	25.2	26.8
IA Small-Cap Value TR	27.2	21.0	17.2	18.7	19.2
IA All Growth TR	19.6	21.4	17.9	16.9	18.9
IA All Value TR	17.6	18.3	15.2	14.5	15.7

*Based on the period 2000–2007

Presentation of the Annual Data

Table 8-4 shows year-by-year total annual returns from 1969 to 2007. This table compares the performance of large-cap growth, large-cap value, mid-cap growth, mid-cap value, small-cap growth, small-cap value, all growth, and all value. Table 8-5 shows the growth of $1.00 invested in each of the categories at year-end 1968.

In addition to the large differences in annual returns between large and small stocks (as noted in Table 7-2 of this book), there are large differences between the returns of growth stocks and value stocks. Table 8-4 shows that value stocks have generally outperformed growth stocks. Most recently, from 2000 to 2006, value stocks outperformed growth stocks in each year, although in 2007 the tables were turned and growth stocks outperformed value stocks 11.3 percent to 1.7 percent.

Table 8-4
Growth and Value Series
Year-by-Year Returns

from 1969 to 2007

	IA Large-cap Growth Stocks	IA Large-cap Value Stocks	IA Mid-cap Growth Stocks	IA Mid-cap Value Stocks	IA Small-cap Growth Stocks	IA Small-cap Value Stocks	IA All Growth Stocks	IA All Value Stocks
1969	0.0440	−0.1686	−0.1358	−0.1857	−0.1956	−0.1971	−0.0032	−0.1732
1970	−0.0514	0.1109	−0.0640	0.0709	−0.1372	0.0354	−0.0579	0.0994
1971	0.2316	0.0553	0.2903	0.1500	0.2630	0.1791	0.2436	0.0773
1972	0.2524	0.1408	0.0832	0.1023	0.0512	0.1012	0.2101	0.1328
1973	−0.1870	−0.1018	−0.3247	−0.1569	−0.4060	−0.2438	−0.2205	−0.1186
1974	−0.3241	−0.2207	−0.3303	−0.2081	−0.2889	−0.2043	−0.3235	−0.2179
1975	0.3137	0.3780	0.4880	0.6122	0.6051	0.5822	0.3515	0.4163
1976	0.1081	0.3407	0.3037	0.4871	0.4285	0.5828	0.1514	0.3731
1977	−0.1199	−0.0479	0.0072	0.0722	0.1848	0.1687	−0.0839	−0.0180
1978	0.0674	0.0511	0.0921	0.0916	0.1580	0.1989	0.0768	0.0662
1979	0.1481	0.2087	0.3796	0.2773	0.5045	0.4156	0.2091	0.2327
1980	0.3571	0.2935	0.4730	0.1707	0.4410	0.2732	0.3840	0.2688
1981	−0.0882	−0.0335	−0.0310	0.1138	−0.0495	0.1161	−0.0736	0.0019
1982	0.1847	0.1865	0.1793	0.3513	0.2640	0.3924	0.1885	0.2307
1983	0.1489	0.2518	0.1839	0.3096	0.3030	0.3888	0.1660	0.2723
1984	0.0266	0.1146	−0.0613	0.0369	−0.0742	0.0502	−0.0006	0.0929
1985	0.3480	0.2987	0.2949	0.3304	0.3096	0.3318	0.3329	0.3086
1986	0.1552	0.2026	0.1393	0.1873	0.0555	0.1286	0.1430	0.1936
1987	0.0577	0.0316	0.0260	−0.0152	−0.0789	−0.0474	0.0393	0.0153
1988	0.1233	0.2006	0.1627	0.2430	0.1803	0.2918	0.1356	0.2155
1989	0.3289	0.3159	0.2727	0.2278	0.2233	0.1910	0.3086	0.2874
1990	0.0327	−0.0835	−0.0510	−0.1558	−0.1634	−0.1871	0.0009	−0.1052
1991	0.4144	0.2173	0.4159	0.3876	0.4841	0.4481	0.4191	0.2631
1992	0.0471	0.1014	0.1041	0.2215	0.0857	0.2695	0.0605	0.1353
1993	0.0044	0.1698	0.1351	0.1846	0.1474	0.2265	0.0400	0.1773
1994	0.0331	−0.0085	−0.0227	−0.0170	−0.0189	−0.0093	0.0173	−0.0103
1995	0.3826	0.3936	0.3163	0.3439	0.2570	0.3001	0.3592	0.3764
1996	0.2274	0.2304	0.1615	0.2116	0.1158	0.2146	0.2070	0.2255
1997	0.3471	0.3422	0.1537	0.3137	0.1247	0.3480	0.2973	0.3375
1998	0.4763	0.1656	0.0643	0.0075	0.0235	−0.0408	0.3817	0.1286
1999	0.2976	0.1309	0.5135	0.0477	0.3927	0.0460	0.3254	0.1159
2000	−0.2201	−0.0300	−0.1847	0.2539	−0.2260	0.2269	−0.2157	0.0078
2001	−0.2012	−0.0882	−0.0724	0.0393	−0.0044	0.1484	−0.1801	−0.0635
2002	−0.2387	−0.2011	−0.2151	−0.1276	−0.2782	−0.1333	−0.2383	−0.1876
2003	0.2477	0.2988	0.4029	0.4386	0.4842	0.4790	0.2809	0.3270
2004	0.0669	0.1343	0.1307	0.2082	0.1958	0.2111	0.0841	0.1492
2005	0.0327	0.0695	0.0876	0.1404	0.0474	0.0923	0.0419	0.0817
2006	0.0891	0.2211	0.1386	0.1305	0.1080	0.2316	0.0982	0.2077
2007	0.1215	0.0254	0.0865	0.0036	0.0738	−0.0562	0.1128	0.0168

Table 8-5
Growth and Value Series
Indices of Year-End Cumulative Wealth
Year-End 1925 = $1.00

from 1968 to 2007

	IA Large-cap Growth Stocks	IA Large-cap Value Stocks	IA Mid-cap Growth Stocks	IA Mid-cap Value Stocks	IA Small-cap Growth Stocks	IA Small-cap Value Stocks	IA All Growth Stocks	IA All Value Stocks
1968	1.000	1.000	1.000	1.000	1.000	1.000	1.000	1.000
1969	1.044	0.831	0.864	0.814	0.804	0.803	0.997	0.827
1970	0.990	0.924	0.809	0.872	0.694	0.831	0.939	0.909
1971	1.220	0.975	1.044	1.003	0.877	0.980	1.168	0.979
1972	1.528	1.112	1.131	1.105	0.922	1.079	1.413	1.109
1973	1.242	0.999	0.763	0.932	0.547	0.816	1.102	0.978
1974	0.839	0.778	0.511	0.738	0.389	0.649	0.745	0.765
1975	1.103	1.072	0.761	1.190	0.625	1.028	1.007	1.083
1976	1.222	1.438	0.992	1.770	0.893	1.626	1.160	1.487
1977	1.076	1.369	0.999	1.897	1.058	1.901	1.062	1.460
1978	1.148	1.439	1.091	2.071	1.225	2.279	1.144	1.557
1979	1.318	1.739	1.505	2.645	1.843	3.226	1.383	1.920
1980	1.789	2.250	2.217	3.097	2.655	4.107	1.914	2.436
1981	1.631	2.175	2.148	3.449	2.524	4.584	1.773	2.440
1982	1.932	2.580	2.533	4.661	3.190	6.383	2.107	3.003
1983	2.220	3.230	2.999	6.104	4.156	8.864	2.457	3.821
1984	2.279	3.600	2.815	6.329	3.848	9.309	2.456	4.176
1985	3.072	4.675	3.646	8.421	5.039	12.398	3.273	5.464
1986	3.549	5.623	4.154	9.998	5.319	13.992	3.742	6.522
1987	3.754	5.800	4.261	9.846	4.899	13.329	3.889	6.622
1988	4.217	6.964	4.955	12.240	5.783	17.219	4.416	8.049
1989	5.604	9.164	6.306	15.028	7.074	20.507	5.779	10.362
1990	5.787	8.399	5.984	12.687	5.918	16.669	5.784	9.272
1991	8.185	10.224	8.474	17.603	8.783	24.138	8.208	11.711
1992	8.570	11.261	9.356	21.503	9.536	30.642	8.705	13.296
1993	8.608	13.172	10.620	25.472	10.941	37.583	9.053	15.653
1994	8.893	13.060	10.379	25.040	10.734	37.235	9.210	15.492
1995	12.296	18.200	13.662	33.651	13.492	48.410	12.518	21.324
1996	15.093	22.392	15.869	40.770	15.056	58.798	15.109	26.133
1997	20.332	30.054	18.309	53.562	16.933	79.258	19.601	34.952
1998	30.015	35.031	19.487	53.964	17.330	76.021	27.083	39.449
1999	38.948	39.616	29.494	56.537	24.136	79.521	35.896	44.023
2000	30.377	38.429	24.046	70.894	18.682	97.569	28.153	44.365
2001	24.265	35.038	22.305	73.678	18.599	112.046	23.081	41.547
2002	18.474	27.992	17.508	64.275	13.425	97.105	17.581	33.754
2003	23.049	36.357	24.561	92.464	19.925	143.619	22.521	44.791
2004	24.590	41.239	27.770	111.718	23.827	173.942	24.413	51.475
2005	25.395	44.106	30.203	127.405	24.956	190.002	25.436	55.682
2006	27.657	53.858	34.391	144.027	27.651	233.999	27.935	67.248
2007	31.017	55.225	37.367	144.541	29.692	220.84	31.085	68.377

Correlation of Growth and Value Series

Table 8-6 presents the annual cross-correlations and serial correlations for the growth and value series. Both large-cap value and large-cap growth are nearly perfectly positively correlated to all value and all growth, respectively. Large-cap growth posted the highest serial correlation out of the different size groupings.

Table 8-6
Growth and Value Series
Serial and Cross Correlations of Historical Annual Returns from 1969 to 2007

Series	IA Large-cap Growth Stocks	IA Large-cap Value Stocks	IA Mid-cap Growth Stocks	IA Mid-cap Value Stocks	IA Small-cap Growth Stocks	IA Small-cap Value Stocks	IA All Growth Stocks	IA All Value Stocks
IA Large-Cap Growth Stocks	1.00							
IA Large-Cap Value Stocks	0.80	1.00						
IA Mid-Cap Growth Stocks	0.81	0.82	1.00					
IA Mid-Cap Value Stocks	0.55	0.84	0.74	1.00				
IA Small-Cap Growth Stocks	0.70	0.78	0.96	0.81	1.00			
IA Small-Cap Value Stocks	0.49	0.80	0.75	0.97	0.84	1.00		
IA All Growth Stocks	0.99	0.84	0.89	0.63	0.80	0.59	1.00	
IA All Value Stocks	0.76	0.99	0.83	0.91	0.82	0.87	0.81	1.00
Serial Correlations	0.14	−0.01	−0.07	−0.07	−0.05	−0.03	0.07	−0.04

Fama-French (FF) Growth and (FF) Value Series

The following commentary and corresponding data make use of the Fama-French growth and value data series.

Historical Returns on Growth and Value

Using the Fama-French series, Graph 8-3 depicts the growth of $1.00 invested in FF small growth, small value, large growth, and large value stocks from the end of 1927 to the end of 2007. All results assume reinvestment of dividends and exclude transaction costs. The top two performers during this time period were small value and large value stocks followed by small growth and large growth stocks. Over the period from 1928 to 2007, small value stocks outperformed all other stock series in the graph. One dollar invested in small value stocks at the end of 1927 grew to $46,602.85 by year-end 2007, falling from $54,965.75 at the end of 2006.

Graph 8-3
FF Small Value Stocks, FF Small Growth Stocks, FF Large Value Stocks, FF Large Growth Stocks
Year-End 1927 = $1.00

from 1927 to 2007

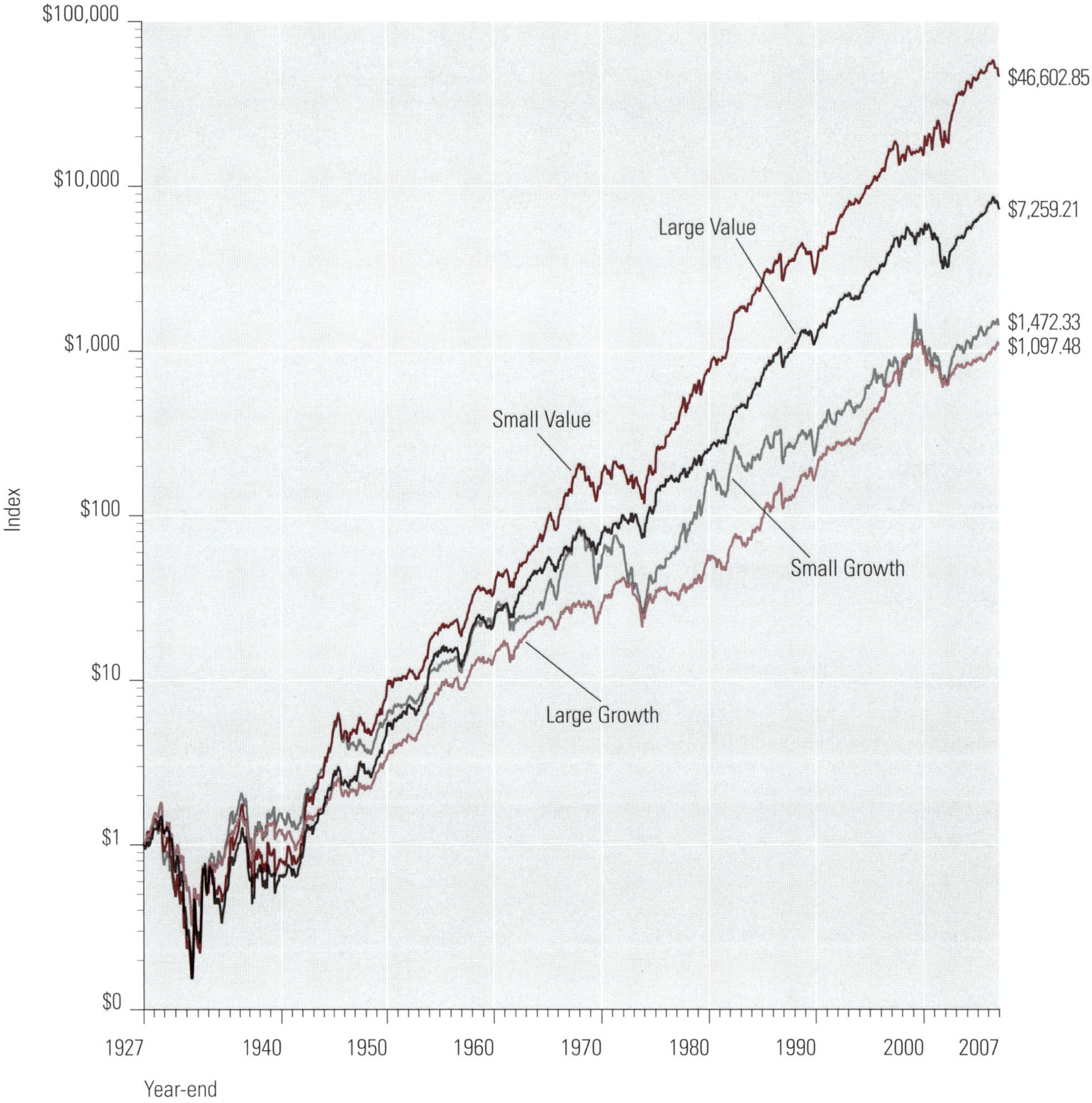

Summary Statistics for Growth and Value Series

Table 8-7 shows summary statistics of annual total returns for all of the Fama-French growth and value series. The summary statistics presented are geometric mean, arithmetic mean, and standard deviation.

Value significantly outperformed growth across the market capitalization spectrum. In the large capitalization arena, the extra return of value over growth was at the expense of increased risk, as the standard deviation of large value was 27.2 percent versus 20.0 percent for large growth. Among the small cap series, small value significantly outperformed small growth and did so with lower volatility (32.1 percent versus 33.2 percent).

Table 8-7
Total Returns and Standard Deviation of Value and Growth
Summary Statistics of Annual Returns
from 1928 to 2007

Series	Geometric Mean (%)	Arithmetic Mean (%)	Standard Deviation (%)
FF Large Growth Stocks	9.1	11.0	20.0
FF Large Value Stocks	11.8	15.1	27.2
FF Small Growth Stocks	9.5	14.2	33.2
FF Small Value Stocks	14.4	18.9	32.1

Returns by Decade

Table 8-8 shows the compound returns by decade for the growth and value series. Small value stocks beat small growth stocks in all decades except the 1930s and the 1990s. It is also interesting to note that in any decade small value stocks were never the worst performing among all four stock series. In this table, the 1920s cover the period 1928 to 1929 and the 2000s cover the period 2000 to 2007.

Table 8-8
Compound Annual Rates of Return by Decade

	1920s*	1930s	1940s	1950s	1960s	1970s	1980s	1990s	2000s**	1998-07
FF Large Growth Stocks	8.1%	1.5%	7.3%	17.6%	7.9%	3.4%	15.8%	19.9%	–0.2%	5.5%
FF Large Value Stocks	9.0	–5.5	17.2	22.2	10.7	12.2	20.2	13.9	4.8	5.4
FF Small Growth Stocks	–13.3	7.4	11.6	17.7	10.7	5.8	10.8	15.0	1.7	6.2
FF Small Value Stocks	–4.8	–0.3	21.0	20.0	15.4	15.0	21.1	14.5	14.1	10.8

*Based on the period 1928–1929

**Based on the period 2000–2007

Presentation of the Annual Data

Table 8-10 shows year-by-year total annual returns from 1928 to 2007. This table compares the performance of large growth, large value, small growth, and small value.

Correlation of Growth and Value Series

Table 8-9 presents the annual cross-correlations and serial correlations for the growth and value series.

Table 8-9
Growth and Value Series
Serial and Cross Correlations of Historical Annual Returns from 1928 to 2007

Series	FF Large Growth Stocks	FF Large Value Stocks	FF Small Growth Stocks	FF Small Value Stocks	U.S. Treasury Bills	Inflation
FF Large Growth Stocks	1.00					
FF Large Value Stocks	0.79	1.00				
FF Small Growth Stocks	0.81	0.81	1.00			
FF Small Value Stocks	0.72	0.90	0.87	1.00		
U.S. Treasury Bills	−0.01	−0.05	−0.11	−0.09	1.00	
Inflation	−0.03	0.05	−0.01	0.04	0.41	1.00
Serial Correlations	0.06	−0.08	0.02	0.04	0.91	0.64

Conclusion

What can explain this value effect? Readers of Graham and Dodd's Security Analysis,[1] first published in 1934, would say that the outperformance of value stocks is due to the market coming to realize the full value of a company's securities that were once undervalued. The Graham and Dodd approach to security analysis is to do an independent valuation of a company using accounting data and common market multiples, then look at the stock price to see if the stock is under- or overvalued. Several academic studies have shown that the market overreacts to bad news and underreacts to good news. This would lead us to conclude that there is more room for value stocks (which are more likely to have reported bad news) to improve and outperform growth stocks, which already have high expectations built into them.

Possibly a larger question is what does the future hold as far as growth and value investing goes? Advocates of growth investing would argue that technology- and innovation-oriented companies will continue to dominate as the Internet changes the way the world communicates and does business. Stalwarts of value investing would argue that there are still companies and industries that continue to be ignored and represent long-term investment bargains. Only time will tell.

1 Cottle, Sidney, Murray, Roger F., and Block, Frank E. "Graham and Dodd's Security Analysis," Fifth Edition, McGraw-Hill, 1988.

Table 8-10
Growth and Value Series
Year-by-Year Returns

from 1928 to 1970

	FF Large Growth Stocks	FF Large Value Stocks	FF Small Growth Stocks	FF Small Value Stocks
1928	0.4805	0.2363	0.3486	0.4096
1929	–0.2107	–0.0393	–0.4423	–0.3577
1930	–0.2644	–0.4316	–0.3585	–0.4638
1931	–0.3696	–0.5824	–0.4270	–0.5187
1932	–0.0793	–0.0326	–0.0525	0.0135
1933	0.4465	1.1691	1.5941	1.1869
1934	0.1106	–0.2151	0.3589	0.0851
1935	0.4222	0.5114	0.4834	0.5316
1936	0.2646	0.4812	0.3710	0.7319
1937	–0.3412	–0.4107	–0.4864	–0.5147
1938	0.3320	0.2520	0.4381	0.2621
1939	0.0773	–0.1251	0.1072	–0.0355
1940	–0.0981	–0.0262	0.0057	–0.0983
1941	–0.1267	–0.0088	–0.1734	–0.0482
1942	0.1317	0.3371	0.1676	0.3500
1943	0.2204	0.4402	0.4508	0.9182
1944	0.1611	0.4198	0.4123	0.4971
1945	0.3195	0.4906	0.6428	0.7461
1946	–0.0829	–0.0829	–0.1240	–0.0736
1947	0.0410	0.0866	–0.0838	0.0534
1948	0.0335	0.0509	–0.0716	–0.0230
1949	0.2331	0.1871	0.2352	0.2104
1950	0.2311	0.5522	0.3101	0.5216
1951	0.2005	0.1436	0.1626	0.1227
1952	0.1338	0.1954	0.0855	0.0859
1953	0.0229	–0.0704	–0.0068	–0.0692
1954	0.4779	0.7732	0.4320	0.6343
1955	0.2850	0.2978	0.1395	0.2347
1956	0.0652	0.0337	0.0765	0.0598
1957	–0.0914	–0.2272	–0.1699	–0.1590
1958	0.4162	0.7230	0.7522	0.6967
1959	0.1315	0.1882	0.2142	0.1742
1960	–0.0236	–0.0856	–0.0178	–0.0602
1961	0.2643	0.2889	0.2220	0.3085
1962	–0.1089	–0.0309	–0.2233	–0.0947
1963	0.2188	0.3235	0.0798	0.2834
1964	0.1448	0.1916	0.0813	0.2290
1965	0.1336	0.2242	0.3999	0.4250
1966	–0.1077	–0.1021	–0.0532	–0.0776
1967	0.2917	0.3174	0.8842	0.6755
1968	0.0403	0.2708	0.3273	0.4581
1969	0.0288	–0.1639	–0.2368	–0.2584
1970	–0.0565	0.1063	–0.2025	0.0662

Source: Eugene Fama and Ken French

Table 8-10 (continued)

Growth and Value Series

Year-by-Year Returns

from 1971 to 2007

	FF Large Growth Stocks	FF Large Value Stocks	FF Small Growth Stocks	FF Small Value Stocks
1971	0.2394	0.1255	0.2586	0.1447
1972	0.2132	0.1862	0.0039	0.0728
1973	−0.2179	−0.0367	−0.4507	−0.2723
1974	−0.2924	−0.2340	−0.3190	−0.1902
1975	0.3444	0.5590	0.6132	0.5712
1976	0.1754	0.4462	0.3820	0.5913
1977	−0.0946	0.0164	0.1935	0.2382
1978	0.0700	0.0348	0.1765	0.2212
1979	0.1659	0.2267	0.4884	0.3833
1980	0.3520	0.1645	0.5266	0.2228
1981	−0.0713	0.1280	−0.1153	0.1768
1982	0.2148	0.2767	0.1972	0.3986
1983	0.1467	0.2692	0.2212	0.4758
1984	−0.0072	0.1617	−0.1284	0.0752
1985	0.3264	0.3175	0.2891	0.3212
1986	0.1438	0.2182	0.0195	0.1450
1987	0.0743	−0.0276	−0.1224	−0.0712
1988	0.1253	0.2596	0.1663	0.3076
1989	0.3611	0.2970	0.2058	0.1570
1990	0.0106	−0.1275	−0.1774	−0.2513
1991	0.4333	0.2735	0.5473	0.4056
1992	0.0641	0.2357	0.0582	0.3476
1993	0.0238	0.1951	0.1264	0.2941
1994	0.0195	−0.0578	−0.0436	0.0321
1995	0.3716	0.3768	0.3513	0.2769
1996	0.2125	0.1335	0.1236	0.2071
1997	0.3161	0.3188	0.1529	0.3729
1998	0.3464	0.1623	0.0304	−0.0863
1999	0.2943	−0.0022	0.5475	0.0559
2000	−0.1363	0.0580	−0.2415	−0.0080
2001	−0.1559	−0.0118	0.0016	0.4024
2002	−0.2150	−0.3253	−0.3087	−0.1241
2003	0.2629	0.3507	0.5320	0.7469
2004	0.0653	0.1891	0.1254	0.2659
2005	0.0282	0.1217	0.0545	0.0353
2006	0.0888	0.2261	0.1167	0.2176
2007	0.1408	−0.0645	0.0736	−0.1521

Source: Eugene Fama and Ken French

Chapter 9

Using Historical Data in Forecasting and Optimization

Probabilistic Forecasts

When forecasting the return on an asset or a portfolio, investors are (or should be) interested in the entire probability distribution of future outcomes, not just the mean or "point estimate." An example of a point estimate forecast is that large company stocks will have a return of 13 percent in 2008. It is more helpful to know the uncertainty surrounding this point estimate than to know the point estimate itself. One measure of uncertainty is standard deviation. The large company stock return forecast can be expressed as 13 percent representing the mean with 20 percent representing the standard deviation.

If the returns on large company stocks are normally distributed, the mean (expected return) and the standard deviation provide enough information to forecast the likelihood of any return. Suppose one wants to ascertain the likelihood that large company stocks will have a return of –25 percent or lower in 2008. Given the above example, a return of –25 percent is $[13 - (-25)]/20 = 1.9$ standard deviations below the mean. The likelihood of an observation 1.9 or more standard deviations below the mean is 2.9 percent. (This can be looked up in any statistics textbook, in the table showing values of the cumulative probability function for a normal distribution.) Thus, the likelihood that the stock market will fall by 25 percent or more in 2008 is 2.9 percent. This is valuable information, both to the investor who believes that stocks are a sure thing and to the investor who is certain that they will crash tomorrow.

In fact, the historical returns of large company stocks are not exactly normally distributed, and a slightly different method needs to be used to make probabilistic forecasts. The actual model used to forecast the distribution of stock returns is described later in this chapter.

Some people are wary of probabilistic forecasts because they seem too wide to be useful, or because they lack punch. (The most widely quoted forecasters, after all, make very specific predictions.) However, the forecast of a probability distribution actually reveals much more than the point estimate. The point estimate reflects what statisticians call an "expected value"—but one does not actually expect this particular outcome to happen. The actual return will likely be higher or lower than the point estimate. By knowing the extent to which actual returns are likely to deviate from the point estimate, the investor can assess the risk of every asset, and thus compare investment opportunities in terms of their risks as well as their expected returns. As Harry Markowitz showed nearly a half-century ago in his Nobel Prize-winning work on portfolio theory, investors care about avoiding risk as well as seeking return. Probabilistic forecasts enable investors to quantify these concepts.

The Lognormal Distribution

In the lognormal model, the natural logarithms of asset return relatives are assumed to be normally distributed. (A return relative is one plus the return. That is, if an asset has a return of 15 percent in a given period, its return relative is 1.15.)

The lognormal distribution is skewed to the right. That is, the expected value, or mean, is greater than the median. Furthermore, if return relatives are lognormally distributed, returns cannot fall below negative 100 percent. These properties of the lognormal distribution make it a more accurate characterization of the behavior of market returns than does the normal distribution.

In all normal distributions, moreover, the probability of an observation falling below the mean by as much as one standard deviation equals the probability of falling above the mean by as much as one standard deviation; both probabilities are about 34 percent. In a lognormal distribution, these probabilities differ and depend on the parameters of the distribution.

Forecasting Wealth Values and Rates of Return

Using the lognormal model, it is fairly simple to form probabilistic forecasts of both compound rates of return and ending period wealth values. Wealth at time **n** (assuming reinvestment of all income and no taxes) is:

$$W_n = W_0(1+r_1)(1+r_2)\ldots(1+r_n) \qquad (30)$$

where,

W_n = the wealth value at time **n**;

W_0 = the initial investment at time **0**; and,

r_1, r_2, etc. = the total returns on the portfolio for the rebalancing period ending at times 1, 2, and so forth.

The compound rate of return or geometric mean return over the same period, r_G, is:

$$r_G = \left(\frac{W_n}{W_0}\right)^{\frac{1}{n}} - 1 \qquad (31)$$

where,

r_G = the geometric mean return;

W_n = the ending period wealth value at time **n**;

W_0 = the initial wealth value at time **0**; and,

n = the inclusive number of periods.

By assuming that all of the $(1+r_n)$s are lognormally distributed with the same expected value and standard deviation and are all statistically independent of each other, it follows that W_n and $(1+r_G)$ are lognormally distributed. In fact, even if the $(1+r_n)$s are not themselves lognormally distributed but are independent and identically distributed, W_n and $(1+r_G)$ are approximately lognormal for large enough values of **n**. This "central-limit theorem" means that the lognormal model can be useful in long-term forecasting even if short-term returns are not well described by a lognormal distribution.

Calculating Parameters of the Lognormal Model

To use the lognormal model, we must first calculate the expected value and standard deviation of the natural logarithm of the return relative of the portfolio. These parameters, denoted **m** and **s** respectively, can be calculated from the expected return (μ) and standard deviation (σ) of the portfolio as follows:

$$m = \ln(1+\mu) - \left(\frac{s^2}{2}\right) \qquad (32)$$

$$s = \sqrt{\ln\left[1+\left(\frac{\sigma}{1+\mu}\right)^2\right]} \quad (33)$$

where,
ln = the natural logarithm function.

To calculate a particular percentile of wealth or return for a given time horizon, the only remaining parameter needed is the z-score of the percentile. The z-score of a percentile ranking is that percentile ranking expressed as the number of standard deviations that it is above or below the mean of a normal distribution. For example, the z-score of the 95th percentile is 1.645 because in a normal distribution, the 95th percentile is 1.645 standard deviations above the 50th percentile or median, which is also the mean. Z-scores can be obtained from a table of cumulative values of the standard normal distribution or from software that produces such values.

Given the logarithmic parameters of a portfolio (**m** and **s**), a time horizon (**n**), and the z-score of a percentile (**z**), the percentile in question in terms of cumulative wealth at the end of the time horizon (W_n) is:

$$e^{(mn + zs\sqrt{n})} \quad (34)$$

Similarly, the percentile in question in terms of the compound rate of return for the period (r_G) is:

$$e^{\left(m + z\frac{s}{\sqrt{n}}\right)} - 1 \quad (35)$$

Mean-Variance Optimization

One important application of the probability forecasts of asset returns is mean-variance optimization. Optimization is the process of identifying portfolios that have the highest possible expected return for a given level of risk, or the lowest possible risk for a given expected return. Such a portfolio is considered "efficient," and the locus of all efficient portfolios is called the efficient frontier. An efficient frontier constructed from large company stocks, long-term government bonds, and Treasury bills is shown in Graph 9-1. All investors should hold portfolios that are efficient with respect to the assets in their opportunity set.

The most widely accepted framework for optimization is Markowitz or mean-variance optimization (MVO), which makes the following assumptions: 1) the forecast mean, or expected return, describes the attribute that investors consider to be desirable about an asset; 2) the risk of the asset is measured by its expected standard deviation of returns; and 3) the interaction between one asset and another is captured by the expected correlation coefficient of the two assets' returns. MVO thus requires forecasts of the return and standard deviation of each asset, and the correlation of each asset with every other asset.[1]

1 The standard deviation is the square root of the variance; hence the term "mean-variance" in describing this form of the optimization problem.

In the 1950s, Harry Markowitz developed both the concept of the efficient frontier and the mathematical means of constructing it (mean-variance optimization)[2]. Currently, there are a number of commercially available mean-variance optimization software tools available, including Morningstar *EnCorr*®[3]. This advanced analytical software unites proven financial models, sophisticated Ibbotson methodologies, and comprehensive Morningstar investment data.

Graph 9-1
Efficient Frontier
Large Company Stocks, Long-Term Government Bonds, and U.S. Treasury Bills

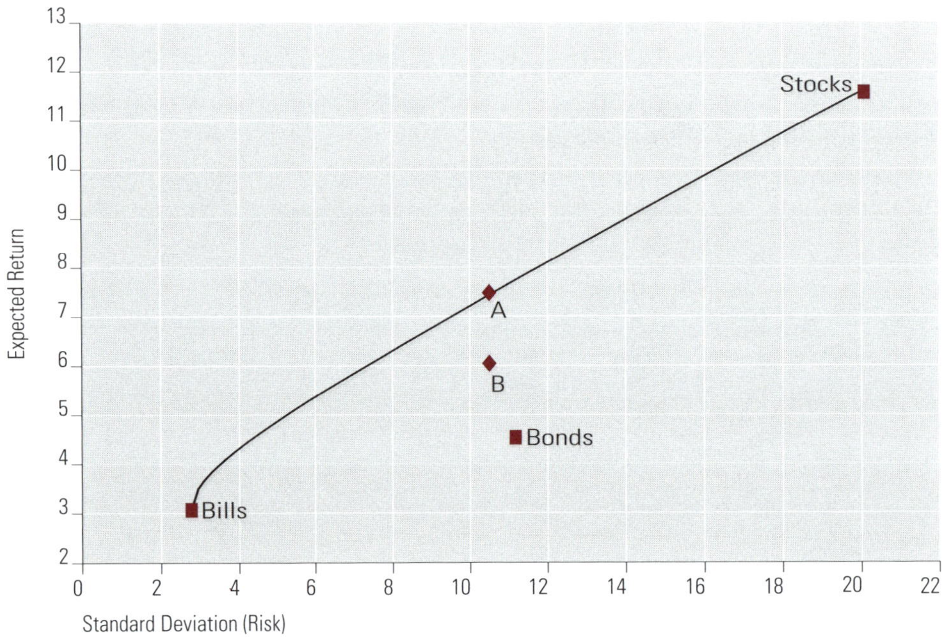

Estimating the Means, Standard Deviations, and Correlations of Asset Returns

To simulate future probability distributions of asset and portfolio returns, one typically estimates parameters of the historical return data. The parameters that are required to simulate returns on an asset are its mean and standard deviation. To simulate returns on portfolios of assets, one must also estimate the correlation of each asset in the portfolio with every other asset. Thus, the parameters required to conduct a simulation are the same as those required as inputs into a mean-variance optimization.[4]

To illustrate how to estimate the parameters of asset class returns relevant to optimization and forecasting, we construct an example using large company stocks, long-term government bonds, and

2 Markowitz, Harry M., Portfolio Selection: Efficient Diversification of Investments, New York: John Wiley & Sons, 1959.

3 For more information about Morningstar *EnCorr*® software refer to the Investment Tools and Resources page at the back of this book, or within the United States, call +1 866 910-0840. Outside the United States, call +44 020 3107-0020.

4 It is also possible to conduct a simulation using entire data sets, that is, without estimating the statistical parameters of the data sets. Typically, in such a nonparametric simulation, the frequency of an event occurring in the simulated history is equal to the frequency of the event occurring in the actual history used to construct the data set.

Treasury bills. The techniques used to estimate these parameters are described below. These are similar techniques as those used in Morningstar *EnCorr*® software.

Means, or Expected Returns

The mean return (forecast mean, or expected return) on an asset is the probability-weighted average of all possible returns on the asset over a future period. Estimates of expected returns are based on models of asset returns. While many models of asset returns incorporate estimates of GNP, the money supply, and other macroeconomic variables, the model employed in this chapter does not. This is because we assume (for the present purpose) that asset markets are informationally efficient, with all relevant and available information fully incorporated in asset prices. If this assumption holds, investor expectations (forecasts) can be discerned from market-observable data. Such forecasts are not attempts to outguess, or beat, the market. They are attempts to discern the market's expectations, i.e., to read what the market itself is forecasting.

For some assets, expected returns can be estimated using current market data alone. For example, the yield on a riskless bond is an estimate of its expected return. For other assets, current data are not sufficient. Stocks, for example, have no exact analogue to the yield on a bond. In such cases, we use the statistical time series properties of historical data in forming the estimates.

To know which data to use in estimating expected returns, we need to know the rebalancing frequency of the portfolios and the planning horizon. In our example, we will assume an annual rebalancing frequency and a twenty-year planning horizon. The rebalancing frequency gives the time units in which returns are measured.

With a twenty-year planning horizon, the relevant riskless rate is the yield on a twenty-year coupon bond. At the end of 2007, the yield on a twenty-year coupon bond was 4.5 percent. This riskless rate is the baseline, from which the expected return on every other asset class is derived by adding or subtracting risk premia.

Large Company Stocks

The expected return on large company stocks is the riskless rate, plus the expected risk premium of large company stocks over bonds that are riskless over the planning horizon. With a twenty-year planning horizon, this risk premium is 7.1 percent, shown as the long-horizon expected equity risk premium in Table 9-1. Hence, the expected return on large company stocks is 4.5 (the riskless rate) plus 7.1 (the risk premium) for a total of 11.6 percent.

Bonds and Bills

For default-free bonds with a maturity equal to the planning horizon, the expected return is the yield on the bond; that is, the expected return is the riskless rate of 4.5 percent. For bonds with other maturities, the expected bond horizon premium should be added to the riskless rate (for longer maturities) or subtracted from the riskless rate (for shorter maturities). Since expected capital gains on a bond are zero, the expected horizon premium is estimated by the historical average difference of the income returns on the bonds.[5]

5 The expected capital gain on a par bond is self-evidently zero. For a zero-coupon (or other discount) bond, investors expect the price to rise as the bond ages, but the expected portion of this price increase should not be considered a capital gain. It is a form of income return.

For Treasury bills, the expected return over a given time horizon is equal to the expected return on a Treasury bond of a similar horizon, less the expected horizon premium of bonds over bills. This premium is estimated by the historical average of the difference of the income return on bonds and the return on bills. From Table 9-1, this is 1.5 percent. Subtracting this from the riskless rate gives us an expected return on bills of 3.0 percent. Of course, this forecast typically differs from the current yield on a Treasury bill, since a portfolio of Treasury bills is rolled over (the proceeds of maturing bills are invested in new bills, at yields not yet known) during the time horizon described.

Standard Deviations

Standard deviations are estimated from historical data as described in Chapter 6. Since there is no evidence of a major change in the variability of returns on large company stocks, we use the entire period 1926–2007 to estimate the standard deviation of these asset classes. For bonds and bills, we use the period 1970–2007. The use of this more recent period reflects the fact that the volatility of bonds has increased over time.

Table 9-1
Building Blocks for Expected Return Construction

	Value (in percent)
Yields (Riskless Rates)[1]	
Long-Term (20-year) U.S. Treasury Coupon Bond Yield	4.5
Intermediate-Term (5-year) U.S. Treasury Coupon Note Yield	3.3
Short-Term (30-day) U.S. Treasury Bill Yield	2.8
Fixed Income Risk Premia[2]	
Expected default premium: *long-term corporate bond total returns minus long-term government bond total returns*	0.0
Expected long-term horizon premium: *long-term government bond income returns minus U.S. Treasury bill total returns**	1.5
Expected intermediate-term horizon premium: *intermediate-term government bond income returns minus U.S. Treasury bill total returns**	1.0
Equity Risk Premia[3]	
Long-horizon expected equity risk premium: *large company stock total returns minus long-term government bond income returns*	7.1
Intermediate-horizon expected equity risk premium: *large company stock total returns minus intermediate-term government bond income returns*	7.5
Short-horizon expected equity risk premium: *large company stock total returns minus U.S. Treasury bill total returns**	8.5
Small Stock Premium: *small company stock total return minus large company stock total return*	4.8

1 As of December 31, 2007. Maturities are approximate.

2 Expected risk premia for fixed income are based on the differences of historical arithmetic mean returns from 1970–2007.

3 Expected risk premia for equities are based on the differences of historical arithmetic mean returns from 1926–2007.

*For U.S. Treasury bills, the income return and total return are the same.

Correlations

Correlations between the asset classes are estimated from historical data as described in Chapter 6. Correlation coefficients for stocks, bonds, and bills are derived from 1970–2007. Correlations between major asset classes change over time. Graph 9-2 shows the historical correlation of annual returns on large company stocks and long-term bonds over 20 year rolling periods from 1926–1945 through 1988–2007.

Graph 9-2
Twenty Year Rolling Period Correlations of Annual Returns
Large Company Stocks and Long-Term Government Bonds
from 1926–1945 through 1988–2007

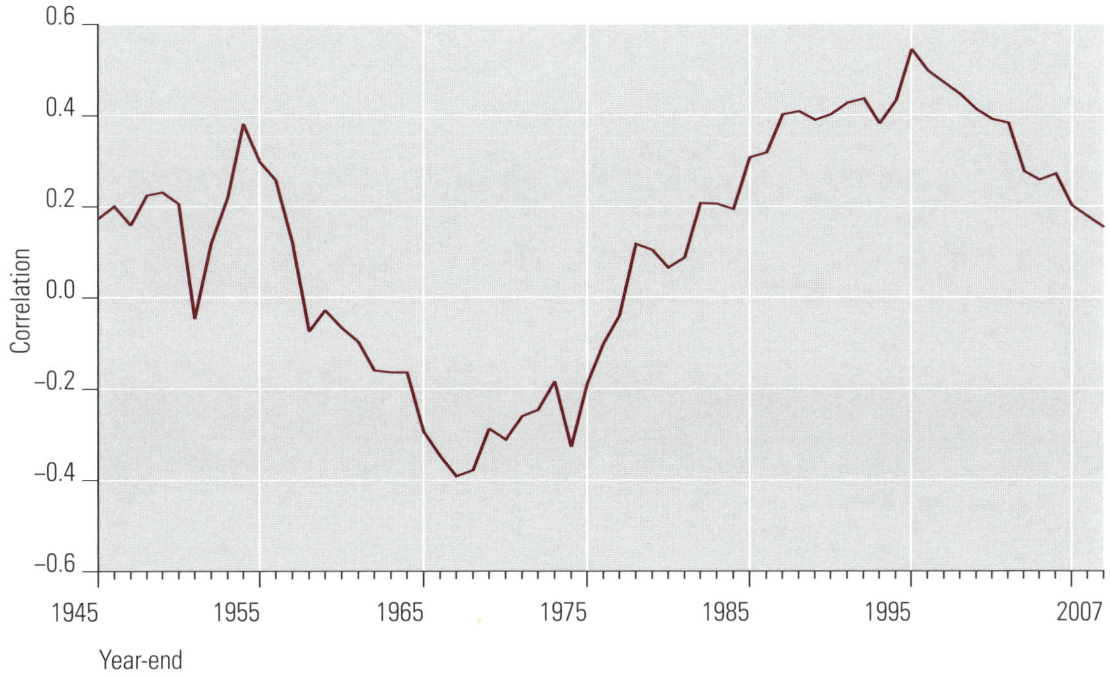

Generating Probabilistic Forecasts

For large company stocks in Table 9-2, the logarithmic parameters are calculated to be **m** = 0.0936 and **s** = 0.1776 based on equations (32) and (33). The z-scores of the 95th, 50th, and 5th percentile are 1.645, 0, and –1.645, respectively. Using these parameters, we can calculate the 95th, 50th, and 5th percentiles of cumulative wealth and compound returns over various time horizons using equations (34) and (35). Graph 9-3 shows percentiles of compound returns over the entire range of one to twenty year horizons in graphical form. This type of graph is sometimes called a "trumpet" graph because the high and low percentile curves taken together make the shape of a trumpet. The "mouthpiece" of the trumpet is on the right side of the graph because for long time horizons, all percentiles converge to the median (50th percentile).

Graph 9-3

Forecast Total Return Distribution

100 Percent Large Stocks from 2008 to 2027

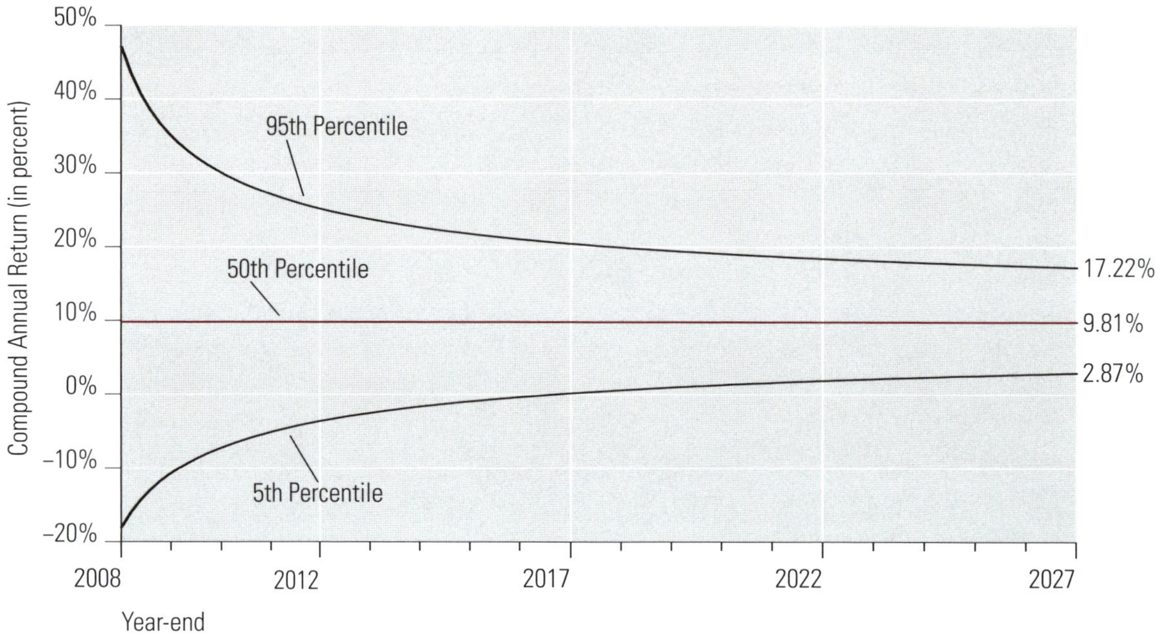

Graph 9-4

Forecast Distribution of Wealth Index Value

100 Percent Large Stocks from 2008 to 2027

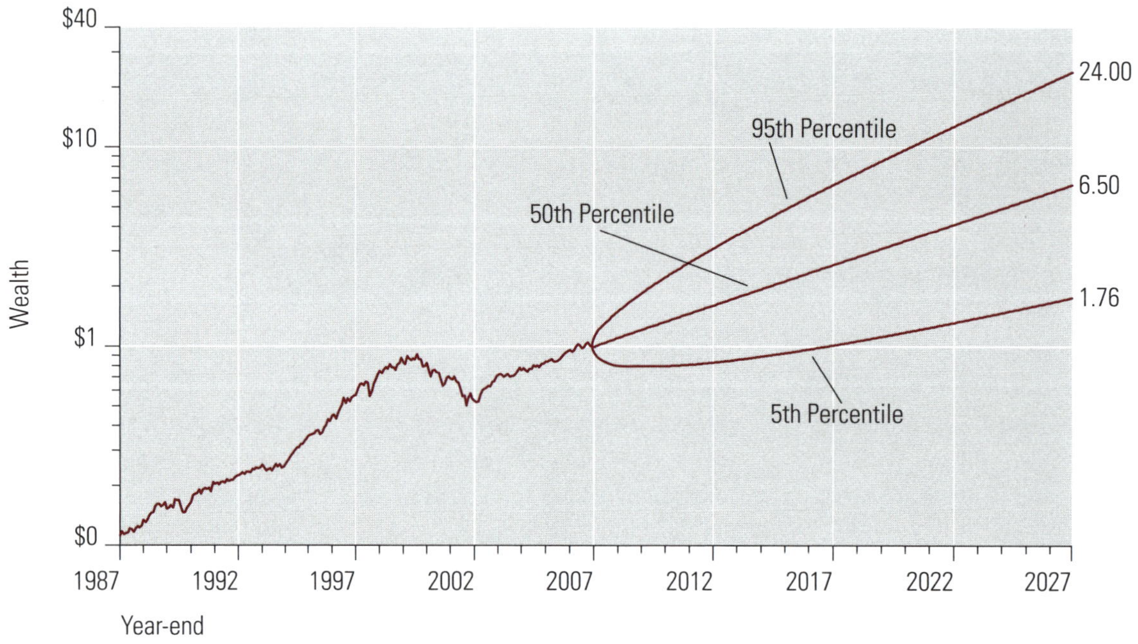

Table 9-2
Optimization Inputs: Year-End 2007 Large Company Stocks, Long-Term Government Bonds, and U.S. Treasury Bills (in percent)

	Expected Return	Standard Deviation	Correlation with Stocks	Bonds	Bills
Stocks	11.6	20.0	1.00		
Bonds	4.5	11.2	0.27	1.00	
Bills	3.0	2.9	0.05	0.04	1.00

Graph 9-4 is a graph showing percentiles of cumulative wealth over the entire range of zero to twenty year time horizons, along with the back history of the portfolio's performance. The past and forecasted (future) values on the graph are connected by setting the wealth index to \$1.00 at the end of 2007. The past index values show how much wealth one would have had to hold in large company stocks to have \$1.00 at the end of 2007; the percentiles of future value show the probability distribution of future growth of \$1.00 invested in large company stocks. This type of graph is sometimes called a "tulip" graph because of its overall shape.

Table 9-3 shows (in the top panel) the probability distribution of compound annual returns on large company stocks over the next 20 years. The top line shows the 95th percentile or optimistic case, the middle line the 50th percentile or median case, and the bottom line the 5th percentile or pessimistic case. The bottom panel shows the same projections, redrawn as cumulative values of \$1.00 invested at the beginning of the period simulated. Simulations such as these are used for asset allocation, funding of liabilities, and other portfolio management-related applications; Morningstar *EnCorr*® mean-variance optimization software can produce these forecasts.

Table 9-3
Forecast Distributions of Compound Annual Returns and End of Period Wealth
Large Company Stocks: Year-End 2007

	Compound Annual Return (in percent)				
Percentile	2008	2012	2017	2022	2027
95th	47.06	25.13	20.44	18.41	17.22
90th	37.87	21.58	18.00	16.46	15.54
75th	23.78	15.85	14.05	13.26	12.79
50th	9.81	9.81	9.81	9.81	9.81
25th	–2.59	4.08	5.73	6.47	6.91
10th	–12.54	–0.82	2.19	3.54	4.36
5th	–18.00	–3.64	0.12	1.83	2.87

	End of Period Wealth (\$1 Invested on 12/31/07)				
Percentile	2008	2012	2017	2022	2027
95th	1.47	3.07	6.42	12.62	24.00
90th	1.38	2.66	5.24	9.83	17.99
75th	1.24	2.09	3.72	6.47	11.11
50th	1.10	1.60	2.55	4.07	6.50
25th	0.97	1.22	1.75	2.56	3.80
10th	0.87	0.96	1.24	1.69	2.35
5th	0.82	0.83	1.01	1.31	1.76

Constructing Efficient Portfolios

A mean-variance optimizer uses the complete set of optimizer inputs (the expected return and standard deviation of each asset class and the correlation of returns for each pair of asset classes) to generate an efficient frontier. The efficient frontier shown in Graph 9-1 was generated from the inputs described above and summarized in Table 9-2. Each point on the frontier represents a portfolio mix that is mean-variance efficient. The point labeled A represents a portfolio that contains 50 percent in large company stocks, 9 percent in long-term bonds, and 41 percent in Treasury bills. (Recall that other asset classes were not considered in this example.) From the location of point A on the grid, we can find its expected return (7.44 percent) and standard deviation (10.52 percent).

Using Inputs to Form Other Portfolios

Given a complete set of inputs, the expected return and standard deviation of any portfolio (efficient or other) of the asset classes can be calculated. The expected return of a portfolio is the weighted average of the expected returns of the asset classes:

$$r_p = \sum_{i=1}^{n} x_i r_i \qquad (36)$$

where,

r_p = the expected return of the portfolio **p**;

n = the number of asset classes;

x_i = the portfolio weight of asset class **i**, scaled such that:

$\sum_{i=1}^{n} x_i = 1$; and,

r_i = the expected return of asset class **i**.

The point labeled B in Graph 9-1 represents a portfolio that contains 22 percent in large company stocks (asset class 1), 76 percent in long-term bonds (asset class 2), and 2 percent in Treasury bills (asset class 3). Applying the above formula to this portfolio using the inputs in Table 9-2, we calculate the expected return to be 6.0 percent as follows:

$$(0.22 \times 0.116) + (0.76 \times 0.045) + (0.02 \times 0.03) = 0.060$$

The standard deviation of the portfolio depends not only on the standard deviations of the asset classes, but on all of the correlations as well. It is given by:

$$\sigma_p = \sqrt{\sum_{i=1}^{n} \sum_{i=1}^{n} x_i x_j \sigma_i \sigma_j \rho_{ij}} \tag{37}$$

where,

σ_p	=	the standard deviation of the portfolio;
x_i and x_j	=	the portfolio weights of asset classes **i** and **j**;
σ_i and σ_j	=	the standard deviations of returns on asset classes **i** and **j**; and,
ρ_{ij}	=	the correlation between returns on asset classes **i** and **j**. (Note that ρ_{ii} equals one and that ρ_{ij} is equal to ρ_{ji}).

The standard deviation for point B in Graph 9-1 (containing three asset classes) would be calculated as follows:

	Stocks (asset class 1)	Bonds (asset class 2)	Bills (asset class 3)
Stocks	$x_1^2 \sigma_1^2 \rho_{1,1}$ = (0.22)²(0.200)²(1) = 0.001930	$x_1 x_2 \sigma_1 \sigma_2 \rho_{1,2}$ = (0.22)(0.76)(0.200)(0.112)(0.27)= 0.000995	$x_1 x_3 \sigma_1 \sigma_3 \rho_{1,3}$ = (0.22)(0.02)(0.200)(0.029)(0.05) = 0.000001
Bonds	$x_1 x_2 \sigma_1 \sigma_2 \rho_{1,2}$ = (0.22)(0.76)(0.200)(0.112)(0.27) = 0.000995	$x_2^2 \sigma_2^2 \rho_{2,2}$ = (0.76)²(0.112)²(1)= 0.007241	$x_2 x_3 \sigma_2 \sigma_3 \rho_{2,3}$ = (0.76)(0.02)(0.112)(0.029)(0.04) = 0.000002
Bills	$x_1 x_3 \sigma_1 \sigma_3 \rho_{1,3}$ = (0.22)(0.02)(0.200)(0.029)(0.05) = 0.000001	$x_2 x_3 \sigma_2 \sigma_3 \rho_{2,3}$ = (0.76)(0.02)(0.112)(0.029)(0.04) = 0.000002	$x_3^2 \sigma_3^2 \rho_{3,3}$ = (0.02)²(0.029)²(1) = 0.000000

By summing these terms and taking the square root of the total, the result is a standard deviation of 10.57 percent.

All of the previous tables and graphs presented in this chapter were prepared using Morningstar *EnCorr*® asset allocation software. Using these tools, similar analyses can be performed for a wide variety of asset classes, historical time periods, percentiles, and planning horizons. Additionally, Morningstar, Inc. offers a returns-based style analysis product to aid in the evaluation of mutual funds for use in implementing an optimal asset mix.[6]

6 For more information about Morningstar *EnCorr*® software and other Morningstar products, refer to the Investment Tools and Resources page at the back of this book, or within the United States, call +1 866 910-0840. Outside the United States, call +44 020 3107-0020.

Enhancements to Mean-Variance Optimization

Ibbotson Associates creates asset class model guidelines on the basis of mean-variance optimization, a Nobel Prize-winning economic theory. Optimization has three inputs: the expected risk and return of each asset class and the correlation among the asset classes. Using these three inputs, optimization models then determine which combination of asset classes will provide either the highest return for a given risk level or the lowest risk for a given return level. Over the last-half century, the Markowitz mean-variance optimization (MVO) framework has become the textbook approach for creating these optimal asset allocations, but the approach has several shortcomings.

Shortcomings of Traditional Optimization Techniques

One notable shortcoming is that the output (optimal asset allocation weights) is very sensitive to the inputs (expected returns, standard deviations, and correlations). Input sensitivity oftentimes can lead to highly concentrated allocations in only a small number of the available asset classes. For example, if a typical optimization starts with around 10 asset classes to choose from, it wouldn't be uncommon to see just a few of these asset choices ending up in the resulting optimal allocation, with the remaining asset choices not even getting a mention. An example of this is shown in Graph 9-5, where only three of the nine asset classes originally considered made it into the final optimized mix (Point A).

Graph 9-5 highlights the potential pitfalls of blindly following mean-variance optimization results. Mean-variance optimization is a powerful tool, but it needs to be used with caution. For instance, basing mean-variance optimization inputs on shorter time periods, as was done in Graph 9-5, can contribute to the extreme results. Basing the mean-variance optimization inputs on longer time periods, such as those presented elsewhere in this book, can help mitigate the extreme asset allocations mixes. The reason that longer time periods are preferred is that with longer time periods there is usually a more consistent ratio of return to risk amongst the different asset classes.

In addition to basing inputs on longer term histories, the most common solution to the problem of the highly concentrated asset allocations is to place maximum and minimum allocation constraints on each asset. For instance, in the example shown in Graph 9-5, we could specify a minimum allocation of 5 percent and a maximum allocation of 15 percent for each of the nine asset choices. This would ensure that each asset gets represented in the final allocation and also that no single asset completely dominates in the final allocation mix. Unfortunately, these artificial minimums and maximums are arbitrary, and usually end up limiting the ability of the optimizer to properly act on the information contained in the inputs.

Graph 9-5
Efficient Frontier: Traditional Optimization*
1998 to 2007

from 1998 to 2007

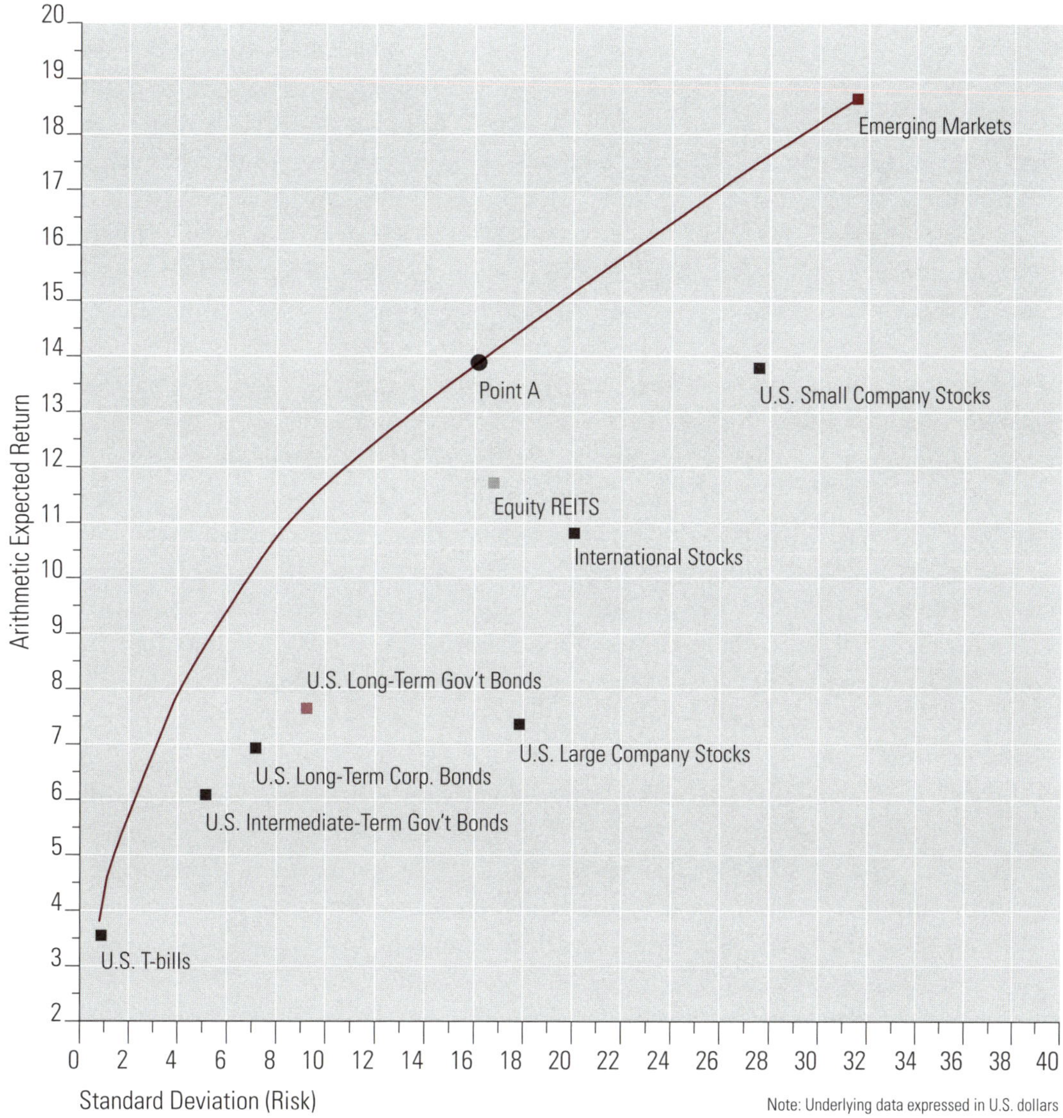

Point A.

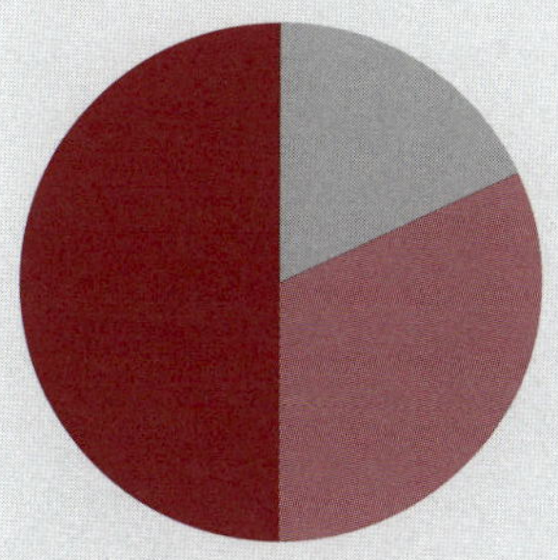

Emerging Markets	50%
Equity REITs	18%
U.S. Long-Term Gov't Bonds	32%

*The inputs for Graph 9-5 were estimated using 10 years of quarterly data.
**International stocks are represented by the Morgan Stanley Capital International Europe, Australasia, and Far East (EAFE®) Index; REITs are represented by the FTSE NAREIT Equity REIT Index®; emerging markets are represented by the Morgan Stanley Capital International Emerging Markets Index.

Two Popular Enhancements to Traditional Optimization Techniques

Two popular enhancements to traditional optimization techniques have emerged in recent years that can help overcome these difficulties. While both of these methods can help develop well-diversified asset allocations, they approach the problem in very different ways. The first of these, the Black-Litterman model, attempts to create better inputs. The second, resampled mean-variance optimization, attempts to build a better optimizer.

The Black-Litterman model was created by Fischer Black and Robert Litterman in the late 1980s. The Black-Litterman model combines investors' views regarding expected returns and the expected returns predicted by the capital asset pricing model CAPM to form a single blended estimate of expected returns. When this new combined estimate is used as an input within a traditional mean-variance optimization framework, it produces well-diversified portfolios that include not only market-based asset allocations but also allocations in assets that received favorable views.

The second approach, resampled mean-variance optimization, is an attempt to build a better optimizer. Resampling grew out of the work of a number of authors, but is most closely associated with the work of Richard Michaud. While traditional mean-variance optimization treats the capital market assumptions as if they were known with 100 percent certainty, resampled mean-variance optimization recognizes that the capital market assumptions are forecasts, and are therefore not known with 100 percent certainty. Conceptually, resampled mean-variance optimization is a combination of Monte Carlo simulation[7] and the more traditional Markowitz mean-variance optimization approach. The simulation randomly resamples possible returns from a forecasted return distribution or randomly resamples possible returns from a historical distribution. The simulated returns lead to a simulated set of capital market assumptions that are used in a traditional mean-variance optimizer, and the asset allocations are recorded. After combining the asset allocations from the numerous intermediate optimizations, the resulting asset allocations are those that, on average, are predicted to perform best over the range of potential outcomes implied by the capital market assumptions. Research has shown that asset allocations selected from a resampled efficient frontier may outperform those from a traditional efficient frontier.[8]

In addition to the problem of getting results that are highly concentrated in just a few of the assets available, there are two more criticisms of the traditional mean-variance optimization framework.

First, the traditional approach focuses on a subset of the total portfolio. Traditionally, the focus is on finding a mix of asset classes that maximizes the expected return, subject to a risk constraint. However, because the purpose of most asset portfolios is to fund a specified future cash-flow stream—a liability—the true risk for the portfolio is not the standard deviation of the assets or the performance of the assets relative to that of peers—the true risk is not being able to fund the future liability.

An asset allocation approach that takes the future liability into account is called liability-relative optimization (or surplus optimization). The usual method employed to accomplish this is to constrain the optimizer to hold an asset class representing the liability short.

7 See Chapter 10, "Wealth Forecasting with Monte Carlo Simulation" for more information.

8 See Markowitz and Usmen [2003].

Second, the traditional mean-variance optimization framework assumes that the returns of the assets in the optimization are normally distributed. As illustrated in Table 2-1, the return distributions of different asset classes don't always follow a standard, symmetrical bell-shaped curve. Some assets have distributions that are skewed to the left or right, while others have distributions that are skinnier or fatter than others. These more complicated characteristics are called skewness and kurtosis, respectively. The next wave of enhancements to the traditional mean-variance optimization are frameworks that incorporate these additional types of non-normalities into the optimization.

The Debate over Future Stock Market Returns

The impressive performance of the stock market over the last two decades and the resultant increase in investor expectations have spurred numerous articles that call attention to the historical market return and caution investors about their overly optimistic expectations. The articles point to the recent stock market performance which was well below its historical average, while the bond market, on the contrary, has performed quite well. In fact, many studies are predicting stock returns that are much lower when compared to the historical average. A few even predict that stocks won't outperform bonds in the future.

Approaches to Calculating the Equity Risk Premium

The expected return on stocks over bonds, the equity risk premium, has been estimated by a number of authors who have utilized a variety of different approaches. Such studies can be categorized into four groups based on the approaches they have taken. The first group of studies derive the equity risk premium from historical returns between stocks and bonds. Supply side models, using fundamental information such as earnings, dividends, or overall productivity, are used by the second group to measure the expected equity risk premium. A third group adopts demand side models that derive the expected returns of equities through the payoff demanded by equity investors for bearing the additional risk. The opinions of financial professionals through broad surveys are relied upon by the fourth and final group.

This section is based upon the work by Roger G. Ibbotson and Peng Chen, who combined the first and second approaches to arrive at their forecast of the equity risk premium.[9] By proposing a new supply side methodology, the Ibbotson-Chen study challenges current arguments that future returns on stocks over bonds will be negative or close to zero. The results affirm the relationship between the stock market and the overall economy.

9 "Long-Run Stock Returns: Participating in the Real Economy," Roger G. Ibbotson and Peng Chen, *Financial Analysts Journal*, January/February 2003.

Graph 9-6
Capital Gains, GDP Per Capita, Earnings, and Dividends
Year-End 1925 = $1.00

from 1925 to 2007

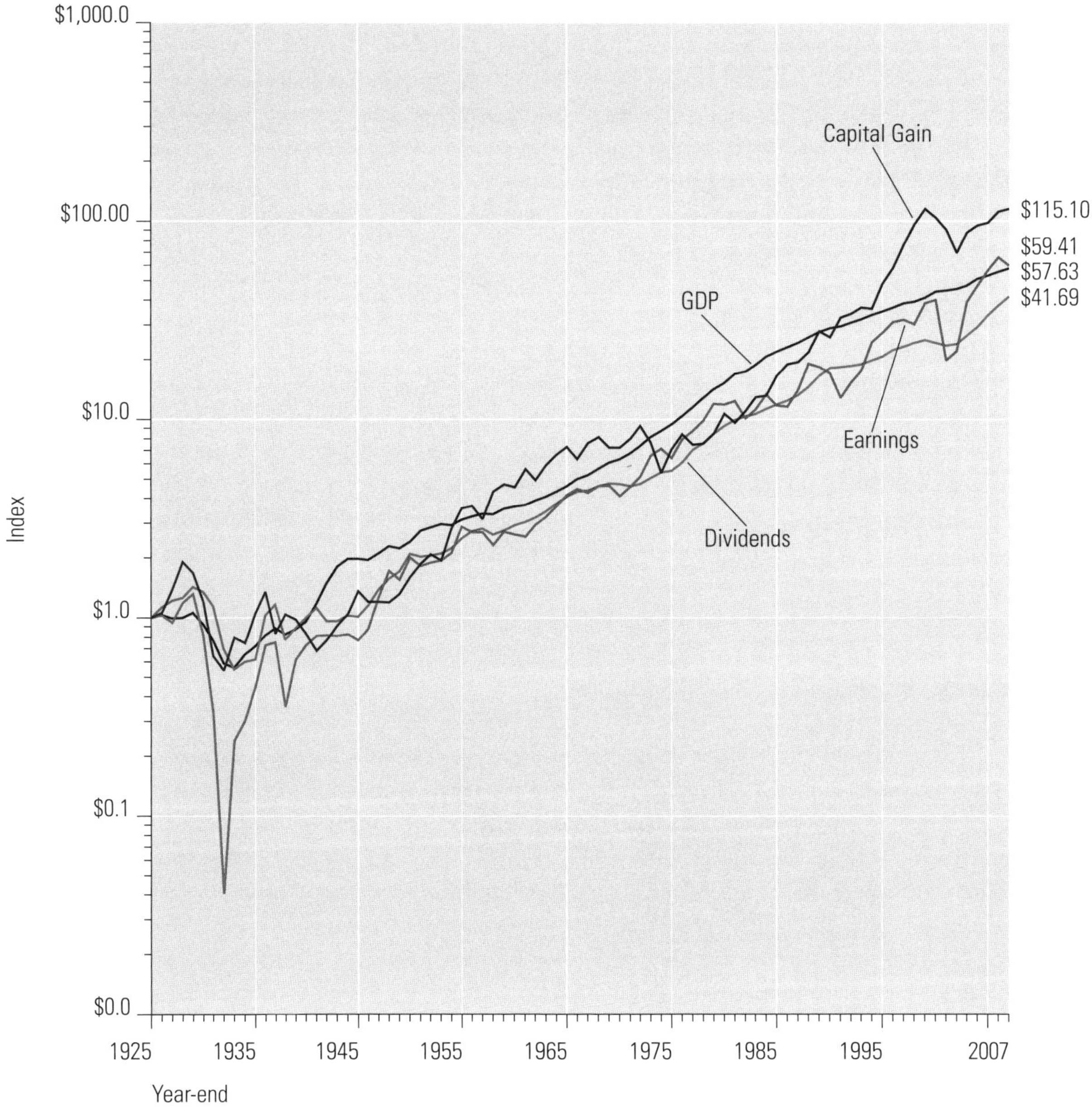

Supply Model

Long-term expected equity returns can be forecasted by the use of supply side models. The supply of stock market returns is generated by the productivity of the corporations in the real economy. Investors should not expect a much higher or lower return than that produced by the companies in the real economy. Thus, over the long run, equity return should be close to the long-run supply estimate.

Earnings, dividends, and capital gains are supplied by corporate productivity. Graph 9-6 illustrates that earnings and dividends have historically grown in tandem with the overall economy (GDP per capita). However, GDP per capita did not outpace the stock market. This is primarily because the P/E ratio increased 1.94 times during the same period. So, assuming that the economy will continue to grow, all three should continue to grow as well.

Forward-Looking Earnings Model

Roger G. Ibbotson and Peng Chen forecast the equity risk premium through a supply side model using historical data. They utilized an earnings model as the basis for their suppy side estimate. The earnings model breaks the historical equity return into four pieces, with only three historically being supplied by companies: inflation, income return, and growth in real earnings per share. The growth in the P/E ratio, the fourth piece, is a reflection of investors' changing prediction of future earnings growth. The past supply of corporate growth is forecasted to continue; however, a change in investors' predictions is not. P/E rose dramatically from 1980 through 2001 because people believed that corporate earnings were going to grow faster in the future. This growth in P/E drove a small portion of the rise in equity returns over the same period.

Graph 9-7 illustrates the price to earnings ratio from 1926 to 2007. The P/E ratio, using one-year average earnings, was 10.22 at the beginning of 1926 and ended the year 2007 at 19.80, an average increase of 0.81 percent per year. The highest P/E was 136.52 recorded in 1932, while the lowest was 7.07 recorded in 1948. Ibbotson Associates revised the calculation of the P/E ratio from a one-year to a three-year average earnings for use in equity forecasting. This is because reported earnings are affected not only by the long-term productivity, but also by "one-time" items that do not necessarily have the same consistent impact year after year. The three-year average is more reflective of the long-term trend than the year-by-year numbers. The P/E ratio calculated using the three-year average of earnings had an increase of 0.67 percent per year.

Graph 9-7
Large Company Stocks
P/E Ratio

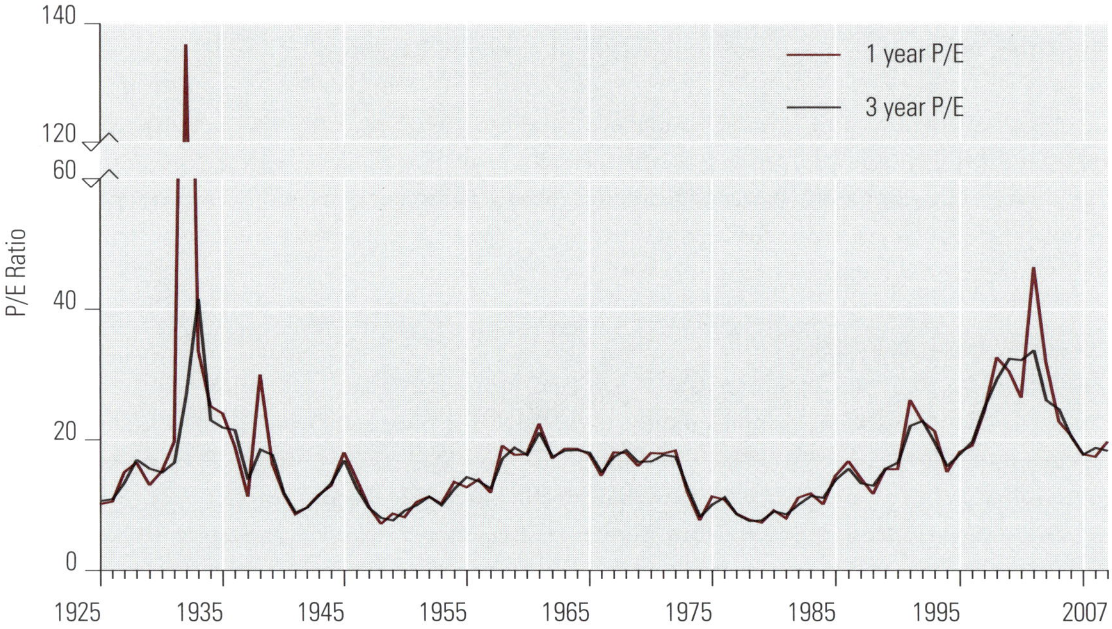

The historical P/E growth factor, using three-year earnings, of 0.67 percent per year is subtracted from the equity forecast, because it is not believed that P/E will continue to increase in the future. The market serves as the cue. The current P/E ratio is the market's best guess for the future of corporate earnings and there is no reason to believe, at this time, that the market will change its mind.

Thus, the supply of equity return only includes inflation, the growth in real earnings per share, and income return. The forward-looking earnings model calculates the long-term supply of U.S. equity returns to be 9.66 percent:

$$SR = [(1 + CPI) \times (1 + g_{REPS}) - 1] + Inc + Rinv$$

$$9.66\%^{*} = [(1 + 3.05\%) \times (1 + 2.14\%) - 1] + 4.18\% + 0.23\%$$ *Difference due to rounding

where:

SR	=	the supply of the equity return;
CPI	=	Consumer Price Index (inflation);
g_{REPS}	=	the growth in real earning per share;
Inc	=	the income return;
Rinv	=	the reinvestment return.

The equity risk premium, based on the supply side earnings model, is calculated to be 4.24 percent on a geometric basis:

$$SERP = \frac{1+SR}{(1+CPI)\times(1+RRf)} - 1$$

$$4.24\%^{*} = \frac{1+9.66\%}{(1+3.05\%)\times(1+2.06\%)} - 1$$

*Difference due to rounding

where:
SERP = the supply side equity risk premium;
SR = the supply of the equity return;
CPI = Consumer Price Index (inflation);
RRf = the real risk-free rate.

Converting the geometric average into an arithmetic average results in an equity risk premium of 6.23%:

$$R_A = R_G + \frac{\sigma^2}{2}$$

$$6.23\% = 4.24\% + \frac{19.97\%^2}{2}$$

where:
R_A = the arithmetic average;
R_G = the geometric average;
σ = the standard deviation of equity returns.

Long-Term Market Predictions

The supply side model estimates that stocks will continue to provide significant returns over the long run, averaging around 9.66 percent per year, assuming historical inflation rates. The equity risk premium, based on the supply side earnings model, is calculated to be 4.24 percent on a geometric basis and 6.23 percent on an arithmetic basis.

In the future, Ibbotson and Chen predict increased earnings growth that will offset lower dividend yields. The fact that earnings will grow as dividend payouts shrink is in line with Miller and Modigliani Theory.

The forecasts for the market are in line with both the historical supply measures of public corporations (i.e. earnings) and overall economic productivity (GDP per capita).

Chapter 10

Wealth Forecasting with Monte Carlo Simulation

Meeting Today's Challenges

Comprehending and communicating various types of risk is one of the most challenging tasks facing advisors before, during, and after the planning process. With the number of complicated products growing and investors' level of sophistication increasing, advisors confront difficult issues each day in understanding and conveying risk effectively.

What Is Monte Carlo Simulation?

Monte Carlo simulation is a problem-solving technique utilized to approximate the probability of certain outcomes by performing multiple trial runs, called simulations, using random variables. The probability distribution of the results is calculated and analyzed in order to infer which outcomes are most likely to be produced. Monte Carlo derives its name from the city in Monaco, where casinos, which contain games of chance, serve as the primary attractions. Random behavior is exhibited in gambling games such as roulette, dice, and slot machines. The random behavior evident in games of chance is comparable to how Monte Carlo simulation selects variable values at random to simulate a model. When a die is rolled, it is certain that a 1, 2, 3, 4, 5, or 6 will result, but it is not known which for any particular roll. It's similar for variables that have a known range of values but an uncertain value for any particular time or event (e.g., interest rates, stock prices, weather conditions, or insurance).

Monte Carlo methods have been used for hundreds of years; however, it wasn't until the past several decades that they grew in popularity and application. Monte Carlo is currently utilized regularly in many different fields; it has particularly been widely embraced in fields that specialize in analyzing the financial markets.

Why Use Monte Carlo Simulation?

Real-life investing involves all sorts of interrelated decisions, ranging from saving, to spending, to tax issues, and more. When all of these complexities need to be considered, Monte Carlo simulation can be quite useful. The process starts with a set of assumptions about the estimated means, standard deviations, and correlations for a set of asset classes or investments. These assumptions are used to randomly generate thousands of possible future return scenarios—somewhat similar to drawing numbers out of a hat. When these returns are used in conjunction with a client's year-by-year cash flows, taxes, asset allocation, and financial product selections, a large number of possible "financial lives" for the client are produced. These "financial lives" can be used to answer a number of questions pertaining to the risk of the client's investment decisions. For example, how many times out of all of these lives did the client reach his goal versus running out of money? Used in this fashion, Monte Carlo techniques can calculate and display risk in a personalized way that is easy for investors to understand. The results from simulation are often used to construct and evaluate an appropriate asset allocation policy.

Types of Monte Carlo Simulation

The most crucial factor in simulation-based techniques is the generation of the future return scenarios. There are quite a few ways to generate simulations, some better than others. Certain methods use only historical data. Other techniques take into account just the mean and standard deviation of the assets involved, while ignoring the correlations. In other words, the value of a Monte Carlo-based tool is only as good as the quality and richness of the return scenarios it generates.

Non-Parametric

This method of Monte Carlo simulation uses purely historical data. The easiest way to describe it is to use this book as an example. Imagine if you were to take a page in this book that shows the annual returns for all of the asset classes (Appendix A) and create pieces of paper so that each piece has one year's total return numbers on it for all of the asset classes considered. The pieces are subsequently put into a hat. One of the pieces is drawn out of the hat, the return numbers on the piece are written down, the piece is dropped back into the hat, and the process is repeated for as many years in the future as you want to forecast. No distribution parameter assumptions are made and no parameter is estimated. Obviously, this method is very simple and takes no real thinking on the part of the user. The biggest problem is that this technique provides a limited amount of information because only what has happened in the past can be drawn out of the hat. It is assumed that the future will resemble the past.

Parametric

A parametric model is based on the means, standard deviations, and correlations of the assets being forecast. These are the parameters that give this method its name. Once these parameters are set, a computer program is used to generate random samples from the bell curve that these parameters define. This provides a much richer set of results, since the program can draw from any number under the curve, not just numbers that have occurred in the past. It is very important to maintain the correlation across all asset classes in the simulation. This process generates a set of random numbers for all of the asset classes, thus maintaining the correlations.

Economic Modeling

This is the most complex method because it involves modeling the movements of the yield curve through time and then layering on various equity and fixed-income risk premia to derive returns. It is the most realistic simulation method, but unfortunately cannot be easily customized by each user.

In general, most Monte Carlo simulation models are constructed on the asset-class level, utilizing parametric modeling assumptions.

Wealth Forecasting

Simulation is used when a statistical property of the estimated variable is unknown or impossible to derive—in other words, when no analytical solution exists. Asset allocation policies are developed for the purpose of meeting financial needs, obligations, and goals. But because uncertainty is prevalent in the financial markets, it is not always clear whether these needs, obligations, and goals will be met. Monte Carlo simulation can help to illustrate this uncertainty with regard to wealth forecasting.

Wealth Forecasting without Cash Flows

When forecasting the ending wealth level for a particular asset class or portfolio, the sequence of returns may or may not play a critical role in determining the ending wealth level. One situation in which the sequence of returns has no impact on the ending wealth value is when there are no cash flows in the analysis. Tables 10-1 and 10-2 illustrate this situation. In both cases the ending wealth value is $1,000,000. This case would not require the use of a simulation model. The use of a lognormal distribution model would be most appropriate. Using the lognormal model, it is fairly simple to form probabilistic forecasts of both compound rates of return and ending period wealth values. Please refer to Chapter 9, Using Historical Data in Forecasting and Optimization, for more information.

Table 10-1
Wealth Forecasting without Cash Flows

Initial Investment		**$1,000,000**
Period 1	25% Return	+$250,000
Ending Wealth		**$1,250,000**
Period 2	–20% Return	−$250,000
Ending Wealth		**$1,000,000**

Table 10-2
Wealth Forecasting without Cash Flows

Initial Investment		**$1,000,000**
Period 1	–20% Return	−$200,000
Ending Wealth		**$800,000**
Period 2	25% Return	+$200,000
Ending Wealth		**$1,000,000**

Wealth Forecasting with Cash Flows

A situation in which the sequence of returns has an impact on the ending wealth value is when cash flows are present in the analysis. Tables 10-3 and 10-4 show a $1,000,000 investment with an outflow of $50,000 at the end of each period. In this situation the sequence of returns does have an impact on the ending wealth value. In Table 10-3 the ending wealth value in period 2 is $910,000, while in

Table 10-4, the ending wealth value in period 2 is $887,500. That amounts to a $22,500 difference—when more years are taken into consideration, the difference can be greater. A simulation model would be required for situations of this nature.

Table 10-3
Wealth Forecasting with Cash Flows

Initial Investment		**$1,000,000**
Period 1	25% Return	+$250,000
	Cash Flow	−$50,000
Ending Wealth		**$1,200,000**
Period 2	−20% Return	−$240,000
	Cash Flow	−$50,000
Ending Wealth		**$910,000**

Table 10-4
Wealth Forecasting with Cash Flows

Initial Investment		**$1,000,000**
Period 1	−20% Return	−$200,000
	Cash Flow	−$50,000
Ending Wealth		**750,000**
Period 2	25% Return	+$187,500
	Cash Flow	−$50,000
Ending Wealth		**$887,500**

Steps in Monte Carlo Simulation

There are four key steps to follow when conducting a Monte Carlo simulation based on parametric modeling assumptions. The first step is to determine whether the random returns are to be generated on the asset class level or on the individual security level. An example of an asset class would be a large company stock index represented by the S&P 500 index, while an example of an individual security can be ABC International Growth Fund or IBM stock.

The fundamental characteristics of asset classes have remained fairly stable over time. Historically, equities have had a higher standard deviation than fixed income. Corporate bonds have had a higher level of default risk than their government counterparts. Due to this stability and consistency, a long historical data stream can be collected and analyzed in order to estimate the risk and return characteristics and the relationships across these asset classes. Conversely, the risk and return characteristics and the relationships across individual securities are highly dynamic and there is typically a rather short historical data stream. This dynamic nature of security-level data, as well as the limitation on available data, makes modeling their future returns extremely difficult. Confidence in security-level models and their ability to estimate risk and return is low when compared to asset class-level models.

Once this has been decided, the second step is to calculate the inputs around which the simulation will be run. These inputs consist of the arithmetic means, standard deviations, and correlations of the asset classes or portfolios for which the simulation results will be produced. The returns for each asset or portfolio are assumed to be lognormally distributed. The lognormal distribution is skewed to the right. That is, the expected value, or mean, is greater than the median. Furthermore, if returns are lognormally distributed, returns cannot fall below negative 100 percent.

The third step is to actually generate the random return scenarios. At this point the number of simulated runs to be conducted for each asset class or portfolio, for each period, needs to be determined. Some experts maintain that 500 simulations are sufficient; others prefer to run thousands or even hundreds of thousands of simulations. The fourth step is to analyze and evaluate the output and to make any necessary adjustments to the inputs. This is an extremely important step that should not be overlooked.

Case Study: Establishing Returns and Wealth Values

As mentioned earlier in the chapter, Monte Carlo simulation is a problem-solving technique utilized to approximate the probability of certain outcomes by performing multiple trial runs using random variables. Once the arithmetic means, standard deviations, and correlations for a set of asset classes or portfolios have been established, these assumptions are used to randomly generate thousands of possible future return scenarios.

Table 10-5 presents a snapshot from a parametric simulation that was run 100 times and produced 100 possible 35-year scenarios for the performance of a sample equity index. Table 10-6 shows a snapshot of the wealth values that were produced corresponding to the return values presented in Table 10-5. The entire table would consist of Year 1 through Year 35 and Simulation Run 1 through Simulation Run 100. The initial value of the portfolio is $1,000,000 and non-inflation-adjusted annual withdrawals of $50,000 are taken from the portfolio.

Calculation of Projected Wealth Values

The wealth values located in column Year 1 in Table 10-6 were calculated from the total returns found in column Year 1 in Table 10-5 using the following equation:

$$W_t = [(1 + r_t)(W_0 - aw)] \qquad (38)$$

where:
W_t = the wealth value as of year-end **t**;
r_t = the total return in period **t**;
W_0 = the wealth value as of year-end **0**;
aw = the annual withdrawal.

For example, the wealth value of $878,415, located in Table 10-6 under column Year 1 and next to row Simulation Run 1, was calculated using the total return –0.0754, found in the same location in Table 10-5, using equation 38 as follows:

$$\$878{,}415^{*} = [(1 + (-0.0754))(\$1{,}000{,}000 - \$50{,}000)]$$ *difference due to rounding

Please keep in mind it is assumed that the investor retires at year zero and withdraws the required income need of $50,000 at the beginning of each year, beginning in year 1, in order to fund the investor's cash flow needs throughout the remainder of the year.

The wealth values located in columns Year 2 through Year 35 in Table 10-6 were calculated from the total returns found in columns Year 2 through Year 35 in Table 10-5 using the following equation:

$$w_t = [(1 + r_t)(w_{t-1} - aw)] \qquad (39)$$

where:
w_t = the wealth value as of year-end **t**;
r_t = the total return in period **t**;
w_{t-1} = the wealth value as of the previous year-end, **t−1**;
aw = the annual withdrawal.

For example, the wealth value of $1,037,492 located in Table 10-6 under column Year 2 and next to row Simulation Run 1 was calculated using the total return 0.2524, found in the same location in Table 10-5, using equation 39 as follows:

$$\$1{,}037{,}492^{*} = [(1 + 0.2524)(\$878{,}415 - \$50{,}000)]$$ *difference due to rounding

Establishing Wealth Percentiles

The values calculated and presented in Table 10-6 are the future projections of an investor's wealth level, and help determine whether or not the investor will be able to successfully fund his or her goal. The values for each year are subsequently sorted from smallest to largest and can be presented according to various wealth percentiles or probabilities.

For example, if you wanted to take the values from Table 10-6 and illustrate at certain probabilities how long the sample equity index may last into the future, you would start by sorting each column from the smallest wealth value to the largest wealth value. Table 10-7 shows the results after each column was sorted (keep in mind the table represents only a snapshot—the entire table actually has 100 simulation runs and 35 years). Since the table illustrates a snapshot of a simulation that was run 100 times, once the columns are sorted, each value alongside each percentile represents the corresponding probability. Take Percentile 25, for example. The investor has a 25 percent chance that the portfolio's future value will be less than $6,091,678 at the end of year 35. Correspondingly, there is a 75 percent chance that the portfolio's future value will be greater than $6,091,678 at the end of year 35.

Table 10-5
Forecast Annual Returns
Sample Equity Index

	Year 1	Year 2	Year 3	Year 4	Year 5	Year 6	Year 7	Year 8	Year 9	Year 35
Simulation Run 1	–0.0754	0.2524	0.1827	0.0842	0.0950	–0.0925	0.1166	0.1146	0.2139	0.2907
Simulation Run 2	0.1865	0.0541	0.1773	0.2970	0.2218	1.0607	0.1327	0.3441	0.1397	0.1374
Simulation Run 3	0.1701	0.4364	0.1221	0.2549	0.1967	0.1539	0.0511	–0.0292	0.1635	0.0622
Simulation Run 4	0.0368	0.3025	–0.2503	0.4014	–0.1414	0.1534	–0.1514	–0.0515	–0.0635	0.3114
Simulation Run 5	0.3224	0.1309	–0.2599	0.2620	0.2388	0.7875	0.3036	0.0374	0.3083	0.1464
Simulation Run 6	0.2752	0.2132	0.2938	–0.0371	0.0342	0.1362	0.0697	0.0387	–0.0119	0.1234
Simulation Run 7	0.2451	–0.0448	0.1971	0.3289	–0.1216	0.4075	–0.0932	–0.0870	–0.0270	0.2237
Simulation Run 8	–0.0480	0.1497	–0.2298	–0.2061	0.2806	0.0880	–0.0082	0.3472	–0.1521	0.6757
Simulation Run 9	0.1787	0.3177	0.1369	0.0607	0.5120	0.1581	0.0036	0.6578	–0.0763	0.1451
Simulation Run 10	0.1450	0.1429	–0.0827	0.8323	–0.0329	–0.0667	0.1182	–0.3860	–0.0451	–0.0613
Simulation Run 11	0.1569	–0.2948	0.2674	0.2127	0.0886	0.3753	–0.0389	0.4661	0.0758	0.2714
Simulation Run 12	0.2089	–0.0721	0.0127	0.1586	0.0321	–0.1330	0.1249	–0.0184	0.0148	0.1049
Simulation Run 13	0.0107	0.1359	0.3664	–0.1981	0.0896	0.0380	0.0067	0.8158	0.2484	0.4472
Simulation Run 14	0.3133	0.1726	–0.1113	0.4109	0.1228	–0.0531	–0.1191	0.2090	0.1820	0.5457
Simulation Run 15	0.0688	–0.0568	0.1192	0.0068	0.1872	0.1569	0.4707	–0.3096	0.0816	0.6448
Simulation Run 16	0.4183	0.6020	0.3403	0.2832	0.0921	0.3127	0.1903	–0.1487	0.0065	–0.0028
Simulation Run 17	0.0514	0.0119	0.4563	0.0510	–0.0063	0.0128	–0.0459	0.0618	–0.1273	–0.1585
Simulation Run 18	0.2719	0.0989	0.1417	0.1515	0.0694	–0.0261	0.2491	–0.0870	0.2254	0.2519
Simulation Run 19	–0.1400	–0.1043	0.2768	0.0005	–0.0777	0.0717	0.1493	0.1903	0.1870	0.1663
Simulation Run 20	0.0711	0.1136	0.0008	–0.0232	–0.0309	0.4534	0.5248	0.0126	0.1532	0.5104
Simulation Run 21	–0.0932	0.1126	0.1298	0.1455	0.1095	0.0822	0.3742	–0.0533	0.1024	–0.1248
Simulation Run 22	–0.1041	0.1269	0.3474	0.0950	–0.1730	–0.0536	0.1758	0.1418	0.3296	0.3067
Simulation Run 23	–0.0280	0.5103	–0.1427	0.0595	0.1295	–0.0485	0.1837	0.1009	0.2509	0.3010
Simulation Run 24	0.0455	–0.0402	–0.0452	0.0671	0.0702	0.4112	0.0559	0.4625	0.1773	0.1596
Simulation Run 25	–0.1260	0.1818	0.0777	–0.0618	0.0239	–0.0798	0.0830	0.1357	0.1453	0.1953
Simulation Run 26	0.2686	0.3095	–0.1414	0.2832	0.0897	0.1435	0.5043	0.2364	0.4723	0.1597
Simulation Run 27	0.3364	0.2791	0.2487	0.0640	0.1010	–0.0006	0.0944	0.4223	0.1866	0.2138
Simulation Run 28	–0.4396	0.5082	0.2486	0.0342	0.0932	0.2892	0.1190	0.0374	0.1115	0.1361
Simulation Run 29	0.1313	–0.1274	0.4559	–0.1672	0.6067	0.2241	0.1144	0.3091	0.3113	0.2477
Simulation Run 30	0.0320	0.0828	0.0167	0.1964	0.2948	0.1488	0.4105	–0.1476	0.0681	–0.0656
Simulation Run 31	0.0022	0.4128	0.3914	0.0289	0.0534	0.1060	0.0347	0.1012	0.0603	0.3040
Simulation Run 32	0.2097	0.1281	0.0103	0.3079	0.0256	–0.0600	0.0024	0.1973	0.2868	–0.0769
Simulation Run 33	–0.0172	0.5292	–0.1352	0.0797	–0.1516	0.0465	0.1206	0.3026	0.4455	0.0600
Simulation Run 34	–0.0576	0.3827	–0.1661	0.2505	0.0777	–0.1225	–0.0393	0.0295	0.2415	0.1377
Simulation Run 35	–0.0289	0.2309	0.0897	0.1857	0.2211	–0.1236	0.0175	0.1141	–0.2313	0.1541
Simulation Run 36	0.2804	0.2117	0.1062	–0.0017	0.4904	0.2071	–0.0166	0.3037	–0.0121	–0.0420
Simulation Run 37	–0.0720	0.0868	0.4504	–0.0057	0.2503	0.1050	–0.0208	0.3299	–0.1124	–0.0501
Simulation Run 38	–0.0109	0.1069	0.1638	0.0466	0.3125	0.2196	0.2321	0.5205	–0.0165	–0.1110
Simulation Run 39	0.0518	0.1604	–0.1607	0.2610	0.9691	0.2388	1.0059	0.0611	0.1051	–0.1133
Simulation Run 40	0.1708	–0.0394	0.2588	0.2144	0.2097	0.1935	–0.0519	–0.0414	0.1983	0.2551
Simulation Run 41	–0.1296	–0.0717	0.0700	0.2603	0.3072	0.2349	–0.0975	0.2951	0.1789	–0.0271
Simulation Run 42	0.0215	0.6383	0.5198	0.1583	–0.2028	0.1958	0.0733	–0.1419	0.1263	0.0276
Simulation Run 43	0.0602	–0.0951	0.5618	0.0910	–0.1409	–0.1385	0.1628	–0.1560	0.0988	0.3294
Simulation Run 44	0.3155	0.0319	0.0848	0.2336	0.0402	0.3832	0.2140	0.3270	–0.3015	0.3105
Simulation Run 100	–0.1174	0.1001	0.0997	–0.2605	0.2291	0.4450	0.0453	0.1409	0.0662	0.0012

Table 10-6
Forecast Wealth Values
Sample Equity Index

	Year 1	Year 2	Year 3	Year 4	Year 5	Year 6	Year 7	Year 8	Year 9	Year 35
Simulation Run 1	878415	1037492	1167907	1212008	1272410	1109286	1182757	1262579	1471957	11485008
Simulation Run 2	1127176	1135500	1277910	1592550	1884636	3780668	4225713	5612449	6339296	12360234
Simulation Run 3	1111636	1524922	1654959	2014004	2350415	2654343	2737534	2609027	2977506	33408922
Simulation Run 4	984937	1217759	875473	1156831	950292	1038420	838750	748121	653787	2602245
Simulation Run 5	1256251	1364161	972614	1164311	1380388	2378084	3034777	3096447	3985741	29040376
Simulation Run 6	1211447	1409051	1758402	1644982	1649503	1817368	1890526	1911724	1839623	86957234
Simulation Run 7	1182830	1082057	1235507	1575445	1339922	1815616	1601102	1416112	1329224	17638080
Simulation Run 8	904375	982311	718042	530389	615185	614942	560285	687465	540511	1459496
Simulation Run 9	1119764	1409614	1545765	1586484	2323156	2632440	2591833	4213856	3845949	59881337
Simulation Run 10	1087744	1186005	1042102	1817868	1709755	1549082	1676292	998611	905794	7405906
Simulation Run 11	1099061	739849	874331	999679	1033845	1353080	1252369	1762846	1842731	10732157
Simulation Run 12	1148480	1019294	981607	1079371	1062464	877762	931165	864973	827073	10609743
Simulation Run 13	960212	1033880	1344408	1038032	1076518	1065496	1022270	1765451	2141606	34394958
Simulation Run 14	1247642	1404330	1203588	1627541	1771247	1629914	1391714	1622163	1858322	45384224
Simulation Run 15	1015318	910504	963094	919287	1032002	1136126	1597367	1068320	1101390	39749116
Simulation Run 16	1347424	2078499	2718801	3424477	3685299	4772118	5620589	4742480	4722980	20942013
Simulation Run 17	998830	960129	1325422	1340495	1282412	1248129	1143189	1160724	969328	37026556
Simulation Run 18	1208299	1272819	1396105	1550020	1604155	1513638	1828217	1623518	1928141	10108490
Simulation Run 19	817038	687043	813379	763746	658255	651894	691761	763892	847387	820370
Simulation Run 20	1017574	1077529	1028337	955663	877715	1203004	1758095	1729693	1937034	8545263
Simulation Run 21	861472	902883	963586	1046529	1105693	1142468	1501265	1373881	1459496	16865388
Simulation Run 22	851131	902782	1149003	1203438	953947	855528	947146	1024364	1295500	84809665
Simulation Run 23	923384	1319109	1088067	1099877	1185848	1080794	1220143	1288201	1548820	19510961
Simulation Run 24	993181	905269	816618	818082	821965	1089403	1097538	1532020	1744755	16726718
Simulation Run 25	830337	922219	939985	834975	803702	693549	696938	734738	784198	1194366
Simulation Run 26	1205159	1512703	1255819	1547318	1631651	1808583	2645387	3208866	4650904	20304481
Simulation Run 27	1269621	1559988	1885526	1953045	2095240	2043956	2182225	3032597	3539252	140687007
Simulation Run 28	532406	727546	845970	823213	845278	1025261	1091345	1080258	1145118	5391290
Simulation Run 29	1074734	894215	1229112	981918	1497339	1771714	1918653	2446209	3142171	22957151
Simulation Run 30	980367	1007427	973382	1104733	1365668	1511497	2061390	1714609	1778015	10469031
Simulation Run 31	952114	1274493	1703792	1701531	1739731	1868782	1881828	2017176	2085893	31703627
Simulation Run 32	1149230	1240021	1202264	1507093	1494349	1357651	1310804	1509507	1878061	54396437
Simulation Run 33	933706	1351339	1125456	1161120	942706	934216	990865	1225538	1699220	16104234
Simulation Run 34	895243	1168682	932834	1103949	1135858	952814	867378	841518	982674	0
Simulation Run 35	922559	1074030	1115933	1263907	1482259	1255272	1226403	1310594	969079	48965451
Simulation Run 36	1216375	1413324	1508051	1455569	2094890	2468358	2378269	3035328	2949294	35767563
Simulation Run 37	881557	903699	1238178	1181365	1414530	1507738	1427364	1831769	1581548	6826945
Simulation Run 38	939601	984707	1087826	1086149	1359896	1597600	1906875	2823325	2727663	4488298
Simulation Run 39	999191	1101482	882525	1049845	1968744	2377008	4667807	4900159	5360111	15169874
Simulation Run 40	1112280	1020391	1221497	1422610	1660499	1922085	1775010	1653576	1921618	29447832
Simulation Run 41	826861	721175	718139	842040	1035327	1216747	1052977	1298914	1472369	5434527
Simulation Run 42	970450	1507951	2215808	2508699	1960179	2284219	2397984	2014767	2212890	14389186
Simulation Run 43	1007226	866150	1274703	1336144	1104924	908821	998611	800581	824775	3664996
Simulation Run 44	1249743	1238027	1288799	1528135	1537539	2057512	2437090	3167580	2177488	122689863
Simulation Run 100	838492	867457	898959	627797	710147	953919	944876	1020925	1035233	4112592

Table 10-7
Wealth Percentiles
Sample Equity Index

Percentile	Year 1	Year 2	Year 3	Year 4	Year 5	Year 6	Year 7	Year 8	Year 9	Year 35
1	532406	598632	598431	503836	457332	371335	347321	321507	321907	0
2	600382	600719	635116	530389	585581	536771	440322	322947	368750	0
3	635013	671649	656676	556723	607811	614942	557917	529390	398119	215667
4	657177	687043	676242	627134	615185	647794	560285	535385	540511	246149
5	731704	719790	718042	627797	628094	651894	633621	687465	579742	474625
6	817038	721175	718139	642835	658255	668827	658715	717940	653787	596261
7	823512	726443	721957	742706	667003	693549	691761	723491	712149	610313
8	826861	727546	753912	763746	710147	755603	696938	725242	754593	820370
9	830337	737471	813379	779747	730395	793727	710028	734738	784198	1194366
10	838492	739849	816618	805885	803702	797838	768875	748121	824775	1459496
11	851131	758977	825668	818082	821965	804115	808446	758237	827073	1674488
12	861342	794002	839643	823213	839346	829271	835900	761264	838335	2368736
13	861472	799988	845970	834975	845278	855528	838750	763892	847387	2602245
14	870865	819097	858408	842040	845939	856736	845884	800581	886611	3664996
15	878415	866150	874331	852432	864039	877762	867378	841518	905794	4112592
16	880740	867457	875473	869286	877715	882850	883198	854127	909996	4238216
17	881557	879838	881788	897169	918066	901423	891515	864973	924523	4472993
18	882399	894215	882525	919287	942706	908821	920516	922952	969079	4488298
19	892093	902782	885821	930489	950292	934216	931165	929904	969328	4602185
20	895243	902883	898959	935808	953947	952814	944876	998611	982674	4632233
21	903737	903699	920153	955663	960795	953919	947146	1013774	1022811	4735245
22	904375	905269	922012	964302	976064	958589	971362	1020925	1035233	5391290
23	922559	908630	929725	972852	980595	996960	990865	1024364	1045861	5428908
24	923384	910504	932834	974093	992540	1005116	998611	1068320	1058341	5434527
25	929407	913707	939985	981918	1015896	1025261	1022270	1069755	1066995	6091678
26	933706	922219	963094	999679	1032002	1038420	1046480	1080258	1076384	6407204
27	936943	935711	963586	1019508	1033845	1065496	1052977	1104064	1099511	6826945
28	937223	960129	967494	1038032	1035327	1080794	1062199	1128597	1101390	6919011
29	939601	965407	972614	1046529	1052661	1089403	1091345	1141710	1104935	7405906
30	945778	975982	973382	1049845	1062464	1109286	1097538	1149718	1145118	8189432
31	949218	976805	975250	1071999	1076518	1136032	1135355	1160724	1192081	8545263
32	951510	982311	981607	1079371	1104924	1136126	1143189	1213059	1194728	9156191
33	952114	982896	985789	1086149	1105693	1142468	1158889	1225209	1295500	10108490
34	953424	984707	1020923	1092018	1124033	1177957	1182757	1225538	1311854	10245298
35	960212	989615	1028337	1099877	1135858	1203004	1220143	1262579	1316939	10469031
36	970450	990034	1042102	1103949	1174954	1212537	1226403	1288201	1329224	10609743
37	971154	1007427	1047608	1104733	1175409	1216747	1252369	1298914	1361817	10732157
38	978366	1008305	1058564	1106179	1185848	1220204	1279959	1310594	1444679	11485008
39	980367	1010937	1070842	1119305	1195181	1224687	1310804	1314588	1459496	12360234
40	984937	1019294	1082646	1156831	1197462	1247995	1338627	1341126	1471957	12608064
41	987907	1020391	1087826	1158004	1212175	1248129	1366189	1373881	1472369	13083948
42	993181	1033880	1088067	1160277	1220986	1255272	1374382	1404937	1518455	13268599
43	997603	1037492	1106360	1161120	1254259	1309561	1374631	1416112	1548820	13514684
44	998830	1038340	1107362	1164120	1272410	1351806	1391714	1496631	1568947	13997319
100	1509963	2078499	2718801	3424477	3823593	4790714	5620589	5862164	7523731	211427351

Case Study: Asset Class Forecasts

Which asset classes are chosen by an investor can affect how long his or her wealth may last or whether or not a particular goal may be sufficiently funded. Graph 10-1 is generated by means of a parametric simulation method using the asset class input values displayed in Table 10-8. The table shows the arithmetic mean and standard deviation of each asset class from 1926 to 2007. For each asset class, the correlation to itself is 1.00.

Each simulation produces 35 randomly selected return estimates consistent with the characteristics of each individual asset class to estimate the return distribution over a 35-year time horizon. Each simulation is run 5,000 times, to give 5,000 possible 35-year scenarios, which in turn, provide the probability estimates for asset class shortfall—or falling short of funding a particular need. The procedure used is similar to the previous example in which each simulation was run 100 times, only this time 5,000 runs are conducted.

Graph 10-1 illustrates at a 50 percent probability how long each asset class, with 100% allocation, may last. Each hypothetical portfolio has an initial starting value of $1,000,000. It is assumed that a person retires at year zero and withdraws a required income need each year beginning in year 1. The initial annual withdrawal is $50,000, which is adjusted by the historical 1926–2007 inflation rate of 3.1 percent each year.

There is a 50 percent chance that the value of the portfolios that contain 100% cash (represented by U.S. Treasury bills), 100% long-term government bonds, and 100% long-term corporate bonds would fall below the required income need before the time depicted. The investor in one of these portfolios may have to look into adding more money to the investment, shifting investment dollars into a different allocation, or explore withdrawing less in order to have a better chance of funding this need. Notice that in this scenario, the portfolios with a 100% allocation to stocks, both large company stocks and small company stocks, potentially last the longest. However, keep in mind that there is also a 50 percent chance that they will not last as long as the graph depicts.

Table 10-8
Simulation Inputs
Arithmetic Mean and Standard Deviation from 1926 to 2007

Asset Class	Arithmetic Mean	Standard Deviation
Large Company Stocks	12.3%	20.0%
Small Company Stocks	17.1	32.6
Long-Term Corporate Bonds	6.2	8.4
Long-Term Government Bonds	5.8	9.2
Cash (Treasury Bills)	3.8	3.1

Graph 10-1
Simulated Asset Class Performance
50th Percentile

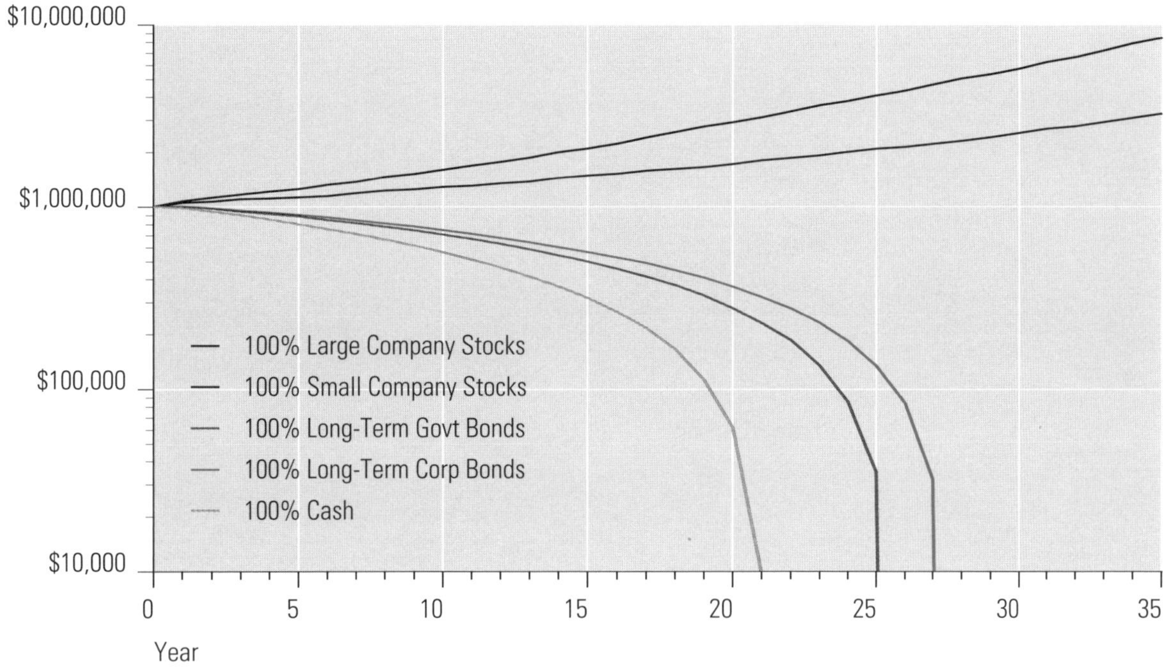

With the same underlying simulation assumptions used to generate Graph 10-1, Graph 10-2 illustrates at a 25 percent probability how long the various asset classes may last. Once again, there is a 25 percent chance that the value of the portfolios that contain 100% cash, 100% long-term government bonds, and 100% long-term corporate bonds would fall below the required income need before the time depicted. However, there is a 75 percent chance that the portfolios will last longer than the years depicted in the graph. The portfolios with a 100% allocation to stocks, both large company stocks and small company stocks, once again potentially last the longest.

Graph 10-3 illustrates at a 10 percent probability how long the various portfolios may last. By looking at such an extreme scenario, it becomes possible to truly convey and understand the risk of the capital markets. Once again, the same underlying simulation assumptions used to generate Graphs 10-1 and 10-2 are used to produce Graph 10-3. Notice that in this case, each portfolio would fall below the required income need before the time depicted. The 100% small company stock and the 100% long-term government bond portfolios are depleted the quickest, followed by the portfolio of 100% long-term corporate bonds and 100% cash. The portfolio comprised of 100% large company stocks potentially lasts the longest. However, there is a 90 percent chance that the portfolios will last longer than the years depicted in the graph.

Graph 10-2
Simulated Asset Class Performance
25th Percentile

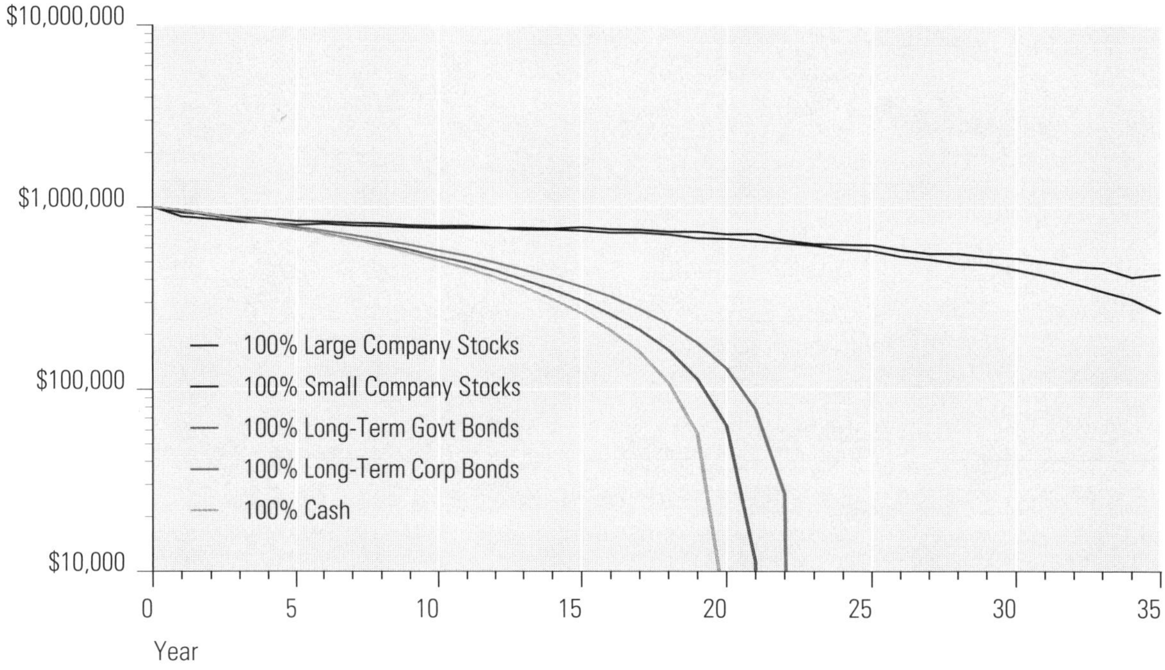

Graph 10-3
Simulated Asset Class Performance
10th Percentile

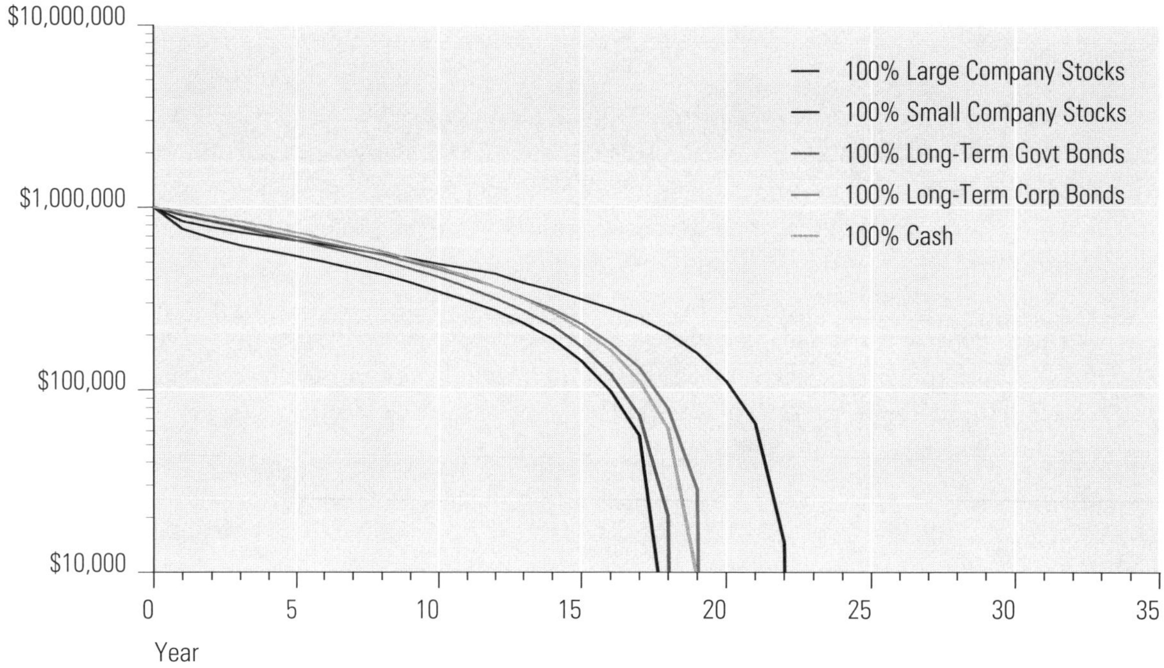

Case Study: Portfolio Forecasts

The combination of asset classes that comprise a particular portfolio can also affect how long an investor's portfolio may last or whether or not a particular goal may be sufficiently funded. Graph 10-4 is also generated by means of a parametric simulation method. The simulated returns on the various portfolios are constructed from the asset-class-level simulated returns. The correlation between large company stocks and long-term government bonds is 0.12.

Similar to Graphs 10-1, 10-2, and 10-3, each simulation for Graphs 10-4, 10-5, and 10-6 produces 35 randomly selected return estimates consistent with the characteristics of each portfolio to estimate the return distribution over a 35-year time horizon. Each simulation is run 5,000 times, to give 5,000 possible 35-year scenarios, which in turn, provide the probability estimates for portfolio shortfall. The beginning portfolio balance is assumed to be $1,000,000 and $50,000 inflation-adjusted annual withdrawals are taken at the beginning of each year.

Graph 10-4 shows that there is a 50 percent chance that the value of the portfolio comprised of 100% long-term government bonds would fall below the required income need before the time depicted. Notice that in this scenario the remaining four portfolios, consisting of 25% stocks/75% bonds, 50% stocks/50% bonds, 75% stocks/25% bonds, and 100% large company stocks, last throughout the time depicted. However, keep in mind that there is also a 50 percent chance that they will not last as long as the graph depicts. As the allocation to stocks increases so does the possibility of the portfolio meeting the needs of the investor. The higher the percentage of bonds allocated to the portfolio, the lower the possibility of the portfolio meeting the investor's needs. While portfolios allocated more heavily toward stocks exhibit higher risk, they historically have offered higher returns as compensation.

Graph 10-4
Simulated Portfolio Performance
50th Percentile

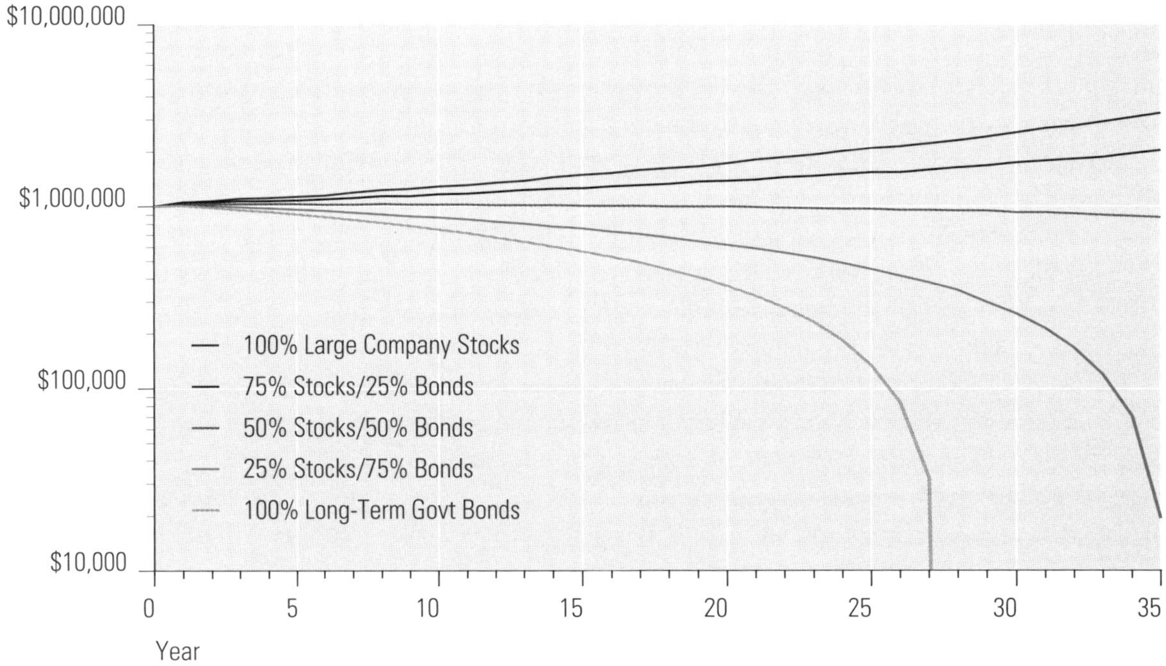

With the same underlying simulation assumptions used to generate Graph 10-4, Graph 10-5 illustrates at a 25 percent probability how long the various portfolio allocations may last. There is a 25 percent chance that the value of the portfolios that contain 100% long-term government bonds, 25% stocks/75% bonds, and 50% stocks/50% bonds would fall below the required income need before the time depicted. However, there is a 75 percent chance that the portfolios will last longer than the years depicted in the graph. At the 25 percent probability level, the portfolios with 75% stocks/25% bonds and 100% large company stocks potentially last the longest.

Graph 10-6 illustrates at a 10 percent probability how long the various portfolios may last. As mentioned earlier, by looking at such an extreme scenario, it becomes possible to truly convey and understand the risk of the capital markets. Once again, the same underlying simulation assumptions used to generate graphs 10-4 and 10-5 are used to produce Graph 10-6. Notice that in this case, each of the five portfolios would fall below the required income need before the time depicted. The 100% long-term government bond portfolio is depleted the quickest, followed by the 25% stock/75% bond portfolio. The portfolio comprised of 50% stocks/50% bonds lasts the longest. However, there is a 90 percent chance that the portfolios will last longer than the years depicted in the graph.

Graph 10-5
Simulated Portfolio Performance
25th Percentile

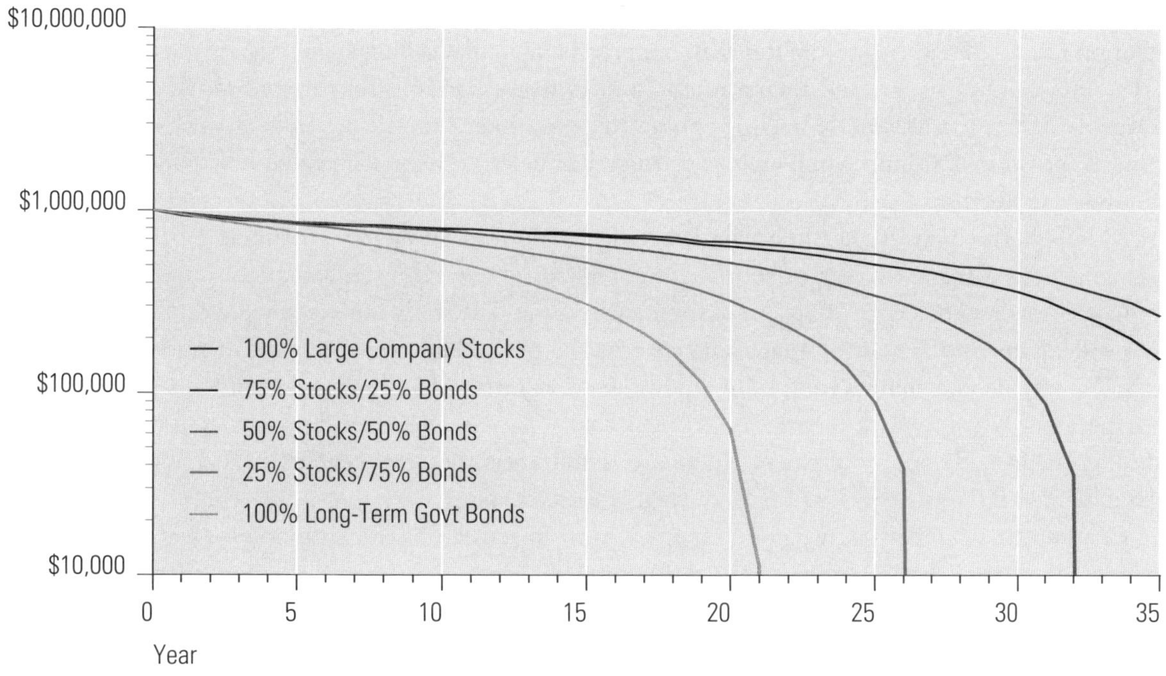

Graph 10-6
Simulated Portfolio Performance
10th Percentile

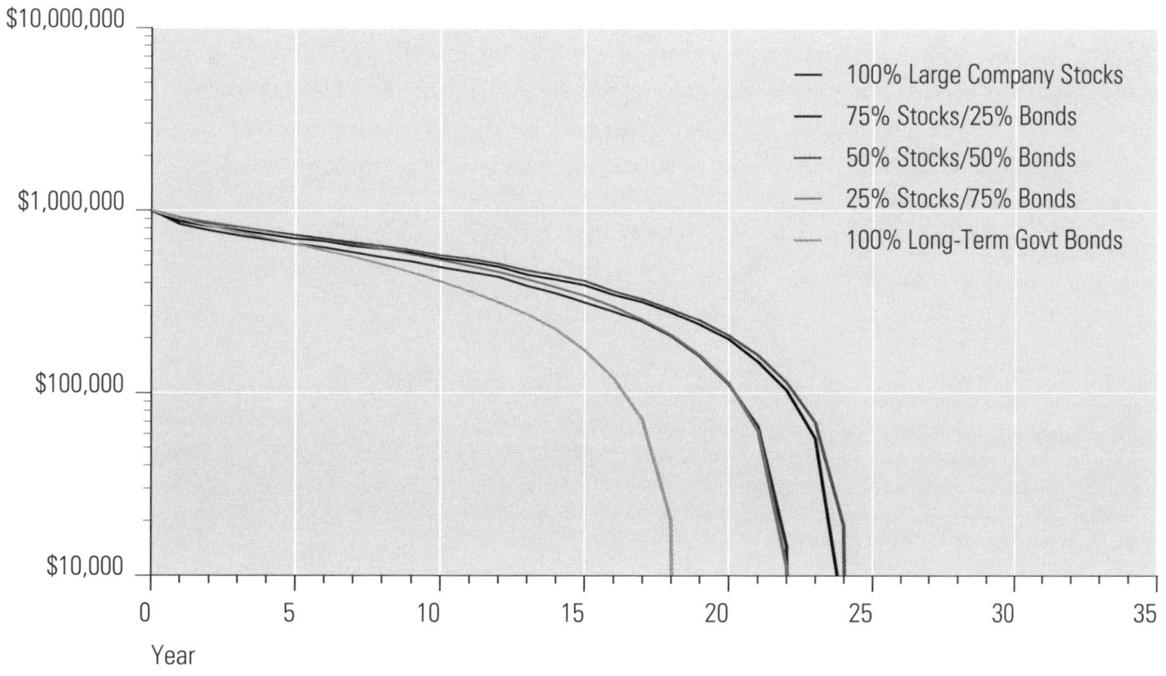

Case Study: Ibbotson's National Savings Rate Guidelines for Individuals

New research by a team led by Professor Roger Ibbotson creates retirement savings guidelines for individuals based on age, current income level, and current savings.[1] The study utilizes Monte Carlo simulation to provide superior estimates than are possible with deterministic modeling, where parameters are determined by averages (and therefore not subject to the random fluctuations that are seen in the real world). Monte Carlo simulation, as opposed to deterministic modeling, enables savers to view projections of possible best- and worst-case scenarios, thus helping them achieve better financial decisions over long time horizons.

Although savers are typically advised that they will need about 80% of their gross annual pre-retirement income for each year of retirement[2], Ibbotson's new research calculates annual retirement income needs as a percentage of net pre-retirement income. The study fairly assumes that the prospective retiree will continue to live off of approximately what he or she had been living off of prior to retiring—in other words, income minus savings. The study also takes into account Social Security income, inflation[3], and expected salary increases (limited to the expected inflation rate), but does not consider late-in-life medical costs. In addition, a retirement age of 65 at full Social Security benefits is also assumed[4], and a probability mortality rate model is used to calculate life expectancy.[5]

Creation of this analysis was very complex both in terms of the methodology and the selection of data used, but the results provide straightforward guidelines for annual retirement income requirements. The study addresses three major issues: retirement income needed (Table 10-9), savings rates guidelines (Table 10-10), and benchmarks against which savers can check their progress (Table 10-11).

Retirement Income Needed

Table 10-9 calculates the post-retirement income needed by future retirees based on what their pre-retirement income is, and also the total assets they will need to have saved to provide that income. Step 1 of Table 10-9 assumes that the annual post-retirement income needed is 80% of net pre-retirement income (gross pre-retirement income minus savings). Step 2 of Table 10-9 goes on to show how much of the required post-retirement income is forecast to come from Social Security benefits, with any annual income deficit necessarily being generated by the retirement portfolio. Finally, the total amount of assets needed in the retirement portfolio to generate the annual income deficit is calculated.[6]

1 Roger Ibbotson, James Xiong, Robert P. Kreitler, Charles F. Kreitler, and Peng Chen. "National Savings Rate Guidelines for Individuals," *Journal of Financial Planning*, April 2007, pp. 50–61. To read the full research paper, go to: global.morningstar.com/US/IbbotsonResearch.

2 Based on the AON Consulting/Georgia State University 2004 Retirement Income Replacement Ratio Study.

3 Forecasted inflation of 2.5% was used, as assumed by Ibbotson Associates, December 2005.

Table 10-9
Calculation of Assets Needed at Age 65 to Provide Required Retirement Income.

Step 1: Determine Annual Income Needed In Retirement

Pre-Retirement								Post-Retirement
Income (Gross)		Annual savings		Income (Net)				Income Needed (80% of Net)
$20,000	–	$1,720	=	$18,280	×	80%	=	$14,624
$40,000	–	$4,880	=	$35,120	×	80%	=	$28,096
$60,000	–	$8,760	=	$51,240	×	80%	=	$40,992
$80,000	–	$13,120	=	$66,880	×	80%	=	$53,504
$100,000	–	$17,600	=	$82,400	×	80%	=	$65,920
$120,000	–	$23,040	=	$96,960	×	80%	=	$77,568

Step 2: Determine Income Needed From Retirement Portfolio

Post-Retirement						Retirement Portfolio
Income Needed* (80% of Net)		Social Security Income (Estimated)		Annual Retirement Deficit		Assets Needed to Generate Deficit
$14,624	–	$11,242	=	$3,382		$64,946
$28,096	–	$17,798	=	$10,298		$190,647
$40,992	–	$22,177	=	$18,815	◀	$343,847
$53,504	–	$25,252	=	$28,252		$512,821
$65,920	–	$27,343	=	$38,577		$697,144
$77,568	–	$27,343	=	$50,225		$904,063

*80% of net, as determined in step 1.

Determining A Savings Rate

The study suggests adoption of the national savings rate guidelines shown in Table 10-10, which shows suggested savings rates for prospective retirees delineated by age, gross income, and the amount already saved. To determine the savings rate suggested for an individual's situation, locate the guideline savings rate in the row with their current age and income. Then, deduct the amount shown in column 4 for each $10,000 of retirement assets already accumulated.

For example, a 35 year old with no current savings and gross income of $40,000 per year needs to save 12.2 percent of his gross income. If, however, he had already saved $10,000, he could reduce the savings rate by 0.86 percent of his gross income (12.2% - 0.86%), or 11.34 percent.

When the savings guidelines in Table 10-10 were used, 90 percent of the Monte Carlo simulations in the study resulted in total savings at age 65 capable of generating the retirement income deficit not covered by Social Security benefits.

4 Age 65 was chosen to match the commonly accepted retirement age. Individuals should strongly consider delaying taking Social Security until they become eligible to receive the full benefit (currently age 67).

5 Mortality rates calculated as the average of female and male mortality rates from the Society of Actuaries' 2000 mortality rate table.

6 Total amount of assets needed in the retirement portfolio was calculated as the purchase price of an inflation-indexed lifetime fixed-payout annuity that would generate an annual income equal to annual income deficit (post-retirement income needed minus estimated Social Security benefits).

Table 10-10

Savings Rates for Different Gross Income Levels with 80% Replacement of Net Pre-Retirement Income

(90% probability of success)

Age	Gross Income ($)	Guideline Savings Rate (%)	Deductions for Each $10,000 of Current Savings(%)
25	**20000**	**5.8**	**1.60**
25	40000	8.2	0.78
25	60000	10.0	0.55
25	80000	11.2	0.40
30	**20000**	**7.0**	**1.65**
30	40000	10.0	0.79
30	60000	11.8	0.54
30	80000	13.6	0.42
35	**20000**	**8.6**	**1.75**
35	40000	12.2	0.86
35	60000	14.6	0.55
35	80000	16.4	0.43
35	100000	17.6	0.34
40	**20000**	**10.2**	**1.67**
40	40000	14.8	0.86
40	60000	17.6	0.57
40	80000	19.8	0.42
40	100000	21.4	0.35
45	**20000**	**12.4**	**1.76**
45	40000	18.0	0.90
45	60000	21.4	0.59
45	80000	24.0	0.45
45	100000	26.2	0.37
45	120000	28.2	0.31
50	**20000**	**15.0**	**1.87**
50	40000	22.0	0.97
50	60000	26.2	0.64
50	80000	29.8	0.48
50	100000	32.2	0.39
50	120000	35.0	0.33
55	**20000**	**18.6**	**2.11**
55	40000	27.2	1.04
55	60000	32.6	0.71
55	80000	36.6	0.53
55	100000	40.2	0.43
55	120000	43.6	0.36
60	**20000**	**23.8**	**2.39**
60	40000	34.4	1.23
60	60000	41.2	0.81
60	80000	46.8	0.61
60	100000	51.4	0.50
60	120000	55.4	0.41

Benchmarks for Checking Progress

Table 10-11 provides benchmarks against which future retirees can check their progress. The table shows the projected capital an individual should have accumulated depending on their current age and income level, and assumes that they had started saving at age 35 and followed the savings guidelines shown in Table 10-10.

The projections in Table 10-11 show the expected capital appreciated for the 90 percent confidence level, and should be considered the minimum someone should have accumulated (due to poor investment performance). In other words, 90 percent of the Monte Carlo simulations in the study resulted in a larger capital accumulation than is shown in Table 10-11, and ten percent resulted in a smaller capital accumulation than is shown.

For example, for 50 year old savers who started saving at age 35 and now have $80,000 in gross income, 90% will have saved more than $198,497 and 10 percent will have saved less than $198,497.

Table 10-11
Minimum Projected Accumulated Wealth by Current Age for Various Income Levels with 80% Replacement of Net Pre-Retirement Income

	Income					
Age	**$20,000**	**$40,000**	**$60,000**	**$80,000**	**$100,000**	**$120,000**
35	0	0	0	0	0	0
40	7,692	21,824	39,176	58,674	78,710	103,038
45	16,005	45,408	81,512	122,082	163,768	214,387
50	26,023	73,831	132,533	198,497	266,277	348,581
55	37,434	106,207	190,650	285,540	383,042	501,436
60	51,562	146,292	262,607	393,310	527,612	690,691
65	68,650	194,775	349,637	523,658	702,467	919,594

Limitations of Monte Carlo Simulation

While Monte Carlo simulation has its fair share of benefits, as with other mathematical models, it also has its limitations. Simulations can lead to misleading results if inappropriate inputs are entered into the model. As discussed earlier, in order to run simulations, the process begins with the entering of asset class returns, standard deviations, and correlations. When cash flows are added to the analysis they may be adjusted for inflation, which can present another possible problem if an unrealistic inflation rate is assumed. The burden clearly lies on the individual who sets up the simulation. The individual should be prepared to make the necessary adjustments if the results that are generated seem out of line.

Some critics contend that Monte Carlo simulations cannot be taken too seriously because they make use of random numbers. They question how accurate Monte Carlo is in replicating the actual behavior of the capital markets. While Monte Carlo does a fine job of illustrating the wide variance of possible results and the probability of success or failure over thousands of "different market environments," it may not consider the consequences based on the "applicable market environment" that exists over an investor's lifetime. Investors rarely spend exactly what they say they will spend when they retire. Tax laws are highly unpredictable as well. Critics argue that there are a number of unknown factors that cannot truly be accounted for.

Conclusion

Monte Carlo simulation has been available for many years, but the forecasting method only recently grew in popularity and application due primarily to high-powered computers that are able to quickly handle the required calculations. One thing to keep in mind is that projecting the future is no easy task—the future is unknowable. While Monte Carlo simulation can produce possible scenarios of the future and help investors make better decisions, it does not help investors make perfect decisions. It would be wise to use this type of simulation in conjunction with other forecasting techniques and compare the results. But there is an important point to remember when contemplating and choosing among the various simulation-based products. The quality of the forecast is directly related to the quality of the technique and the inputs used.

Chapter 11

Stock Market Returns from 1815 to 1925

Introduction

Studies on the long-horizon predictability of stock returns, by necessity, require a database of return information that dates as far back as possible. Ibbotson Associates® has been the leading producer and supplier of a broad set of historical returns on asset classes dating back to 1926. Researchers interested in the dynamics of the U.S. capital markets over earlier decades have had to rely upon indices of uneven quality. Roger Ibbotson and William N. Goetzmann, professors of finance, and Liang Peng, then a Ph.D. candidate in finance, all at Yale School of Management, have assembled a New York Stock Exchange database for the period prior to 1926. This chapter covers the sources and construction of this database extending back to 1815.

We firmly believe that a 1926 starting date was approximately when quality financial data became available. However, the hope is that the new data will allow modern researchers of pre-1926 stock returns, along with future researchers, to test a broad range of hypotheses about the U.S. capital markets as well as open up new areas for more accurate analysis.

Data Sources and Collection Methods

Share Price Collection

End-of-month equity prices for companies listed on the New York Stock Exchange (NYSE) were hand-collected from three different sources published over the period January 1815 to December 1870. For the time period 1871 through 1925, end-of-month NYSE stock prices were collected from the major New York newspapers.

The New York Shipping List, later called *The New York Shipping and Commercial*, served as the "official" source for NYSE share price collection up until the early 1850s. In the mid-1850s, *The New York Shipping List* reported prices for fewer and fewer stocks. This led to the collection of price quotes from *The New York Herald* and *The New York Times*. While neither claimed to be the official list for the NYSE, the number of securities quoted by each far exceeded the number quoted by *The New York Shipping List*.

It is important to note that in instances where no transaction took place in December, the latest bid and ask prices were averaged to obtain a year-end price. In total, at least two prices from 664 companies were collected. From a low number of eight firms in 1815, the number of firms in the index reached a high point in May of 1883 with 114 listed firms.

One interesting observation was the fact that share prices for much of the period of analysis remained around 100. Graph 11-1 illustrates this point. The graph shows that the typical price of a share of stock was around 100. The distribution of stock prices is significantly skewed to the left with only a few trading above 200. Such a distribution suggests that management maintained a ceiling on stock prices by paying out most of earnings as dividends. No reports of stock splits over the period of data were discovered.

Graph 11-1
Distribution of Raw Stock Prices
from 1815 to 1925

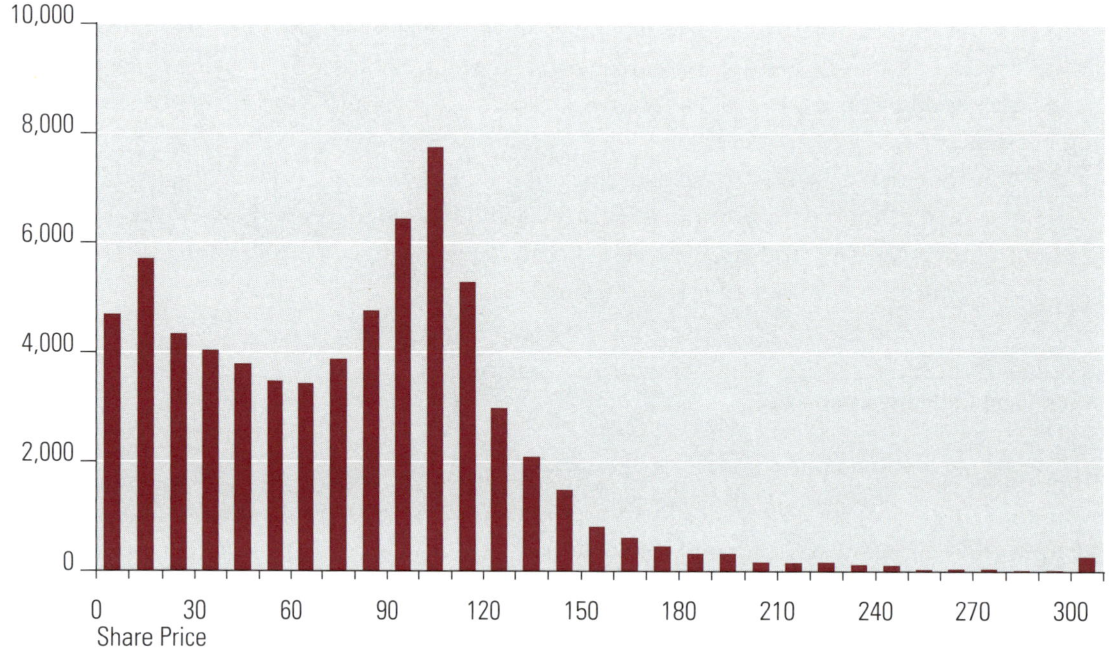

Dividend Collection

Dividend data was collected for the period 1825–1870 by identifying the semi-annual dividend announcements for equity securities as reported in *The New York Commercial*, *The Banker's Magazine*, *The New York Times*, and *The New York Herald*. From 1871 to 1925, aggregate dividend data from the Alfred Cowles[1] series was used. Whether or not the above publications reported dividends for all NYSE stocks is unknown. As a result, there is no way of knowing whether missing dividends meant that they were not paid or possibly not reported. Dividend records were collected for more than 500 stocks in the sample, and most stocks paid dividends semiannually.

In order to estimate the income return for each year, two approaches were implemented. The first approach, the low dividend return estimate, consisted of the summation of all of the dividends paid in a given year by firms whose prices were observed in the preceding year. This number is then divided by the sum of the last available preceding year prices for those firms. The second approach, the high dividend return estimate, focused solely on firms that paid regular dividends and for which price data was collected. The sample is restricted to firms that have two years of dividend payments (four semiannual dividends) and for which there was a price observation. Using the second approach, dividend yields tend to be quite high by modern standards.

1 Cowles, Alfred. (1939). *Common Stock Indices*. Principia Press, Bloomington.

It is important to note that when both a high and a low income return series were present, the average was computed. This holds true for the summary statistics table in this chapter as well as the graphs/tables presented throughout. Also, due to missing income return data for the year 1868, an average of the previous forty-three years was computed and used.

Price Index Estimation

Index Calculation Concerns

When attempting to construct an index without having market capitalization data readily available, one is left with one of two options: an equal-weighted index or a price-weighted index. One key concern with an equal-weighted index is the effect of a bid-ask bounce. Take for example an illiquid stock that trades at either $1.00 or $2.00 per share. When it rises in price from $1.00 to $2.00, it goes up by 100 percent. When it decreases in price from $2.00 to $1.00, it drops by 50 percent. Equally weighting these returns can produce a substantial upward bias. This led us to the construction of a price-weighted index.

Calculation of the Price-Weighted Index

The procedure used for calculating the price-weighted index is rather simple. For each month, returns are calculated for all stocks that trade in two consecutive periods. These returns are weighted by the price at the beginning of the two periods.

The return of the price-weighted index closely approximates the return to a "buy and hold" portfolio over the period. Buy and hold portfolios are not sensitive to bid-ask bounce bias. We believe that the price-weighted index does a fairly good job of avoiding such an upward bias.

It was found that companies were rather concentrated into specific industries. In 1815, the index was about evenly split between banks and insurance companies. Banks, transportation firms (primarily canals and railroads), and insurance companies made up the index by the 1850s. By the end of the sample period, the index was dominated by transport companies and other industrials.

A Look at the Historical Results

It is important to note that there are a few missing months of data that create gaps in the analysis. The NYSE was closed from July 1914 to December 1914 due to World War I. This is obviously an institutional gap. There are additional gaps. We are missing returns for 1822, part of 1848 and 1849, parts of 1866, all of 1867 and January 1868. We do not know whether the late 1860's missing records are due to the Civil War, but the NYSE was certainly open at that time—among other things, it was the era of heated speculation and stock price manipulation by legendary financiers Gould, Fisk and Drew. The number of available security records was quite lower after 1871. A change in the range of coverage by the financial press is the likely culprit for this. Further data collection efforts hopefully will allow these missing records to be filled in.

Table 11-1 illustrates summary statistics of annual returns of large company stocks for three different time periods. Note that the three different periods cover the pre-1926 data, the familiar 1926 to 2007 time period, and a combination of the two.

Table 11-1
Large Company Stocks
Summary Statistics of Annual Returns
from 1825 to 1925

	Geometric Mean	Arithmetic Mean	Standard Deviation
Total Return	7.3%	8.4%	16.3%
Income Return	5.9%	5.9%	1.9%
Capital Appreciation	1.3%	2.5%	16.1%

from 1926 to 2007

	Geometric Mean	Arithmetic Mean	Standard Deviation
Total Return	10.4%	12.3%	20.0%
Income Return	4.2%	4.2%	1.6%
Capital Appreciation	6.0%	7.8%	19.3%

from 1825 to 2007

	Geometric Mean	Arithmetic Mean	Standard Deviation
Total Return	8.6%	10.1%	18.1%
Income Return	5.1%	5.1%	1.9%
Capital Appreciation	3.4%	4.9%	17.7%

Price Returns

It is interesting to note that the price-weighted index in Table 11-1 has an annual geometric capital appreciation return from 1825 through 1925 of 1.3 percent. This number is significantly lower when compared to the 6.0 percent annual capital appreciation return experienced by large company stocks over the period 1926 through 2007. This once again alludes to the suggestion that dividend policies have evolved over the past two centuries, and that management of old most likely paid out earnings and kept their stock prices lower. In today's financial world, capital appreciation is accepted as a substitute for dividend payments.

Graph 11-2 shows the annual capital appreciation returns for the period 1825 to 2007. The rise in capital appreciation returns over the years is more evident when viewing returns on a twenty-year rolling period basis, as Graph 11-3 demonstrates.

Graph 11-2
Large Company Stocks Annual Capital Appreciation Returns (in percent)
from 1825 to 2007

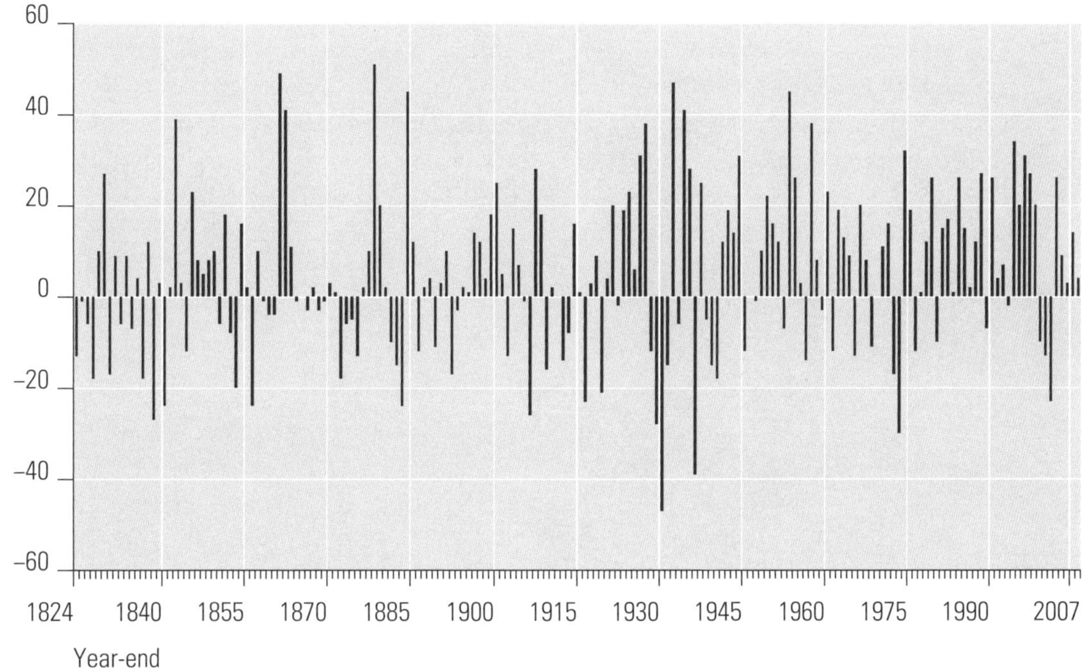

Graph 11-3
20-Year Rolling Capital Appreciation Returns for Large Company Stocks (in percent)
from 1844 to 2007

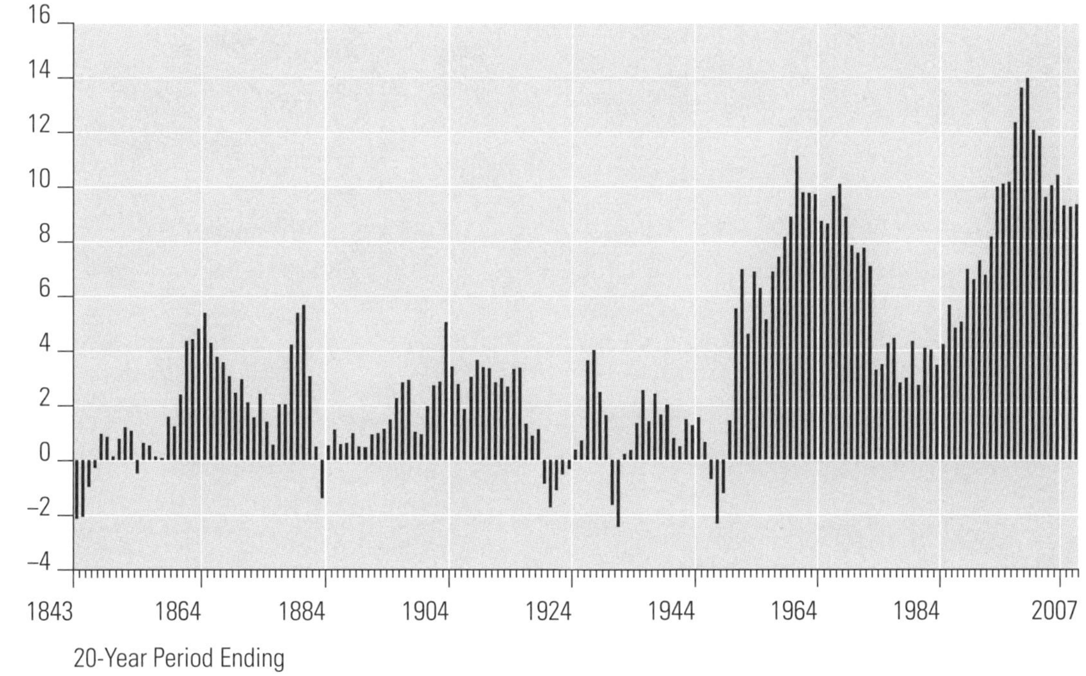

Income Returns

Table 11-1 also illustrates the summary statistics for the annual income return series. The higher income return of 5.9 percent in the earlier period, and the fact the many stocks traded near par, once again suggest that most companies paid out a large share of their profits rather than retaining them.

Graph 11-4 shows the annual income returns for the period 1825 to 2007. In fact, when looking at the time distribution of dividend changes over the new time period, dividend decreases were only slightly less common than increases, suggesting that managers may have been less averse to cutting dividends than they are today. Perhaps in the pre-income tax environment of the nineteenth century, investors had a preference for income returns, as opposed to capital appreciation.

Graph 11-4
Large Company Stocks Annual Income Returns (in percent)
from 1825 to 2007

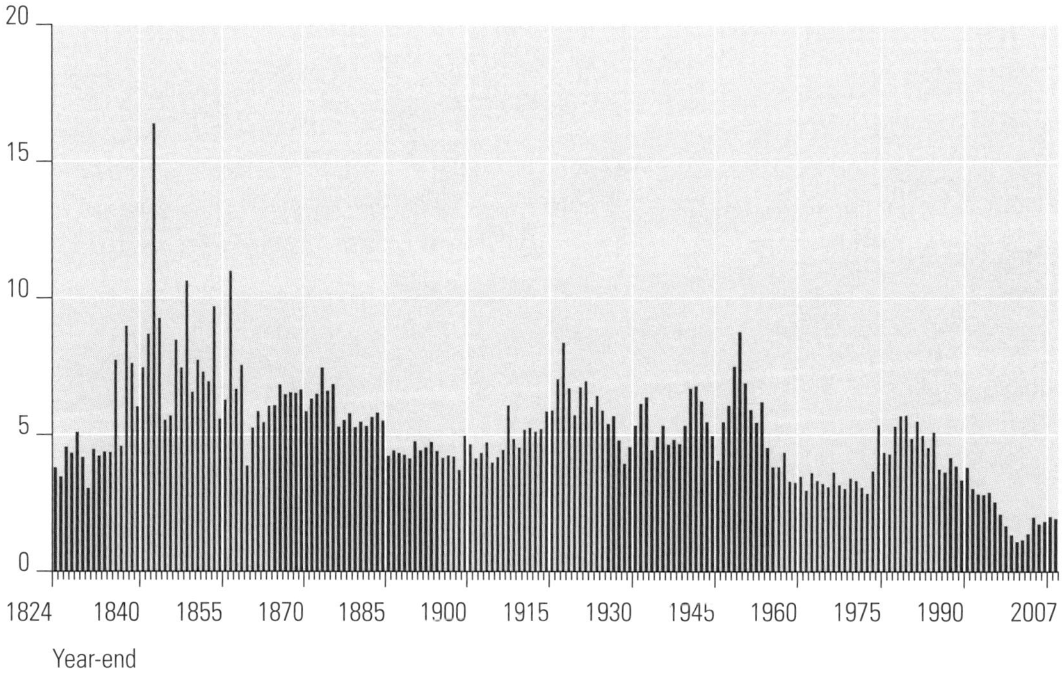

Total Returns

Looking once again at the summary statistics in Table 11-1, it is interesting to notice that the annual geometric total return for large company stocks from 1825 to 1925 was 7.3 percent. This is quite low when compared to the 10.4 percent annual geometric total return of the commonly used 1926 to 2007 time period. For the entire period, the total return seems to fall somewhere in between.

Graph 11-5 illustrates the annual total returns for the period 1825 to 2007.

Graph 11-5
Large Company Stocks Annual Total Returns (in percent)
from 1825 to 2007

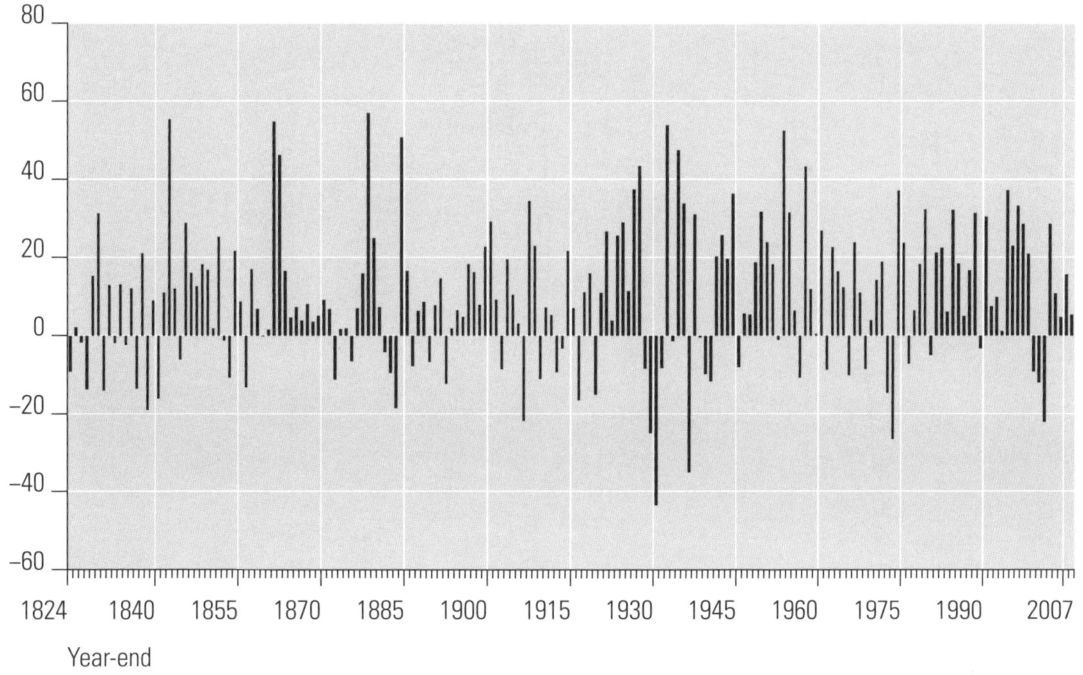

The standard deviation of total returns is also slightly lower for the 1825 to 1925 time period (16.3 percent) versus the time period of 1926 to 2007 (20.0 percent). Graph 11-6 illustrates a five-year rolling period standard deviation for periods ending 1829 to 2007.

Graph 11-6
5-Year Rolling Standard Deviation for Large Company Stocks (in percent)
from 1829 to 2007

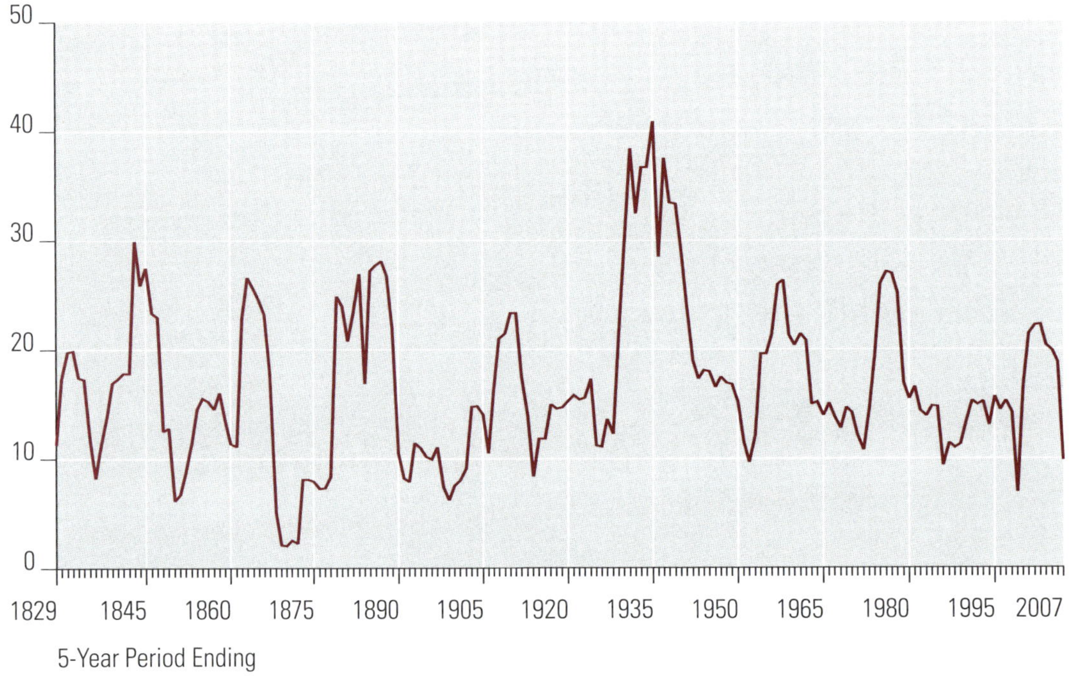

How much would a dollar be worth today if invested around the beginning of the New York Stock Exchange? Graph 11-7 depicts the growth of $1.00 invested in large company stocks over the period from the end of 1824 to the end of 2007.

Table 11-2 shows year-by-year capital appreciation, average income, and total returns from 1815 to 1925 of large company stocks. Table 11-3 shows the growth of a dollar invested in large company stocks over the period from the end of 1824 to the end of 2007.

Graph 11-7
Large Company Stocks
Year-End 1824 = $1.00

from 1824 to 2007

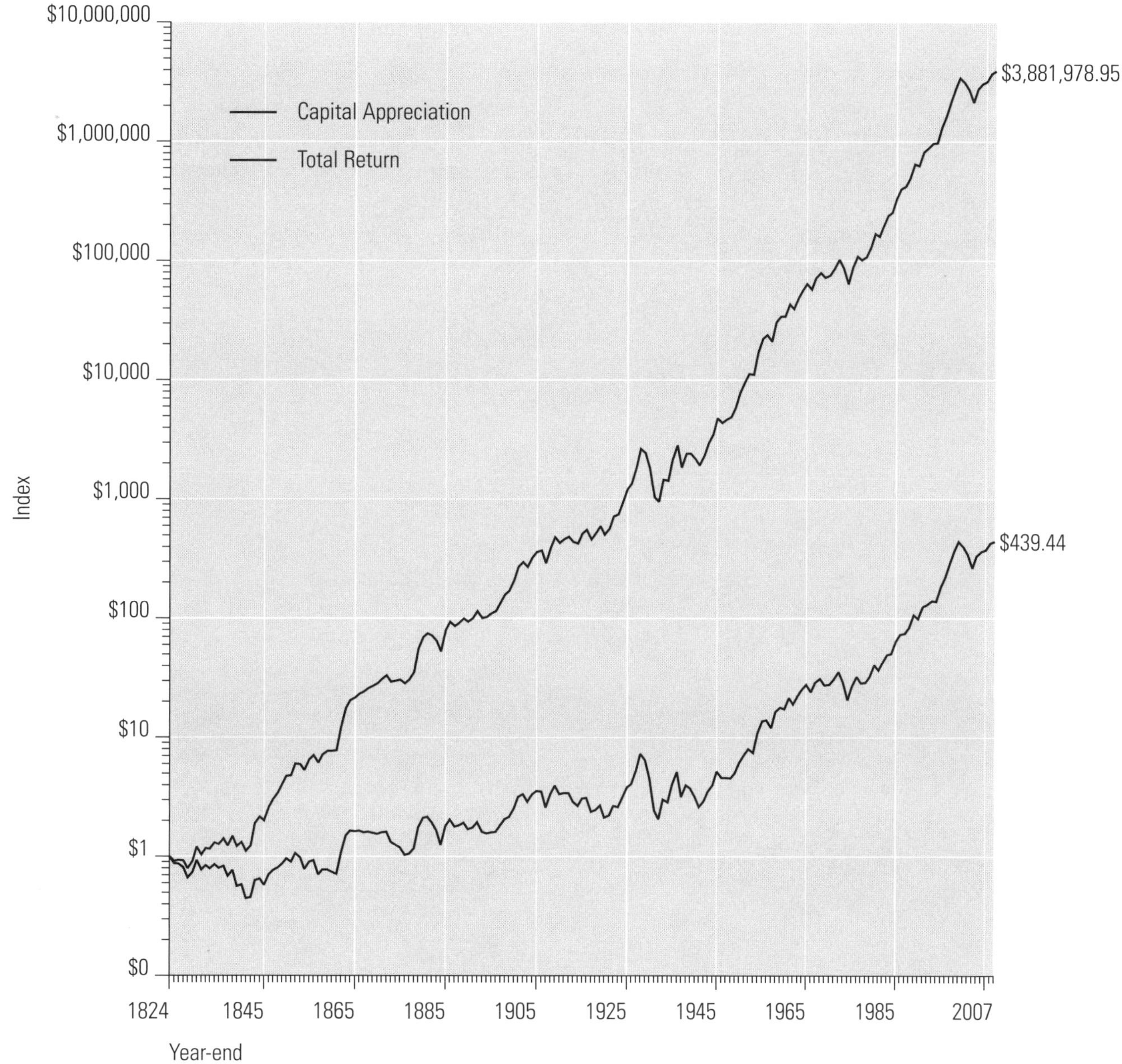

Conclusion

Data collection efforts have yielded a comprehensive database of New York Stock Exchange security prices for nearly the entire history of the NYSE. The goal of the study is to assemble an NYSE database for the period prior to 1926. The 1926 starting date was approximately when high-quality financial data became available. However, with a pre-1926 database assembled, researchers can expand their analysis back to the early 1800s. It is our hope that the long time series outlined in this chapter will lead to a better understanding of how the New York Stock Exchange evolved from an emerging market at the turn of the eighteenth century to the largest capital market in the world today.

Table 11-2

Large Company Stocks

Annual Capital Appreciation, Income, and Total Returns (in perce

from 1815 to 1925

Year	Cap App	Average Income Return	Total Return
1815	−6.65	—	—
1816	−1.93	—	—
1817	19.43	—	—
1818	−3.76	—	—
1819	−8.82	—	—
1820	9.59	—	—
1821	3.34	—	—
1822	−12.85	—	—
1823	5.29	—	—
1824	3.70	—	—
1825	−12.99	3.81	−9.18
1826	−1.22	3.48	2.27
1827	−6.24	4.57	−1.67
1828	−17.95	4.34	−13.61
1829	10.33	5.10	15.43
1830	27.31	4.20	31.51
1831	−17.05	3.07	−13.98
1832	8.60	4.48	13.08
1833	−6.09	4.24	−1.85
1834	8.84	4.40	13.24
1835	−6.74	4.38	−2.36
1836	4.33	7.76	12.09
1837	−18.02	4.60	−13.43
1838	12.20	8.99	21.19
1839	−26.62	7.64	−18.97
1840	3.01	6.03	9.04
1841	−23.52	7.46	−16.06
1842	2.34	8.71	11.05
1843	39.16	16.40	55.56
1844	2.81	9.29	12.11
1845	−11.61	5.56	−6.05
1846	23.21	5.70	28.91
1847	7.65	8.48	16.13
1848	5.28	7.45	12.72
1849	7.80	10.64	18.44
1850	10.48	6.57	17.05
1851	−5.78	7.74	1.95
1852	[illegible]	[illegible]	[illegible]
1853	[illegible]	[illegible]	[illegible]
1854	[illegible]	[illegible]	[illegible]
185	[illegible]	[illegible]	[illegible]
[illegible]	[illegible]	[illegible]	[illegible]
[illegible]	[illegible]	[illegible]	[illegible]
[illegible]	[illegible]	[illegible]	[illegible]
[illegible]	[illegible]	[illegible]	[illegible]
[illegible]	[illegible]	[illegible]	[illegible]
[illegible]	[illegible]	[illegible]	[illegible]
[illegible]	[illegible]	[illegible]	[illegible]
1864	[illegible]	[illegible]	[illegible]
1865	−1.33	[illegible]	[illegible]
1866	0.46	6.85	7.31
1867	−2.61	6.48	3.87
1868	1.52	6.56	8.08
1869	−2.85	6.53	3.67
1870	−1.44	6.66	5.22
1871	3.34	5.86	9.20
1872	0.50	6.33	6.83
1873	−17.70	6.51	−11.19
1874	−5.77	7.47	1.70
1875	−4.72	6.61	1.89
1876	−13.31	6.86	−6.45
1877	1.74	5.31	7.05
1878	10.50	5.54	16.04
1879	51.31	5.80	57.10
1880	19.83	5.28	25.12
1881	1.88	5.48	7.36
1882	−9.54	5.32	−4.22
1883	−15.04	5.65	−9.39
1884	−24.28	5.81	−18.47
1885	45.32	5.53	50.85
1886	12.46	4.23	16.69
1887	−12.13	4.43	−7.70
1888	2.09	4.36	6.45
[illegible]	[illegible]	4.28	8.77
[illegible]	[illegible]	4.14	−6.59
[illegible]	[illegible]	4.78	7.74
[illegible]	[illegible]	4.44	14.79
[illegible]	[illegible]	4.54	−12.33
[illegible]	2.82	4.76	1.94
[illegible]	2.14	4.42	6.56
[illegible]	0.69	4.17	4.86
[illegible]	14.15	4.27	18.41
[illegible]	12.17	4.21	16.38
[illegible]	4.17	3.72	7.89
[illegible]	17.99	4.98	22.97
[illegible]	24.60	4.66	29.26
[illegible]	5.29	4.15	9.44
[illegible]	−12.88	4.35	−8.53
1904	14.94	4.72	19.66
1905	6.67	4.00	10.67
1906	−1.09	4.19	3.10
1907	−26.26	4.47	−21.79
1908	28.47	6.09	34.56
1909	18.12	4.87	22.99
1910	−15.50	4.56	−10.94
1911	2.17	5.19	7.37
1912	0.03	5.27	5.30
1913	−14.44	5.12	−9.32
1914	−8.47	5.22	−3.25
1915	15.88	5.85	21.73
1916	1.29	5.91	7.19
1917	−23.48	7.04	−16.44
1918	2.88	8.38	11.27
1919	9.38	6.71	16.09
1920	−20.74	5.72	−15.02
1921	4.26	6.75	11.02
1922	19.74	6.98	26.72
1923	−2.13	6.04	3.90
1924	19.34	6.43	25.77
1925	23.22	5.91	29.12

buckconsultants.
an ACS company
Henry K. To, CFA
Consultant, Investment
1801 Century Park East, Suite 500 • Los Angeles, CA 90067
310.282.8232 • 310.282.0881 (fax)
henry.to@buckconsultants.com

Table 11-3

Large Company Stocks

Annual Capital Appreciation and Total Return Index Values

from 1824 to 1943

Year	Cap App	Total Return	Year	Cap App	Total Return	Year	Cap App	Total Return
1824	1.00	1.00	1864	1.65	20.48	1904	3.32	322.65
1825	0.87	0.91	1865	1.63	21.45	1905	3.54	357.07
1826	0.86	0.93	1866	1.64	23.02	1906	3.51	368.14
1827	0.81	0.91	1867	1.59	23.91	1907	2.58	287.92
1828	0.66	0.79	1868	1.62	25.84	1908	3.32	387.42
1829	0.73	0.91	1869	1.57	26.79	1909	3.92	476.49
1830	0.93	1.20	1870	1.55	28.19	1910	3.31	424.37
1831	0.77	1.03	1871	1.60	30.78	1911	3.39	455.63
1832	0.84	1.16	1872	1.61	32.89	1912	3.39	479.76
1833	0.79	1.14	1873	1.32	29.21	1913	2.90	435.04
1834	0.86	1.29	1874	1.25	29.70	1914	2.65	420.90
1835	0.80	1.26	1875	1.19	30.26	1915	3.07	512.38
1836	0.83	1.42	1876	1.03	28.31	1916	3.11	549.24
1837	0.68	1.23	1877	1.05	30.31	1917	2.38	458.96
1838	0.77	1.49	1878	1.16	35.17	1918	2.45	510.66
1839	0.56	1.20	1879	1.75	55.25	1919	2.68	592.84
1840	0.58	1.31	1880	2.10	69.13	1920	2.13	503.78
1841	0.44	1.10	1881	2.14	74.22	1921	2.22	559.27
1842	0.45	1.22	1882	1.93	71.09	1922	2.65	708.68
1843	0.63	1.90	1883	1.64	64.41	1923	2.60	736.34
1844	0.65	2.14	1884	1.24	52.51	1924	3.10	926.09
1845	0.57	2.01	1885	1.81	79.21	1925	3.82	1195.79
1846	0.71	2.59	1886	2.03	92.44	1926	4.04	1334.79
1847	0.76	3.00	1887	1.79	85.32	1927	5.28	1835.18
1848	0.80	3.39	1888	1.82	90.83	1928	7.29	2635.47
1849	0.86	4.01	1889	1.91	98.79	1929	6.42	2413.68
1850	0.95	4.69	1890	1.70	92.28	1930	4.59	1812.75
1851	0.90	4.78	1891	1.75	99.42	1931	2.43	1027.17
1852	1.06	6.00	1892	1.93	114.12	1932	2.06	943.01
1853	0.97	5.93	1893	1.61	100.06	1933	3.02	1452.15
1854	0.78	5.30	1894	1.56	102.00	1934	2.84	1431.20
1855	0.90	6.45	1895	1.60	108.69	1935	4.02	2113.43
1856	0.92	7.02	1896	1.61	113.97	1936	5.14	2830.34
1857	0.70	6.09	1897	1.83	134.96	1937	3.16	1838.97
1858	0.77	7.13	1898	2.06	157.07	1938	3.95	2411.28
1859	0.77	7.63	1899	2.14	169.45	1939	3.74	2401.38
1860	0.74	7.62	1900	2.53	208.38	1940	3.17	2166.42
1861	0.71	7.74	1901	3.15	269.34	1941	2.60	1915.29
1862	1.06	12.00	1902	3.32	294.77	1942	2.92	2304.86
1863	1.49	17.56	1903	2.89	269.63	1943	3.49	2901.81

Table 11-3 (continued)

Large Company Stocks

Annual Capital Appreciation and Total Return Index Values

from 1944 to 2007

Year	Cap App	Total Return	Year	Cap App	Total Return
1944	3.97	3474.99	1984	50.04	252548.89
1945	5.19	4741.14	1985	63.22	333763.56
1946	4.58	4358.47	1986	72.47	395411.36
1947	4.58	4607.25	1987	73.94	416094.53
1948	4.55	4860.71	1988	83.11	486037.11
1949	5.01	5774.16	1989	105.76	639094.09
1950	6.11	7605.31	1990	98.83	618817.55
1951	7.11	9431.84	1991	124.82	807863.22
1952	7.95	11164.23	1992	130.40	869827.94
1953	7.42	11053.79	1993	139.60	956722.01
1954	10.77	16870.70	1994	137.45	969229.24
1955	13.61	22195.54	1995	184.33	1332006.90
1956	13.96	23650.66	1996	221.69	1639356.83
1957	11.97	21100.53	1997	290.43	2186285.62
1958	16.52	30250.48	1998	367.88	2811163.21
1959	17.92	33866.95	1999	439.71	3402761.27
1960	17.39	34025.99	2000	395.13	3092926.24
1961	21.41	43175.07	2001	343.59	2725344.33
1962	18.88	39406.53	2002	263.31	2122923.32
1963	22.45	48391.69	2003	332.77	2732108.90
1964	25.36	56367.95	2004	362.70	3029162.91
1965	27.66	63386.32	2005	373.58	3177864.63
1966	24.03	57007.57	2006	424.46	3679817.89
1967	28.86	70675.53	2007	439.44	3881978.95
1968	31.08	78493.24			
1969	27.53	71817.70			
1970	27.57	74695.15			
1971	30.55	85386.04			
1972	35.32	101588.98			
1973	29.19	86694.82			
1974	20.51	63748.52			
1975	26.98	87464.94			
1976	32.15	108319.39			
1977	28.45	100537.72			
1978	28.76	107133.20			
1979	32.30	126888.02			
1980	40.62	168024.36			
1981	36.67	159776.38			
1982	42.08	193983.54			
1983	49.35	237656.61			

Chapter 12

International Equity Investing

Discussion of International Investing

With the disappearance of trade barriers and the opening of foreign markets, the level of global business has increased considerably. Communism and other systems have essentially been discredited, leading to increasingly open markets in nations around the world. Investing internationally literally offers a world of opportunity. The opportunities available today are growing rapidly, encouraged by open markets and the accelerating economies of many nations. The evidence in favor of taking a global approach to investing, and the possible rewards an investor can reap, is plentiful. However, significant risks are present as well—risks that apply strictly to the international marketplace. In this chapter, we consider both the rewards and the risks associated with international investments.

Construction of the International Indices

Our analysis of international investing uses the indices created by Morgan Stanley Capital International, Inc. (MSCI®). The MSCI indices are designed to measure the performance of the developed and emerging stock markets of such countries and regions as the United States, Europe, Canada, Australasia, and the Far East, and that of industry groups. MSCI indices are designed to reflect the performance of the entire range of stocks available to investors in each local market.

From January 1970 to October 2001, inclusion in the MSCI indices was based upon market capitalization. Stocks chosen for the indices were required to have a target market representation of 60 percent of total market capitalization. MSCI has enhanced its index construction methodology by free float-adjusting constituents' index weights and increasing the target market representation. Target market representation is increased from 60 percent of total market capitalization to 85 percent of free float-adjusted market capitalization within each industry group, within each country. MSCI defines the free float of a security as the proportion of shares outstanding that is deemed to be available for purchase in the public equity markets by international investors.

The international stock series presented throughout this chapter is represented by the MSCI EAFE® (Europe, Australasia, Far East) index. The MSCI EAFE index consists of 21 developed equity markets outside of North America.

Benefits of Investing Internationally

The arguments for adding international investments to an investment portfolio can be rather powerful. Examples include participation in the more than 50 percent of the world's investable assets that exist outside the U.S., growth potential, diversification, and the improvement of the risk/reward trade-off.

Investment Opportunities

An investor who chooses to ignore investment opportunities outside of the United States is missing out on over half of the investable developed stock market opportunities in the world. Graph 12-1 presents the relative size of international and domestic markets as of year-end 2007. The international markets represented in the graph constitute countries having developed economies. In 2007, the total developed world stock market capitalization was $39.1 trillion, with $22.3 trillion representing international stock market capitalization.[1]

Graph 12-1
World Stock Market Capitalization
Year-End 2007

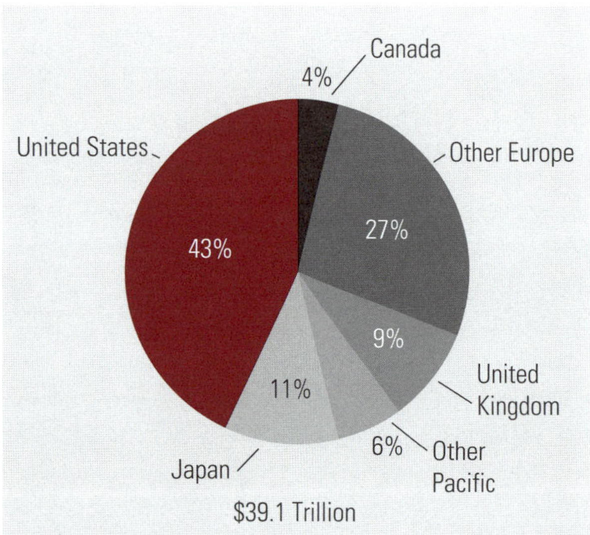

Note: Underlying data expressed in U.S. dollars

Although the domestic (U.S.) stock market continues to account for the largest part of world stock market capitalization, an investor who chooses to exclude international investments from his or her portfolio is ignoring over half of the world's investable assets.

Many of the possible investment choices available to you outside the United States are with companies you already know and whose products you may in fact be using on a daily basis. From the car you drive to the technology you use, many of these products are produced by companies that call other countries home. Some examples include: Daimler (Germany), Toyota (Japan), Nokia (Finland), and Samsung (Korea). If an investor were to limit the scope of his or her investments strictly to the U.S., many countries that are home to world class industries would be excluded. Switzerland has a major presence in the pharmaceutical industry, Germany in the automotive industry, and Japan in the consumer electronics industry. Globalization has helped to increase brand awareness with investors across the world. When looking at the names listed above, international investing suddenly seems a little less foreign.

1 World Market Capitalization by County—Morgan Stanley Capital International Blue Book℠.

Growth Potential

As markets have grown and international companies have thrived, the performance of many international stock markets has been impressive. Graph 12-2 depicts the growth of $1.00 invested in international stocks as well as U.S. large company stocks, long-term government bonds, Treasury bills, and a hypothetical asset returning the inflation rate over the period from the end of 1969 to the end of 2007. Of the asset classes shown, International stocks accumulated the highest ending wealth by year-end 2007. International stocks have outperformed U.S. large company stocks for the past six years.

Graph 12-2
Global Investing
Year-End 1969 = $1.00
from 1969 to 2007

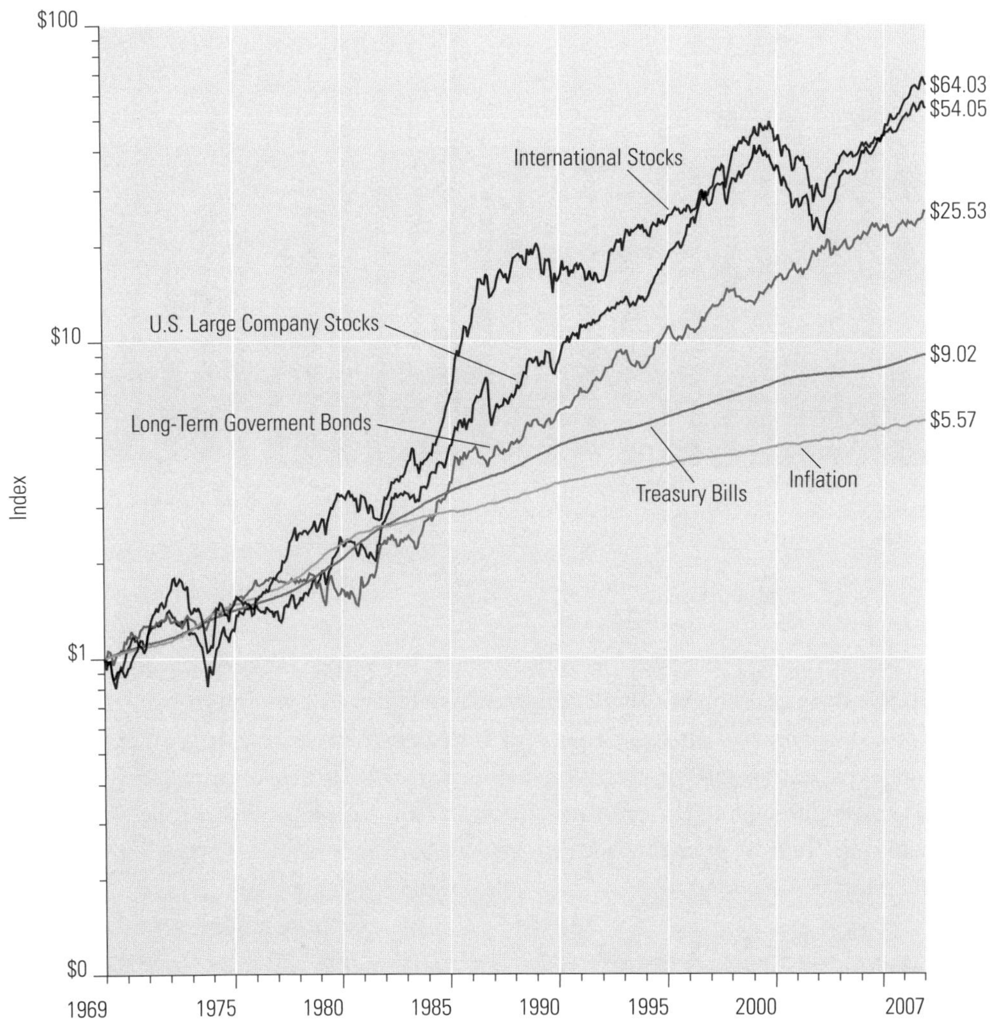

Note: Underlying data expressed in U.S. dollars

Graph 12-3 compares the performance of international and U.S. large company stocks over rolling 10-year holding periods ending 1979 through 2007. Although international stocks outperformed U.S. stocks in each of the ten-year holding periods ending 1979 to 1994, U.S. stocks have outperformed international stocks in each of the ten-year holding periods since 1995 (with the exception of the ten-year holding period ending in 2007).

Graph 12-3
Total Return of U.S. Large Company Stocks and International Stocks
10-Year Rolling Periods

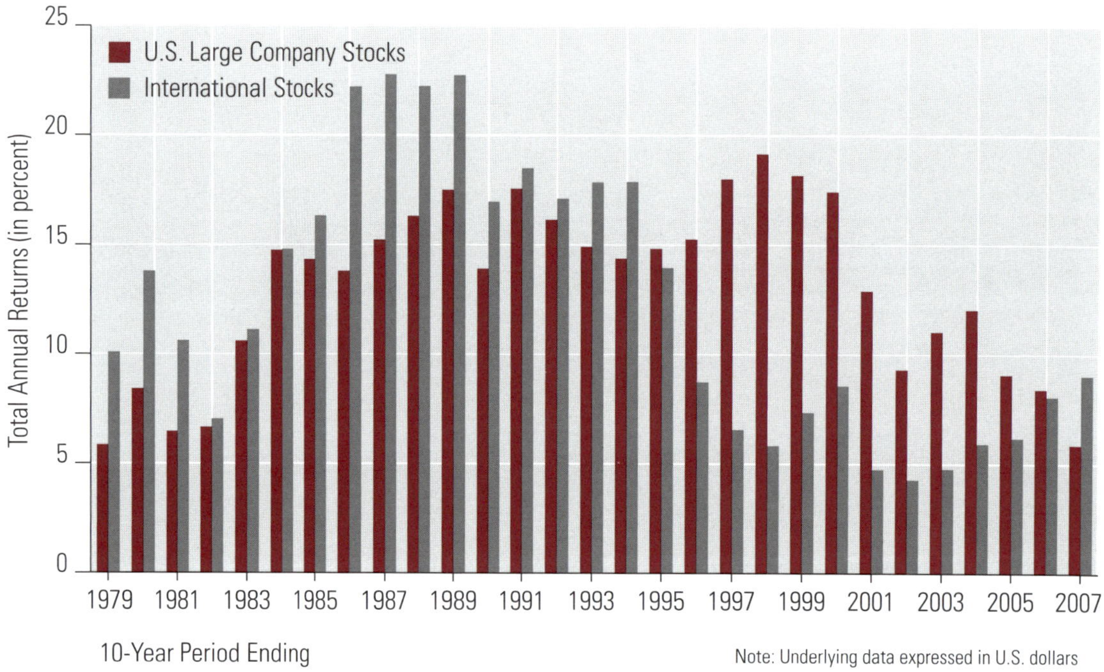

Diversification

Diversification can be another important benefit of international investing. By spreading risks among foreign and U.S. stocks, investors can potentially lower overall investment risk and/or improve investment returns. Fluctuations may occur at different times for different markets, and if growth is slow in one country, international investing provides a means of seeking healthier prospects elsewhere. Investing abroad may help an investor balance such fluctuations. Since it is almost impossible to fore-cast which markets will be top performers in any given year, it can be very valuable to be invested in a portfolio diversified across several countries.

Graph 12-4 presents the best-performing developed stock markets worldwide compared to the U.S. market over the past 10 years. The graph clearly indicates that by taking advantage of opportunities abroad, one may experience higher returns than by investing solely in the U.S. market.

Graph 12-4
Best Performing Developed Stock Markets vs. U.S. Market
from 1998 to 2007

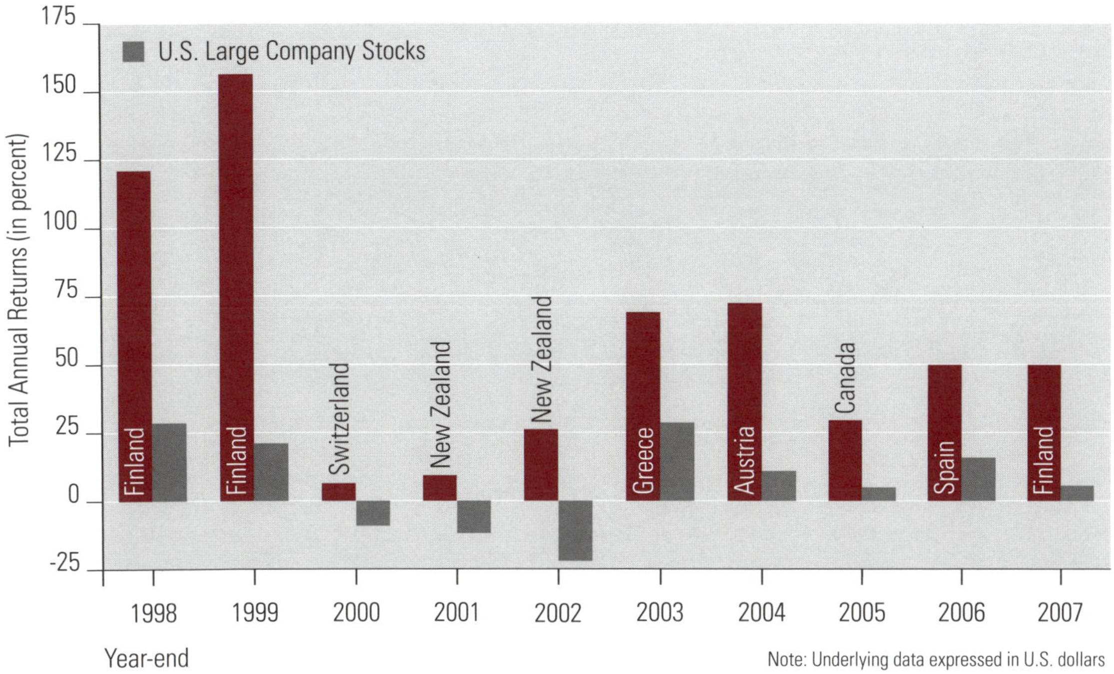

Graph 12-5 depicts the growth of $1,000 invested in U.S. large company stocks, European, and Pacific stocks as well as a global portfolio that represents an equally weighted mix of the aforementioned stocks. Notice that the European portfolio was the top performer, followed in order of performance by the Global, U.S., and Pacific stock indices at the end of the 38-year period. In local terms, the European portfolio did only marginally better than the U.S. portfolio in 2007, but in U.S. dollar terms, the European portfolio significantly outperformed the U.S. portfolio due to appreciation of the Euro.

Graph 12-5
Benefits of Global Diversification
Year-End 1969 = $1,000.00
from 1969 to 2007-

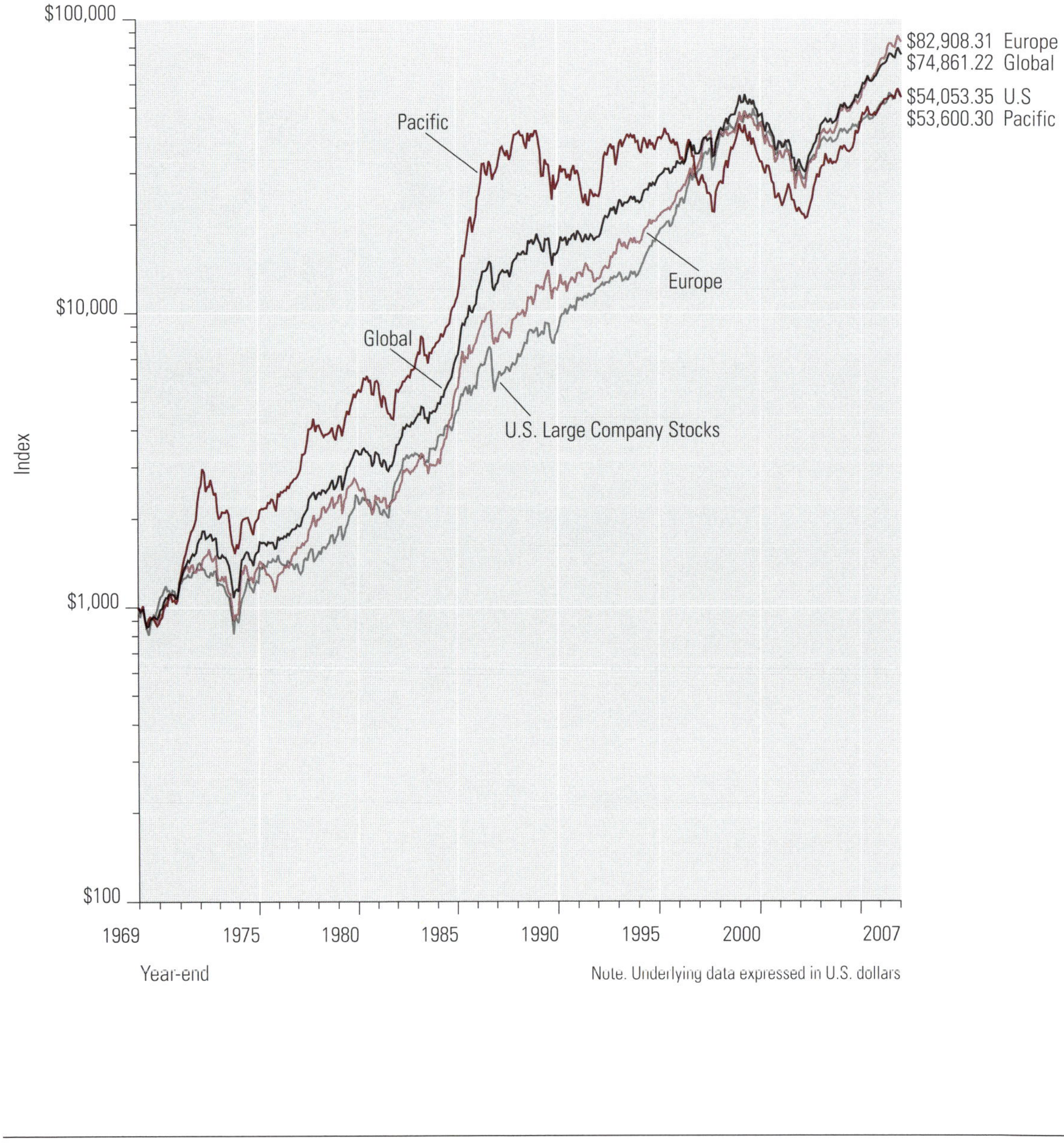

Note. Underlying data expressed in U.S. dollars

The cross-correlation coefficient between two series, covered in Chapter 6, measures the extent to which they are linearly related. The correlation coefficient measures the sensitivity of returns on one asset class or portfolio to the returns of another.

Graph 12-6 examines a 60-month rolling period correlation between international and U.S. large company stocks. This graph illustrates the recent rise in cross-correlation between the two, suggesting that the benefit of diversification has suffered in recent years. The maximum benefit to an investor would have come in the 60-month period ending July 1987, where the cross-correlation was 0.26. The least amount of diversification benefit would have come in the 60-month period ending April 2007, where the cross-correlation was 0.86. The monthly average over the entire time horizon has been 0.55.

Graph 12-6
Rolling 60-Month Correlations
U.S Large Company Stocks and International Stocks

60-Month Period Ending

Note: Underlying data expressed in U.S. dollars

Expanding the Efficient Range

Expanding a set of domestic portfolios to include securities from specific countries and regions can possibly improve the risk/return trade-off of investment opportunities. How would an efficient frontier be affected by such an expansion?

Graph 12-7 shows two efficient frontiers—one constructed entirely of domestic portfolios and the other constructed of global portfolios for the period 1970 to 1986. The comparison of the two efficient frontiers in this image makes a strong case for global diversification. An investor could have achieved higher returns at given levels of risk by expanding the set of domestic portfolios to include international stocks.

Graph 12-7
Efficient Frontier
U.S. Large Company Stocks, Long-Term Government Bonds, and International Stocks from 1970 to 1986

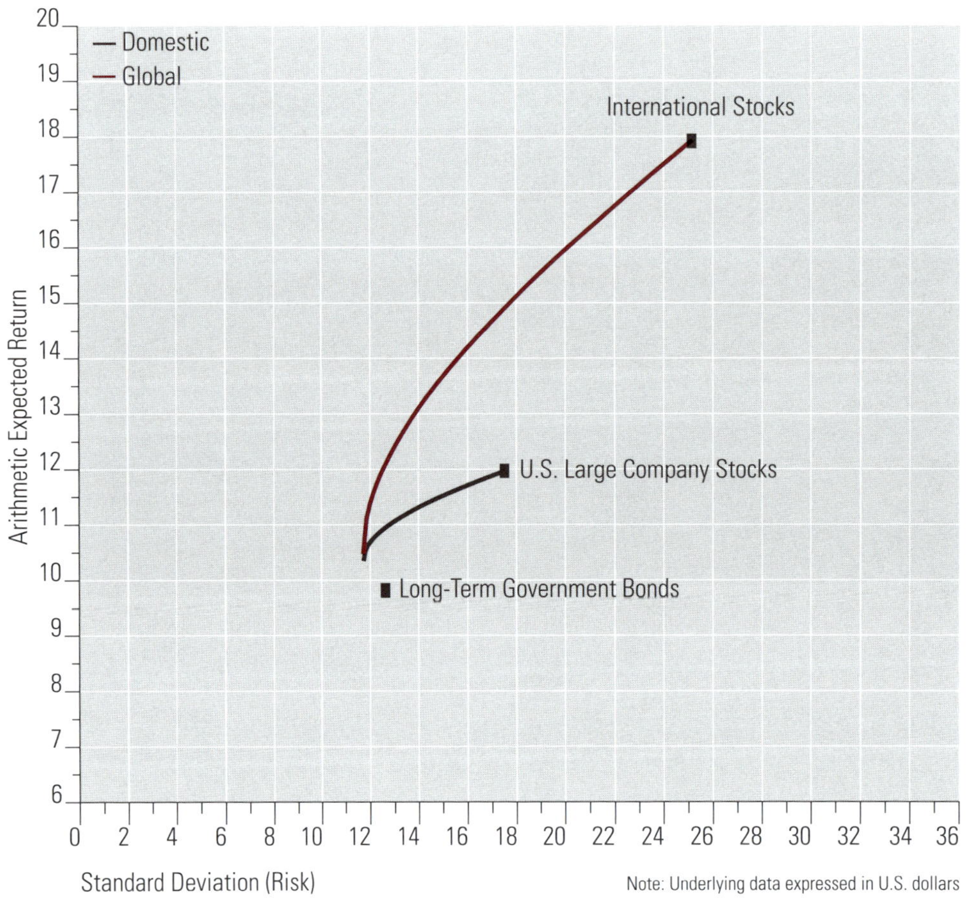

Note: Underlying data expressed in U.S. dollars

The time horizon is changed to cover the period 1987 to 2007 to construct the two efficient frontiers found in Graph 12-8. The comparison of the two efficient frontiers in this image makes somewhat of a weak case for global diversification. Although the diversification benefit and the risk/return trade-off have suffered of late, recent trends may not be indicative of future performance.

Graph 12-8
Efficient Frontier
U.S. Large Company Stocks, Long-Term Government Bonds, and International Stocks from 1987 to 2007

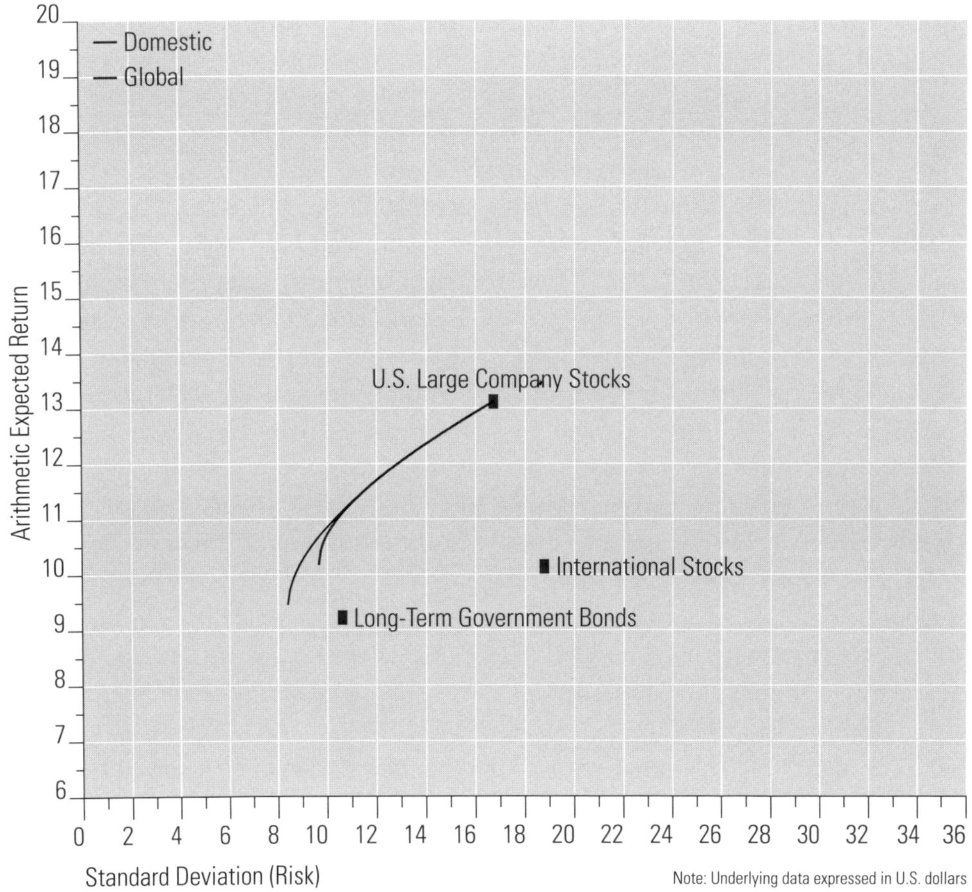

Note: Underlying data expressed in U.S. dollars

Risk Associated with International Investing

In addition to the potential rewards offered through international investing, significant risks apply as well. An investor assumes risk when investing in any type of stock. International investing, however, encompasses special risks—risks that should be carefully evaluated. Examples include currency risk, political and economic risk, liquidity risk, company information and accounting standards, market risk, and perhaps higher expenses.

Currency Risk

The risk of losing money when gains and losses are exchanged from foreign currencies into U.S. dollars is called currency risk. Exchange rates need to be considered with international stocks, and an investor should weigh the exchange rate risk (currency risk) in relation to the return benefit. Foreign exchange rates are continually fluctuating with changes in the supply and demand of each country's currency. Thus, returns realized by local investors are often quite different from the returns that U.S. investors attained—even though they are invested in the same security.

An investor purchases and trades foreign securities in the foreign country's local currency. When these securities are purchased by a U.S. investor, the investor's U.S. dollars must be converted to the foreign currency. When it is time to sell the securities or receive dividends, the currency is converted back to U.S. dollars. Movements in the foreign currency in relation to the U.S. dollar change the value of the foreign investment for the U.S. investor. Thus, a strengthening dollar diminishes the value of foreign assets owned by U.S. investors, while a weakening dollar increases the value of the foreign investment owned by U.S. investors.

Table 12-1 illustrates the impact of currency conversion. Both the Canadian dollar and the Japanese yen appreciated relative to the U.S. dollar in 2004, translating into more dollars and a higher return for U.S. investors. For example, a local investor in Japan had a 10.87 percent return in 2004, while a U.S. investor would have realized a 16.23 percent return. Why? Because of the yen's increased value, the U.S. investor could purchase a greater number of U.S. dollars at the end of 2004 than he could have at the beginning of 2004 (with the same number of yen). In 2006 the opposite happened; both the Canadian dollar and the Japanese yen lost value relative to the U.S. dollar, and U.S. investors did not fare as well as their local counterparts. U.S. investors' yen purchased fewer dollars at the end of 2006 than they did at the beginning of 2006, thus lowering U.S. investors' return.

Table 12-1
Impact of Currency Conversion

Country	Year	Return to Local Investors (%)	Return to U.S. Investors (%)	Currency Impact (%)
Canada	2004	13.84	23.02	9.19
Japan	2004	10.87	16.23	5.37
Canada	2006	17.90	17.58	−0.32
Japan	2006	7.35	6.38	−0.97

Political/Economic Risk

Governmental and political environments abroad can be quite unstable at times. Political events pose a considerable hazard to the stability of returns from foreign markets. In emerging markets, macroeconomic conditions remain exceptionally volatile and political risk is a fact of life. U.S. investors could be affected by economic policy changes such as currency controls, changes in taxation, restrictive trade policies, or seizure of foreigners' assets. Political instability and economic risk can lead to greater volatility, which can negatively affect investment markets/values.

Liquidity Risk

Liquidity risk refers to the potential that an asset will be difficult to buy or sell quickly and in large volume without substantially affecting the asset's price. Shares in large blue-chip stocks such as General Electric are liquid because they are actively traded and, therefore, the stock price will not be dramatically moved by a few buy or sell orders.

International markets, however, normally have much lower daily trading volumes when compared to the stock exchanges of the United States. Thus, a few large orders can have the potential to move the price of a security up or down rather sharply. This would go almost unnoticed in a large, established market. Also, a number of developing countries allow foreigners to buy only limited quantities of specified classes of shares.

Company Information/Accounting Standards

The type of information provided to investors from foreign companies often differs from the information U.S. public companies supply. Financial information concerning specific foreign companies can be much more difficult to obtain, since accounting and financial disclosure practices can vary widely from U.S. standards. Moreover, once the information is obtained, it may not be in English.

Market Risk

Just as U.S. stock prices fluctuate from one period to the next, prices of foreign stocks are subject to significant gains and declines. However, past returns from international stocks have fluctuated even more so than the returns of U.S. stocks. Annual ranges of returns provide an indication of the historical volatility (risk) experienced by investments in various markets.

Graph 12-9 illustrates the range of annual returns for domestic and international composites, as well as the Europe and Pacific regional composites, over the period 1970 through 2007. All three international composites exhibit more volatility when compared to the domestic composite. However, when one compares the compounded average return of each composite over the same period, the numbers seem to be more in line with one another. International investments have the potential for significant short-term declines; however, a long-term approach to investing may help reduce the pain of volatility. Investors should plan on holding international stock investments for much longer time periods to reap the potential rewards.

Graph 12-9
Global Stock Market Returns
Highest and Lowest Historical Annual Returns for Each Region
from 1970 to 2007

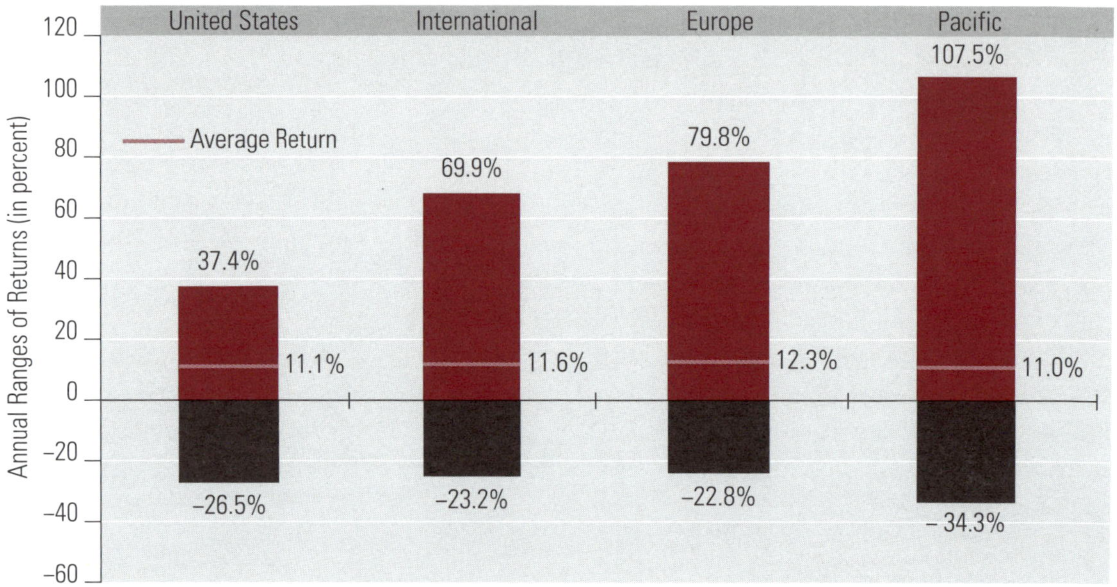

Note: Underlying data expressed in U.S. dollars

Expenses

Lastly, for the reasons stated earlier, investments in foreign securities generally have higher associated expenses compared to investments in domestic securities, including transaction costs as well as sales charges. All of these expenses work to reduce the investor's return on the foreign security.

The risks associated with international investing should be carefully examined by an investor interested in or already partaking in the international marketplace. While the potential rewards of investing internationally are quite clear, an investor should weigh those along with the added risks.

Summary Statistics for International and Domestic Series

Table 12-2 shows summary statistics of annual total returns for various international regions and composites. The summary statistics presented are geometric mean, arithmetic mean, and standard deviation.

Over the period 1970 to 2007, the Pacific regional composite was the riskiest, with a standard deviation of 31.2 percent. The geometric mean of the Pacific regional composite was 11.0 percent, similar to EAFE and the World composite, which were considerably less risky.

Table 12-2

Summary Statistics of Annual Returns (in percent)
from 1970 to 2007

Series	Geometric Mean	Arithmetic Mean	Standard Deviation
Canada	11.4	13.0	19.4
Europe	12.3	14.1	20.7
Pacific	11.0	14.9	31.2
EAFE (Europe, Australasia, Far East)	11.6	13.6	21.6
World	10.8	12.1	16.8
United States	11.1	12.4	16.6

Note: Underlying data expressed in U.S. dollars

Table 12-3 shows the compound returns by decade for the various international regions and composites. The Pacific regional composite provided the highest compound annual rate of return in the first two decades but performed rather poorly in the 1990s as well as in the last two time periods. The 1990s were a good time period in which to be a domestic investor, with a compound annual rate of return of 18.2 percent.

Table 12-3

Compound Annual Rates of Return by Decade (in percent)

	1970s	1980s	1990s	2000s*	1998-07
Canada	11.0	11.6	9.9	13.5	15.0
Europe	8.6	18.5	14.5	7.1	10.0
Pacific	14.8	26.4	0.5	2.6	7.1
EAFE (Europe, Australasia, Far East)	10.1	22.8	7.3	5.6	9.0
World	7.0	19.9	12.0	3.4	7.4
United States	5.9	17.5	18.2	1.7	5.9

*Based on the period 2000–2007.

Note: Underlying data expressed in U.S. dollars

Table 12-4 shows the annualized monthly standard deviations by decade for the various international regions and composites. The World composite was the least risky asset in the first three decades as well as during the time period of 1998 to 2007. The Pacific regional composite was the riskiest asset in the 1970s, 1980s, and 1990s, but Canada has experienced the most risk in the 2000s and over the time period 1998 to 2007.

Table 12-4
Annualized Monthly Standard Deviation by Decade (in percent)

	1970s	1980s	1990s	2000s*	1998-07
Canada	20.7	24.7	18.7	22.1	24.0
Europe	18.6	21.5	16.8	16.8	17.5
Pacific	22.1	26.6	24.8	16.1	18.7
EAFE (Europe, Australasia, Far East)	17.4	21.6	18.7	15.0	16.0
World	15.1	17.6	15.7	14.0	15.2
United States	17.1	19.4	15.8	14.2	15.7

*Based on the period 2000–2007.

Note: Underlying data expressed in U.S. dollars

Table 12-5 presents annual cross-correlations and serial correlations from 1970 to 2007 for the six basic series and inflation as well as international stocks. International stocks, when compared to U.S. large company stocks, provided a higher cross-correlation than when compared to U.S. small company stocks. The serial correlation of international stocks suggests no pattern, and the return from period to period can best be interpreted as random or unpredictable.

Table 12-5
Basic Series and International Stocks
Serial and Cross-Correlations of Historical Annual Returns from 1970 to 2007

Series	International Stocks	Large Company Stocks	Small Company Stocks	Long-Term Corp Bonds	Long-Term Govt Bonds	Intermediate Govt Bonds	U.S Treasury Bills	Inflation
International Stocks	1.00							
Large Company Stocks	0.59	1.00						
Small Company Stocks	0.41	0.66	1.00					
Long-Term Corp Bonds	0.08	0.34	0.14	1.00				
Long-Term Govt Bonds	0.06	0.27	0.04	0.94	1.00			
Intermediate Govt Bonds	–0.07	0.19	–0.01	0.90	0.91	1.00		
Treasury Bills	–0.12	0.05	–0.01	0.02	0.04	0.31	1.00	
Inflation	–0.21	–0.22	–0.02	–0.42	–0.37	–0.18	0.63	1.00
Serial Correlations	0.15	0.05	0.07	–0.09	–0.25	–0.06	0.81	0.74

Note: Underlying data expressed in U.S. dollars

Conclusion

International investments are no different than any other investment when it comes to information gathering. Investors interested in or already taking part in the international marketplace should learn as much as possible about the corresponding risks and rewards. International investments are not for everyone, and the most appropriate mix for an individual investor depends on his or her risk tolerance, investment goals, time horizon, and financial resources.

Table 12-6
U.S. Large Company Stocks, International Stocks, Pacific Stocks, and Europe Stocks
Annual Total Returns (in percent)
from 1970 to 2007

Year	U.S. Large Company Stocks	International Stocks	Pacific Stocks	Europe Stocks
1970	4.01	–10.51	–11.99	–9.35
1971	14.31	31.21	38.75	28.04
1972	18.98	37.60	107.55	15.62
1973	–14.66	–14.17	–20.95	–7.73
1974	–26.47	–22.15	–20.94	–22.78
1975	37.20	37.10	26.73	43.90
1976	23.84	3.74	21.64	–6.37
1977	–7.18	19.42	13.69	23.92
1978	6.56	34.30	48.77	24.30
1979	18.44	6.18	–3.48	14.67
1980	32.42	24.43	36.38	14.53
1981	–4.91	–1.03	8.31	–10.45
1982	21.41	–0.86	–6.26	5.69
1983	22.51	24.61	26.42	22.38
1984	6.27	7.86	13.48	1.26
1985	32.16	56.72	39.39	79.79
1986	18.47	69.94	93.82	44.46
1987	5.23	24.93	39.85	4.10
1988	16.81	28.59	35.19	16.35
1989	31.49	10.80	2.68	29.06
1990	–3.17	–23.19	–34.29	–3.37
1991	30.55	12.49	11.54	13.66
1992	7.67	–11.85	–18.20	–4.25
1993	9.99	32.94	35.97	29.79
1994	1.31	8.06	13.03	2.66
1995	37.43	11.55	2.99	22.13
1996	23.07	6.36	–8.40	21.57
1997	33.36	2.06	–25.34	24.20
1998	28.58	20.33	2.69	28.91
1999	21.04	27.30	57.96	16.23
2000	–9.11	–13.96	–25.64	–8.14
2001	–11.88	–21.21	–25.22	–19.64
2002	–22.10	–15.66	–9.01	–18.09
2003	28.70	39.17	38.98	39.14
2004	10.87	20.70	19.30	21.39
2005	4.91	14.02	23.01	9.93
2006	15.80	26.86	12.51	34.36
2007	5.49	11.63	5.61	14.39

Note: Underlying data expressed in U.S. dollars

Appendix A

Appendix A

Monthly and Annual Returns on Basic Series

Basic Series

Real Riskless Rate of Return

Table A-1

Large Company Stocks: Total Returns

from January 1926 to December 1970

Year	Jan	Feb	Mar	Apr	May	Jun	Jul	Aug	Sep	Oct	Nov	Dec	Year	Jan–Dec*
1926	0.0000	−0.0385	−0.0575	0.0253	0.0179	0.0457	0.0479	0.0248	0.0252	−0.0284	0.0347	0.0196	1926	0.1162
1927	−0.0193	0.0537	0.0087	0.0201	0.0607	−0.0067	0.0670	0.0515	0.0450	−0.0502	0.0721	0.0279	1927	0.3749
1928	−0.0040	−0.0125	0.1101	0.0345	0.0197	−0.0385	0.0141	0.0803	0.0259	0.0168	0.1292	0.0049	1928	0.4361
1929	0.0583	−0.0019	−0.0012	0.0176	−0.0362	0.1140	0.0471	0.1028	−0.0476	−0.1973	−0.1246	0.0282	1929	−0.0842
1930	0.0639	0.0259	0.0812	−0.0080	−0.0096	−0.1625	0.0386	0.0141	−0.1282	−0.0855	−0.0089	−0.0706	1930	−0.2490
1931	0.0502	0.1193	−0.0675	−0.0935	−0.1279	0.1421	−0.0722	0.0182	−0.2973	0.0896	−0.0798	−0.1400	1931	−0.4334
1932	−0.0271	0.0570	−0.1158	−0.1997	−0.2196	−0.0022	0.3815	0.3869	−0.0346	−0.1349	−0.0417	0.0565	1932	−0.0819
1933	0.0087	−0.1772	0.0353	0.4256	0.1683	0.1338	−0.0862	0.1206	−0.1118	−0.0855	0.1127	0.0253	1933	0.5399
1934	0.1069	−0.0322	0.0000	−0.0251	−0.0736	0.0229	−0.1132	0.0611	−0.0033	−0.0286	0.0942	−0.0010	1934	−0.0144
1935	−0.0411	−0.0341	−0.0286	0.0980	0.0409	0.0699	0.0850	0.0280	0.0256	0.0777	0.0474	0.0394	1935	0.4767
1936	0.0670	0.0224	0.0268	−0.0751	0.0545	0.0333	0.0701	0.0151	0.0031	0.0775	0.0134	−0.0029	1936	0.3392
1937	0.0390	0.0191	−0.0077	−0.0809	−0.0024	−0.0504	0.1045	−0.0483	−0.1403	−0.0981	−0.0866	−0.0459	1937	−0.3503
1938	0.0152	0.0674	−0.2487	0.1447	−0.0330	0.2503	0.0744	−0.0226	0.0166	0.0776	−0.0273	0.0401	1938	0.3112
1939	−0.0674	0.0390	−0.1339	−0.0027	0.0733	−0.0612	0.1105	−0.0648	0.1673	−0.0123	−0.0398	0.0270	1939	−0.0041
1940	−0.0336	0.0133	0.0124	−0.0024	−0.2289	0.0809	0.0341	0.0350	0.0123	0.0422	−0.0316	0.0009	1940	−0.0978
1941	−0.0463	−0.0060	0.0071	−0.0612	0.0183	0.0578	0.0579	0.0010	−0.0068	−0.0657	−0.0284	−0.0407	1941	−0.1159
1942	0.0161	−0.0159	−0.0652	−0.0399	0.0796	0.0221	0.0337	0.0164	0.0290	0.0678	−0.0021	0.0549	1942	0.2034
1943	0.0737	0.0583	0.0545	0.0035	0.0552	0.0223	−0.0526	0.0171	0.0263	−0.0108	−0.0654	0.0617	1943	0.2590
1944	0.0171	0.0042	0.0195	−0.0100	0.0505	0.0543	−0.0193	0.0157	−0.0008	0.0023	0.0133	0.0374	1944	0.1975
1945	0.0158	0.0683	−0.0441	0.0902	0.0195	−0.0007	−0.0180	0.0641	0.0438	0.0322	0.0396	0.0116	1945	0.3644
1946	0.0714	−0.0641	0.0480	0.0393	0.0288	−0.0370	−0.0239	−0.0674	−0.0997	−0.0060	−0.0027	0.0457	1946	−0.0807
1947	0.0255	−0.0077	−0.0149	−0.0363	0.0014	0.0554	0.0381	−0.0203	−0.0111	0.0238	−0.0175	0.0233	1947	0.0571
1948	−0.0379	−0.0388	0.0793	0.0292	0.0879	0.0054	−0.0508	0.0158	−0.0276	0.0710	−0.0961	0.0346	1948	0.0550
1949	0.0039	−0.0296	0.0328	−0.0179	−0.0258	0.0014	0.0650	0.0219	0.0263	0.0340	0.0175	0.0486	1949	0.1879
1950	0.0197	0.0199	0.0070	0.0486	0.0509	−0.0548	0.0119	0.0443	0.0592	0.0093	0.0169	0.0513	1950	0.3171
1951	0.0637	0.0157	−0.0156	0.0509	−0.0299	−0.0228	0.0711	0.0478	0.0013	−0.0103	0.0096	0.0424	1951	0.2402
1952	0.0181	−0.0282	0.0503	−0.0402	0.0343	0.0490	0.0196	−0.0071	−0.0176	0.0020	0.0571	0.0382	1952	0.1837
1953	−0.0049	−0.0106	−0.0212	−0.0237	0.0077	−0.0134	0.0273	−0.0501	0.0034	0.0540	0.0204	0.0052	1953	−0.0099
1954	0.0536	0.0111	0.0325	0.0516	0.0418	0.0031	0.0589	−0.0275	0.0851	−0.0167	0.0909	0.0534	1954	0.5262
1955	0.0197	0.0098	−0.0030	0.0396	0.0055	0.0841	0.0622	−0.0025	0.0130	−0.0284	0.0827	0.0015	1955	0.3156
1956	−0.0347	0.0413	0.0710	−0.0004	−0.0593	0.0409	0.0530	−0.0328	−0.0440	0.0066	−0.0050	0.0370	1956	0.0656
1957	−0.0401	−0.0264	0.0215	0.0388	0.0437	0.0004	0.0131	−0.0505	−0.0602	−0.0302	0.0231	−0.0395	1957	−0.1078
1958	0.0445	−0.0141	0.0328	0.0337	0.0212	0.0279	0.0449	0.0176	0.0501	0.0270	0.0284	0.0535	1958	0.4336
1959	0.0053	0.0049	0.0020	0.0402	0.0240	−0.0022	0.0363	−0.0102	−0.0443	0.0128	0.0186	0.0292	1959	0.1196
1960	−0.0700	0.0147	−0.0123	−0.0161	0.0326	0.0211	−0.0234	0.0317	−0.0590	−0.0007	0.0465	0.0479	1960	0.0047
1961	0.0645	0.0319	0.0270	0.0051	0.0239	−0.0275	0.0342	0.0243	−0.0184	0.0298	0.0447	0.0046	1961	0.2689
1962	−0.0366	0.0209	−0.0046	−0.0607	−0.0811	−0.0803	0.0652	0.0208	−0.0465	0.0064	0.1086	0.0153	1962	−0.0873
1963	0.0506	−0.0239	0.0370	0.0500	0.0193	−0.0188	−0.0022	0.0535	−0.0097	0.0339	−0.0046	0.0262	1963	0.2280
1964	0.0283	0.0147	0.0165	0.0075	0.0162	0.0178	0.0195	−0.0118	0.0301	0.0096	0.0005	0.0056	1964	0.1648
1965	0.0345	0.0031	−0.0133	0.0356	−0.0030	−0.0473	0.0147	0.0272	0.0334	0.0289	−0.0031	0.0106	1965	0.1245
1966	0.0062	−0.0131	−0.0205	0.0220	−0.0492	−0.0146	−0.0120	−0.0725	−0.0053	0.0494	0.0095	0.0002	1966	−0.1006
1967	0.0798	0.0072	0.0409	0.0437	−0.0477	0.0190	0.0468	−0.0070	0.0342	−0.0276	0.0065	0.0278	1967	0.2398
1968	−0.0425	−0.0261	0.0110	0.0834	0.0161	0.0105	−0.0172	0.0164	0.0400	0.0087	0.0531	−0.0402	1968	0.1106
1969	−0.0068	−0.0426	0.0359	0.0229	0.0026	−0.0542	−0.0587	0.0454	−0.0236	0.0459	−0.0297	−0.0177	1969	−0.0850
1970	−0.0743	0.0586	0.0030	−0.0889	−0.0547	−0.0482	0.0752	0.0509	0.0347	−0.0097	0.0536	0.0584	1970	0.0401

* Compound annual return

Table A-1 (Continued)

Large Company Stocks: Total Returns

from January 1971 to December 2007

Year	Jan	Feb	Mar	Apr	May	Jun	Jul	Aug	Sep	Oct	Nov	Dec	Year	Jan–Dec*
1971	0.0419	0.0141	0.0382	0.0377	−0.0367	0.0021	−0.0399	0.0412	−0.0056	−0.0404	0.0027	0.0877	1971	0.1431
1972	0.0194	0.0299	0.0072	0.0057	0.0219	−0.0205	0.0036	0.0391	−0.0036	0.0107	0.0505	0.0131	1972	0.1898
1973	−0.0159	−0.0333	−0.0002	−0.0395	−0.0139	−0.0051	0.0394	−0.0318	0.0415	0.0003	−0.1082	0.0183	1973	−0.1466
1974	−0.0085	0.0019	−0.0217	−0.0373	−0.0272	−0.0128	−0.0759	−0.0828	−0.1170	0.1657	−0.0448	−0.0177	1974	−0.2647
1975	0.1251	0.0674	0.0237	0.0493	0.0509	0.0462	−0.0659	−0.0144	−0.0328	0.0637	0.0313	−0.0096	1975	0.3720
1976	0.1199	−0.0058	0.0326	−0.0099	−0.0073	0.0427	−0.0068	0.0014	0.0247	−0.0206	−0.0009	0.0540	1976	0.2384
1977	−0.0489	−0.0151	−0.0119	0.0014	−0.0150	0.0475	−0.0151	−0.0133	0.0000	−0.0415	0.0370	0.0048	1977	−0.0718
1978	−0.0596	−0.0161	0.0276	0.0870	0.0136	−0.0152	0.0560	0.0340	−0.0048	−0.0891	0.0260	0.0172	1978	0.0656
1979	0.0421	−0.0284	0.0575	0.0036	−0.0168	0.0410	0.0110	0.0611	0.0025	−0.0656	0.0514	0.0192	1979	0.1844
1980	0.0610	0.0031	−0.0987	0.0429	0.0562	0.0296	0.0676	0.0131	0.0281	0.0187	0.1095	−0.0315	1980	0.3242
1981	−0.0438	0.0208	0.0380	−0.0213	0.0062	−0.0080	0.0007	−0.0554	−0.0502	0.0528	0.0441	−0.0265	1981	−0.0491
1982	−0.0163	−0.0512	−0.0060	0.0414	−0.0288	−0.0174	−0.0215	0.1267	0.0110	0.1126	0.0438	0.0173	1982	0.2141
1983	0.0348	0.0260	0.0365	0.0758	−0.0052	0.0382	−0.0313	0.0170	0.0136	−0.0134	0.0233	−0.0061	1983	0.2251
1984	−0.0065	−0.0328	0.0171	0.0069	−0.0534	0.0221	−0.0143	0.1125	0.0002	0.0026	−0.0101	0.0253	1984	0.0627
1985	0.0768	0.0137	0.0018	−0.0032	0.0615	0.0159	−0.0026	−0.0061	−0.0321	0.0447	0.0716	0.0467	1985	0.3216
1986	0.0044	0.0761	0.0554	−0.0124	0.0549	0.0166	−0.0569	0.0748	−0.0822	0.0556	0.0256	−0.0264	1986	0.1847
1987	0.1343	0.0413	0.0272	−0.0088	0.0103	0.0499	0.0498	0.0385	−0.0220	−0.2152	−0.0819	0.0738	1987	0.0523
1988	0.0427	0.0470	−0.0302	0.0108	0.0078	0.0464	−0.0040	−0.0331	0.0424	0.0273	−0.0142	0.0181	1988	0.1681
1989	0.0723	−0.0249	0.0236	0.0516	0.0402	−0.0054	0.0898	0.0193	−0.0039	−0.0233	0.0208	0.0236	1989	0.3149
1990	−0.0671	0.0129	0.0263	−0.0247	0.0975	−0.0070	−0.0032	−0.0903	−0.0492	−0.0037	0.0644	0.0274	1990	−0.0317
1991	0.0442	0.0716	0.0238	0.0028	0.0428	−0.0457	0.0468	0.0235	−0.0164	0.0134	−0.0404	0.1143	1991	0.3055
1992	−0.0186	0.0128	−0.0196	0.0291	0.0054	−0.0145	0.0403	−0.0202	0.0115	0.0036	0.0337	0.0131	1992	0.0767
1993	0.0073	0.0135	0.0215	−0.0245	0.0270	0.0033	−0.0047	0.0381	−0.0074	0.0203	−0.0094	0.0123	1993	0.0999
1994	0.0335	−0.0270	−0.0435	0.0130	0.0163	−0.0247	0.0331	0.0407	−0.0241	0.0229	−0.0367	0.0146	1994	0.0131
1995	0.0260	0.0388	0.0296	0.0291	0.0395	0.0235	0.0333	0.0027	0.0419	−0.0035	0.0440	0.0185	1995	0.3743
1996	0.0344	0.0096	0.0096	0.0147	0.0258	0.0041	−0.0445	0.0212	0.0562	0.0274	0.0759	−0.0196	1996	0.2307
1997	0.0621	0.0081	−0.0416	0.0597	0.0614	0.0446	0.0794	−0.0556	0.0548	−0.0334	0.0463	0.0172	1997	0.3336
1998	0.0111	0.0721	0.0512	0.0101	−0.0172	0.0406	−0.0106	−0.1446	0.0641	0.0813	0.0606	0.0576	1998	0.2858
1999	0.0418	−0.0311	0.0400	0.0387	−0.0236	0.0555	−0.0312	−0.0050	−0.0274	0.0633	0.0203	0.0589	1999	0.2104
2000	−0.0502	−0.0189	0.0978	−0.0301	−0.0205	0.0246	−0.0156	0.0621	−0.0528	−0.0042	−0.0788	0.0049	2000	−0.0911
2001	0.0355	−0.0912	−0.0634	0.0777	0.0067	−0.0243	−0.0098	−0.0626	−0.0808	0.0191	0.0767	0.0088	2001	−0.1188
2002	−0.0146	−0.0193	0.0376	−0.0606	−0.0074	−0.0712	−0.0780	0.0066	−0.1087	0.0880	0.0589	−0.0588	2002	−0.2210
2003	−0.0262	−0.0150	0.0097	0.0824	0.0527	0.0128	0.0176	0.0195	−0.0106	0.0566	0.0088	0.0524	2003	0.2870
2004	0.0184	0.0139	−0.0151	−0.0157	0.0137	0.0194	−0.0331	0.0040	0.0108	0.0153	0.0405	0.0340	2004	0.1087
2005	−0.0244	0.0210	−0.0177	−0.0190	0.0318	0.0014	0.0372	−0.0091	0.0081	−0.0167	0.0378	0.0003	2005	0.0491
2006	0.0265	0.0027	0.0124	0.0134	−0.0288	0.0014	0.0062	0.0238	0.0258	0.0326	0.0190	0.0140	2006	0.1580
2007	0.0151	−0.0196	0.0112	0.0443	0.0349	−0.0166	−0.0310	0.0150	0.0374	0.0159	−0.0418	−0.0069	2007	0.0549

Compound annual return

Table A-2
Large Company Stocks: Income Returns

from January 1926 to December 1970

Year	Jan	Feb	Mar	Apr	May	Jun	Jul	Aug	Sep	Oct	Nov	Dec	Year	Jan–De
1926	0.0016	0.0055	0.0016	0.0026	0.0102	0.0025	0.0024	0.0078	0.0023	0.0030	0.0123	0.0030	1926	0.054
1927	0.0015	0.0061	0.0022	0.0029	0.0085	0.0027	0.0020	0.0070	0.0018	0.0029	0.0105	0.0029	1927	0.057
1928	0.0011	0.0051	0.0017	0.0021	0.0071	0.0020	0.0016	0.0062	0.0019	0.0023	0.0092	0.0021	1928	0.048
1929	0.0012	0.0039	0.0012	0.0016	0.0066	0.0016	0.0014	0.0048	0.0013	0.0020	0.0091	0.0029	1929	0.039
1930	0.0014	0.0044	0.0013	0.0016	0.0068	0.0020	0.0020	0.0066	0.0019	0.0032	0.0130	0.0036	1930	0.045
1931	0.0013	0.0050	0.0017	0.0024	0.0093	0.0031	0.0020	0.0087	0.0022	0.0051	0.0180	0.0053	1931	0.053
1932	0.0012	0.0063	0.0024	0.0027	0.0137	0.0067	0.0045	0.0115	0.0024	0.0037	0.0172	0.0046	1932	0.061
1933	0.0015	0.0072	0.0018	0.0034	0.0096	0.0021	0.0018	0.0060	0.0018	0.0031	0.0100	0.0030	1933	0.063
1934	0.0010	0.0045	0.0009	0.0019	0.0076	0.0021	0.0020	0.0069	0.0022	0.0033	0.0114	0.0031	1934	0.044
1935	0.0011	0.0055	0.0023	0.0024	0.0086	0.0021	0.0020	0.0063	0.0018	0.0026	0.0080	0.0023	1935	0.049
1936	0.0015	0.0056	0.0014	0.0020	0.0087	0.0028	0.0020	0.0063	0.0019	0.0025	0.0093	0.0029	1936	0.053
1937	0.0012	0.0045	0.0017	0.0022	0.0079	0.0025	0.0019	0.0071	0.0019	0.0036	0.0146	0.0045	1937	0.046
1938	0.0019	0.0065	0.0018	0.0035	0.0113	0.0032	0.0017	0.0048	0.0017	0.0016	0.0061	0.0024	1938	0.048
1939	0.0015	0.0065	0.0016	0.0027	0.0110	0.0026	0.0018	0.0066	0.0027	0.0023	0.0094	0.0033	1939	0.046
1940	0.0016	0.0066	0.0025	0.0024	0.0107	0.0043	0.0030	0.0087	0.0028	0.0028	0.0108	0.0038	1940	0.053
1941	0.0019	0.0089	0.0030	0.0040	0.0140	0.0043	0.0030	0.0096	0.0029	0.0029	0.0137	0.0044	1941	0.067
1942	0.0023	0.0091	0.0023	0.0037	0.0157	0.0037	0.0024	0.0093	0.0023	0.0034	0.0117	0.0032	1942	0.067
1943	0.0020	0.0076	0.0018	0.0026	0.0104	0.0025	0.0016	0.0068	0.0025	0.0025	0.0101	0.0027	1943	0.062
1944	0.0017	0.0068	0.0025	0.0025	0.0101	0.0032	0.0015	0.0071	0.0023	0.0023	0.0094	0.0023	1944	0.054
1945	0.0015	0.0067	0.0021	0.0022	0.0081	0.0027	0.0020	0.0061	0.0019	0.0019	0.0072	0.0017	1945	0.049
1946	0.0017	0.0054	0.0017	0.0017	0.0064	0.0021	0.0016	0.0056	0.0018	0.0020	0.0088	0.0027	1946	0.040
1947	0.0020	0.0070	0.0019	0.0026	0.0103	0.0028	0.0020	0.0076	0.0026	0.0026	0.0110	0.0027	1947	0.054
1948	0.0020	0.0082	0.0021	0.0027	0.0097	0.0024	0.0024	0.0082	0.0025	0.0032	0.0121	0.0041	1948	0.060
1949	0.0026	0.0099	0.0027	0.0033	0.0115	0.0035	0.0028	0.0100	0.0026	0.0045	0.0162	0.0050	1949	0.075
1950	0.0024	0.0100	0.0029	0.0035	0.0116	0.0032	0.0034	0.0118	0.0033	0.0051	0.0179	0.0051	1950	0.087
1951	0.0025	0.0092	0.0028	0.0028	0.0107	0.0033	0.0024	0.0085	0.0021	0.0034	0.0122	0.0035	1951	0.069
1952	0.0025	0.0083	0.0026	0.0029	0.0111	0.0029	0.0020	0.0075	0.0020	0.0029	0.0106	0.0027	1952	0.059
1953	0.0023	0.0076	0.0023	0.0028	0.0110	0.0029	0.0021	0.0077	0.0021	0.0030	0.0114	0.0032	1953	0.054
1954	0.0024	0.0084	0.0023	0.0026	0.0088	0.0024	0.0017	0.0065	0.0020	0.0028	0.0101	0.0026	1954	0.062
1955	0.0017	0.0063	0.0019	0.0019	0.0068	0.0018	0.0015	0.0053	0.0016	0.0021	0.0078	0.0022	1955	0.045
1956	0.0018	0.0066	0.0018	0.0017	0.0064	0.0018	0.0015	0.0053	0.0015	0.0015	0.0059	0.0018	1956	0.038
1957	0.0017	0.0063	0.0018	0.0018	0.0068	0.0017	0.0017	0.0056	0.0018	0.0019	0.0071	0.0019	1957	0.038
1958	0.0017	0.0065	0.0020	0.0019	0.0062	0.0018	0.0018	0.0057	0.0017	0.0016	0.0060	0.0015	1958	0.043
1959	0.0014	0.0051	0.0014	0.0014	0.0050	0.0014	0.0014	0.0048	0.0013	0.0016	0.0054	0.0015	1959	0.033
1960	0.0015	0.0056	0.0016	0.0014	0.0057	0.0016	0.0014	0.0056	0.0014	0.0017	0.0062	0.0016	1960	0.032
1961	0.0014	0.0050	0.0014	0.0012	0.0047	0.0014	0.0014	0.0046	0.0013	0.0015	0.0054	0.0014	1961	0.034
1962	0.0013	0.0046	0.0013	0.0013	0.0049	0.0015	0.0016	0.0055	0.0017	0.0020	0.0071	0.0018	1962	0.029
1963	0.0014	0.0050	0.0016	0.0015	0.0050	0.0014	0.0013	0.0048	0.0014	0.0017	0.0059	0.0018	1963	0.0361
1964	0.0013	0.0048	0.0013	0.0014	0.0048	0.0014	0.0012	0.0044	0.0013	0.0015	0.0057	0.0017	1964	0.033
1965	0.0013	0.0046	0.0013	0.0014	0.0047	0.0014	0.0013	0.0047	0.0014	0.0016	0.0056	0.0016	1965	0.0321
1966	0.0013	0.0047	0.0013	0.0015	0.0049	0.0015	0.0014	0.0053	0.0017	0.0018	0.0064	0.0017	1966	0.0311
1967	0.0016	0.0052	0.0015	0.0014	0.0048	0.0015	0.0014	0.0047	0.0014	0.0014	0.0054	0.0015	1967	0.0364
1968	0.0013	0.0051	0.0016	0.0014	0.0049	0.0014	0.0013	0.0049	0.0014	0.0015	0.0051	0.0014	1968	0.031
1969	0.0013	0.0048	0.0014	0.0014	0.0048	0.0014	0.0014	0.0053	0.0015	0.0016	0.0056	0.0016	1969	0.0304
1970	0.0015	0.0059	0.0016	0.0016	0.0063	0.0018	0.0019	0.0064	0.0017	0.0017	0.0061	0.0016	1970	0.0341

* Compound annual return

Table A-2 (Continued)

Large Company Stocks: Income Returns

from January 1971 to December 2007

Year	Jan	Feb	Mar	Apr	May	Jun	Jul	Aug	Sep	Oct	Nov	Dec	Year	Jan–Dec*
1971	0.0014	0.0050	0.0014	0.0014	0.0048	0.0014	0.0014	0.0051	0.0014	0.0014	0.0052	0.0015	1971	0.0333
1972	0.0013	0.0046	0.0013	0.0013	0.0046	0.0013	0.0013	0.0047	0.0013	0.0014	0.0048	0.0013	1972	0.0309
1973	0.0012	0.0042	0.0013	0.0013	0.0050	0.0014	0.0014	0.0049	0.0014	0.0016	0.0056	0.0018	1973	0.0286
1974	0.0015	0.0055	0.0016	0.0017	0.0063	0.0018	0.0019	0.0074	0.0024	0.0027	0.0084	0.0024	1974	0.0369
1975	0.0023	0.0075	0.0020	0.0020	0.0068	0.0019	0.0018	0.0066	0.0018	0.0020	0.0066	0.0019	1975	0.0537
1976	0.0016	0.0056	0.0019	0.0011	0.0071	0.0018	0.0012	0.0065	0.0020	0.0017	0.0069	0.0015	1976	0.0438
1977	0.0016	0.0065	0.0021	0.0012	0.0086	0.0021	0.0011	0.0078	0.0025	0.0019	0.0100	0.0020	1977	0.0431
1978	0.0019	0.0086	0.0027	0.0016	0.0094	0.0023	0.0020	0.0081	0.0024	0.0025	0.0093	0.0023	1978	0.0533
1979	0.0024	0.0081	0.0024	0.0020	0.0095	0.0023	0.0022	0.0080	0.0025	0.0030	0.0088	0.0024	1979	0.0571
1980	0.0034	0.0075	0.0031	0.0018	0.0096	0.0026	0.0026	0.0073	0.0029	0.0026	0.0072	0.0024	1980	0.0573
1981	0.0019	0.0075	0.0020	0.0022	0.0079	0.0021	0.0032	0.0066	0.0036	0.0036	0.0075	0.0036	1981	0.0489
1982	0.0012	0.0093	0.0042	0.0014	0.0104	0.0029	0.0015	0.0107	0.0034	0.0022	0.0077	0.0021	1982	0.0550
1983	0.0017	0.0070	0.0034	0.0009	0.0071	0.0030	0.0017	0.0057	0.0034	0.0018	0.0059	0.0027	1983	0.0500
1984	0.0027	0.0061	0.0036	0.0014	0.0060	0.0046	0.0022	0.0062	0.0037	0.0027	0.0050	0.0029	1984	0.0456
1985	0.0027	0.0051	0.0047	0.0014	0.0074	0.0038	0.0022	0.0059	0.0026	0.0022	0.0065	0.0016	1985	0.0510
1986	0.0020	0.0046	0.0026	0.0017	0.0047	0.0025	0.0018	0.0036	0.0032	0.0009	0.0041	0.0019	1986	0.0374
1987	0.0025	0.0044	0.0008	0.0027	0.0043	0.0020	0.0016	0.0035	0.0022	0.0024	0.0034	0.0009	1987	0.0364
1988	0.0023	0.0052	0.0031	0.0014	0.0046	0.0031	0.0014	0.0055	0.0027	0.0013	0.0047	0.0034	1988	0.0417
1989	0.0012	0.0040	0.0028	0.0015	0.0051	0.0025	0.0014	0.0038	0.0026	0.0019	0.0043	0.0022	1989	0.0385
1990	0.0017	0.0044	0.0020	0.0022	0.0055	0.0019	0.0020	0.0040	0.0020	0.0030	0.0045	0.0026	1990	0.0336
1991	0.0027	0.0043	0.0016	0.0025	0.0042	0.0022	0.0019	0.0039	0.0027	0.0015	0.0035	0.0027	1991	0.0382
1992	0.0013	0.0032	0.0022	0.0012	0.0044	0.0028	0.0009	0.0038	0.0024	0.0015	0.0034	0.0030	1992	0.0303
1993	0.0003	0.0030	0.0028	0.0009	0.0043	0.0025	0.0006	0.0037	0.0026	0.0009	0.0035	0.0022	1993	0.0283
1994	0.0010	0.0030	0.0022	0.0015	0.0039	0.0021	0.0016	0.0031	0.0028	0.0020	0.0028	0.0023	1994	0.0282
1995	0.0017	0.0027	0.0023	0.0011	0.0032	0.0022	0.0015	0.0030	0.0018	0.0015	0.0030	0.0011	1995	0.0291
1996	0.0018	0.0027	0.0017	0.0013	0.0029	0.0018	0.0012	0.0024	0.0020	0.0013	0.0025	0.0019	1996	0.0254
1997	0.0008	0.0022	0.0010	0.0013	0.0028	0.0011	0.0013	0.0018	0.0016	0.0011	0.0017	0.0014	1997	0.0211
1998	0.0009	0.0017	0.0013	0.0010	0.0016	0.0012	0.0010	0.0012	0.0017	0.0010	0.0015	0.0012	1998	0.0168
1999	0.0008	0.0012	0.0012	0.0008	0.0014	0.0011	0.0008	0.0013	0.0011	0.0007	0.0013	0.0011	1999	0.0136
2000	0.0007	0.0012	0.0011	0.0007	0.0014	0.0007	0.0007	0.0014	0.0007	0.0007	0.0012	0.0008	2000	0.0110
2001	0.0008	0.0011	0.0009	0.0009	0.0016	0.0007	0.0009	0.0015	0.0010	0.0010	0.0015	0.0012	2001	0.0118
2002	0.0010	0.0015	0.0009	0.0008	0.0017	0.0012	0.0011	0.0017	0.0013	0.0016	0.0018	0.0015	2002	0.0139
2003	0.0012	0.0020	0.0013	0.0014	0.0018	0.0015	0.0014	0.0016	0.0013	0.0016	0.0017	0.0017	2003	0.0200
2004	0.0011	0.0017	0.0013	0.0011	0.0016	0.0014	0.0012	0.0017	0.0014	0.0013	0.0019	0.0015	2004	0.0175
2005	0.0009	0.0021	0.0014	0.0011	0.0019	0.0016	0.0012	0.0021	0.0012	0.0011	0.0026	0.0013	2005	0.0184
2006	0.0010	0.0023	0.0014	0.0012	0.0021	0.0013	0.0011	0.0025	0.0012	0.0011	0.0025	0.0014	2006	0.0201
2007	0.0011	0.0023	0.0012	0.0010	0.0023	0.0012	0.0010	0.0021	0.0016	0.0011	0.0022	0.0017	2007	0.0196

Compound annual return

Table A-3
Large Company Stocks: Capital Appreciation Returns

from January 1926 to December 1970

Year	Jan	Feb	Mar	Apr	May	Jun	Jul	Aug	Sep	Oct	Nov	Dec	Year	Jan–Dec*
1926	–0.0016	–0.0440	–0.0591	0.0227	0.0077	0.0432	0.0455	0.0171	0.0229	–0.0313	0.0223	0.0166	1926	0.0572
1927	–0.0208	0.0477	0.0065	0.0172	0.0522	–0.0094	0.0650	0.0445	0.0432	–0.0531	0.0616	0.0250	1927	0.3091
1928	–0.0051	–0.0176	0.1083	0.0324	0.0127	–0.0405	0.0125	0.0741	0.0240	0.0145	0.1199	0.0029	1928	0.3788
1929	0.0571	–0.0058	–0.0023	0.0161	–0.0428	0.1124	0.0456	0.0980	–0.0489	–0.1993	–0.1337	0.0253	1929	–0.1191
1930	0.0625	0.0215	0.0799	–0.0095	–0.0165	–0.1646	0.0367	0.0075	–0.1301	–0.0888	–0.0218	–0.0742	1930	–0.2848
1931	0.0489	0.1144	–0.0692	–0.0959	–0.1372	0.1390	–0.0742	0.0095	–0.2994	0.0844	–0.0978	–0.1453	1931	–0.4707
1932	–0.0283	0.0507	–0.1182	–0.2025	–0.2333	–0.0089	0.3770	0.3754	–0.0369	–0.1386	–0.0589	0.0519	1932	–0.1515
1933	0.0073	–0.1844	0.0336	0.4222	0.1587	0.1317	–0.0880	0.1146	–0.1136	–0.0885	0.1027	0.0223	1933	0.4659
1934	0.1059	–0.0367	–0.0009	–0.0270	–0.0813	0.0208	–0.1152	0.0541	–0.0055	–0.0319	0.0829	–0.0042	1934	–0.0594
1935	–0.0421	–0.0396	–0.0309	0.0956	0.0323	0.0679	0.0831	0.0217	0.0239	0.0751	0.0393	0.0371	1935	0.4137
1936	0.0655	0.0168	0.0254	–0.0771	0.0458	0.0306	0.0681	0.0088	0.0013	0.0750	0.0041	–0.0058	1936	0.2792
1937	0.0378	0.0146	–0.0094	–0.0831	–0.0103	–0.0529	0.1026	–0.0554	–0.1421	–0.1017	–0.1011	–0.0504	1937	–0.3859
1938	0.0133	0.0608	–0.2504	0.1412	–0.0443	0.2470	0.0727	–0.0274	0.0149	0.0760	–0.0334	0.0377	1938	0.2521
1939	–0.0689	0.0325	–0.1354	–0.0055	0.0623	–0.0638	0.1087	–0.0714	0.1646	–0.0146	–0.0491	0.0238	1939	–0.0545
1940	–0.0352	0.0066	0.0099	–0.0049	–0.2395	0.0766	0.0311	0.0262	0.0095	0.0394	–0.0424	–0.0028	1940	–0.1529
1941	–0.0482	–0.0149	0.0040	–0.0653	0.0043	0.0535	0.0548	–0.0087	–0.0097	–0.0686	–0.0421	–0.0451	1941	–0.1786
1942	0.0138	–0.0250	–0.0675	–0.0437	0.0640	0.0184	0.0313	0.0070	0.0267	0.0644	–0.0138	0.0517	1942	0.1243
1943	0.0716	0.0506	0.0527	0.0009	0.0449	0.0198	–0.0543	0.0103	0.0237	–0.0132	–0.0755	0.0590	1943	0.1945
1944	0.0154	–0.0025	0.0169	–0.0125	0.0404	0.0510	–0.0208	0.0087	–0.0031	0.0000	0.0039	0.0351	1944	0.1380
1945	0.0143	0.0616	–0.0462	0.0880	0.0115	–0.0033	–0.0201	0.0580	0.0419	0.0303	0.0324	0.0099	1945	0.3072
1946	0.0697	–0.0695	0.0463	0.0376	0.0224	–0.0391	–0.0255	–0.0729	–0.1015	–0.0080	–0.0115	0.0429	1946	–0.1187
1947	0.0235	–0.0147	–0.0169	–0.0389	–0.0089	0.0526	0.0362	–0.0279	–0.0137	0.0212	–0.0285	0.0207	1947	0.0000
1948	–0.0399	–0.0470	0.0771	0.0265	0.0782	0.0030	–0.0532	0.0076	–0.0301	0.0678	–0.1082	0.0305	1948	–0.0065
1949	0.0013	–0.0394	0.0301	–0.0212	–0.0373	–0.0021	0.0621	0.0120	0.0237	0.0295	0.0012	0.0436	1949	0.1026
1950	0.0173	0.0100	0.0041	0.0451	0.0393	–0.0580	0.0085	0.0325	0.0559	0.0041	–0.0010	0.0461	1950	0.2178
1951	0.0612	0.0065	–0.0183	0.0481	–0.0406	–0.0260	0.0687	0.0393	–0.0009	–0.0138	–0.0026	0.0389	1951	0.1646
1952	0.0156	–0.0365	0.0477	–0.0431	0.0232	0.0461	0.0176	–0.0146	–0.0196	–0.0008	0.0465	0.0355	1952	0.1178
1953	–0.0072	–0.0182	–0.0236	–0.0265	–0.0032	–0.0163	0.0253	–0.0578	0.0013	0.0510	0.0090	0.0020	1953	–0.0662
1954	0.0512	0.0027	0.0302	0.0490	0.0329	0.0007	0.0572	–0.0340	0.0831	–0.0195	0.0808	0.0508	1954	0.4502
1955	0.0181	0.0035	–0.0049	0.0377	–0.0013	0.0823	0.0607	–0.0078	0.0113	–0.0305	0.0749	–0.0007	1955	0.2640
1956	–0.0365	0.0347	0.0693	–0.0021	–0.0657	0.0392	0.0515	–0.0381	–0.0455	0.0051	–0.0110	0.0353	1956	0.0262
1957	–0.0418	–0.0326	0.0196	0.0370	0.0369	–0.0013	0.0114	–0.0561	–0.0619	–0.0321	0.0161	–0.0415	1957	–0.1431
1958	0.0428	–0.0206	0.0309	0.0318	0.0150	0.0261	0.0431	0.0119	0.0484	0.0254	0.0224	0.0520	1958	0.3806
1959	0.0038	–0.0002	0.0005	0.0388	0.0189	–0.0036	0.0349	–0.0150	–0.0456	0.0113	0.0132	0.0276	1959	0.0848
1960	–0.0715	0.0092	–0.0139	–0.0175	0.0269	0.0195	–0.0248	0.0261	–0.0604	–0.0024	0.0403	0.0463	1960	–0.0297
1961	0.0632	0.0269	0.0255	0.0038	0.0191	–0.0288	0.0328	0.0196	–0.0197	0.0283	0.0393	0.0032	1961	0.2313
1962	–0.0379	0.0163	–0.0059	–0.0620	–0.0860	–0.0818	0.0636	0.0153	–0.0482	0.0044	0.1016	0.0135	1962	–0.1181
1963	0.0491	–0.0289	0.0355	0.0485	0.0143	–0.0202	–0.0035	0.0487	–0.0110	0.0322	–0.0105	0.0244	1963	0.1889
1964	0.0269	0.0099	0.0152	0.0061	0.0115	0.0164	0.0182	–0.0162	0.0287	0.0081	–0.0052	0.0039	1964	0.1297
1965	0.0332	–0.0015	–0.0145	0.0342	–0.0077	–0.0486	0.0134	0.0225	0.0320	0.0273	–0.0088	0.0090	1965	0.0906
1966	0.0049	–0.0179	–0.0218	0.0205	–0.0541	–0.0161	–0.0135	–0.0778	–0.0070	0.0475	0.0031	–0.0015	1966	–0.1309
1967	0.0782	0.0020	0.0394	0.0422	–0.0524	0.0175	0.0453	–0.0117	0.0328	–0.0291	0.0011	0.0263	1967	0.2009
1968	–0.0438	–0.0312	0.0094	0.0819	0.0112	0.0091	–0.0185	0.0115	0.0385	0.0072	0.0480	–0.0416	1968	0.0766
1969	–0.0082	–0.0474	0.0344	0.0215	–0.0022	–0.0556	–0.0602	0.0401	–0.0250	0.0442	–0.0353	–0.0193	1969	–0.1142
1970	–0.0759	0.0527	0.0015	–0.0905	–0.0610	–0.0500	0.0733	0.0445	0.0330	–0.0114	0.0474	0.0568	1970	0.0016

* Compound annual return

Table A-3 (Continued)

Large Company Stocks: Capital Appreciation Returns

from January 1971 to December 2007

Year	Jan	Feb	Mar	Apr	May	Jun	Jul	Aug	Sep	Oct	Nov	Dec	Year	Jan–Dec*
1971	0.0405	0.0091	0.0368	0.0363	−0.0416	0.0007	−0.0413	0.0361	−0.0070	−0.0418	−0.0025	0.0862	1971	0.1079
1972	0.0181	0.0253	0.0059	0.0044	0.0173	−0.0218	0.0023	0.0345	−0.0049	0.0093	0.0456	0.0118	1972	0.1563
1973	−0.0171	−0.0375	−0.0014	−0.0408	−0.0189	−0.0066	0.0380	−0.0367	0.0401	−0.0013	−0.1139	0.0166	1973	−0.1737
1974	−0.0100	−0.0036	−0.0233	−0.0391	−0.0336	−0.0147	−0.0778	−0.0903	−0.1193	0.1630	−0.0532	−0.0202	1974	−0.2972
1975	0.1228	0.0599	0.0217	0.0473	0.0441	0.0443	−0.0677	−0.0211	−0.0346	0.0616	0.0247	−0.0115	1975	0.3155
1976	0.1183	−0.0114	0.0307	−0.0110	−0.0144	0.0409	−0.0081	−0.0051	0.0226	−0.0222	−0.0078	0.0525	1976	0.1915
1977	−0.0505	−0.0217	−0.0140	0.0002	−0.0236	0.0454	−0.0162	−0.0210	−0.0025	−0.0434	0.0270	0.0028	1977	−0.1150
1978	−0.0615	−0.0248	0.0249	0.0854	0.0042	−0.0176	0.0539	0.0259	−0.0073	−0.0916	0.0166	0.0149	1978	0.0106
1979	0.0397	−0.0365	0.0551	0.0017	−0.0263	0.0387	0.0088	0.0531	0.0000	−0.0686	0.0426	0.0168	1979	0.1231
1980	0.0576	−0.0044	−0.1018	0.0411	0.0466	0.0270	0.0650	0.0058	0.0252	0.0160	0.1023	−0.0339	1980	0.2577
1981	−0.0457	0.0133	0.0360	−0.0235	−0.0017	−0.0101	−0.0025	−0.0620	−0.0538	0.0492	0.0366	−0.0301	1981	−0.0972
1982	−0.0175	−0.0605	−0.0102	0.0400	−0.0392	−0.0203	−0.0230	0.1160	0.0076	0.1104	0.0361	0.0152	1982	0.1476
1983	0.0331	0.0190	0.0331	0.0749	−0.0123	0.0352	−0.0330	0.0113	0.0102	−0.0152	0.0174	−0.0088	1983	0.1727
1984	−0.0092	−0.0389	0.0135	0.0055	−0.0594	0.0175	−0.0165	0.1063	−0.0035	−0.0001	−0.0151	0.0224	1984	0.0139
1985	0.0741	0.0086	−0.0029	−0.0046	0.0541	0.0121	−0.0048	−0.0120	−0.0347	0.0425	0.0651	0.0451	1985	0.2634
1986	0.0024	0.0715	0.0528	−0.0141	0.0502	0.0141	−0.0587	0.0712	−0.0854	0.0547	0.0215	−0.0283	1986	0.1463
1987	0.1318	0.0369	0.0264	−0.0115	0.0060	0.0479	0.0482	0.0350	−0.0242	−0.2176	−0.0853	0.0729	1987	0.0203
1988	0.0404	0.0418	−0.0333	0.0094	0.0032	0.0433	−0.0054	−0.0386	0.0397	0.0260	−0.0189	0.0147	1988	0.1241
1989	0.0711	−0.0289	0.0208	0.0501	0.0351	−0.0079	0.0884	0.0155	−0.0065	−0.0252	0.0165	0.0214	1989	0.2726
1990	−0.0688	0.0085	0.0243	−0.0269	0.0920	−0.0089	−0.0052	−0.0943	−0.0512	−0.0067	0.0599	0.0248	1990	−0.0656
1991	0.0415	0.0673	0.0222	0.0003	0.0386	−0.0479	0.0449	0.0196	−0.0191	0.0119	−0.0439	0.1116	1991	0.2631
1992	−0.0199	0.0096	−0.0218	0.0279	0.0010	−0.0174	0.0394	−0.0240	0.0091	0.0021	0.0303	0.0101	1992	0.0446
1993	0.0070	0.0105	0.0187	−0.0254	0.0227	0.0008	−0.0053	0.0344	−0.0100	0.0194	−0.0129	0.0101	1993	0.0706
1994	0.0325	−0.0300	−0.0457	0.0115	0.0124	−0.0268	0.0315	0.0376	−0.0269	0.0209	−0.0395	0.0123	1994	−0.0154
1995	0.0243	0.0361	0.0273	0.0280	0.0363	0.0213	0.0318	−0.0003	0.0401	−0.0050	0.0410	0.0174	1995	0.3411
1996	0.0326	0.0069	0.0079	0.0134	0.0229	0.0023	−0.0457	0.0188	0.0542	0.0261	0.0734	−0.0215	1996	0.2026
1997	0.0613	0.0059	−0.0426	0.0584	0.0586	0.0435	0.0781	−0.0574	0.0532	−0.0345	0.0446	0.0157	1997	0.3101
1998	0.0102	0.0704	0.0499	0.0091	−0.0188	0.0394	−0.0116	−0.1458	0.0624	0.0803	0.0591	0.0564	1998	0.2667
1999	0.0410	−0.0323	0.0388	0.0379	−0.0250	0.0544	−0.0320	−0.0063	−0.0286	0.0625	0.0191	0.0578	1999	0.1953
2000	−0.0509	−0.0201	0.0967	−0.0308	−0.0219	0.0239	−0.0163	0.0607	−0.0535	−0.0049	−0.0801	0.0041	2000	−0.1014
2001	0.0346	−0.0923	−0.0642	0.0768	0.0051	−0.0250	−0.0108	−0.0641	−0.0817	0.0181	0.0752	0.0076	2001	−0.1304
2002	−0.0156	−0.0208	0.0367	−0.0614	−0.0091	−0.0725	−0.0790	0.0049	−0.1100	0.0865	0.0571	−0.0603	2002	−0.2337
2003	−0.0274	−0.0170	0.0084	0.0810	0.0509	0.0113	0.0162	0.0179	−0.0119	0.0550	0.0071	0.0508	2003	0.2638
2004	0.0173	0.0122	−0.0164	−0.0168	0.0121	0.0180	−0.0343	0.0023	0.0094	0.0140	0.0386	0.0325	2004	0.0899
2005	−0.0253	0.0189	−0.0191	−0.0201	0.0300	−0.0001	0.0360	−0.0112	0.0069	−0.0177	0.0352	−0.0010	2005	0.0300
2006	0.0255	0.0005	0.0111	0.0122	−0.0309	0.0001	0.0051	0.0213	0.0246	0.0315	0.0165	0.0126	2006	0.1362
2007	0.0141	−0.0218	0.0100	0.0433	0.0325	−0.0178	−0.0320	0.0129	0.0358	0.0148	−0.0440	−0.0086	2007	0.0353

* Compound annual return

Table A-4
Small Company Stocks: Total Returns

from January 1926 to December 1970

Year	Jan	Feb	Mar	Apr	May	Jun	Jul	Aug	Sep	Oct	Nov	Dec	Jan–Dec*
1926	0.0699	–0.0639	–0.1073	0.0179	–0.0066	0.0378	0.0112	0.0256	–0.0001	–0.0227	0.0207	0.0332	0.0028
1927	0.0296	0.0547	–0.0548	0.0573	0.0734	–0.0303	0.0516	–0.0178	0.0047	–0.0659	0.0808	0.0316	0.2210
1928	0.0482	–0.0236	0.0531	0.0910	0.0438	–0.0842	0.0059	0.0442	0.0890	0.0276	0.1147	–0.0513	0.3969
1929	0.0035	–0.0026	–0.0200	0.0306	–0.1336	0.0533	0.0114	–0.0164	–0.0922	–0.2768	–0.1500	–0.0501	–0.5136
1930	0.1293	0.0643	0.1007	–0.0698	–0.0542	–0.2168	0.0301	–0.0166	–0.1459	–0.1097	–0.0028	–0.1166	–0.3815
1931	0.2103	0.2566	–0.0708	–0.2164	–0.1379	0.1819	–0.0557	–0.0763	–0.3246	0.0770	–0.1008	–0.2195	–0.4975
1932	0.1019	0.0291	–0.1311	–0.2220	–0.1193	0.0033	0.3523	0.7346	–0.1320	–0.1775	–0.1227	–0.0492	–0.0539
1933	–0.0083	–0.1278	0.1118	0.5038	0.6339	0.2617	–0.0550	0.0924	–0.1595	–0.1236	0.0654	0.0055	1.4287
1934	0.3891	0.0166	–0.0012	0.0240	–0.1275	–0.0024	–0.2259	0.1546	–0.0167	0.0097	0.0948	0.0172	0.2422
1935	–0.0328	–0.0592	–0.1189	0.0791	–0.0024	0.0305	0.0855	0.0545	0.0357	0.0994	0.1412	0.0598	0.4019
1936	0.3009	0.0602	0.0066	–0.1795	0.0272	–0.0231	0.0873	0.0210	0.0542	0.0635	0.1400	0.0160	0.6480
1937	0.1267	0.0658	0.0120	–0.1679	–0.0408	–0.1183	0.1235	–0.0736	–0.2539	–0.1093	–0.1453	–0.1694	–0.5801
1938	0.0534	0.0343	–0.3600	0.2776	–0.0849	0.3498	0.1499	–0.1001	–0.0157	0.2136	–0.0689	0.0487	0.3280
1939	–0.0848	0.0107	–0.2466	0.0142	0.1088	–0.1042	0.2535	–0.1590	0.5145	–0.0397	–0.1053	0.0422	0.0035
1940	0.0009	0.0821	0.0632	0.0654	–0.3674	0.1051	0.0231	0.0255	0.0213	0.0545	0.0245	–0.0447	–0.0516
1941	0.0025	–0.0288	0.0319	–0.0669	0.0044	0.0753	0.2165	–0.0060	–0.0469	–0.0672	–0.0495	–0.1204	–0.0900
1942	0.1894	–0.0073	–0.0709	–0.0353	–0.0032	0.0336	0.0737	0.0325	0.0912	0.1087	–0.0511	0.0413	0.4451
1943	0.2132	0.1931	0.1445	0.0933	0.1156	–0.0083	–0.1083	–0.0002	0.0428	0.0123	–0.1113	0.1241	0.8837
1944	0.0641	0.0295	0.0749	–0.0532	0.0740	0.1384	–0.0299	0.0318	–0.0020	–0.0108	0.0499	0.0869	0.5372
1945	0.0482	0.1009	–0.0861	0.1157	0.0500	0.0855	–0.0556	0.0557	0.0679	0.0701	0.1172	0.0171	0.7361
1946	0.1562	–0.0637	0.0273	0.0696	0.0591	–0.0462	–0.0530	–0.0849	–0.1603	–0.0118	–0.0141	0.0373	–0.1163
1947	0.0421	–0.0041	–0.0336	–0.1031	–0.0534	0.0552	0.0789	–0.0037	0.0115	0.0282	–0.0303	0.0359	0.0092
1948	–0.0154	–0.0783	0.0986	0.0368	0.1059	0.0048	–0.0578	0.0006	–0.0526	0.0647	–0.1116	0.0088	–0.0211
1949	0.0182	–0.0481	0.0629	–0.0336	–0.0564	–0.0096	0.0671	0.0256	0.0489	0.0472	0.0016	0.0690	0.1975
1950	0.0492	0.0221	–0.0037	0.0411	0.0255	–0.0777	0.0591	0.0530	0.0521	–0.0059	0.0322	0.0953	0.3875
1951	0.0830	0.0061	–0.0477	0.0367	–0.0331	–0.0529	0.0373	0.0605	0.0215	–0.0222	–0.0083	0.0044	0.0780
1952	0.0191	–0.0300	0.0175	–0.0519	0.0032	0.0272	0.0112	–0.0006	–0.0161	–0.0103	0.0485	0.0160	0.0303
1953	0.0409	0.0269	–0.0067	–0.0287	0.0141	–0.0486	0.0152	–0.0628	–0.0262	0.0292	0.0126	–0.0266	–0.0649
1954	0.0756	0.0094	0.0183	0.0140	0.0451	0.0086	0.0808	0.0014	0.0410	0.0068	0.0779	0.1112	0.6058
1955	0.0201	0.0479	0.0085	0.0150	0.0078	0.0293	0.0064	–0.0028	0.0109	–0.0170	0.0468	0.0163	0.2044
1956	–0.0047	0.0278	0.0431	0.0047	–0.0398	0.0056	0.0283	–0.0134	–0.0260	0.0104	0.0053	0.0038	0.0428
1957	0.0236	–0.0200	0.0167	0.0248	0.0075	0.0073	–0.0060	–0.0386	–0.0452	–0.0832	0.0113	–0.0481	–0.1457
1958	0.1105	–0.0170	0.0471	0.0376	0.0387	0.0324	0.0492	0.0428	0.0518	0.0407	0.0496	0.0313	0.6489
1959	0.0575	0.0295	0.0027	0.0117	0.0014	–0.0042	0.0327	–0.0088	–0.0431	0.0227	0.0222	0.0322	0.1640
1960	–0.0306	0.0050	–0.0315	–0.0187	0.0204	0.0340	–0.0189	0.0525	–0.0738	–0.0401	0.0437	0.0332	–0.0329
1961	0.0915	0.0589	0.0619	0.0127	0.0427	–0.0543	0.0031	0.0130	–0.0339	0.0262	0.0613	0.0079	0.3209
1962	0.0136	0.0187	0.0057	–0.0777	–0.1009	–0.0785	0.0763	0.0289	–0.0659	–0.0373	0.1248	–0.0089	–0.1190
1963	0.0906	0.0034	0.0149	0.0312	0.0436	–0.0118	0.0033	0.0517	–0.0163	0.0236	–0.0106	–0.0048	0.2357
1964	0.0274	0.0365	0.0219	0.0093	0.0157	0.0163	0.0398	–0.0029	0.0402	0.0205	0.0011	–0.0112	0.2352
1965	0.0529	0.0390	0.0238	0.0509	–0.0078	–0.0901	0.0449	0.0595	0.0347	0.0572	0.0371	0.0622	0.4175
1966	0.0756	0.0311	–0.0192	0.0343	–0.0961	–0.0012	–0.0012	–0.1080	–0.0164	–0.0107	0.0491	0.0065	–0.0701
1967	0.1838	0.0450	0.0615	0.0271	–0.0085	0.1017	0.0951	0.0020	0.0565	–0.0311	0.0117	0.0965	0.8357
1968	0.0154	–0.0709	–0.0109	0.1461	0.0999	0.0030	–0.0345	0.0367	0.0599	0.0030	0.0764	0.0062	0.3597
1969	–0.0166	–0.0990	0.0396	0.0395	0.0173	–0.1165	–0.1070	0.0732	–0.0261	0.0610	–0.0557	–0.0687	–0.2505
1970	–0.0608	0.0387	–0.0285	–0.1728	–0.1031	–0.0929	0.0554	0.0949	0.1086	–0.0706	0.0137	0.0726	–0.1743

* Compound annual return

Table A-4 (Continued)

Small Company Stocks: Total Returns

from January 1971 to December 2007

Year	Jan	Feb	Mar	Apr	May	Jun	Jul	Aug	Sep	Oct	Nov	Dec	Year	Jan–Dec*
1971	0.1592	0.0317	0.0564	0.0247	−0.0605	−0.0319	−0.0563	0.0583	−0.0226	−0.0551	−0.0373	0.1144	1971	0.1650
1972	0.1130	0.0296	−0.0143	0.0129	−0.0191	−0.0305	−0.0413	0.0186	−0.0349	−0.0175	0.0592	−0.0214	1972	0.0443
1973	−0.0432	−0.0799	−0.0208	−0.0621	−0.0811	−0.0290	0.1194	−0.0445	0.1064	0.0084	−0.1962	−0.0014	1973	−0.3090
1974	0.1326	−0.0085	−0.0074	−0.0464	−0.0793	−0.0147	−0.0219	−0.0681	−0.0653	0.1063	−0.0438	−0.0788	1974	−0.1995
1975	0.2767	0.0285	0.0618	0.0531	0.0663	0.0750	−0.0254	−0.0574	−0.0182	−0.0050	0.0320	−0.0197	1975	0.5282
1976	0.2684	0.1390	−0.0015	−0.0359	−0.0361	0.0459	0.0045	−0.0290	0.0104	−0.0209	0.0404	0.1180	1976	0.5738
1977	0.0450	−0.0039	0.0131	0.0228	−0.0028	0.0772	0.0030	−0.0107	0.0092	−0.0330	0.1086	0.0081	1977	0.2538
1978	−0.0189	0.0347	0.1032	0.0788	0.0820	−0.0189	0.0684	0.0939	−0.0032	−0.2427	0.0732	0.0168	1978	0.2346
1979	0.1321	−0.0282	0.1120	0.0387	0.0035	0.0472	0.0171	0.0756	−0.0344	−0.1154	0.0858	0.0588	1979	0.4346
1980	0.0836	−0.0284	−0.1778	0.0694	0.0750	0.0452	0.1323	0.0604	0.0418	0.0333	0.0766	−0.0338	1980	0.3988
1981	0.0207	0.0094	0.0943	0.0657	0.0422	0.0076	−0.0316	−0.0684	−0.0733	0.0742	0.0276	−0.0220	1981	0.1388
1982	−0.0196	−0.0296	−0.0086	0.0383	−0.0248	−0.0159	−0.0015	0.0698	0.0327	0.1305	0.0779	0.0132	1982	0.2801
1983	0.0628	0.0712	0.0525	0.0767	0.0870	0.0348	−0.0088	−0.0197	0.0133	−0.0568	0.0516	−0.0145	1983	0.3967
1984	−0.0008	−0.0645	0.0174	−0.0085	−0.0521	0.0300	−0.0420	0.0998	0.0027	−0.0217	−0.0336	0.0150	1984	−0.0667
1985	0.1059	0.0272	−0.0214	−0.0174	0.0276	0.0106	0.0260	−0.0072	−0.0544	0.0261	0.0620	0.0470	1985	0.2466
1986	0.0112	0.0719	0.0477	0.0064	0.0360	0.0026	−0.0710	0.0218	−0.0559	0.0346	−0.0031	−0.0262	1986	0.0685
1987	0.0943	0.0809	0.0233	−0.0313	−0.0039	0.0266	0.0364	0.0287	−0.0081	−0.2919	−0.0397	0.0520	1987	−0.0930
1988	0.0556	0.0760	0.0408	0.0209	−0.0179	0.0612	−0.0025	−0.0246	0.0227	−0.0123	−0.0437	0.0394	1988	0.2287
1989	0.0404	0.0083	0.0358	0.0279	0.0362	−0.0201	0.0407	0.0122	0.0000	−0.0604	−0.0051	−0.0134	1989	0.1018
1990	−0.0764	0.0187	0.0368	−0.0266	0.0561	0.0144	−0.0382	−0.1296	−0.0829	−0.0572	0.0450	0.0194	1990	−0.2156
1991	0.0841	0.1113	0.0680	0.0034	0.0334	−0.0485	0.0407	0.0261	0.0032	0.0317	−0.0276	0.0601	1991	0.4463
1992	0.1128	0.0452	−0.0249	−0.0403	−0.0014	−0.0519	0.0370	−0.0228	0.0131	0.0259	0.0885	0.0441	1992	0.2335
1993	0.0543	−0.0180	0.0289	−0.0306	0.0342	−0.0038	0.0166	0.0339	0.0316	0.0471	−0.0175	0.0194	1993	0.2098
1994	0.0618	−0.0023	−0.0446	0.0060	−0.0012	−0.0262	0.0184	0.0337	0.0105	0.0115	−0.0326	0.0002	1994	0.0311
1995	0.0283	0.0252	0.0145	0.0352	0.0298	0.0568	0.0645	0.0358	0.0195	−0.0487	0.0192	0.0239	1995	0.3446
1996	0.0028	0.0369	0.0228	0.0848	0.0749	−0.0582	−0.0943	0.0476	0.0291	−0.0175	0.0288	0.0204	1996	0.1762
1997	0.0420	−0.0206	−0.0490	−0.0276	0.1022	0.0498	0.0605	0.0509	0.0844	−0.0386	−0.0155	−0.0171	1997	0.2278
1998	−0.0059	0.0649	0.0481	0.0168	−0.0497	−0.0206	−0.0671	−0.2010	0.0369	0.0356	0.0758	0.0252	1998	−0.0731
1999	0.0279	−0.0687	−0.0379	0.0949	0.0387	0.0568	0.0092	−0.0191	−0.0221	−0.0087	0.0971	0.1137	1999	0.2979
2000	0.0595	0.2358	−0.0751	−0.1251	−0.0808	0.1368	−0.0322	0.0925	−0.0217	−0.0706	−0.1110	0.0189	2000	−0.0359
2001	0.1380	−0.0702	−0.0480	0.0731	0.0960	0.0359	−0.0254	−0.0295	−0.1278	0.0645	0.0674	0.0672	2001	0.2277
2002	0.0110	−0.0277	0.0884	0.0243	−0.0273	−0.0356	−0.1448	−0.0057	−0.0674	0.0257	0.0836	−0.0429	2002	−0.1328
2003	−0.0223	−0.0288	0.0111	0.0928	0.1162	0.0440	0.0738	0.0473	0.0009	0.0894	0.0430	0.0277	2003	0.6070
2004	0.0578	0.0050	0.0014	−0.0409	0.0000	0.0441	−0.0747	−0.0152	0.0501	0.0184	0.0897	0.0458	2004	0.1839
2005	−0.0410	0.0083	−0.0323	−0.0622	0.0603	0.0452	0.0763	−0.0139	0.0061	−0.0281	0.0453	0.0018	2005	0.0569
2006	0.0914	0.0025	0.0455	−0.0041	−0.0589	−0.0089	−0.0345	0.0278	0.0056	0.0545	0.0225	0.0161	2006	0.1617
2007	0.0115	−0.0050	0.0102	0.0150	0.0315	−0.0033	−0.0651	0.0116	0.0148	0.0170	−0.0842	−0.0006	2007	−0.0522

* Compound annual return

Table A-5

Long-Term Corporate Bonds: Total Returns

from January 1926 to December 1970

Year	Jan	Feb	Mar	Apr	May	Jun	Jul	Aug	Sep	Oct	Nov	Dec	Year	Jan–Dec*
1926	0.0072	0.0045	0.0084	0.0097	0.0044	0.0004	0.0057	0.0044	0.0057	0.0097	0.0057	0.0056	1926	0.0737
1927	0.0056	0.0069	0.0083	0.0055	–0.0011	0.0043	0.0003	0.0083	0.0149	0.0055	0.0068	0.0068	1927	0.0744
1928	0.0027	0.0068	0.0041	0.0014	–0.0078	–0.0024	–0.0010	0.0083	0.0030	0.0083	–0.0036	0.0084	1928	0.0284
1929	0.0043	0.0030	–0.0087	0.0019	0.0045	–0.0046	0.0020	0.0020	0.0034	0.0073	–0.0018	0.0192	1929	0.0327
1930	0.0059	0.0072	0.0138	0.0084	0.0057	0.0110	0.0056	0.0136	0.0108	0.0054	–0.0012	–0.0090	1930	0.0798
1931	0.0203	0.0068	0.0094	0.0067	0.0134	0.0052	0.0052	0.0012	–0.0014	–0.0363	–0.0189	–0.0286	1931	–0.0185
1932	–0.0052	–0.0238	0.0356	–0.0176	0.0107	–0.0009	0.0043	0.0436	0.0301	0.0074	0.0073	0.0139	1932	0.1082
1933	0.0547	–0.0523	0.0047	–0.0095	0.0588	0.0190	0.0161	0.0093	–0.0014	0.0040	–0.0248	0.0257	1933	0.1038
1934	0.0257	0.0146	0.0187	0.0104	0.0090	0.0158	0.0047	0.0047	–0.0061	0.0102	0.0129	0.0101	1934	0.1384
1935	0.0211	0.0141	0.0043	0.0112	0.0042	0.0112	0.0111	–0.0042	0.0000	0.0042	0.0069	0.0083	1935	0.0961
1936	0.0082	0.0054	0.0082	0.0026	0.0040	0.0082	0.0011	0.0067	0.0067	0.0025	0.0109	0.0010	1936	0.0674
1937	0.0024	–0.0046	–0.0114	0.0068	0.0040	0.0053	0.0039	–0.0017	0.0025	0.0067	0.0067	0.0067	1937	0.0275
1938	0.0038	0.0010	–0.0087	0.0138	0.0010	0.0095	0.0066	–0.0019	0.0109	0.0080	0.0037	0.0122	1938	0.0613
1939	0.0022	0.0064	0.0022	0.0064	0.0049	0.0035	–0.0007	–0.0392	0.0151	0.0237	0.0079	0.0078	1939	0.0397
1940	0.0049	0.0021	0.0049	–0.0092	–0.0021	0.0121	0.0021	0.0007	0.0092	0.0049	0.0063	–0.0023	1940	0.0339
1941	0.0006	0.0006	–0.0022	0.0078	0.0049	0.0063	0.0063	0.0034	0.0048	0.0034	–0.0094	0.0006	1941	0.0273
1942	0.0006	–0.0008	0.0063	0.0006	0.0020	0.0034	0.0020	0.0035	0.0020	0.0006	0.0006	0.0049	1942	0.0260
1943	0.0049	0.0006	0.0020	0.0049	0.0048	0.0048	0.0019	0.0019	0.0005	–0.0009	–0.0023	0.0049	1943	0.0283
1944	0.0020	0.0034	0.0048	0.0034	0.0005	0.0020	0.0034	0.0034	0.0019	0.0019	0.0048	0.0149	1944	0.0473
1945	0.0076	0.0046	0.0018	0.0018	–0.0011	0.0032	–0.0011	0.0004	0.0032	0.0032	0.0032	0.0133	1945	0.0408
1946	0.0128	0.0034	0.0034	–0.0043	0.0019	0.0019	–0.0012	–0.0088	–0.0026	0.0020	–0.0025	0.0113	1946	0.0172
1947	0.0005	0.0005	0.0067	0.0020	0.0020	0.0004	0.0020	–0.0071	–0.0131	–0.0099	–0.0098	0.0024	1947	–0.0234
1948	0.0024	0.0039	0.0115	0.0038	0.0008	–0.0083	–0.0052	0.0055	0.0024	0.0024	0.0085	0.0131	1948	0.0414
1949	0.0038	0.0038	0.0007	0.0023	0.0038	0.0084	0.0099	0.0037	0.0021	0.0067	0.0021	–0.0145	1949	0.0331
1950	0.0037	0.0007	0.0022	–0.0008	–0.0008	0.0023	0.0069	0.0038	–0.0039	–0.0008	0.0054	0.0023	1950	0.0212
1951	0.0019	–0.0044	–0.0237	–0.0009	–0.0015	–0.0093	0.0205	0.0114	–0.0057	–0.0145	–0.0061	0.0058	1951	–0.0269
1952	0.0199	–0.0085	0.0076	–0.0004	0.0031	0.0016	0.0016	0.0063	–0.0018	0.0039	0.0108	–0.0091	1952	0.0352
1953	–0.0080	–0.0040	–0.0033	–0.0248	–0.0030	0.0109	0.0177	–0.0085	0.0253	0.0227	–0.0073	0.0172	1953	0.0341
1954	0.0124	0.0198	0.0039	–0.0034	–0.0042	0.0063	0.0040	0.0018	0.0040	0.0040	0.0025	0.0017	1954	0.0539
1955	–0.0097	–0.0063	0.0092	–0.0001	–0.0018	0.0029	–0.0041	–0.0038	0.0076	0.0078	–0.0030	0.0063	1955	0.0048
1956	0.0104	0.0026	–0.0146	–0.0115	0.0052	–0.0018	–0.0093	–0.0208	0.0012	–0.0105	–0.0126	–0.0082	1956	–0.0681
1957	0.0197	0.0093	0.0050	–0.0066	–0.0075	–0.0322	–0.0110	–0.0009	0.0095	0.0023	0.0311	0.0685	1957	0.0871
1958	0.0099	–0.0008	–0.0046	0.0163	0.0031	–0.0038	–0.0153	–0.0320	–0.0096	0.0107	0.0105	–0.0058	1958	–0.0222
1959	–0.0028	0.0126	–0.0083	–0.0172	–0.0114	0.0044	0.0089	–0.0068	–0.0088	0.0165	0.0135	–0.0096	1959	–0.0097
1960	0.0107	0.0128	0.0191	–0.0022	–0.0021	0.0141	0.0257	0.0117	–0.0063	0.0008	–0.0070	0.0104	1960	0.0907
1961	0.0148	0.0210	–0.0029	–0.0116	0.0049	–0.0080	0.0040	–0.0018	0.0144	0.0127	0.0028	–0.0026	1961	0.0482
1962	0.0080	0.0052	0.0151	0.0142	0.0000	–0.0026	–0.0015	0.0143	0.0089	0.0068	0.0062	0.0023	1962	0.0795
1963	0.0059	0.0023	0.0026	–0.0051	0.0048	0.0043	0.0028	0.0035	–0.0023	0.0049	0.0015	–0.0034	1963	0.0219
1964	0.0087	0.0054	–0.0062	0.0040	0.0057	0.0048	0.0052	0.0037	0.0021	0.0050	–0.0004	0.0088	1964	0.0477
1965	0.0081	0.0009	0.0012	0.0021	–0.0008	0.0003	0.0019	–0.0006	–0.0015	0.0046	–0.0057	–0.0149	1965	–0.0046
1966	0.0022	–0.0113	–0.0059	0.0013	–0.0026	0.0030	–0.0098	–0.0259	0.0078	0.0261	–0.0020	0.0201	1966	0.0020
1967	0.0450	–0.0201	0.0117	–0.0071	–0.0254	–0.0223	0.0041	–0.0007	0.0094	–0.0281	–0.0272	0.0127	1967	–0.0495
1968	0.0361	0.0037	–0.0197	0.0048	0.0032	0.0122	0.0341	0.0206	–0.0053	–0.0160	–0.0226	–0.0233	1968	0.0257
1969	0.0139	–0.0160	–0.0200	0.0335	–0.0227	0.0035	0.0005	–0.0020	–0.0244	0.0127	–0.0471	–0.0134	1969	–0.0809
1970	0.0141	0.0401	–0.0045	–0.0250	–0.0163	0.0001	0.0556	0.0100	0.0139	–0.0096	0.0584	0.0372	1970	0.1837

* Compound annual return

Table A-5 (Continued)
Long-Term Corporate Bonds: Total Returns

from January 1971 to December 2007

Year	Jan	Feb	Mar	Apr	May	Jun	Jul	Aug	Sep	Oct	Nov	Dec	Year	Jan–Dec*
1971	0.0532	–0.0366	0.0258	–0.0236	–0.0161	0.0107	–0.0025	0.0554	–0.0102	0.0282	0.0029	0.0223	1971	0.1101
1972	–0.0033	0.0107	0.0024	0.0035	0.0163	–0.0068	0.0030	0.0072	0.0031	0.0101	0.0249	–0.0004	1972	0.0726
1973	–0.0054	0.0023	0.0045	0.0061	–0.0039	–0.0056	–0.0476	0.0356	0.0356	–0.0066	0.0078	–0.0089	1973	0.0114
1974	–0.0053	0.0009	–0.0307	–0.0341	0.0105	–0.0285	–0.0211	–0.0268	0.0174	0.0885	0.0117	–0.0075	1974	–0.0306
1975	0.0596	0.0137	–0.0247	–0.0052	0.0106	0.0304	–0.0030	–0.0175	–0.0126	0.0553	–0.0088	0.0442	1975	0.1464
1976	0.0188	0.0061	0.0167	–0.0015	–0.0103	0.0150	0.0149	0.0231	0.0167	0.0070	0.0319	0.0347	1976	0.1865
1977	–0.0303	–0.0020	0.0094	0.0100	0.0106	0.0175	–0.0005	0.0136	–0.0022	–0.0038	0.0061	–0.0105	1977	0.0171
1978	–0.0089	0.0051	0.0042	–0.0023	–0.0108	0.0023	0.0101	0.0257	–0.0048	–0.0205	0.0134	–0.0133	1978	–0.0007
1979	0.0184	–0.0128	0.0106	–0.0052	0.0228	0.0269	–0.0031	0.0006	–0.0179	–0.0890	0.0222	–0.0108	1979	–0.0418
1980	–0.0645	–0.0665	–0.0062	0.1376	0.0560	0.0341	–0.0429	–0.0445	–0.0237	–0.0159	0.0017	0.0248	1980	–0.0276
1981	–0.0130	–0.0269	0.0311	–0.0769	0.0595	0.0023	–0.0372	–0.0345	–0.0199	0.0521	0.1267	–0.0580	1981	–0.0124
1982	–0.0129	0.0312	0.0306	0.0338	0.0245	–0.0468	0.0540	0.0837	0.0623	0.0759	0.0201	0.0108	1982	0.4256
1983	–0.0094	0.0428	0.0072	0.0548	–0.0324	–0.0046	–0.0455	0.0051	0.0392	–0.0025	0.0142	–0.0033	1983	0.0626
1984	0.0270	–0.0172	–0.0235	–0.0073	–0.0483	0.0199	0.0586	0.0307	0.0314	0.0572	0.0212	0.0128	1984	0.1686
1985	0.0325	–0.0373	0.0179	0.0296	0.0820	0.0083	–0.0121	0.0260	0.0071	0.0329	0.0370	0.0469	1985	0.3009
1986	0.0045	0.0752	0.0256	0.0016	–0.0164	0.0218	0.0031	0.0275	–0.0114	0.0189	0.0233	0.0117	1986	0.1985
1987	0.0216	0.0058	–0.0087	–0.0502	–0.0052	0.0155	–0.0119	–0.0075	–0.0422	0.0507	0.0125	0.0212	1987	–0.0027
1988	0.0517	0.0138	–0.0188	–0.0149	–0.0057	0.0379	–0.0111	0.0054	0.0326	0.0273	–0.0169	0.0039	1988	0.1070
1989	0.0202	–0.0129	0.0064	0.0213	0.0379	0.0395	0.0178	–0.0163	0.0040	0.0276	0.0070	0.0006	1989	0.1623
1990	–0.0191	–0.0012	–0.0011	–0.0191	0.0385	0.0216	0.0102	–0.0292	0.0091	0.0132	0.0285	0.0167	1990	0.0678
1991	0.0150	0.0121	0.0108	0.0138	0.0039	–0.0018	0.0167	0.0275	0.0271	0.0043	0.0106	0.0436	1991	0.1989
1992	–0.0173	0.0096	–0.0073	0.0016	0.0254	0.0156	0.0308	0.0090	0.0099	–0.0156	0.0069	0.0228	1992	0.0939
1993	0.0250	0.0256	0.0025	0.0052	0.0020	0.0293	0.0100	0.0287	0.0043	0.0051	–0.0188	0.0067	1993	0.1319
1994	0.0202	–0.0286	–0.0383	–0.0097	–0.0062	–0.0081	0.0309	–0.0031	–0.0265	–0.0050	0.0018	0.0157	1994	–0.0576
1995	0.0256	0.0289	0.0095	0.0175	0.0631	0.0079	–0.0101	0.0214	0.0153	0.0185	0.0242	0.0228	1995	0.2720
1996	0.0014	–0.0373	–0.0130	–0.0160	0.0005	0.0172	0.0010	–0.0070	0.0259	0.0361	0.0263	–0.0186	1996	0.0140
1997	–0.0028	0.0028	–0.0221	0.0184	0.0128	0.0187	0.0528	–0.0240	0.0226	0.0191	0.0101	0.0163	1997	0.1295
1998	0.0137	–0.0007	0.0038	0.0053	0.0167	0.0115	–0.0056	0.0089	0.0413	–0.0190	0.0270	0.0010	1998	0.1076
1999	0.0123	–0.0401	0.0002	–0.0024	–0.0176	–0.0160	–0.0113	–0.0026	0.0093	0.0047	–0.0024	–0.0102	1999	–0.0745
2000	–0.0021	0.0092	0.0169	–0.0115	–0.0161	0.0326	0.0179	0.0135	0.0046	0.0045	0.0263	0.0270	2000	0.1287
2001	0.0359	0.0127	–0.0029	–0.0128	0.0132	0.0055	0.0361	0.0157	–0.0152	0.0437	–0.0188	–0.0090	2001	0.1065
2002	0.0175	0.0130	–0.0295	0.0253	0.0113	0.0073	0.0094	0.0452	0.0330	–0.0240	0.0103	0.0361	2002	0.1633
2003	0.0021	0.0264	–0.0080	0.0229	0.0471	–0.0143	–0.0881	0.0219	0.0503	–0.0203	0.0052	0.0139	2003	0.0527
2004	0.0187	0.0178	0.0118	–0.0534	–0.0071	0.0093	0.0184	0.0395	0.0101	0.0164	–0.0200	0.0257	2004	0.0872
2005	0.0277	–0.0112	–0.0125	0.0327	0.0295	0.0141	–0.0244	0.0233	–0.0310	–0.0204	0.0099	0.0225	2005	0.0587
2006	–0.0093	0.0128	–0.0404	–0.0224	–0.0020	0.0039	0.0237	0.0361	0.0183	0.0127	0.0246	–0.0232	2006	0.0324
2007	–0.0051	0.0287	–0.0231	0.0140	–0.0178	–0.0148	–0.0032	0.0152	0.0135	0.0088	0.0079	0.0028	2007	0.0260

Compound annual return

Table A-6

Long-Term Government Bonds: Total Returns

from January 1926 to December 1970

Year	Jan	Feb	Mar	Apr	May	Jun	Jul	Aug	Sep	Oct	Nov	Dec	Year	Jan–Dec*
1926	0.0138	0.0063	0.0041	0.0076	0.0014	0.0038	0.0004	0.0000	0.0038	0.0102	0.0160	0.0078	1926	0.0777
1927	0.0075	0.0088	0.0253	–0.0005	0.0109	–0.0069	0.0050	0.0076	0.0018	0.0099	0.0097	0.0072	1927	0.0893
1928	–0.0036	0.0061	0.0045	–0.0004	–0.0077	0.0041	–0.0217	0.0076	–0.0041	0.0158	0.0003	0.0004	1928	0.0010
1929	–0.0090	–0.0157	–0.0144	0.0275	–0.0162	0.0110	0.0000	–0.0034	0.0027	0.0382	0.0236	–0.0089	1929	0.0342
1930	–0.0057	0.0129	0.0083	–0.0016	0.0139	0.0051	0.0034	0.0013	0.0074	0.0035	0.0042	–0.0070	1930	0.0466
1931	–0.0121	0.0085	0.0104	0.0086	0.0145	0.0004	–0.0042	0.0012	–0.0281	–0.0330	0.0027	–0.0220	1931	–0.0531
1932	0.0034	0.0413	–0.0018	0.0604	–0.0188	0.0065	0.0481	0.0003	0.0057	–0.0017	0.0032	0.0131	1932	0.1684
1933	0.0148	–0.0258	0.0097	–0.0032	0.0303	0.0050	–0.0017	0.0044	0.0023	–0.0091	–0.0149	–0.0113	1933	–0.0007
1934	0.0257	0.0081	0.0197	0.0126	0.0131	0.0067	0.0040	–0.0118	–0.0146	0.0182	0.0037	0.0112	1934	0.1003
1935	0.0182	0.0092	0.0041	0.0079	–0.0057	0.0092	0.0046	–0.0133	0.0009	0.0061	0.0010	0.0070	1935	0.0498
1936	0.0055	0.0081	0.0106	0.0035	0.0040	0.0021	0.0060	0.0111	–0.0031	0.0006	0.0205	0.0038	1936	0.0752
1937	–0.0013	0.0086	–0.0411	0.0039	0.0053	–0.0018	0.0138	–0.0104	0.0045	0.0042	0.0096	0.0082	1937	0.0023
1938	0.0057	0.0052	–0.0037	0.0210	0.0044	0.0004	0.0043	0.0000	0.0022	0.0087	–0.0022	0.0080	1938	0.0553
1939	0.0059	0.0080	0.0125	0.0118	0.0171	–0.0027	0.0113	–0.0201	–0.0545	0.0410	0.0162	0.0145	1939	0.0594
1940	–0.0017	0.0027	0.0177	–0.0035	–0.0299	0.0258	0.0052	0.0028	0.0110	0.0031	0.0205	0.0067	1940	0.0609
1941	–0.0201	0.0020	0.0096	0.0129	0.0027	0.0066	0.0022	0.0018	–0.0012	0.0140	–0.0029	–0.0177	1941	0.0093
1942	0.0069	0.0011	0.0092	–0.0029	0.0075	0.0003	0.0018	0.0038	0.0003	0.0024	–0.0035	0.0049	1942	0.0322
1943	0.0033	–0.0005	0.0009	0.0048	0.0050	0.0018	–0.0001	0.0021	0.0011	0.0005	0.0000	0.0018	1943	0.0208
1944	0.0021	0.0032	0.0021	0.0013	0.0028	0.0008	0.0036	0.0027	0.0014	0.0012	0.0024	0.0042	1944	0.0281
1945	0.0127	0.0077	0.0021	0.0160	0.0056	0.0169	–0.0086	0.0026	0.0054	0.0104	0.0125	0.0194	1945	0.1073
1946	0.0025	0.0032	0.0010	–0.0135	–0.0012	0.0070	–0.0040	–0.0111	–0.0009	0.0074	–0.0054	0.0145	1946	–0.0010
1947	–0.0006	0.0021	0.0020	–0.0037	0.0033	0.0010	0.0063	0.0081	–0.0044	–0.0037	–0.0174	–0.0192	1947	–0.0262
1948	0.0020	0.0046	0.0034	0.0045	0.0141	–0.0084	–0.0021	0.0001	0.0014	0.0007	0.0076	0.0056	1948	0.0340
1949	0.0082	0.0049	0.0074	0.0011	0.0019	0.0167	0.0033	0.0111	–0.0011	0.0019	0.0021	0.0052	1949	0.0645
1950	–0.0061	0.0021	0.0008	0.0030	0.0033	–0.0025	0.0055	0.0014	–0.0072	–0.0048	0.0035	0.0016	1950	0.0006
1951	0.0058	–0.0074	–0.0157	–0.0063	–0.0069	–0.0062	0.0138	0.0099	–0.0080	0.0010	–0.0136	–0.0061	1951	–0.0393
1952	0.0028	0.0014	0.0111	0.0171	–0.0033	0.0003	–0.0020	–0.0070	–0.0130	0.0148	–0.0015	–0.0086	1952	0.0116
1953	0.0012	–0.0087	–0.0088	–0.0105	–0.0148	0.0223	0.0039	–0.0008	0.0299	0.0074	–0.0049	0.0206	1953	0.0364
1954	0.0089	0.0240	0.0058	0.0104	–0.0087	0.0163	0.0134	–0.0036	–0.0010	0.0006	–0.0025	0.0064	1954	0.0719
1955	–0.0241	–0.0078	0.0087	0.0001	0.0073	–0.0076	–0.0102	0.0004	0.0073	0.0144	–0.0045	0.0037	1955	–0.0129
1956	0.0083	–0.0002	–0.0149	–0.0113	0.0225	0.0027	–0.0209	–0.0187	0.0050	–0.0054	–0.0057	–0.0179	1956	–0.0559
1957	0.0346	0.0025	–0.0024	–0.0222	–0.0023	–0.0180	–0.0041	0.0002	0.0076	–0.0050	0.0533	0.0307	1957	0.0746
1958	–0.0084	0.0100	0.0102	0.0186	0.0001	–0.0160	–0.0278	–0.0435	–0.0117	0.0138	0.0120	–0.0181	1958	–0.0609
1959	–0.0080	0.0117	0.0017	–0.0117	–0.0005	0.0010	0.0060	–0.0041	–0.0057	0.0150	–0.0119	–0.0159	1959	–0.0226
1960	0.0112	0.0204	0.0282	–0.0170	0.0152	0.0173	0.0368	–0.0067	0.0075	–0.0028	–0.0066	0.0279	1960	0.1378
1961	–0.0107	0.0200	–0.0037	0.0115	–0.0046	–0.0075	0.0035	–0.0038	0.0129	0.0071	–0.0020	–0.0125	1961	0.0097
1962	–0.0014	0.0103	0.0253	0.0082	0.0046	–0.0076	–0.0109	0.0187	0.0061	0.0084	0.0021	0.0035	1962	0.0689
1963	–0.0001	0.0008	0.0009	–0.0012	0.0023	0.0019	0.0031	0.0021	0.0004	–0.0026	0.0051	–0.0006	1963	0.0121
1964	–0.0014	–0.0011	0.0037	0.0047	0.0050	0.0069	0.0008	0.0020	0.0050	0.0043	0.0017	0.0030	1964	0.0351
1965	0.0040	0.0014	0.0054	0.0036	0.0018	0.0047	0.0022	–0.0013	–0.0034	0.0027	–0.0062	–0.0078	1965	0.0071
1966	–0.0104	–0.0250	0.0296	–0.0063	–0.0059	–0.0016	–0.0037	–0.0206	0.0332	0.0228	–0.0148	0.0413	1966	0.0365
1967	0.0154	–0.0221	0.0198	–0.0291	–0.0039	–0.0312	0.0068	–0.0084	–0.0004	–0.0400	–0.0196	0.0192	1967	–0.0918
1968	0.0328	–0.0033	–0.0212	0.0227	0.0043	0.0230	0.0289	–0.0003	–0.0102	–0.0132	–0.0269	–0.0363	1968	–0.0026
1969	–0.0206	0.0042	0.0010	0.0427	–0.0490	0.0214	0.0079	–0.0069	–0.0531	0.0365	–0.0243	–0.0068	1969	–0.0507
1970	–0.0021	0.0587	–0.0068	–0.0413	–0.0468	0.0486	0.0319	–0.0019	0.0228	–0.0109	0.0791	–0.0084	1970	0.1211

* Compound annual return

Table A-6 (Continued)

Long-Term Government Bonds: Total Returns

from January 1971 to December 2007

Year	Jan	Feb	Mar	Apr	May	Jun	Jul	Aug	Sep	Oct	Nov	Dec	Year	Jan–Dec*
1971	0.0506	−0.0163	0.0526	−0.0283	−0.0006	−0.0159	0.0030	0.0471	0.0204	0.0167	−0.0047	0.0044	1971	0.1323
1972	−0.0063	0.0088	−0.0082	0.0027	0.0270	−0.0065	0.0216	0.0029	−0.0083	0.0234	0.0226	−0.0229	1972	0.0569
1973	−0.0321	0.0014	0.0082	0.0046	−0.0105	−0.0021	−0.0433	0.0391	0.0318	0.0215	−0.0183	−0.0082	1973	−0.0111
1974	−0.0083	−0.0024	−0.0292	−0.0253	0.0123	0.0045	−0.0029	−0.0232	0.0247	0.0489	0.0295	0.0171	1974	0.0435
1975	0.0225	0.0131	−0.0267	−0.0182	0.0212	0.0292	−0.0087	−0.0068	−0.0098	0.0475	−0.0109	0.0390	1975	0.0920
1976	0.0090	0.0062	0.0166	0.0018	−0.0158	0.0208	0.0078	0.0211	0.0145	0.0084	0.0339	0.0327	1976	0.1675
1977	−0.0388	−0.0049	0.0091	0.0071	0.0125	0.0164	−0.0070	0.0198	−0.0029	−0.0093	0.0093	−0.0168	1977	−0.0069
1978	−0.0080	0.0004	−0.0021	−0.0005	−0.0058	−0.0062	0.0143	0.0218	−0.0106	−0.0200	0.0189	−0.0130	1978	−0.0118
1979	0.0191	−0.0135	0.0129	−0.0112	0.0261	0.0311	−0.0085	−0.0035	−0.0122	−0.0841	0.0311	0.0057	1979	−0.0123
1980	−0.0741	−0.0467	−0.0315	0.1523	0.0419	0.0359	−0.0476	−0.0432	−0.0262	−0.0263	0.0100	0.0352	1980	−0.0395
1981	−0.0115	−0.0435	0.0384	−0.0518	0.0622	−0.0179	−0.0353	−0.0386	−0.0145	0.0829	0.1410	−0.0713	1981	0.0186
1982	0.0046	0.0182	0.0231	0.0373	0.0034	−0.0223	0.0501	0.0781	0.0618	0.0634	−0.0002	0.0312	1982	0.4036
1983	−0.0309	0.0492	−0.0094	0.0350	−0.0386	0.0039	−0.0486	0.0020	0.0505	−0.0132	0.0183	−0.0059	1983	0.0065
1984	0.0244	−0.0178	−0.0156	−0.0105	−0.0516	0.0150	0.0693	0.0266	0.0342	0.0561	0.0118	0.0091	1984	0.1548
1985	0.0364	−0.0493	0.0307	0.0242	0.0896	0.0142	−0.0180	0.0259	−0.0021	0.0338	0.0401	0.0541	1985	0.3097
1986	−0.0025	0.1145	0.0770	−0.0080	−0.0505	0.0613	−0.0108	0.0499	−0.0500	0.0289	0.0267	−0.0018	1986	0.2453
1987	0.0161	0.0202	−0.0223	−0.0473	−0.0105	0.0098	−0.0178	−0.0165	−0.0369	0.0623	0.0037	0.0165	1987	−0.0271
1988	0.0666	0.0052	−0.0307	−0.0160	−0.0102	0.0368	−0.0170	0.0058	0.0345	0.0308	−0.0196	0.0110	1988	0.0967
1989	0.0203	−0.0179	0.0122	0.0159	0.0401	0.0550	0.0238	−0.0259	0.0019	0.0379	0.0078	−0.0006	1989	0.1811
1990	−0.0343	−0.0025	−0.0044	−0.0202	0.0415	0.0230	0.0107	−0.0419	0.0117	0.0215	0.0402	0.0187	1990	0.0618
1991	0.0130	0.0030	0.0038	0.0140	0.0000	−0.0063	0.0157	0.0340	0.0303	0.0054	0.0082	0.0581	1991	0.1930
1992	−0.0324	0.0051	−0.0094	0.0016	0.0243	0.0200	0.0398	0.0067	0.0185	−0.0198	0.0010	0.0246	1992	0.0805
1993	0.0280	0.0354	0.0021	0.0072	0.0047	0.0449	0.0191	0.0434	0.0005	0.0096	−0.0259	0.0020	1993	0.1824
1994	0.0257	−0.0450	−0.0395	−0.0150	−0.0082	−0.0100	0.0363	−0.0086	−0.0331	−0.0025	0.0066	0.0161	1994	−0.0777
1995	0.0273	0.0287	0.0091	0.0169	0.0790	0.0139	−0.0168	0.0236	0.0175	0.0294	0.0249	0.0272	1995	0.3167
1996	−0.0011	−0.0483	−0.0210	−0.0165	−0.0054	0.0203	0.0018	−0.0139	0.0290	0.0404	0.0351	−0.0256	1996	−0.0093
1997	−0.0079	0.0005	−0.0252	0.0255	0.0095	0.0197	0.0626	−0.0317	0.0316	0.0341	0.0148	0.0184	1997	0.1585
1998	0.0200	−0.0072	0.0025	0.0026	0.0182	0.0228	−0.0040	0.0465	0.0395	−0.0218	0.0097	−0.0032	1998	0.1306
1999	0.0121	−0.0520	−0.0008	0.0021	−0.0185	−0.0078	−0.0079	−0.0051	0.0084	−0.0012	−0.0061	−0.0155	1999	−0.0896
2000	0.0228	0.0264	0.0367	−0.0076	−0.0054	0.0244	0.0173	0.0240	−0.0157	0.0187	0.0319	0.0243	2000	0.2148
2001	0.0005	0.0191	−0.0074	−0.0313	0.0037	0.0085	0.0376	0.0206	0.0081	0.0464	−0.0471	−0.0183	2001	0.0370
2002	0.0138	0.0115	−0.0436	0.0410	0.0015	0.0187	0.0303	0.0464	0.0417	−0.0294	−0.0122	0.0507	2002	0.1784
2003	−0.0106	0.0329	−0.0135	0.0102	0.0592	−0.0154	−0.0982	0.0166	0.0546	−0.0283	0.0027	0.0139	2003	0.0145
2004	0.0187	0.0230	0.0141	−0.0588	−0.0051	0.0121	0.0155	0.0395	0.0096	0.0154	−0.0234	0.0250	2004	0.0851
2005	0.0300	−0.0128	−0.0072	0.0373	0.0297	0.0167	−0.0288	0.0333	−0.0338	−0.0196	0.0076	0.0267	2005	0.0781
2006	−0.0118	0.0238	−0.0539	−0.0247	0.0010	0.0092	0.0199	0.0299	0.0170	0.0077	0.0207	−0.0236	2006	0.0119
2007	−0.0102	0.0335	−0.0145	0.0085	−0.0200	−0.0091	0.0284	0.0199	0.0012	0.0155	0.0468	−0.0029	2007	0.0988

* Compound annual return

Table A-7

Long-Term Government Bonds: Income Returns

from January 1926 to December 1970

Year	Jan	Feb	Mar	Apr	May	Jun	Jul	Aug	Sep	Oct	Nov	Dec	Year	Jan–Dec*
1926	0.0031	0.0028	0.0032	0.0030	0.0028	0.0033	0.0031	0.0031	0.0030	0.0030	0.0031	0.0030	1926	0.0373
1927	0.0030	0.0027	0.0029	0.0027	0.0028	0.0027	0.0027	0.0029	0.0027	0.0028	0.0027	0.0027	1927	0.0341
1928	0.0027	0.0025	0.0027	0.0026	0.0027	0.0027	0.0027	0.0029	0.0027	0.0030	0.0027	0.0029	1928	0.0322
1929	0.0029	0.0027	0.0028	0.0034	0.0030	0.0029	0.0032	0.0030	0.0032	0.0031	0.0026	0.0031	1929	0.0347
1930	0.0029	0.0026	0.0029	0.0027	0.0027	0.0029	0.0028	0.0026	0.0029	0.0027	0.0026	0.0028	1930	0.0332
1931	0.0028	0.0026	0.0029	0.0027	0.0026	0.0028	0.0027	0.0027	0.0027	0.0029	0.0031	0.0032	1931	0.0333
1932	0.0032	0.0032	0.0031	0.0030	0.0028	0.0028	0.0028	0.0028	0.0026	0.0027	0.0026	0.0027	1932	0.0369
1933	0.0027	0.0023	0.0027	0.0025	0.0028	0.0025	0.0026	0.0026	0.0025	0.0026	0.0025	0.0028	1933	0.0312
1934	0.0029	0.0024	0.0027	0.0025	0.0025	0.0024	0.0024	0.0024	0.0023	0.0027	0.0025	0.0025	1934	0.0318
1935	0.0025	0.0021	0.0022	0.0023	0.0023	0.0022	0.0024	0.0023	0.0023	0.0023	0.0024	0.0024	1935	0.0281
1936	0.0024	0.0023	0.0024	0.0022	0.0022	0.0024	0.0023	0.0023	0.0021	0.0023	0.0022	0.0022	1936	0.0277
1937	0.0021	0.0020	0.0022	0.0023	0.0022	0.0025	0.0024	0.0023	0.0023	0.0023	0.0024	0.0023	1937	0.0266
1938	0.0023	0.0021	0.0023	0.0022	0.0022	0.0021	0.0021	0.0022	0.0021	0.0022	0.0021	0.0022	1938	0.0264
1939	0.0021	0.0019	0.0021	0.0019	0.0020	0.0018	0.0019	0.0018	0.0019	0.0023	0.0020	0.0019	1939	0.0240
1940	0.0020	0.0018	0.0019	0.0018	0.0019	0.0019	0.0020	0.0019	0.0018	0.0018	0.0018	0.0017	1940	0.0223
1941	0.0016	0.0016	0.0018	0.0017	0.0017	0.0016	0.0016	0.0016	0.0016	0.0016	0.0014	0.0016	1941	0.0194
1942	0.0021	0.0019	0.0021	0.0020	0.0019	0.0021	0.0021	0.0021	0.0020	0.0021	0.0020	0.0021	1942	0.0246
1943	0.0020	0.0019	0.0021	0.0020	0.0019	0.0021	0.0021	0.0021	0.0020	0.0020	0.0021	0.0021	1943	0.0244
1944	0.0021	0.0020	0.0021	0.0020	0.0022	0.0020	0.0021	0.0021	0.0020	0.0021	0.0020	0.0020	1944	0.0246
1945	0.0021	0.0018	0.0020	0.0019	0.0019	0.0019	0.0018	0.0019	0.0018	0.0019	0.0018	0.0018	1945	0.0234
1946	0.0017	0.0015	0.0016	0.0017	0.0018	0.0016	0.0019	0.0017	0.0018	0.0019	0.0018	0.0019	1946	0.0204
1947	0.0018	0.0016	0.0018	0.0017	0.0017	0.0019	0.0018	0.0017	0.0018	0.0018	0.0017	0.0021	1947	0.0213
1948	0.0020	0.0019	0.0022	0.0020	0.0018	0.0021	0.0019	0.0021	0.0020	0.0019	0.0021	0.0020	1948	0.0240
1949	0.0020	0.0018	0.0019	0.0018	0.0020	0.0019	0.0017	0.0019	0.0017	0.0018	0.0017	0.0017	1949	0.0225
1950	0.0018	0.0016	0.0018	0.0016	0.0019	0.0017	0.0018	0.0018	0.0017	0.0019	0.0018	0.0018	1950	0.0212
1951	0.0020	0.0017	0.0019	0.0020	0.0021	0.0020	0.0023	0.0021	0.0019	0.0023	0.0021	0.0022	1951	0.0238
1952	0.0023	0.0021	0.0023	0.0022	0.0020	0.0022	0.0022	0.0021	0.0023	0.0023	0.0021	0.0024	1952	0.0266
1953	0.0023	0.0021	0.0025	0.0024	0.0024	0.0027	0.0025	0.0025	0.0025	0.0023	0.0024	0.0024	1953	0.0284
1954	0.0023	0.0022	0.0025	0.0022	0.0020	0.0025	0.0022	0.0023	0.0022	0.0021	0.0023	0.0023	1954	0.0279
1955	0.0022	0.0022	0.0024	0.0022	0.0025	0.0023	0.0023	0.0027	0.0024	0.0025	0.0024	0.0024	1955	0.0275
1956	0.0025	0.0023	0.0023	0.0026	0.0026	0.0023	0.0026	0.0026	0.0025	0.0029	0.0027	0.0028	1956	0.0299
1957	0.0029	0.0025	0.0026	0.0029	0.0029	0.0025	0.0033	0.0030	0.0031	0.0031	0.0029	0.0029	1957	0.0344
1958	0.0027	0.0025	0.0027	0.0026	0.0024	0.0027	0.0027	0.0027	0.0032	0.0032	0.0028	0.0033	1958	0.0327
1959	0.0031	0.0031	0.0035	0.0033	0.0033	0.0036	0.0035	0.0035	0.0034	0.0035	0.0035	0.0036	1959	0.0401
1960	0.0035	0.0037	0.0036	0.0032	0.0037	0.0034	0.0032	0.0034	0.0032	0.0033	0.0032	0.0033	1960	0.0426
1961	0.0033	0.0030	0.0031	0.0031	0.0034	0.0032	0.0033	0.0033	0.0032	0.0034	0.0032	0.0031	1961	0.0383
1962	0.0037	0.0032	0.0033	0.0033	0.0032	0.0030	0.0034	0.0034	0.0030	0.0035	0.0031	0.0032	1962	0.0400
1963	0.0032	0.0029	0.0031	0.0034	0.0033	0.0030	0.0036	0.0033	0.0034	0.0034	0.0032	0.0036	1963	0.0389
1964	0.0035	0.0032	0.0037	0.0035	0.0032	0.0038	0.0035	0.0035	0.0034	0.0034	0.0035	0.0035	1964	0.0415
1965	0.0033	0.0032	0.0038	0.0033	0.0033	0.0038	0.0034	0.0037	0.0035	0.0034	0.0037	0.0037	1965	0.0419
1966	0.0038	0.0034	0.0040	0.0036	0.0041	0.0039	0.0038	0.0043	0.0041	0.0040	0.0038	0.0039	1966	0.0449
1967	0.0040	0.0034	0.0039	0.0035	0.0043	0.0039	0.0043	0.0042	0.0040	0.0045	0.0045	0.0044	1967	0.0459
1968	0.0050	0.0042	0.0043	0.0049	0.0046	0.0042	0.0048	0.0042	0.0044	0.0045	0.0043	0.0049	1968	0.0550
1969	0.0050	0.0046	0.0047	0.0055	0.0047	0.0055	0.0052	0.0048	0.0055	0.0057	0.0049	0.0060	1969	0.0595
1970	0.0056	0.0052	0.0056	0.0054	0.0055	0.0064	0.0059	0.0057	0.0056	0.0055	0.0058	0.0053	1970	0.0674

* Compound annual return

Table A-7 (Continued)

Long-Term Government Bonds: Income Returns

from January 1971 to December 2007

Year	Jan	Feb	Mar	Apr	May	Jun	Jul	Aug	Sep	Oct	Nov	Dec	Year	Jan–Dec*
1971	0.0051	0.0046	0.0056	0.0048	0.0047	0.0056	0.0052	0.0055	0.0049	0.0047	0.0051	0.0050	1971	0.0632
1972	0.0050	0.0047	0.0049	0.0048	0.0055	0.0049	0.0051	0.0049	0.0047	0.0052	0.0048	0.0045	1972	0.0587
1973	0.0054	0.0051	0.0056	0.0057	0.0058	0.0055	0.0061	0.0062	0.0055	0.0063	0.0056	0.0060	1973	0.0651
1974	0.0061	0.0055	0.0058	0.0068	0.0068	0.0061	0.0072	0.0065	0.0071	0.0070	0.0062	0.0067	1974	0.0727
1975	0.0068	0.0060	0.0066	0.0067	0.0067	0.0070	0.0068	0.0065	0.0073	0.0072	0.0061	0.0074	1975	0.0799
1976	0.0065	0.0060	0.0071	0.0064	0.0059	0.0073	0.0065	0.0069	0.0064	0.0061	0.0066	0.0063	1976	0.0789
1977	0.0059	0.0057	0.0065	0.0061	0.0067	0.0062	0.0059	0.0067	0.0061	0.0063	0.0063	0.0062	1977	0.0714
1978	0.0069	0.0060	0.0069	0.0063	0.0075	0.0069	0.0073	0.0070	0.0065	0.0073	0.0071	0.0068	1978	0.0790
1979	0.0079	0.0065	0.0074	0.0076	0.0077	0.0071	0.0076	0.0073	0.0068	0.0082	0.0083	0.0083	1979	0.0886
1980	0.0083	0.0084	0.0099	0.0100	0.0087	0.0086	0.0084	0.0081	0.0097	0.0097	0.0091	0.0108	1980	0.0997
1981	0.0094	0.0088	0.0111	0.0101	0.0104	0.0109	0.0109	0.0110	0.0114	0.0117	0.0113	0.0100	1981	0.1155
1982	0.0108	0.0103	0.0124	0.0112	0.0101	0.0120	0.0114	0.0112	0.0100	0.0091	0.0094	0.0093	1982	0.1350
1983	0.0087	0.0081	0.0089	0.0085	0.0091	0.0090	0.0088	0.0103	0.0096	0.0095	0.0094	0.0094	1983	0.1038
1984	0.0103	0.0092	0.0098	0.0104	0.0103	0.0106	0.0116	0.0106	0.0094	0.0108	0.0091	0.0098	1984	0.1174
1985	0.0096	0.0082	0.0094	0.0102	0.0097	0.0080	0.0094	0.0085	0.0088	0.0089	0.0081	0.0086	1985	0.1125
1986	0.0079	0.0073	0.0071	0.0063	0.0062	0.0070	0.0066	0.0063	0.0065	0.0069	0.0059	0.0070	1986	0.0898
1987	0.0064	0.0059	0.0066	0.0065	0.0066	0.0075	0.0073	0.0075	0.0075	0.0079	0.0075	0.0078	1987	0.0792
1988	0.0072	0.0071	0.0072	0.0070	0.0078	0.0076	0.0071	0.0083	0.0076	0.0076	0.0070	0.0075	1988	0.0897
1989	0.0080	0.0069	0.0079	0.0070	0.0080	0.0070	0.0068	0.0066	0.0065	0.0072	0.0064	0.0064	1989	0.0881
1990	0.0073	0.0066	0.0071	0.0075	0.0075	0.0068	0.0074	0.0071	0.0069	0.0081	0.0071	0.0072	1990	0.0819
1991	0.0071	0.0064	0.0064	0.0076	0.0068	0.0063	0.0076	0.0068	0.0068	0.0065	0.0060	0.0068	1991	0.0822
1992	0.0061	0.0059	0.0067	0.0065	0.0061	0.0067	0.0063	0.0060	0.0058	0.0057	0.0061	0.0063	1992	0.0726
1993	0.0059	0.0055	0.0063	0.0057	0.0052	0.0062	0.0054	0.0056	0.0050	0.0049	0.0053	0.0055	1993	0.0717
1994	0.0055	0.0049	0.0058	0.0057	0.0063	0.0061	0.0060	0.0066	0.0061	0.0066	0.0064	0.0066	1994	0.0659
1995	0.0070	0.0059	0.0064	0.0058	0.0065	0.0054	0.0056	0.0057	0.0052	0.0057	0.0051	0.0049	1995	0.0760
1996	0.0054	0.0048	0.0052	0.0059	0.0058	0.0054	0.0062	0.0057	0.0060	0.0058	0.0052	0.0056	1996	0.0618
1997	0.0056	0.0051	0.0059	0.0059	0.0058	0.0059	0.0058	0.0049	0.0058	0.0054	0.0047	0.0054	1997	0.0664
1998	0.0048	0.0044	0.0052	0.0049	0.0048	0.0052	0.0049	0.0048	0.0044	0.0042	0.0045	0.0045	1998	0.0583
1999	0.0042	0.0040	0.0053	0.0048	0.0045	0.0055	0.0051	0.0054	0.0052	0.0050	0.0056	0.0055	1999	0.0557
2000	0.0057	0.0051	0.0054	0.0047	0.0056	0.0052	0.0052	0.0050	0.0046	0.0053	0.0048	0.0045	2000	0.0650
2001	0.0049	0.0042	0.0045	0.0047	0.0050	0.0047	0.0052	0.0046	0.0041	0.0048	0.0041	0.0046	2001	0.0553
2002	0.0048	0.0043	0.0043	0.0054	0.0049	0.0044	0.0051	0.0044	0.0042	0.0040	0.0040	0.0045	2002	0.0559
2003	0.0041	0.0038	0.0040	0.0040	0.0039	0.0036	0.0038	0.0042	0.0046	0.0041	0.0039	0.0047	2003	0.0480
2004	0.0042	0.0038	0.0043	0.0039	0.0040	0.0048	0.0043	0.0045	0.0040	0.0038	0.0041	0.0043	2004	0.0502
2005	0.0041	0.0035	0.0041	0.0039	0.0040	0.0036	0.0034	0.0040	0.0035	0.0039	0.0039	0.0039	2005	0.0469
2006	0.0040	0.0036	0.0039	0.0039	0.0048	0.0044	0.0045	0.0043	0.0039	0.0042	0.0039	0.0036	2006	0.0468
2007	0.0043	0.0038	0.0039	0.0042	0.0041	0.0040	0.0046	0.0042	0.0037	0.0043	0.0039	0.0037	2007	0.0486

* Compound annual return

Table A-8
Long-Term Government Bonds: Capital Appreciation Returns

from January 1926 to December 1970

Year	Jan	Feb	Mar	Apr	May	Jun	Jul	Aug	Sep	Oct	Nov	Dec	Year	Jan–Dec*
1926	0.0106	0.0035	0.0009	0.0046	−0.0014	0.0005	−0.0027	−0.0031	0.0007	0.0072	0.0129	0.0048	1926	0.0391
1927	0.0045	0.0061	0.0224	−0.0032	0.0081	−0.0096	0.0022	0.0047	−0.0009	0.0071	0.0071	0.0045	1927	0.0540
1928	−0.0063	0.0036	0.0019	−0.0029	−0.0104	0.0015	−0.0245	0.0047	−0.0067	0.0128	−0.0024	−0.0024	1928	−0.0312
1929	−0.0119	−0.0183	−0.0171	0.0242	−0.0192	0.0081	−0.0032	−0.0064	−0.0004	0.0351	0.0211	−0.0120	1929	−0.0020
1930	−0.0086	0.0102	0.0055	−0.0043	0.0113	0.0022	0.0007	−0.0013	0.0045	0.0008	0.0017	−0.0098	1930	0.0128
1931	−0.0149	0.0059	0.0076	0.0059	0.0119	−0.0024	−0.0069	−0.0015	−0.0307	−0.0360	−0.0004	−0.0252	1931	−0.0846
1932	0.0002	0.0382	−0.0049	0.0574	−0.0216	0.0037	0.0453	−0.0025	0.0031	−0.0044	0.0006	0.0104	1932	0.1294
1933	0.0122	−0.0282	0.0070	−0.0057	0.0274	0.0025	−0.0043	0.0018	−0.0002	−0.0117	−0.0174	−0.0140	1933	−0.0314
1934	0.0228	0.0057	0.0170	0.0101	0.0106	0.0043	0.0016	−0.0143	−0.0169	0.0155	0.0013	0.0087	1934	0.0676
1935	0.0157	0.0070	0.0019	0.0056	−0.0079	0.0070	0.0022	−0.0156	−0.0014	0.0038	−0.0014	0.0047	1935	0.0214
1936	0.0031	0.0059	0.0083	0.0013	0.0019	−0.0003	0.0037	0.0088	−0.0053	−0.0017	0.0183	0.0017	1936	0.0464
1937	−0.0034	0.0067	−0.0433	0.0016	0.0031	−0.0043	0.0114	−0.0128	0.0022	0.0019	0.0072	0.0059	1937	−0.0248
1938	0.0034	0.0031	−0.0059	0.0187	0.0022	−0.0016	0.0022	−0.0022	0.0001	0.0065	−0.0043	0.0059	1938	0.0283
1939	0.0038	0.0061	0.0105	0.0099	0.0151	−0.0045	0.0095	−0.0219	−0.0564	0.0386	0.0142	0.0125	1939	0.0348
1940	−0.0037	0.0009	0.0158	−0.0053	−0.0318	0.0239	0.0032	0.0009	0.0092	0.0013	0.0187	0.0050	1940	0.0377
1941	−0.0217	0.0004	0.0078	0.0112	0.0011	0.0050	0.0005	0.0002	−0.0028	0.0124	−0.0044	−0.0194	1941	−0.0101
1942	0.0048	−0.0008	0.0071	−0.0049	0.0056	−0.0018	−0.0003	0.0017	−0.0016	0.0004	−0.0055	0.0028	1942	0.0074
1943	0.0013	−0.0024	−0.0012	0.0028	0.0031	−0.0003	−0.0021	0.0000	−0.0009	−0.0015	−0.0021	−0.0003	1943	−0.0037
1944	0.0000	0.0012	0.0000	−0.0006	0.0006	−0.0012	0.0015	0.0006	−0.0006	−0.0009	0.0003	0.0022	1944	0.0032
1945	0.0105	0.0058	0.0001	0.0141	0.0037	0.0150	−0.0104	0.0007	0.0037	0.0085	0.0108	0.0177	1945	0.0827
1946	0.0008	0.0017	−0.0006	−0.0152	−0.0030	0.0054	−0.0058	−0.0129	−0.0028	0.0055	−0.0072	0.0126	1946	−0.0215
1947	−0.0024	0.0005	0.0002	−0.0054	0.0016	−0.0009	0.0044	0.0064	−0.0062	−0.0055	−0.0191	−0.0213	1947	−0.0470
1948	0.0000	0.0028	0.0013	0.0025	0.0123	−0.0105	−0.0041	−0.0019	−0.0006	−0.0012	0.0055	0.0036	1948	0.0096
1949	0.0062	0.0031	0.0055	−0.0006	0.0000	0.0148	0.0016	0.0092	−0.0029	0.0001	0.0004	0.0035	1949	0.0415
1950	−0.0080	0.0005	−0.0010	0.0014	0.0014	−0.0042	0.0037	−0.0004	−0.0089	−0.0067	0.0017	−0.0001	1950	−0.0206
1951	0.0038	−0.0091	−0.0176	−0.0083	−0.0090	−0.0082	0.0116	0.0077	−0.0098	−0.0012	−0.0157	−0.0083	1951	−0.0627
1952	0.0005	−0.0007	0.0088	0.0149	−0.0054	−0.0019	−0.0041	−0.0091	−0.0153	0.0124	−0.0036	−0.0110	1952	−0.0148
1953	−0.0011	−0.0108	−0.0113	−0.0129	−0.0171	0.0195	0.0014	−0.0033	0.0275	0.0051	−0.0073	0.0182	1953	0.0067
1954	0.0066	0.0218	0.0034	0.0081	−0.0107	0.0138	0.0113	−0.0059	−0.0031	−0.0015	−0.0048	0.0042	1954	0.0435
1955	−0.0264	−0.0100	0.0063	−0.0022	0.0048	−0.0099	−0.0125	−0.0022	0.0049	0.0119	−0.0069	0.0013	1955	−0.0407
1956	0.0058	−0.0025	−0.0172	−0.0139	0.0199	0.0004	−0.0234	−0.0213	0.0025	−0.0083	−0.0084	−0.0206	1956	−0.0846
1957	0.0317	0.0000	−0.0050	−0.0250	−0.0052	−0.0206	−0.0074	−0.0028	0.0045	−0.0081	0.0504	0.0277	1957	0.0382
1958	−0.0112	0.0075	0.0075	0.0160	−0.0023	−0.0187	−0.0305	−0.0463	−0.0149	0.0106	0.0092	−0.0213	1958	−0.0923
1959	−0.0111	0.0087	−0.0018	−0.0150	−0.0038	−0.0026	0.0025	−0.0076	−0.0091	0.0115	−0.0154	−0.0195	1959	−0.0620
1960	0.0077	0.0167	0.0246	−0.0202	0.0115	0.0139	0.0335	−0.0101	0.0043	−0.0061	−0.0098	0.0247	1960	0.0929
1961	−0.0140	0.0170	−0.0069	0.0085	−0.0080	−0.0106	0.0001	−0.0071	0.0097	0.0037	−0.0052	−0.0156	1961	−0.0286
1962	−0.0051	0.0071	0.0220	0.0049	0.0014	−0.0106	−0.0143	0.0153	0.0031	0.0049	−0.0010	0.0003	1962	0.0278
1963	−0.0033	−0.0022	−0.0022	−0.0046	−0.0010	−0.0011	−0.0005	−0.0011	−0.0029	−0.0060	0.0019	−0.0042	1963	−0.0270
1964	−0.0048	−0.0043	0.0000	0.0012	0.0018	0.0031	−0.0027	−0.0015	0.0015	0.0009	−0.0018	−0.0005	1964	−0.0072
1965	0.0007	−0.0018	0.0016	0.0003	−0.0015	0.0009	−0.0012	−0.0050	−0.0069	−0.0007	−0.0099	−0.0115	1965	−0.0345
1966	−0.0142	−0.0284	0.0256	−0.0099	−0.0100	−0.0054	−0.0074	−0.0249	0.0292	0.0188	−0.0187	0.0374	1966	−0.0106
1967	0.0115	−0.0255	0.0159	−0.0326	−0.0082	−0.0351	0.0026	−0.0126	−0.0045	−0.0445	−0.0241	0.0148	1967	−0.1355
1968	0.0278	−0.0075	−0.0254	0.0178	−0.0003	0.0188	0.0241	−0.0044	−0.0146	−0.0177	−0.0312	−0.0412	1968	−0.0551
1969	−0.0256	−0.0004	−0.0036	0.0371	−0.0537	0.0159	0.0027	−0.0117	−0.0586	0.0309	−0.0293	−0.0129	1969	−0.1083
1970	−0.0077	0.0535	−0.0124	−0.0467	−0.0523	0.0422	0.0260	−0.0076	0.0172	−0.0164	0.0733	−0.0137	1970	0.0484

* Compound annual return

Table A-8 (Continued)

Long-Term Government Bonds: Capital Appreciation Returns

from January 1971 to December 2007

Year	Jan	Feb	Mar	Apr	May	Jun	Jul	Aug	Sep	Oct	Nov	Dec	Year	Jan–Dec*
1971	0.0455	−0.0209	0.0470	−0.0331	−0.0053	−0.0214	−0.0022	0.0416	0.0154	0.0120	−0.0098	−0.0006	1971	0.0661
1972	−0.0114	0.0041	−0.0131	−0.0021	0.0215	−0.0113	0.0165	−0.0021	−0.0129	0.0182	0.0178	−0.0275	1972	−0.0035
1973	−0.0375	−0.0037	0.0026	−0.0012	−0.0162	−0.0076	−0.0495	0.0329	0.0263	0.0153	−0.0238	−0.0142	1973	−0.0770
1974	−0.0144	−0.0079	−0.0350	−0.0320	0.0055	−0.0016	−0.0101	−0.0298	0.0176	0.0419	0.0233	0.0105	1974	−0.0345
1975	0.0157	0.0071	−0.0333	−0.0248	0.0145	0.0222	−0.0155	−0.0133	−0.0171	0.0403	−0.0170	0.0316	1975	0.0073
1976	0.0025	0.0001	0.0094	−0.0046	−0.0217	0.0135	0.0013	0.0142	0.0081	0.0023	0.0273	0.0265	1976	0.0807
1977	−0.0447	−0.0106	0.0026	0.0010	0.0058	0.0102	−0.0130	0.0131	−0.0089	−0.0156	0.0031	−0.0230	1977	−0.0786
1978	−0.0149	−0.0056	−0.0090	−0.0068	−0.0133	−0.0132	0.0070	0.0148	−0.0171	−0.0273	0.0117	−0.0198	1978	−0.0905
1979	0.0112	−0.0200	0.0056	−0.0188	0.0184	0.0240	−0.0161	−0.0108	−0.0190	−0.0922	0.0229	−0.0026	1979	−0.0984
1980	−0.0824	−0.0551	−0.0413	0.1424	0.0332	0.0272	−0.0560	−0.0513	−0.0358	−0.0360	0.0009	0.0244	1980	−0.1400
1981	−0.0209	−0.0524	0.0274	−0.0618	0.0518	−0.0288	−0.0462	−0.0496	−0.0259	0.0712	0.1297	−0.0813	1981	−0.1033
1982	−0.0062	0.0079	0.0107	0.0262	−0.0067	−0.0343	0.0387	0.0669	0.0519	0.0543	−0.0097	0.0219	1982	0.2395
1983	−0.0396	0.0410	−0.0183	0.0265	−0.0477	−0.0051	−0.0574	−0.0083	0.0408	−0.0227	0.0089	−0.0152	1983	−0.0982
1984	0.0141	−0.0270	−0.0254	−0.0210	−0.0619	0.0044	0.0577	0.0160	0.0248	0.0453	0.0027	−0.0007	1984	0.0232
1985	0.0268	−0.0575	0.0212	0.0140	0.0798	0.0061	−0.0274	0.0173	−0.0109	0.0248	0.0320	0.0455	1985	0.1784
1986	−0.0105	0.1073	0.0699	−0.0142	−0.0567	0.0543	−0.0173	0.0437	−0.0565	0.0220	0.0208	−0.0087	1986	0.1499
1987	0.0096	0.0143	−0.0289	−0.0538	−0.0171	0.0023	−0.0251	−0.0239	−0.0443	0.0544	−0.0038	0.0088	1987	−0.1069
1988	0.0595	−0.0019	−0.0378	−0.0230	−0.0180	0.0292	−0.0241	−0.0025	0.0269	0.0232	−0.0266	0.0035	1988	0.0036
1989	0.0124	−0.0248	0.0044	0.0088	0.0321	0.0480	0.0170	−0.0325	−0.0046	0.0307	0.0014	−0.0070	1989	0.0862
1990	−0.0416	−0.0090	−0.0115	−0.0277	0.0340	0.0162	0.0033	−0.0490	0.0048	0.0135	0.0331	0.0114	1990	−0.0261
1991	0.0059	−0.0033	−0.0026	0.0065	−0.0068	−0.0126	0.0082	0.0272	0.0236	−0.0011	0.0022	0.0513	1991	0.1010
1992	−0.0385	−0.0008	−0.0161	−0.0049	0.0181	0.0133	0.0334	0.0007	0.0127	−0.0255	−0.0051	0.0183	1992	0.0034
1993	0.0222	0.0299	−0.0042	0.0015	−0.0006	0.0387	0.0138	0.0378	−0.0045	0.0048	−0.0312	−0.0035	1993	0.1071
1994	0.0202	−0.0498	−0.0453	−0.0208	−0.0146	−0.0161	0.0303	−0.0152	−0.0392	−0.0091	0.0002	0.0095	1994	−0.1429
1995	0.0203	0.0227	0.0028	0.0112	0.0725	0.0084	−0.0223	0.0179	0.0122	0.0237	0.0198	0.0223	1995	0.2304
1996	−0.0065	−0.0530	−0.0262	−0.0224	−0.0112	0.0149	−0.0045	−0.0196	0.0230	0.0345	0.0299	−0.0312	1996	−0.0737
1997	−0.0135	−0.0046	−0.0311	0.0196	0.0037	0.0138	0.0567	−0.0367	0.0258	0.0287	0.0101	0.0130	1997	0.0851
1998	0.0152	−0.0116	−0.0028	−0.0023	0.0135	0.0176	−0.0088	0.0416	0.0350	−0.0260	0.0052	−0.0077	1998	0.0689
1999	0.0079	−0.0560	−0.0061	−0.0028	−0.0230	−0.0133	−0.0130	−0.0105	0.0032	−0.0062	−0.0117	−0.0210	1999	−0.1435
2000	0.0171	0.0213	0.0312	−0.0123	−0.0111	0.0192	0.0120	0.0190	−0.0203	0.0135	0.0270	0.0198	2000	0.1436
2001	−0.0044	0.0149	−0.0119	−0.0360	−0.0013	0.0038	0.0324	0.0159	0.0040	0.0416	−0.0512	−0.0229	2001	−0.0189
2002	0.0090	0.0072	−0.0479	0.0355	−0.0034	0.0143	0.0252	0.0420	0.0374	−0.0334	−0.0161	0.0462	2002	0.1169
2003	−0.0147	0.0291	−0.0175	0.0062	0.0553	−0.0190	−0.1020	0.0124	0.0501	−0.0324	−0.0012	0.0093	2003	−0.0336
2004	0.0146	0.0192	0.0098	−0.0627	−0.0090	0.0074	0.0113	0.0350	0.0057	0.0115	−0.0275	0.0207	2004	0.0326
2005	0.0260	−0.0163	−0.0112	0.0334	0.0256	0.0131	−0.0322	0.0292	−0.0373	−0.0235	0.0037	0.0228	2005	0.0302
2006	−0.0157	0.0203	−0.0578	−0.0285	−0.0038	0.0048	0.0154	0.0256	0.0132	0.0035	0.0169	−0.0272	2006	−0.0364
2007	−0.0146	0.0297	−0.0184	0.0043	−0.0242	−0.0131	0.0238	0.0157	−0.0025	0.0112	0.0429	−0.0066	2007	0.0469

* Compound annual return

Table A-9
Long-Term Government Bonds: Yields

from January 1926 to December 1970

Year	Jan	Feb	Mar	Apr	May	Jun	Jul	Aug	Sep	Oct	Nov	Dec	Yr-end	Yield
1926	0.0374	0.0372	0.0371	0.0368	0.0369	0.0368	0.0370	0.0373	0.0372	0.0367	0.0358	0.0354	1926	0.0354
1927	0.0351	0.0347	0.0331	0.0333	0.0327	0.0334	0.0333	0.0329	0.0330	0.0325	0.0320	0.0316	1927	0.0316
1928	0.0321	0.0318	0.0317	0.0319	0.0327	0.0326	0.0344	0.0341	0.0346	0.0336	0.0338	0.0340	1928	0.0340
1929	0.0349	0.0363	0.0377	0.0358	0.0373	0.0367	0.0369	0.0375	0.0375	0.0347	0.0331	0.0340	1929	0.0340
1930	0.0347	0.0339	0.0335	0.0338	0.0329	0.0328	0.0327	0.0328	0.0324	0.0324	0.0322	0.0330	1930	0.0330
1931	0.0343	0.0338	0.0332	0.0327	0.0317	0.0319	0.0325	0.0326	0.0353	0.0385	0.0385	0.0407	1931	0.0407
1932	0.0390	0.0367	0.0370	0.0336	0.0349	0.0347	0.0320	0.0321	0.0319	0.0322	0.0322	0.0315	1932	0.0315
1933	0.0308	0.0325	0.0321	0.0325	0.0308	0.0306	0.0309	0.0308	0.0308	0.0315	0.0327	0.0336	1933	0.0336
1934	0.0321	0.0317	0.0307	0.0300	0.0292	0.0289	0.0288	0.0299	0.0310	0.0300	0.0299	0.0293	1934	0.0293
1935	0.0281	0.0275	0.0274	0.0269	0.0276	0.0270	0.0268	0.0281	0.0282	0.0279	0.0280	0.0276	1935	0.0276
1936	0.0285	0.0281	0.0275	0.0274	0.0273	0.0273	0.0271	0.0264	0.0268	0.0269	0.0257	0.0255	1936	0.0255
1937	0.0258	0.0253	0.0285	0.0284	0.0282	0.0285	0.0277	0.0286	0.0284	0.0283	0.0278	0.0273	1937	0.0273
1938	0.0271	0.0268	0.0273	0.0259	0.0257	0.0259	0.0257	0.0259	0.0259	0.0254	0.0257	0.0252	1938	0.0252
1939	0.0249	0.0245	0.0237	0.0229	0.0217	0.0221	0.0213	0.0231	0.0278	0.0247	0.0236	0.0226	1939	0.0226
1940	0.0229	0.0228	0.0215	0.0220	0.0246	0.0227	0.0224	0.0223	0.0215	0.0214	0.0199	0.0194	1940	0.0194
1941	0.0213	0.0213	0.0206	0.0196	0.0195	0.0191	0.0191	0.0190	0.0193	0.0182	0.0186	0.0204	1941	0.0204
1942	0.0247	0.0247	0.0244	0.0246	0.0243	0.0244	0.0244	0.0244	0.0244	0.0244	0.0247	0.0246	1942	0.0246
1943	0.0245	0.0246	0.0247	0.0246	0.0244	0.0244	0.0245	0.0245	0.0246	0.0247	0.0248	0.0248	1943	0.0248
1944	0.0248	0.0247	0.0247	0.0248	0.0247	0.0248	0.0247	0.0247	0.0247	0.0247	0.0247	0.0246	1944	0.0246
1945	0.0240	0.0236	0.0236	0.0228	0.0226	0.0217	0.0224	0.0223	0.0221	0.0216	0.0210	0.0199	1945	0.0199
1946	0.0199	0.0198	0.0198	0.0207	0.0209	0.0206	0.0209	0.0217	0.0219	0.0216	0.0220	0.0212	1946	0.0212
1947	0.0214	0.0214	0.0213	0.0217	0.0216	0.0216	0.0214	0.0210	0.0213	0.0217	0.0229	0.0243	1947	0.0243
1948	0.0243	0.0241	0.0241	0.0239	0.0231	0.0238	0.0241	0.0242	0.0242	0.0243	0.0239	0.0237	1948	0.0237
1949	0.0233	0.0231	0.0227	0.0227	0.0227	0.0217	0.0216	0.0210	0.0212	0.0212	0.0212	0.0209	1949	0.0209
1950	0.0215	0.0214	0.0215	0.0214	0.0213	0.0216	0.0214	0.0214	0.0220	0.0225	0.0224	0.0224	1950	0.0224
1951	0.0221	0.0228	0.0241	0.0248	0.0254	0.0259	0.0252	0.0246	0.0253	0.0254	0.0264	0.0269	1951	0.0269
1952	0.0268	0.0269	0.0263	0.0254	0.0257	0.0259	0.0261	0.0267	0.0277	0.0269	0.0272	0.0279	1952	0.0279
1953	0.0279	0.0287	0.0294	0.0303	0.0314	0.0301	0.0301	0.0303	0.0284	0.0281	0.0286	0.0274	1953	0.0274
1954	0.0291	0.0279	0.0278	0.0273	0.0279	0.0272	0.0266	0.0269	0.0271	0.0271	0.0274	0.0272	1954	0.0272
1955	0.0286	0.0292	0.0288	0.0290	0.0287	0.0293	0.0300	0.0301	0.0298	0.0292	0.0295	0.0295	1955	0.0295
1956	0.0292	0.0293	0.0303	0.0311	0.0299	0.0299	0.0313	0.0325	0.0324	0.0329	0.0333	0.0345	1956	0.0345
1957	0.0328	0.0328	0.0331	0.0345	0.0348	0.0361	0.0365	0.0367	0.0364	0.0369	0.0340	0.0323	1957	0.0323
1958	0.0330	0.0325	0.0321	0.0311	0.0313	0.0324	0.0343	0.0371	0.0380	0.0374	0.0368	0.0382	1958	0.0382
1959	0.0408	0.0402	0.0403	0.0414	0.0417	0.0419	0.0417	0.0423	0.0429	0.0421	0.0432	0.0447	1959	0.0447
1960	0.0441	0.0429	0.0411	0.0426	0.0417	0.0407	0.0382	0.0390	0.0387	0.0391	0.0399	0.0380	1960	0.0380
1961	0.0404	0.0392	0.0397	0.0391	0.0397	0.0404	0.0404	0.0410	0.0403	0.0400	0.0404	0.0415	1961	0.0415
1962	0.0419	0.0414	0.0398	0.0394	0.0393	0.0401	0.0412	0.0401	0.0398	0.0395	0.0396	0.0395	1962	0.0395
1963	0.0398	0.0400	0.0401	0.0405	0.0406	0.0407	0.0407	0.0408	0.0410	0.0415	0.0414	0.0417	1963	0.0417
1964	0.0421	0.0424	0.0424	0.0423	0.0422	0.0419	0.0421	0.0423	0.0421	0.0421	0.0422	0.0423	1964	0.0423
1965	0.0422	0.0424	0.0422	0.0422	0.0423	0.0423	0.0424	0.0428	0.0433	0.0433	0.0441	0.0450	1965	0.0450
1966	0.0457	0.0477	0.0460	0.0467	0.0473	0.0477	0.0482	0.0499	0.0480	0.0467	0.0480	0.0455	1966	0.0455
1967	0.0448	0.0465	0.0455	0.0477	0.0482	0.0507	0.0505	0.0514	0.0517	0.0549	0.0567	0.0556	1967	0.0556
1968	0.0536	0.0542	0.0560	0.0547	0.0547	0.0534	0.0517	0.0520	0.0531	0.0543	0.0566	0.0598	1968	0.0598
1969	0.0617	0.0618	0.0620	0.0593	0.0635	0.0623	0.0621	0.0630	0.0677	0.0653	0.0676	0.0687	1969	0.0687
1970	0.0693	0.0651	0.0661	0.0699	0.0743	0.0709	0.0687	0.0694	0.0680	0.0693	0.0637	0.0648	1970	0.0648

Table A-9 (Continued)

Long-Term Government Bonds: Yields

from January 1971 to December 2007

Year	Jan	Feb	Mar	Apr	May	Jun	Jul	Aug	Sep	Oct	Nov	Dec	Yr-end	Yield
1971	0.0612	0.0629	0.0593	0.0619	0.0624	0.0641	0.0643	0.0610	0.0598	0.0588	0.0596	0.0597	1971	0.0597
1972	0.0606	0.0602	0.0613	0.0615	0.0597	0.0607	0.0593	0.0595	0.0606	0.0591	0.0577	0.0599	1972	0.0599
1973	0.0685	0.0688	0.0686	0.0687	0.0703	0.0710	0.0760	0.0728	0.0703	0.0689	0.0712	0.0726	1973	0.0726
1974	0.0740	0.0748	0.0783	0.0816	0.0810	0.0812	0.0823	0.0855	0.0837	0.0795	0.0771	0.0760	1974	0.0760
1975	0.0796	0.0788	0.0824	0.0852	0.0836	0.0813	0.0829	0.0844	0.0862	0.0819	0.0838	0.0805	1975	0.0805
1976	0.0802	0.0802	0.0792	0.0797	0.0821	0.0807	0.0805	0.0790	0.0781	0.0779	0.0749	0.0721	1976	0.0721
1977	0.0764	0.0775	0.0772	0.0771	0.0765	0.0754	0.0768	0.0754	0.0764	0.0781	0.0777	0.0803	1977	0.0803
1978	0.0816	0.0822	0.0831	0.0838	0.0852	0.0865	0.0858	0.0843	0.0860	0.0889	0.0877	0.0898	1978	0.0898
1979	0.0886	0.0908	0.0902	0.0922	0.0903	0.0877	0.0895	0.0907	0.0927	0.1034	0.1009	0.1012	1979	0.1012
1980	0.1114	0.1186	0.1239	0.1076	0.1037	0.1006	0.1074	0.1140	0.1185	0.1231	0.1230	0.1199	1980	0.1199
1981	0.1211	0.1283	0.1248	0.1332	0.1265	0.1304	0.1370	0.1445	0.1482	0.1384	0.1220	0.1334	1981	0.1334
1982	0.1415	0.1402	0.1387	0.1348	0.1358	0.1412	0.1352	0.1254	0.1183	0.1112	0.1125	0.1095	1982	0.1095
1983	0.1113	0.1060	0.1083	0.1051	0.1112	0.1119	0.1198	0.1210	0.1157	0.1188	0.1176	0.1197	1983	0.1197
1984	0.1180	0.1217	0.1253	0.1284	0.1381	0.1374	0.1293	0.1270	0.1235	0.1173	0.1169	0.1170	1984	0.1170
1985	0.1127	0.1209	0.1181	0.1162	0.1062	0.1055	0.1091	0.1068	0.1082	0.1051	0.1011	0.0956	1985	0.0956
1986	0.0958	0.0841	0.0766	0.0782	0.0848	0.0790	0.0809	0.0763	0.0827	0.0803	0.0779	0.0789	1986	0.0789
1987	0.0778	0.0763	0.0795	0.0859	0.0880	0.0877	0.0907	0.0936	0.0992	0.0926	0.0931	0.0920	1987	0.0920
1988	0.0852	0.0854	0.0901	0.0929	0.0952	0.0917	0.0947	0.0950	0.0917	0.0889	0.0923	0.0918	1988	0.0918
1989	0.0903	0.0935	0.0929	0.0918	0.0878	0.0821	0.0801	0.0841	0.0847	0.0810	0.0808	0.0816	1989	0.0816
1990	0.0865	0.0876	0.0889	0.0924	0.0883	0.0864	0.0860	0.0920	0.0914	0.0898	0.0858	0.0844	1990	0.0844
1991	0.0837	0.0841	0.0844	0.0837	0.0845	0.0860	0.0850	0.0818	0.0790	0.0791	0.0789	0.0730	1991	0.0730
1992	0.0776	0.0777	0.0797	0.0803	0.0781	0.0765	0.0726	0.0725	0.0710	0.0741	0.0748	0.0726	1992	0.0726
1993	0.0725	0.0698	0.0702	0.0701	0.0701	0.0668	0.0656	0.0623	0.0627	0.0623	0.0651	0.0654	1993	0.0654
1994	0.0637	0.0682	0.0725	0.0745	0.0759	0.0774	0.0746	0.0761	0.0800	0.0809	0.0808	0.0799	1994	0.0799
1995	0.0780	0.0758	0.0755	0.0745	0.0677	0.0670	0.0691	0.0674	0.0663	0.0641	0.0623	0.0603	1995	0.0603
1996	0.0609	0.0659	0.0684	0.0706	0.0717	0.0703	0.0707	0.0726	0.0704	0.0671	0.0643	0.0673	1996	0.0673
1997	0.0689	0.0694	0.0723	0.0705	0.0701	0.0688	0.0637	0.0672	0.0649	0.0623	0.0614	0.0602	1997	0.0602
1998	0.0589	0.0599	0.0602	0.0604	0.0592	0.0576	0.0584	0.0547	0.0517	0.0540	0.0535	0.0542	1998	0.0542
1999	0.0536	0.0587	0.0592	0.0594	0.0615	0.0627	0.0639	0.0649	0.0646	0.0651	0.0662	0.0682	1999	0.0682
2000	0.0666	0.0646	0.0618	0.0630	0.0640	0.0622	0.0611	0.0594	0.0612	0.0600	0.0576	0.0558	2000	0.0558
2001	0.0562	0.0549	0.0559	0.0593	0.0594	0.0590	0.0561	0.0546	0.0542	0.0506	0.0553	0.0575	2001	0.0575
2002	0.0569	0.0563	0.0604	0.0575	0.0578	0.0566	0.0544	0.0510	0.0480	0.0508	0.0521	0.0484	2002	0.0484
2003	0.0495	0.0472	0.0486	0.0481	0.0436	0.0452	0.0542	0.0532	0.0490	0.0518	0.0519	0.0511	2003	0.0511
2004	0.0499	0.0483	0.0474	0.0531	0.0539	0.0532	0.0523	0.0493	0.0488	0.0478	0.0502	0.0484	2004	0.0484
2005	0.0465	0.0479	0.0488	0.0461	0.0440	0.0429	0.0456	0.0432	0.0464	0.0484	0.0481	0.0461	2005	0.0461
2006	0.0474	0.0457	0.0507	0.0532	0.0535	0.0531	0.0518	0.0496	0.0484	0.0481	0.0467	0.0491	2006	0.0491
2007	0.0502	0.0477	0.0493	0.0489	0.0510	0.0521	0.0501	0.0487	0.0489	0.0480	0.0445	0.0450	2007	0.0450

Table A-10
Intermediate-Term Government Bonds: Total Returns

from January 1926 to December 1970

Year	Jan	Feb	Mar	Apr	May	Jun	Jul	Aug	Sep	Oct	Nov	Dec	Year	Jan–Dec*
1926	0.0068	0.0032	0.0041	0.0090	0.0008	0.0027	0.0013	0.0009	0.0050	0.0054	0.0045	0.0089	1926	0.0538
1927	0.0057	0.0038	0.0038	0.0016	0.0020	0.0029	0.0043	0.0056	0.0060	−0.0034	0.0083	0.0037	1927	0.0452
1928	0.0046	−0.0004	0.0010	−0.0003	−0.0006	0.0017	−0.0089	0.0050	0.0028	0.0032	0.0019	−0.0007	1928	0.0092
1929	−0.0029	−0.0018	0.0005	0.0089	−0.0061	0.0107	0.0066	0.0052	−0.0014	0.0168	0.0180	0.0044	1929	0.0601
1930	−0.0041	0.0094	0.0161	−0.0071	0.0061	0.0142	0.0054	0.0022	0.0063	0.0076	0.0070	0.0024	1930	0.0672
1931	−0.0071	0.0099	0.0052	0.0083	0.0119	−0.0214	0.0016	0.0017	−0.0113	−0.0105	0.0049	−0.0159	1931	−0.0232
1932	−0.0032	0.0128	0.0078	0.0194	−0.0090	0.0108	0.0120	0.0124	0.0027	0.0045	0.0031	0.0118	1932	0.0881
1933	−0.0016	−0.0001	0.0099	0.0057	0.0199	0.0008	−0.0006	0.0073	0.0026	−0.0025	0.0027	−0.0253	1933	0.0183
1934	0.0130	0.0052	0.0189	0.0182	0.0120	0.0091	−0.0024	−0.0092	−0.0138	0.0190	0.0046	0.0125	1934	0.0900
1935	0.0114	0.0105	0.0125	0.0107	−0.0035	0.0113	0.0037	−0.0071	−0.0057	0.0109	0.0014	0.0120	1935	0.0701
1936	−0.0003	0.0069	0.0031	0.0024	0.0038	0.0012	0.0022	0.0050	0.0010	0.0025	0.0081	−0.0057	1936	0.0306
1937	−0.0031	0.0007	−0.0164	0.0047	0.0080	−0.0012	0.0059	−0.0043	0.0081	0.0032	0.0042	0.0062	1937	0.0156
1938	0.0085	0.0052	−0.0012	0.0230	0.0023	0.0075	0.0010	0.0015	−0.0013	0.0093	−0.0001	0.0052	1938	0.0623
1939	0.0029	0.0082	0.0081	0.0038	0.0095	0.0002	0.0040	−0.0147	−0.0262	0.0315	0.0074	0.0108	1939	0.0452
1940	−0.0014	0.0035	0.0088	0.0002	−0.0214	0.0187	0.0003	0.0043	0.0047	0.0036	0.0056	0.0028	1940	0.0296
1941	0.0001	−0.0047	0.0069	0.0033	0.0012	0.0056	0.0000	0.0011	0.0000	0.0023	−0.0092	−0.0016	1941	0.0050
1942	0.0074	0.0015	0.0023	0.0022	0.0016	0.0013	0.0000	0.0017	−0.0023	0.0017	0.0017	0.0000	1942	0.0194
1943	0.0039	0.0013	0.0021	0.0024	0.0057	0.0033	0.0021	0.0002	0.0014	0.0017	0.0015	0.0021	1943	0.0281
1944	0.0011	0.0016	0.0019	0.0028	0.0005	0.0007	0.0029	0.0024	0.0011	0.0011	0.0009	0.0010	1944	0.0180
1945	0.0052	0.0038	0.0004	0.0014	0.0012	0.0019	0.0000	0.0016	0.0017	0.0016	0.0010	0.0021	1945	0.0222
1946	0.0039	0.0048	−0.0038	−0.0020	0.0006	0.0033	−0.0010	0.0004	−0.0011	0.0026	−0.0008	0.0032	1946	0.0100
1947	0.0023	0.0006	0.0024	−0.0013	0.0008	0.0008	0.0006	0.0026	0.0000	−0.0023	0.0006	0.0021	1947	0.0091
1948	0.0015	0.0018	0.0018	0.0019	0.0053	−0.0008	−0.0002	−0.0004	0.0010	0.0013	0.0021	0.0032	1948	0.0185
1949	0.0028	0.0011	0.0025	0.0015	0.0023	0.0050	0.0020	0.0031	0.0008	0.0006	0.0002	0.0012	1949	0.0232
1950	−0.0005	0.0008	0.0000	0.0008	0.0020	0.0003	0.0020	−0.0007	−0.0004	0.0001	0.0018	0.0008	1950	0.0070
1951	0.0022	0.0007	−0.0127	0.0057	−0.0040	0.0050	0.0058	0.0036	−0.0057	0.0016	0.0032	−0.0016	1951	0.0036
1952	0.0038	−0.0020	0.0067	0.0054	0.0019	−0.0035	−0.0034	−0.0024	0.0019	0.0066	−0.0006	0.0019	1952	0.0163
1953	−0.0002	0.0003	−0.0017	−0.0096	−0.0117	0.0155	0.0056	−0.0008	0.0194	0.0038	0.0014	0.0103	1953	0.0323
1954	0.0065	0.0100	0.0027	0.0043	−0.0073	0.0125	−0.0005	0.0011	−0.0020	−0.0009	−0.0001	0.0005	1954	0.0268
1955	−0.0032	−0.0052	0.0024	0.0004	0.0001	−0.0036	−0.0071	0.0007	0.0082	0.0072	−0.0053	−0.0011	1955	−0.0065
1956	0.0105	0.0003	−0.0100	−0.0001	0.0112	0.0003	−0.0095	−0.0103	0.0092	−0.0019	−0.0047	0.0011	1956	−0.0042
1957	0.0237	−0.0012	0.0018	−0.0101	−0.0017	−0.0106	−0.0015	0.0109	0.0002	0.0043	0.0396	0.0215	1957	0.0784
1958	0.0034	0.0139	0.0053	0.0052	0.0060	−0.0068	−0.0091	−0.0356	−0.0017	0.0002	0.0132	−0.0061	1958	−0.0129
1959	−0.0013	0.0107	−0.0037	−0.0052	−0.0001	−0.0077	0.0034	−0.0078	0.0020	0.0174	−0.0092	−0.0020	1959	−0.0039
1960	0.0154	0.0072	0.0292	−0.0064	0.0031	0.0217	0.0267	−0.0004	0.0029	0.0016	−0.0094	0.0210	1960	0.1176
1961	−0.0059	0.0090	0.0037	0.0054	−0.0028	−0.0025	0.0007	0.0019	0.0079	0.0014	−0.0019	0.0018	1961	0.0185
1962	−0.0045	0.0155	0.0089	0.0025	0.0049	−0.0028	−0.0012	0.0125	0.0021	0.0051	0.0060	0.0056	1962	0.0556
1963	−0.0029	0.0017	0.0027	0.0030	0.0014	0.0014	0.0003	0.0019	0.0014	0.0011	0.0040	0.0003	1963	0.0164
1964	0.0033	0.0012	0.0016	0.0033	0.0081	0.0036	0.0027	0.0027	0.0045	0.0032	−0.0004	0.0058	1964	0.0404
1965	0.0042	0.0018	0.0043	0.0026	0.0035	0.0049	0.0017	0.0019	−0.0005	0.0000	0.0007	−0.0149	1965	0.0102
1966	0.0003	−0.0083	0.0187	−0.0019	0.0011	−0.0024	−0.0025	−0.0125	0.0216	0.0075	0.0027	0.0223	1966	0.0469
1967	0.0118	−0.0013	0.0183	−0.0089	0.0044	−0.0227	0.0133	−0.0036	0.0007	−0.0049	0.0028	0.0007	1967	0.0101
1968	0.0145	0.0040	−0.0026	−0.0016	0.0064	0.0167	0.0176	0.0021	0.0055	0.0009	−0.0013	−0.0173	1968	0.0454
1969	0.0086	−0.0013	0.0097	0.0079	−0.0082	−0.0084	0.0082	−0.0018	−0.0300	0.0333	−0.0047	−0.0193	1969	−0.0074
1970	0.0030	0.0439	0.0087	−0.0207	0.0110	0.0061	0.0152	0.0116	0.0196	0.0095	0.0451	0.0054	1970	0.1686

* Compound annual return

Table A-10 (Continued)
Intermediate-Term Government Bonds: Total Returns

from January 1971 to December 2007

Year	Jan	Feb	Mar	Apr	May	Jun	Jul	Aug	Sep	Oct	Nov	Dec	Year	Jan–Dec*
1971	0.0168	0.0224	0.0186	−0.0327	0.0011	−0.0187	0.0027	0.0350	0.0026	0.0220	0.0052	0.0110	1971	0.0872
1972	0.0106	0.0014	0.0015	0.0014	0.0016	0.0045	0.0015	0.0015	0.0014	0.0016	0.0045	0.0192	1972	0.0516
1973	−0.0006	−0.0075	0.0046	0.0064	0.0057	−0.0006	−0.0276	0.0254	0.0250	0.0050	0.0064	0.0040	1973	0.0461
1974	0.0009	0.0035	−0.0212	−0.0152	0.0130	−0.0087	0.0007	−0.0012	0.0319	0.0109	0.0236	0.0185	1974	0.0569
1975	0.0053	0.0148	−0.0059	−0.0186	0.0260	0.0027	−0.0030	−0.0009	0.0010	0.0366	−0.0010	0.0198	1975	0.0783
1976	0.0057	0.0084	0.0075	0.0116	−0.0145	0.0159	0.0119	0.0189	0.0076	0.0147	0.0321	0.0026	1976	0.1287
1977	−0.0190	0.0048	0.0055	0.0051	0.0056	0.0102	0.0001	0.0008	0.0015	−0.0060	0.0079	−0.0023	1977	0.0141
1978	0.0013	0.0017	0.0037	0.0024	−0.0002	−0.0021	0.0098	0.0079	0.0057	−0.0112	0.0092	0.0063	1978	0.0349
1979	0.0055	−0.0059	0.0112	0.0033	0.0193	0.0205	−0.0011	−0.0091	0.0006	−0.0468	0.0363	0.0087	1979	0.0409
1980	−0.0135	−0.0641	0.0143	0.1198	0.0490	−0.0077	−0.0106	−0.0387	−0.0038	−0.0152	0.0029	0.0171	1980	0.0391
1981	0.0032	−0.0235	0.0263	−0.0216	0.0245	0.0060	−0.0270	−0.0178	0.0164	0.0611	0.0624	−0.0142	1981	0.0945
1982	0.0050	0.0148	0.0042	0.0299	0.0146	−0.0135	0.0464	0.0469	0.0325	0.0531	0.0080	0.0185	1982	0.2910
1983	0.0007	0.0252	−0.0049	0.0259	−0.0122	0.0016	−0.0198	0.0081	0.0315	0.0019	0.0103	0.0047	1983	0.0741
1984	0.0177	−0.0064	−0.0035	−0.0003	−0.0250	0.0099	0.0393	0.0101	0.0202	0.0383	0.0192	0.0143	1984	0.1402
1985	0.0206	−0.0179	0.0166	0.0264	0.0485	0.0108	−0.0045	0.0148	0.0113	0.0162	0.0195	0.0257	1985	0.2033
1986	0.0082	0.0275	0.0338	0.0081	−0.0215	0.0276	0.0157	0.0266	−0.0110	0.0162	0.0113	0.0007	1986	0.1514
1987	0.0107	0.0059	−0.0031	−0.0244	−0.0038	0.0122	0.0025	−0.0038	−0.0141	0.0299	0.0083	0.0093	1987	0.0290
1988	0.0316	0.0123	−0.0086	−0.0044	−0.0049	0.0181	−0.0047	−0.0009	0.0196	0.0148	−0.0115	−0.0010	1988	0.0610
1989	0.0121	−0.0051	0.0049	0.0220	0.0212	0.0324	0.0235	−0.0246	0.0069	0.0237	0.0084	0.0012	1989	0.1329
1990	−0.0104	0.0007	0.0002	−0.0077	0.0261	0.0151	0.0174	−0.0092	0.0094	0.0171	0.0193	0.0161	1990	0.0973
1991	0.0107	0.0048	0.0023	0.0117	0.0059	−0.0023	0.0129	0.0247	0.0216	0.0134	0.0128	0.0265	1991	0.1546
1992	−0.0195	0.0022	−0.0079	0.0098	0.0222	0.0177	0.0242	0.0150	0.0194	−0.0182	−0.0084	0.0146	1992	0.0719
1993	0.0270	0.0243	0.0043	0.0088	−0.0009	0.0201	0.0005	0.0223	0.0056	0.0018	−0.0093	0.0032	1993	0.1124
1994	0.0138	−0.0258	−0.0257	−0.0105	−0.0002	−0.0028	0.0169	0.0026	−0.0158	−0.0023	−0.0070	0.0053	1994	−0.0514
1995	0.0182	0.0234	0.0063	0.0143	0.0369	0.0079	−0.0016	0.0086	0.0064	0.0121	0.0149	0.0095	1995	0.1680
1996	0.0006	−0.0138	−0.0118	−0.0050	−0.0032	0.0117	0.0025	−0.0005	0.0155	0.0183	0.0149	−0.0078	1996	0.0210
1997	0.0025	0.0002	−0.0114	0.0148	0.0077	0.0103	0.0264	−0.0098	0.0151	0.0150	−0.0001	0.0106	1997	0.0838
1998	0.0180	−0.0039	0.0026	0.0061	0.0070	0.0079	0.0027	0.0271	0.0330	0.0041	−0.0098	0.0037	1998	0.1021
1999	0.0055	−0.0262	0.0086	0.0021	−0.0147	0.0032	−0.0005	0.0015	0.0097	−0.0008	−0.0008	−0.0048	1999	−0.0177
2000	−0.0053	0.0078	0.0203	−0.0043	0.0052	0.0191	0.0072	0.0134	0.0096	0.0079	0.0174	0.0214	2000	0.1259
2001	0.0098	0.0105	0.0076	−0.0114	−0.0007	0.0066	0.0247	0.0095	0.0253	0.0180	−0.0171	−0.0082	2001	0.0762
2002	0.0036	0.0108	−0.0242	0.0239	0.0118	0.0169	0.0272	0.0167	0.0288	−0.0024	−0.0169	0.0279	2002	0.1293
2003	−0.0089	0.0179	−0.0007	0.0013	0.0273	−0.0035	−0.0319	−0.0027	0.0307	−0.0136	−0.0014	0.0109	2003	0.0240
2004	0.0052	0.0124	0.0100	−0.0334	−0.0049	0.0049	0.0082	0.0195	0.0012	0.0064	−0.0127	0.0067	2004	0.0225
2005	0.0026	−0.0111	−0.0038	0.0167	0.0103	0.0043	−0.0144	0.0161	−0.0124	−0.0063	0.0059	0.0061	2005	0.0136
2006	−0.0036	−0.0017	−0.0056	−0.0008	−0.0004	0.0022	0.0125	0.0135	0.0079	0.0052	0.0088	−0.0067	2006	0.0314
2007	−0.0020	0.0170	0.0024	0.0047	−0.0102	0.0011	0.0175	0.0185	0.0057	−0.0048	0.0425	0.0048	2007	0.1005

* Compound annual return

Table A-11

Intermediate-Term Government Bonds: Income Returns

from January 1926 to December 1970

Year	Jan	Feb	Mar	Apr	May	Jun	Jul	Aug	Sep	Oct	Nov	Dec	Year	Jan–Dec*
1926	0.0032	0.0032	0.0032	0.0031	0.0031	0.0031	0.0032	0.0032	0.0032	0.0031	0.0031	0.0030	1926	0.0378
1927	0.0029	0.0029	0.0029	0.0029	0.0029	0.0029	0.0029	0.0029	0.0028	0.0029	0.0028	0.0028	1927	0.0349
1928	0.0028	0.0028	0.0029	0.0029	0.0030	0.0030	0.0032	0.0032	0.0032	0.0032	0.0032	0.0033	1928	0.0364
1929	0.0034	0.0035	0.0036	0.0035	0.0037	0.0035	0.0035	0.0034	0.0035	0.0033	0.0030	0.0030	1929	0.0407
1930	0.0031	0.0030	0.0028	0.0030	0.0029	0.0027	0.0026	0.0026	0.0026	0.0025	0.0024	0.0024	1930	0.0330
1931	0.0026	0.0025	0.0024	0.0023	0.0021	0.0026	0.0026	0.0026	0.0028	0.0031	0.0031	0.0034	1931	0.0316
1932	0.0035	0.0034	0.0033	0.0030	0.0032	0.0031	0.0029	0.0027	0.0027	0.0027	0.0027	0.0025	1932	0.0363
1933	0.0026	0.0026	0.0025	0.0025	0.0021	0.0022	0.0022	0.0021	0.0021	0.0022	0.0022	0.0027	1933	0.0283
1934	0.0030	0.0024	0.0027	0.0024	0.0023	0.0021	0.0021	0.0021	0.0021	0.0026	0.0022	0.0023	1934	0.0293
1935	0.0021	0.0018	0.0018	0.0017	0.0016	0.0015	0.0015	0.0014	0.0015	0.0016	0.0015	0.0016	1935	0.0202
1936	0.0014	0.0013	0.0013	0.0012	0.0012	0.0013	0.0012	0.0012	0.0011	0.0011	0.0011	0.0010	1936	0.0144
1937	0.0010	0.0010	0.0012	0.0015	0.0013	0.0014	0.0014	0.0013	0.0014	0.0012	0.0012	0.0011	1937	0.0148
1938	0.0018	0.0016	0.0017	0.0017	0.0015	0.0014	0.0013	0.0014	0.0013	0.0014	0.0013	0.0013	1938	0.0182
1939	0.0013	0.0011	0.0012	0.0010	0.0011	0.0009	0.0009	0.0009	0.0011	0.0015	0.0010	0.0009	1939	0.0131
1940	0.0009	0.0008	0.0008	0.0007	0.0007	0.0010	0.0008	0.0008	0.0007	0.0007	0.0006	0.0005	1940	0.0090
1941	0.0006	0.0006	0.0008	0.0006	0.0006	0.0006	0.0005	0.0005	0.0005	0.0005	0.0004	0.0007	1941	0.0067
1942	0.0008	0.0006	0.0007	0.0006	0.0006	0.0006	0.0006	0.0006	0.0006	0.0006	0.0006	0.0006	1942	0.0076
1943	0.0014	0.0013	0.0014	0.0013	0.0013	0.0013	0.0013	0.0012	0.0012	0.0012	0.0012	0.0012	1943	0.0156
1944	0.0013	0.0012	0.0013	0.0012	0.0013	0.0012	0.0012	0.0012	0.0011	0.0012	0.0011	0.0011	1944	0.0144
1945	0.0012	0.0010	0.0010	0.0010	0.0010	0.0010	0.0010	0.0010	0.0009	0.0010	0.0009	0.0009	1945	0.0119
1946	0.0009	0.0008	0.0007	0.0009	0.0009	0.0009	0.0009	0.0009	0.0010	0.0010	0.0009	0.0010	1946	0.0108
1947	0.0010	0.0009	0.0010	0.0009	0.0010	0.0011	0.0010	0.0010	0.0010	0.0010	0.0010	0.0012	1947	0.0121
1948	0.0013	0.0012	0.0014	0.0013	0.0012	0.0013	0.0012	0.0013	0.0013	0.0013	0.0014	0.0013	1948	0.0156
1949	0.0013	0.0012	0.0013	0.0012	0.0013	0.0012	0.0010	0.0011	0.0010	0.0010	0.0010	0.0010	1949	0.0136
1950	0.0011	0.0010	0.0011	0.0010	0.0012	0.0011	0.0012	0.0011	0.0011	0.0013	0.0013	0.0013	1950	0.0139
1951	0.0016	0.0014	0.0015	0.0018	0.0017	0.0017	0.0018	0.0017	0.0015	0.0019	0.0017	0.0018	1951	0.0198
1952	0.0018	0.0017	0.0019	0.0017	0.0016	0.0017	0.0018	0.0018	0.0021	0.0020	0.0017	0.0021	1952	0.0219
1953	0.0019	0.0018	0.0021	0.0021	0.0022	0.0027	0.0024	0.0023	0.0023	0.0020	0.0020	0.0020	1953	0.0255
1954	0.0016	0.0014	0.0014	0.0013	0.0011	0.0016	0.0011	0.0012	0.0011	0.0012	0.0014	0.0014	1954	0.0160
1955	0.0018	0.0017	0.0020	0.0019	0.0021	0.0020	0.0020	0.0025	0.0023	0.0023	0.0021	0.0022	1955	0.0245
1956	0.0025	0.0021	0.0022	0.0026	0.0026	0.0023	0.0025	0.0027	0.0026	0.0030	0.0028	0.0030	1956	0.0305
1957	0.0030	0.0025	0.0026	0.0029	0.0030	0.0027	0.0036	0.0032	0.0032	0.0033	0.0031	0.0028	1957	0.0359
1958	0.0024	0.0021	0.0022	0.0021	0.0019	0.0021	0.0021	0.0022	0.0032	0.0032	0.0029	0.0032	1958	0.0293
1959	0.0031	0.0030	0.0033	0.0032	0.0033	0.0037	0.0038	0.0037	0.0039	0.0039	0.0038	0.0041	1959	0.0418
1960	0.0039	0.0039	0.0039	0.0032	0.0037	0.0035	0.0031	0.0030	0.0028	0.0029	0.0028	0.0031	1960	0.0415
1961	0.0030	0.0028	0.0029	0.0027	0.0030	0.0029	0.0031	0.0031	0.0030	0.0032	0.0030	0.0030	1961	0.0354
1962	0.0035	0.0031	0.0031	0.0031	0.0031	0.0029	0.0033	0.0032	0.0028	0.0033	0.0029	0.0030	1962	0.0373
1963	0.0030	0.0028	0.0029	0.0032	0.0031	0.0029	0.0034	0.0031	0.0033	0.0033	0.0031	0.0034	1963	0.0371
1964	0.0034	0.0030	0.0035	0.0033	0.0031	0.0036	0.0034	0.0033	0.0033	0.0033	0.0034	0.0034	1964	0.0400
1965	0.0033	0.0031	0.0037	0.0033	0.0033	0.0037	0.0034	0.0036	0.0034	0.0034	0.0038	0.0037	1965	0.0415
1966	0.0040	0.0036	0.0043	0.0038	0.0042	0.0040	0.0040	0.0047	0.0046	0.0044	0.0042	0.0042	1966	0.0493
1967	0.0041	0.0035	0.0039	0.0033	0.0042	0.0038	0.0045	0.0042	0.0041	0.0047	0.0046	0.0044	1967	0.0488
1968	0.0051	0.0043	0.0043	0.0049	0.0048	0.0043	0.0049	0.0042	0.0044	0.0044	0.0041	0.0047	1968	0.0549
1969	0.0054	0.0048	0.0049	0.0057	0.0050	0.0058	0.0059	0.0054	0.0061	0.0067	0.0056	0.0068	1969	0.0665
1970	0.0066	0.0061	0.0063	0.0059	0.0062	0.0067	0.0065	0.0062	0.0060	0.0057	0.0058	0.0050	1970	0.0749

* Compound annual return

Table A-11 (Continued)

Intermediate-Term Government Bonds: Income Returns

from January 1971 to December 2007

Year	Jan	Feb	Mar	Apr	May	Jun	Jul	Aug	Sep	Oct	Nov	Dec	Year	Jan–Dec*
1971	0.0047	0.0043	0.0047	0.0040	0.0044	0.0053	0.0053	0.0056	0.0048	0.0046	0.0047	0.0046	1971	0.0575
1972	0.0048	0.0044	0.0046	0.0044	0.0052	0.0048	0.0049	0.0050	0.0047	0.0053	0.0051	0.0049	1972	0.0575
1973	0.0056	0.0048	0.0054	0.0056	0.0056	0.0053	0.0059	0.0064	0.0055	0.0060	0.0055	0.0056	1973	0.0658
1974	0.0057	0.0051	0.0054	0.0065	0.0067	0.0059	0.0073	0.0067	0.0072	0.0067	0.0061	0.0064	1974	0.0724
1975	0.0061	0.0055	0.0059	0.0060	0.0063	0.0063	0.0063	0.0061	0.0069	0.0068	0.0055	0.0067	1975	0.0735
1976	0.0060	0.0055	0.0066	0.0059	0.0054	0.0069	0.0060	0.0062	0.0056	0.0054	0.0058	0.0050	1976	0.0710
1977	0.0051	0.0050	0.0056	0.0053	0.0058	0.0055	0.0052	0.0059	0.0056	0.0059	0.0059	0.0059	1977	0.0649
1978	0.0066	0.0057	0.0066	0.0060	0.0071	0.0066	0.0070	0.0068	0.0065	0.0072	0.0072	0.0069	1978	0.0783
1979	0.0079	0.0066	0.0075	0.0077	0.0077	0.0070	0.0074	0.0073	0.0070	0.0084	0.0089	0.0086	1979	0.0904
1980	0.0086	0.0083	0.0107	0.0103	0.0081	0.0075	0.0079	0.0076	0.0097	0.0094	0.0096	0.0111	1980	0.1055
1981	0.0101	0.0095	0.0117	0.0106	0.0110	0.0118	0.0116	0.0120	0.0130	0.0129	0.0121	0.0108	1981	0.1297
1982	0.0107	0.0102	0.0122	0.0112	0.0101	0.0118	0.0113	0.0109	0.0097	0.0089	0.0087	0.0085	1982	0.1281
1983	0.0084	0.0079	0.0084	0.0081	0.0086	0.0085	0.0082	0.0103	0.0094	0.0092	0.0091	0.0091	1983	0.1035
1984	0.0096	0.0088	0.0095	0.0101	0.0104	0.0105	0.0113	0.0105	0.0095	0.0110	0.0093	0.0093	1984	0.1168
1985	0.0090	0.0081	0.0089	0.0097	0.0090	0.0073	0.0083	0.0081	0.0082	0.0081	0.0074	0.0078	1985	0.1029
1986	0.0071	0.0066	0.0068	0.0060	0.0060	0.0068	0.0062	0.0057	0.0058	0.0060	0.0052	0.0060	1986	0.0772
1987	0.0055	0.0052	0.0060	0.0058	0.0062	0.0071	0.0066	0.0068	0.0068	0.0073	0.0070	0.0070	1987	0.0747
1988	0.0065	0.0066	0.0064	0.0063	0.0072	0.0070	0.0064	0.0077	0.0072	0.0071	0.0067	0.0071	1988	0.0824
1989	0.0077	0.0066	0.0078	0.0071	0.0080	0.0070	0.0067	0.0061	0.0065	0.0071	0.0063	0.0060	1989	0.0846
1990	0.0071	0.0064	0.0069	0.0071	0.0075	0.0067	0.0072	0.0068	0.0065	0.0074	0.0067	0.0067	1990	0.0815
1991	0.0064	0.0059	0.0059	0.0070	0.0065	0.0059	0.0069	0.0062	0.0061	0.0058	0.0052	0.0056	1991	0.0743
1992	0.0052	0.0052	0.0060	0.0058	0.0056	0.0058	0.0053	0.0050	0.0047	0.0044	0.0050	0.0053	1992	0.0627
1993	0.0049	0.0045	0.0049	0.0045	0.0041	0.0050	0.0041	0.0044	0.0041	0.0038	0.0042	0.0043	1993	0.0553
1994	0.0045	0.0039	0.0048	0.0049	0.0058	0.0055	0.0055	0.0060	0.0055	0.0060	0.0061	0.0063	1994	0.0607
1995	0.0067	0.0056	0.0060	0.0054	0.0062	0.0050	0.0051	0.0051	0.0047	0.0052	0.0047	0.0043	1995	0.0669
1996	0.0046	0.0041	0.0045	0.0053	0.0054	0.0050	0.0058	0.0052	0.0056	0.0053	0.0047	0.0050	1996	0.0582
1997	0.0052	0.0047	0.0054	0.0055	0.0054	0.0055	0.0054	0.0046	0.0054	0.0050	0.0043	0.0052	1997	0.0614
1998	0.0046	0.0041	0.0049	0.0046	0.0045	0.0049	0.0047	0.0046	0.0041	0.0035	0.0036	0.0039	1998	0.0529
1999	0.0037	0.0035	0.0048	0.0043	0.0041	0.0052	0.0048	0.0051	0.0048	0.0046	0.0052	0.0052	1999	0.0530
2000	0.0054	0.0052	0.0056	0.0048	0.0059	0.0054	0.0053	0.0051	0.0047	0.0051	0.0047	0.0043	2000	0.0619
2001	0.0032	0.0026	0.0027	0.0033	0.0042	0.0040	0.0044	0.0039	0.0034	0.0035	0.0030	0.0035	2001	0.0427
2002	0.0038	0.0034	0.0034	0.0045	0.0039	0.0034	0.0037	0.0029	0.0027	0.0022	0.0022	0.0028	2002	0.0398
2003	0.0024	0.0024	0.0024	0.0023	0.0023	0.0019	0.0020	0.0025	0.0029	0.0022	0.0023	0.0029	2003	0.0285
2004	0.0026	0.0024	0.0026	0.0023	0.0027	0.0034	0.0030	0.0031	0.0026	0.0026	0.0027	0.0030	2004	0.0328
2005	0.0031	0.0028	0.0034	0.0033	0.0034	0.0031	0.0030	0.0037	0.0031	0.0035	0.0036	0.0036	2005	0.0392
2006	0.0037	0.0034	0.0039	0.0037	0.0044	0.0041	0.0043	0.0040	0.0036	0.0039	0.0036	0.0034	2006	0.0454
2007	0.0041	0.0036	0.0037	0.0038	0.0038	0.0038	0.0043	0.0038	0.0032	0.0037	0.0035	0.0028	2007	0.0444

* Compound annual return

Table A-12

Intermediate-Term Government Bonds: Capital Appreciation Returns

from January 1926 to December 1970

Year	Jan	Feb	Mar	Apr	May	Jun	Jul	Aug	Sep	Oct	Nov	Dec	Year	Jan–Dec*
1926	0.0036	0.0000	0.0009	0.0059	–0.0023	–0.0004	–0.0018	–0.0023	0.0018	0.0023	0.0014	0.0059	1926	0.0151
1927	0.0027	0.0009	0.0009	–0.0014	–0.0009	0.0000	0.0014	0.0027	0.0032	–0.0064	0.0055	0.0009	1927	0.0096
1928	0.0018	–0.0032	–0.0018	–0.0032	–0.0036	–0.0014	–0.0122	0.0018	–0.0004	0.0000	–0.0014	–0.0041	1928	–0.0273
1929	–0.0063	–0.0054	–0.0031	0.0054	–0.0098	0.0072	0.0031	0.0018	–0.0049	0.0135	0.0150	0.0014	1929	0.0177
1930	–0.0072	0.0064	0.0133	–0.0100	0.0032	0.0115	0.0028	–0.0005	0.0037	0.0051	0.0046	0.0000	1930	0.0330
1931	–0.0097	0.0074	0.0028	0.0060	0.0098	–0.0240	–0.0009	–0.0009	–0.0142	–0.0136	0.0018	–0.0193	1931	–0.0540
1932	–0.0067	0.0094	0.0045	0.0164	–0.0122	0.0077	0.0091	0.0096	0.0000	0.0018	0.0005	0.0092	1932	0.0502
1933	–0.0041	–0.0028	0.0074	0.0032	0.0178	–0.0014	–0.0028	0.0051	0.0005	–0.0047	0.0005	–0.0280	1933	–0.0099
1934	0.0100	0.0028	0.0162	0.0158	0.0097	0.0070	–0.0044	–0.0113	–0.0160	0.0164	0.0024	0.0102	1934	0.0597
1935	0.0093	0.0088	0.0107	0.0090	–0.0050	0.0098	0.0022	–0.0086	–0.0072	0.0093	–0.0002	0.0105	1935	0.0494
1936	–0.0017	0.0056	0.0018	0.0012	0.0026	–0.0001	0.0010	0.0038	–0.0001	0.0014	0.0070	–0.0067	1936	0.0160
1937	–0.0041	–0.0003	–0.0176	0.0032	0.0067	–0.0027	0.0045	–0.0056	0.0068	0.0020	0.0030	0.0051	1937	0.0005
1938	0.0067	0.0036	–0.0030	0.0214	0.0008	0.0061	–0.0003	0.0000	–0.0026	0.0079	–0.0014	0.0039	1938	0.0437
1939	0.0016	0.0071	0.0069	0.0028	0.0084	–0.0007	0.0030	–0.0155	–0.0273	0.0300	0.0063	0.0098	1939	0.0318
1940	–0.0023	0.0027	0.0080	–0.0005	–0.0221	0.0177	–0.0005	0.0035	0.0040	0.0030	0.0050	0.0023	1940	0.0204
1941	–0.0006	–0.0052	0.0061	0.0027	0.0006	0.0051	–0.0004	0.0006	–0.0004	0.0018	–0.0096	–0.0023	1941	–0.0017
1942	0.0066	0.0009	0.0016	0.0016	0.0010	0.0006	–0.0006	0.0011	–0.0029	0.0011	0.0011	–0.0006	1942	0.0117
1943	0.0025	0.0001	0.0007	0.0010	0.0044	0.0020	0.0008	–0.0010	0.0002	0.0005	0.0002	0.0008	1943	0.0123
1944	–0.0002	0.0004	0.0007	0.0016	–0.0008	–0.0005	0.0016	0.0012	0.0000	–0.0001	–0.0003	–0.0001	1944	0.0035
1945	0.0040	0.0028	–0.0005	0.0005	0.0002	0.0009	–0.0010	0.0006	0.0008	0.0006	0.0001	0.0012	1945	0.0102
1946	0.0030	0.0040	–0.0045	–0.0028	–0.0003	0.0024	–0.0019	–0.0005	–0.0020	0.0015	–0.0018	0.0022	1946	–0.0008
1947	0.0012	–0.0003	0.0014	–0.0022	–0.0002	–0.0003	–0.0004	0.0016	–0.0010	–0.0033	–0.0004	0.0008	1947	–0.0030
1948	0.0002	0.0006	0.0003	0.0006	0.0042	–0.0021	–0.0014	–0.0018	–0.0003	0.0000	0.0006	0.0019	1948	0.0027
1949	0.0015	0.0000	0.0012	0.0003	0.0010	0.0038	0.0010	0.0019	–0.0002	–0.0004	–0.0008	0.0002	1949	0.0095
1950	–0.0016	–0.0002	–0.0011	–0.0003	0.0007	–0.0008	0.0009	–0.0019	–0.0015	–0.0012	0.0005	–0.0004	1950	–0.0069
1951	0.0006	–0.0007	–0.0142	0.0040	–0.0058	0.0033	0.0040	0.0019	–0.0072	–0.0003	0.0015	–0.0033	1951	–0.0163
1952	0.0019	–0.0037	0.0048	0.0037	0.0004	–0.0052	–0.0052	–0.0042	–0.0002	0.0046	–0.0023	–0.0002	1952	–0.0057
1953	–0.0022	–0.0016	–0.0038	–0.0117	–0.0138	0.0129	0.0032	–0.0031	0.0171	0.0018	–0.0006	0.0083	1953	0.0061
1954	0.0049	0.0086	0.0013	0.0031	–0.0084	0.0109	–0.0016	–0.0001	–0.0032	–0.0021	–0.0015	–0.0010	1954	0.0108
1955	–0.0050	–0.0070	0.0004	–0.0014	–0.0019	–0.0057	–0.0091	–0.0018	0.0059	0.0050	–0.0074	–0.0033	1955	–0.0310
1956	0.0080	–0.0018	–0.0122	–0.0027	0.0086	–0.0020	–0.0120	–0.0130	0.0066	–0.0049	–0.0075	–0.0019	1956	–0.0345
1957	0.0207	–0.0037	–0.0009	–0.0130	–0.0047	–0.0133	–0.0051	0.0077	–0.0030	0.0010	0.0365	0.0188	1957	0.0405
1958	0.0010	0.0117	0.0031	0.0031	0.0041	–0.0088	–0.0112	–0.0378	–0.0048	–0.0029	0.0103	–0.0093	1958	–0.0417
1959	–0.0045	0.0078	–0.0070	–0.0084	–0.0033	–0.0113	–0.0004	–0.0116	–0.0019	0.0134	–0.0130	–0.0060	1959	–0.0456
1960	0.0115	0.0032	0.0253	–0.0096	–0.0006	0.0182	0.0236	–0.0034	0.0001	–0.0012	–0.0122	0.0180	1960	0.0742
1961	–0.0089	0.0063	0.0008	0.0026	–0.0058	–0.0054	–0.0024	–0.0012	0.0049	–0.0018	–0.0049	–0.0012	1961	–0.0172
1962	–0.0080	0.0124	0.0058	–0.0006	0.0018	–0.0056	–0.0045	0.0092	–0.0007	0.0018	0.0031	0.0026	1962	0.0173
1963	–0.0059	–0.0011	–0.0002	–0.0002	–0.0017	–0.0015	–0.0030	–0.0012	–0.0019	–0.0022	0.0008	–0.0032	1963	–0.0210
1964	–0.0001	–0.0019	–0.0019	0.0000	0.0049	0.0000	–0.0006	–0.0006	0.0012	0.0000	–0.0037	0.0024	1964	–0.0003
1965	0.0009	–0.0013	0.0006	–0.0007	0.0002	0.0012	–0.0016	–0.0017	–0.0039	–0.0033	–0.0031	–0.0186	1965	–0.0310
1966	–0.0037	–0.0120	0.0145	–0.0056	–0.0032	–0.0064	–0.0065	–0.0171	0.0170	0.0031	–0.0015	0.0180	1966	–0.0041
1967	0.0077	–0.0048	0.0144	–0.0122	0.0002	–0.0265	0.0089	–0.0078	–0.0035	–0.0095	–0.0018	–0.0038	1967	–0.0385
1968	0.0095	–0.0003	–0.0069	–0.0065	0.0015	0.0123	0.0128	–0.0021	0.0011	–0.0034	–0.0054	–0.0220	1968	–0.0099
1969	0.0032	–0.0061	0.0048	0.0021	–0.0131	–0.0142	0.0024	–0.0072	–0.0361	0.0266	–0.0103	–0.0260	1969	–0.0727
1970	–0.0035	0.0378	0.0024	–0.0266	0.0049	–0.0006	0.0087	0.0054	0.0136	0.0037	0.0393	0.0005	1970	0.0871

* Compound annual return

le A-12 (Continued)

ermediate-Term Government Bonds: Capital Appreciation Returns

m January 1971 to December 2007

r	Jan	Feb	Mar	Apr	May	Jun	Jul	Aug	Sep	Oct	Nov	Dec	Year	Jan–Dec*
1	0.0121	0.0181	0.0139	−0.0367	−0.0034	−0.0240	−0.0027	0.0294	−0.0022	0.0173	0.0005	0.0064	1971	0.0272
2	0.0058	−0.0030	−0.0031	−0.0030	−0.0035	−0.0003	−0.0034	−0.0035	−0.0033	−0.0037	−0.0006	0.0143	1972	−0.0075
3	−0.0062	−0.0123	−0.0008	0.0007	0.0001	−0.0059	−0.0336	0.0190	0.0195	−0.0010	0.0009	−0.0016	1973	−0.0219
4	−0.0048	−0.0016	−0.0266	−0.0217	0.0063	−0.0147	−0.0066	−0.0078	0.0247	0.0043	0.0175	0.0120	1974	−0.0199
5	−0.0008	0.0092	−0.0119	−0.0246	0.0197	−0.0035	−0.0093	−0.0070	−0.0059	0.0298	−0.0065	0.0131	1975	0.0012
6	−0.0003	0.0028	0.0010	0.0057	−0.0200	0.0090	0.0059	0.0127	0.0019	0.0093	0.0264	−0.0024	1976	0.0525
7	−0.0241	−0.0002	−0.0001	−0.0001	−0.0002	0.0048	−0.0051	−0.0052	−0.0041	−0.0118	0.0019	−0.0082	1977	−0.0515
8	−0.0053	−0.0041	−0.0029	−0.0036	−0.0073	−0.0087	0.0028	0.0010	−0.0008	−0.0184	0.0020	−0.0005	1978	−0.0449
9	−0.0024	−0.0125	0.0038	−0.0044	0.0116	0.0135	−0.0086	−0.0163	−0.0065	−0.0553	0.0274	0.0001	1979	−0.0507
30	−0.0221	−0.0724	0.0036	0.1095	0.0409	−0.0152	−0.0185	−0.0463	−0.0135	−0.0246	−0.0067	0.0060	1980	−0.0681
31	−0.0069	−0.0331	0.0146	−0.0322	0.0135	−0.0058	−0.0386	−0.0298	0.0034	0.0482	0.0502	−0.0250	1981	−0.0455
32	−0.0057	0.0046	−0.0080	0.0186	0.0045	−0.0253	0.0351	0.0359	0.0228	0.0442	−0.0007	0.0100	1982	0.1423
33	−0.0076	0.0173	−0.0133	0.0177	−0.0208	−0.0069	−0.0280	−0.0022	0.0220	−0.0073	0.0012	−0.0043	1983	−0.0330
34	0.0081	−0.0153	−0.0129	−0.0104	−0.0353	−0.0007	0.0280	−0.0005	0.0106	0.0274	0.0099	0.0050	1984	0.0122
35	0.0116	−0.0260	0.0077	0.0167	0.0395	0.0035	−0.0129	0.0067	0.0031	0.0081	0.0121	0.0178	1985	0.0901
36	0.0011	0.0210	0.0270	0.0021	−0.0274	0.0208	0.0095	0.0209	−0.0168	0.0102	0.0061	−0.0053	1986	0.0699
37	0.0051	0.0007	−0.0091	−0.0302	−0.0100	0.0051	−0.0040	−0.0105	−0.0209	0.0226	0.0013	0.0023	1987	−0.0475
88	0.0251	0.0057	−0.0151	−0.0107	−0.0121	0.0111	−0.0111	−0.0086	0.0124	0.0077	−0.0182	−0.0081	1988	−0.0226
89	0.0044	−0.0117	−0.0029	0.0149	0.0132	0.0254	0.0168	−0.0307	0.0004	0.0166	0.0021	−0.0048	1989	0.0434
90	−0.0176	−0.0057	−0.0067	−0.0148	0.0186	0.0084	0.0102	−0.0160	0.0030	0.0096	0.0126	0.0095	1990	0.0102
91	0.0042	−0.0011	−0.0036	0.0046	−0.0006	−0.0081	0.0060	0.0184	0.0155	0.0077	0.0076	0.0209	1991	0.0736
92	−0.0247	−0.0030	−0.0139	0.0039	0.0166	0.0118	0.0189	0.0100	0.0147	−0.0226	−0.0134	0.0093	1992	0.0064
93	0.0221	0.0198	−0.0006	0.0043	−0.0051	0.0152	−0.0036	0.0179	0.0015	−0.0020	−0.0135	−0.0011	1993	0.0556
94	0.0093	−0.0297	−0.0306	−0.0154	−0.0060	−0.0084	0.0115	−0.0034	−0.0213	−0.0084	−0.0131	−0.0010	1994	−0.1114
95	0.0115	0.0178	0.0003	0.0090	0.0307	0.0030	−0.0066	0.0035	0.0017	0.0069	0.0102	0.0052	1995	0.0966
96	−0.0040	−0.0178	−0.0164	−0.0103	−0.0086	0.0067	−0.0033	−0.0057	0.0100	0.0129	0.0102	−0.0128	1996	−0.0390
97	−0.0027	−0.0045	−0.0168	0.0093	0.0024	0.0048	0.0210	−0.0143	0.0098	0.0100	−0.0045	0.0054	1997	0.0195
98	0.0134	−0.0080	−0.0024	0.0015	0.0025	0.0030	−0.0020	0.0225	0.0289	0.0006	−0.0134	−0.0002	1998	0.0466
99	0.0018	−0.0297	0.0038	−0.0023	−0.0188	−0.0020	−0.0053	−0.0035	0.0049	−0.0054	−0.0060	−0.0100	1999	−0.0706
00	−0.0107	0.0026	0.0147	−0.0091	−0.0007	0.0138	0.0019	0.0083	0.0049	0.0028	0.0127	0.0171	2000	0.0594
01	0.0066	0.0079	0.0049	−0.0146	−0.0049	0.0025	0.0203	0.0056	0.0219	0.0145	−0.0201	−0.0117	2001	0.0323
02	−0.0003	0.0073	−0.0276	0.0193	0.0079	0.0135	0.0234	0.0138	0.0261	−0.0046	−0.0191	0.0251	2002	0.0865
03	−0.0113	0.0155	−0.0031	−0.0010	0.0250	−0.0054	−0.0339	−0.0053	0.0279	−0.0158	−0.0038	0.0080	2003	−0.0048
04	0.0025	0.0100	0.0074	−0.0357	−0.0076	0.0015	0.0051	0.0164	−0.0014	0.0039	−0.0154	0.0036	2004	−0.0107
05	−0.0005	−0.0139	−0.0073	0.0134	0.0069	0.0012	−0.0173	0.0124	−0.0155	−0.0098	0.0023	0.0026	2005	−0.0258
06	−0.0073	−0.0051	−0.0095	−0.0045	−0.0049	−0.0019	0.0082	0.0095	0.0042	0.0012	0.0052	−0.0102	2006	−0.0151
07	−0.0061	0.0134	−0.0012	0.0009	−0.0141	−0.0028	0.0132	0.0147	0.0026	−0.0085	0.0390	0.0021	2007	0.0533

Compound annual return

Table A-13

Intermediate-Term Government Bonds: Yields

from January 1926 to December 1970

Year	Jan	Feb	Mar	Apr	May	Jun	Jul	Aug	Sep	Oct	Nov	Dec	Yr-end	Yiel
1926	0.0386	0.0386	0.0384	0.0371	0.0376	0.0377	0.0381	0.0386	0.0382	0.0377	0.0374	0.0361	1926	0.036
1927	0.0355	0.0353	0.0351	0.0354	0.0356	0.0356	0.0353	0.0347	0.0340	0.0354	0.0342	0.0340	1927	0.034
1928	0.0336	0.0343	0.0347	0.0354	0.0362	0.0365	0.0392	0.0388	0.0389	0.0389	0.0392	0.0401	1928	0.040
1929	0.0415	0.0427	0.0434	0.0422	0.0444	0.0428	0.0421	0.0417	0.0428	0.0398	0.0365	0.0362	1929	0.0362
1930	0.0378	0.0364	0.0335	0.0357	0.0350	0.0325	0.0319	0.0320	0.0312	0.0301	0.0291	0.0291	1930	0.029
1931	0.0312	0.0296	0.0290	0.0277	0.0256	0.0308	0.0310	0.0312	0.0343	0.0373	0.0369	0.0412	1931	0.0412
1932	0.0427	0.0406	0.0396	0.0360	0.0387	0.0370	0.0350	0.0329	0.0329	0.0325	0.0324	0.0304	1932	0.0304
1933	0.0313	0.0319	0.0303	0.0296	0.0258	0.0261	0.0267	0.0256	0.0255	0.0265	0.0264	0.0325	1933	0.0325
1934	0.0325	0.0321	0.0296	0.0272	0.0257	0.0246	0.0253	0.0271	0.0298	0.0271	0.0267	0.0249	1934	0.0249
1935	0.0233	0.0218	0.0199	0.0184	0.0193	0.0175	0.0171	0.0187	0.0201	0.0183	0.0183	0.0163	1935	0.0163
1936	0.0166	0.0155	0.0151	0.0149	0.0143	0.0143	0.0141	0.0133	0.0133	0.0130	0.0114	0.0129	1936	0.0129
1937	0.0134	0.0135	0.0184	0.0175	0.0156	0.0164	0.0151	0.0168	0.0147	0.0141	0.0131	0.0114	1937	0.0114
1938	0.0205	0.0200	0.0204	0.0174	0.0173	0.0164	0.0164	0.0164	0.0168	0.0156	0.0158	0.0152	1938	0.0152
1939	0.0149	0.0138	0.0127	0.0122	0.0108	0.0110	0.0105	0.0131	0.0180	0.0127	0.0116	0.0098	1939	0.0098
1940	0.0103	0.0098	0.0083	0.0084	0.0127	0.0092	0.0093	0.0086	0.0078	0.0072	0.0061	0.0057	1940	0.0057
1941	0.0077	0.0089	0.0075	0.0069	0.0067	0.0055	0.0056	0.0055	0.0056	0.0051	0.0076	0.0082	1941	0.0082
1942	0.0083	0.0081	0.0077	0.0074	0.0071	0.0070	0.0071	0.0069	0.0076	0.0073	0.0070	0.0072	1942	0.0072
1943	0.0166	0.0166	0.0164	0.0162	0.0153	0.0149	0.0147	0.0149	0.0149	0.0147	0.0147	0.0145	1943	0.0145
1944	0.0150	0.0150	0.0148	0.0143	0.0146	0.0147	0.0142	0.0139	0.0139	0.0139	0.0140	0.0140	1944	0.0140
1945	0.0127	0.0118	0.0120	0.0118	0.0117	0.0114	0.0118	0.0115	0.0112	0.0109	0.0109	0.0103	1945	0.0103
1946	0.0099	0.0087	0.0101	0.0111	0.0112	0.0103	0.0110	0.0112	0.0120	0.0114	0.0121	0.0112	1946	0.0112
1947	0.0116	0.0117	0.0112	0.0120	0.0121	0.0122	0.0124	0.0117	0.0121	0.0136	0.0138	0.0134	1947	0.0134
1948	0.0160	0.0158	0.0157	0.0155	0.0142	0.0149	0.0154	0.0160	0.0161	0.0161	0.0158	0.0151	1948	0.0151
1949	0.0153	0.0153	0.0148	0.0147	0.0144	0.0129	0.0125	0.0117	0.0118	0.0120	0.0124	0.0123	1949	0.0123
1950	0.0131	0.0132	0.0137	0.0138	0.0134	0.0139	0.0134	0.0145	0.0154	0.0162	0.0159	0.0162	1950	0.0162
1951	0.0179	0.0180	0.0211	0.0202	0.0215	0.0208	0.0199	0.0194	0.0212	0.0212	0.0209	0.0217	1951	0.0217
1952	0.0212	0.0222	0.0209	0.0199	0.0198	0.0213	0.0228	0.0241	0.0242	0.0227	0.0235	0.0235	1952	0.0235
1953	0.0242	0.0245	0.0253	0.0277	0.0307	0.0279	0.0272	0.0279	0.0241	0.0237	0.0238	0.0218	1953	0.0218
1954	0.0187	0.0157	0.0153	0.0142	0.0173	0.0131	0.0138	0.0138	0.0152	0.0161	0.0168	0.0172	1954	0.0172
1955	0.0227	0.0240	0.0240	0.0242	0.0246	0.0257	0.0276	0.0280	0.0267	0.0257	0.0273	0.0280	1955	0.0280
1956	0.0271	0.0275	0.0300	0.0305	0.0287	0.0292	0.0317	0.0346	0.0331	0.0342	0.0359	0.0363	1956	0.0363
1957	0.0326	0.0333	0.0334	0.0357	0.0366	0.0390	0.0399	0.0385	0.0390	0.0388	0.0320	0.0284	1957	0.0284
1958	0.0282	0.0259	0.0253	0.0246	0.0238	0.0250	0.0281	0.0365	0.0376	0.0382	0.0359	0.0381	1958	0.0381
1959	0.0395	0.0378	0.0393	0.0413	0.0420	0.0447	0.0448	0.0477	0.0482	0.0448	0.0482	0.0498	1959	0.0498
1960	0.0471	0.0464	0.0409	0.0431	0.0432	0.0390	0.0334	0.0343	0.0343	0.0346	0.0377	0.0331	1960	0.0331
1961	0.0363	0.0350	0.0348	0.0342	0.0355	0.0368	0.0373	0.0376	0.0365	0.0369	0.0381	0.0384	1961	0.0384
1962	0.0402	0.0377	0.0366	0.0367	0.0363	0.0375	0.0384	0.0365	0.0366	0.0362	0.0355	0.0350	1962	0.0350
1963	0.0368	0.0370	0.0370	0.0371	0.0374	0.0378	0.0385	0.0388	0.0392	0.0398	0.0396	0.0404	1963	0.0404
1964	0.0402	0.0407	0.0411	0.0411	0.0399	0.0399	0.0401	0.0402	0.0399	0.0399	0.0409	0.0403	1964	0.0403
1965	0.0413	0.0416	0.0414	0.0416	0.0415	0.0413	0.0416	0.0420	0.0429	0.0437	0.0444	0.0490	1965	0.0490
1966	0.0482	0.0507	0.0477	0.0489	0.0496	0.0510	0.0525	0.0565	0.0526	0.0519	0.0522	0.0479	1966	0.0479
1967	0.0459	0.0470	0.0437	0.0466	0.0465	0.0530	0.0508	0.0528	0.0537	0.0562	0.0566	0.0577	1967	0.0577
1968	0.0548	0.0549	0.0563	0.0577	0.0574	0.0547	0.0518	0.0523	0.0520	0.0528	0.0541	0.0596	1968	0.0596
1969	0.0637	0.0651	0.0640	0.0636	0.0666	0.0699	0.0693	0.0711	0.0799	0.0735	0.0761	0.0829	1969	0.0829
1970	0.0820	0.0730	0.0724	0.0790	0.0778	0.0780	0.0757	0.0743	0.0707	0.0697	0.0591	0.0590	1970	0.0590

Table A-13 (Continued)

Intermediate-Term Government Bonds: Yields

from January 1971 to December 2007

Year	Jan	Feb	Mar	Apr	May	Jun	Jul	Aug	Sep	Oct	Nov	Dec	Yr-end	Yield
1971	0.0570	0.0526	0.0493	0.0585	0.0593	0.0656	0.0663	0.0585	0.0591	0.0545	0.0543	0.0525	1971	0.0525
1972	0.0556	0.0563	0.0570	0.0577	0.0586	0.0587	0.0595	0.0604	0.0613	0.0623	0.0625	0.0585	1972	0.0585
1973	0.0641	0.0671	0.0673	0.0671	0.0671	0.0686	0.0776	0.0725	0.0674	0.0677	0.0674	0.0679	1973	0.0679
1974	0.0687	0.0691	0.0751	0.0801	0.0786	0.0822	0.0838	0.0857	0.0797	0.0787	0.0743	0.0712	1974	0.0712
1975	0.0730	0.0709	0.0737	0.0798	0.0749	0.0758	0.0782	0.0800	0.0815	0.0736	0.0754	0.0719	1975	0.0719
1976	0.0743	0.0736	0.0733	0.0719	0.0771	0.0747	0.0732	0.0697	0.0692	0.0667	0.0594	0.0600	1976	0.0600
1977	0.0673	0.0673	0.0673	0.0674	0.0674	0.0662	0.0675	0.0689	0.0700	0.0733	0.0727	0.0751	1977	0.0751
1978	0.0773	0.0784	0.0791	0.0800	0.0820	0.0843	0.0836	0.0833	0.0835	0.0887	0.0882	0.0883	1978	0.0883
1979	0.0895	0.0928	0.0918	0.0929	0.0899	0.0864	0.0887	0.0933	0.0951	0.1112	0.1033	0.1033	1979	0.1033
1980	0.1093	0.1294	0.1285	0.1009	0.0903	0.0944	0.0996	0.1133	0.1171	0.1244	0.1264	0.1245	1980	0.1245
1981	0.1275	0.1371	0.1328	0.1427	0.1385	0.1404	0.1533	0.1636	0.1625	0.1472	0.1311	0.1396	1981	0.1396
1982	0.1397	0.1385	0.1406	0.1355	0.1343	0.1417	0.1315	0.1209	0.1144	0.1018	0.1020	0.0990	1982	0.0990
1983	0.1057	0.1010	0.1048	0.0997	0.1059	0.1080	0.1168	0.1175	0.1108	0.1131	0.1127	0.1141	1983	0.1141
1984	0.1137	0.1181	0.1219	0.1251	0.1363	0.1365	0.1274	0.1276	0.1242	0.1154	0.1121	0.1104	1984	0.1104
1985	0.1081	0.1152	0.1131	0.1084	0.0974	0.0963	0.1002	0.0982	0.0973	0.0949	0.0911	0.0855	1985	0.0855
1986	0.0870	0.0815	0.0743	0.0737	0.0816	0.0756	0.0728	0.0668	0.0718	0.0687	0.0669	0.0685	1986	0.0685
1987	0.0685	0.0683	0.0708	0.0793	0.0821	0.0806	0.0818	0.0849	0.0912	0.0844	0.0840	0.0832	1987	0.0832
1988	0.0782	0.0768	0.0807	0.0836	0.0870	0.0839	0.0871	0.0895	0.0859	0.0837	0.0892	0.0917	1988	0.0917
1989	0.0896	0.0927	0.0934	0.0895	0.0860	0.0791	0.0745	0.0834	0.0833	0.0786	0.0779	0.0794	1989	0.0794
1990	0.0842	0.0855	0.0871	0.0907	0.0864	0.0843	0.0819	0.0859	0.0851	0.0826	0.0795	0.0770	1990	0.0770
1991	0.0772	0.0774	0.0783	0.0772	0.0773	0.0793	0.0778	0.0732	0.0693	0.0673	0.0653	0.0597	1991	0.0597
1992	0.0683	0.0690	0.0720	0.0711	0.0674	0.0647	0.0604	0.0581	0.0547	0.0601	0.0634	0.0611	1992	0.0611
1993	0.0588	0.0547	0.0549	0.0540	0.0551	0.0517	0.0526	0.0486	0.0483	0.0488	0.0519	0.0522	1993	0.0522
1994	0.0515	0.0575	0.0638	0.0670	0.0682	0.0699	0.0675	0.0683	0.0730	0.0749	0.0778	0.0780	1994	0.0780
1995	0.0754	0.0708	0.0707	0.0685	0.0606	0.0598	0.0616	0.0606	0.0601	0.0582	0.0553	0.0538	1995	0.0538
1996	0.0528	0.0573	0.0614	0.0640	0.0663	0.0645	0.0654	0.0670	0.0643	0.0607	0.0578	0.0616	1996	0.0616
1997	0.0629	0.0639	0.0677	0.0656	0.0650	0.0639	0.0589	0.0624	0.0601	0.0576	0.0587	0.0573	1997	0.0573
1998	0.0545	0.0562	0.0567	0.0564	0.0558	0.0551	0.0556	0.0503	0.0435	0.0434	0.0467	0.0468	1998	0.0468
1999	0.0467	0.0535	0.0526	0.0532	0.0576	0.0581	0.0594	0.0602	0.0590	0.0604	0.0619	0.0645	1999	0.0645
2000	0.0675	0.0669	0.0636	0.0657	0.0658	0.0626	0.0621	0.0601	0.0589	0.0582	0.0551	0.0507	2000	0.0507
2001	0.0499	0.0482	0.0471	0.0504	0.0515	0.0510	0.0464	0.0450	0.0399	0.0365	0.0413	0.0442	2001	0.0442
2002	0.0459	0.0442	0.0504	0.0461	0.0443	0.0412	0.0358	0.0325	0.0265	0.0276	0.0323	0.0261	2002	0.0261
2003	0.0310	0.0276	0.0283	0.0285	0.0228	0.0240	0.0322	0.0335	0.0267	0.0307	0.0317	0.0297	2003	0.0297
2004	0.0315	0.0293	0.0276	0.0360	0.0378	0.0374	0.0362	0.0322	0.0326	0.0316	0.0356	0.0347	2004	0.0347
2005	0.0375	0.0405	0.0421	0.0392	0.0377	0.0374	0.0415	0.0385	0.0422	0.0446	0.0440	0.0434	2005	0.0434
2006	0.0449	0.0460	0.0481	0.0491	0.0502	0.0506	0.0487	0.0465	0.0455	0.0452	0.0439	0.0465	2006	0.0465
2007	0.0479	0.0448	0.0451	0.0449	0.0483	0.0490	0.0457	0.0420	0.0413	0.0435	0.0333	0.0328	2007	0.0328

Table A-14

U.S. Treasury Bills: Total Returns

from January 1926 to December 1970

Year	Jan	Feb	Mar	Apr	May	Jun	Jul	Aug	Sep	Oct	Nov	Dec	Year	Jan–Dec*
1926	0.0034	0.0027	0.0030	0.0034	0.0001	0.0035	0.0022	0.0025	0.0023	0.0032	0.0031	0.0028	1926	0.0327
1927	0.0025	0.0026	0.0030	0.0025	0.0030	0.0026	0.0030	0.0028	0.0021	0.0025	0.0021	0.0022	1927	0.0312
1928	0.0025	0.0033	0.0029	0.0022	0.0032	0.0031	0.0032	0.0032	0.0027	0.0041	0.0038	0.0006	1928	0.0356
1929	0.0034	0.0036	0.0034	0.0036	0.0044	0.0052	0.0033	0.0040	0.0035	0.0046	0.0037	0.0037	1929	0.0475
1930	0.0014	0.0030	0.0035	0.0021	0.0026	0.0027	0.0020	0.0009	0.0022	0.0009	0.0013	0.0014	1930	0.0241
1931	0.0015	0.0004	0.0013	0.0008	0.0009	0.0008	0.0006	0.0003	0.0003	0.0010	0.0017	0.0012	1931	0.0107
1932	0.0023	0.0023	0.0016	0.0011	0.0006	0.0002	0.0003	0.0003	0.0003	0.0002	0.0002	0.0001	1932	0.0096
1933	0.0001	−0.0003	0.0004	0.0010	0.0004	0.0002	0.0002	0.0003	0.0002	0.0001	0.0002	0.0002	1933	0.0030
1934	0.0005	0.0002	0.0002	0.0001	0.0001	0.0001	0.0001	0.0001	0.0001	0.0001	0.0001	0.0001	1934	0.0016
1935	0.0001	0.0002	0.0001	0.0001	0.0001	0.0001	0.0001	0.0001	0.0001	0.0001	0.0002	0.0001	1935	0.0017
1936	0.0001	0.0001	0.0002	0.0002	0.0002	0.0003	0.0001	0.0002	0.0001	0.0002	0.0001	0.0000	1936	0.0018
1937	0.0001	0.0002	0.0001	0.0003	0.0006	0.0003	0.0003	0.0002	0.0004	0.0002	0.0002	0.0000	1937	0.0031
1938	0.0000	0.0000	−0.0001	0.0001	0.0000	0.0000	−0.0001	0.0000	0.0002	0.0001	−0.0006	0.0000	1938	−0.0002
1939	−0.0001	0.0001	−0.0001	0.0000	0.0001	0.0001	0.0000	−0.0001	0.0001	0.0000	0.0000	0.0000	1939	0.0002
1940	0.0000	0.0000	0.0000	0.0000	−0.0002	0.0000	0.0001	−0.0001	0.0000	0.0000	0.0000	0.0000	1940	0.0000
1941	−0.0001	−0.0001	0.0001	−0.0001	0.0000	0.0000	0.0003	0.0001	0.0001	0.0000	0.0000	0.0001	1941	0.0006
1942	0.0002	0.0001	0.0001	0.0001	0.0003	0.0002	0.0003	0.0003	0.0003	0.0003	0.0003	0.0003	1942	0.0027
1943	0.0003	0.0003	0.0003	0.0003	0.0003	0.0003	0.0003	0.0003	0.0003	0.0003	0.0003	0.0003	1943	0.0035
1944	0.0003	0.0003	0.0002	0.0003	0.0003	0.0003	0.0003	0.0003	0.0002	0.0003	0.0003	0.0002	1944	0.0033
1945	0.0003	0.0002	0.0002	0.0003	0.0003	0.0002	0.0003	0.0003	0.0003	0.0003	0.0002	0.0003	1945	0.0033
1946	0.0003	0.0003	0.0003	0.0003	0.0003	0.0003	0.0003	0.0003	0.0003	0.0003	0.0003	0.0003	1946	0.0035
1947	0.0003	0.0003	0.0003	0.0003	0.0003	0.0003	0.0003	0.0003	0.0006	0.0006	0.0006	0.0008	1947	0.0050
1948	0.0007	0.0007	0.0009	0.0008	0.0008	0.0009	0.0008	0.0009	0.0004	0.0004	0.0004	0.0004	1948	0.0081
1949	0.0010	0.0009	0.0010	0.0009	0.0010	0.0010	0.0009	0.0009	0.0009	0.0009	0.0008	0.0009	1949	0.0110
1950	0.0009	0.0009	0.0010	0.0009	0.0010	0.0010	0.0010	0.0010	0.0010	0.0012	0.0011	0.0011	1950	0.0120
1951	0.0013	0.0010	0.0011	0.0013	0.0012	0.0012	0.0013	0.0013	0.0012	0.0016	0.0011	0.0012	1951	0.0149
1952	0.0015	0.0012	0.0011	0.0012	0.0013	0.0015	0.0015	0.0015	0.0016	0.0014	0.0010	0.0016	1952	0.0166
1953	0.0016	0.0014	0.0018	0.0016	0.0017	0.0018	0.0015	0.0017	0.0016	0.0013	0.0008	0.0013	1953	0.0182
1954	0.0011	0.0007	0.0008	0.0009	0.0005	0.0006	0.0005	0.0005	0.0009	0.0007	0.0006	0.0008	1954	0.0086
1955	0.0008	0.0009	0.0010	0.0010	0.0014	0.0010	0.0010	0.0016	0.0016	0.0018	0.0017	0.0018	1955	0.0157
1956	0.0022	0.0019	0.0015	0.0019	0.0023	0.0020	0.0022	0.0017	0.0018	0.0025	0.0020	0.0024	1956	0.0246
1957	0.0027	0.0024	0.0023	0.0025	0.0026	0.0024	0.0030	0.0025	0.0026	0.0029	0.0028	0.0024	1957	0.0314
1958	0.0028	0.0012	0.0009	0.0008	0.0011	0.0003	0.0007	0.0004	0.0019	0.0018	0.0011	0.0022	1958	0.0154
1959	0.0021	0.0019	0.0022	0.0020	0.0022	0.0025	0.0025	0.0019	0.0031	0.0030	0.0026	0.0034	1959	0.0295
1960	0.0033	0.0029	0.0035	0.0019	0.0027	0.0024	0.0013	0.0017	0.0016	0.0022	0.0013	0.0016	1960	0.0266
1961	0.0019	0.0014	0.0020	0.0017	0.0018	0.0020	0.0018	0.0014	0.0017	0.0019	0.0015	0.0019	1961	0.0213
1962	0.0024	0.0020	0.0020	0.0022	0.0024	0.0020	0.0027	0.0023	0.0021	0.0026	0.0020	0.0023	1962	0.0273
1963	0.0025	0.0023	0.0023	0.0025	0.0024	0.0023	0.0027	0.0025	0.0027	0.0029	0.0027	0.0029	1963	0.0312
1964	0.0030	0.0026	0.0031	0.0029	0.0026	0.0030	0.0030	0.0028	0.0028	0.0029	0.0029	0.0031	1964	0.0354
1965	0.0028	0.0030	0.0036	0.0031	0.0031	0.0035	0.0031	0.0033	0.0031	0.0031	0.0035	0.0033	1965	0.0393
1966	0.0038	0.0035	0.0038	0.0034	0.0041	0.0038	0.0035	0.0041	0.0040	0.0045	0.0040	0.0040	1966	0.0476
1967	0.0043	0.0036	0.0039	0.0032	0.0033	0.0027	0.0032	0.0031	0.0032	0.0039	0.0036	0.0033	1967	0.0421
1968	0.0040	0.0039	0.0038	0.0043	0.0045	0.0043	0.0048	0.0042	0.0043	0.0044	0.0042	0.0043	1968	0.0521
1969	0.0053	0.0046	0.0046	0.0053	0.0048	0.0051	0.0053	0.0050	0.0062	0.0060	0.0052	0.0064	1969	0.0658
1970	0.0060	0.0062	0.0057	0.0050	0.0053	0.0058	0.0052	0.0053	0.0054	0.0046	0.0046	0.0042	1970	0.0652

* Compound annual return

Table A-14 (Continued)

U.S. Treasury Bills: Total Returns

from January 1971 to December 2007

Year	Jan	Feb	Mar	Apr	May	Jun	Jul	Aug	Sep	Oct	Nov	Dec	Year	Jan–Dec*
1971	0.0038	0.0033	0.0030	0.0028	0.0029	0.0037	0.0040	0.0047	0.0037	0.0037	0.0037	0.0037	1971	0.0439
1972	0.0029	0.0025	0.0027	0.0029	0.0030	0.0029	0.0031	0.0029	0.0034	0.0040	0.0037	0.0037	1972	0.0384
1973	0.0044	0.0041	0.0046	0.0052	0.0051	0.0051	0.0064	0.0070	0.0068	0.0065	0.0056	0.0064	1973	0.0693
1974	0.0063	0.0058	0.0056	0.0075	0.0075	0.0060	0.0070	0.0060	0.0081	0.0051	0.0054	0.0070	1974	0.0800
1975	0.0058	0.0043	0.0041	0.0044	0.0044	0.0041	0.0048	0.0048	0.0053	0.0056	0.0041	0.0048	1975	0.0580
1976	0.0047	0.0034	0.0040	0.0042	0.0037	0.0043	0.0047	0.0042	0.0044	0.0041	0.0040	0.0040	1976	0.0508
1977	0.0036	0.0035	0.0038	0.0038	0.0037	0.0040	0.0042	0.0044	0.0043	0.0049	0.0050	0.0049	1977	0.0512
1978	0.0049	0.0046	0.0053	0.0054	0.0051	0.0054	0.0056	0.0055	0.0062	0.0068	0.0070	0.0078	1978	0.0718
1979	0.0077	0.0073	0.0081	0.0080	0.0082	0.0081	0.0077	0.0077	0.0083	0.0087	0.0099	0.0095	1979	0.1038
1980	0.0080	0.0089	0.0121	0.0126	0.0081	0.0061	0.0053	0.0064	0.0075	0.0095	0.0096	0.0131	1980	0.1124
1981	0.0104	0.0107	0.0121	0.0108	0.0115	0.0135	0.0124	0.0128	0.0124	0.0121	0.0107	0.0087	1981	0.1471
1982	0.0080	0.0092	0.0098	0.0113	0.0106	0.0096	0.0105	0.0076	0.0051	0.0059	0.0063	0.0067	1982	0.1054
1983	0.0069	0.0062	0.0063	0.0071	0.0069	0.0067	0.0074	0.0076	0.0076	0.0076	0.0070	0.0073	1983	0.0880
1984	0.0076	0.0071	0.0073	0.0081	0.0078	0.0075	0.0082	0.0083	0.0086	0.0100	0.0073	0.0064	1984	0.0985
1985	0.0065	0.0058	0.0062	0.0072	0.0066	0.0055	0.0062	0.0055	0.0060	0.0065	0.0061	0.0065	1985	0.0772
1986	0.0056	0.0053	0.0060	0.0052	0.0049	0.0052	0.0052	0.0046	0.0045	0.0046	0.0039	0.0049	1986	0.0616
1987	0.0042	0.0043	0.0047	0.0044	0.0038	0.0048	0.0046	0.0047	0.0045	0.0060	0.0035	0.0039	1987	0.0547
1988	0.0029	0.0046	0.0044	0.0046	0.0051	0.0049	0.0051	0.0059	0.0062	0.0061	0.0057	0.0063	1988	0.0635
1989	0.0055	0.0061	0.0067	0.0067	0.0079	0.0071	0.0070	0.0074	0.0065	0.0068	0.0069	0.0061	1989	0.0837
1990	0.0057	0.0057	0.0064	0.0069	0.0068	0.0063	0.0068	0.0066	0.0060	0.0068	0.0057	0.0060	1990	0.0781
1991	0.0052	0.0048	0.0044	0.0053	0.0047	0.0042	0.0049	0.0046	0.0046	0.0042	0.0039	0.0038	1991	0.0560
1992	0.0034	0.0028	0.0034	0.0032	0.0028	0.0032	0.0031	0.0026	0.0026	0.0023	0.0023	0.0028	1992	0.0351
1993	0.0023	0.0022	0.0025	0.0024	0.0022	0.0025	0.0024	0.0025	0.0026	0.0022	0.0025	0.0023	1993	0.0290
1994	0.0025	0.0021	0.0027	0.0027	0.0032	0.0031	0.0028	0.0037	0.0037	0.0038	0.0037	0.0044	1994	0.0390
1995	0.0042	0.0040	0.0046	0.0044	0.0054	0.0047	0.0045	0.0047	0.0043	0.0047	0.0042	0.0049	1995	0.0560
1996	0.0043	0.0039	0.0039	0.0046	0.0042	0.0040	0.0045	0.0041	0.0044	0.0042	0.0041	0.0046	1996	0.0521
1997	0.0045	0.0039	0.0043	0.0043	0.0049	0.0037	0.0043	0.0041	0.0044	0.0042	0.0039	0.0048	1997	0.0526
1998	0.0043	0.0039	0.0039	0.0043	0.0040	0.0041	0.0040	0.0043	0.0046	0.0032	0.0031	0.0038	1998	0.0486
1999	0.0035	0.0035	0.0043	0.0037	0.0034	0.0040	0.0038	0.0039	0.0039	0.0039	0.0036	0.0044	1999	0.0468
2000	0.0041	0.0043	0.0047	0.0046	0.0050	0.0040	0.0048	0.0050	0.0051	0.0056	0.0051	0.0050	2000	0.0589
2001	0.0054	0.0038	0.0042	0.0039	0.0032	0.0028	0.0030	0.0031	0.0028	0.0022	0.0017	0.0015	2001	0.0383
2002	0.0014	0.0013	0.0013	0.0015	0.0014	0.0013	0.0015	0.0014	0.0014	0.0014	0.0012	0.0011	2002	0.0165
2003	0.0010	0.0009	0.0010	0.0010	0.0009	0.0010	0.0007	0.0007	0.0008	0.0007	0.0007	0.0008	2003	0.0102
2004	0.0007	0.0006	0.0009	0.0008	0.0006	0.0008	0.0010	0.0011	0.0011	0.0011	0.0015	0.0016	2004	0.0120
2005	0.0016	0.0016	0.0021	0.0021	0.0024	0.0023	0.0024	0.0030	0.0029	0.0027	0.0031	0.0032	2005	0.0298
2006	0.0035	0.0034	0.0037	0.0036	0.0043	0.0040	0.0040	0.0042	0.0041	0.0041	0.0042	0.0040	2006	0.0480
2007	0.0044	0.0038	0.0043	0.0044	0.0041	0.0040	0.0040	0.0042	0.0032	0.0032	0.0034	0.0027	2007	0.0466

Compound annual return

Table A-15
Inflation

from January 1926 to December 1970

Year	Jan	Feb	Mar	Apr	May	Jun	Jul	Aug	Sep	Oct	Nov	Dec	Year	Jan–De
1926	0.0000	−0.0037	−0.0056	0.0094	−0.0056	−0.0075	−0.0094	−0.0057	0.0057	0.0038	0.0038	0.0000	1926	−0.014
1927	−0.0076	−0.0076	−0.0058	0.0000	0.0077	0.0096	−0.0190	−0.0058	0.0058	0.0058	−0.0019	−0.0019	1927	−0.020
1928	−0.0019	−0.0097	0.0000	0.0020	0.0058	−0.0078	0.0000	0.0020	0.0078	−0.0019	−0.0019	−0.0039	1928	−0.009
1929	−0.0019	−0.0020	−0.0039	−0.0039	0.0059	0.0039	0.0098	0.0039	−0.0019	0.0000	−0.0019	−0.0058	1929	0.002
1930	−0.0039	−0.0039	−0.0059	0.0059	−0.0059	−0.0059	−0.0139	−0.0060	0.0061	−0.0060	−0.0081	−0.0143	1930	−0.060
1931	−0.0145	−0.0147	−0.0064	−0.0064	−0.0108	−0.0109	−0.0022	−0.0022	−0.0044	−0.0067	−0.0112	−0.0091	1931	−0.095
1932	−0.0206	−0.0140	−0.0047	−0.0071	−0.0144	−0.0073	0.0000	−0.0123	−0.0050	−0.0075	−0.0050	−0.0101	1932	−0.103
1933	−0.0153	−0.0155	−0.0079	−0.0027	0.0027	0.0106	0.0289	0.0102	0.0000	0.0000	0.0000	−0.0051	1933	0.005
1934	0.0051	0.0076	0.0000	−0.0025	0.0025	0.0025	0.0000	0.0025	0.0150	−0.0074	−0.0025	−0.0025	1934	0.020
1935	0.0149	0.0074	−0.0024	0.0098	−0.0048	−0.0024	−0.0049	0.0000	0.0049	0.0000	0.0049	0.0024	1935	0.029
1936	0.0000	−0.0048	−0.0049	0.0000	0.0000	0.0098	0.0048	0.0072	0.0024	−0.0024	0.0000	0.0000	1936	0.012
1937	0.0072	0.0024	0.0071	0.0047	0.0047	0.0023	0.0046	0.0023	0.0092	−0.0046	−0.0069	−0.0023	1937	0.031
1938	−0.0139	−0.0094	0.0000	0.0047	−0.0047	0.0000	0.0024	−0.0024	0.0000	−0.0047	−0.0024	0.0024	1938	−0.027
1939	−0.0048	−0.0048	−0.0024	−0.0024	0.0000	0.0000	0.0000	0.0000	0.0193	−0.0047	0.0000	−0.0048	1939	−0.004
1940	−0.0024	0.0072	−0.0024	0.0000	0.0024	0.0024	−0.0024	−0.0024	0.0024	0.0000	0.0000	0.0048	1940	0.009
1941	0.0000	0.0000	0.0047	0.0094	0.0070	0.0186	0.0046	0.0091	0.0180	0.0110	0.0087	0.0022	1941	0.097
1942	0.0130	0.0085	0.0127	0.0063	0.0104	0.0021	0.0041	0.0061	0.0020	0.0101	0.0060	0.0080	1942	0.092
1943	0.0000	0.0020	0.0158	0.0116	0.0077	−0.0019	−0.0076	−0.0038	0.0039	0.0038	−0.0019	0.0019	1943	0.031
1944	−0.0019	−0.0019	0.0000	0.0058	0.0038	0.0019	0.0057	0.0038	0.0000	0.0000	0.0000	0.0038	1944	0.021
1945	0.0000	−0.0019	0.0000	0.0019	0.0075	0.0093	0.0018	0.0000	−0.0037	0.0000	0.0037	0.0037	1945	0.022
1946	0.0000	−0.0037	0.0074	0.0055	0.0055	0.0109	0.0590	0.0220	0.0116	0.0196	0.0240	0.0078	1946	0.181
1947	0.0000	−0.0016	0.0218	0.0000	−0.0030	0.0076	0.0091	0.0105	0.0238	0.0000	0.0058	0.0130	1947	0.0901
1948	0.0114	−0.0085	−0.0028	0.0142	0.0070	0.0070	0.0125	0.0041	0.0000	−0.0041	−0.0068	−0.0069	1948	0.0271
1949	−0.0014	−0.0111	0.0028	0.0014	−0.0014	0.0014	−0.0070	0.0028	0.0042	−0.0056	0.0014	−0.0056	1949	−0.018
1950	−0.0042	−0.0028	0.0043	0.0014	0.0042	0.0056	0.0098	0.0083	0.0069	0.0055	0.0041	0.0135	1950	0.057
1951	0.0160	0.0118	0.0039	0.0013	0.0039	−0.0013	0.0013	0.0000	0.0064	0.0051	0.0051	0.0038	1951	0.058
1952	0.0000	−0.0063	0.0000	0.0038	0.0013	0.0025	0.0076	0.0012	−0.0012	0.0012	0.0000	−0.0012	1952	0.008
1953	−0.0025	−0.0050	0.0025	0.0013	0.0025	0.0038	0.0025	0.0025	0.0012	0.0025	−0.0037	−0.0012	1953	0.006
1954	0.0025	−0.0012	−0.0012	−0.0025	0.0037	0.0012	0.0000	−0.0012	−0.0025	−0.0025	0.0012	−0.0025	1954	−0.005
1955	0.0000	0.0000	0.0000	0.0000	0.0000	0.0000	0.0037	−0.0025	0.0037	0.0000	0.0012	−0.0025	1955	0.003
1956	−0.0012	0.0000	0.0012	0.0012	0.0050	0.0062	0.0074	−0.0012	0.0012	0.0061	0.0000	0.0024	1956	0.028
1957	0.0012	0.0036	0.0024	0.0036	0.0024	0.0060	0.0047	0.0012	0.0012	0.0000	0.0035	0.0000	1957	0.030
1958	0.0059	0.0012	0.0070	0.0023	0.0000	0.0012	0.0012	−0.0012	0.0000	0.0000	0.0012	−0.0012	1958	0.017
1959	0.0012	−0.0012	0.0000	0.0012	0.0012	0.0046	0.0023	−0.0011	0.0034	0.0034	0.0000	0.0000	1959	0.015
1960	−0.0011	0.0011	0.0000	0.0057	0.0000	0.0023	0.0000	0.0000	0.0011	0.0045	0.0011	0.0000	1960	0.014
1961	0.0000	0.0000	0.0000	0.0000	0.0000	0.0011	0.0045	−0.0011	0.0022	0.0000	0.0000	0.0000	1961	0.0067
1962	0.0000	0.0022	0.0022	0.0022	0.0000	0.0000	0.0022	0.0000	0.0055	−0.0011	0.0000	−0.0011	1962	0.0122
1963	0.0011	0.0011	0.0011	0.0000	0.0000	0.0044	0.0044	0.0000	0.0000	0.0011	0.0011	0.0022	1963	0.0165
1964	0.0011	−0.0011	0.0011	0.0011	0.0000	0.0022	0.0022	−0.0011	0.0022	0.0011	0.0021	0.0011	1964	0.0119
1965	0.0000	0.0000	0.0011	0.0032	0.0021	0.0053	0.0011	−0.0021	0.0021	0.0011	0.0021	0.0032	1965	0.0192
1966	0.0000	0.0063	0.0031	0.0042	0.0010	0.0031	0.0031	0.0051	0.0020	0.0041	0.0000	0.0010	1966	0.0335
1967	0.0000	0.0010	0.0020	0.0020	0.0030	0.0030	0.0050	0.0030	0.0020	0.0030	0.0030	0.0030	1967	0.0304
1968	0.0039	0.0029	0.0049	0.0029	0.0029	0.0058	0.0048	0.0029	0.0029	0.0057	0.0038	0.0028	1968	0.0472
1969	0.0028	0.0037	0.0084	0.0065	0.0028	0.0064	0.0046	0.0045	0.0045	0.0036	0.0054	0.0062	1969	0.0611
1970	0.0035	0.0053	0.0053	0.0061	0.0043	0.0052	0.0034	0.0017	0.0051	0.0051	0.0034	0.0051	1970	0.0549

* Compound annual return

Table A-15 (Continued)
Inflation

from January 1971 to December 2007

Year	Jan	Feb	Mar	Apr	May	Jun	Jul	Aug	Sep	Oct	Nov	Dec	Year	Jan–Dec*
1971	0.0008	0.0017	0.0033	0.0033	0.0050	0.0058	0.0025	0.0025	0.0008	0.0016	0.0016	0.0041	1971	0.0336
1972	0.0008	0.0049	0.0016	0.0024	0.0032	0.0024	0.0040	0.0016	0.0040	0.0032	0.0024	0.0032	1972	0.0341
1973	0.0031	0.0070	0.0093	0.0069	0.0061	0.0068	0.0023	0.0181	0.0030	0.0081	0.0073	0.0065	1973	0.0880
1974	0.0087	0.0129	0.0113	0.0056	0.0111	0.0096	0.0075	0.0128	0.0120	0.0086	0.0085	0.0071	1974	0.1220
1975	0.0045	0.0070	0.0038	0.0051	0.0044	0.0082	0.0106	0.0031	0.0049	0.0061	0.0061	0.0042	1975	0.0701
1976	0.0024	0.0024	0.0024	0.0042	0.0059	0.0053	0.0059	0.0047	0.0041	0.0041	0.0029	0.0029	1976	0.0481
1977	0.0057	0.0103	0.0062	0.0079	0.0056	0.0066	0.0044	0.0038	0.0038	0.0027	0.0049	0.0038	1977	0.0677
1978	0.0054	0.0069	0.0069	0.0090	0.0099	0.0103	0.0072	0.0051	0.0071	0.0080	0.0055	0.0055	1978	0.0903
1979	0.0089	0.0117	0.0097	0.0115	0.0123	0.0093	0.0130	0.0100	0.0104	0.0090	0.0093	0.0105	1979	0.1331
1980	0.0144	0.0137	0.0144	0.0113	0.0099	0.0110	0.0008	0.0065	0.0092	0.0087	0.0091	0.0086	1980	0.1240
1981	0.0081	0.0104	0.0072	0.0064	0.0082	0.0086	0.0114	0.0077	0.0101	0.0021	0.0029	0.0029	1981	0.0894
1982	0.0036	0.0032	–0.0011	0.0042	0.0098	0.0122	0.0055	0.0021	0.0017	0.0027	–0.0017	–0.0041	1982	0.0387
1983	0.0024	0.0003	0.0007	0.0072	0.0054	0.0034	0.0040	0.0033	0.0050	0.0027	0.0017	0.0013	1983	0.0380
1984	0.0056	0.0046	0.0023	0.0049	0.0029	0.0032	0.0032	0.0042	0.0048	0.0025	0.0000	0.0006	1984	0.0395
1985	0.0019	0.0041	0.0044	0.0041	0.0037	0.0031	0.0016	0.0022	0.0031	0.0031	0.0034	0.0025	1985	0.0377
1986	0.0031	–0.0027	–0.0046	–0.0021	0.0031	0.0049	0.0003	0.0018	0.0049	0.0009	0.0009	0.0009	1986	0.0113
1987	0.0060	0.0039	0.0045	0.0054	0.0030	0.0041	0.0021	0.0056	0.0050	0.0026	0.0014	–0.0003	1987	0.0441
1988	0.0026	0.0026	0.0043	0.0052	0.0034	0.0043	0.0042	0.0042	0.0067	0.0033	0.0008	0.0017	1988	0.0442
1989	0.0050	0.0041	0.0058	0.0065	0.0057	0.0024	0.0024	0.0016	0.0032	0.0048	0.0024	0.0016	1989	0.0465
1990	0.0103	0.0047	0.0055	0.0016	0.0023	0.0054	0.0038	0.0092	0.0084	0.0060	0.0022	0.0000	1990	0.0611
1991	0.0060	0.0015	0.0015	0.0015	0.0030	0.0029	0.0015	0.0029	0.0044	0.0015	0.0029	0.0007	1991	0.0306
1992	0.0015	0.0036	0.0051	0.0014	0.0014	0.0036	0.0021	0.0028	0.0028	0.0035	0.0014	–0.0007	1992	0.0290
1993	0.0049	0.0035	0.0035	0.0028	0.0014	0.0014	0.0000	0.0028	0.0021	0.0041	0.0007	0.0000	1993	0.0275
1994	0.0027	0.0034	0.0034	0.0014	0.0007	0.0034	0.0027	0.0040	0.0027	0.0007	0.0013	0.0000	1994	0.0267
1995	0.0040	0.0040	0.0033	0.0033	0.0020	0.0020	0.0000	0.0026	0.0020	0.0033	–0.0007	–0.0007	1995	0.0254
1996	0.0059	0.0032	0.0052	0.0039	0.0019	0.0006	0.0019	0.0019	0.0032	0.0032	0.0019	0.0000	1996	0.0332
1997	0.0032	0.0031	0.0025	0.0013	–0.0006	0.0012	0.0012	0.0019	0.0025	0.0025	–0.0006	–0.0012	1997	0.0170
1998	0.0019	0.0019	0.0019	0.0018	0.0018	0.0012	0.0012	0.0012	0.0012	0.0024	0.0000	–0.0006	1998	0.0161
1999	0.0024	0.0012	0.0030	0.0073	0.0000	0.0000	0.0030	0.0024	0.0048	0.0018	0.0006	0.0000	1999	0.0268
2000	0.0024	0.0059	0.0082	0.0006	0.0006	0.0058	0.0017	0.0012	0.0052	0.0017	0.0006	–0.0006	2000	0.0339
2001	0.0063	0.0040	0.0023	0.0040	0.0045	0.0017	–0.0028	0.0000	0.0045	–0.0034	–0.0017	–0.0039	2001	0.0155
2002	0.0023	0.0040	0.0056	0.0056	0.0000	0.0006	0.0011	0.0033	0.0017	0.0017	0.0000	–0.0022	2002	0.0238
2003	0.0044	0.0077	0.0060	–0.0022	–0.0016	0.0011	0.0011	0.0038	0.0033	–0.0011	–0.0027	–0.0011	2003	0.0188
2004	0.0049	0.0054	0.0064	0.0032	0.0059	0.0032	–0.0016	0.0005	0.0021	0.0053	0.0005	–0.0037	2004	0.0326
2005	0.0021	0.0058	0.0078	0.0067	–0.0010	0.0005	0.0046	0.0051	0.0122	0.0020	–0.0080	–0.0040	2005	0.0342
2006	0.0076	0.0020	0.0055	0.0085	0.0050	0.0020	0.0030	0.0020	–0.0049	–0.0054	–0.0015	0.0015	2006	0.0254
2007	0.0031	0.0054	0.0091	0.0065	0.0061	0.0019	–0.0003	–0.0018	0.0028	0.0021	0.0059	–0.0007	2007	0.0408

Compound annual return

Table A-16
U.S. Treasury Bills: Inflation-Adjusted Total Returns

from January 1926 to December 1970

Year	Jan	Feb	Mar	Apr	May	Jun	Jul	Aug	Sep	Oct	Nov	Dec	Year	Jan–Dec*
1926	0.0034	0.0064	0.0086	–0.0059	0.0057	0.0110	0.0118	0.0083	–0.0035	–0.0006	–0.0007	0.0028	1926	0.0483
1927	0.0101	0.0103	0.0088	0.0025	–0.0047	–0.0069	0.0224	0.0086	–0.0037	–0.0033	0.0040	0.0042	1927	0.0531
1928	0.0045	0.0131	0.0029	0.0003	–0.0026	0.0110	0.0032	0.0013	–0.0051	0.0060	0.0058	0.0045	1928	0.0457
1929	0.0054	0.0055	0.0074	0.0075	–0.0015	0.0013	–0.0064	0.0002	0.0055	0.0046	0.0057	0.0095	1929	0.0454
1930	0.0053	0.0069	0.0094	–0.0038	0.0085	0.0087	0.0161	0.0070	–0.0039	0.0069	0.0095	0.0159	1930	0.0898
1931	0.0162	0.0153	0.0077	0.0072	0.0118	0.0118	0.0028	0.0026	0.0047	0.0078	0.0130	0.0104	1931	0.1171
1932	0.0234	0.0166	0.0064	0.0083	0.0152	0.0076	0.0003	0.0127	0.0053	0.0077	0.0052	0.0103	1932	0.1255
1933	0.0157	0.0155	0.0084	0.0036	–0.0022	–0.0103	–0.0279	–0.0098	0.0002	0.0001	0.0002	0.0053	1933	–0.0021
1934	–0.0046	–0.0073	0.0002	0.0026	–0.0024	–0.0024	0.0001	–0.0024	–0.0147	0.0075	0.0026	0.0026	1934	–0.0183
1935	–0.0146	–0.0071	0.0026	–0.0095	0.0050	0.0026	0.0050	0.0001	–0.0047	0.0001	–0.0046	–0.0023	1935	–0.0273
1936	0.0001	0.0050	0.0051	0.0002	0.0002	–0.0094	–0.0047	–0.0070	–0.0023	0.0026	0.0001	0.0000	1936	–0.0102
1937	–0.0070	–0.0022	–0.0069	–0.0043	–0.0040	–0.0020	–0.0043	–0.0021	–0.0088	0.0048	0.0071	0.0024	1937	–0.0271
1938	0.0141	0.0095	–0.0001	–0.0046	0.0048	0.0000	–0.0024	0.0024	0.0002	0.0049	0.0018	–0.0024	1938	0.0284
1939	0.0047	0.0049	0.0023	0.0024	0.0001	0.0001	0.0000	–0.0001	–0.0189	0.0048	0.0000	0.0048	1939	0.0050
1940	0.0024	–0.0071	0.0024	0.0000	–0.0025	–0.0023	0.0025	0.0023	–0.0024	0.0000	0.0000	–0.0047	1940	–0.0094
1941	–0.0001	–0.0001	–0.0046	–0.0094	–0.0069	–0.0182	–0.0042	–0.0089	–0.0176	–0.0109	–0.0086	–0.0021	1941	–0.0880
1942	–0.0126	–0.0083	–0.0124	–0.0062	–0.0100	–0.0018	–0.0038	–0.0058	–0.0017	–0.0097	–0.0057	–0.0076	1942	–0.0825
1943	0.0003	–0.0017	–0.0152	–0.0112	–0.0074	0.0022	0.0080	0.0042	–0.0036	–0.0035	0.0022	–0.0016	1943	–0.0273
1944	0.0022	0.0022	0.0002	–0.0055	–0.0036	–0.0016	–0.0054	–0.0035	0.0002	0.0003	0.0003	–0.0035	1944	–0.0174
1945	0.0003	0.0021	0.0002	–0.0016	–0.0072	–0.0090	–0.0015	0.0003	0.0040	0.0003	–0.0034	–0.0034	1945	–0.0188
1946	0.0003	0.0040	–0.0070	–0.0052	–0.0051	–0.0105	–0.0554	–0.0212	–0.0111	–0.0189	–0.0232	–0.0075	1946	–0.1507
1947	0.0003	0.0018	–0.0210	0.0003	0.0033	–0.0073	–0.0087	–0.0101	–0.0226	0.0006	–0.0052	–0.0120	1947	–0.0780
1948	–0.0105	0.0093	0.0037	–0.0132	–0.0062	–0.0060	–0.0115	–0.0032	0.0004	0.0045	0.0073	0.0074	1948	–0.0185
1949	0.0023	0.0121	–0.0018	–0.0005	0.0024	–0.0004	0.0079	–0.0019	–0.0033	0.0065	–0.0006	0.0065	1949	0.0296
1950	0.0052	0.0037	–0.0033	–0.0006	–0.0032	–0.0046	–0.0087	–0.0073	–0.0058	–0.0043	–0.0030	–0.0123	1950	–0.0434
1951	–0.0145	–0.0107	–0.0028	0.0000	–0.0026	0.0025	0.0001	0.0013	–0.0052	–0.0035	–0.0040	–0.0026	1951	–0.0414
1952	0.0015	0.0075	0.0011	–0.0026	0.0000	–0.0010	–0.0060	0.0002	0.0029	0.0001	0.0010	0.0029	1952	0.0077
1953	0.0041	0.0064	–0.0007	0.0004	–0.0008	–0.0019	–0.0010	–0.0008	0.0004	–0.0012	0.0045	0.0025	1953	0.0119
1954	–0.0014	0.0019	0.0020	0.0034	–0.0032	–0.0007	0.0005	0.0017	0.0034	0.0032	–0.0006	0.0033	1954	0.0137
1955	0.0008	0.0009	0.0010	0.0010	0.0014	0.0010	–0.0027	0.0041	–0.0021	0.0018	0.0005	0.0043	1955	0.0119
1956	0.0035	0.0019	0.0003	0.0006	–0.0027	–0.0042	–0.0052	0.0029	0.0006	–0.0036	0.0020	0.0000	1956	–0.0039
1957	0.0015	–0.0012	–0.0001	–0.0011	0.0002	–0.0035	–0.0018	0.0013	0.0014	0.0029	–0.0008	0.0024	1957	0.0011
1958	–0.0031	0.0000	–0.0060	–0.0015	0.0011	–0.0009	–0.0005	0.0016	0.0019	0.0018	–0.0001	0.0034	1958	–0.0022
1959	0.0009	0.0030	0.0022	0.0008	0.0010	–0.0021	0.0002	0.0030	–0.0003	–0.0004	0.0026	0.0034	1959	0.0143
1960	0.0045	0.0017	0.0035	–0.0037	0.0027	0.0001	0.0013	0.0017	0.0005	–0.0023	0.0002	0.0016	1960	0.0117
1961	0.0019	0.0014	0.0020	0.0017	0.0018	0.0009	–0.0026	0.0025	–0.0006	0.0019	0.0015	0.0019	1961	0.0144
1962	0.0024	–0.0002	–0.0002	0.0000	0.0024	0.0020	0.0005	0.0023	–0.0034	0.0037	0.0020	0.0034	1962	0.0149
1963	0.0014	0.0012	0.0012	0.0025	0.0024	–0.0021	–0.0017	0.0025	0.0027	0.0018	0.0016	0.0008	1963	0.0144
1964	0.0019	0.0037	0.0020	0.0018	0.0026	0.0009	0.0008	0.0039	0.0006	0.0019	0.0008	0.0020	1964	0.0232
1965	0.0028	0.0030	0.0025	–0.0001	0.0010	–0.0018	0.0020	0.0054	0.0010	0.0021	0.0014	0.0002	1965	0.0197
1966	0.0038	–0.0028	0.0007	–0.0007	0.0031	0.0007	0.0005	–0.0010	0.0020	0.0005	0.0040	0.0030	1966	0.0136
1967	0.0043	0.0026	0.0019	0.0012	0.0003	–0.0004	–0.0019	0.0001	0.0012	0.0010	0.0006	0.0004	1967	0.0113
1968	0.0001	0.0009	–0.0011	0.0014	0.0015	–0.0015	0.0000	0.0013	0.0014	–0.0013	0.0005	0.0014	1968	0.0046
1969	0.0024	0.0009	–0.0037	–0.0011	0.0021	–0.0013	0.0008	0.0005	0.0017	0.0024	–0.0002	0.0002	1969	0.0045
1970	0.0025	0.0009	0.0004	–0.0011	0.0009	0.0006	0.0018	0.0036	0.0002	–0.0005	0.0012	–0.0008	1970	0.0098

* Compound annual return

Table A-16 (Continued)

U.S. Treasury Bills: Inflation-Adjusted Total Returns

from January 1971 to December 2007

Year	Jan	Feb	Mar	Apr	May	Jun	Jul	Aug	Sep	Oct	Nov	Dec	Year	Jan–Dec*
1971	0.0030	0.0016	–0.0004	–0.0006	–0.0020	–0.0020	0.0015	0.0022	0.0029	0.0020	0.0021	–0.0004	1971	0.0099
1972	0.0021	–0.0024	0.0011	0.0005	–0.0002	0.0005	–0.0009	0.0013	–0.0006	0.0008	0.0013	0.0006	1972	0.0041
1973	0.0012	–0.0029	–0.0047	–0.0017	–0.0010	–0.0017	0.0041	–0.0109	0.0038	–0.0016	–0.0017	–0.0002	1973	–0.0172
1974	–0.0024	–0.0070	–0.0057	0.0019	–0.0035	–0.0036	–0.0004	–0.0068	–0.0039	–0.0035	–0.0031	–0.0002	1974	–0.0374
1975	0.0013	–0.0027	0.0003	–0.0007	–0.0001	–0.0040	–0.0057	0.0017	0.0004	–0.0006	–0.0020	0.0006	1975	–0.0113
1976	0.0023	0.0010	0.0016	0.0000	–0.0022	–0.0010	–0.0012	–0.0005	0.0003	0.0000	0.0011	0.0012	1976	0.0026
1977	–0.0021	–0.0067	–0.0024	–0.0041	–0.0018	–0.0026	–0.0002	0.0006	0.0005	0.0022	0.0001	0.0011	1977	–0.0155
1978	–0.0005	–0.0023	–0.0016	–0.0036	–0.0048	–0.0049	–0.0016	0.0005	–0.0009	–0.0012	0.0015	0.0024	1978	–0.0169
1979	–0.0011	–0.0043	–0.0015	–0.0035	–0.0041	–0.0012	–0.0052	–0.0024	–0.0021	–0.0002	0.0005	–0.0010	1979	–0.0259
1980	–0.0063	–0.0048	–0.0023	0.0013	–0.0018	–0.0049	0.0045	–0.0001	–0.0017	0.0008	0.0005	0.0044	1980	–0.0103
1981	0.0022	0.0003	0.0048	0.0043	0.0033	0.0049	0.0010	0.0051	0.0023	0.0099	0.0078	0.0059	1981	0.0530
1982	0.0044	0.0060	0.0109	0.0070	0.0007	–0.0026	0.0050	0.0056	0.0034	0.0032	0.0081	0.0109	1982	0.0642
1983	0.0045	0.0058	0.0056	0.0000	0.0015	0.0033	0.0034	0.0043	0.0026	0.0049	0.0054	0.0059	1983	0.0482
1984	0.0020	0.0025	0.0050	0.0032	0.0049	0.0043	0.0050	0.0041	0.0038	0.0074	0.0073	0.0058	1984	0.0567
1985	0.0046	0.0017	0.0017	0.0031	0.0029	0.0024	0.0047	0.0033	0.0029	0.0034	0.0027	0.0040	1985	0.0381
1986	0.0025	0.0081	0.0106	0.0074	0.0019	0.0003	0.0049	0.0028	–0.0004	0.0037	0.0030	0.0040	1986	0.0498
1987	–0.0019	0.0004	0.0002	–0.0009	0.0008	0.0007	0.0025	–0.0009	–0.0004	0.0034	0.0020	0.0042	1987	0.0101
1988	0.0003	0.0020	0.0001	–0.0005	0.0016	0.0006	0.0008	0.0017	–0.0006	0.0028	0.0048	0.0047	1988	0.0185
1989	0.0005	0.0020	0.0009	0.0002	0.0022	0.0047	0.0045	0.0058	0.0033	0.0020	0.0045	0.0045	1989	0.0356
1990	–0.0046	0.0010	0.0010	0.0053	0.0044	0.0008	0.0029	–0.0026	–0.0024	0.0008	0.0034	0.0060	1990	0.0161
1991	–0.0008	0.0033	0.0029	0.0038	0.0018	0.0012	0.0034	0.0017	0.0002	0.0028	0.0010	0.0031	1991	0.0246
1992	0.0019	–0.0008	–0.0017	0.0018	0.0013	–0.0004	0.0009	–0.0002	–0.0003	–0.0012	0.0009	0.0035	1992	0.0059
1993	–0.0026	–0.0013	–0.0010	–0.0004	0.0008	0.0011	0.0024	–0.0003	0.0005	–0.0019	0.0018	0.0023	1993	0.0014
1994	–0.0002	–0.0013	–0.0007	0.0014	0.0025	–0.0003	0.0000	–0.0004	0.0010	0.0032	0.0023	0.0044	1994	0.0120
1995	0.0001	0.0000	0.0013	0.0011	0.0034	0.0027	0.0045	0.0020	0.0023	0.0014	0.0049	0.0055	1995	0.0298
1996	–0.0016	0.0007	–0.0012	0.0007	0.0023	0.0034	0.0026	0.0022	0.0012	0.0011	0.0022	0.0046	1996	0.0182
1997	0.0013	0.0007	0.0018	0.0031	0.0056	0.0024	0.0030	0.0022	0.0019	0.0017	0.0045	0.0060	1997	0.0349
1998	0.0024	0.0020	0.0021	0.0024	0.0022	0.0029	0.0028	0.0031	0.0033	0.0008	0.0031	0.0044	1998	0.0319
1999	0.0011	0.0023	0.0012	–0.0035	0.0034	0.0040	0.0008	0.0015	–0.0009	0.0021	0.0030	0.0044	1999	0.0195
2000	0.0017	–0.0016	–0.0035	0.0040	0.0045	–0.0018	0.0031	0.0039	–0.0001	0.0039	0.0045	0.0056	2000	0.0242
2001	–0.0009	–0.0002	0.0019	0.0000	–0.0013	0.0011	0.0058	0.0031	–0.0017	0.0056	0.0034	0.0054	2001	0.0224
2002	–0.0009	–0.0026	–0.0043	–0.0040	0.0014	0.0007	0.0004	–0.0019	–0.0002	–0.0003	0.0012	0.0033	2002	–0.0071
2003	–0.0034	–0.0068	–0.0050	0.0032	0.0025	–0.0001	–0.0004	–0.0031	–0.0024	0.0018	0.0034	0.0019	2003	–0.0084
2004	–0.0042	–0.0048	–0.0055	–0.0024	–0.0052	–0.0023	0.0026	0.0006	–0.0010	–0.0041	0.0010	0.0053	2004	–0.0199
2005	–0.0005	–0.0041	–0.0057	–0.0046	0.0034	0.0018	–0.0022	–0.0021	–0.0093	0.0007	0.0113	0.0072	2005	–0.0042
2006	–0.0041	0.0013	–0.0019	–0.0049	–0.0006	0.0020	0.0010	0.0023	0.0090	0.0095	0.0057	0.0025	2006	0.0220
2007	0.0014	–0.0015	–0.0048	–0.0021	–0.0020	0.0020	0.0042	0.0060	0.0005	0.0011	–0.0025	0.0034	2007	0.0056

Compound annual return

Appendix B

Appendix B

Cumulative Wealth Indices of Basic Series

Basic Series

Table B-1

Large Company Stocks: Total Return Index

from December 1925 to December 1970

Year	Jan	Feb	Mar	Apr	May	Jun	Jul	Aug	Sep	Oct	Nov	Dec	Yr-end	Index
1925												1.000	1925	1.000
1926	1.000	0.962	0.906	0.929	0.946	0.989	1.036	1.062	1.089	1.058	1.095	1.116	1926	1.116
1927	1.095	1.154	1.164	1.187	1.259	1.251	1.334	1.403	1.466	1.393	1.493	1.535	1927	1.535
1928	1.529	1.509	1.676	1.733	1.768	1.700	1.724	1.862	1.910	1.942	2.193	2.204	1928	2.204
1929	2.332	2.328	2.325	2.366	2.280	2.540	2.660	2.933	2.794	2.243	1.963	2.018	1929	2.018
1930	2.147	2.203	2.382	2.363	2.340	1.960	2.035	2.064	1.800	1.646	1.631	1.516	1930	1.516
1931	1.592	1.782	1.662	1.506	1.314	1.500	1.392	1.418	0.996	1.085	0.999	0.859	1931	0.859
1932	0.836	0.883	0.781	0.625	0.488	0.487	0.672	0.933	0.900	0.779	0.746	0.789	1932	0.789
1933	0.795	0.654	0.678	0.966	1.129	1.280	1.169	1.310	1.164	1.064	1.184	1.214	1933	1.214
1934	1.344	1.301	1.301	1.268	1.175	1.202	1.066	1.131	1.127	1.095	1.198	1.197	1934	1.197
1935	1.148	1.109	1.077	1.182	1.231	1.317	1.429	1.469	1.507	1.624	1.700	1.767	1935	1.767
1936	1.886	1.928	1.980	1.831	1.931	1.995	2.135	2.167	2.174	2.342	2.374	2.367	1936	2.367
1937	2.459	2.506	2.487	2.286	2.280	2.165	2.391	2.276	1.957	1.765	1.612	1.538	1937	1.538
1938	1.561	1.666	1.252	1.433	1.386	1.733	1.862	1.820	1.850	1.993	1.939	2.016	1938	2.016
1939	1.881	1.954	1.692	1.688	1.811	1.701	1.889	1.766	2.062	2.036	1.955	2.008	1939	2.008
1940	1.941	1.966	1.991	1.986	1.531	1.655	1.712	1.772	1.793	1.869	1.810	1.812	1940	1.812
1941	1.728	1.718	1.730	1.624	1.653	1.749	1.850	1.852	1.839	1.718	1.670	1.602	1941	1.602
1942	1.627	1.602	1.497	1.437	1.552	1.586	1.640	1.666	1.715	1.831	1.827	1.927	1942	1.927
1943	2.070	2.190	2.310	2.318	2.446	2.500	2.368	2.409	2.472	2.446	2.286	2.427	1943	2.427
1944	2.468	2.479	2.527	2.502	2.628	2.771	2.717	2.760	2.758	2.764	2.801	2.906	1944	2.906
1945	2.952	3.154	3.015	3.287	3.351	3.349	3.288	3.499	3.652	3.770	3.919	3.965	1945	3.965
1946	4.248	3.976	4.167	4.330	4.455	4.290	4.188	3.906	3.516	3.495	3.486	3.645	1946	3.645
1947	3.738	3.709	3.654	3.521	3.526	3.721	3.863	3.785	3.743	3.832	3.765	3.853	1947	3.853
1948	3.707	3.563	3.846	3.958	4.305	4.329	4.109	4.174	4.059	4.347	3.929	4.065	1948	4.065
1949	4.081	3.960	4.090	4.017	3.913	3.919	4.174	4.265	4.377	4.526	4.605	4.829	1949	4.829
1950	4.924	5.022	5.057	5.303	5.573	5.267	5.330	5.566	5.895	5.949	6.050	6.360	1950	6.360
1951	6.765	6.871	6.764	7.109	6.896	6.739	7.218	7.563	7.573	7.495	7.567	7.888	1951	7.888
1952	8.030	7.804	8.197	7.867	8.137	8.536	8.703	8.642	8.490	8.507	8.993	9.336	1952	9.336
1953	9.291	9.192	8.997	8.783	8.851	8.732	8.971	8.521	8.551	9.012	9.196	9.244	1953	9.244
1954	9.739	9.848	10.168	10.693	11.139	11.173	11.831	11.506	12.485	12.277	13.393	14.108	1954	14.108
1955	14.387	14.528	14.485	15.059	15.142	16.416	17.437	17.393	17.618	17.118	18.533	18.561	1955	18.561
1956	17.917	18.657	19.982	19.973	18.788	19.557	20.594	19.919	19.043	19.169	19.072	19.778	1956	19.778
1957	18.986	18.485	18.882	19.614	20.472	20.481	20.749	19.701	18.516	17.957	18.372	17.646	1957	17.646
1958	18.431	18.170	18.767	19.400	19.810	20.363	21.277	21.651	22.735	23.348	24.012	25.298	1958	25.298
1959	25.430	25.554	25.605	26.635	27.273	27.213	28.199	27.911	26.674	27.017	27.519	28.322	1959	28.322
1960	26.340	26.729	26.400	25.976	26.821	27.388	26.748	27.596	25.968	25.949	27.154	28.455	1960	28.455
1961	30.291	31.257	32.100	32.262	33.033	32.125	33.223	34.029	33.404	34.401	35.940	36.106	1961	36.106
1962	34.784	35.511	35.349	33.204	30.512	28.061	29.891	30.512	29.092	29.279	32.459	32.954	1962	32.954
1963	34.620	33.794	35.045	36.798	37.510	36.805	36.726	38.692	38.318	39.617	39.435	40.469	1963	40.469
1964	41.612	42.222	42.917	43.238	43.940	44.721	45.592	45.055	46.409	46.856	46.878	47.139	1964	47.139
1965	48.763	48.913	48.264	49.984	49.833	47.477	48.177	49.488	51.140	52.618	52.453	53.008	1965	53.008
1966	53.335	52.634	51.555	52.688	50.096	49.363	48.769	45.234	44.993	47.214	47.662	47.674	1966	47.674
1967	51.478	51.846	53.967	56.325	53.641	54.658	57.215	56.817	58.758	57.136	57.507	59.104	1967	59.104
1968	56.592	55.113	55.718	60.363	61.334	61.980	60.916	61.913	64.387	64.945	68.393	65.642	1968	65.642
1969	65.193	62.414	64.653	66.131	66.303	62.708	59.024	61.705	60.251	63.014	61.141	60.059	1969	60.059
1970	55.594	58.850	59.028	53.779	50.837	48.386	52.026	54.672	56.570	56.019	59.020	62.465	1970	62.465

Table B-1 (Continued)

Large Company Stocks: Total Return Index

from January 1971 to December 2007

Year	Jan	Feb	Mar	Apr	May	Jun	Jul	Aug	Sep	Oct	Nov	Dec	Yr-end	Index
1971	65.082	65.998	68.522	71.104	68.491	68.636	65.896	68.612	68.231	65.477	65.650	71.406	1971	71.406
1972	72.791	74.969	75.510	75.940	77.605	76.010	76.287	79.271	78.985	79.828	83.856	84.956	1972	84.956
1973	83.603	80.822	80.807	77.619	76.538	76.144	79.146	76.630	79.813	79.835	71.194	72.500	1973	72.500
1974	71.883	72.017	70.453	67.822	65.974	65.127	60.183	55.197	48.740	56.818	54.273	53.311	1974	53.311
1975	59.983	64.027	65.541	68.773	72.270	75.608	70.628	69.610	67.326	71.613	73.857	73.144	1975	73.144
1976	81.916	81.441	84.095	83.262	82.654	86.185	85.596	85.717	87.830	86.025	85.946	90.584	1976	90.584
1977	86.151	84.849	83.841	83.956	82.699	86.626	85.317	84.186	84.187	80.690	83.675	84.077	1977	84.077
1978	79.062	77.786	79.933	86.888	88.072	86.730	91.583	94.696	94.240	85.847	88.078	89.592	1978	89.592
1979	93.368	90.717	95.934	96.280	94.661	98.541	99.620	105.703	105.970	99.022	104.113	106.113	1979	106.113
1980	112.589	112.934	101.792	106.162	112.130	115.445	123.249	124.865	128.369	130.763	145.085	140.514	1980	140.514
1981	134.359	137.154	142.366	139.333	140.197	139.076	139.173	131.463	124.863	131.456	137.253	133.616	1981	133.616
1982	131.438	124.709	123.960	129.092	125.374	123.193	120.544	135.817	137.311	152.772	159.464	162.223	1982	162.223
1983	167.868	172.233	178.519	192.051	191.052	198.350	192.142	195.408	198.066	195.412	199.965	198.745	1983	198.745
1984	197.453	190.977	194.242	195.583	185.139	189.230	186.524	207.508	207.550	208.089	205.988	211.199	1984	211.199
1985	227.419	230.535	230.950	230.211	244.369	248.254	247.609	246.098	238.199	248.846	266.663	279.117	1985	279.117
1986	280.345	301.679	318.392	314.444	331.707	337.213	318.026	341.814	313.717	331.160	339.637	330.671	1986	330.671
1987	375.080	390.571	401.194	397.664	401.760	421.808	442.814	459.862	449.745	352.960	324.052	347.967	1987	347.967
1988	362.826	379.878	368.406	372.385	375.290	392.703	391.132	378.186	394.221	404.983	399.232	406.458	1988	406.458
1989	435.845	424.993	435.023	457.470	475.860	473.290	515.792	525.747	523.696	511.494	522.133	534.455	1989	534.455
1990	498.594	505.025	518.308	505.505	554.792	550.909	549.146	499.558	474.980	473.222	503.698	517.499	1990	517.499
1991	540.372	579.063	592.845	594.505	619.950	591.618	619.306	633.859	623.464	631.818	606.293	675.592	1991	675.592
1992	663.026	671.513	658.351	677.509	681.168	671.291	698.344	684.237	692.106	694.598	718.006	727.412	1992	727.412
1993	732.722	742.613	758.580	739.994	759.974	762.482	758.898	787.812	781.983	797.857	790.357	800.078	1993	800.078
1994	826.881	804.555	769.557	779.561	792.268	772.699	798.276	830.765	810.744	829.310	798.874	810.538	1994	810.538
1995	831.612	863.878	889.449	915.332	951.488	973.848	1006.277	1008.994	1051.271	1047.591	1093.685	1113.918	1995	1113.918
1996	1152.237	1163.299	1174.466	1191.731	1222.478	1227.490	1172.867	1197.731	1265.044	1299.706	1398.354	1370.946	1996	1370.946
1997	1456.082	1467.876	1406.812	1490.799	1582.334	1652.906	1784.147	1684.948	1777.233	1717.873	1797.411	1828.326	1997	1828.326
1998	1848.621	1981.943	2083.439	2104.398	2068.223	2152.235	2129.313	1821.457	1938.140	2095.788	2222.814	2350.892	1998	2350.892
1999	2449.207	2373.085	2468.032	2563.619	2503.092	2642.014	2559.530	2546.861	2477.051	2633.799	2687.344	2845.629	1999	2845.629
2000	2702.664	2651.503	2910.899	2823.310	2765.376	2833.543	2789.254	2962.495	2806.105	2794.235	2573.937	2586.524	2000	2586.524
2001	2678.294	2434.087	2279.888	2457.058	2473.520	2413.315	2389.567	2239.981	2059.102	2098.369	2259.335	2279.127	2001	2279.127
2002	2245.874	2202.574	2285.413	2146.848	2131.026	1979.212	1824.932	1836.922	1637.285	1781.399	1886.252	1775.341	2002	1775.341
2003	1728.827	1702.894	1719.412	1861.092	1959.171	1984.249	2019.172	2058.545	2036.725	2152.004	2170.941	2284.785	2003	2284.785
2004	2326.825	2359.168	2323.545	2287.065	2318.398	2363.375	2285.147	2294.288	2319.066	2354.548	2449.907	2533.204	2004	2533.204
2005	2471.470	2523.370	2478.682	2431.661	2509.036	2512.599	2606.068	2582.301	2603.217	2559.822	2656.634	2657.559	2005	2657.559
2006	2727.931	2735.324	2769.378	2806.571	2725.798	2729.505	2746.342	2811.686	2884.143	2978.126	3034.758	3077.329	2006	3077.329
2007	3123.868	3062.769	3097.026	3234.210	3347.068	3291.462	3189.411	3237.220	3358.292	3411.722	3269.078	3246.391	2007	3246.391

Table B-2

Large Company Stocks: Capital Appreciation Index

from December 1925 to December 1970

Year	Jan	Feb	Mar	Apr	May	Jun	Jul	Aug	Sep	Oct	Nov	Dec	Yr-end	Index
1925												1.000	1925	1.000
1926	0.998	0.955	0.898	0.918	0.926	0.966	1.009	1.027	1.050	1.017	1.040	1.057	1926	1.057
1927	1.035	1.085	1.092	1.111	1.168	1.158	1.233	1.288	1.343	1.272	1.350	1.384	1927	1.384
1928	1.377	1.353	1.499	1.548	1.567	1.504	1.523	1.636	1.675	1.699	1.903	1.908	1928	1.908
1929	2.017	2.005	2.001	2.033	1.946	2.165	2.263	2.485	2.364	1.893	1.640	1.681	1929	1.681
1930	1.786	1.824	1.970	1.951	1.919	1.603	1.662	1.675	1.457	1.328	1.299	1.202	1930	1.202
1931	1.261	1.405	1.308	1.183	1.020	1.162	1.076	1.086	0.761	0.825	0.745	0.636	1931	0.636
1932	0.618	0.650	0.573	0.457	0.350	0.347	0.478	0.658	0.633	0.545	0.513	0.540	1932	0.540
1933	0.544	0.444	0.458	0.652	0.755	0.855	0.780	0.869	0.770	0.702	0.774	0.792	1933	0.792
1934	0.875	0.843	0.842	0.820	0.753	0.769	0.680	0.717	0.713	0.690	0.748	0.745	1934	0.745
1935	0.713	0.685	0.664	0.727	0.751	0.802	0.868	0.887	0.908	0.976	1.015	1.053	1935	1.053
1936	1.121	1.140	1.169	1.079	1.129	1.163	1.242	1.253	1.255	1.349	1.354	1.346	1936	1.346
1937	1.397	1.418	1.404	1.288	1.274	1.207	1.331	1.257	1.078	0.969	0.871	0.827	1937	0.827
1938	0.838	0.889	0.666	0.760	0.726	0.906	0.972	0.945	0.959	1.032	0.998	1.035	1938	1.035
1939	0.964	0.995	0.861	0.856	0.909	0.851	0.944	0.876	1.020	1.005	0.956	0.979	1939	0.979
1940	0.944	0.951	0.960	0.955	0.726	0.782	0.806	0.828	0.835	0.868	0.832	0.829	1940	0.829
1941	0.789	0.777	0.781	0.730	0.733	0.772	0.814	0.807	0.799	0.745	0.713	0.681	1941	0.681
1942	0.690	0.673	0.628	0.600	0.639	0.650	0.671	0.676	0.694	0.738	0.728	0.766	1942	0.766
1943	0.821	0.862	0.908	0.908	0.949	0.968	0.915	0.925	0.947	0.934	0.864	0.915	1943	0.915
1944	0.929	0.926	0.942	0.930	0.968	1.017	0.996	1.005	1.002	1.002	1.005	1.041	1944	1.041
1945	1.056	1.121	1.069	1.163	1.176	1.172	1.149	1.216	1.266	1.305	1.347	1.361	1945	1.361
1946	1.455	1.354	1.417	1.470	1.503	1.444	1.408	1.305	1.172	1.163	1.150	1.199	1946	1.199
1947	1.227	1.209	1.189	1.143	1.132	1.192	1.235	1.201	1.184	1.209	1.175	1.199	1947	1.199
1948	1.151	1.097	1.182	1.213	1.308	1.312	1.242	1.252	1.214	1.296	1.156	1.191	1948	1.191
1949	1.193	1.146	1.180	1.155	1.112	1.110	1.179	1.193	1.221	1.257	1.259	1.313	1949	1.313
1950	1.336	1.350	1.355	1.416	1.472	1.386	1.398	1.444	1.524	1.531	1.529	1.600	1950	1.600
1951	1.697	1.708	1.677	1.758	1.687	1.643	1.755	1.824	1.823	1.798	1.793	1.863	1951	1.863
1952	1.892	1.823	1.910	1.828	1.870	1.956	1.991	1.962	1.923	1.922	2.011	2.082	1952	2.082
1953	2.067	2.030	1.982	1.929	1.923	1.892	1.940	1.828	1.830	1.923	1.940	1.944	1953	1.944
1954	2.044	2.049	2.111	2.215	2.288	2.289	2.420	2.338	2.532	2.483	2.683	2.820	1954	2.820
1955	2.871	2.881	2.867	2.975	2.971	3.216	3.411	3.384	3.422	3.318	3.567	3.564	1955	3.564
1956	3.434	3.553	3.799	3.792	3.542	3.681	3.871	3.723	3.554	3.572	3.533	3.658	1956	3.658
1957	3.505	3.390	3.457	3.585	3.717	3.712	3.755	3.544	3.324	3.218	3.270	3.134	1957	3.134
1958	3.268	3.201	3.299	3.404	3.455	3.545	3.698	3.742	3.923	4.023	4.113	4.327	1958	4.327
1959	4.343	4.342	4.345	4.513	4.599	4.582	4.742	4.671	4.458	4.508	4.567	4.694	1959	4.694
1960	4.358	4.398	4.337	4.261	4.375	4.461	4.350	4.464	4.194	4.184	4.353	4.554	1960	4.554
1961	4.842	4.972	5.099	5.118	5.216	5.066	5.232	5.335	5.230	5.378	5.589	5.607	1961	5.607
1962	5.395	5.483	5.451	5.113	4.673	4.291	4.563	4.633	4.410	4.429	4.879	4.945	1962	4.945
1963	5.188	5.038	5.217	5.470	5.549	5.437	5.418	5.682	5.619	5.800	5.739	5.879	1963	5.879
1964	6.038	6.097	6.190	6.227	6.299	6.402	6.519	6.413	6.597	6.650	6.616	6.642	1964	6.642
1965	6.862	6.852	6.752	6.984	6.929	6.592	6.681	6.832	7.050	7.243	7.179	7.244	1965	7.244
1966	7.279	7.149	6.993	7.136	6.750	6.641	6.552	6.042	6.000	6.285	6.305	6.295	1966	6.295
1967	6.788	6.801	7.069	7.368	6.981	7.103	7.426	7.339	7.579	7.359	7.367	7.560	1967	7.560
1968	7.229	7.003	7.069	7.648	7.734	7.804	7.660	7.748	8.046	8.104	8.493	8.139	1968	8.139
1969	8.073	7.690	7.955	8.126	8.108	7.658	7.197	7.485	7.298	7.621	7.352	7.210	1969	7.210
1970	6.663	7.014	7.024	6.389	5.999	5.699	6.117	6.389	6.600	6.524	6.834	7.222	1970	7.222

Table B-2 (Continued)

Large Company Stocks: Capital Appreciation Index

from January 1971 to December 2007

Year	Jan	Feb	Mar	Apr	May	Jun	Jul	Aug	Sep	Oct	Nov	Dec	Yr-end	Index
1971	7.514	7.582	7.861	8.147	7.808	7.813	7.491	7.761	7.707	7.385	7.366	8.001	1971	8.001
1972	8.146	8.352	8.401	8.438	8.584	8.397	8.416	8.706	8.664	8.744	9.143	9.252	1972	9.252
1973	9.093	8.752	8.740	8.383	8.225	8.171	8.481	8.170	8.498	8.487	7.520	7.645	1973	7.645
1974	7.568	7.541	7.365	7.078	6.840	6.740	6.215	5.654	4.980	5.792	5.484	5.373	1974	5.373
1975	6.033	6.394	6.533	6.842	7.143	7.460	6.955	6.809	6.573	6.978	7.150	7.068	1975	7.068
1976	7.904	7.814	8.054	7.965	7.851	8.172	8.107	8.065	8.248	8.064	8.002	8.422	1976	8.422
1977	7.996	7.823	7.713	7.715	7.533	7.875	7.747	7.584	7.565	7.237	7.432	7.453	1977	7.453
1978	6.995	6.821	6.991	7.589	7.621	7.487	7.890	8.095	8.036	7.300	7.422	7.532	1978	7.532
1979	7.831	7.545	7.962	7.975	7.765	8.065	8.135	8.567	8.567	7.980	8.320	8.459	1979	8.459
1980	8.947	8.907	8.001	8.330	8.718	8.953	9.535	9.591	9.832	9.989	11.012	10.639	1980	10.639
1981	10.153	10.288	10.658	10.407	10.390	10.285	10.259	9.623	9.105	9.553	9.903	9.605	1981	9.605
1982	9.436	8.865	8.775	9.126	8.769	8.591	8.393	9.367	9.438	10.480	10.858	11.023	1982	11.023
1983	11.388	11.604	11.988	12.886	12.727	13.175	12.741	12.885	13.016	12.818	13.041	12.926	1983	12.926
1984	12.807	12.309	12.475	12.544	11.799	12.005	11.807	13.062	13.017	13.015	12.819	13.106	1984	13.106
1985	14.077	14.198	14.157	14.092	14.854	15.034	14.962	14.783	14.269	14.876	15.844	16.559	1985	16.559
1986	16.598	17.785	18.724	18.460	19.387	19.660	18.506	19.824	18.131	19.123	19.534	18.981	1986	18.981
1987	21.483	22.275	22.864	22.601	22.736	23.825	24.974	25.848	25.222	19.734	18.051	19.366	1987	19.366
1988	20.149	20.991	20.292	20.483	20.548	21.438	21.322	20.499	21.313	21.867	21.454	21.769	1988	21.769
1989	23.317	22.643	23.114	24.272	25.124	24.926	27.129	27.550	27.370	26.680	27.122	27.703	1989	27.703
1990	25.796	26.016	26.648	25.931	28.316	28.065	27.918	25.285	23.991	23.830	25.259	25.886	1990	25.886
1991	26.961	28.774	29.413	29.424	30.559	29.095	30.400	30.998	30.404	30.765	29.413	32.695	1991	32.695
1992	32.045	32.351	31.645	32.528	32.559	31.994	33.254	32.456	32.751	32.820	33.813	34.155	1992	34.155
1993	34.396	34.756	35.406	34.506	35.290	35.317	35.129	36.338	35.975	36.673	36.199	36.565	1993	36.565
1994	37.753	36.619	34.944	35.347	35.785	34.826	35.923	37.273	36.270	37.027	35.565	36.002	1994	36.002
1995	36.876	38.206	39.250	40.348	41.814	42.703	44.060	44.045	45.812	45.583	47.455	48.282	1995	48.282
1996	49.857	50.203	50.600	51.280	52.452	52.570	50.165	51.109	53.878	55.286	59.342	58.066	1996	58.066
1997	61.627	61.992	59.350	62.817	66.496	69.386	74.806	70.509	74.257	71.697	74.893	76.071	1997	76.071
1998	76.844	82.257	86.366	87.149	85.509	88.881	87.849	75.041	79.723	86.124	91.216	96.359	1998	96.359
1999	100.310	97.072	100.838	104.664	102.050	107.606	104.158	103.506	100.551	106.839	108.876	115.174	1999	115.174
2000	109.311	107.113	117.473	113.855	111.360	114.025	112.162	118.970	112.607	112.050	103.078	103.496	2000	103.496
2001	107.081	97.198	90.958	97.944	98.443	95.982	94.948	88.861	81.599	83.076	89.321	89.997	2001	89.997
2002	88.596	86.756	89.943	84.419	83.652	77.591	71.461	71.810	63.909	69.435	73.397	68.969	2002	68.969
2003	67.078	65.937	66.488	71.877	75.535	76.390	77.630	79.017	78.073	82.365	82.952	87.163	2003	87.163
2004	88.669	89.751	88.283	86.801	87.849	89.430	86.363	86.561	87.371	88.596	92.015	95.002	2004	95.002
2005	92.599	94.349	92.546	90.685	93.401	93.388	96.747	95.661	96.326	94.617	97.946	97.853	2005	97.853
2006	100.345	100.390	101.501	102.738	99.562	99.570	100.077	102.206	104.716	108.016	109.795	111.180	2006	111.180
2007	112.743	110.280	111.380	116.202	119.984	117.847	114.078	115.545	119.681	121.455	116.106	115.104	2007	115.104

Table B-3

Small Company Stocks: Total Return Index

from December 1925 to December 1970

Year	Jan	Feb	Mar	Apr	May	Jun	Jul	Aug	Sep	Oct	Nov	Dec	Yr-end	Index
1925												1.000	1925	1.000
1926	1.070	1.001	0.894	0.910	0.904	0.938	0.949	0.973	0.973	0.951	0.971	1.003	1926	1.003
1927	1.032	1.089	1.029	1.088	1.168	1.133	1.191	1.170	1.176	1.098	1.187	1.224	1927	1.224
1928	1.283	1.253	1.319	1.440	1.503	1.376	1.384	1.445	1.574	1.617	1.803	1.710	1928	1.710
1929	1.716	1.712	1.677	1.729	1.498	1.578	1.596	1.569	1.425	1.030	0.876	0.832	1929	0.832
1930	0.939	1.000	1.101	1.024	0.968	0.758	0.781	0.768	0.656	0.584	0.583	0.515	1930	0.515
1931	0.623	0.783	0.727	0.570	0.491	0.581	0.548	0.507	0.342	0.368	0.331	0.259	1931	0.259
1932	0.285	0.293	0.255	0.198	0.175	0.175	0.237	0.411	0.357	0.293	0.257	0.245	1932	0.245
1933	0.243	0.212	0.235	0.354	0.578	0.729	0.689	0.753	0.633	0.555	0.591	0.594	1933	0.594
1934	0.825	0.839	0.838	0.858	0.749	0.747	0.578	0.667	0.656	0.663	0.726	0.738	1934	0.738
1935	0.714	0.672	0.592	0.639	0.637	0.656	0.713	0.751	0.778	0.855	0.976	1.035	1935	1.035
1936	1.346	1.427	1.436	1.179	1.211	1.183	1.286	1.313	1.384	1.472	1.678	1.705	1936	1.705
1937	1.921	2.047	2.072	1.724	1.654	1.458	1.638	1.517	1.132	1.008	0.862	0.716	1937	0.716
1938	0.754	0.780	0.499	0.638	0.584	0.788	0.906	0.815	0.802	0.974	0.907	0.951	1938	0.951
1939	0.870	0.879	0.663	0.672	0.745	0.667	0.837	0.704	1.066	1.023	0.915	0.954	1939	0.954
1940	0.955	1.033	1.099	1.171	0.741	0.818	0.837	0.859	0.877	0.925	0.947	0.905	1940	0.905
1941	0.907	0.881	0.909	0.848	0.852	0.916	1.115	1.108	1.056	0.985	0.936	0.823	1941	0.823
1942	0.979	0.972	0.903	0.872	0.869	0.898	0.964	0.995	1.086	1.204	1.143	1.190	1942	1.190
1943	1.444	1.723	1.971	2.155	2.404	2.384	2.126	2.126	2.217	2.244	1.994	2.242	1943	2.242
1944	2.385	2.456	2.640	2.499	2.684	3.055	2.964	3.059	3.053	3.020	3.170	3.446	1944	3.446
1945	3.612	3.977	3.634	4.055	4.257	4.621	4.364	4.607	4.920	5.265	5.882	5.983	1945	5.983
1946	6.917	6.476	6.653	7.117	7.537	7.189	6.808	6.230	5.232	5.170	5.097	5.287	1946	5.287
1947	5.509	5.487	5.303	4.756	4.502	4.750	5.125	5.106	5.165	5.311	5.150	5.335	1947	5.335
1948	5.254	4.842	5.320	5.515	6.099	6.128	5.774	5.778	5.474	5.828	5.177	5.223	1948	5.223
1949	5.318	5.062	5.380	5.199	4.906	4.859	5.185	5.318	5.578	5.841	5.851	6.254	1949	6.254
1950	6.562	6.706	6.682	6.956	7.134	6.580	6.969	7.338	7.720	7.675	7.922	8.677	1950	8.677
1951	9.398	9.455	9.004	9.334	9.026	8.548	8.867	9.403	9.606	9.392	9.314	9.355	1951	9.355
1952	9.533	9.248	9.410	8.922	8.950	9.193	9.296	9.291	9.142	9.047	9.486	9.638	1952	9.638
1953	10.032	10.302	10.233	9.939	10.079	9.589	9.735	9.123	8.884	9.143	9.258	9.013	1953	9.013
1954	9.694	9.786	9.965	10.104	10.561	10.651	11.512	11.528	12.000	12.082	13.024	14.473	1954	14.473
1955	14.764	15.471	15.602	15.837	15.960	16.428	16.533	16.487	16.667	16.384	17.152	17.431	1955	17.431
1956	17.348	17.830	18.598	18.685	17.942	18.042	18.552	18.303	17.827	18.013	18.108	18.177	1956	18.177
1957	18.607	18.234	18.540	19.000	19.143	19.283	19.167	18.427	17.595	16.131	16.314	15.529	1957	15.529
1958	17.245	16.952	17.750	18.418	19.131	19.752	20.722	21.610	22.730	23.655	24.828	25.605	1958	25.605
1959	27.076	27.875	27.951	28.277	28.315	28.196	29.118	28.863	27.619	28.245	28.873	29.804	1959	29.804
1960	28.891	29.034	28.120	27.594	28.158	29.116	28.565	30.064	27.844	26.728	27.896	28.823	1960	28.823
1961	31.460	33.314	35.376	35.825	37.355	35.326	35.436	35.898	34.682	35.590	37.772	38.072	1961	38.072
1962	38.591	39.314	39.537	36.464	32.786	30.213	32.518	33.458	31.254	30.087	33.842	33.540	1962	33.540
1963	36.580	36.705	37.251	38.412	40.088	39.613	39.744	41.799	41.118	42.090	41.642	41.444	1963	41.444
1964	42.581	44.134	45.099	45.520	46.234	46.985	48.857	48.715	50.676	51.716	51.772	51.193	1964	51.193
1965	53.902	56.003	57.335	60.252	59.782	54.398	56.837	60.220	62.310	65.876	68.319	72.567	1965	72.567
1966	78.051	80.479	78.935	81.645	73.797	73.709	73.617	65.669	64.595	63.902	67.041	67.479	1966	67.479
1967	79.884	83.475	88.606	91.003	90.232	99.411	108.862	109.085	115.244	111.662	112.965	123.870	1967	123.870
1968	125.779	116.861	115.586	132.468	145.698	146.137	141.088	146.266	155.034	155.505	167.388	168.429	1968	168.429
1969	165.634	149.238	155.142	161.265	164.063	144.954	129.449	138.925	135.301	143.552	135.552	126.233	1969	126.233
1970	118.554	123.145	119.641	98.970	88.762	80.519	84.975	93.037	103.140	95.856	97.170	104.226	1970	104.226

Table B-3 (Continued)
Small Company Stocks: Total Return Index

from January 1971 to December 2007

Year	Jan	Feb	Mar	Apr	May	Jun	Jul	Aug	Sep	Oct	Nov	Dec	Yr-end	Index
1971	120.820	124.647	131.676	134.923	126.760	122.710	115.802	122.555	119.780	113.180	108.954	121.423	1971	121.423
1972	135.142	139.141	137.144	138.912	136.257	132.100	126.645	129.005	124.506	122.329	129.576	126.807	1972	126.807
1973	121.329	111.635	109.318	102.527	94.211	91.476	102.398	97.837	108.242	109.155	87.737	87.618	1973	87.618
1974	99.238	98.393	97.661	93.129	85.745	84.485	82.637	77.009	71.978	79.629	76.143	70.142	1974	70.142
1975	89.551	92.105	97.799	102.990	109.821	118.053	115.056	108.456	106.488	105.954	109.341	107.189	1975	107.189
1976	135.960	154.854	154.626	149.081	143.698	150.298	150.976	146.592	148.123	145.028	150.881	168.691	1976	168.691
1977	176.275	175.587	177.880	181.941	181.434	195.445	196.028	193.924	195.715	189.249	209.804	211.500	1977	211.500
1978	207.502	214.707	236.868	255.528	276.484	271.254	289.807	317.010	316.002	239.303	256.811	261.120	1978	261.120
1979	295.623	287.279	319.448	331.805	332.955	348.676	354.642	381.457	368.351	325.827	353.796	374.614	1979	374.614
1980	405.926	394.411	324.303	346.795	372.814	389.666	441.224	467.894	487.473	503.725	542.326	523.992	1980	523.992
1981	534.839	539.866	590.776	629.590	656.158	661.145	640.253	596.460	552.739	593.752	610.140	596.717	1981	596.717
1982	585.021	567.705	562.822	584.378	569.886	560.825	559.983	599.070	618.660	699.395	753.878	763.829	1982	763.829
1983	811.793	869.617	915.267	985.448	1071.150	1108.462	1098.662	1077.054	1091.419	1029.455	1082.532	1066.828	1983	1066.828
1984	1065.974	997.219	1014.571	1005.947	953.537	982.143	940.893	1034.794	1037.588	1015.072	980.966	995.680	1984	995.680
1985	1101.123	1131.074	1106.869	1087.609	1117.627	1129.474	1158.840	1150.497	1087.910	1116.304	1185.515	1241.234	1985	1241.234
1986	1255.136	1345.380	1409.555	1418.576	1469.645	1473.466	1368.850	1398.691	1320.504	1366.193	1361.958	1326.275	1986	1326.275
1987	1451.342	1568.756	1605.308	1555.062	1548.997	1590.201	1648.084	1695.384	1681.651	1190.777	1143.503	1202.966	1987	1202.966
1988	1269.850	1366.359	1422.107	1451.829	1425.841	1513.102	1509.320	1472.190	1505.609	1487.090	1422.104	1478.135	1988	1478.135
1989	1537.852	1550.616	1606.128	1650.939	1710.703	1676.318	1744.544	1765.827	1765.827	1659.171	1650.710	1628.590	1989	1628.590
1990	1504.166	1532.294	1588.682	1546.423	1633.178	1656.695	1593.410	1386.904	1271.929	1199.175	1253.138	1277.449	1990	1277.449
1991	1384.882	1539.020	1643.673	1649.261	1704.347	1621.686	1687.688	1731.737	1737.279	1792.350	1742.882	1847.629	1991	1847.629
1992	2056.041	2148.974	2095.465	2011.018	2008.202	1903.977	1974.424	1929.407	1954.682	2005.308	2182.778	2279.039	1992	2279.039
1993	2402.790	2359.540	2427.731	2353.442	2433.930	2424.681	2464.931	2548.492	2629.024	2752.851	2704.676	2757.147	1993	2757.147
1994	2927.539	2920.806	2790.538	2807.281	2803.912	2730.450	2780.690	2874.399	2904.580	2937.983	2842.205	2842.773	1994	2842.773
1995	2923.224	2996.889	3040.344	3147.364	3241.155	3425.253	3646.182	3776.715	3850.361	3662.848	3733.175	3822.398	1995	3822.398
1996	3833.101	3974.542	4065.162	4409.887	4740.188	4464.309	4043.325	4235.787	4359.048	4282.765	4406.109	4495.993	1996	4495.993
1997	4684.825	4588.318	4363.490	4243.058	4676.698	4909.598	5206.628	5471.646	5933.453	5704.421	5616.003	5519.969	1997	5519.969
1998	5487.401	5843.534	6124.608	6227.501	5917.994	5796.084	5407.166	4320.326	4479.746	4639.225	4990.878	5116.648	1998	5116.648
1999	5259.403	4898.082	4712.445	5159.656	5359.334	5663.744	5715.851	5606.678	5482.771	5435.070	5962.816	6640.788	1999	6640.788
2000	7035.915	8694.984	8041.990	7035.937	6467.434	7352.179	7115.438	7773.616	7604.929	7068.021	6283.471	6402.228	2000	6402.228
2001	7285.736	6774.277	6449.112	6920.542	7584.914	7857.212	7657.639	7431.739	6481.963	6900.049	7365.112	7860.048	2001	7860.048
2002	7946.508	7726.390	8409.403	8613.752	8378.596	8080.318	6910.288	6870.899	6407.801	6572.481	7121.941	6816.409	2002	6816.409
2003	6664.404	6472.469	6544.313	7151.625	7982.644	8333.881	8948.921	9372.205	9380.640	10219.269	10658.698	10953.944	2003	10953.944
2004	11587.082	11645.017	11661.320	11184.372	11184.372	11677.603	10805.286	10641.046	11174.162	11379.767	12400.532	12968.476	2004	12968.476
2005	12436.768	12539.994	12134.952	11380.158	12066.381	12611.782	13574.061	13385.381	13467.032	13088.608	13681.522	13706.149	2005	13706.149
2006	14958.891	14996.288	15678.620	15614.337	14694.653	14563.870	14061.417	14452.324	14533.257	15325.320	15670.139	15922.429	2006	15922.429
2007	16105.537	16025.009	16188.464	16431.291	16948.877	16892.945	15793.215	15976.416	16212.867	16488.486	15100.155	15091.095	2007	15091.095

Table B-4
Long-Term Corporate Bonds: Total Return Index

from December 1925 to December 1970

Year	Jan	Feb	Mar	Apr	May	Jun	Jul	Aug	Sep	Oct	Nov	Dec	Yr-end	Index
1925												1.000	1925	1.000
1926	1.007	1.012	1.020	1.030	1.035	1.035	1.041	1.046	1.052	1.062	1.068	1.074	1926	1.074
1927	1.080	1.087	1.096	1.102	1.101	1.106	1.106	1.115	1.132	1.138	1.146	1.154	1927	1.154
1928	1.157	1.165	1.169	1.171	1.162	1.159	1.158	1.168	1.171	1.181	1.177	1.186	1928	1.186
1929	1.192	1.195	1.185	1.187	1.192	1.187	1.189	1.192	1.196	1.204	1.202	1.225	1929	1.225
1930	1.233	1.241	1.259	1.269	1.276	1.290	1.298	1.315	1.329	1.337	1.335	1.323	1930	1.323
1931	1.350	1.359	1.372	1.381	1.400	1.407	1.414	1.416	1.414	1.362	1.337	1.299	1931	1.299
1932	1.292	1.261	1.306	1.283	1.297	1.295	1.301	1.358	1.399	1.409	1.419	1.439	1932	1.439
1933	1.518	1.438	1.445	1.431	1.516	1.544	1.569	1.584	1.582	1.588	1.549	1.588	1933	1.588
1934	1.629	1.653	1.684	1.701	1.717	1.744	1.752	1.760	1.749	1.767	1.790	1.808	1934	1.808
1935	1.846	1.872	1.880	1.901	1.909	1.931	1.952	1.944	1.944	1.952	1.966	1.982	1935	1.982
1936	1.998	2.009	2.026	2.031	2.039	2.056	2.058	2.072	2.086	2.091	2.114	2.116	1936	2.116
1937	2.121	2.111	2.087	2.101	2.110	2.121	2.129	2.125	2.131	2.145	2.159	2.174	1937	2.174
1938	2.182	2.184	2.165	2.195	2.197	2.218	2.233	2.229	2.253	2.271	2.279	2.307	1938	2.307
1939	2.312	2.327	2.332	2.347	2.359	2.367	2.365	2.272	2.307	2.361	2.380	2.399	1939	2.399
1940	2.410	2.415	2.427	2.405	2.400	2.429	2.434	2.436	2.458	2.470	2.486	2.480	1940	2.480
1941	2.482	2.483	2.478	2.497	2.509	2.525	2.541	2.550	2.562	2.570	2.546	2.548	1941	2.548
1942	2.549	2.547	2.563	2.565	2.570	2.579	2.584	2.593	2.598	2.600	2.601	2.614	1942	2.614
1943	2.627	2.628	2.634	2.647	2.659	2.672	2.677	2.682	2.684	2.681	2.675	2.688	1943	2.688
1944	2.693	2.703	2.716	2.725	2.726	2.732	2.741	2.750	2.755	2.761	2.774	2.815	1944	2.815
1945	2.837	2.850	2.855	2.860	2.857	2.866	2.863	2.864	2.873	2.882	2.892	2.930	1945	2.930
1946	2.968	2.978	2.988	2.975	2.981	2.986	2.983	2.956	2.949	2.955	2.947	2.980	1946	2.980
1947	2.982	2.983	3.003	3.009	3.015	3.017	3.023	3.001	2.962	2.933	2.904	2.911	1947	2.911
1948	2.918	2.929	2.963	2.974	2.977	2.952	2.936	2.953	2.960	2.967	2.992	3.031	1948	3.031
1949	3.043	3.054	3.056	3.063	3.075	3.101	3.132	3.143	3.150	3.171	3.178	3.132	1949	3.132
1950	3.143	3.145	3.152	3.150	3.147	3.154	3.176	3.188	3.176	3.173	3.190	3.198	1950	3.198
1951	3.204	3.190	3.114	3.111	3.107	3.078	3.141	3.177	3.159	3.113	3.094	3.112	1951	3.112
1952	3.174	3.147	3.171	3.169	3.179	3.184	3.189	3.209	3.204	3.216	3.251	3.221	1952	3.221
1953	3.196	3.183	3.172	3.094	3.084	3.118	3.173	3.146	3.226	3.299	3.275	3.331	1953	3.331
1954	3.373	3.439	3.453	3.441	3.427	3.448	3.462	3.468	3.482	3.496	3.505	3.511	1954	3.511
1955	3.477	3.455	3.486	3.486	3.480	3.490	3.476	3.462	3.489	3.516	3.505	3.527	1955	3.527
1956	3.564	3.573	3.521	3.481	3.499	3.493	3.460	3.388	3.392	3.357	3.314	3.287	1956	3.287
1957	3.352	3.383	3.400	3.377	3.352	3.244	3.209	3.206	3.236	3.244	3.344	3.573	1957	3.573
1958	3.609	3.606	3.589	3.648	3.659	3.645	3.590	3.475	3.441	3.478	3.515	3.494	1958	3.494
1959	3.484	3.528	3.499	3.439	3.400	3.415	3.445	3.422	3.392	3.447	3.494	3.460	1959	3.460
1960	3.498	3.542	3.610	3.602	3.594	3.645	3.739	3.783	3.759	3.762	3.735	3.774	1960	3.774
1961	3.830	3.911	3.899	3.854	3.873	3.842	3.857	3.850	3.906	3.955	3.966	3.956	1961	3.956
1962	3.988	4.008	4.069	4.127	4.127	4.116	4.110	4.169	4.206	4.234	4.261	4.270	1962	4.270
1963	4.296	4.305	4.317	4.295	4.315	4.334	4.346	4.361	4.351	4.372	4.379	4.364	1963	4.364
1964	4.402	4.426	4.398	4.416	4.441	4.463	4.486	4.502	4.512	4.534	4.533	4.572	1964	4.572
1965	4.609	4.614	4.619	4.629	4.625	4.627	4.635	4.633	4.626	4.647	4.620	4.552	1965	4.552
1966	4.562	4.510	4.483	4.489	4.478	4.491	4.447	4.332	4.366	4.480	4.471	4.560	1966	4.560
1967	4.766	4.670	4.724	4.691	4.572	4.470	4.488	4.485	4.527	4.400	4.280	4.335	1967	4.335
1968	4.491	4.508	4.419	4.440	4.454	4.509	4.662	4.758	4.733	4.658	4.552	4.446	1968	4.446
1969	4.508	4.436	4.347	4.493	4.391	4.406	4.408	4.400	4.292	4.347	4.142	4.086	1969	4.086
1970	4.144	4.310	4.291	4.184	4.115	4.116	4.345	4.388	4.449	4.406	4.664	4.837	1970	4.837

Table B-4 (Continued)

Long-Term Corporate Bonds: Total Return Index

from January 1971 to December 2007

Year	Jan	Feb	Mar	Apr	May	Jun	Jul	Aug	Sep	Oct	Nov	Dec	Yr-end	Index
1971	5.095	4.908	5.035	4.916	4.837	4.889	4.876	5.146	5.094	5.238	5.253	5.370	1971	5.370
1972	5.352	5.409	5.422	5.441	5.530	5.493	5.509	5.549	5.566	5.622	5.762	5.760	1972	5.760
1973	5.729	5.742	5.768	5.803	5.780	5.748	5.474	5.669	5.871	5.832	5.878	5.825	1973	5.825
1974	5.795	5.800	5.622	5.430	5.487	5.331	5.218	5.078	5.167	5.624	5.690	5.647	1974	5.647
1975	5.984	6.066	5.916	5.885	5.947	6.128	6.110	6.003	5.927	6.255	6.200	6.474	1975	6.474
1976	6.596	6.636	6.747	6.737	6.667	6.767	6.868	7.027	7.144	7.194	7.424	7.681	1976	7.681
1977	7.448	7.434	7.503	7.579	7.659	7.793	7.789	7.895	7.878	7.848	7.895	7.813	1977	7.813
1978	7.743	7.783	7.815	7.797	7.713	7.731	7.809	8.010	7.971	7.808	7.912	7.807	1978	7.807
1979	7.951	7.849	7.932	7.892	8.072	8.289	8.263	8.269	8.121	7.398	7.563	7.481	1979	7.481
1980	6.998	6.533	6.492	7.386	7.799	8.065	7.719	7.376	7.201	7.086	7.098	7.274	1980	7.274
1981	7.180	6.987	7.204	6.650	7.046	7.062	6.799	6.565	6.434	6.769	7.627	7.185	1981	7.185
1982	7.092	7.313	7.537	7.792	7.983	7.609	8.020	8.691	9.233	9.933	10.133	10.242	1982	10.242
1983	10.146	10.580	10.657	11.241	10.876	10.826	10.334	10.386	10.794	10.767	10.920	10.883	1983	10.883
1984	11.177	10.985	10.727	10.649	10.134	10.336	10.942	11.278	11.632	12.297	12.558	12.718	1984	12.718
1985	13.132	12.642	12.868	13.249	14.336	14.455	14.280	14.651	14.755	15.240	15.804	16.546	1985	16.546
1986	16.620	17.870	18.327	18.357	18.056	18.449	18.506	19.015	18.799	19.154	19.600	19.829	1986	19.829
1987	20.258	20.375	20.198	19.184	19.084	19.380	19.149	19.006	18.204	19.127	19.366	19.776	1987	19.776
1988	20.799	21.086	20.689	20.381	20.265	21.033	20.800	20.912	21.594	22.183	21.808	21.893	1988	21.893
1989	22.335	22.047	22.188	22.661	23.520	24.449	24.884	24.479	24.576	25.255	25.432	25.447	1989	25.447
1990	24.961	24.931	24.903	24.428	25.368	25.916	26.181	25.416	25.647	25.986	26.726	27.173	1990	27.173
1991	27.580	27.914	28.216	28.605	28.717	28.665	29.144	29.945	30.757	30.889	31.216	32.577	1991	32.577
1992	32.014	32.321	32.085	32.136	32.953	33.467	34.497	34.808	35.153	34.604	34.843	35.637	1992	35.637
1993	36.528	37.463	37.557	37.752	37.828	38.936	39.326	40.454	40.628	40.835	40.068	40.336	1993	40.336
1994	41.151	39.974	38.443	38.070	37.834	37.528	38.687	38.567	37.545	37.358	37.425	38.012	1994	38.012
1995	38.985	40.112	40.493	41.202	43.802	44.148	43.702	44.637	45.320	46.158	47.275	48.353	1995	48.353
1996	48.421	46.615	46.009	45.273	45.295	46.074	46.121	45.798	46.984	48.680	49.960	49.031	1996	49.031
1997	48.894	49.031	47.947	48.829	49.454	50.379	53.039	51.766	52.936	53.947	54.492	55.380	1997	55.380
1998	56.139	56.100	56.313	56.611	57.557	58.219	57.893	58.408	60.820	59.664	61.275	61.339	1998	61.339
1999	62.091	59.603	59.617	59.473	58.427	57.493	56.843	56.693	57.221	57.492	57.356	56.772	1999	56.772
2000	56.652	57.174	58.142	57.476	56.552	58.396	59.442	60.245	60.525	60.797	62.394	64.077	2000	64.077
2001	66.377	67.222	67.026	66.166	67.041	67.412	69.844	70.937	69.858	72.913	71.542	70.900	2001	70.900
2002	72.139	73.080	70.925	72.720	73.542	74.079	74.772	78.152	80.729	78.794	79.605	82.480	2002	82.480
2003	82.651	84.830	84.152	86.083	90.135	88.845	81.016	82.788	86.954	85.192	85.634	86.824	2003	86.824
2004	88.445	90.023	91.081	86.215	85.600	86.400	87.993	91.468	92.391	93.905	92.028	94.396	2004	94.396
2005	97.007	95.924	94.730	97.824	100.711	102.132	99.640	101.959	98.794	96.778	97.734	99.937	2005	99.937
2006	99.012	100.277	96.223	94.068	93.877	94.242	96.478	99.958	101.791	103.085	105.625	103.178	2006	103.178
2007	102.652	105.602	103.167	104.616	102.756	101.231	100.905	102.437	103.825	104.735	105.559	105.858	2007	105.858

Table B-5
Long-Term Government Bonds: Total Return Index

from December 1925 to December 1970

Year	Jan	Feb	Mar	Apr	May	Jun	Jul	Aug	Sep	Oct	Nov	Dec	Yr-end	Index
1925												1.000	1925	1.000
1926	1.014	1.020	1.024	1.032	1.034	1.038	1.038	1.038	1.042	1.053	1.069	1.078	1926	1.078
1927	1.086	1.095	1.123	1.122	1.135	1.127	1.132	1.141	1.143	1.154	1.166	1.174	1927	1.174
1928	1.170	1.177	1.182	1.182	1.173	1.178	1.152	1.161	1.156	1.174	1.175	1.175	1928	1.175
1929	1.165	1.146	1.130	1.161	1.142	1.155	1.155	1.151	1.154	1.198	1.226	1.215	1929	1.215
1930	1.208	1.224	1.234	1.232	1.249	1.256	1.260	1.262	1.271	1.276	1.281	1.272	1930	1.272
1931	1.257	1.267	1.280	1.291	1.310	1.311	1.305	1.307	1.270	1.228	1.231	1.204	1931	1.204
1932	1.208	1.258	1.256	1.332	1.307	1.315	1.379	1.379	1.387	1.385	1.389	1.407	1932	1.407
1933	1.428	1.391	1.405	1.400	1.443	1.450	1.447	1.454	1.457	1.444	1.422	1.406	1933	1.406
1934	1.442	1.454	1.483	1.501	1.521	1.531	1.537	1.519	1.497	1.524	1.530	1.547	1934	1.547
1935	1.575	1.590	1.596	1.609	1.600	1.615	1.622	1.600	1.602	1.611	1.613	1.624	1935	1.624
1936	1.633	1.647	1.664	1.670	1.677	1.680	1.690	1.709	1.704	1.705	1.740	1.746	1936	1.746
1937	1.744	1.759	1.687	1.693	1.702	1.699	1.723	1.705	1.712	1.720	1.736	1.750	1937	1.750
1938	1.760	1.770	1.763	1.800	1.808	1.809	1.817	1.817	1.821	1.837	1.833	1.847	1938	1.847
1939	1.858	1.873	1.896	1.919	1.951	1.946	1.968	1.929	1.824	1.898	1.929	1.957	1939	1.957
1940	1.954	1.959	1.994	1.987	1.927	1.977	1.987	1.993	2.015	2.021	2.062	2.076	1940	2.076
1941	2.034	2.039	2.058	2.085	2.090	2.104	2.109	2.113	2.110	2.140	2.133	2.096	1941	2.096
1942	2.110	2.112	2.132	2.126	2.142	2.142	2.146	2.154	2.155	2.160	2.152	2.163	1942	2.163
1943	2.170	2.169	2.171	2.181	2.192	2.196	2.196	2.201	2.203	2.204	2.204	2.208	1943	2.208
1944	2.213	2.220	2.224	2.227	2.234	2.235	2.243	2.249	2.253	2.255	2.261	2.270	1944	2.270
1945	2.299	2.317	2.321	2.358	2.372	2.412	2.391	2.397	2.410	2.435	2.466	2.514	1945	2.514
1946	2.520	2.528	2.531	2.497	2.493	2.511	2.501	2.473	2.471	2.489	2.475	2.511	1946	2.511
1947	2.510	2.515	2.520	2.511	2.519	2.522	2.537	2.558	2.547	2.537	2.493	2.445	1947	2.445
1948	2.450	2.462	2.470	2.481	2.516	2.495	2.490	2.490	2.494	2.496	2.514	2.529	1948	2.529
1949	2.549	2.562	2.581	2.584	2.589	2.632	2.641	2.670	2.667	2.672	2.678	2.692	1949	2.692
1950	2.675	2.681	2.683	2.691	2.700	2.693	2.708	2.712	2.692	2.679	2.689	2.693	1950	2.693
1951	2.709	2.689	2.646	2.630	2.612	2.596	2.632	2.657	2.636	2.639	2.603	2.587	1951	2.587
1952	2.595	2.598	2.627	2.672	2.663	2.664	2.658	2.640	2.606	2.644	2.640	2.617	1952	2.617
1953	2.620	2.598	2.575	2.548	2.510	2.566	2.576	2.574	2.651	2.671	2.658	2.713	1953	2.713
1954	2.737	2.802	2.819	2.848	2.823	2.869	2.908	2.897	2.894	2.896	2.889	2.907	1954	2.907
1955	2.837	2.815	2.840	2.840	2.861	2.839	2.810	2.811	2.832	2.872	2.859	2.870	1955	2.870
1956	2.894	2.893	2.850	2.818	2.881	2.889	2.829	2.776	2.790	2.775	2.759	2.710	1956	2.710
1957	2.803	2.810	2.804	2.741	2.735	2.686	2.675	2.675	2.696	2.682	2.825	2.912	1957	2.912
1958	2.887	2.916	2.946	3.001	3.001	2.953	2.871	2.746	2.714	2.751	2.785	2.734	1958	2.734
1959	2.712	2.744	2.749	2.717	2.715	2.718	2.734	2.723	2.708	2.748	2.716	2.673	1959	2.673
1960	2.702	2.757	2.835	2.787	2.829	2.878	2.984	2.964	2.986	2.978	2.958	3.041	1960	3.041
1961	3.008	3.068	3.057	3.092	3.078	3.055	3.065	3.054	3.093	3.115	3.109	3.070	1961	3.070
1962	3.066	3.098	3.176	3.202	3.217	3.192	3.158	3.217	3.236	3.263	3.270	3.282	1962	3.282
1963	3.281	3.284	3.287	3.283	3.290	3.297	3.307	3.314	3.315	3.307	3.324	3.322	1963	3.322
1964	3.317	3.313	3.326	3.341	3.358	3.381	3.384	3.390	3.407	3.422	3.428	3.438	1964	3.438
1965	3.452	3.457	3.475	3.488	3.494	3.511	3.518	3.514	3.502	3.511	3.490	3.462	1965	3.462
1966	3.427	3.341	3.440	3.418	3.398	3.393	3.380	3.310	3.420	3.498	3.447	3.589	1966	3.589
1967	3.644	3.564	3.634	3.528	3.515	3.405	3.428	3.399	3.398	3.262	3.198	3.259	1967	3.259
1968	3.366	3.355	3.284	3.359	3.373	3.451	3.550	3.549	3.513	3.466	3.373	3.251	1968	3.251
1969	3.184	3.197	3.201	3.337	3.174	3.242	3.267	3.245	3.073	3.185	3.107	3.086	1969	3.086
1970	3.079	3.260	3.238	3.104	2.959	3.103	3.202	3.196	3.269	3.233	3.489	3.460	1970	3.460

Table B-5 (Continued)

Long-Term Government Bonds: Total Return Index

from January 1971 to December 2007

Year	Jan	Feb	Mar	Apr	May	Jun	Jul	Aug	Sep	Oct	Nov	Dec	Yr-end	Index
1971	3.634	3.575	3.763	3.657	3.655	3.597	3.607	3.777	3.854	3.918	3.900	3.917	1971	3.917
1972	3.892	3.927	3.895	3.905	4.011	3.985	4.071	4.082	4.049	4.143	4.237	4.140	1972	4.140
1973	4.007	4.013	4.046	4.064	4.021	4.013	3.839	3.989	4.116	4.205	4.128	4.094	1973	4.094
1974	4.060	4.050	3.932	3.833	3.880	3.897	3.886	3.796	3.890	4.080	4.200	4.272	1974	4.272
1975	4.368	4.426	4.308	4.229	4.319	4.445	4.407	4.377	4.334	4.539	4.490	4.665	1975	4.665
1976	4.707	4.736	4.815	4.824	4.747	4.846	4.884	4.987	5.059	5.102	5.274	5.447	1976	5.447
1977	5.236	5.210	5.257	5.295	5.361	5.449	5.411	5.518	5.502	5.451	5.502	5.410	1977	5.410
1978	5.366	5.368	5.357	5.355	5.323	5.290	5.366	5.483	5.425	5.316	5.416	5.346	1978	5.346
1979	5.448	5.375	5.444	5.383	5.524	5.696	5.647	5.627	5.559	5.091	5.250	5.280	1979	5.280
1980	4.889	4.660	4.514	5.201	5.419	5.613	5.346	5.115	4.982	4.851	4.899	5.071	1980	5.071
1981	5.013	4.795	4.979	4.721	5.015	4.925	4.751	4.568	4.502	4.875	5.562	5.166	1981	5.166
1982	5.189	5.284	5.406	5.608	5.627	5.501	5.777	6.228	6.613	7.033	7.031	7.251	1982	7.251
1983	7.027	7.372	7.303	7.558	7.267	7.295	6.940	6.954	7.305	7.209	7.341	7.298	1983	7.298
1984	7.476	7.343	7.228	7.152	6.782	6.884	7.361	7.557	7.816	8.254	8.352	8.427	1984	8.427
1985	8.734	8.304	8.558	8.766	9.551	9.686	9.512	9.759	9.738	10.067	10.471	11.037	1985	11.037
1986	11.009	12.270	13.215	13.109	12.447	13.210	13.068	13.720	13.034	13.410	13.769	13.745	1986	13.745
1987	13.966	14.247	13.930	13.271	13.132	13.260	13.024	12.810	12.337	13.106	13.154	13.372	1987	13.372
1988	14.263	14.337	13.897	13.675	13.536	14.035	13.797	13.876	14.355	14.796	14.506	14.665	1988	14.665
1989	14.963	14.695	14.875	15.111	15.717	16.582	16.977	16.537	16.569	17.198	17.332	17.322	1989	17.322
1990	16.728	16.686	16.613	16.278	16.954	17.344	17.530	16.796	16.992	17.358	18.056	18.392	1990	18.392
1991	18.632	18.689	18.760	19.023	19.024	18.904	19.202	19.855	20.458	20.569	20.738	21.942	1991	21.942
1992	21.231	21.339	21.140	21.173	21.687	22.121	23.001	23.155	23.584	23.117	23.140	23.709	1992	23.709
1993	24.374	25.237	25.290	25.472	25.591	26.739	27.251	28.433	28.448	28.722	27.979	28.034	1993	28.034
1994	28.755	27.462	26.378	25.981	25.767	25.508	26.435	26.209	25.342	25.280	25.447	25.856	1994	25.856
1995	26.561	27.322	27.572	28.039	30.255	30.675	30.161	30.873	31.413	32.337	33.143	34.044	1995	34.044
1996	34.007	32.366	31.687	31.163	30.994	31.622	31.678	31.237	32.142	33.440	34.612	33.727	1996	33.727
1997	33.459	33.476	32.633	33.465	33.783	34.448	36.603	35.441	36.560	37.807	38.366	39.074	1997	39.074
1998	39.856	39.570	39.668	39.771	40.497	41.421	41.256	43.173	44.876	43.896	44.320	44.178	1998	44.178
1999	44.713	42.390	42.355	42.444	41.660	41.337	41.012	40.803	41.147	41.099	40.849	40.218	1999	40.218
2000	41.135	42.220	43.768	43.437	43.200	44.254	45.018	46.100	45.376	46.227	47.699	48.856	2000	48.856
2001	48.882	49.816	49.447	47.899	48.079	48.488	50.309	51.343	51.758	54.160	51.607	50.662	2001	50.662
2002	51.361	51.951	49.686	51.721	51.798	52.769	54.368	56.888	59.258	57.517	56.817	59.699	2002	59.699
2003	59.065	61.011	60.186	60.798	64.397	63.406	57.178	58.129	61.306	59.573	59.732	60.564	2003	60.564
2004	61.699	63.117	64.007	60.244	59.939	60.666	61.609	64.040	64.657	65.649	64.115	65.717	2004	65.717
2005	67.691	66.826	66.348	68.820	70.862	72.047	69.973	72.302	69.860	68.489	69.010	70.852	2005	70.852
2006	70.018	71.687	67.821	66.148	66.213	66.819	68.148	70.186	71.383	71.932	73.425	71.694	2006	71.694
2007	70.961	73.335	72.272	72.887	71.428	70.782	72.790	74.235	74.323	75.476	79.009	78.779	2007	78.779

Table B-6
Long-Term Government Bonds: Capital Appreciation Index

from December 1925 to December 1970

Year	Jan	Feb	Mar	Apr	May	Jun	Jul	Aug	Sep	Oct	Nov	Dec	Yr-end	Index
1925												1.000	1925	1.000
1926	1.011	1.014	1.015	1.020	1.018	1.019	1.016	1.013	1.014	1.021	1.034	1.039	1926	1.039
1927	1.044	1.050	1.074	1.070	1.079	1.069	1.071	1.076	1.075	1.083	1.090	1.095	1927	1.095
1928	1.088	1.092	1.094	1.091	1.080	1.081	1.055	1.060	1.053	1.066	1.064	1.061	1928	1.061
1929	1.048	1.029	1.011	1.036	1.016	1.024	1.021	1.014	1.014	1.050	1.072	1.059	1929	1.059
1930	1.050	1.061	1.066	1.062	1.074	1.076	1.077	1.075	1.080	1.081	1.083	1.072	1930	1.072
1931	1.056	1.063	1.071	1.077	1.090	1.087	1.080	1.078	1.045	1.007	1.007	0.982	1931	0.982
1932	0.982	1.019	1.014	1.072	1.049	1.053	1.101	1.098	1.101	1.097	1.097	1.109	1932	1.109
1933	1.122	1.091	1.098	1.092	1.122	1.124	1.120	1.122	1.122	1.108	1.089	1.074	1933	1.074
1934	1.098	1.105	1.123	1.135	1.147	1.152	1.153	1.137	1.118	1.135	1.137	1.146	1934	1.146
1935	1.164	1.173	1.175	1.181	1.172	1.180	1.183	1.164	1.163	1.167	1.166	1.171	1935	1.171
1936	1.175	1.182	1.191	1.193	1.195	1.195	1.199	1.210	1.203	1.201	1.223	1.225	1936	1.225
1937	1.221	1.229	1.176	1.178	1.182	1.176	1.190	1.175	1.177	1.180	1.188	1.195	1937	1.195
1938	1.199	1.203	1.196	1.218	1.221	1.219	1.222	1.219	1.219	1.227	1.222	1.229	1938	1.229
1939	1.233	1.241	1.254	1.266	1.285	1.280	1.292	1.263	1.192	1.238	1.256	1.272	1939	1.272
1940	1.267	1.268	1.288	1.281	1.241	1.270	1.274	1.275	1.287	1.289	1.313	1.319	1940	1.319
1941	1.291	1.291	1.301	1.316	1.317	1.324	1.325	1.325	1.321	1.338	1.332	1.306	1941	1.306
1942	1.312	1.311	1.321	1.314	1.322	1.319	1.319	1.321	1.319	1.319	1.312	1.316	1942	1.316
1943	1.317	1.314	1.313	1.316	1.320	1.320	1.317	1.317	1.316	1.314	1.311	1.311	1943	1.311
1944	1.311	1.312	1.312	1.312	1.312	1.311	1.313	1.314	1.313	1.312	1.312	1.315	1944	1.315
1945	1.329	1.337	1.337	1.356	1.361	1.381	1.367	1.368	1.373	1.384	1.399	1.424	1945	1.424
1946	1.425	1.427	1.427	1.405	1.401	1.408	1.400	1.382	1.378	1.386	1.376	1.393	1946	1.393
1947	1.390	1.390	1.391	1.383	1.385	1.384	1.390	1.399	1.391	1.383	1.357	1.328	1947	1.328
1948	1.328	1.332	1.333	1.337	1.353	1.339	1.333	1.331	1.330	1.328	1.336	1.341	1948	1.341
1949	1.349	1.353	1.360	1.360	1.360	1.380	1.382	1.395	1.391	1.391	1.391	1.396	1949	1.396
1950	1.385	1.386	1.384	1.386	1.388	1.382	1.387	1.387	1.374	1.365	1.367	1.367	1950	1.367
1951	1.372	1.360	1.336	1.325	1.313	1.302	1.317	1.328	1.315	1.313	1.292	1.282	1951	1.282
1952	1.282	1.281	1.293	1.312	1.305	1.302	1.297	1.285	1.266	1.281	1.277	1.263	1952	1.263
1953	1.261	1.248	1.233	1.218	1.197	1.220	1.222	1.218	1.251	1.258	1.248	1.271	1953	1.271
1954	1.280	1.307	1.312	1.322	1.308	1.326	1.341	1.333	1.329	1.327	1.321	1.326	1954	1.326
1955	1.291	1.279	1.287	1.284	1.290	1.277	1.261	1.258	1.265	1.280	1.271	1.272	1955	1.272
1956	1.280	1.277	1.255	1.237	1.262	1.262	1.233	1.207	1.210	1.200	1.189	1.165	1956	1.165
1957	1.202	1.202	1.196	1.166	1.160	1.136	1.127	1.124	1.129	1.120	1.177	1.209	1957	1.209
1958	1.196	1.205	1.214	1.233	1.230	1.207	1.170	1.116	1.100	1.111	1.122	1.098	1958	1.098
1959	1.085	1.095	1.093	1.076	1.072	1.070	1.072	1.064	1.054	1.067	1.050	1.030	1959	1.030
1960	1.038	1.055	1.081	1.059	1.071	1.086	1.122	1.111	1.116	1.109	1.098	1.125	1960	1.125
1961	1.109	1.128	1.121	1.130	1.121	1.109	1.109	1.101	1.112	1.116	1.110	1.093	1961	1.093
1962	1.088	1.095	1.119	1.125	1.126	1.115	1.099	1.115	1.119	1.124	1.123	1.124	1962	1.124
1963	1.120	1.117	1.115	1.110	1.109	1.107	1.107	1.106	1.102	1.096	1.098	1.093	1963	1.093
1964	1.088	1.083	1.083	1.085	1.087	1.090	1.087	1.085	1.087	1.088	1.086	1.085	1964	1.085
1965	1.086	1.084	1.086	1.086	1.085	1.086	1.084	1.079	1.072	1.071	1.060	1.048	1965	1.048
1966	1.033	1.004	1.030	1.019	1.009	1.004	0.996	0.971	1.000	1.019	1.000	1.037	1966	1.037
1967	1.049	1.022	1.038	1.005	0.996	0.961	0.964	0.952	0.947	0.905	0.883	0.896	1967	0.896
1968	0.921	0.914	0.891	0.907	0.907	0.924	0.946	0.942	0.928	0.912	0.883	0.847	1968	0.847
1969	0.825	0.825	0.822	0.853	0.807	0.820	0.822	0.812	0.765	0.788	0.765	0.755	1969	0.755
1970	0.750	0.790	0.780	0.743	0.705	0.734	0.753	0.748	0.761	0.748	0.803	0.792	1970	0.792

Table B-6 (Continued)
Long-Term Government Bonds: Capital Appreciation Index

from January 1971 to December 2007

Year	Jan	Feb	Mar	Apr	May	Jun	Jul	Aug	Sep	Oct	Nov	Dec	Yr-end	Index
1971	0.828	0.811	0.849	0.821	0.816	0.799	0.797	0.830	0.843	0.853	0.845	0.844	1971	0.844
1972	0.835	0.838	0.827	0.825	0.843	0.834	0.847	0.846	0.835	0.850	0.865	0.841	1972	0.841
1973	0.810	0.807	0.809	0.808	0.795	0.789	0.750	0.774	0.795	0.807	0.788	0.777	1973	0.777
1974	0.765	0.759	0.733	0.709	0.713	0.712	0.705	0.684	0.696	0.725	0.742	0.750	1974	0.750
1975	0.761	0.767	0.741	0.723	0.733	0.750	0.738	0.728	0.716	0.745	0.732	0.755	1975	0.755
1976	0.757	0.757	0.764	0.761	0.744	0.754	0.755	0.766	0.772	0.774	0.795	0.816	1976	0.816
1977	0.780	0.771	0.773	0.774	0.779	0.787	0.776	0.787	0.780	0.767	0.770	0.752	1977	0.752
1978	0.741	0.737	0.730	0.725	0.715	0.706	0.711	0.721	0.709	0.690	0.698	0.684	1978	0.684
1979	0.692	0.678	0.682	0.669	0.681	0.697	0.686	0.679	0.666	0.604	0.618	0.617	1979	0.617
1980	0.566	0.535	0.512	0.585	0.605	0.621	0.587	0.556	0.537	0.517	0.518	0.530	1980	0.530
1981	0.519	0.492	0.505	0.474	0.499	0.484	0.462	0.439	0.428	0.458	0.518	0.476	1981	0.476
1982	0.473	0.476	0.481	0.494	0.491	0.474	0.492	0.525	0.552	0.582	0.577	0.589	1982	0.589
1983	0.566	0.589	0.578	0.594	0.565	0.563	0.530	0.526	0.547	0.535	0.540	0.532	1983	0.532
1984	0.539	0.524	0.511	0.500	0.469	0.472	0.499	0.507	0.519	0.543	0.544	0.544	1984	0.544
1985	0.558	0.526	0.538	0.545	0.589	0.592	0.576	0.586	0.580	0.594	0.613	0.641	1985	0.641
1986	0.634	0.702	0.751	0.741	0.699	0.737	0.724	0.755	0.713	0.728	0.743	0.737	1986	0.737
1987	0.744	0.755	0.733	0.693	0.682	0.683	0.666	0.650	0.621	0.655	0.652	0.658	1987	0.658
1988	0.697	0.696	0.670	0.654	0.642	0.661	0.645	0.644	0.661	0.676	0.658	0.661	1988	0.661
1989	0.669	0.652	0.655	0.661	0.682	0.715	0.727	0.703	0.700	0.722	0.723	0.718	1989	0.718
1990	0.688	0.681	0.674	0.655	0.677	0.688	0.691	0.657	0.660	0.669	0.691	0.699	1990	0.699
1991	0.703	0.701	0.699	0.703	0.699	0.690	0.695	0.714	0.731	0.730	0.732	0.769	1991	0.769
1992	0.740	0.739	0.727	0.724	0.737	0.747	0.772	0.772	0.782	0.762	0.758	0.772	1992	0.772
1993	0.789	0.813	0.809	0.811	0.810	0.841	0.853	0.885	0.881	0.885	0.858	0.855	1993	0.855
1994	0.872	0.829	0.791	0.775	0.763	0.751	0.774	0.762	0.732	0.726	0.726	0.733	1994	0.733
1995	0.748	0.765	0.767	0.775	0.831	0.838	0.820	0.834	0.845	0.865	0.882	0.901	1995	0.901
1996	0.896	0.848	0.826	0.807	0.798	0.810	0.807	0.791	0.809	0.837	0.862	0.835	1996	0.835
1997	0.824	0.820	0.794	0.810	0.813	0.824	0.871	0.839	0.861	0.885	0.894	0.906	1997	0.906
1998	0.920	0.909	0.907	0.904	0.917	0.933	0.925	0.963	0.997	0.971	0.976	0.968	1998	0.968
1999	0.976	0.921	0.916	0.913	0.892	0.880	0.869	0.860	0.863	0.857	0.847	0.829	1999	0.829
2000	0.844	0.862	0.889	0.878	0.868	0.885	0.895	0.912	0.894	0.906	0.930	0.949	2000	0.949
2001	0.944	0.958	0.947	0.913	0.912	0.915	0.945	0.960	0.964	1.004	0.952	0.931	2001	0.931
2002	0.939	0.946	0.900	0.932	0.929	0.943	0.966	1.007	1.045	1.010	0.993	1.039	2002	1.039
2003	1.024	1.054	1.036	1.042	1.100	1.079	0.969	0.981	1.030	0.996	0.995	1.004	2003	1.004
2004	1.019	1.039	1.049	0.983	0.974	0.981	0.992	1.027	1.033	1.045	1.016	1.037	2004	1.037
2005	1.064	1.047	1.035	1.070	1.097	1.111	1.076	1.107	1.066	1.041	1.045	1.069	2005	1.069
2006	1.052	1.073	1.011	0.982	0.978	0.983	0.998	1.024	1.037	1.041	1.058	1.030	2006	1.030
2007	1.015	1.045	1.026	1.030	1.005	0.992	1.016	1.032	1.029	1.040	1.085	1.078	2007	1.078

Table B-7
Intermediate-Term Government Bonds: Total Return Index

from December 1925 to December 1970

Year	Jan	Feb	Mar	Apr	May	Jun	Jul	Aug	Sep	Oct	Nov	Dec	Yr-end	Index
1925												1.000	1925	1.000
1926	1.007	1.010	1.014	1.023	1.024	1.027	1.028	1.029	1.034	1.040	1.044	1.054	1926	1.054
1927	1.060	1.064	1.068	1.070	1.072	1.075	1.079	1.086	1.092	1.088	1.097	1.101	1927	1.101
1928	1.107	1.106	1.107	1.107	1.106	1.108	1.098	1.104	1.107	1.110	1.112	1.112	1928	1.112
1929	1.108	1.106	1.107	1.117	1.110	1.122	1.129	1.135	1.133	1.153	1.173	1.178	1929	1.178
1930	1.174	1.185	1.204	1.195	1.202	1.219	1.226	1.229	1.236	1.246	1.255	1.258	1930	1.258
1931	1.249	1.261	1.267	1.278	1.293	1.266	1.268	1.270	1.255	1.242	1.248	1.228	1931	1.228
1932	1.224	1.240	1.250	1.274	1.263	1.276	1.292	1.307	1.311	1.317	1.321	1.337	1932	1.337
1933	1.335	1.334	1.348	1.355	1.382	1.383	1.382	1.393	1.396	1.393	1.396	1.361	1933	1.361
1934	1.379	1.386	1.412	1.438	1.455	1.468	1.465	1.451	1.431	1.458	1.465	1.483	1934	1.483
1935	1.500	1.516	1.535	1.552	1.546	1.564	1.570	1.558	1.550	1.566	1.569	1.587	1935	1.587
1936	1.587	1.598	1.603	1.607	1.613	1.615	1.618	1.626	1.628	1.632	1.645	1.636	1936	1.636
1937	1.631	1.632	1.605	1.613	1.625	1.623	1.633	1.626	1.639	1.644	1.651	1.661	1937	1.661
1938	1.676	1.684	1.682	1.721	1.725	1.738	1.740	1.742	1.740	1.756	1.756	1.765	1938	1.765
1939	1.770	1.785	1.799	1.806	1.823	1.823	1.831	1.804	1.756	1.812	1.825	1.845	1939	1.845
1940	1.842	1.849	1.865	1.865	1.825	1.860	1.860	1.868	1.877	1.884	1.894	1.899	1940	1.899
1941	1.900	1.891	1.904	1.910	1.912	1.923	1.923	1.925	1.925	1.930	1.912	1.909	1941	1.909
1942	1.923	1.926	1.930	1.935	1.938	1.940	1.940	1.944	1.939	1.943	1.946	1.946	1942	1.946
1943	1.953	1.956	1.960	1.965	1.976	1.983	1.987	1.987	1.990	1.993	1.996	2.000	1943	2.000
1944	2.003	2.006	2.010	2.015	2.016	2.017	2.023	2.028	2.030	2.033	2.034	2.036	1944	2.036
1945	2.047	2.055	2.056	2.059	2.061	2.065	2.065	2.068	2.072	2.075	2.077	2.082	1945	2.082
1946	2.090	2.100	2.092	2.088	2.089	2.096	2.094	2.094	2.092	2.098	2.096	2.102	1946	2.102
1947	2.107	2.109	2.114	2.111	2.112	2.114	2.115	2.121	2.121	2.116	2.117	2.122	1947	2.122
1948	2.125	2.129	2.132	2.136	2.148	2.146	2.146	2.145	2.147	2.149	2.154	2.161	1948	2.161
1949	2.167	2.169	2.175	2.178	2.183	2.194	2.198	2.205	2.207	2.208	2.208	2.211	1949	2.211
1950	2.210	2.212	2.212	2.213	2.218	2.218	2.223	2.221	2.220	2.221	2.225	2.227	1950	2.227
1951	2.231	2.233	2.205	2.217	2.208	2.219	2.232	2.240	2.227	2.231	2.238	2.235	1951	2.235
1952	2.243	2.239	2.253	2.266	2.270	2.262	2.254	2.249	2.253	2.268	2.267	2.271	1952	2.271
1953	2.271	2.271	2.267	2.246	2.219	2.254	2.266	2.265	2.309	2.317	2.321	2.345	1953	2.345
1954	2.360	2.383	2.390	2.400	2.382	2.412	2.411	2.414	2.409	2.406	2.406	2.407	1954	2.407
1955	2.400	2.387	2.393	2.394	2.394	2.386	2.369	2.370	2.390	2.407	2.394	2.392	1955	2.392
1956	2.417	2.418	2.393	2.393	2.420	2.421	2.398	2.373	2.395	2.390	2.379	2.382	1956	2.382
1957	2.438	2.435	2.439	2.415	2.411	2.385	2.382	2.408	2.408	2.418	2.514	2.568	1957	2.568
1958	2.577	2.613	2.627	2.640	2.656	2.638	2.614	2.521	2.517	2.518	2.551	2.535	1958	2.535
1959	2.532	2.559	2.550	2.536	2.536	2.517	2.525	2.505	2.510	2.554	2.530	2.525	1959	2.525
1960	2.564	2.583	2.658	2.641	2.649	2.707	2.779	2.778	2.786	2.790	2.764	2.822	1960	2.822
1961	2.805	2.831	2.841	2.856	2.848	2.841	2.843	2.848	2.871	2.875	2.869	2.874	1961	2.874
1962	2.861	2.906	2.932	2.939	2.953	2.945	2.941	2.978	2.984	3.000	3.018	3.034	1962	3.034
1963	3.026	3.031	3.039	3.048	3.053	3.057	3.058	3.064	3.068	3.071	3.083	3.084	1963	3.084
1964	3.094	3.098	3.103	3.113	3.138	3.150	3.158	3.167	3.181	3.191	3.190	3.209	1964	3.209
1965	3.222	3.228	3.242	3.250	3.262	3.278	3.283	3.290	3.288	3.288	3.290	3.242	1965	3.242
1966	3.242	3.215	3.275	3.269	3.273	3.265	3.257	3.216	3.286	3.311	3.320	3.394	1966	3.394
1967	3.434	3.429	3.492	3.461	3.476	3.397	3.443	3.430	3.433	3.416	3.425	3.428	1967	3.428
1968	3.478	3.491	3.482	3.477	3.499	3.557	3.620	3.628	3.648	3.651	3.646	3.583	1968	3.583
1969	3.614	3.609	3.644	3.673	3.643	3.613	3.642	3.636	3.527	3.644	3.627	3.557	1969	3.557
1970	3.568	3.724	3.757	3.679	3.720	3.742	3.799	3.843	3.919	3.956	4.134	4.156	1970	4.156

Table B-7 (Continued)

Intermediate-Term Government Bonds: Total Return Index

from January 1971 to December 2007

Year	Jan	Feb	Mar	Apr	May	Jun	Jul	Aug	Sep	Oct	Nov	Dec	Yr-end	Index
1971	4.226	4.321	4.401	4.257	4.262	4.182	4.193	4.340	4.351	4.447	4.470	4.519	1971	4.519
1972	4.567	4.573	4.580	4.586	4.594	4.614	4.621	4.628	4.635	4.642	4.662	4.752	1972	4.752
1973	4.749	4.713	4.735	4.765	4.792	4.790	4.657	4.776	4.895	4.920	4.951	4.971	1973	4.971
1974	4.975	4.993	4.887	4.813	4.876	4.833	4.837	4.831	4.985	5.040	5.159	5.254	1974	5.254
1975	5.282	5.360	5.328	5.229	5.365	5.380	5.363	5.359	5.364	5.561	5.555	5.665	1975	5.665
1976	5.697	5.745	5.788	5.855	5.770	5.862	5.932	6.044	6.089	6.179	6.378	6.394	1976	6.394
1977	6.273	6.303	6.338	6.371	6.407	6.472	6.473	6.478	6.487	6.449	6.499	6.484	1977	6.484
1978	6.492	6.503	6.527	6.543	6.542	6.528	6.592	6.644	6.682	6.608	6.668	6.710	1978	6.710
1979	6.747	6.707	6.783	6.805	6.936	7.079	7.071	7.006	7.010	6.682	6.925	6.985	1979	6.985
1980	6.891	6.449	6.542	7.325	7.684	7.625	7.544	7.252	7.225	7.115	7.136	7.258	1980	7.258
1981	7.281	7.110	7.297	7.140	7.315	7.358	7.160	7.033	7.148	7.585	8.058	7.944	1981	7.944
1982	7.984	8.102	8.137	8.379	8.502	8.387	8.776	9.188	9.486	9.990	10.070	10.256	1982	10.256
1983	10.263	10.522	10.471	10.742	10.611	10.628	10.417	10.501	10.832	10.852	10.964	11.015	1983	11.015
1984	11.211	11.139	11.100	11.097	10.819	10.926	11.355	11.469	11.701	12.149	12.382	12.560	1984	12.560
1985	12.818	12.588	12.798	13.136	13.772	13.922	13.859	14.064	14.222	14.453	14.735	15.113	1985	15.113
1986	15.238	15.657	16.186	16.318	15.968	16.409	16.667	17.109	16.921	17.195	17.389	17.401	1986	17.401
1987	17.587	17.691	17.636	17.205	17.140	17.350	17.394	17.328	17.085	17.596	17.741	17.906	1987	17.906
1988	18.472	18.698	18.537	18.455	18.364	18.698	18.610	18.593	18.957	19.238	19.017	18.999	1988	18.999
1989	19.230	19.133	19.227	19.650	20.067	20.717	21.203	20.682	20.824	21.318	21.497	21.524	1989	21.524
1990	21.299	21.313	21.318	21.154	21.707	22.035	22.418	22.213	22.422	22.804	23.243	23.618	1990	23.618
1991	23.870	23.984	24.039	24.320	24.464	24.409	24.725	25.335	25.881	26.228	26.565	27.270	1991	27.270
1992	26.737	26.796	26.583	26.843	27.438	27.923	28.600	29.029	29.592	29.054	28.810	29.230	1992	29.230
1993	30.021	30.749	30.883	31.156	31.126	31.753	31.769	32.477	32.657	32.714	32.411	32.516	1993	32.516
1994	32.964	32.113	31.286	30.957	30.951	30.863	31.385	31.466	30.968	30.896	30.680	30.843	1994	30.843
1995	31.404	32.140	32.341	32.805	34.014	34.285	34.231	34.525	34.745	35.164	35.687	36.025	1995	36.025
1996	36.048	35.551	35.131	34.955	34.844	35.253	35.340	35.323	35.872	36.527	37.072	36.782	1996	36.782
1997	36.873	36.880	36.460	37.000	37.286	37.671	38.666	38.289	38.867	39.451	39.446	39.864	1997	39.864
1998	40.583	40.426	40.530	40.777	41.062	41.385	41.495	42.619	44.023	44.203	43.772	43.933	1998	43.933
1999	44.175	43.015	43.387	43.476	42.835	42.972	42.950	43.016	43.435	43.401	43.365	43.155	1999	43.155
2000	42.925	43.260	44.140	43.950	44.179	45.024	45.347	45.953	46.394	46.760	47.573	48.589	2000	48.589
2001	49.066	49.583	49.958	49.390	49.356	49.680	50.907	51.391	52.694	53.642	52.725	52.291	2001	52.291
2002	52.477	53.043	51.761	52.997	53.621	54.526	56.007	56.942	58.583	58.442	57.451	59.054	2002	59.054
2003	58.529	59.576	59.534	59.613	61.239	61.027	59.080	58.918	60.730	59.906	59.820	60.469	2003	60.469
2004	60.781	61.533	62.148	60.072	59.777	60.067	60.558	61.740	61.815	62.211	61.422	61.832	2004	61.832
2005	61.995	61.308	61.075	62.095	62.735	63.005	62.099	63.100	62.320	61.930	62.293	62.674	2005	62.674
2006	62.448	62.342	61.992	61.942	61.915	62.054	62.831	63.682	64.183	64.513	65.081	64.643	2006	64.643
2007	64.515	65.615	65.775	66.084	65.407	65.477	66.620	67.852	68.241	67.911	70.799	71.142	2007	71.142

Table B-8
Intermediate-Term Government Bonds: Capital Appreciation Index

from December 1925 to December 1970

Year	Jan	Feb	Mar	Apr	May	Jun	Jul	Aug	Sep	Oct	Nov	Dec	Yr-end	Index
1925												1.000	1925	1.000
1926	1.004	1.004	1.005	1.010	1.008	1.008	1.006	1.004	1.005	1.008	1.009	1.015	1926	1.015
1927	1.018	1.019	1.020	1.018	1.017	1.017	1.019	1.022	1.025	1.018	1.024	1.025	1927	1.025
1928	1.027	1.023	1.022	1.018	1.015	1.013	1.001	1.003	1.002	1.002	1.001	0.997	1928	0.997
1929	0.991	0.985	0.982	0.987	0.978	0.985	0.988	0.990	0.985	0.998	1.013	1.014	1929	1.014
1930	1.007	1.013	1.027	1.017	1.020	1.032	1.034	1.034	1.038	1.043	1.048	1.048	1930	1.048
1931	1.038	1.045	1.048	1.055	1.065	1.040	1.039	1.038	1.023	1.009	1.011	0.991	1931	0.991
1932	0.985	0.994	0.998	1.015	1.002	1.010	1.019	1.029	1.029	1.031	1.032	1.041	1932	1.041
1933	1.037	1.034	1.042	1.045	1.063	1.062	1.059	1.064	1.065	1.060	1.061	1.031	1933	1.031
1934	1.041	1.044	1.061	1.078	1.088	1.096	1.091	1.079	1.061	1.079	1.081	1.092	1934	1.092
1935	1.103	1.112	1.124	1.134	1.129	1.140	1.142	1.132	1.124	1.135	1.134	1.146	1935	1.146
1936	1.144	1.151	1.153	1.154	1.157	1.157	1.158	1.163	1.163	1.164	1.172	1.165	1936	1.165
1937	1.160	1.159	1.139	1.143	1.150	1.147	1.152	1.146	1.154	1.156	1.159	1.165	1937	1.165
1938	1.173	1.177	1.174	1.199	1.200	1.207	1.207	1.207	1.204	1.213	1.211	1.216	1938	1.216
1939	1.218	1.227	1.235	1.239	1.249	1.248	1.252	1.232	1.199	1.235	1.243	1.255	1939	1.255
1940	1.252	1.255	1.265	1.265	1.237	1.259	1.258	1.262	1.267	1.271	1.278	1.280	1940	1.280
1941	1.280	1.273	1.281	1.284	1.285	1.292	1.291	1.292	1.291	1.294	1.281	1.278	1941	1.278
1942	1.287	1.288	1.290	1.292	1.293	1.294	1.293	1.295	1.291	1.293	1.294	1.293	1942	1.293
1943	1.296	1.297	1.297	1.299	1.304	1.307	1.308	1.307	1.307	1.308	1.308	1.309	1943	1.309
1944	1.309	1.309	1.310	1.312	1.311	1.311	1.313	1.314	1.314	1.314	1.314	1.314	1944	1.314
1945	1.319	1.323	1.322	1.323	1.323	1.324	1.323	1.324	1.325	1.325	1.326	1.327	1945	1.327
1946	1.331	1.336	1.330	1.327	1.326	1.329	1.327	1.326	1.324	1.326	1.323	1.326	1946	1.326
1947	1.328	1.327	1.329	1.326	1.326	1.326	1.325	1.327	1.326	1.322	1.321	1.322	1947	1.322
1948	1.322	1.323	1.323	1.324	1.330	1.327	1.325	1.323	1.322	1.322	1.323	1.326	1948	1.326
1949	1.328	1.328	1.329	1.330	1.331	1.336	1.337	1.340	1.340	1.339	1.338	1.338	1949	1.338
1950	1.336	1.336	1.334	1.334	1.335	1.334	1.335	1.333	1.331	1.329	1.330	1.329	1950	1.329
1951	1.330	1.329	1.310	1.315	1.308	1.312	1.317	1.320	1.310	1.310	1.312	1.307	1951	1.307
1952	1.310	1.305	1.311	1.316	1.317	1.310	1.303	1.297	1.297	1.303	1.300	1.300	1952	1.300
1953	1.297	1.295	1.290	1.275	1.257	1.274	1.278	1.274	1.295	1.298	1.297	1.308	1953	1.308
1954	1.314	1.326	1.327	1.331	1.320	1.334	1.332	1.332	1.328	1.325	1.323	1.322	1954	1.322
1955	1.315	1.306	1.307	1.305	1.302	1.295	1.283	1.281	1.288	1.295	1.285	1.281	1955	1.281
1956	1.291	1.289	1.273	1.270	1.281	1.278	1.263	1.246	1.255	1.248	1.239	1.237	1956	1.237
1957	1.262	1.258	1.257	1.240	1.234	1.218	1.212	1.221	1.217	1.219	1.263	1.287	1957	1.287
1958	1.288	1.303	1.307	1.311	1.317	1.305	1.290	1.242	1.236	1.232	1.245	1.233	1958	1.233
1959	1.228	1.237	1.228	1.218	1.214	1.200	1.200	1.186	1.184	1.200	1.184	1.177	1959	1.177
1960	1.190	1.194	1.224	1.213	1.212	1.234	1.263	1.259	1.259	1.257	1.242	1.264	1960	1.264
1961	1.253	1.261	1.262	1.265	1.258	1.251	1.248	1.246	1.252	1.250	1.244	1.243	1961	1.243
1962	1.233	1.248	1.255	1.254	1.257	1.250	1.244	1.255	1.255	1.257	1.261	1.264	1962	1.264
1963	1.257	1.255	1.255	1.255	1.253	1.251	1.247	1.246	1.243	1.240	1.241	1.237	1963	1.237
1964	1.237	1.235	1.233	1.233	1.239	1.239	1.238	1.237	1.239	1.239	1.234	1.237	1964	1.237
1965	1.238	1.237	1.237	1.236	1.237	1.238	1.236	1.234	1.229	1.225	1.221	1.199	1965	1.199
1966	1.194	1.180	1.197	1.190	1.186	1.179	1.171	1.151	1.171	1.174	1.173	1.194	1966	1.194
1967	1.203	1.197	1.214	1.200	1.200	1.168	1.178	1.169	1.165	1.154	1.152	1.148	1967	1.148
1968	1.159	1.158	1.150	1.143	1.145	1.159	1.173	1.171	1.172	1.168	1.162	1.136	1968	1.136
1969	1.140	1.133	1.139	1.141	1.126	1.110	1.113	1.105	1.065	1.093	1.082	1.054	1969	1.054
1970	1.050	1.090	1.092	1.063	1.068	1.068	1.077	1.083	1.098	1.102	1.145	1.145	1970	1.145

Table B-8 (Continued)

Intermediate-Term Government Bonds: Capital Appreciation Index

from January 1971 to December 2007

Year	Jan	Feb	Mar	Apr	May	Jun	Jul	Aug	Sep	Oct	Nov	Dec	Yr-end	Index
1971	1.159	1.180	1.197	1.153	1.149	1.121	1.118	1.151	1.149	1.169	1.169	1.177	1971	1.177
1972	1.183	1.180	1.176	1.173	1.169	1.168	1.164	1.160	1.156	1.152	1.151	1.168	1972	1.168
1973	1.161	1.146	1.145	1.146	1.146	1.140	1.101	1.122	1.144	1.143	1.144	1.142	1973	1.142
1974	1.137	1.135	1.105	1.081	1.088	1.072	1.065	1.056	1.083	1.087	1.106	1.120	1974	1.120
1975	1.119	1.129	1.116	1.088	1.110	1.106	1.095	1.088	1.081	1.114	1.106	1.121	1975	1.121
1976	1.121	1.124	1.125	1.131	1.109	1.119	1.125	1.139	1.142	1.152	1.183	1.180	1976	1.180
1977	1.151	1.151	1.151	1.151	1.151	1.156	1.150	1.144	1.140	1.126	1.128	1.119	1977	1.119
1978	1.113	1.109	1.105	1.101	1.093	1.084	1.087	1.088	1.087	1.067	1.069	1.069	1978	1.069
1979	1.066	1.053	1.057	1.052	1.064	1.079	1.069	1.052	1.045	0.987	1.015	1.015	1979	1.015
1980	0.992	0.920	0.924	1.025	1.067	1.051	1.031	0.983	0.970	0.946	0.940	0.946	1980	0.946
1981	0.939	0.908	0.921	0.892	0.904	0.898	0.864	0.838	0.841	0.881	0.926	0.903	1981	0.903
1982	0.897	0.902	0.894	0.911	0.915	0.892	0.923	0.956	0.978	1.021	1.021	1.031	1982	1.031
1983	1.023	1.041	1.027	1.045	1.023	1.016	0.988	0.986	1.007	1.000	1.001	0.997	1983	0.997
1984	1.005	0.990	0.977	0.967	0.933	0.932	0.958	0.958	0.968	0.994	1.004	1.009	1984	1.009
1985	1.021	0.994	1.002	1.019	1.059	1.063	1.049	1.056	1.059	1.068	1.081	1.100	1985	1.100
1986	1.101	1.124	1.155	1.157	1.125	1.149	1.160	1.184	1.164	1.176	1.183	1.177	1986	1.177
1987	1.183	1.184	1.173	1.138	1.126	1.132	1.127	1.116	1.092	1.117	1.118	1.121	1987	1.121
1988	1.149	1.156	1.138	1.126	1.112	1.125	1.112	1.103	1.116	1.125	1.105	1.096	1988	1.096
1989	1.100	1.088	1.085	1.101	1.115	1.144	1.163	1.127	1.128	1.146	1.149	1.143	1989	1.143
1990	1.123	1.117	1.109	1.093	1.113	1.122	1.134	1.116	1.119	1.130	1.144	1.155	1990	1.155
1991	1.160	1.158	1.154	1.160	1.159	1.150	1.156	1.178	1.196	1.205	1.214	1.240	1991	1.240
1992	1.209	1.206	1.189	1.193	1.213	1.228	1.251	1.263	1.282	1.253	1.236	1.248	1992	1.248
1993	1.275	1.301	1.300	1.305	1.299	1.318	1.314	1.337	1.339	1.336	1.318	1.317	1993	1.317
1994	1.329	1.290	1.250	1.231	1.224	1.213	1.227	1.223	1.197	1.187	1.171	1.170	1994	1.170
1995	1.184	1.205	1.205	1.216	1.253	1.257	1.249	1.253	1.255	1.264	1.277	1.283	1995	1.283
1996	1.278	1.255	1.235	1.222	1.212	1.220	1.216	1.209	1.221	1.237	1.249	1.233	1996	1.233
1997	1.230	1.225	1.204	1.215	1.218	1.224	1.250	1.232	1.244	1.256	1.251	1.257	1997	1.257
1998	1.274	1.264	1.261	1.263	1.266	1.270	1.267	1.296	1.333	1.334	1.316	1.316	1998	1.316
1999	1.318	1.279	1.284	1.281	1.257	1.255	1.248	1.244	1.250	1.243	1.235	1.223	1999	1.223
2000	1.210	1.213	1.231	1.220	1.219	1.236	1.238	1.248	1.254	1.258	1.274	1.296	2000	1.296
2001	1.304	1.315	1.321	1.302	1.295	1.298	1.325	1.332	1.361	1.381	1.353	1.338	2001	1.338
2002	1.337	1.347	1.310	1.335	1.346	1.364	1.396	1.415	1.452	1.445	1.418	1.453	2002	1.453
2003	1.437	1.459	1.455	1.453	1.489	1.481	1.431	1.424	1.463	1.440	1.435	1.446	2003	1.446
2004	1.450	1.464	1.475	1.423	1.412	1.414	1.421	1.444	1.442	1.448	1.426	1.431	2004	1.431
2005	1.430	1.410	1.400	1.419	1.429	1.430	1.405	1.423	1.401	1.387	1.390	1.394	2005	1.394
2006	1.384	1.377	1.364	1.357	1.351	1.348	1.359	1.372	1.378	1.380	1.387	1.373	2006	1.373
2007	1.364	1.383	1.381	1.382	1.363	1.359	1.377	1.397	1.401	1.389	1.443	1.446	2007	1.446

Table B-9
U.S. Treasury Bills: Total Return Index

from December 1925 to December 1970

Year	Jan	Feb	Mar	Apr	May	Jun	Jul	Aug	Sep	Oct	Nov	Dec	Yr-end	Index
1925												1.000	1925	1.000
1926	1.003	1.006	1.009	1.013	1.013	1.016	1.018	1.021	1.023	1.027	1.030	1.033	1926	1.033
1927	1.035	1.038	1.041	1.044	1.047	1.049	1.053	1.055	1.058	1.060	1.063	1.065	1927	1.065
1928	1.068	1.071	1.074	1.077	1.080	1.084	1.087	1.091	1.093	1.098	1.102	1.103	1928	1.103
1929	1.107	1.111	1.114	1.118	1.123	1.129	1.133	1.137	1.141	1.147	1.151	1.155	1929	1.155
1930	1.157	1.160	1.164	1.167	1.170	1.173	1.175	1.176	1.179	1.180	1.181	1.183	1930	1.183
1931	1.185	1.185	1.187	1.188	1.189	1.190	1.190	1.191	1.191	1.192	1.194	1.196	1931	1.196
1932	1.198	1.201	1.203	1.205	1.205	1.206	1.206	1.206	1.207	1.207	1.207	1.207	1932	1.207
1933	1.207	1.207	1.208	1.209	1.209	1.210	1.210	1.210	1.210	1.210	1.211	1.211	1933	1.211
1934	1.211	1.212	1.212	1.212	1.212	1.212	1.212	1.212	1.212	1.213	1.213	1.213	1934	1.213
1935	1.213	1.213	1.213	1.213	1.214	1.214	1.214	1.214	1.214	1.214	1.215	1.215	1935	1.215
1936	1.215	1.215	1.215	1.216	1.216	1.216	1.216	1.216	1.217	1.217	1.217	1.217	1936	1.217
1937	1.217	1.217	1.218	1.218	1.219	1.219	1.219	1.220	1.220	1.220	1.221	1.221	1937	1.221
1938	1.221	1.221	1.221	1.221	1.221	1.221	1.221	1.221	1.221	1.221	1.221	1.221	1938	1.221
1939	1.220	1.221	1.220	1.220	1.220	1.221	1.221	1.221	1.221	1.221	1.221	1.221	1939	1.221
1940	1.221	1.221	1.221	1.221	1.221	1.221	1.221	1.221	1.221	1.221	1.221	1.221	1940	1.221
1941	1.221	1.221	1.221	1.221	1.221	1.221	1.221	1.221	1.221	1.221	1.221	1.222	1941	1.222
1942	1.222	1.222	1.222	1.222	1.222	1.223	1.223	1.223	1.224	1.224	1.225	1.225	1942	1.225
1943	1.225	1.226	1.226	1.226	1.227	1.227	1.227	1.228	1.228	1.228	1.229	1.229	1943	1.229
1944	1.229	1.230	1.230	1.230	1.231	1.231	1.231	1.232	1.232	1.233	1.233	1.233	1944	1.233
1945	1.233	1.234	1.234	1.234	1.235	1.235	1.235	1.236	1.236	1.237	1.237	1.237	1945	1.237
1946	1.238	1.238	1.238	1.239	1.239	1.239	1.240	1.240	1.240	1.241	1.241	1.242	1946	1.242
1947	1.242	1.242	1.243	1.243	1.243	1.244	1.244	1.244	1.245	1.246	1.247	1.248	1947	1.248
1948	1.249	1.250	1.251	1.252	1.253	1.254	1.255	1.256	1.256	1.257	1.257	1.258	1948	1.258
1949	1.259	1.260	1.262	1.263	1.264	1.265	1.266	1.267	1.269	1.270	1.271	1.272	1949	1.272
1950	1.273	1.274	1.275	1.276	1.278	1.279	1.280	1.281	1.283	1.284	1.286	1.287	1950	1.287
1951	1.289	1.290	1.291	1.293	1.295	1.296	1.298	1.300	1.301	1.303	1.305	1.306	1951	1.306
1952	1.308	1.310	1.311	1.313	1.314	1.316	1.318	1.320	1.322	1.324	1.326	1.328	1952	1.328
1953	1.330	1.332	1.334	1.337	1.339	1.341	1.343	1.345	1.348	1.349	1.350	1.352	1953	1.352
1954	1.354	1.355	1.356	1.357	1.357	1.358	1.359	1.360	1.361	1.362	1.363	1.364	1954	1.364
1955	1.365	1.366	1.367	1.369	1.371	1.372	1.373	1.376	1.378	1.380	1.383	1.385	1955	1.385
1956	1.388	1.391	1.393	1.396	1.399	1.402	1.405	1.407	1.410	1.413	1.416	1.419	1956	1.419
1957	1.423	1.426	1.430	1.433	1.437	1.441	1.445	1.448	1.452	1.456	1.460	1.464	1957	1.464
1958	1.468	1.470	1.471	1.472	1.474	1.474	1.475	1.476	1.479	1.481	1.483	1.486	1958	1.486
1959	1.489	1.492	1.496	1.499	1.502	1.505	1.509	1.512	1.517	1.521	1.525	1.530	1959	1.530
1960	1.535	1.540	1.545	1.548	1.552	1.556	1.558	1.561	1.563	1.567	1.569	1.571	1960	1.571
1961	1.574	1.576	1.579	1.582	1.585	1.588	1.591	1.593	1.596	1.599	1.601	1.604	1961	1.604
1962	1.608	1.612	1.615	1.618	1.622	1.626	1.630	1.634	1.637	1.641	1.645	1.648	1962	1.648
1963	1.652	1.656	1.660	1.664	1.668	1.672	1.677	1.681	1.685	1.690	1.695	1.700	1963	1.700
1964	1.705	1.709	1.715	1.720	1.724	1.729	1.734	1.739	1.744	1.749	1.754	1.760	1964	1.760
1965	1.765	1.770	1.776	1.782	1.787	1.794	1.799	1.805	1.811	1.817	1.823	1.829	1965	1.829
1966	1.836	1.842	1.849	1.856	1.863	1.870	1.877	1.885	1.892	1.901	1.908	1.916	1966	1.916
1967	1.924	1.931	1.939	1.945	1.951	1.957	1.963	1.969	1.975	1.983	1.990	1.997	1967	1.997
1968	2.005	2.012	2.020	2.029	2.038	2.046	2.056	2.065	2.074	2.083	2.092	2.101	1968	2.101
1969	2.112	2.121	2.131	2.143	2.153	2.164	2.175	2.186	2.200	2.213	2.225	2.239	1969	2.239
1970	2.252	2.266	2.279	2.291	2.303	2.316	2.328	2.341	2.353	2.364	2.375	2.385	1970	2.385

Table B-9 (Continued)
U.S. Treasury Bills: Total Return Index

from January 1971 to December 2007

Year	Jan	Feb	Mar	Apr	May	Jun	Jul	Aug	Sep	Oct	Nov	Dec	Yr-end	Index
1971	2.394	2.402	2.409	2.416	2.423	2.432	2.442	2.453	2.462	2.471	2.480	2.490	1971	2.490
1972	2.497	2.503	2.510	2.517	2.525	2.532	2.540	2.547	2.556	2.566	2.575	2.585	1972	2.585
1973	2.596	2.607	2.619	2.633	2.646	2.660	2.677	2.695	2.714	2.732	2.747	2.764	1973	2.764
1974	2.782	2.798	2.813	2.835	2.856	2.873	2.893	2.911	2.934	2.949	2.965	2.986	1974	2.986
1975	3.003	3.016	3.028	3.042	3.055	3.067	3.082	3.097	3.113	3.131	3.144	3.159	1975	3.159
1976	3.174	3.184	3.197	3.210	3.222	3.237	3.252	3.265	3.280	3.293	3.306	3.319	1976	3.319
1977	3.331	3.343	3.356	3.368	3.381	3.394	3.408	3.423	3.438	3.455	3.472	3.489	1977	3.489
1978	3.506	3.522	3.541	3.560	3.578	3.597	3.618	3.638	3.660	3.685	3.711	3.740	1978	3.740
1979	3.769	3.796	3.827	3.858	3.889	3.921	3.951	3.981	4.014	4.049	4.089	4.128	1979	4.128
1980	4.161	4.198	4.248	4.302	4.336	4.363	4.386	4.414	4.447	4.489	4.532	4.592	1980	4.592
1981	4.639	4.689	4.746	4.797	4.852	4.917	4.978	5.042	5.105	5.166	5.221	5.267	1981	5.267
1982	5.309	5.358	5.411	5.472	5.530	5.583	5.641	5.684	5.713	5.747	5.783	5.822	1982	5.822
1983	5.862	5.899	5.936	5.978	6.020	6.060	6.105	6.151	6.198	6.245	6.289	6.335	1983	6.335
1984	6.383	6.428	6.475	6.528	6.579	6.629	6.683	6.738	6.796	6.864	6.914	6.959	1984	6.959
1985	7.004	7.044	7.088	7.138	7.186	7.225	7.271	7.311	7.355	7.403	7.448	7.496	1985	7.496
1986	7.538	7.578	7.623	7.663	7.700	7.741	7.781	7.817	7.852	7.889	7.919	7.958	1986	7.958
1987	7.991	8.025	8.063	8.099	8.129	8.169	8.206	8.245	8.282	8.331	8.360	8.393	1987	8.393
1988	8.418	8.456	8.493	8.532	8.576	8.617	8.661	8.712	8.766	8.819	8.869	8.926	1988	8.926
1989	8.975	9.030	9.090	9.152	9.224	9.289	9.354	9.423	9.485	9.549	9.614	9.673	1989	9.673
1990	9.728	9.783	9.846	9.914	9.981	10.043	10.111	10.178	10.238	10.308	10.366	10.429	1990	10.429
1991	10.483	10.533	10.579	10.635	10.685	10.730	10.782	10.832	10.881	10.928	10.970	11.012	1991	11.012
1992	11.049	11.081	11.118	11.154	11.185	11.221	11.255	11.285	11.314	11.340	11.366	11.398	1992	11.398
1993	11.425	11.450	11.479	11.506	11.531	11.561	11.588	11.617	11.647	11.673	11.702	11.728	1993	11.728
1994	11.758	11.783	11.814	11.846	11.884	11.921	11.954	11.998	12.042	12.088	12.132	12.186	1994	12.186
1995	12.237	12.286	12.342	12.397	12.464	12.522	12.579	12.638	12.692	12.752	12.806	12.868	1995	12.868
1996	12.923	12.974	13.025	13.084	13.140	13.192	13.252	13.306	13.365	13.421	13.476	13.538	1996	13.538
1997	13.599	13.652	13.710	13.769	13.837	13.888	13.948	14.005	14.067	14.127	14.182	14.250	1997	14.250
1998	14.311	14.367	14.423	14.485	14.544	14.603	14.662	14.725	14.792	14.840	14.886	14.942	1998	14.942
1999	14.994	15.048	15.112	15.168	15.219	15.280	15.338	15.397	15.457	15.517	15.573	15.641	1999	15.641
2000	15.706	15.774	15.848	15.920	16.001	16.064	16.141	16.223	16.305	16.397	16.480	16.563	2000	16.563
2001	16.652	16.715	16.784	16.850	16.905	16.952	17.004	17.056	17.103	17.142	17.172	17.197	2001	17.197
2002	17.221	17.243	17.266	17.293	17.318	17.340	17.367	17.391	17.416	17.440	17.460	17.480	2002	17.480
2003	17.497	17.512	17.530	17.547	17.563	17.580	17.592	17.604	17.619	17.631	17.644	17.659	2003	17.659
2004	17.671	17.682	17.697	17.711	17.722	17.737	17.754	17.774	17.794	17.814	17.842	17.871	2004	17.871
2005	17.900	17.930	17.968	18.005	18.048	18.089	18.132	18.186	18.238	18.288	18.345	18.403	2005	18.403
2006	18.468	18.530	18.598	18.664	18.745	18.819	18.894	18.974	19.051	19.128	19.209	19.287	2006	19.287
2007	19.372	19.447	19.529	19.615	19.694	19.773	19.851	19.934	19.998	20.063	20.131	20.186	2007	20.186

Table B-10
Inflation Index

from December 1925 to December 1970

Year	Jan	Feb	Mar	Apr	May	Jun	Jul	Aug	Sep	Oct	Nov	Dec	Yr-end	Index
1925												1.000	1925	1.000
1926	1.000	0.996	0.991	1.000	0.994	0.987	0.978	0.972	0.978	0.981	0.985	0.985	1926	0.985
1927	0.978	0.970	0.965	0.965	0.972	0.981	0.963	0.957	0.963	0.968	0.966	0.965	1927	0.965
1928	0.963	0.953	0.953	0.955	0.961	0.953	0.953	0.955	0.963	0.961	0.959	0.955	1928	0.955
1929	0.953	0.952	0.948	0.944	0.950	0.953	0.963	0.966	0.965	0.965	0.963	0.957	1929	0.957
1930	0.953	0.950	0.944	0.950	0.944	0.939	0.926	0.920	0.926	0.920	0.912	0.899	1930	0.899
1931	0.886	0.873	0.868	0.862	0.853	0.844	0.842	0.840	0.836	0.831	0.821	0.814	1931	0.814
1932	0.797	0.786	0.782	0.777	0.765	0.760	0.760	0.750	0.747	0.741	0.737	0.730	1932	0.730
1933	0.719	0.708	0.702	0.700	0.702	0.709	0.730	0.737	0.737	0.737	0.737	0.734	1933	0.734
1934	0.737	0.743	0.743	0.741	0.743	0.745	0.745	0.747	0.758	0.752	0.750	0.749	1934	0.749
1935	0.760	0.765	0.764	0.771	0.767	0.765	0.762	0.762	0.765	0.765	0.769	0.771	1935	0.771
1936	0.771	0.767	0.764	0.764	0.764	0.771	0.775	0.780	0.782	0.780	0.780	0.780	1936	0.780
1937	0.786	0.788	0.793	0.797	0.801	0.803	0.806	0.808	0.816	0.812	0.806	0.804	1937	0.804
1938	0.793	0.786	0.786	0.790	0.786	0.786	0.788	0.786	0.786	0.782	0.780	0.782	1938	0.782
1939	0.778	0.775	0.773	0.771	0.771	0.771	0.771	0.771	0.786	0.782	0.782	0.778	1939	0.778
1940	0.777	0.782	0.780	0.780	0.782	0.784	0.782	0.780	0.782	0.782	0.782	0.786	1940	0.786
1941	0.786	0.786	0.790	0.797	0.803	0.818	0.821	0.829	0.844	0.853	0.860	0.862	1941	0.862
1942	0.873	0.881	0.892	0.898	0.907	0.909	0.912	0.918	0.920	0.929	0.935	0.942	1942	0.942
1943	0.942	0.944	0.959	0.970	0.978	0.976	0.968	0.965	0.968	0.972	0.970	0.972	1943	0.972
1944	0.970	0.968	0.968	0.974	0.978	0.980	0.985	0.989	0.989	0.989	0.989	0.993	1944	0.993
1945	0.993	0.991	0.991	0.993	1.000	1.009	1.011	1.011	1.007	1.007	1.011	1.015	1945	1.015
1946	1.015	1.011	1.019	1.024	1.030	1.041	1.102	1.127	1.140	1.162	1.190	1.199	1946	1.199
1947	1.199	1.197	1.223	1.223	1.220	1.229	1.240	1.253	1.283	1.283	1.291	1.307	1947	1.307
1948	1.322	1.311	1.307	1.326	1.335	1.345	1.361	1.367	1.367	1.361	1.352	1.343	1948	1.343
1949	1.341	1.326	1.330	1.331	1.330	1.331	1.322	1.326	1.331	1.324	1.326	1.318	1949	1.318
1950	1.313	1.309	1.315	1.317	1.322	1.330	1.343	1.354	1.363	1.371	1.376	1.395	1950	1.395
1951	1.417	1.434	1.439	1.441	1.447	1.445	1.447	1.447	1.456	1.464	1.471	1.477	1951	1.477
1952	1.477	1.467	1.467	1.473	1.475	1.479	1.490	1.492	1.490	1.492	1.492	1.490	1952	1.490
1953	1.486	1.479	1.482	1.484	1.488	1.493	1.497	1.501	1.503	1.507	1.501	1.499	1953	1.499
1954	1.503	1.501	1.499	1.495	1.501	1.503	1.503	1.501	1.497	1.493	1.495	1.492	1954	1.492
1955	1.492	1.492	1.492	1.492	1.492	1.492	1.497	1.493	1.499	1.499	1.501	1.497	1955	1.497
1956	1.495	1.495	1.497	1.499	1.507	1.516	1.527	1.525	1.527	1.536	1.536	1.540	1956	1.540
1957	1.542	1.547	1.551	1.557	1.561	1.570	1.577	1.579	1.581	1.581	1.587	1.587	1957	1.587
1958	1.596	1.598	1.609	1.613	1.613	1.615	1.616	1.615	1.615	1.615	1.616	1.615	1958	1.615
1959	1.616	1.615	1.615	1.616	1.618	1.626	1.629	1.628	1.633	1.639	1.639	1.639	1959	1.639
1960	1.637	1.639	1.639	1.648	1.648	1.652	1.652	1.652	1.654	1.661	1.663	1.663	1960	1.663
1961	1.663	1.663	1.663	1.663	1.663	1.665	1.672	1.670	1.674	1.674	1.674	1.674	1961	1.674
1962	1.674	1.678	1.682	1.685	1.685	1.685	1.689	1.689	1.698	1.696	1.696	1.695	1962	1.695
1963	1.696	1.698	1.700	1.700	1.700	1.708	1.715	1.715	1.715	1.717	1.719	1.723	1963	1.723
1964	1.724	1.723	1.724	1.726	1.726	1.730	1.734	1.732	1.736	1.737	1.741	1.743	1964	1.743
1965	1.743	1.743	1.745	1.750	1.754	1.764	1.765	1.762	1.765	1.767	1.771	1.777	1965	1.777
1966	1.777	1.788	1.793	1.801	1.803	1.808	1.814	1.823	1.827	1.834	1.834	1.836	1966	1.836
1967	1.836	1.838	1.842	1.845	1.851	1.857	1.866	1.872	1.875	1.881	1.886	1.892	1967	1.892
1968	1.899	1.905	1.914	1.920	1.926	1.937	1.946	1.952	1.957	1.968	1.976	1.981	1968	1.981
1969	1.987	1.994	2.011	2.024	2.030	2.043	2.052	2.061	2.071	2.078	2.089	2.102	1969	2.102
1970	2.110	2.121	2.132	2.145	2.155	2.166	2.173	2.177	2.188	2.199	2.207	2.218	1970	2.218

Table B-10 (Continued)

Inflation Index

from January 1971 to December 2007

Year	Jan	Feb	Mar	Apr	May	Jun	Jul	Aug	Sep	Oct	Nov	Dec	Yr-end	Index
1971	2.220	2.223	2.231	2.238	2.250	2.263	2.268	2.274	2.276	2.279	2.283	2.292	1971	2.292
1972	2.294	2.305	2.309	2.315	2.322	2.328	2.337	2.341	2.350	2.358	2.363	2.371	1972	2.371
1973	2.378	2.395	2.417	2.434	2.449	2.466	2.471	2.516	2.523	2.544	2.562	2.579	1973	2.579
1974	2.602	2.635	2.665	2.680	2.710	2.736	2.756	2.791	2.825	2.849	2.873	2.894	1974	2.894
1975	2.907	2.927	2.939	2.953	2.967	2.991	3.022	3.032	3.047	3.065	3.084	3.097	1975	3.097
1976	3.104	3.112	3.119	3.132	3.151	3.168	3.186	3.201	3.214	3.227	3.237	3.246	1976	3.246
1977	3.264	3.298	3.318	3.345	3.363	3.386	3.400	3.413	3.426	3.436	3.453	3.466	1977	3.466
1978	3.484	3.508	3.533	3.564	3.600	3.637	3.663	3.682	3.708	3.737	3.758	3.778	1978	3.778
1979	3.812	3.857	3.894	3.939	3.987	4.024	4.076	4.117	4.160	4.197	4.237	4.281	1979	4.281
1980	4.343	4.402	4.466	4.516	4.561	4.611	4.615	4.644	4.687	4.728	4.771	4.812	1980	4.812
1981	4.851	4.901	4.937	4.968	5.009	5.052	5.110	5.149	5.201	5.212	5.227	5.242	1981	5.242
1982	5.261	5.278	5.272	5.294	5.346	5.412	5.441	5.453	5.462	5.477	5.467	5.445	1982	5.445
1983	5.458	5.460	5.464	5.503	5.533	5.551	5.574	5.592	5.620	5.635	5.644	5.652	1983	5.652
1984	5.683	5.710	5.723	5.750	5.767	5.786	5.805	5.829	5.857	5.872	5.872	5.875	1984	5.875
1985	5.886	5.911	5.937	5.961	5.983	6.002	6.011	6.024	6.043	6.061	6.082	6.097	1985	6.097
1986	6.115	6.099	6.071	6.058	6.076	6.106	6.108	6.119	6.149	6.155	6.160	6.166	1986	6.166
1987	6.203	6.227	6.255	6.289	6.307	6.333	6.346	6.382	6.413	6.430	6.439	6.438	1987	6.438
1988	6.454	6.471	6.499	6.532	6.555	6.583	6.610	6.638	6.683	6.705	6.711	6.722	1988	6.722
1989	6.756	6.783	6.822	6.867	6.906	6.923	6.940	6.951	6.973	7.007	7.023	7.034	1989	7.034
1990	7.107	7.140	7.180	7.191	7.207	7.246	7.274	7.341	7.403	7.447	7.464	7.464	1990	7.464
1991	7.509	7.520	7.531	7.542	7.564	7.587	7.598	7.620	7.654	7.665	7.687	7.693	1991	7.693
1992	7.704	7.732	7.771	7.782	7.793	7.821	7.838	7.860	7.882	7.910	7.921	7.916	1992	7.916
1993	7.955	7.983	8.011	8.033	8.044	8.055	8.055	8.078	8.094	8.128	8.133	8.133	1993	8.133
1994	8.156	8.184	8.212	8.223	8.228	8.256	8.278	8.312	8.334	8.340	8.351	8.351	1994	8.351
1995	8.384	8.418	8.446	8.474	8.490	8.507	8.507	8.530	8.546	8.574	8.569	8.563	1995	8.563
1996	8.613	8.641	8.686	8.719	8.736	8.741	8.758	8.775	8.803	8.831	8.847	8.847	1996	8.847
1997	8.875	8.903	8.926	8.937	8.931	8.942	8.953	8.970	8.993	9.015	9.009	8.998	1997	8.998
1998	9.015	9.032	9.048	9.065	9.082	9.093	9.104	9.115	9.126	9.149	9.149	9.143	1998	9.143
1999	9.165	9.177	9.204	9.271	9.271	9.271	9.299	9.322	9.366	9.383	9.389	9.389	1999	9.389
2000	9.411	9.467	9.545	9.550	9.556	9.612	9.628	9.640	9.690	9.707	9.712	9.707	2000	9.707
2001	9.768	9.807	9.829	9.868	9.913	9.930	9.902	9.902	9.946	9.913	9.896	9.857	2001	9.857
2002	9.879	9.919	9.974	10.030	10.030	10.036	10.047	10.080	10.097	10.114	10.114	10.091	2002	10.091
2003	10.136	10.214	10.276	10.253	10.237	10.248	10.259	10.298	10.331	10.320	10.292	10.281	2003	10.281
2004	10.331	10.387	10.454	10.488	10.549	10.582	10.566	10.571	10.594	10.649	10.655	10.616	2004	10.616
2005	10.638	10.700	10.783	10.856	10.845	10.850	10.900	10.956	11.090	11.112	11.023	10.978	2005	10.978
2006	11.062	11.084	11.146	11.241	11.296	11.319	11.352	11.375	11.319	11.257	11.241	11.257	2006	11.257
2007	11.292	11.352	11.456	11.530	11.600	11.623	11.620	11.599	11.631	11.655	11.725	11.717	2007	11.717

Appendix C

Appendix C

Rates of Return for All Yearly Holding Periods: 1926–2007

Basic Series: Total Rates of Return for All Holding Periods

Each table in this section consists of six pages.

Table C-1 (page 1 of 6)

Large Company Stocks Total Returns

Rates of Return for all holding periods
Percent per annum compounded annually

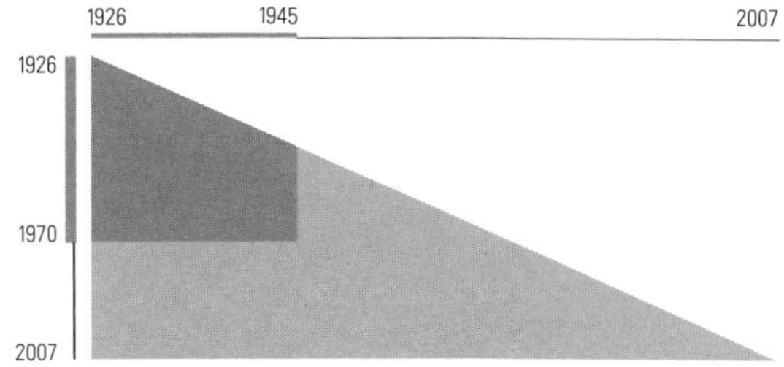

from 1926 to 2007

To the end of	From the beginning of 1926	1927	1928	1929	1930	1931	1932	1933	1934	1935	1936	1937	1938	1939	1940	1941	1942	1943	1944	1945
1926	11.6																			
1927	23.9	37.5																		
1928	30.1	40.5	43.6																	
1929	19.2	21.8	14.7	−8.4																
1930	8.7	8.0	−0.4	−17.1	−24.9															
1931	−2.5	−5.1	−13.5	−27.0	−34.8	−43.3														
1932	−3.3	−5.6	−12.5	−22.7	−26.9	−27.9	−8.2													
1933	2.5	1.2	−3.8	−11.2	−11.9	−7.1	18.9	54.0												
1934	2.0	0.9	−3.5	−9.7	−9.9	−5.7	11.7	23.2	−1.4											
1935	5.9	5.2	1.8	−3.1	−2.2	3.1	19.8	30.9	20.6	47.7										
1936	8.1	7.8	4.9	0.9	2.3	7.7	22.5	31.6	24.9	40.6	33.9									
1937	3.7	3.0	0.0	−3.9	−3.3	0.2	10.2	14.3	6.1	8.7	−6.7	−35.0								
1938	5.5	5.1	2.5	−0.9	0.0	3.6	13.0	16.9	10.7	13.9	4.5	−7.7	31.1							
1939	5.1	4.6	2.3	−0.8	−0.1	3.2	11.2	14.3	8.7	10.9	3.2	−5.3	14.3	−0.4						
1940	4.0	3.5	1.3	−1.6	−1.0	1.8	8.6	11.0	5.9	7.2	0.5	−6.5	5.6	−5.2	−9.8					
1941	3.0	2.4	0.3	−2.4	−1.9	0.5	6.4	8.2	3.5	4.3	−1.6	−7.5	1.0	−7.4	−10.7	−11.6				
1942	3.9	3.5	1.5	−1.0	−0.4	2.0	7.6	9.3	5.3	6.1	1.2	−3.4	4.6	−1.1	−1.4	3.1	20.3			
1943	5.0	4.7	2.9	0.6	1.3	3.7	9.0	10.8	7.2	8.2	4.0	0.4	7.9	3.8	4.8	10.2	23.1	25.9		
1944	5.8	5.5	3.8	1.7	2.5	4.8	9.8	11.5	8.3	9.3	5.7	2.6	9.5	6.3	7.7	12.5	22.0	22.8	19.8	
1945	7.1	6.9	5.4	3.5	4.3	6.6	11.5	13.2	10.4	11.5	8.4	5.9	12.6	10.1	12.0	17.0	25.4	27.2	27.8	36.4
1946	6.4	6.1	4.7	2.8	3.5	5.6	10.1	11.6	8.8	9.7	6.8	4.4	10.1	7.7	8.9	12.4	17.9	17.3	14.5	12.0
1947	6.3	6.1	4.7	3.0	3.7	5.6	9.8	11.2	8.6	9.4	6.7	4.5	9.6	7.5	8.5	11.4	15.8	14.9	12.3	9.9
1948	6.3	6.1	4.7	3.1	3.8	5.6	9.6	10.8	8.4	9.1	6.6	4.6	9.2	7.3	8.2	10.6	14.2	13.2	10.9	8.8
1949	6.8	6.6	5.3	3.8	4.5	6.3	10.1	11.2	9.0	9.7	7.4	5.6	10.0	8.3	9.2	11.5	14.8	14.0	12.2	10.7
1950	7.7	7.5	6.4	4.9	5.6	7.4	11.1	12.3	10.2	11.0	8.9	7.3	11.5	10.0	11.0	13.4	16.6	16.1	14.8	13.9
1951	8.3	8.1	7.1	5.7	6.4	8.2	11.7	12.9	11.0	11.7	9.8	8.4	12.4	11.1	12.1	14.3	17.3	16.9	15.9	15.3
1952	8.6	8.5	7.5	6.2	6.9	8.6	12.0	13.2	11.3	12.1	10.3	9.0	12.8	11.6	12.5	14.6	17.4	17.1	16.1	15.7
1953	8.3	8.1	7.2	5.9	6.5	8.2	11.4	12.4	10.7	11.4	9.6	8.3	11.9	10.7	11.5	13.4	15.7	15.3	14.3	13.7
1954	9.6	9.5	8.6	7.4	8.1	9.7	12.9	14.0	12.4	13.1	11.6	10.4	13.9	12.9	13.9	15.8	18.2	18.0	17.4	17.1
1955	10.2	10.2	9.3	8.2	8.9	10.5	13.7	14.7	13.2	13.9	12.5	11.4	14.8	13.9	14.9	16.8	19.1	19.0	18.5	18.4
1956	10.1	10.1	9.2	8.2	8.8	10.4	13.4	14.4	12.9	13.6	12.2	11.2	14.4	13.5	14.4	16.1	18.2	18.1	17.5	17.3
1957	9.4	9.3	8.5	7.4	8.1	9.5	12.3	13.2	11.8	12.4	11.0	10.0	13.0	12.1	12.8	14.3	16.2	15.9	15.2	14.9
1958	10.3	10.2	9.5	8.5	9.1	10.6	13.3	14.3	12.9	13.6	12.3	11.4	14.3	13.5	14.3	15.8	17.6	17.5	16.9	16.7
1959	10.3	10.3	9.5	8.6	9.2	10.6	13.3	14.2	12.9	13.5	12.3	11.4	14.2	13.4	14.1	15.6	17.3	17.1	16.6	16.4
1960	10.0	10.0	9.3	8.3	8.9	10.3	12.8	13.7	12.4	13.0	11.8	10.9	13.5	12.8	13.5	14.8	16.4	16.1	15.6	15.3
1961	10.5	10.4	9.7	8.8	9.4	10.8	13.3	14.1	12.9	13.4	12.3	11.5	14.1	13.4	14.0	15.3	16.9	16.7	16.2	16.0
1962	9.9	9.9	9.2	8.3	8.8	10.1	12.5	13.2	12.1	12.6	11.4	10.7	13.0	12.3	12.9	14.1	15.5	15.3	14.7	14.4
1963	10.2	10.2	9.5	8.7	9.2	10.5	12.8	13.5	12.4	12.9	11.8	11.1	13.4	12.7	13.3	14.5	15.8	15.6	15.1	14.9
1964	10.4	10.4	9.7	8.9	9.4	10.6	12.9	13.6	12.5	13.0	12.0	11.3	13.5	12.9	13.5	14.5	15.8	15.6	15.2	14.9
1965	10.4	10.4	9.8	9.0	9.5	10.7	12.9	13.6	12.5	13.0	12.0	11.3	13.5	12.9	13.4	14.5	15.7	15.5	15.0	14.8
1966	9.9	9.8	9.2	8.4	8.9	10.1	12.2	12.8	11.8	12.2	11.2	10.5	12.6	12.0	12.4	13.4	14.5	14.3	13.8	13.6
1967	10.2	10.2	9.6	8.8	9.3	10.4	12.5	13.1	12.1	12.5	11.6	10.9	12.9	12.4	12.8	13.8	14.9	14.7	14.2	14.0
1968	10.2	10.2	9.6	8.9	9.3	10.4	12.4	13.1	12.1	12.5	11.6	10.9	12.9	12.3	12.8	13.7	14.7	14.5	14.1	13.9
1969	9.8	9.7	9.1	8.4	8.9	9.9	11.8	12.4	11.4	11.8	10.9	10.3	12.1	11.6	12.0	12.8	13.0	13.6	13.1	12.9
1970	9.6	9.6	9.0	8.3	8.7	9.7	11.6	12.2	11.2	11.6	10.7	10.1	11.9	11.3	11.7	12.5	13.5	13.2	12.8	12.5

Table C-1 (page 2 of 6)

Large Company Stocks Total Returns

Rates of Return for all holding periods

Percent per annum compounded annually

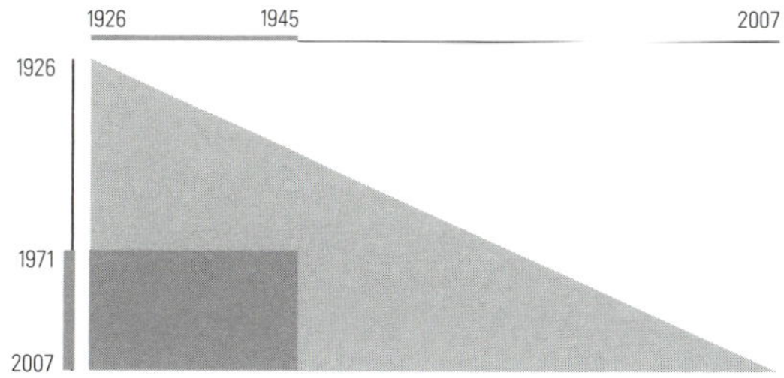

from 1926 to 2007

To the end of	From the beginning of 1926	1927	1928	1929	1930	1931	1932	1933	1934	1935	1936	1937	1938	1939	1940	1941	1942	1943	1944	1945
1971	9.7	9.7	9.1	8.4	8.9	9.9	11.7	12.2	11.3	11.7	10.8	10.2	11.9	11.4	11.8	12.6	13.5	13.3	12.8	12.6
1972	9.9	9.9	9.3	8.7	9.1	10.1	11.9	12.4	11.5	11.9	11.0	10.5	12.1	11.6	12.0	12.8	13.7	13.5	13.0	12.8
1973	9.3	9.3	8.7	8.1	8.5	9.4	11.1	11.7	10.8	11.1	10.3	9.7	11.3	10.8	11.1	11.8	12.7	12.4	12.0	11.7
1974	8.5	8.4	7.8	7.2	7.5	8.4	10.1	10.6	9.7	10.0	9.1	8.5	10.1	9.5	9.8	10.5	11.2	10.9	10.5	10.2
1975	9.0	8.9	8.4	7.7	8.1	9.0	10.6	11.1	10.2	10.6	9.8	9.2	10.7	10.2	10.5	11.1	11.9	11.6	11.2	11.0
1976	9.2	9.2	8.7	8.0	8.4	9.3	10.9	11.4	10.5	10.9	10.1	9.5	11.0	10.5	10.8	11.5	12.2	12.0	11.6	11.3
1977	8.9	8.8	8.3	7.7	8.1	8.9	10.5	10.9	10.1	10.4	9.6	9.1	10.5	10.0	10.3	10.9	11.6	11.4	11.0	10.7
1978	8.9	8.8	8.3	7.7	8.0	8.9	10.4	10.8	10.0	10.3	9.6	9.0	10.4	9.9	10.2	10.8	11.5	11.3	10.9	10.6
1979	9.0	9.0	8.5	7.9	8.2	9.1	10.6	11.0	10.2	10.5	9.8	9.2	10.6	10.1	10.4	11.0	11.7	11.4	11.1	10.8
1980	9.4	9.4	8.9	8.3	8.7	9.5	11.0	11.4	10.6	10.9	10.2	9.7	11.1	10.6	10.9	11.5	12.2	11.9	11.6	11.4
1981	9.1	9.1	8.6	8.1	8.4	9.2	10.6	11.0	10.3	10.6	9.9	9.4	10.7	10.2	10.5	11.1	11.7	11.5	11.1	10.9
1982	9.3	9.3	8.8	8.3	8.6	9.4	10.8	11.2	10.5	10.8	10.1	9.6	10.9	10.5	10.8	11.3	11.9	11.7	11.4	11.2
1983	9.6	9.5	9.1	8.5	8.9	9.6	11.0	11.5	10.7	11.0	10.3	9.9	11.1	10.7	11.0	11.5	12.2	12.0	11.6	11.4
1984	9.5	9.5	9.0	8.5	8.8	9.6	10.9	11.3	10.6	10.9	10.3	9.8	11.0	10.6	10.9	11.4	12.0	11.8	11.5	11.3
1985	9.8	9.8	9.4	8.9	9.2	9.9	11.3	11.7	11.0	11.3	10.7	10.2	11.4	11.1	11.3	11.8	12.4	12.3	12.0	11.8
1986	10.0	9.9	9.5	9.0	9.4	10.1	11.4	11.8	11.2	11.4	10.8	10.4	11.6	11.2	11.5	12.0	12.6	12.4	12.1	11.9
1987	9.9	9.9	9.5	9.0	9.3	10.0	11.3	11.7	11.0	11.3	10.7	10.3	11.5	11.1	11.3	11.8	12.4	12.2	11.9	11.8
1988	10.0	10.0	9.6	9.1	9.4	10.1	11.4	11.8	11.1	11.4	10.8	10.4	11.6	11.2	11.4	11.9	12.5	12.3	12.1	11.9
1989	10.3	10.3	9.9	9.4	9.7	10.5	11.7	12.1	11.5	11.7	11.2	10.8	11.9	11.6	11.8	12.3	12.9	12.7	12.4	12.3
1990	10.1	10.1	9.7	9.2	9.5	10.2	11.5	11.8	11.2	11.4	10.9	10.5	11.6	11.3	11.5	12.0	12.5	12.4	12.1	11.9
1991	10.4	10.4	10.0	9.5	9.8	10.5	11.8	12.1	11.5	11.8	11.2	10.8	11.9	11.6	11.8	12.3	12.9	12.7	12.4	12.3
1992	10.3	10.3	9.9	9.5	9.8	10.5	11.7	12.1	11.4	11.7	11.1	10.8	11.8	11.5	11.8	12.2	12.7	12.6	12.3	12.2
1993	10.3	10.3	9.9	9.5	9.8	10.5	11.7	12.0	11.4	11.7	11.1	10.8	11.8	11.5	11.7	12.2	12.7	12.5	12.3	12.1
1994	10.2	10.2	9.8	9.4	9.7	10.3	11.5	11.8	11.3	11.5	10.9	10.6	11.6	11.3	11.5	12.0	12.5	12.3	12.1	11.9
1995	10.5	10.5	10.2	9.7	10.0	10.7	11.9	12.2	11.6	11.9	11.3	11.0	12.0	11.7	11.9	12.4	12.9	12.7	12.5	12.4
1996	10.7	10.7	10.3	9.9	10.2	10.9	12.0	12.4	11.8	12.0	11.5	11.2	12.2	11.9	12.1	12.6	13.1	12.9	12.7	12.6
1997	11.0	11.0	10.6	10.2	10.5	11.2	12.3	12.7	12.1	12.3	11.8	11.5	12.5	12.2	12.5	12.9	13.4	13.3	13.1	12.9
1998	11.2	11.2	10.9	10.5	10.8	11.4	12.5	12.9	12.3	12.6	12.1	11.8	12.8	12.5	12.7	13.2	13.6	13.5	13.3	13.2
1999	11.3	11.3	11.0	10.6	10.9	11.5	12.7	13.0	12.5	12.7	12.2	11.9	12.9	12.6	12.9	13.3	13.8	13.7	13.5	13.3
2000	11.0	11.0	10.7	10.3	10.6	11.2	12.3	12.6	12.1	12.3	11.9	11.6	12.5	12.2	12.5	12.9	13.3	13.2	13.0	12.9
2001	10.7	10.7	10.4	10.0	10.3	10.9	11.9	12.2	11.7	11.9	11.5	11.1	12.1	11.8	12.0	12.4	12.9	12.7	12.5	12.4
2002	10.2	10.2	9.9	9.5	9.7	10.3	11.4	11.7	11.1	11.3	10.9	10.6	11.5	11.2	11.4	11.7	12.2	12.0	11.8	11.7
2003	10.4	10.4	10.1	9.7	10.0	10.5	11.6	11.9	11.4	11.6	11.1	10.8	11.7	11.4	11.6	12.0	12.4	12.3	12.1	12.0
2004	10.4	10.4	10.1	9.7	10.0	10.5	11.6	11.9	11.4	11.6	11.1	10.8	11.7	11.4	11.6	12.0	12.4	12.3	12.1	11.9
2005	10.4	10.3	10.0	9.7	9.9	10.5	11.5	11.8	11.3	11.5	11.0	10.7	11.6	11.3	11.5	11.9	12.3	12.2	11.9	11.8
2006	10.4	10.4	10.1	9.7	10.0	10.5	11.5	11.8	11.3	11.5	11.1	10.8	11.6	11.4	11.6	11.9	12.3	12.2	12.0	11.9
2007	10.4	10.3	10.0	9.7	9.9	10.5	11.4	11.7	11.3	11.4	11.0	10.7	11.6	11.3	11.5	11.8	12.2	12.1	11.9	11.8

Table C-1 (page 3 of 6)

Large Company Stocks Total Returns

Rates of Return for all holding periods

Percent per annum compounded annually

from 1926 to 2007

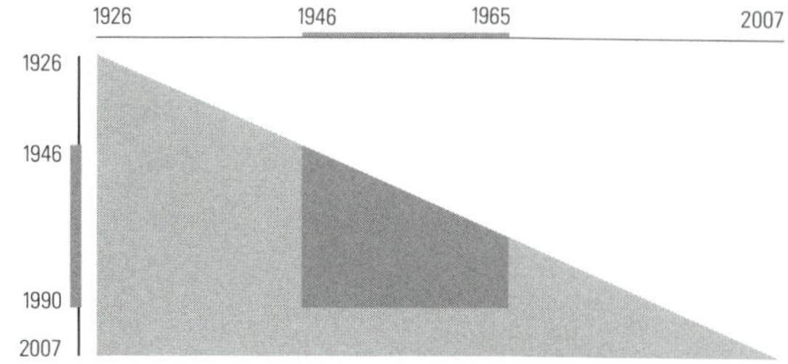

To the end of	From the beginning of 1946	1947	1948	1949	1950	1951	1952	1953	1954	1955	1956	1957	1958	1959	1960	1961	1962	1963	1964	1965
1946	−8.1																			
1947	−1.4	5.7																		
1948	0.8	5.6	5.5																	
1949	5.1	9.8	11.9	18.8																
1950	9.9	14.9	18.2	25.1	31.7															
1951	12.1	16.7	19.6	24.7	27.8	24.0														
1952	13.0	17.0	19.4	23.1	24.6	21.2	18.4													
1953	11.2	14.2	15.7	17.9	17.6	13.3	8.3	−1.0												
1954	15.1	18.4	20.4	23.0	23.9	22.0	21.4	22.9	52.6											
1955	16.7	19.8	21.7	24.2	25.2	23.9	23.9	25.7	41.7	31.6										
1956	15.7	18.4	19.9	21.9	22.3	20.8	20.2	20.6	28.9	18.4	6.6									
1957	13.2	15.4	16.4	17.7	17.6	15.7	14.4	13.6	17.5	7.7	−2.5	−10.8								
1958	15.3	17.5	18.7	20.1	20.2	18.8	18.1	18.1	22.3	15.7	10.9	13.1	43.4							
1959	15.1	17.1	18.1	19.3	19.4	18.1	17.3	17.2	20.5	15.0	11.1	12.7	26.7	12.0						
1960	14.0	15.8	16.6	17.6	17.5	16.2	15.3	14.9	17.4	12.4	8.9	9.5	17.3	6.1	0.5					
1961	14.8	16.5	17.3	18.3	18.3	17.1	16.4	16.2	18.6	14.4	11.7	12.8	19.6	12.6	12.9	26.9				
1962	13.3	14.8	15.4	16.1	15.9	14.7	13.9	13.4	15.2	11.2	8.5	8.9	13.3	6.8	5.2	7.6	−8.7			
1963	13.8	15.2	15.8	16.6	16.4	15.3	14.6	14.3	15.9	12.4	10.2	10.8	14.8	9.9	9.3	12.5	5.9	22.8		
1964	13.9	15.3	15.9	16.6	16.4	15.4	14.7	14.4	16.0	12.8	10.9	11.5	15.1	10.9	10.7	13.5	9.3	19.6	16.5	
1965	13.8	15.1	15.7	16.3	16.2	15.2	14.6	14.3	15.7	12.8	11.1	11.6	14.7	11.1	11.0	13.2	10.1	17.2	14.4	12.5
1966	12.6	13.7	14.2	14.7	14.4	13.4	12.7	12.4	13.4	10.7	9.0	9.2	11.7	8.2	7.7	9.0	5.7	9.7	5.6	0.6
1967	13.1	14.2	14.6	15.1	14.9	14.0	13.4	13.1	14.2	11.6	10.1	10.5	12.8	9.9	9.6	11.0	8.6	12.4	9.9	7.8
1968	13.0	14.0	14.5	14.9	14.7	13.8	13.3	13.0	14.0	11.6	10.2	10.5	12.7	10.0	9.8	11.0	8.9	12.2	10.2	8.6
1969	12.0	13.0	13.3	13.7	13.4	12.5	11.9	11.6	12.4	10.1	8.7	8.9	10.7	8.2	7.8	8.7	6.6	9.0	6.8	5.0
1970	11.7	12.6	12.9	13.2	13.0	12.1	11.5	11.1	11.9	9.7	8.4	8.6	10.2	7.8	7.5	8.2	6.3	8.3	6.4	4.8
1971	11.8	12.6	12.9	13.3	13.0	12.2	11.6	11.3	12.0	10.0	8.8	8.9	10.5	8.3	8.0	8.7	7.1	9.0	7.4	6.1
1972	12.0	12.9	13.2	13.5	13.3	12.5	12.0	11.7	12.4	10.5	9.4	9.5	11.0	9.0	8.8	9.5	8.1	9.9	8.6	7.6
1973	10.9	11.7	11.9	12.2	11.9	11.2	10.6	10.3	10.8	9.0	7.9	7.9	9.2	7.3	6.9	7.5	6.0	7.4	6.0	4.9
1974	9.4	10.1	10.2	10.4	10.1	9.3	8.7	8.2	8.7	6.9	5.7	5.7	6.7	4.8	4.3	4.6	3.0	4.1	2.5	1.2
1975	10.2	10.9	11.1	11.3	11.0	10.3	9.7	9.4	9.9	8.2	7.1	7.1	8.2	6.4	6.1	6.5	5.2	6.3	5.1	4.1
1976	10.6	11.3	11.5	11.7	11.5	10.8	10.3	9.9	10.4	8.8	7.8	7.9	9.0	7.3	7.1	7.5	6.3	7.5	6.4	5.6
1977	10.0	10.7	10.8	11.0	10.7	10.0	9.5	9.2	9.6	8.1	7.1	7.1	8.1	6.5	6.2	6.6	5.4	6.4	5.4	4.6
1978	9.9	10.5	10.7	10.9	10.6	9.9	9.4	9.1	9.5	8.0	7.1	7.1	8.0	6.5	6.2	6.6	5.5	6.5	5.4	4.7
1979	10.2	10.8	10.9	11.1	10.8	10.2	9.7	9.4	9.8	8.4	7.5	7.6	8.5	7.1	6.8	7.2	6.2	7.1	6.2	5.6
1980	10.7	11.3	11.5	11.7	11.5	10.9	10.4	10.2	10.6	9.2	8.4	8.5	9.4	8.1	7.9	8.3	7.4	8.4	7.6	7.1
1981	10.3	10.8	11.0	11.2	10.9	10.3	9.9	9.6	10.0	8.7	7.9	7.9	8.8	7.5	7.3	7.6	6.8	7.6	6.9	6.3
1982	10.6	11.1	11.3	11.5	11.2	10.7	10.2	10.0	10.4	9.1	8.4	8.4	9.3	8.1	7.9	8.2	7.4	8.3	7.6	7.1
1983	10.9	11.4	11.6	11.8	11.6	11.0	10.6	10.4	10.8	9.6	8.8	8.9	9.8	8.6	8.5	8.8	8.1	8.9	8.3	7.9
1984	10.7	11.3	11.4	11.6	11.4	10.9	10.5	10.2	10.6	9.4	8.7	8.8	9.6	8.5	8.4	8.7	8.0	8.8	8.2	7.8
1985	11.2	11.8	11.9	12.1	11.9	11.4	11.1	10.8	11.2	10.1	9.5	9.6	10.4	9.3	9.2	9.6	8.9	9.7	9.2	8.8
1986	11.4	11.9	12.1	12.3	12.1	11.6	11.3	11.1	11.4	10.4	9.7	9.8	10.6	9.6	9.5	9.9	9.3	10.1	9.6	9.3
1987	11.2	11.8	11.9	12.1	11.9	11.4	11.1	10.9	11.3	10.2	9.6	9.7	10.4	9.5	9.4	9.7	9.1	9.9	9.4	9.1
1988	11.4	11.9	12.0	12.2	12.0	11.6	11.2	11.1	11.4	10.4	9.8	9.9	10.6	9.7	9.6	10.0	9.4	10.1	9.7	9.4
1989	11.8	12.3	12.5	12.6	12.5	12.0	11.7	11.6	11.9	10.9	10.4	10.5	11.2	10.3	10.3	10.6	10.1	10.9	10.4	10.2
1990	11.4	11.9	12.1	12.2	12.1	11.6	11.3	11.1	11.5	10.5	10.0	10.1	10.8	9.9	9.8	10.2	9.6	10.3	9.9	9.7

Table C-1 (page 4 of 6)

Large Company Stocks Total Returns

Rates of Return for all holding periods

Percent per annum compounded annually

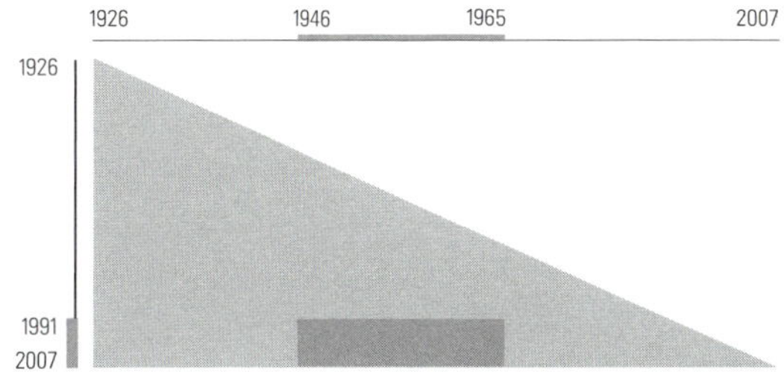

from 1926 to 2007

To the end of	From the beginning of 1946	1947	1948	1949	1950	1951	1952	1953	1954	1955	1956	1957	1958	1959	1960	1961	1962	1963	1964	1965
1991	11.8	12.3	12.5	12.6	12.5	12.1	11.8	11.6	12.0	11.0	10.5	10.6	11.3	10.5	10.4	10.8	10.3	11.0	10.6	10.4
1992	11.7	12.2	12.4	12.5	12.4	11.9	11.7	11.5	11.8	10.9	10.4	10.5	11.2	10.4	10.3	10.7	10.2	10.9	10.5	10.3
1993	11.7	12.2	12.3	12.5	12.3	11.9	11.6	11.5	11.8	10.9	10.4	10.5	11.2	10.4	10.3	10.6	10.2	10.8	10.5	10.3
1994	11.5	11.9	12.1	12.2	12.1	11.6	11.4	11.2	11.5	10.7	10.2	10.3	10.9	10.1	10.1	10.4	9.9	10.5	10.2	9.9
1995	11.9	12.4	12.5	12.7	12.6	12.2	11.9	11.8	12.1	11.2	10.8	10.9	11.5	10.8	10.7	11.0	10.6	11.3	10.9	10.7
1996	12.1	12.6	12.7	12.9	12.8	12.4	12.1	12.0	12.3	11.5	11.1	11.2	11.8	11.1	11.1	11.4	10.9	11.6	11.3	11.1
1997	12.5	13.0	13.1	13.3	13.2	12.8	12.6	12.4	12.8	12.0	11.5	11.7	12.3	11.6	11.6	11.9	11.5	12.2	11.9	11.7
1998	12.8	13.2	13.4	13.6	13.5	13.1	12.9	12.8	13.1	12.3	11.9	12.0	12.7	12.0	12.0	12.3	11.9	12.6	12.3	12.2
1999	13.0	13.4	13.5	13.7	13.6	13.3	13.1	12.9	13.3	12.5	12.1	12.2	12.9	12.2	12.2	12.5	12.2	12.8	12.5	12.4
2000	12.5	12.9	13.1	13.2	13.1	12.8	12.5	12.4	12.7	12.0	11.6	11.7	12.3	11.6	11.6	11.9	11.6	12.2	11.9	11.8
2001	12.0	12.4	12.5	12.7	12.6	12.2	12.0	11.9	12.2	11.4	11.0	11.1	11.7	11.0	11.0	11.3	10.9	11.5	11.2	11.1
2002	11.3	11.7	11.8	11.9	11.8	11.4	11.2	11.1	11.3	10.6	10.2	10.3	10.8	10.1	10.1	10.3	10.0	10.5	10.2	10.0
2003	11.6	12.0	12.1	12.2	12.1	11.7	11.5	11.4	11.7	10.9	10.5	10.6	11.2	10.5	10.5	10.7	10.4	10.9	10.6	10.5
2004	11.6	11.9	12.1	12.2	12.1	11.7	11.5	11.4	11.6	10.9	10.6	10.6	11.1	10.5	10.5	10.7	10.4	10.9	10.6	10.5
2005	11.5	11.8	11.9	12.0	11.9	11.6	11.4	11.3	11.5	10.8	10.4	10.5	11.0	10.4	10.4	10.6	10.3	10.7	10.5	10.3
2006	11.5	11.9	12.0	12.1	12.0	11.7	11.5	11.3	11.6	10.9	10.5	10.6	11.1	10.5	10.5	10.7	10.4	10.9	10.6	10.5
2007	11.4	11.8	11.9	12.0	11.9	11.6	11.3	11.2	11.5	10.8	10.4	10.5	11.0	10.4	10.4	10.6	10.3	10.7	10.5	10.3

Table C-1 (page 5 of 6)

Large Company Stocks Total Returns

Rates of Return for all holding periods

Percent per annum compounded annually

from 1926 to 2007

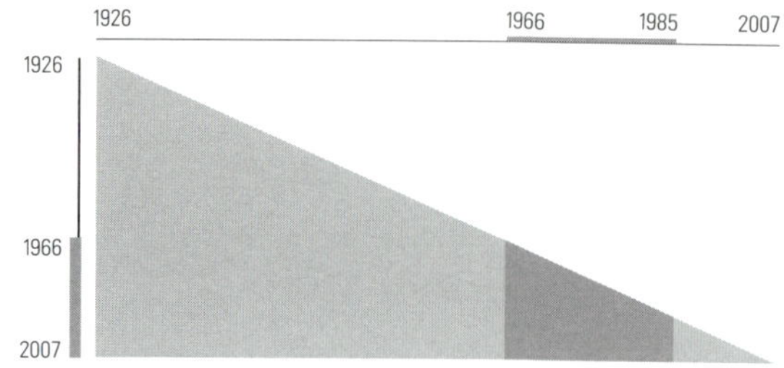

To the end of	From the beginning of 1966	1967	1968	1969	1970	1971	1972	1973	1974	1975	1976	1977	1978	1979	1980	1981	1982	1983	1984	1985
1966	−10.1																			
1967	5.6	24.0																		
1968	7.4	17.3	11.1																	
1969	3.2	8.0	0.8	−8.5																
1970	3.3	7.0	1.9	−2.4	4.0															
1971	5.1	8.4	4.8	2.8	9.0	14.3														
1972	7.0	10.1	7.5	6.7	12.3	16.6	19.0													
1973	4.0	6.2	3.5	2.0	4.8	5.1	0.8	−14.7												
1974	0.1	1.4	−1.5	−3.4	−2.4	−3.9	−9.3	−20.8	−26.5											
1975	3.3	4.9	2.7	1.6	3.3	3.2	0.6	−4.9	0.4	37.2										
1976	5.0	6.6	4.9	4.1	6.0	6.4	4.9	1.6	7.7	30.4	23.8									
1977	3.9	5.3	3.6	2.8	4.3	4.3	2.8	−0.2	3.8	16.4	7.2	−7.2								
1978	4.1	5.4	3.9	3.2	4.5	4.6	3.3	0.9	4.3	13.9	7.0	−0.5	6.6							
1979	5.1	6.3	5.0	4.5	5.9	6.1	5.1	3.2	6.6	14.8	9.7	5.4	12.3	18.4						
1980	6.7	8.0	6.9	6.5	8.0	8.4	7.8	6.5	9.9	17.5	13.9	11.6	18.7	25.2	32.4					
1981	5.9	7.1	6.0	5.6	6.9	7.2	6.5	5.2	7.9	14.0	10.6	8.1	12.3	14.3	12.2	−4.9				
1982	6.8	8.0	7.0	6.7	7.9	8.3	7.7	6.7	9.4	14.9	12.1	10.2	14.0	16.0	15.2	7.4	21.4			
1983	7.6	8.8	7.9	7.7	8.9	9.3	8.9	8.0	10.6	15.7	13.3	11.9	15.4	17.3	17.0	12.3	22.0	22.5		
1984	7.5	8.6	7.8	7.6	8.7	9.1	8.7	7.9	10.2	14.8	12.5	11.2	14.1	15.4	14.8	10.7	16.5	14.1	6.3	
1985	8.7	9.7	9.0	8.9	10.1	10.5	10.2	9.6	11.9	16.2	14.3	13.3	16.2	17.6	17.5	14.7	20.2	19.8	18.5	32.2
1986	9.1	10.2	9.5	9.4	10.6	11.0	10.8	10.2	12.4	16.4	14.7	13.8	16.4	17.7	17.6	15.3	19.9	19.5	18.5	25.1
1987	8.9	9.9	9.3	9.2	10.3	10.6	10.4	9.9	11.9	15.5	13.9	13.0	15.3	16.3	16.0	13.8	17.3	16.5	15.0	18.1
1988	9.3	10.2	9.6	9.5	10.6	11.0	10.8	10.3	12.2	15.6	14.1	13.3	15.4	16.3	16.1	14.2	17.2	16.5	15.4	17.8
1989	10.1	11.1	10.5	10.5	11.5	12.0	11.8	11.4	13.3	16.6	15.3	14.6	16.7	17.6	17.5	16.0	18.9	18.6	17.9	20.4
1990	9.5	10.4	9.9	9.8	10.8	11.2	11.0	10.6	12.3	15.3	13.9	13.3	15.0	15.7	15.5	13.9	16.2	15.6	14.6	16.1
1991	10.3	11.2	10.7	10.7	11.6	12.0	11.9	11.5	13.2	16.1	14.9	14.3	16.0	16.8	16.7	15.3	17.6	17.2	16.5	18.1
1992	10.2	11.1	10.6	10.5	11.5	11.8	11.7	11.3	12.9	15.6	14.5	13.9	15.5	16.1	16.0	14.7	16.7	16.2	15.5	16.7
1993	10.2	11.0	10.5	10.5	11.4	11.7	11.6	11.3	12.8	15.3	14.2	13.7	15.1	15.7	15.5	14.3	16.1	15.6	14.9	16.0
1994	9.9	10.6	10.2	10.1	11.0	11.3	11.1	10.8	12.2	14.6	13.5	12.9	14.3	14.8	14.5	13.3	14.9	14.3	13.6	14.4
1995	10.7	11.5	11.1	11.1	11.9	12.2	12.1	11.8	13.2	15.6	14.6	14.1	15.4	16.0	15.8	14.8	16.4	16.0	15.4	16.3
1996	11.1	11.8	11.5	11.5	12.3	12.6	12.5	12.3	13.6	15.9	15.0	14.6	15.8	16.4	16.2	15.3	16.8	16.5	16.0	16.9
1997	11.7	12.5	12.1	12.2	13.0	13.3	13.3	13.1	14.4	16.6	15.8	15.4	16.6	17.2	17.1	16.3	17.8	17.5	17.2	18.1
1998	12.2	13.0	12.6	12.7	13.5	13.8	13.8	13.6	14.9	17.1	16.3	16.0	17.2	17.7	17.7	16.9	18.4	18.2	17.9	18.8
1999	12.4	13.2	12.9	12.9	13.7	14.1	14.1	13.9	15.2	17.2	16.5	16.2	17.4	17.9	17.9	17.2	18.5	18.4	18.1	18.9
2000	11.7	12.5	12.1	12.2	12.9	13.2	13.2	13.0	14.2	16.1	15.3	15.0	16.1	16.5	16.4	15.7	16.9	16.6	16.3	17.0
2001	11.0	11.7	11.3	11.3	12.0	12.3	12.2	12.0	13.1	14.9	14.1	13.8	14.7	15.1	15.0	14.2	15.2	14.9	14.5	15.0
2002	10.0	10.6	10.2	10.2	10.8	11.0	10.9	10.7	11.7	13.3	12.5	12.1	13.0	13.3	13.0	12.2	13.1	12.7	12.2	12.6
2003	10.4	11.0	10.7	10.7	11.3	11.5	11.4	11.2	12.2	13.8	13.1	12.7	13.5	13.8	13.6	12.9	13.8	13.4	13.0	13.4
2004	10.4	11.0	10.7	10.7	11.3	11.5	11.4	11.2	12.1	13.7	13.0	12.6	13.4	13.7	13.5	12.8	13.6	13.3	12.9	13.2
2005	10.3	10.9	10.5	10.5	11.1	11.3	11.2	11.0	11.9	13.4	12.7	12.4	13.1	13.4	13.2	12.5	13.3	12.9	12.5	12.8
2006	10.4	11.0	10.7	10.7	11.2	11.4	11.4	11.1	12.0	13.5	12.8	12.5	13.2	13.5	13.3	12.6	13.4	13.0	12.7	12.9
2007	10.3	10.8	10.5	10.5	11.1	11.3	11.2	11.0	11.8	13.3	12.6	12.2	13.0	13.2	13.0	12.3	13.1	12.7	12.3	12.6

Table C-1 (page 6 of 6)-a

Large Company Stocks Total Returns

Rates of Return for all holding periods

Percent per annum compounded annually

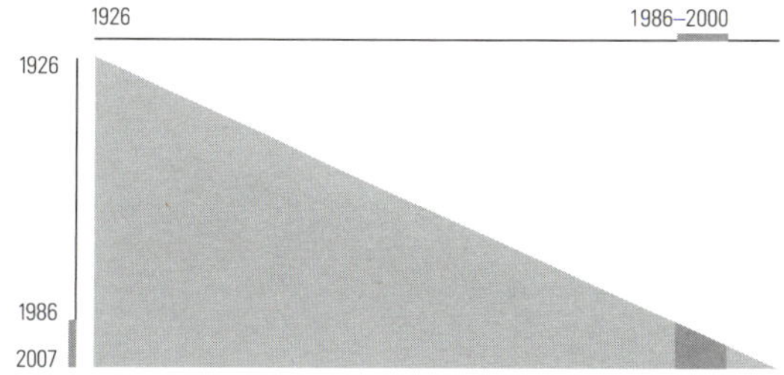

from 1926 to 2007

To the end of	From the beginning of 1986	1987	1988	1989	1990	1991	1992	1993	1994	1995	1996	1997	1998	1999	2000
1986	18.5														
1987	11.7	5.2													
1988	13.3	10.9	16.8												
1989	17.6	17.4	23.9	31.5											
1990	13.1	11.8	14.1	12.8	−3.2										
1991	15.9	15.4	18.0	18.5	12.4	30.5									
1992	14.7	14.0	15.9	15.7	10.8	18.6	7.7								
1993	14.1	13.5	14.9	14.5	10.6	15.6	8.8	10.0							
1994	12.6	11.9	12.8	12.2	8.7	11.9	6.3	5.6	1.3						
1995	14.8	14.4	15.7	15.5	13.0	16.6	13.3	15.3	18.0	37.4					
1996	15.6	15.3	16.5	16.4	14.4	17.6	15.2	17.2	19.7	30.1	23.1				
1997	17.0	16.8	18.0	18.2	16.6	19.8	18.0	20.2	23.0	31.1	28.1	33.4			
1998	17.8	17.8	19.0	19.2	17.9	20.8	19.5	21.6	24.1	30.5	28.3	31.0	28.6		
1999	18.0	18.0	19.1	19.4	18.2	20.9	19.7	21.5	23.5	28.6	26.4	27.6	24.8	21.0	
2000	16.0	15.8	16.7	16.7	15.4	17.5	16.1	17.2	18.2	21.3	18.4	17.2	12.3	4.9	−9.1
2001	14.0	13.7	14.4	14.2	12.8	14.4	12.9	13.5	14.0	15.9	12.7	10.7	5.7	−1.0	−10.5
2002	11.5	11.1	11.5	11.1	9.7	10.8	9.2	9.3	9.3	10.3	6.9	4.4	−0.6	−6.8	−14.6
2003	12.4	12.0	12.5	12.2	10.9	12.1	10.7	11.0	11.1	12.2	9.4	7.6	3.8	−0.6	−5.3
2004	12.3	12.0	12.4	12.1	10.9	12.0	10.7	11.0	11.0	12.1	9.6	8.0	4.8	1.3	−2.3
2005	11.9	11.6	12.0	11.7	10.5	11.5	10.3	10.5	10.5	11.4	9.1	7.6	4.8	1.8	−1.1
2006	12.1	11.8	12.2	11.9	10.8	11.8	10.6	10.9	10.9	11.8	9.7	8.4	6.0	3.4	1.1
2007	11.8	11.5	11.8	11.6	10.5	11.4	10.3	10.5	10.5	11.3	9.3	8.2	5.9	3.7	1.7

Table C-1 (page 6 of 6)-b

Large Company Stocks Total Returns

Rates of Return for all holding periods

Percent per annum compounded annually

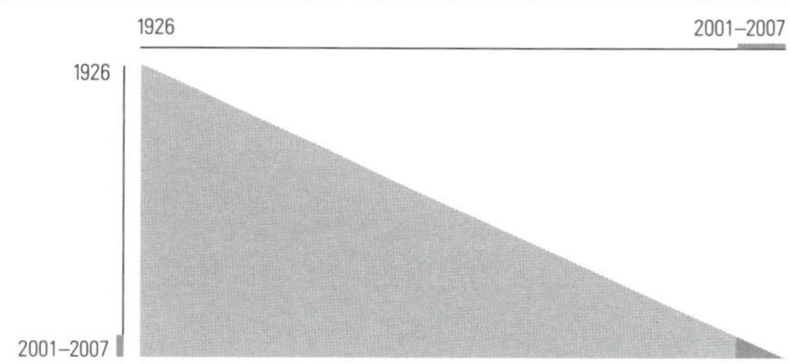

from 1926 to 2007

To the end of	From the beginning of 2001	2002	2003	2004	2005	2006	2007
2001	−11.9						
2002	−17.2	−22.1					
2003	−4.1	0.1	28.7				
2004	−0.5	3.6	19.5	10.9			
2005	0.5	3.9	14.4	7.8	4.9		
2006	2.9	6.2	14.7	10.4	10.2	15.8	
2007	3.3	6.1	12.8	9.2	8.6	10.5	5.5

Table C-2 (page 1 of 6)

Small Company Stocks Total Returns

Rates of Return for all holding periods

Percent per annum compounded annually

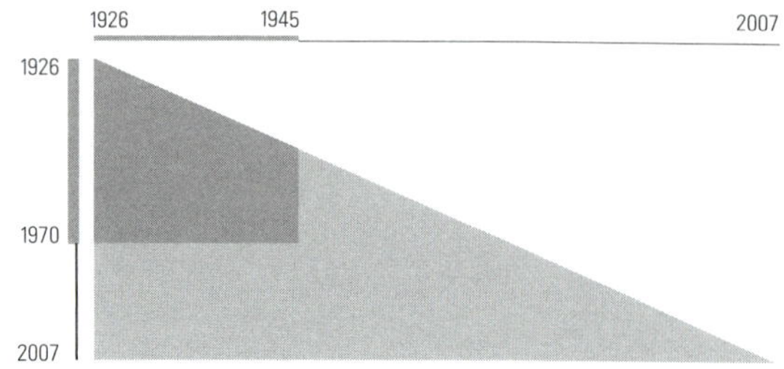

from 1926 to 2007

To the end of	From the beginning of 1926	1927	1928	1929	1930	1931	1932	1933	1934	1935	1936	1937	1938	1939	1940	1941	1942	1943	1944	1945
1926	0.3																			
1927	10.7	22.1																		
1928	19.6	30.6	39.7																	
1929	−4.5	−6.0	−17.6	−51.4																
1930	−12.4	−15.4	−25.1	−45.1	−38.1															
1931	−20.2	−23.7	−32.2	−46.7	−44.3	−49.8														
1932	−18.2	−21.0	−27.5	−38.5	−33.5	−31.1	−5.4													
1933	−6.3	−7.2	−11.4	−19.1	−8.1	4.9	51.6	142.9												
1934	−3.3	−3.8	−7.0	−13.1	−2.4	9.4	41.9	73.7	24.2											
1935	0.3	0.3	−2.1	−6.9	3.7	15.0	41.4	61.7	32.0	40.2										
1936	5.0	5.5	3.7	0.0	10.8	22.1	45.8	62.5	42.1	52.0	64.8									
1937	−2.7	−3.0	−5.2	−9.2	−1.9	4.8	18.5	24.0	4.8	−1.0	−16.8	−58.0								
1938	−0.4	−0.4	−2.3	−5.7	1.5	8.0	20.4	25.4	9.9	6.5	−2.8	−25.3	32.8							
1939	−0.3	−0.4	−2.1	−5.2	1.4	7.1	17.7	21.5	8.2	5.3	−2.0	−17.6	15.4	0.3						
1940	−0.7	−0.7	−2.3	−5.2	0.8	5.8	14.9	17.8	6.2	3.5	−2.6	−14.6	8.1	−2.4	−5.2					
1941	−1.2	−1.3	−2.8	−5.5	−0.1	4.4	12.3	14.4	4.2	1.6	−3.7	−13.5	3.6	−4.7	−7.1	−9.0				
1942	1.0	1.1	−0.2	−2.6	2.8	7.2	14.9	17.1	8.0	6.2	2.0	−5.8	10.7	5.8	7.6	14.7	44.5			
1943	4.6	4.8	3.9	1.8	7.3	12.0	19.7	22.3	14.2	13.1	10.1	4.0	21.0	18.7	23.8	35.3	65.0	88.4		
1944	6.7	7.1	6.3	4.5	9.9	14.5	22.0	24.7	17.3	16.7	14.3	9.2	25.2	23.9	29.3	39.7	61.1	70.2	53.7	
1945	9.4	9.9	9.2	7.6	13.1	17.8	25.2	27.9	21.2	21.0	19.2	15.0	30.4	30.1	35.8	45.9	64.2	71.3	63.4	73.6
1946	8.3	8.7	8.0	6.5	11.5	15.7	22.3	24.5	18.3	17.8	16.0	12.0	24.9	23.9	27.7	34.2	45.0	45.2	33.1	23.9
1947	7.9	8.3	7.6	6.2	10.9	14.7	20.8	22.8	17.0	16.4	14.6	10.9	22.2	21.1	24.0	28.8	36.5	35.0	24.2	15.7
1948	7.5	7.8	7.2	5.7	10.2	13.7	19.3	21.1	15.6	15.0	13.3	9.8	19.8	18.6	20.8	24.5	30.2	28.0	18.4	11.0
1949	7.9	8.3	7.7	6.4	10.6	14.0	19.4	21.0	15.8	15.3	13.7	10.5	19.8	18.7	20.7	24.0	28.8	26.7	18.6	12.7
1950	9.0	9.4	8.9	7.7	11.8	15.2	20.3	21.9	17.1	16.7	15.2	12.3	21.2	20.2	22.2	25.4	29.9	28.2	21.3	16.6
1951	9.0	9.3	8.8	7.7	11.6	14.8	19.7	21.1	16.5	16.1	14.8	12.0	20.1	19.2	21.0	23.7	27.5	25.7	19.6	15.3
1952	8.8	9.1	8.6	7.5	11.2	14.2	18.8	20.2	15.8	15.3	14.0	11.4	18.9	18.0	19.5	21.8	25.1	23.3	17.6	13.7
1953	8.2	8.5	8.0	6.9	10.4	13.3	17.5	18.7	14.6	14.1	12.8	10.3	17.2	16.2	17.4	19.3	22.1	20.2	14.9	11.3
1954	9.7	10.0	9.6	8.6	12.1	14.9	19.1	20.4	16.4	16.0	14.9	12.6	19.3	18.6	19.9	21.9	24.7	23.1	18.5	15.4
1955	10.0	10.3	9.9	9.0	12.4	15.1	19.2	20.4	16.6	16.3	15.2	13.0	19.4	18.7	19.9	21.8	24.4	22.9	18.6	15.9
1956	9.8	10.1	9.7	8.8	12.1	14.7	18.5	19.7	16.0	15.7	14.6	12.6	18.6	17.8	18.9	20.6	22.9	21.5	17.5	14.9
1957	8.9	9.2	8.8	7.9	11.0	13.4	17.1	18.1	14.6	14.2	13.1	11.1	16.6	15.8	16.8	18.2	20.1	18.7	14.8	12.3
1958	10.3	10.7	10.3	9.4	12.5	15.0	18.6	19.6	16.2	15.9	15.0	13.1	18.6	17.9	18.9	20.4	22.4	21.1	17.6	15.4
1959	10.5	10.8	10.5	9.7	12.7	15.0	18.5	19.5	16.3	15.9	15.0	13.2	18.5	17.8	18.8	20.2	22.1	20.9	17.6	15.5
1960	10.1	10.4	10.0	9.2	12.1	14.4	17.7	18.6	15.5	15.1	14.2	12.5	17.4	16.8	17.6	18.9	20.6	19.4	16.2	14.2
1961	10.6	10.9	10.6	9.9	12.7	14.9	18.1	19.0	16.0	15.7	14.9	13.2	18.0	17.4	18.2	19.5	21.1	20.0	17.0	15.2
1962	10.0	10.2	9.9	9.1	11.9	13.9	17.0	17.8	14.9	14.6	13.8	12.1	16.6	16.0	16.7	17.8	19.3	18.2	15.3	13.5
1963	10.3	10.6	10.3	9.5	12.2	14.2	17.2	18.0	15.2	14.9	14.1	12.5	16.9	16.3	17.0	18.1	19.5	18.4	15.7	14.0
1964	10.6	10.9	10.6	9.9	12.5	14.5	17.4	18.2	15.5	15.2	14.4	12.9	17.1	16.6	17.3	18.3	19.7	18.6	16.1	14.4
1965	11.3	11.6	11.3	10.7	13.2	15.2	18.0	18.8	16.2	16.0	15.2	13.8	17.9	17.4	18.1	19.2	20.5	19.6	17.1	15.6
1966	10.8	11.1	10.8	10.2	12.6	14.5	17.2	18.0	15.4	15.2	14.4	13.0	17.0	16.4	17.1	18.0	19.3	18.3	16.0	14.5
1967	12.2	12.5	12.2	11.6	14.1	16.0	18.7	19.5	17.0	16.8	16.1	14.8	18.7	18.3	19.0	20.0	21.3	20.4	18.2	16.9
1968	12.7	13.0	12.8	12.2	14.6	16.5	19.1	19.9	17.5	17.3	16.7	15.4	19.3	18.8	19.5	20.5	21.8	21.0	18.9	17.6
1969	11.6	11.9	11.7	11.1	13.4	15.2	17.7	18.4	16.1	15.8	15.2	13.9	17.5	17.1	17.7	18.6	19.7	18.9	16.8	15.5
1970	10.9	11.1	10.9	10.3	12.5	14.2	16.6	17.3	15.0	14.7	14.1	12.9	16.3	15.8	16.3	17.1	18.2	17.3	15.3	14.0

Table C-2 (page 2 of 6)

Small Company Stocks Total Returns

Rates of Return for all holding periods

Percent per annum compounded annually

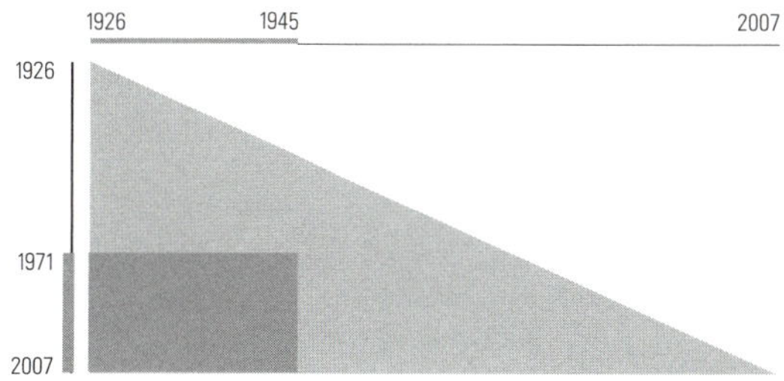

from 1926 to 2007

To the end of	From the beginning of 1926	1927	1928	1929	1930	1931	1932	1933	1934	1935	1936	1937	1938	1939	1940	1941	1942	1943	1944	1945
1971	11.0	11.2	11.0	10.4	12.6	14.3	16.6	17.3	15.0	14.8	14.2	13.0	16.3	15.8	16.4	17.1	18.1	17.3	15.3	14.1
1972	10.9	11.1	10.9	10.3	12.4	14.0	16.3	16.9	14.7	14.5	13.9	12.7	15.9	15.5	16.0	16.7	17.6	16.8	14.9	13.7
1973	9.8	10.0	9.7	9.1	11.2	12.7	14.9	15.4	13.3	13.0	12.4	11.2	14.3	13.8	14.2	14.9	15.7	14.9	13.0	11.8
1974	9.1	9.3	9.0	8.4	10.4	11.8	13.9	14.4	12.3	12.1	11.4	10.3	13.2	12.7	13.1	13.7	14.4	13.6	11.7	10.6
1975	9.8	10.0	9.8	9.2	11.1	12.6	14.7	15.2	13.2	12.9	12.3	11.2	14.1	13.6	14.0	14.6	15.4	14.6	12.8	11.7
1976	10.6	10.8	10.6	10.0	12.0	13.4	15.5	16.0	14.0	13.8	13.2	12.2	15.0	14.6	15.0	15.6	16.4	15.7	14.0	12.9
1977	10.8	11.1	10.9	10.3	12.2	13.7	15.7	16.2	14.3	14.1	13.5	12.5	15.3	14.9	15.3	15.9	16.7	16.0	14.3	13.3
1978	11.1	11.3	11.1	10.6	12.4	13.9	15.9	16.4	14.5	14.3	13.7	12.7	15.5	15.1	15.5	16.1	16.8	16.2	14.6	13.6
1979	11.6	11.8	11.6	11.1	13.0	14.4	16.4	16.9	15.0	14.8	14.3	13.4	16.1	15.7	16.1	16.7	17.5	16.8	15.3	14.3
1980	12.1	12.3	12.1	11.6	13.5	14.9	16.8	17.3	15.5	15.3	14.8	13.9	16.6	16.2	16.6	17.2	18.0	17.4	15.9	15.0
1981	12.1	12.3	12.1	11.7	13.5	14.8	16.8	17.3	15.5	15.3	14.8	13.9	16.5	16.2	16.6	17.2	17.9	17.3	15.8	14.9
1982	12.4	12.6	12.4	12.0	13.7	15.1	17.0	17.5	15.7	15.6	15.1	14.2	16.8	16.4	16.8	17.4	18.1	17.5	16.1	15.3
1983	12.8	13.0	12.9	12.4	14.2	15.5	17.4	17.9	16.2	16.0	15.6	14.7	17.2	16.9	17.3	17.9	18.6	18.0	16.7	15.8
1984	12.4	12.6	12.5	12.0	13.8	15.0	16.9	17.3	15.7	15.5	15.0	14.2	16.6	16.3	16.7	17.3	17.9	17.4	16.0	15.2
1985	12.6	12.8	12.7	12.3	13.9	15.2	17.0	17.5	15.8	15.7	15.2	14.4	16.8	16.5	16.9	17.4	18.1	17.5	16.2	15.4
1986	12.5	12.7	12.6	12.2	13.8	15.1	16.8	17.3	15.7	15.5	15.1	14.2	16.6	16.3	16.6	17.2	17.8	17.3	16.0	15.2
1987	12.1	12.3	12.2	11.8	13.4	14.6	16.3	16.7	15.1	15.0	14.5	13.7	16.0	15.7	16.0	16.5	17.2	16.6	15.4	14.6
1988	12.3	12.5	12.3	11.9	13.5	14.7	16.4	16.8	15.3	15.1	14.7	13.9	16.1	15.8	16.2	16.7	17.3	16.8	15.5	14.8
1989	12.2	12.5	12.3	11.9	13.5	14.6	16.3	16.7	15.2	15.0	14.6	13.8	16.0	15.7	16.0	16.5	17.1	16.6	15.4	14.7
1990	11.6	11.8	11.7	11.3	12.8	13.9	15.5	15.9	14.4	14.2	13.8	13.0	15.2	14.9	15.2	15.6	16.2	15.6	14.5	13.7
1991	12.1	12.3	12.1	11.7	13.2	14.4	15.9	16.3	14.9	14.7	14.3	13.5	15.7	15.4	15.7	16.1	16.7	16.2	15.0	14.3
1992	12.2	12.4	12.3	11.9	13.4	14.5	16.1	16.5	15.0	14.9	14.5	13.7	15.8	15.5	15.8	16.3	16.8	16.3	15.2	14.5
1993	12.4	12.5	12.4	12.0	13.5	14.6	16.1	16.5	15.1	15.0	14.6	13.8	15.9	15.6	15.9	16.3	16.9	16.4	15.3	14.6
1994	12.2	12.4	12.3	11.9	13.3	14.4	15.9	16.3	14.9	14.8	14.4	13.6	15.6	15.4	15.7	16.1	16.6	16.1	15.0	14.4
1995	12.5	12.7	12.6	12.2	13.6	14.7	16.2	16.6	15.2	15.1	14.7	14.0	15.9	15.7	16.0	16.4	16.9	16.5	15.4	14.7
1996	12.6	12.8	12.6	12.3	13.7	14.7	16.2	16.6	15.2	15.1	14.7	14.0	16.0	15.7	16.0	16.4	16.9	16.5	15.4	14.8
1997	12.7	12.9	12.8	12.4	13.8	14.9	16.3	16.7	15.3	15.2	14.8	14.2	16.1	15.8	16.1	16.5	17.0	16.6	15.6	14.9
1998	12.4	12.6	12.5	12.1	13.5	14.5	15.9	16.3	15.0	14.8	14.5	13.8	15.7	15.4	15.7	16.1	16.6	16.1	15.1	14.5
1999	12.6	12.8	12.7	12.3	13.7	14.7	16.1	16.5	15.2	15.0	14.7	14.0	15.9	15.6	15.9	16.3	16.8	16.3	15.3	14.7
2000	12.4	12.6	12.4	12.1	13.4	14.4	15.8	16.1	14.9	14.7	14.4	13.7	15.5	15.3	15.5	15.9	16.4	16.0	15.0	14.4
2001	12.5	12.7	12.6	12.2	13.6	14.5	15.9	16.2	15.0	14.8	14.5	13.9	15.6	15.4	15.7	16.0	16.5	16.1	15.1	14.5
2002	12.1	12.3	12.2	11.9	13.1	14.1	15.4	15.7	14.5	14.4	14.0	13.4	15.1	14.9	15.1	15.5	15.9	15.5	14.6	14.0
2003	12.7	12.8	12.7	12.4	13.7	14.6	15.9	16.3	15.1	14.9	14.6	14.0	15.7	15.5	15.7	16.1	16.6	16.1	15.2	14.6
2004	12.7	12.9	12.8	12.5	13.7	14.7	16.0	16.3	15.1	15.0	14.7	14.0	15.8	15.5	15.8	16.1	16.6	16.2	15.3	14.7
2005	12.6	12.8	12.7	12.4	13.6	14.6	15.8	16.2	15.0	14.8	14.5	13.9	15.6	15.4	15.6	16.0	16.4	16.0	15.1	14.6
2006	12.7	12.9	12.7	12.4	13.7	14.6	15.8	16.2	15.0	14.9	14.5	14.0	15.6	15.4	15.6	16.0	16.4	16.0	15.1	14.6
2007	12.5	12.6	12.5	12.2	13.4	14.3	15.5	15.8	14.7	14.6	14.2	13.7	15.3	15.0	15.3	15.6	16.0	15.6	14.8	14.2

Table C-2 (page 3 of 6)

Small Company Stocks Total Returns

Rates of Return for all holding periods
Percent per annum compounded annually

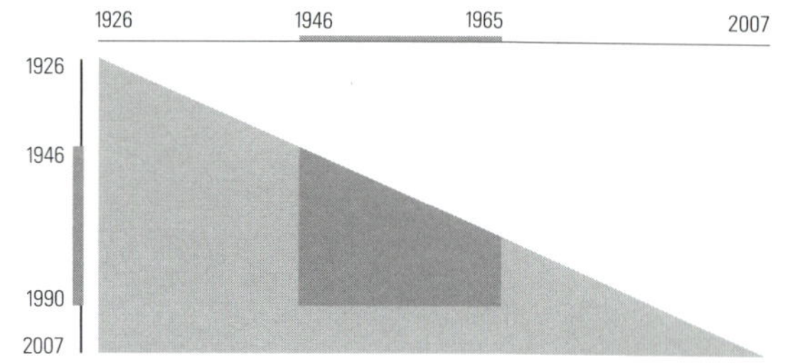

from 1926 to 2007

To the end of	From the beginning of 1946	1947	1948	1949	1950	1951	1952	1953	1954	1955	1956	1957	1958	1959	1960	1961	1962	1963	1964	1965
1946	−11.6																			
1947	−5.6	0.9																		
1948	−4.4	−0.6	−2.1																	
1949	1.1	5.8	8.3	19.7																
1950	7.7	13.2	17.6	28.9	38.7															
1951	7.7	12.1	15.1	21.4	22.3	7.8														
1952	7.0	10.5	12.6	16.6	15.5	5.4	3.0													
1953	5.3	7.9	9.1	11.5	9.6	1.3	−1.8	−6.5												
1954	10.3	13.4	15.3	18.5	18.3	13.6	15.7	22.5	60.6											
1955	11.3	14.2	15.9	18.8	18.6	15.0	16.8	21.8	39.1	20.4										
1956	10.6	13.1	14.6	16.9	16.5	13.1	14.2	17.2	26.3	12.1	4.3									
1957	8.3	10.3	11.3	12.9	12.0	8.7	8.8	10.0	14.6	2.4	−5.6	−14.6								
1958	11.8	14.0	15.3	17.2	17.0	14.5	15.5	17.7	23.2	15.3	13.7	18.7	64.9							
1959	12.2	14.2	15.4	17.2	16.9	14.7	15.6	17.5	22.1	15.5	14.4	17.9	38.5	16.4						
1960	11.1	12.9	13.9	15.3	14.9	12.8	13.3	14.7	18.1	12.2	10.6	12.2	22.9	6.1	−3.3					
1961	12.3	14.1	15.1	16.5	16.2	14.4	15.1	16.5	19.7	14.8	13.9	15.9	25.1	14.1	13.0	32.1				
1962	10.7	12.2	13.0	14.2	13.8	11.9	12.3	13.3	15.7	11.1	9.8	10.7	16.6	7.0	4.0	7.9	−11.9			
1963	11.4	12.9	13.7	14.8	14.5	12.8	13.2	14.2	16.5	12.4	11.4	12.5	17.8	10.1	8.6	12.9	4.3	23.6		
1964	12.0	13.4	14.2	15.3	15.0	13.5	14.0	14.9	17.1	13.5	12.7	13.8	18.6	12.2	11.4	15.4	10.4	23.5	23.5	
1965	13.3	14.8	15.6	16.7	16.6	15.2	15.8	16.8	19.0	15.8	15.3	16.6	21.3	16.0	16.0	20.3	17.5	29.3	32.3	41.8
1966	12.2	13.6	14.3	15.3	15.0	13.7	14.1	14.9	16.7	13.7	13.1	14.0	17.7	12.9	12.4	15.2	12.1	19.1	17.6	14.8
1967	14.8	16.2	17.0	18.1	18.0	16.9	17.5	18.6	20.6	18.0	17.8	19.1	23.1	19.1	19.5	23.2	21.7	29.9	31.5	34.3
1968	15.6	17.0	17.9	19.0	18.9	17.9	18.5	19.6	21.6	19.2	19.1	20.4	24.2	20.7	21.2	24.7	23.7	30.9	32.4	34.7
1969	13.5	14.8	15.5	16.4	16.2	15.1	15.6	16.3	17.9	15.5	15.2	16.1	19.1	15.6	15.5	17.8	16.2	20.8	20.4	19.8
1970	12.1	13.2	13.8	14.6	14.3	13.2	13.5	14.1	15.5	13.1	12.7	13.3	15.8	12.4	12.1	13.7	11.8	15.2	14.1	12.6
1971	12.3	13.4	13.9	14.7	14.4	13.4	13.7	14.3	15.5	13.3	12.9	13.5	15.8	12.7	12.4	14.0	12.3	15.4	14.4	13.1
1972	12.0	13.0	13.5	14.2	14.0	13.0	13.2	13.8	14.9	12.8	12.4	12.9	15.0	12.1	11.8	13.1	11.6	14.2	13.2	12.0
1973	10.1	11.0	11.4	11.9	11.6	10.6	10.7	11.1	12.0	9.9	9.4	9.7	11.4	8.5	8.0	8.9	7.2	9.1	7.8	6.2
1974	8.9	9.7	10.0	10.5	10.2	9.1	9.2	9.4	10.3	8.2	7.6	7.8	9.3	6.5	5.9	6.6	4.8	6.3	4.9	3.2
1975	10.1	10.9	11.3	11.8	11.5	10.6	10.7	11.0	11.9	10.0	9.5	9.8	11.3	8.8	8.3	9.2	7.7	9.3	8.2	6.9
1976	11.4	12.2	12.6	13.2	13.0	12.1	12.3	12.7	13.6	11.8	11.4	11.8	13.4	11.0	10.7	11.7	10.4	12.2	11.4	10.4
1977	11.8	12.6	13.1	13.6	13.4	12.6	12.7	13.1	14.1	12.4	12.0	12.4	13.9	11.8	11.5	12.4	11.3	13.1	12.3	11.5
1978	12.1	13.0	13.4	13.9	13.7	12.9	13.1	13.5	14.4	12.8	12.5	12.9	14.4	12.3	12.1	13.0	12.0	13.7	13.1	12.3
1979	12.9	13.8	14.2	14.8	14.6	13.9	14.1	14.5	15.4	13.9	13.6	14.1	15.6	13.6	13.5	14.5	13.5	15.3	14.8	14.2
1980	13.6	14.5	14.9	15.5	15.4	14.6	14.9	15.3	16.2	14.8	14.6	15.0	16.5	14.7	14.6	15.6	14.8	16.5	16.1	15.6
1981	13.6	14.5	14.9	15.4	15.3	14.6	14.9	15.3	16.2	14.8	14.6	15.0	16.4	14.7	14.6	15.5	14.8	16.4	16.0	15.5
1982	14.0	14.8	15.2	15.8	15.7	15.0	15.3	15.7	16.5	15.2	15.0	15.5	16.9	15.2	15.1	16.1	15.4	16.9	16.6	16.2
1983	14.6	15.4	15.9	16.4	16.3	15.7	16.0	16.4	17.2	16.0	15.8	16.3	17.7	16.1	16.1	17.0	16.4	17.9	17.6	17.3
1984	14.0	14.8	15.2	15.7	15.6	15.0	15.2	15.6	16.4	15.1	15.0	15.4	16.7	15.1	15.1	15.9	15.2	16.7	16.3	16.0
1985	14.3	15.0	15.4	15.9	15.8	15.2	15.5	15.9	16.6	15.4	15.3	15.7	16.9	15.5	15.4	16.2	15.6	17.0	16.7	16.4
1986	14.1	14.8	15.2	15.7	15.6	15.0	15.2	15.6	16.3	15.2	15.0	15.4	16.6	15.1	15.1	15.9	15.3	16.6	16.3	15.9
1987	13.5	14.2	14.5	15.0	14.8	14.3	14.4	14.8	15.5	14.3	14.1	14.5	15.6	14.2	14.1	14.8	14.2	15.4	15.1	14.7
1988	13.7	14.4	14.7	15.2	15.0	14.5	14.7	15.0	15.7	14.6	14.4	14.7	15.8	14.5	14.4	15.1	14.5	15.7	15.4	15.0
1989	13.6	14.3	14.6	15.0	14.9	14.4	14.5	14.9	15.5	14.4	14.3	14.6	15.7	14.3	14.3	14.9	14.4	15.5	15.2	14.8
1990	12.7	13.3	13.6	14.0	13.9	13.3	13.4	13.7	14.3	13.3	13.1	13.3	14.3	13.0	12.9	13.5	12.9	13.9	13.5	13.2

Table C-2 (page 4 of 6)

Small Company Stocks Total Returns

Rates of Return for all holding periods
Percent per annum compounded annually

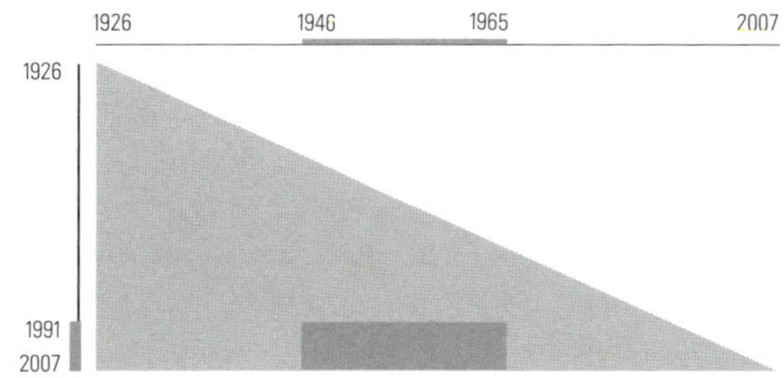

from 1926 to 2007

To the end of	From the beginning of 1946	1947	1948	1949	1950	1951	1952	1953	1954	1955	1956	1957	1958	1959	1960	1961	1962	1963	1964	1965
1991	13.3	13.9	14.2	14.6	14.5	14.0	14.1	14.4	15.0	14.0	13.8	14.1	15.1	13.8	13.8	14.4	13.8	14.8	14.5	14.2
1992	13.5	14.1	14.4	14.8	14.7	14.2	14.3	14.6	15.2	14.2	14.1	14.4	15.3	14.1	14.0	14.6	14.1	15.1	14.8	14.5
1993	13.6	14.2	14.5	14.9	14.8	14.3	14.5	14.8	15.4	14.4	14.3	14.5	15.5	14.3	14.2	14.8	14.3	15.3	15.0	14.7
1994	13.4	14.0	14.3	14.7	14.6	14.1	14.2	14.5	15.1	14.1	14.0	14.2	15.1	14.0	13.9	14.5	14.0	14.9	14.6	14.3
1995	13.8	14.4	14.7	15.1	15.0	14.5	14.6	14.9	15.5	14.6	14.4	14.7	15.6	14.5	14.4	15.0	14.5	15.4	15.2	14.9
1996	13.9	14.4	14.7	15.1	15.0	14.6	14.7	15.0	15.5	14.6	14.5	14.8	15.6	14.6	14.5	15.1	14.6	15.5	15.3	15.0
1997	14.0	14.6	14.9	15.3	15.2	14.7	14.9	15.2	15.7	14.8	14.7	15.0	15.8	14.8	14.7	15.3	14.8	15.7	15.5	15.2
1998	13.6	14.1	14.4	14.8	14.7	14.2	14.4	14.6	15.1	14.3	14.1	14.4	15.2	14.2	14.1	14.6	14.2	15.0	14.8	14.5
1999	13.9	14.4	14.7	15.0	15.0	14.5	14.7	14.9	15.4	14.6	14.5	14.7	15.5	14.5	14.5	15.0	14.5	15.4	15.1	14.9
2000	13.5	14.0	14.3	14.7	14.6	14.1	14.3	14.5	15.0	14.2	14.0	14.3	15.0	14.1	14.0	14.5	14.0	14.8	14.6	14.4
2001	13.7	14.2	14.5	14.8	14.7	14.3	14.4	14.7	15.1	14.3	14.2	14.4	15.2	14.2	14.2	14.7	14.3	15.0	14.8	14.6
2002	13.1	13.6	13.9	14.2	14.1	13.7	13.8	14.0	14.5	13.7	13.5	13.8	14.5	13.5	13.5	13.9	13.5	14.2	14.0	13.7
2003	13.8	14.3	14.6	14.9	14.8	14.4	14.6	14.8	15.3	14.5	14.4	14.6	15.3	14.4	14.4	14.8	14.4	15.2	15.0	14.8
2004	13.9	14.4	14.7	15.0	14.9	14.5	14.6	14.9	15.3	14.6	14.4	14.7	15.4	14.5	14.5	14.9	14.5	15.2	15.0	14.8
2005	13.8	14.3	14.5	14.8	14.7	14.3	14.5	14.7	15.1	14.4	14.3	14.5	15.2	14.3	14.3	14.7	14.3	15.0	14.8	14.6
2006	13.8	14.3	14.5	14.8	14.7	14.4	14.5	14.7	15.2	14.4	14.3	14.5	15.2	14.3	14.3	14.7	14.4	15.0	14.8	14.6
2007	13.5	13.9	14.2	14.5	14.4	14.0	14.1	14.3	14.7	14.0	13.9	14.1	14.7	13.9	13.9	14.2	13.9	14.5	14.3	14.1

Table C-2 (page 5 of 6)

Small Company Stocks Total Returns

Rates of Return for all holding periods

Percent per annum compounded annually

from 1926 to 2007

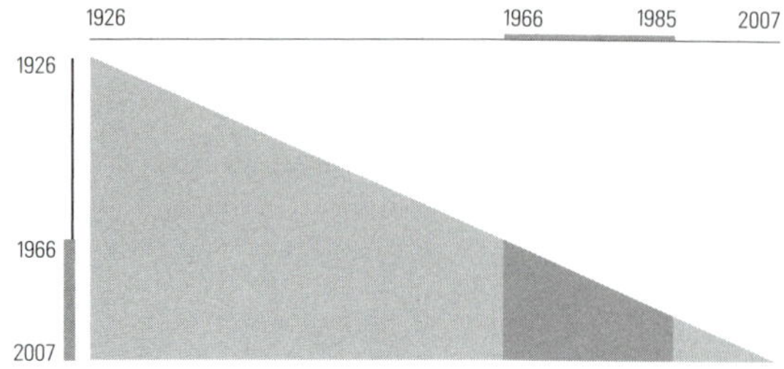

To the end of	From the beginning of 1966	1967	1968	1969	1970	1971	1972	1973	1974	1975	1976	1977	1978	1979	1980	1981	1982	1983	1984	1985
1966	-7.0																			
1967	30.7	83.6																		
1968	32.4	58.0	36.0																	
1969	14.8	23.2	0.9	-25.1																
1970	7.5	11.5	-5.6	-21.3	-17.4															
1971	9.0	12.5	-0.5	-10.3	-1.9	16.5														
1972	8.3	11.1	0.5	-6.9	0.2	10.3	4.4													
1973	2.4	3.8	-5.6	-12.3	-8.7	-5.6	-15.1	-30.9												
1974	-0.4	0.5	-7.8	-13.6	-11.1	-9.4	-16.7	-25.6	-19.9											
1975	4.0	5.3	-1.8	-6.3	-2.7	0.6	-3.1	-5.4	10.6	52.8										
1976	8.0	9.6	3.5	0.0	4.2	8.4	6.8	7.4	24.4	55.1	57.4									
1977	9.3	10.9	5.5	2.6	6.7	10.6	9.7	10.8	24.6	44.5	40.5	25.4								
1978	10.4	11.9	7.0	4.5	8.4	12.2	11.6	12.8	24.4	38.9	34.6	24.4	23.5							
1979	12.4	14.1	9.7	7.5	11.5	15.3	15.1	16.7	27.4	39.8	36.7	30.5	33.1	43.5						
1980	14.1	15.8	11.7	9.9	13.8	17.5	17.6	19.4	29.1	39.8	37.4	32.8	35.3	41.7	39.9					
1981	14.1	15.6	11.9	10.2	13.8	17.2	17.3	18.8	27.1	35.8	33.1	28.7	29.6	31.7	26.2	13.9				
1982	14.9	16.4	12.9	11.4	14.9	18.1	18.2	19.7	27.2	34.8	32.4	28.6	29.3	30.8	26.8	20.7	28.0			
1983	16.1	17.6	14.4	13.1	16.5	19.6	19.9	21.4	28.4	35.3	33.3	30.1	31.0	32.5	29.9	26.7	33.7	39.7		
1984	14.8	16.1	13.0	11.7	14.8	17.5	17.6	18.7	24.7	30.4	28.1	24.8	24.8	25.0	21.6	17.4	18.6	14.2	-6.7	
1985	15.3	16.6	13.7	12.5	15.4	18.0	18.1	19.2	24.7	29.9	27.8	24.8	24.8	24.9	22.1	18.8	20.1	17.6	7.9	24.7
1986	14.8	16.1	13.3	12.1	14.8	17.2	17.3	18.3	23.2	27.8	25.7	22.9	22.6	22.5	19.8	16.7	17.3	14.8	7.5	15.4
1987	13.6	14.7	12.0	10.9	13.3	15.5	15.4	16.2	20.6	24.4	22.3	19.6	19.0	18.5	15.7	12.6	12.4	9.5	3.0	6.5
1988	14.0	15.1	12.5	11.5	13.8	15.9	15.8	16.6	20.7	24.3	22.4	19.8	19.3	18.9	16.5	13.8	13.8	11.6	6.7	10.4
1989	13.8	14.8	12.4	11.4	13.6	15.6	15.5	16.2	20.0	23.3	21.5	19.1	18.5	18.1	15.8	13.4	13.4	11.4	7.3	10.3
1990	12.2	13.0	10.7	9.6	11.7	13.3	13.2	13.7	17.1	19.9	18.0	15.6	14.8	14.1	11.8	9.3	8.8	6.6	2.6	4.2
1991	13.3	14.2	11.9	11.0	13.0	14.7	14.6	15.1	18.5	21.2	19.5	17.3	16.7	16.2	14.2	12.1	12.0	10.3	7.1	9.2
1992	13.6	14.5	12.4	11.5	13.4	15.1	15.0	15.5	18.7	21.3	19.7	17.7	17.2	16.7	14.9	13.0	13.0	11.6	8.8	10.9
1993	13.9	14.7	12.7	11.8	13.7	15.3	15.3	15.8	18.8	21.3	19.8	17.9	17.4	17.0	15.3	13.6	13.6	12.4	10.0	12.0
1994	13.5	14.3	12.3	11.5	13.3	14.8	14.7	15.2	18.0	20.3	18.8	17.0	16.5	16.1	14.5	12.8	12.8	11.6	9.3	11.1
1995	14.1	14.9	13.0	12.3	14.0	15.5	15.5	16.0	18.7	21.0	19.6	17.8	17.4	17.1	15.6	14.2	14.2	13.2	11.2	13.0
1996	14.2	15.0	13.2	12.4	14.1	15.6	15.5	16.0	18.7	20.8	19.5	17.8	17.5	17.1	15.7	14.4	14.4	13.5	11.7	13.4
1997	14.5	15.3	13.5	12.8	14.4	15.8	15.8	16.3	18.8	20.9	19.6	18.1	17.7	17.4	16.1	14.9	14.9	14.1	12.5	14.1
1998	13.8	14.5	12.8	12.1	13.6	14.9	14.9	15.3	17.7	19.6	18.3	16.8	16.4	16.0	14.8	13.5	13.5	12.6	11.0	12.4
1999	14.2	14.9	13.3	12.6	14.1	15.4	15.4	15.8	18.1	20.0	18.8	17.3	17.0	16.7	15.5	14.3	14.3	13.6	12.1	13.5
2000	13.7	14.3	12.7	12.0	13.5	14.7	14.7	15.0	17.2	19.0	17.8	16.4	16.0	15.7	14.5	13.3	13.3	12.5	11.1	12.3
2001	13.9	14.6	13.0	12.4	13.8	15.0	14.9	15.3	17.4	19.1	18.0	16.6	16.3	16.0	14.8	13.8	13.8	13.1	11.7	12.9
2002	13.1	13.7	12.1	11.5	12.8	14.0	13.9	14.2	16.2	17.8	16.6	15.3	14.9	14.6	13.4	12.4	12.3	11.6	10.3	11.3
2003	14.1	14.7	13.3	12.7	14.0	15.1	15.1	15.5	17.5	19.0	18.0	16.7	16.4	16.1	15.1	14.1	14.1	13.5	12.4	13.5
2004	14.2	14.8	13.4	12.8	14.2	15.2	15.2	15.6	17.5	19.0	18.0	16.8	16.5	16.2	15.2	14.3	14.3	13.7	12.6	13.7
2005	14.0	14.6	13.2	12.6	13.9	15.0	14.9	15.2	17.1	18.5	17.6	16.4	16.1	15.8	14.8	13.9	14.0	13.4	12.3	13.3
2006	14.1	14.6	13.3	12.7	14.0	15.0	14.9	15.3	17.1	18.5	17.5	16.4	16.1	15.8	14.9	14.0	14.0	13.5	12.5	13.4
2007	13.6	14.1	12.8	12.2	13.4	14.4	14.3	14.6	16.4	17.7	16.7	15.6	15.3	15.0	14.1	13.3	13.2	12.7	11.7	12.5

Table C-2 (page 6 of 6)-a
Small Company Stocks Total Returns
Rates of Return for all holding periods
Percent per annum compounded annually

from 1926 to 2007

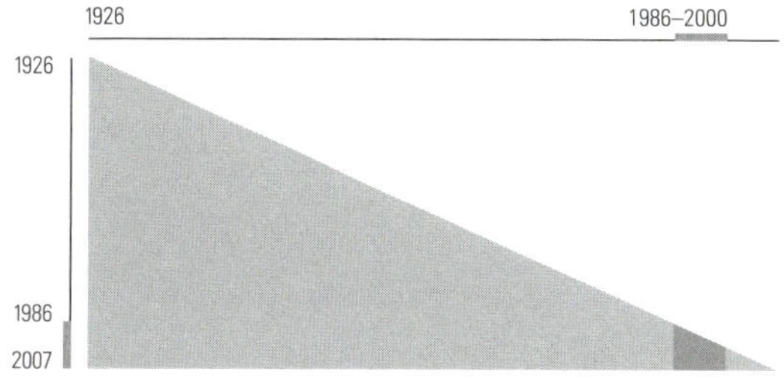

To the end of	From the beginning of 1986	1987	1988	1989	1990	1991	1992	1993	1994	1995	1996	1997	1998	1999	2000
1986	6.9														
1987	−1.6	−9.3													
1988	6.0	5.6	22.9												
1989	7.0	7.1	16.4	10.2											
1990	0.6	−0.9	2.0	−7.0	−21.6										
1991	6.9	6.9	11.3	7.7	6.5	44.6									
1992	9.1	9.4	13.6	11.4	11.9	33.6	23.3								
1993	10.5	11.0	14.8	13.3	14.1	29.2	22.2	21.0							
1994	9.6	10.0	13.1	11.5	11.8	22.1	15.4	11.7	3.1						
1995	11.9	12.5	15.5	14.5	15.3	24.5	19.9	18.8	17.7	34.5					
1996	12.4	13.0	15.8	14.9	15.6	23.3	19.5	18.5	17.7	25.8	17.6				
1997	13.2	13.8	16.5	15.8	16.5	23.3	20.0	19.4	19.0	24.8	20.2	22.8			
1998	11.5	11.9	14.1	13.2	13.6	18.9	15.7	14.4	13.2	15.8	10.2	6.7	−7.3		
1999	12.7	13.2	15.3	14.6	15.1	20.1	17.3	16.5	15.8	18.5	14.8	13.9	9.7	29.8	
2000	11.6	11.9	13.7	13.0	13.3	17.5	14.8	13.8	12.8	14.5	10.9	9.2	5.1	11.9	−3.6
2001	12.2	12.6	14.3	13.7	14.0	18.0	15.6	14.7	14.0	15.6	12.8	11.8	9.2	15.4	8.8
2002	10.5	10.8	12.3	11.5	11.6	15.0	12.6	11.6	10.6	11.6	8.6	7.2	4.3	7.4	0.9
2003	12.9	13.2	14.8	14.3	14.6	18.0	16.0	15.3	14.8	16.2	14.1	13.6	12.1	16.4	13.3
2004	13.1	13.5	15.0	14.5	14.8	18.0	16.2	15.6	15.1	16.4	14.5	14.2	13.0	16.8	14.3
2005	12.8	13.1	14.5	14.0	14.2	17.1	15.4	14.8	14.3	15.4	13.6	13.2	12.0	15.1	12.8
2006	12.9	13.2	14.6	14.1	14.4	17.1	15.4	14.9	14.4	15.4	13.9	13.5	12.5	15.2	13.3
2007	12.0	12.3	13.5	13.0	13.2	15.6	14.0	13.4	12.9	13.7	12.1	11.6	10.6	12.8	10.8

Table C-2 (page 6 of 6)-b
Small Company Stocks Total Returns
Rates of Return for all holding periods
Percent per annum compounded annually

from 1926 to 2007

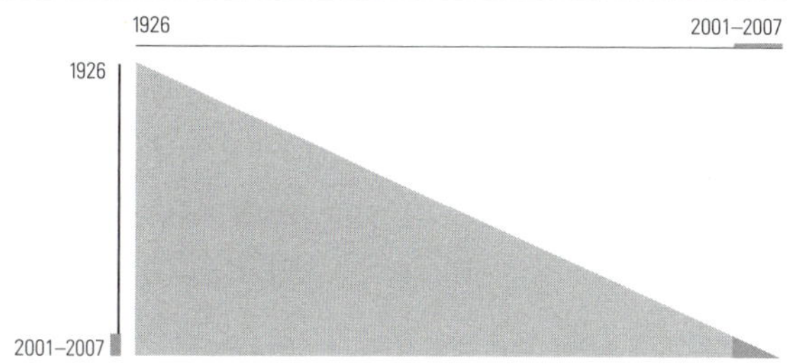

To the end of	From the beginning of 2001	2002	2003	2004	2005	2006	2007
2001	22.8						
2002	3.2	−13.3					
2003	19.6	18.1	60.7				
2004	19.3	18.2	37.9	18.4			
2005	16.4	14.9	26.2	11.9	5.7		
2006	16.4	15.2	23.6	13.3	10.8	16.2	
2007	13.0	11.5	17.2	8.3	5.2	4.9	−5.2

Table C-3 (page 1 of 6)

Long-Term Corporate Bonds Total Returns

Rates of Return for all holding periods
Percent per annum compounded annually

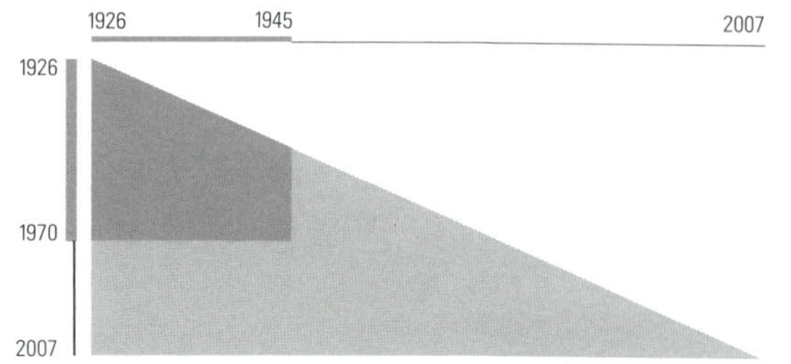

from 1926 to 2007

To the end of	From the beginning of 1926	1927	1928	1929	1930	1931	1932	1933	1934	1935	1936	1937	1938	1939	1940	1941	1942	1943	1944	1945
1926	7.4																			
1927	7.4	7.4																		
1928	5.9	5.1	2.8																	
1929	5.2	4.5	3.1	3.3																
1930	5.8	5.4	4.7	5.6	8.0															
1931	4.4	3.9	3.0	3.1	2.9	-1.9														
1932	5.3	5.0	4.5	4.9	5.5	4.3	10.8													
1933	6.0	5.8	5.5	6.0	6.7	6.3	10.6	10.4												
1934	6.8	6.7	6.6	7.3	8.1	8.1	11.7	12.1	13.8											
1935	7.1	7.0	7.0	7.6	8.3	8.4	11.2	11.3	11.7	9.6										
1936	7.1	7.0	7.0	7.5	8.1	8.1	10.3	10.1	10.0	8.2	6.7									
1937	6.7	6.6	6.5	7.0	7.4	7.4	9.0	8.6	8.2	6.3	4.7	2.7								
1938	6.6	6.6	6.5	6.9	7.3	7.2	8.6	8.2	7.8	6.3	5.2	4.4	6.1							
1939	6.4	6.4	6.3	6.6	6.9	6.8	8.0	7.6	7.1	5.8	4.9	4.3	5.0	4.0						
1940	6.2	6.2	6.1	6.3	6.6	6.5	7.5	7.0	6.6	5.4	4.6	4.1	4.5	3.7	3.4					
1941	6.0	5.9	5.8	6.1	6.3	6.1	7.0	6.6	6.1	5.0	4.3	3.8	4.0	3.4	3.1	2.7				
1942	5.8	5.7	5.6	5.8	6.0	5.8	6.6	6.2	5.7	4.7	4.0	3.6	3.8	3.2	2.9	2.7	2.6			
1943	5.6	5.5	5.4	5.6	5.8	5.6	6.3	5.8	5.4	4.5	3.9	3.5	3.6	3.1	2.9	2.7	2.7	2.8		
1944	5.6	5.5	5.4	5.5	5.7	5.5	6.1	5.8	5.3	4.5	4.0	3.6	3.8	3.4	3.3	3.2	3.4	3.8	4.7	
1945	5.5	5.4	5.3	5.5	5.6	5.4	6.0	5.6	5.2	4.5	4.0	3.7	3.8	3.5	3.4	3.4	3.6	3.9	4.4	4.1
1946	5.3	5.2	5.1	5.3	5.4	5.2	5.7	5.3	5.0	4.3	3.8	3.5	3.6	3.3	3.2	3.1	3.2	3.3	3.5	2.9
1947	5.0	4.9	4.7	4.8	4.9	4.7	5.2	4.8	4.4	3.7	3.3	2.9	3.0	2.6	2.4	2.3	2.2	2.2	2.0	1.1
1948	4.9	4.8	4.7	4.8	4.9	4.7	5.1	4.8	4.4	3.8	3.3	3.0	3.1	2.8	2.6	2.5	2.5	2.5	2.4	1.9
1949	4.9	4.8	4.6	4.7	4.8	4.6	5.0	4.7	4.3	3.7	3.3	3.1	3.1	2.8	2.7	2.6	2.6	2.6	2.6	2.2
1950	4.8	4.7	4.5	4.6	4.7	4.5	4.9	4.5	4.2	3.6	3.2	3.0	3.0	2.8	2.6	2.6	2.6	2.6	2.5	2.1
1951	4.5	4.3	4.2	4.3	4.3	4.2	4.5	4.1	3.8	3.2	2.9	2.6	2.6	2.3	2.2	2.1	2.0	2.0	1.8	1.4
1952	4.4	4.3	4.2	4.2	4.3	4.1	4.4	4.1	3.8	3.3	2.9	2.7	2.7	2.4	2.3	2.2	2.2	2.1	2.0	1.7
1953	4.4	4.3	4.2	4.2	4.3	4.1	4.4	4.1	3.8	3.3	2.9	2.7	2.7	2.5	2.4	2.3	2.3	2.2	2.2	1.9
1954	4.4	4.3	4.2	4.3	4.3	4.2	4.4	4.1	3.8	3.4	3.1	2.9	2.9	2.7	2.6	2.5	2.5	2.5	2.5	2.2
1955	4.3	4.2	4.1	4.1	4.2	4.0	4.3	4.0	3.7	3.2	2.9	2.7	2.7	2.5	2.4	2.4	2.4	2.3	2.3	2.1
1956	3.9	3.8	3.7	3.7	3.7	3.6	3.8	3.5	3.2	2.8	2.4	2.2	2.2	2.0	1.9	1.8	1.7	1.6	1.6	1.3
1957	4.1	4.0	3.8	3.9	3.9	3.7	4.0	3.7	3.4	3.0	2.7	2.5	2.5	2.3	2.2	2.2	2.1	2.1	2.1	1.9
1958	3.9	3.8	3.6	3.7	3.7	3.5	3.7	3.5	3.2	2.8	2.5	2.3	2.3	2.1	2.0	1.9	1.9	1.8	1.8	1.6
1959	3.7	3.6	3.5	3.5	3.5	3.4	3.6	3.3	3.0	2.6	2.3	2.2	2.1	1.9	1.8	1.8	1.7	1.7	1.6	1.4
1960	3.9	3.8	3.7	3.7	3.7	3.6	3.7	3.5	3.3	2.9	2.6	2.4	2.4	2.3	2.2	2.1	2.1	2.1	2.0	1.8
1961	3.9	3.8	3.7	3.7	3.7	3.6	3.8	3.5	3.3	2.9	2.7	2.5	2.5	2.4	2.3	2.2	2.2	2.2	2.2	2.0
1962	4.0	3.9	3.8	3.8	3.9	3.7	3.9	3.7	3.5	3.1	2.9	2.7	2.7	2.6	2.5	2.5	2.5	2.5	2.5	2.3
1963	4.0	3.9	3.8	3.8	3.8	3.7	3.9	3.6	3.4	3.1	2.9	2.7	2.7	2.6	2.5	2.5	2.5	2.5	2.5	2.3
1964	4.0	3.9	3.8	3.8	3.8	3.7	3.9	3.7	3.5	3.1	2.9	2.8	2.8	2.7	2.6	2.6	2.6	2.6	2.6	2.5
1965	3.9	3.8	3.7	3.7	3.7	3.6	3.8	3.6	3.3	3.0	2.8	2.7	2.7	2.5	2.5	2.5	2.4	2.4	2.4	2.3
1966	3.8	3.7	3.6	3.6	3.6	3.5	3.7	3.5	3.2	2.9	2.7	2.6	2.6	2.5	2.4	2.4	2.4	2.3	2.3	2.2
1967	3.6	3.5	3.4	3.4	3.4	3.3	3.4	3.2	3.0	2.7	2.5	2.3	2.3	2.2	2.1	2.1	2.1	2.0	2.0	1.9
1968	3.5	3.4	3.3	3.4	3.4	3.2	3.4	3.2	3.0	2.7	2.5	2.3	2.3	2.2	2.2	2.1	2.1	2.1	2.0	1.9
1969	3.3	3.2	3.1	3.1	3.1	2.9	3.1	2.9	2.7	2.4	2.2	2.0	2.0	1.9	1.8	1.7	1.7	1.7	1.6	1.5
1970	3.6	3.5	3.4	3.4	3.4	3.3	3.4	3.2	3.1	2.8	2.6	2.5	2.5	2.3	2.3	2.3	2.2	2.2	2.2	2.1

Table C-3 (page 2 of 6)

Long-Term Corporate Bonds Total Returns

Rates of Return for all holding periods
Percent per annum compounded annually

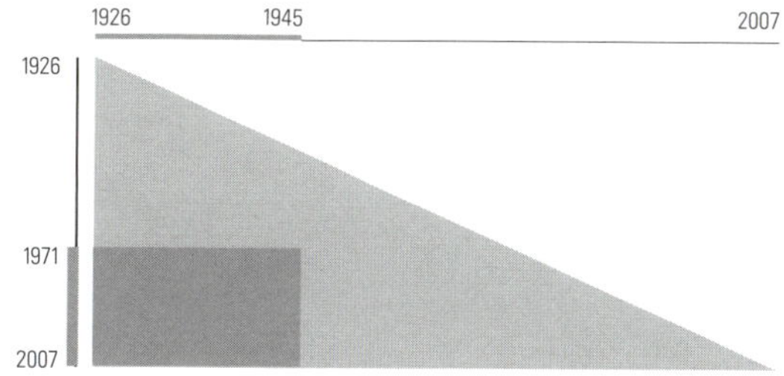

from 1926 to 2007

To the end of	From the beginning of 1926	1927	1928	1929	1930	1931	1932	1933	1934	1935	1936	1937	1938	1939	1940	1941	1942	1943	1944	1945
1971	3.7	3.6	3.6	3.6	3.6	3.5	3.6	3.4	3.3	3.0	2.8	2.7	2.7	2.6	2.6	2.5	2.5	2.5	2.5	2.4
1972	3.8	3.7	3.6	3.7	3.7	3.6	3.7	3.5	3.4	3.1	2.9	2.8	2.8	2.7	2.7	2.7	2.7	2.7	2.7	2.6
1973	3.7	3.7	3.6	3.6	3.6	3.5	3.6	3.5	3.3	3.0	2.9	2.8	2.8	2.7	2.6	2.6	2.6	2.6	2.6	2.5
1974	3.6	3.5	3.4	3.4	3.5	3.4	3.5	3.3	3.1	2.9	2.7	2.6	2.6	2.5	2.5	2.4	2.4	2.4	2.4	2.3
1975	3.8	3.7	3.7	3.7	3.7	3.6	3.7	3.6	3.4	3.2	3.0	2.9	2.9	2.8	2.8	2.8	2.8	2.8	2.8	2.7
1976	4.1	4.0	3.9	4.0	4.0	3.9	4.0	3.9	3.7	3.5	3.4	3.3	3.3	3.2	3.2	3.2	3.2	3.2	3.2	3.2
1977	4.0	4.0	3.9	3.9	3.9	3.9	4.0	3.8	3.7	3.5	3.3	3.2	3.2	3.2	3.2	3.1	3.2	3.2	3.2	3.1
1978	4.0	3.9	3.8	3.8	3.9	3.8	3.9	3.7	3.6	3.4	3.2	3.2	3.2	3.1	3.1	3.1	3.1	3.1	3.1	3.0
1979	3.8	3.7	3.7	3.7	3.7	3.6	3.7	3.6	3.4	3.2	3.1	3.0	3.0	2.9	2.9	2.9	2.9	2.9	2.9	2.8
1980	3.7	3.6	3.5	3.5	3.6	3.5	3.6	3.4	3.3	3.1	2.9	2.8	2.8	2.8	2.7	2.7	2.7	2.7	2.7	2.7
1981	3.6	3.5	3.4	3.5	3.5	3.4	3.5	3.3	3.2	3.0	2.8	2.8	2.8	2.7	2.6	2.6	2.6	2.6	2.6	2.6
1982	4.2	4.1	4.1	4.1	4.1	4.0	4.1	4.0	3.9	3.7	3.6	3.5	3.5	3.4	3.4	3.4	3.5	3.5	3.5	3.5
1983	4.2	4.1	4.1	4.1	4.1	4.1	4.2	4.0	3.9	3.7	3.6	3.5	3.6	3.5	3.5	3.5	3.5	3.5	3.6	3.5
1984	4.4	4.4	4.3	4.3	4.3	4.3	4.4	4.3	4.2	4.0	3.9	3.8	3.8	3.8	3.8	3.8	3.8	3.8	3.9	3.8
1985	4.8	4.7	4.7	4.7	4.8	4.7	4.8	4.7	4.6	4.4	4.3	4.3	4.3	4.3	4.3	4.3	4.3	4.4	4.4	4.4
1986	5.0	5.0	4.9	5.0	5.0	5.0	5.1	5.0	4.9	4.7	4.6	4.6	4.6	4.6	4.6	4.6	4.7	4.7	4.8	4.8
1987	4.9	4.9	4.8	4.9	4.9	4.9	5.0	4.9	4.8	4.6	4.5	4.5	4.5	4.5	4.5	4.5	4.6	4.6	4.6	4.6
1988	5.0	5.0	4.9	5.0	5.0	5.0	5.1	5.0	4.9	4.7	4.6	4.6	4.6	4.6	4.6	4.6	4.7	4.7	4.8	4.8
1989	5.2	5.2	5.1	5.2	5.2	5.1	5.3	5.2	5.1	4.9	4.8	4.8	4.8	4.8	4.8	4.9	4.9	5.0	5.0	5.0
1990	5.2	5.2	5.1	5.2	5.2	5.2	5.3	5.2	5.1	5.0	4.9	4.8	4.9	4.9	4.9	4.9	4.9	5.0	5.0	5.1
1991	5.4	5.4	5.4	5.4	5.4	5.4	5.5	5.4	5.3	5.2	5.1	5.1	5.1	5.1	5.1	5.2	5.2	5.3	5.3	5.3
1992	5.5	5.4	5.4	5.5	5.5	5.5	5.6	5.5	5.4	5.3	5.2	5.2	5.2	5.2	5.2	5.3	5.3	5.4	5.4	5.4
1993	5.6	5.6	5.5	5.6	5.6	5.6	5.7	5.6	5.5	5.4	5.3	5.3	5.4	5.3	5.4	5.4	5.5	5.5	5.6	5.6
1994	5.4	5.4	5.4	5.4	5.4	5.4	5.5	5.4	5.3	5.2	5.1	5.1	5.1	5.1	5.2	5.2	5.2	5.3	5.3	5.3
1995	5.7	5.7	5.6	5.7	5.7	5.7	5.8	5.7	5.7	5.5	5.5	5.4	5.5	5.5	5.5	5.5	5.6	5.7	5.7	5.7
1996	5.6	5.6	5.6	5.6	5.7	5.6	5.7	5.7	5.6	5.5	5.4	5.4	5.4	5.4	5.4	5.5	5.5	5.6	5.6	5.6
1997	5.7	5.7	5.7	5.7	5.8	5.7	5.9	5.8	5.7	5.6	5.5	5.5	5.5	5.5	5.6	5.6	5.7	5.7	5.8	5.8
1998	5.8	5.8	5.8	5.8	5.8	5.8	5.9	5.9	5.8	5.7	5.6	5.6	5.6	5.6	5.6	5.7	5.7	5.8	5.9	5.9
1999	5.6	5.6	5.6	5.6	5.6	5.6	5.7	5.6	5.6	5.4	5.4	5.4	5.4	5.4	5.4	5.4	5.5	5.5	5.6	5.6
2000	5.7	5.7	5.7	5.7	5.7	5.7	5.8	5.7	5.7	5.6	5.5	5.5	5.5	5.5	5.5	5.6	5.6	5.7	5.7	5.7
2001	5.8	5.7	5.7	5.8	5.8	5.8	5.9	5.8	5.7	5.6	5.6	5.6	5.6	5.6	5.6	5.7	5.7	5.8	5.8	5.8
2002	5.9	5.9	5.9	5.9	5.9	5.9	6.0	6.0	5.9	5.8	5.7	5.7	5.8	5.7	5.8	5.8	5.9	5.9	6.0	6.0
2003	5.9	5.9	5.9	5.9	5.9	5.9	6.0	5.9	5.9	5.8	5.7	5.7	5.7	5.7	5.8	5.8	5.9	5.9	6.0	6.0
2004	5.9	5.9	5.9	5.9	6.0	5.9	6.0	6.0	5.9	5.8	5.8	5.7	5.8	5.8	5.8	5.9	5.9	6.0	6.0	6.0
2005	5.9	5.9	5.9	5.9	6.0	5.9	6.0	6.0	5.9	5.8	5.8	5.7	5.8	5.8	5.8	5.9	5.9	6.0	6.0	6.0
2006	5.9	5.9	5.9	5.9	5.9	5.9	6.0	5.9	5.9	5.8	5.7	5.7	5.8	5.7	5.8	5.8	5.9	5.9	6.0	6.0
2007	5.9	5.8	5.8	5.8	5.9	5.9	6.0	5.9	5.8	5.7	5.7	5.7	5.7	5.7	5.7	5.8	5.8	5.9	5.9	5.9

Table C-3 (page 3 of 6)

Long-Term Corporate Bonds Total Returns

Rates of Return for all holding periods

Percent per annum compounded annually

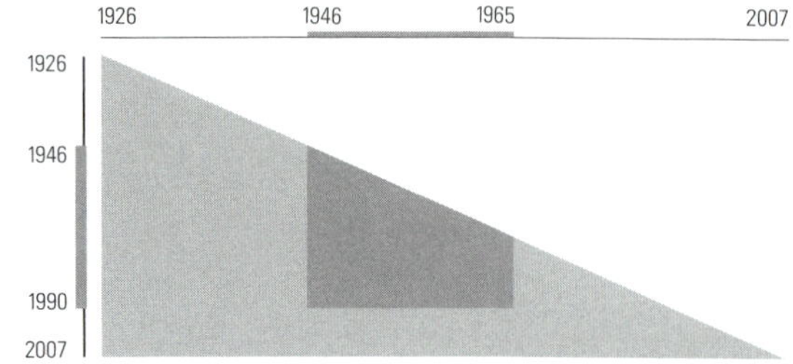

from 1926 to 2007

To the end of	From the beginning of 1946	1947	1948	1949	1950	1951	1952	1953	1954	1955	1956	1957	1958	1959	1960	1961	1962	1963	1964	1965
1946	1.7																			
1947	−0.3	−2.3																		
1948	1.1	0.8	4.1																	
1949	1.7	1.7	3.7	3.3																
1950	1.8	1.8	3.2	2.7	2.1															
1951	1.0	0.9	1.7	0.9	−0.3	−2.7														
1952	1.4	1.3	2.0	1.5	0.9	0.4	3.5													
1953	1.6	1.6	2.3	1.9	1.6	1.4	3.5	3.4												
1954	2.0	2.1	2.7	2.5	2.3	2.4	4.1	4.4	5.4											
1955	1.9	1.9	2.4	2.2	2.0	2.0	3.2	3.1	2.9	0.5										
1956	1.1	1.0	1.4	1.0	0.7	0.5	1.1	0.5	−0.4	−3.2	−6.8									
1957	1.7	1.7	2.1	1.8	1.7	1.6	2.3	2.1	1.8	0.6	0.7	8.7								
1958	1.4	1.3	1.7	1.4	1.2	1.1	1.7	1.4	1.0	−0.1	−0.3	3.1	−2.2							
1959	1.2	1.2	1.5	1.2	1.0	0.9	1.3	1.0	0.6	−0.3	−0.5	1.7	−1.6	−1.0						
1960	1.7	1.7	2.0	1.8	1.7	1.7	2.2	2.0	1.8	1.2	1.4	3.5	1.8	3.9	9.1					
1961	1.9	1.9	2.2	2.1	2.0	2.0	2.4	2.3	2.2	1.7	1.9	3.8	2.6	4.2	6.9	4.8				
1962	2.2	2.3	2.6	2.5	2.4	2.4	2.9	2.9	2.8	2.5	2.8	4.5	3.6	5.1	7.3	6.4	7.9			
1963	2.2	2.3	2.6	2.5	2.4	2.4	2.9	2.8	2.7	2.4	2.7	4.1	3.4	4.5	6.0	5.0	5.0	2.2		
1964	2.4	2.4	2.7	2.6	2.6	2.6	3.0	3.0	2.9	2.7	2.9	4.2	3.6	4.6	5.7	4.9	4.9	3.5	4.8	
1965	2.2	2.3	2.5	2.4	2.4	2.4	2.8	2.7	2.6	2.4	2.6	3.7	3.1	3.8	4.7	3.8	3.6	2.1	2.1	−0.5
1966	2.1	2.1	2.4	2.3	2.2	2.2	2.6	2.5	2.4	2.2	2.4	3.3	2.7	3.4	4.0	3.2	2.9	1.7	1.5	−0.1
1967	1.8	1.8	2.0	1.9	1.8	1.8	2.1	2.0	1.9	1.6	1.7	2.5	1.9	2.4	2.9	2.0	1.5	0.3	−0.2	−1.8
1968	1.8	1.8	2.0	1.9	1.9	1.8	2.1	2.0	1.9	1.7	1.8	2.5	2.0	2.4	2.8	2.1	1.7	0.7	0.4	−0.7
1969	1.4	1.4	1.6	1.4	1.3	1.3	1.5	1.4	1.3	1.0	1.1	1.7	1.1	1.4	1.7	0.9	0.4	−0.6	−1.1	−2.2
1970	2.0	2.0	2.2	2.1	2.1	2.1	2.3	2.3	2.2	2.0	2.1	2.8	2.4	2.7	3.1	2.5	2.3	1.6	1.5	0.9
1971	2.4	2.4	2.6	2.5	2.5	2.5	2.8	2.7	2.7	2.5	2.7	3.3	3.0	3.4	3.7	3.3	3.1	2.6	2.6	2.3
1972	2.5	2.6	2.8	2.7	2.7	2.7	3.0	2.9	2.9	2.8	2.9	3.6	3.2	3.6	4.0	3.6	3.5	3.0	3.1	2.9
1973	2.5	2.5	2.7	2.6	2.6	2.6	2.9	2.9	2.8	2.7	2.8	3.4	3.1	3.5	3.8	3.4	3.3	2.9	2.9	2.7
1974	2.3	2.3	2.5	2.4	2.4	2.4	2.6	2.6	2.5	2.4	2.5	3.1	2.7	3.0	3.3	2.9	2.8	2.4	2.4	2.1
1975	2.7	2.7	2.9	2.9	2.8	2.9	3.1	3.1	3.1	3.0	3.1	3.6	3.4	3.7	4.0	3.7	3.6	3.3	3.3	3.2
1976	3.2	3.2	3.4	3.4	3.4	3.4	3.7	3.7	3.7	3.6	3.8	4.3	4.1	4.5	4.8	4.5	4.5	4.3	4.4	4.4
1977	3.1	3.2	3.3	3.3	3.3	3.4	3.6	3.6	3.6	3.5	3.7	4.2	4.0	4.3	4.6	4.4	4.3	4.1	4.2	4.2
1978	3.0	3.1	3.2	3.2	3.2	3.2	3.5	3.5	3.5	3.4	3.5	4.0	3.8	4.1	4.4	4.1	4.1	3.8	4.0	3.9
1979	2.8	2.8	3.0	3.0	2.9	3.0	3.2	3.2	3.2	3.1	3.2	3.6	3.4	3.7	3.9	3.7	3.6	3.4	3.4	3.3
1980	2.6	2.7	2.8	2.8	2.8	2.8	3.0	3.0	2.9	2.8	2.9	3.4	3.1	3.4	3.6	3.3	3.3	3.0	3.1	2.9
1981	2.5	2.5	2.7	2.6	2.6	2.6	2.8	2.8	2.8	2.7	2.8	3.2	3.0	3.2	3.4	3.1	3.0	2.8	2.8	2.7
1982	3.4	3.5	3.7	3.6	3.7	3.7	3.9	3.9	3.9	3.9	4.0	4.5	4.3	4.6	4.8	4.6	4.6	4.5	4.6	4.6
1983	3.5	3.6	3.7	3.7	3.7	3.8	4.0	4.0	4.0	4.0	4.1	4.5	4.4	4.6	4.9	4.7	4.7	4.6	4.7	4.7
1984	3.8	3.9	4.1	4.1	4.1	4.1	4.4	4.4	4.4	4.4	4.5	5.0	4.8	5.1	5.3	5.2	5.2	5.1	5.2	5.2
1985	4.4	4.5	4.7	4.7	4.7	4.8	5.0	5.1	5.1	5.1	5.3	5.7	5.6	5.9	6.2	6.1	6.1	6.1	6.2	6.3
1986	4.8	4.9	5.0	5.1	5.1	5.2	5.4	5.5	5.6	5.6	5.7	6.2	6.1	6.4	6.7	6.6	6.7	6.6	6.8	6.9
1987	4.7	4.7	4.9	4.9	5.0	5.0	5.3	5.3	5.4	5.4	5.5	6.0	5.9	6.2	6.4	6.3	6.4	6.3	6.5	6.6
1988	4.8	4.9	5.0	5.1	5.1	5.2	5.4	5.5	5.5	5.5	5.7	6.1	6.0	6.3	6.6	6.5	6.5	6.5	6.7	6.7
1989	5.0	5.1	5.3	5.3	5.4	5.5	5.7	5.7	5.8	5.8	6.0	6.4	6.3	6.6	6.9	6.8	6.9	6.8	7.0	7.1
1990	5.1	5.2	5.3	5.4	5.4	5.5	5.7	5.8	5.8	5.8	6.0	6.4	6.3	6.6	6.9	6.8	6.9	6.8	7.0	7.1

Table C-3 (page 4 of 6)

Long-Term Corporate Bonds Total Returns

Rates of Return for all holding periods
Percent per annum compounded annually

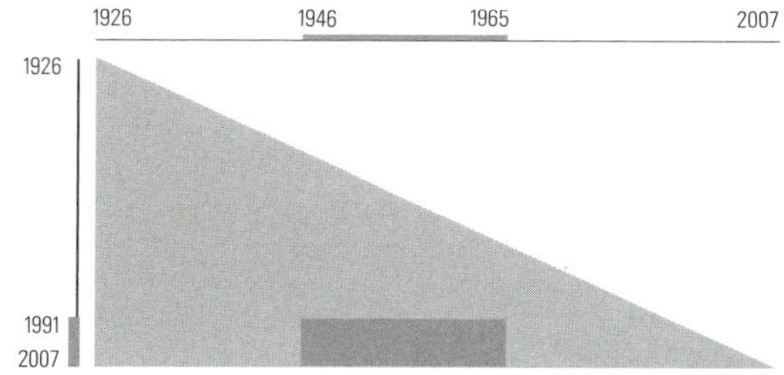

from 1926 to 2007

To the end of	From the beginning of 1946	1947	1948	1949	1950	1951	1952	1953	1954	1955	1956	1957	1958	1959	1960	1961	1962	1963	1964	1965
1991	5.4	5.5	5.6	5.7	5.7	5.8	6.0	6.1	6.2	6.2	6.4	6.8	6.7	7.0	7.3	7.2	7.3	7.3	7.4	7.5
1992	5.5	5.5	5.7	5.8	5.8	5.9	6.1	6.2	6.3	6.3	6.5	6.8	6.8	7.1	7.3	7.3	7.3	7.3	7.5	7.6
1993	5.6	5.7	5.9	5.9	6.0	6.1	6.3	6.4	6.4	6.5	6.6	7.0	7.0	7.2	7.5	7.4	7.5	7.5	7.7	7.8
1994	5.4	5.4	5.6	5.7	5.7	5.8	6.0	6.1	6.1	6.1	6.3	6.7	6.6	6.9	7.1	7.0	7.1	7.1	7.2	7.3
1995	5.8	5.9	6.0	6.1	6.1	6.2	6.4	6.5	6.6	6.6	6.8	7.1	7.1	7.4	7.6	7.6	7.6	7.6	7.8	7.9
1996	5.7	5.8	5.9	6.0	6.0	6.1	6.3	6.4	6.5	6.5	6.6	7.0	6.9	7.2	7.4	7.4	7.5	7.4	7.6	7.7
1997	5.8	5.9	6.1	6.1	6.2	6.3	6.5	6.5	6.6	6.6	6.8	7.1	7.1	7.3	7.6	7.5	7.6	7.6	7.8	7.9
1998	5.9	6.0	6.2	6.2	6.3	6.3	6.5	6.6	6.7	6.7	6.9	7.2	7.2	7.4	7.7	7.6	7.7	7.7	7.8	7.9
1999	5.6	5.7	5.9	5.9	6.0	6.0	6.2	6.3	6.4	6.4	6.5	6.9	6.8	7.0	7.2	7.2	7.3	7.2	7.4	7.5
2000	5.8	5.8	6.0	6.0	6.1	6.2	6.4	6.4	6.5	6.5	6.7	7.0	6.9	7.2	7.4	7.3	7.4	7.4	7.5	7.6
2001	5.9	5.9	6.1	6.1	6.2	6.3	6.5	6.5	6.6	6.6	6.7	7.1	7.0	7.3	7.5	7.4	7.5	7.5	7.6	7.7
2002	6.0	6.1	6.3	6.3	6.4	6.4	6.6	6.7	6.8	6.8	6.9	7.3	7.2	7.4	7.7	7.6	7.7	7.7	7.8	7.9
2003	6.0	6.1	6.3	6.3	6.3	6.4	6.6	6.7	6.7	6.8	6.9	7.2	7.2	7.4	7.6	7.6	7.6	7.6	7.8	7.8
2004	6.1	6.1	6.3	6.3	6.4	6.5	6.7	6.7	6.8	6.8	6.9	7.2	7.2	7.4	7.6	7.6	7.7	7.6	7.8	7.9
2005	6.1	6.1	6.3	6.3	6.4	6.5	6.6	6.7	6.8	6.8	6.9	7.2	7.2	7.4	7.6	7.6	7.6	7.6	7.7	7.8
2006	6.0	6.1	6.2	6.3	6.3	6.4	6.6	6.6	6.7	6.7	6.8	7.1	7.1	7.3	7.5	7.5	7.5	7.5	7.6	7.7
2007	6.0	6.0	6.2	6.2	6.3	6.3	6.5	6.6	6.6	6.6	6.8	7.0	7.0	7.2	7.4	7.4	7.4	7.4	7.5	7.6

Table C-3 (page 5 of 6)

Long-Term Corporate Bonds Total Returns

Rates of Return for all holding periods

Percent per annum compounded annually

from 1926 to 2007

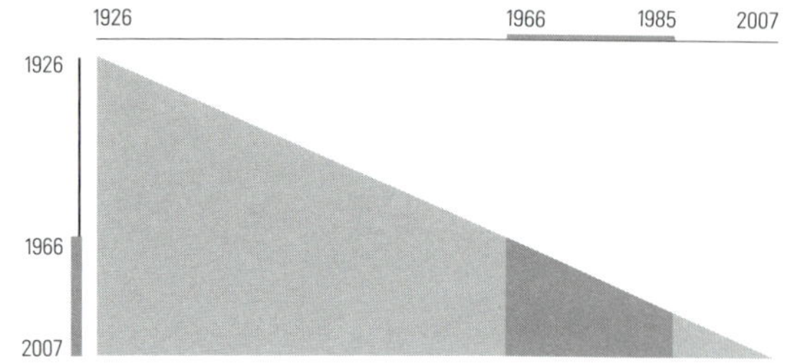

To the end of	From the beginning of 1966	1967	1968	1969	1970	1971	1972	1973	1974	1975	1976	1977	1978	1979	1980	1981	1982	1983	1984	1985
1966	0.2																			
1967	−2.4	−5.0																		
1968	−0.8	−1.3	2.6																	
1969	−2.7	−3.6	−2.9	−8.1																
1970	1.2	1.5	3.7	4.3	18.4															
1971	2.8	3.3	5.5	6.5	14.6	11.0														
1972	3.4	4.0	5.8	6.7	12.1	9.1	7.3													
1973	3.1	3.6	5.0	5.6	9.3	6.4	4.2	1.1												
1974	2.4	2.7	3.9	4.1	6.7	3.9	1.7	−1.0	−3.1											
1975	3.6	4.0	5.1	5.5	8.0	6.0	4.8	4.0	5.4	14.6										
1976	4.9	5.4	6.6	7.1	9.4	8.0	7.4	7.5	9.7	16.6	18.6									
1977	4.6	5.0	6.1	6.5	8.4	7.1	6.4	6.3	7.6	11.4	9.9	1.7								
1978	4.2	4.6	5.5	5.8	7.5	6.2	5.5	5.2	6.0	8.4	6.4	0.8	−0.1							
1979	3.6	3.9	4.7	4.8	6.2	5.0	4.2	3.8	4.3	5.8	3.7	−0.9	−2.1	−4.2						
1980	3.2	3.4	4.1	4.2	5.4	4.2	3.4	3.0	3.2	4.3	2.4	−1.4	−2.4	−3.5	−2.8					
1981	2.9	3.1	3.7	3.8	4.8	3.7	3.0	2.5	2.7	3.5	1.8	−1.3	−2.1	−2.7	−2.0	−1.2				
1982	4.9	5.2	5.9	6.1	7.3	6.5	6.0	5.9	6.5	7.7	6.8	4.9	5.6	7.0	11.0	18.7	42.6			
1983	5.0	5.2	5.9	6.1	7.2	6.4	6.1	6.0	6.4	7.6	6.7	5.1	5.7	6.9	9.8	14.4	23.1	6.3		
1984	5.6	5.9	6.5	6.8	7.9	7.1	6.9	6.8	7.4	8.5	7.8	6.5	7.2	8.5	11.2	15.0	21.0	11.4	16.9	
1985	6.7	7.0	7.7	8.0	9.1	8.5	8.4	8.5	9.1	10.3	9.8	8.9	9.8	11.3	14.1	17.9	23.2	17.3	23.3	30.1
1986	7.3	7.6	8.3	8.7	9.7	9.2	9.1	9.2	9.9	11.0	10.7	9.9	10.9	12.4	14.9	18.2	22.5	18.0	22.1	24.9
1987	6.9	7.2	7.9	8.2	9.2	8.6	8.5	8.6	9.1	10.1	9.8	9.0	9.7	10.9	12.9	15.4	18.4	14.1	16.1	15.9
1988	7.1	7.4	8.0	8.3	9.2	8.7	8.6	8.7	9.2	10.2	9.8	9.1	9.8	10.9	12.7	14.8	17.3	13.5	15.0	14.5
1989	7.4	7.8	8.4	8.7	9.6	9.1	9.0	9.1	9.7	10.6	10.3	9.7	10.3	11.3	13.0	14.9	17.1	13.9	15.2	14.9
1990	7.4	7.7	8.3	8.6	9.4	9.0	8.9	9.0	9.5	10.3	10.0	9.4	10.1	11.0	12.4	14.1	15.9	13.0	14.0	13.5
1991	7.9	8.2	8.8	9.0	9.9	9.5	9.4	9.5	10.0	10.9	10.6	10.1	10.7	11.6	13.0	14.6	16.3	13.7	14.7	14.4
1992	7.9	8.2	8.8	9.1	9.9	9.5	9.4	9.5	10.0	10.8	10.6	10.1	10.6	11.5	12.8	14.2	15.7	13.3	14.1	13.7
1993	8.1	8.4	9.0	9.2	10.0	9.7	9.6	9.7	10.2	10.9	10.7	10.2	10.8	11.6	12.8	14.1	15.5	13.3	14.0	13.7
1994	7.6	7.9	8.4	8.6	9.3	9.0	8.9	9.0	9.3	10.0	9.8	9.3	9.8	10.4	11.4	12.5	13.7	11.5	12.0	11.6
1995	8.2	8.5	9.0	9.2	10.0	9.6	9.6	9.7	10.1	10.8	10.6	10.2	10.7	11.3	12.4	13.5	14.6	12.7	13.2	12.9
1996	8.0	8.2	8.7	9.0	9.6	9.3	9.2	9.3	9.7	10.3	10.1	9.7	10.1	10.7	11.7	12.7	13.7	11.8	12.3	11.9
1997	8.1	8.4	8.9	9.1	9.8	9.4	9.4	9.5	9.8	10.4	10.2	9.9	10.3	10.9	11.8	12.7	13.6	11.9	12.3	12.0
1998	8.2	8.5	8.9	9.1	9.8	9.5	9.4	9.5	9.9	10.4	10.3	9.9	10.3	10.9	11.7	12.6	13.4	11.8	12.2	11.9
1999	7.7	7.9	8.4	8.6	9.2	8.9	8.8	8.8	9.2	9.7	9.5	9.1	9.4	9.9	10.7	11.4	12.2	10.6	10.9	10.5
2000	7.8	8.1	8.5	8.7	9.3	9.0	8.9	9.0	9.3	9.8	9.6	9.2	9.6	10.0	10.8	11.5	12.2	10.7	11.0	10.6
2001	7.9	8.2	8.6	8.8	9.3	9.0	9.0	9.0	9.3	9.8	9.6	9.3	9.6	10.1	10.8	11.5	12.1	10.7	11.0	10.6
2002	8.1	8.4	8.8	9.0	9.5	9.3	9.2	9.3	9.6	10.1	9.9	9.6	9.9	10.3	11.0	11.7	12.3	11.0	11.2	10.9
2003	8.1	8.3	8.7	8.9	9.4	9.1	9.1	9.1	9.4	9.9	9.7	9.4	9.7	10.1	10.8	11.4	12.0	10.7	10.9	10.6
2004	8.1	8.3	8.7	8.9	9.4	9.1	9.1	9.1	9.4	9.8	9.7	9.4	9.7	10.1	10.7	11.3	11.8	10.6	10.8	10.5
2005	8.0	8.2	8.6	8.8	9.3	9.0	9.0	9.0	9.3	9.7	9.6	9.3	9.5	9.9	10.5	11.0	11.6	10.4	10.6	10.3
2006	7.9	8.1	8.5	8.6	9.1	8.9	8.8	8.9	9.1	9.5	9.3	9.0	9.3	9.7	10.2	10.7	11.2	10.1	10.3	10.0
2007	7.8	8.0	8.3	8.5	8.9	8.7	8.6	8.7	8.9	9.3	9.1	8.8	9.1	9.4	9.9	10.4	10.9	9.8	9.9	9.7

Table C-3 (page 6 of 6)-a

Long-Term Corporate Bonds Total Returns

Rates of Return for all holding periods
Percent per annum compounded annually

from 1926 to 2007

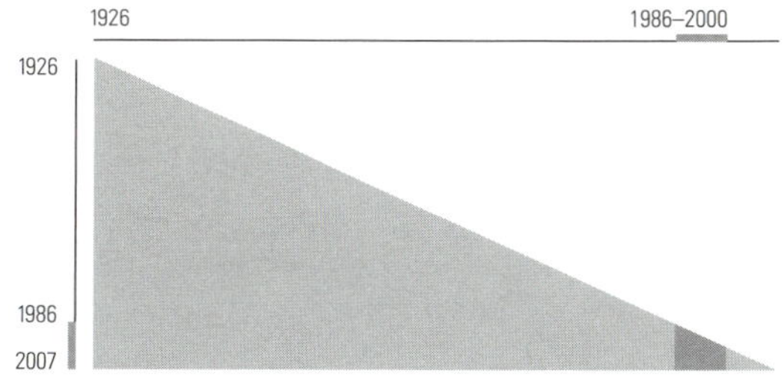

To the end of	From the beginning of 1986	1987	1988	1989	1990	1991	1992	1993	1994	1995	1996	1997	1998	1999	2000
1986	19.8														
1987	9.3	–0.3													
1988	9.8	5.1	10.7												
1989	11.4	8.7	13.4	16.2											
1990	10.4	8.2	11.2	11.4	6.8										
1991	12.0	10.4	13.3	14.2	13.1	19.9									
1992	11.6	10.3	12.5	13.0	11.9	14.5	9.4								
1993	11.8	10.7	12.6	13.0	12.2	14.1	11.3	13.2							
1994	9.7	8.5	9.8	9.6	8.4	8.8	5.3	3.3	–5.8						
1995	11.3	10.4	11.8	12.0	11.3	12.2	10.4	10.7	9.5	27.2					
1996	10.4	9.5	10.6	10.6	9.8	10.3	8.5	8.3	6.7	13.6	1.4				
1997	10.6	9.8	10.8	10.9	10.2	10.7	9.2	9.2	8.2	13.4	7.0	12.9			
1998	10.6	9.9	10.8	10.9	10.3	10.7	9.5	9.5	8.7	12.7	8.3	11.8	10.8		
1999	9.2	8.4	9.2	9.0	8.4	8.5	7.2	6.9	5.9	8.4	4.1	5.0	1.2	–7.4	
2000	9.4	8.7	9.5	9.4	8.8	9.0	7.8	7.6	6.8	9.1	5.8	6.9	5.0	2.2	12.9
2001	9.5	8.9	9.5	9.5	8.9	9.1	8.1	7.9	7.3	9.3	6.6	7.7	6.4	4.9	11.8
2002	9.9	9.3	10.0	9.9	9.5	9.7	8.8	8.8	8.3	10.2	7.9	9.1	8.3	7.7	13.3
2003	9.6	9.1	9.7	9.6	9.2	9.3	8.5	8.4	8.0	9.6	7.6	8.5	7.8	7.2	11.2
2004	9.6	9.1	9.6	9.6	9.1	9.3	8.5	8.5	8.0	9.5	7.7	8.5	7.9	7.4	10.7
2005	9.4	8.9	9.4	9.3	8.9	9.1	8.3	8.3	7.9	9.2	7.5	8.2	7.7	7.2	9.9
2006	9.1	8.6	9.1	9.0	8.6	8.7	8.0	7.9	7.5	8.7	7.1	7.7	7.2	6.7	8.9
2007	8.8	8.3	8.7	8.6	8.2	8.3	7.6	7.5	7.1	8.2	6.7	7.2	6.7	6.3	8.1

Table C-3 (page 6 of 6)-b

Long-Term Corporate Bonds Total Returns

Rates of Return for all holding periods
Percent per annum compounded annually

from 1926 to 2007

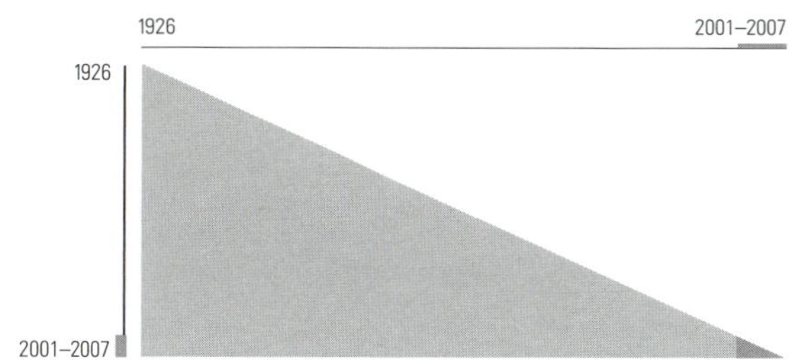

To the end of	From the beginning of 2001	2002	2003	2004	2005	2006	2007
2001	10.6						
2002	13.5	16.3					
2003	10.7	10.7	5.3				
2004	10.2	10.0	7.0	8.7			
2005	9.3	9.0	6.6	7.3	5.9		
2006	8.3	7.8	5.8	5.9	4.5	3.2	
2007	7.4	6.9	5.1	5.1	3.9	2.9	2.6

Table C-4 (page 1 of 6)

Long-Term Government Bonds Total Returns

Rates of Return for all holding periods

Percent per annum compounded annually

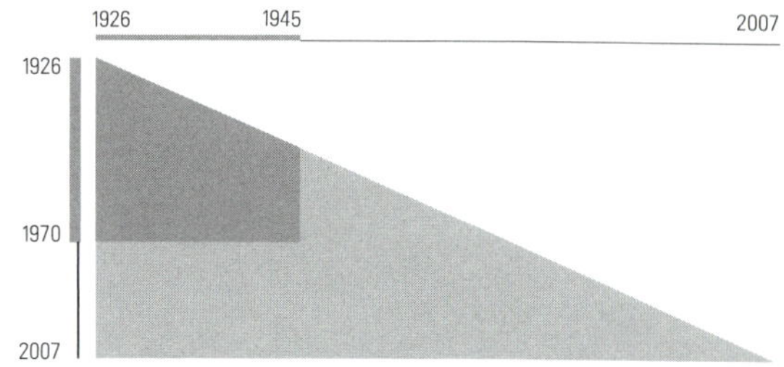

from 1926 to 2007

To the end of	From the beginning of 1926	1927	1928	1929	1930	1931	1932	1933	1934	1935	1936	1937	1938	1939	1940	1941	1942	1943	1944	1945
1926	7.8																			
1927	8.3	8.9																		
1928	5.5	4.4	0.1																	
1929	5.0	4.1	1.7	3.4																
1930	4.9	4.2	2.7	4.0	4.7															
1931	3.1	2.2	0.6	0.8	–0.5	–5.3														
1932	5.0	4.5	3.7	4.6	5.0	5.2	16.8													
1933	4.4	3.9	3.1	3.7	3.7	3.4	8.1	–0.1												
1934	5.0	4.6	4.0	4.7	4.9	5.0	8.7	4.9	10.0											
1935	5.0	4.7	4.1	4.7	5.0	5.0	7.8	4.9	7.5	5.0										
1936	5.2	4.9	4.5	5.1	5.3	5.4	7.7	5.5	7.5	6.2	7.5									
1937	4.8	4.5	4.1	4.5	4.7	4.7	6.4	4.5	5.6	4.2	3.8	0.2								
1938	4.8	4.6	4.2	4.6	4.8	4.8	6.3	4.6	5.6	4.5	4.4	2.8	5.5							
1939	4.9	4.7	4.4	4.7	4.9	4.9	6.3	4.8	5.7	4.8	4.8	3.9	5.7	5.9						
1940	5.0	4.8	4.5	4.9	5.0	5.0	6.2	5.0	5.7	5.0	5.0	4.4	5.9	6.0	6.1					
1941	4.7	4.5	4.2	4.5	4.6	4.6	5.7	4.5	5.1	4.4	4.3	3.7	4.6	4.3	3.5	0.9				
1942	4.6	4.5	4.2	4.5	4.5	4.5	5.5	4.4	4.9	4.3	4.2	3.6	4.3	4.0	3.4	2.1	3.2			
1943	4.5	4.3	4.0	4.3	4.4	4.3	5.2	4.2	4.6	4.0	3.9	3.4	3.9	3.6	3.1	2.1	2.6	2.1		
1944	4.4	4.2	4.0	4.2	4.3	4.2	5.0	4.1	4.5	3.9	3.8	3.3	3.8	3.5	3.0	2.3	2.7	2.4	2.8	
1945	4.7	4.6	4.3	4.6	4.6	4.6	5.4	4.6	5.0	4.5	4.5	4.1	4.6	4.5	4.3	3.9	4.7	5.1	6.7	10.7
1946	4.5	4.3	4.1	4.3	4.4	4.3	5.0	4.2	4.6	4.1	4.0	3.7	4.1	3.9	3.6	3.2	3.7	3.8	4.4	5.2
1947	4.1	4.0	3.7	3.9	4.0	3.9	4.5	3.8	4.0	3.6	3.5	3.1	3.4	3.2	2.8	2.4	2.6	2.5	2.6	2.5
1948	4.1	4.0	3.7	3.9	3.9	3.9	4.5	3.7	4.0	3.6	3.5	3.1	3.4	3.2	2.9	2.5	2.7	2.6	2.7	2.7
1949	4.2	4.1	3.8	4.0	4.1	4.0	4.6	3.9	4.1	3.8	3.7	3.4	3.7	3.5	3.2	2.9	3.2	3.2	3.4	3.5
1950	4.0	3.9	3.7	3.8	3.9	3.8	4.3	3.7	3.9	3.5	3.4	3.1	3.4	3.2	2.9	2.6	2.8	2.8	2.9	2.9
1951	3.7	3.6	3.3	3.5	3.5	3.4	3.9	3.3	3.4	3.1	3.0	2.7	2.8	2.6	2.4	2.0	2.1	2.0	2.0	1.9
1952	3.6	3.5	3.3	3.4	3.4	3.3	3.8	3.2	3.3	3.0	2.8	2.6	2.7	2.5	2.3	1.9	2.0	1.9	1.9	1.8
1953	3.6	3.5	3.3	3.4	3.4	3.3	3.8	3.2	3.3	3.0	2.9	2.6	2.8	2.6	2.4	2.1	2.2	2.1	2.1	2.0
1954	3.7	3.6	3.4	3.5	3.6	3.5	3.9	3.4	3.5	3.2	3.1	2.9	3.0	2.9	2.7	2.4	2.6	2.5	2.5	2.5
1955	3.6	3.4	3.2	3.4	3.4	3.3	3.7	3.1	3.3	3.0	2.9	2.6	2.8	2.6	2.4	2.2	2.3	2.2	2.2	2.2
1956	3.3	3.1	2.9	3.0	3.0	3.0	3.3	2.8	2.9	2.6	2.5	2.2	2.3	2.2	1.9	1.7	1.7	1.6	1.6	1.5
1957	3.4	3.3	3.1	3.2	3.2	3.1	3.5	3.0	3.1	2.8	2.7	2.5	2.6	2.4	2.2	2.0	2.1	2.0	2.0	1.9
1958	3.1	3.0	2.8	2.9	2.8	2.8	3.1	2.6	2.7	2.4	2.3	2.1	2.1	2.0	1.8	1.5	1.6	1.5	1.4	1.3
1959	2.9	2.8	2.6	2.7	2.7	2.6	2.9	2.4	2.5	2.2	2.1	1.9	1.9	1.8	1.6	1.3	1.4	1.3	1.2	1.1
1960	3.2	3.1	2.9	3.0	3.0	2.9	3.2	2.8	2.9	2.6	2.5	2.3	2.4	2.3	2.1	1.9	2.0	1.9	1.9	1.8
1961	3.2	3.0	2.9	3.0	2.9	2.9	3.2	2.7	2.8	2.6	2.5	2.3	2.4	2.2	2.1	1.9	1.9	1.9	1.8	1.8
1962	3.3	3.1	3.0	3.1	3.1	3.0	3.3	2.9	3.0	2.7	2.6	2.5	2.5	2.4	2.3	2.1	2.2	2.1	2.1	2.1
1963	3.2	3.1	2.9	3.0	3.0	3.0	3.2	2.8	2.9	2.7	2.6	2.4	2.5	2.4	2.2	2.1	2.1	2.1	2.1	2.0
1964	3.2	3.1	2.9	3.0	3.0	3.0	3.2	2.8	2.9	2.7	2.6	2.4	2.5	2.4	2.3	2.1	2.2	2.1	2.1	2.1
1965	3.2	3.0	2.9	3.0	3.0	2.9	3.2	2.8	2.9	2.6	2.6	2.4	2.5	2.4	2.2	2.1	2.1	2.1	2.1	2.0
1966	3.2	3.1	2.9	3.0	3.0	2.9	3.2	2.8	2.9	2.7	2.6	2.4	2.5	2.4	2.3	2.1	2.2	2.1	2.1	2.1
1967	2.9	2.7	2.6	2.7	2.6	2.6	2.8	2.4	2.5	2.3	2.2	2.0	2.1	2.0	1.8	1.7	1.7	1.7	1.6	1.6
1968	2.8	2.7	2.5	2.6	2.6	2.5	2.7	2.4	2.4	2.2	2.1	2.0	2.0	1.9	1.8	1.6	1.6	1.6	1.6	1.5
1969	2.6	2.5	2.3	2.4	2.4	2.3	2.5	2.1	2.2	2.0	1.9	1.7	1.8	1.7	1.5	1.4	1.4	1.3	1.3	1.2
1970	2.8	2.7	2.5	2.6	2.6	2.5	2.7	2.4	2.5	2.3	2.2	2.0	2.1	2.0	1.9	1.7	1.7	1.7	1.7	1.6

Table C-4 (page 2 of 6)

Long-Term Government Bonds Total Returns

Rates of Return for all holding periods

Percent per annum compounded annually

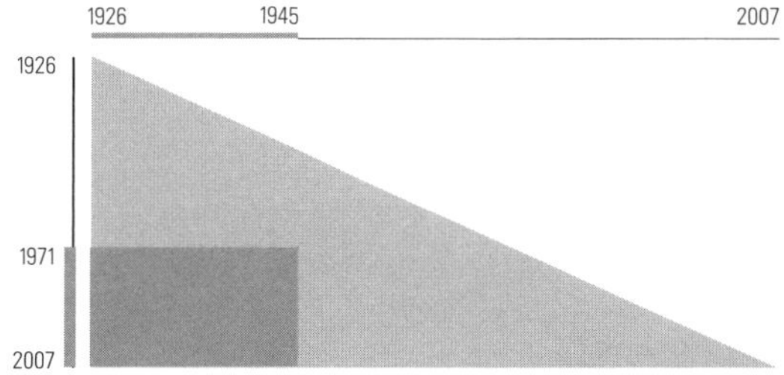

from 1926 to 2007

To the end of	From the beginning of 1926	1927	1928	1929	1930	1931	1932	1933	1934	1935	1936	1937	1938	1939	1940	1941	1942	1943	1944	1945
1971	3.0	2.9	2.8	2.8	2.8	2.8	3.0	2.7	2.7	2.5	2.5	2.3	2.4	2.3	2.2	2.1	2.1	2.1	2.1	2.0
1972	3.1	3.0	2.8	2.9	2.9	2.8	3.1	2.7	2.8	2.6	2.6	2.4	2.5	2.4	2.3	2.2	2.2	2.2	2.2	2.2
1973	3.0	2.9	2.8	2.8	2.8	2.8	3.0	2.6	2.7	2.5	2.5	2.3	2.4	2.3	2.2	2.1	2.1	2.1	2.1	2.1
1974	3.0	2.9	2.8	2.8	2.8	2.8	3.0	2.7	2.7	2.6	2.5	2.4	2.4	2.4	2.3	2.1	2.2	2.2	2.2	2.1
1975	3.1	3.0	2.9	3.0	3.0	2.9	3.1	2.8	2.9	2.7	2.7	2.6	2.6	2.5	2.4	2.3	2.4	2.4	2.4	2.4
1976	3.4	3.3	3.2	3.2	3.2	3.2	3.4	3.1	3.2	3.0	3.0	2.9	3.0	2.9	2.8	2.7	2.8	2.8	2.8	2.8
1977	3.3	3.2	3.1	3.2	3.2	3.1	3.3	3.0	3.1	3.0	2.9	2.8	2.9	2.8	2.7	2.6	2.7	2.7	2.7	2.7
1978	3.2	3.1	3.0	3.1	3.1	3.0	3.2	2.9	3.0	2.9	2.8	2.7	2.8	2.7	2.6	2.5	2.6	2.5	2.6	2.6
1979	3.1	3.0	2.9	3.0	3.0	2.9	3.1	2.9	2.9	2.8	2.7	2.6	2.7	2.6	2.5	2.4	2.5	2.4	2.5	2.4
1980	3.0	2.9	2.8	2.9	2.8	2.8	3.0	2.7	2.8	2.6	2.6	2.5	2.5	2.4	2.3	2.3	2.3	2.3	2.3	2.3
1981	3.0	2.9	2.8	2.8	2.8	2.8	3.0	2.7	2.7	2.6	2.5	2.4	2.5	2.4	2.3	2.2	2.3	2.3	2.3	2.2
1982	3.5	3.5	3.4	3.4	3.4	3.4	3.6	3.3	3.4	3.3	3.2	3.1	3.2	3.2	3.1	3.0	3.1	3.1	3.1	3.1
1983	3.5	3.4	3.3	3.4	3.4	3.4	3.5	3.3	3.3	3.2	3.2	3.1	3.2	3.1	3.0	3.0	3.0	3.0	3.0	3.0
1984	3.7	3.6	3.5	3.6	3.6	3.6	3.7	3.5	3.6	3.4	3.4	3.3	3.4	3.4	3.3	3.2	3.3	3.3	3.3	3.3
1985	4.1	4.0	3.9	4.0	4.0	4.0	4.2	4.0	4.0	3.9	3.9	3.8	3.9	3.9	3.8	3.8	3.8	3.9	3.9	3.9
1986	4.4	4.3	4.3	4.3	4.3	4.3	4.5	4.3	4.4	4.3	4.3	4.2	4.3	4.3	4.2	4.2	4.3	4.3	4.3	4.4
1987	4.3	4.2	4.1	4.2	4.2	4.2	4.4	4.2	4.3	4.2	4.1	4.1	4.2	4.1	4.1	4.0	4.1	4.1	4.2	4.2
1988	4.4	4.3	4.2	4.3	4.3	4.3	4.5	4.3	4.4	4.3	4.2	4.2	4.3	4.2	4.2	4.2	4.2	4.2	4.3	4.3
1989	4.6	4.5	4.4	4.5	4.5	4.5	4.7	4.5	4.6	4.5	4.5	4.4	4.5	4.5	4.5	4.4	4.5	4.5	4.6	4.6
1990	4.6	4.5	4.5	4.5	4.6	4.6	4.7	4.5	4.6	4.5	4.5	4.5	4.5	4.5	4.5	4.5	4.5	4.6	4.6	4.7
1991	4.8	4.7	4.7	4.8	4.8	4.8	5.0	4.8	4.9	4.8	4.8	4.7	4.8	4.8	4.8	4.7	4.8	4.8	4.9	4.9
1992	4.8	4.8	4.7	4.8	4.8	4.8	5.0	4.8	4.9	4.8	4.8	4.8	4.9	4.8	4.8	4.8	4.9	4.9	5.0	5.0
1993	5.0	5.0	4.9	5.0	5.0	5.0	5.2	5.0	5.1	5.0	5.0	5.0	5.1	5.1	5.1	5.0	5.1	5.2	5.2	5.3
1994	4.8	4.8	4.7	4.8	4.8	4.8	5.0	4.8	4.9	4.8	4.8	4.8	4.8	4.8	4.8	4.8	4.9	4.9	4.9	5.0
1995	5.2	5.1	5.1	5.2	5.2	5.2	5.4	5.2	5.3	5.2	5.2	5.2	5.3	5.2	5.2	5.2	5.3	5.3	5.4	5.5
1996	5.1	5.0	5.0	5.1	5.1	5.1	5.3	5.1	5.2	5.1	5.1	5.1	5.1	5.1	5.1	5.1	5.2	5.2	5.3	5.3
1997	5.2	5.2	5.1	5.2	5.2	5.2	5.4	5.2	5.3	5.3	5.3	5.2	5.3	5.3	5.3	5.3	5.4	5.4	5.5	5.5
1998	5.3	5.3	5.2	5.3	5.3	5.4	5.5	5.4	5.4	5.4	5.4	5.3	5.4	5.4	5.4	5.4	5.5	5.5	5.6	5.7
1999	5.1	5.1	5.0	5.1	5.1	5.1	5.3	5.1	5.2	5.1	5.1	5.1	5.2	5.2	5.2	5.2	5.2	5.3	5.3	5.4
2000	5.3	5.3	5.2	5.3	5.3	5.4	5.5	5.4	5.4	5.4	5.4	5.3	5.4	5.4	5.4	5.4	5.5	5.5	5.6	5.6
2001	5.3	5.3	5.2	5.3	5.3	5.3	5.5	5.3	5.4	5.3	5.4	5.3	5.4	5.4	5.4	5.4	5.5	5.5	5.6	5.6
2002	5.5	5.4	5.4	5.5	5.5	5.5	5.7	5.5	5.6	5.5	5.5	5.5	5.6	5.6	5.6	5.6	5.6	5.7	5.7	5.8
2003	5.4	5.4	5.3	5.4	5.4	5.4	5.6	5.4	5.5	5.5	5.5	5.4	5.5	5.5	5.5	5.5	5.6	5.6	5.7	5.7
2004	5.4	5.4	5.4	5.4	5.5	5.5	5.6	5.5	5.6	5.5	5.5	5.5	5.6	5.6	5.6	5.5	5.6	5.7	5.7	5.8
2005	5.5	5.4	5.4	5.5	5.5	5.5	5.7	5.5	5.6	5.5	5.5	5.5	5.6	5.6	5.6	5.6	5.7	5.7	5.8	5.8
2006	5.4	5.4	5.3	5.4	5.4	5.4	5.6	5.5	5.5	5.5	5.5	5.5	5.5	5.5	5.5	5.5	5.6	5.6	5.7	5.7
2007	5.5	5.4	5.4	5.5	5.5	5.5	5.7	5.5	5.6	5.5	5.5	5.5	5.6	5.6	5.6	5.6	5.6	5.7	5.7	5.8

Table C-4 (page 3 of 6)

Long-Term Government Bonds Total Returns

Rates of Return for all holding periods

Percent per annum compounded annually

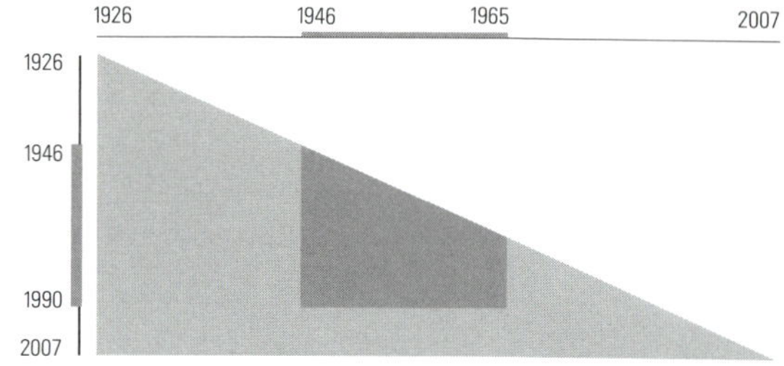

from 1926 to 2007

To the end of	From the beginning of 1946	1947	1948	1949	1950	1951	1952	1953	1954	1955	1956	1957	1958	1959	1960	1961	1962	1963	1964	1965
1946	−0.1																			
1947	−1.4	−2.6																		
1948	0.2	0.3	3.4																	
1949	1.7	2.3	4.9	6.4																
1950	1.4	1.8	3.3	3.2	0.1															
1951	0.5	0.6	1.4	0.8	−2.0	−3.9														
1952	0.6	0.7	1.4	0.9	−0.9	−1.4	1.2													
1953	1.0	1.1	1.7	1.4	0.2	0.2	2.4	3.6												
1954	1.6	1.8	2.5	2.4	1.6	1.9	4.0	5.4	7.2											
1955	1.3	1.5	2.0	1.8	1.1	1.3	2.6	3.1	2.9	−1.3										
1956	0.7	0.8	1.1	0.9	0.1	0.1	0.9	0.9	0.0	−3.5	−5.6									
1957	1.2	1.4	1.8	1.6	1.0	1.1	2.0	2.2	1.8	0.0	0.7	7.5								
1958	0.6	0.7	1.0	0.8	0.2	0.2	0.8	0.7	0.2	−1.5	−1.6	0.5	−6.1							
1959	0.4	0.5	0.7	0.5	−0.1	−0.1	0.4	0.3	−0.2	−1.7	−1.8	−0.5	−4.2	−2.3						
1960	1.3	1.4	1.7	1.5	1.1	1.2	1.8	1.9	1.6	0.7	1.2	2.9	1.5	5.5	13.8					
1961	1.3	1.3	1.6	1.5	1.1	1.2	1.7	1.8	1.6	0.8	1.1	2.5	1.3	3.9	7.2	1.0				
1962	1.6	1.7	2.0	1.9	1.5	1.7	2.2	2.3	2.1	1.5	1.9	3.2	2.4	4.7	7.1	3.9	6.9			
1963	1.6	1.7	1.9	1.8	1.5	1.6	2.1	2.2	2.0	1.5	1.8	3.0	2.2	4.0	5.6	3.0	4.0	1.2		
1964	1.7	1.8	2.0	1.9	1.6	1.8	2.2	2.3	2.2	1.7	2.0	3.0	2.4	3.9	5.2	3.1	3.8	2.4	3.5	
1965	1.6	1.7	2.0	1.9	1.6	1.7	2.1	2.2	2.1	1.6	1.9	2.8	2.2	3.4	4.4	2.6	3.1	1.8	2.1	0.7
1966	1.7	1.8	2.0	2.0	1.7	1.8	2.2	2.3	2.2	1.8	2.1	2.9	2.4	3.5	4.3	2.8	3.2	2.3	2.6	2.2
1967	1.2	1.2	1.4	1.3	1.1	1.1	1.5	1.5	1.3	0.9	1.1	1.7	1.1	2.0	2.5	1.0	1.0	−0.1	−0.5	−1.8
1968	1.1	1.2	1.4	1.3	1.0	1.1	1.4	1.4	1.2	0.8	1.0	1.5	1.0	1.7	2.2	0.8	0.8	−0.2	−0.4	−1.4
1969	0.9	0.9	1.1	1.0	0.7	0.7	1.0	1.0	0.8	0.4	0.5	1.0	0.5	1.1	1.4	0.2	0.1	−0.9	−1.2	−2.1
1970	1.3	1.3	1.5	1.4	1.2	1.3	1.5	1.6	1.4	1.1	1.3	1.8	1.3	2.0	2.4	1.3	1.3	0.7	0.6	0.1
1971	1.7	1.8	2.0	1.9	1.7	1.8	2.1	2.1	2.1	1.8	2.0	2.5	2.1	2.8	3.2	2.3	2.5	2.0	2.1	1.9
1972	1.9	1.9	2.1	2.1	1.9	2.0	2.3	2.3	2.3	2.0	2.2	2.7	2.4	3.0	3.4	2.6	2.8	2.4	2.5	2.3
1973	1.8	1.8	2.0	1.9	1.8	1.8	2.1	2.2	2.1	1.8	2.0	2.5	2.2	2.7	3.1	2.3	2.4	2.0	2.1	2.0
1974	1.8	1.9	2.1	2.0	1.9	1.9	2.2	2.3	2.2	1.9	2.1	2.6	2.3	2.8	3.2	2.5	2.6	2.2	2.3	2.2
1975	2.1	2.2	2.3	2.3	2.1	2.2	2.5	2.5	2.5	2.3	2.5	2.9	2.7	3.2	3.5	2.9	3.0	2.7	2.9	2.8
1976	2.5	2.6	2.8	2.8	2.6	2.7	3.0	3.1	3.1	2.9	3.1	3.6	3.4	3.9	4.3	3.7	3.9	3.7	3.9	3.9
1977	2.4	2.5	2.7	2.7	2.5	2.6	2.9	2.9	2.9	2.7	2.9	3.3	3.1	3.7	4.0	3.4	3.6	3.4	3.5	3.5
1978	2.3	2.4	2.6	2.5	2.4	2.5	2.7	2.8	2.8	2.6	2.7	3.1	2.9	3.4	3.7	3.2	3.3	3.1	3.2	3.2
1979	2.2	2.3	2.4	2.4	2.3	2.3	2.6	2.6	2.6	2.4	2.6	2.9	2.7	3.2	3.5	2.9	3.1	2.8	2.9	2.9
1980	2.0	2.1	2.2	2.2	2.1	2.1	2.3	2.4	2.3	2.2	2.3	2.6	2.4	2.8	3.1	2.6	2.7	2.4	2.5	2.5
1981	2.0	2.1	2.2	2.2	2.1	2.1	2.3	2.4	2.3	2.2	2.3	2.6	2.4	2.8	3.0	2.6	2.6	2.4	2.5	2.4
1982	2.9	3.0	3.2	3.1	3.0	3.1	3.4	3.5	3.4	3.3	3.5	3.9	3.7	4.1	4.4	4.0	4.2	4.0	4.2	4.2
1983	2.8	2.9	3.1	3.1	3.0	3.1	3.3	3.4	3.4	3.2	3.4	3.7	3.6	4.0	4.3	3.9	4.0	3.9	4.0	4.0
1984	3.2	3.2	3.4	3.4	3.3	3.4	3.6	3.7	3.7	3.6	3.8	4.1	4.0	4.4	4.7	4.3	4.5	4.4	4.5	4.6
1985	3.8	3.9	4.0	4.1	4.0	4.1	4.4	4.5	4.5	4.4	4.6	5.0	4.9	5.3	5.6	5.3	5.5	5.4	5.6	5.7
1986	4.2	4.3	4.5	4.6	4.5	4.6	4.9	5.0	5.0	5.0	5.2	5.6	5.5	5.9	6.3	6.0	6.2	6.1	6.4	6.5
1987	4.1	4.2	4.3	4.4	4.3	4.4	4.7	4.8	4.8	4.7	4.9	5.3	5.2	5.6	5.9	5.6	5.8	5.8	6.0	6.1
1988	4.2	4.3	4.5	4.5	4.4	4.6	4.8	4.9	4.9	4.9	5.1	5.4	5.4	5.8	6.0	5.8	6.0	5.9	6.1	6.2
1989	4.5	4.6	4.8	4.8	4.8	4.9	5.1	5.2	5.3	5.2	5.4	5.8	5.7	6.1	6.4	6.2	6.4	6.4	6.6	6.7
1990	4.5	4.6	4.8	4.8	4.8	4.9	5.2	5.3	5.3	5.3	5.5	5.8	5.7	6.1	6.4	6.2	6.4	6.3	6.5	6.7

Table C-4 (page 4 of 6)

Long-Term Government Bonds Total Returns

Rates of Return for all holding periods

Percent per annum compounded annually

from 1926 to 2007

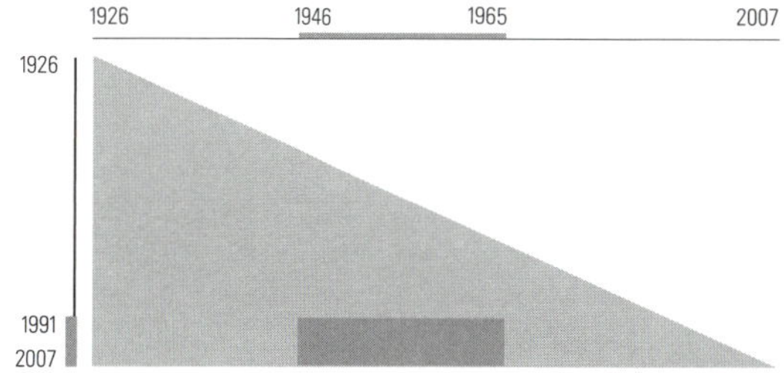

To the end of	From the beginning of 1946	1947	1948	1949	1950	1951	1952	1953	1954	1955	1956	1957	1958	1959	1960	1961	1962	1963	1964	1965
1991	4.8	4.9	5.1	5.2	5.1	5.2	5.5	5.6	5.7	5.6	5.8	6.2	6.1	6.5	6.8	6.6	6.8	6.8	7.0	7.1
1992	4.9	5.0	5.2	5.2	5.2	5.3	5.6	5.7	5.7	5.7	5.9	6.2	6.2	6.6	6.8	6.6	6.8	6.8	7.0	7.1
1993	5.2	5.3	5.4	5.5	5.5	5.6	5.8	6.0	6.0	6.0	6.2	6.5	6.5	6.9	7.2	7.0	7.2	7.2	7.4	7.5
1994	4.9	5.0	5.1	5.2	5.2	5.3	5.5	5.6	5.7	5.6	5.8	6.1	6.1	6.4	6.7	6.5	6.7	6.7	6.8	7.0
1995	5.3	5.5	5.6	5.7	5.7	5.8	6.0	6.1	6.2	6.2	6.4	6.7	6.7	7.1	7.3	7.1	7.3	7.3	7.5	7.7
1996	5.2	5.3	5.5	5.5	5.5	5.6	5.9	6.0	6.0	6.0	6.2	6.5	6.5	6.8	7.1	6.9	7.1	7.1	7.3	7.4
1997	5.4	5.5	5.7	5.7	5.7	5.9	6.1	6.2	6.3	6.2	6.4	6.7	6.7	7.1	7.3	7.1	7.3	7.3	7.5	7.6
1998	5.6	5.7	5.8	5.9	5.9	6.0	6.2	6.3	6.4	6.4	6.6	6.9	6.9	7.2	7.5	7.3	7.5	7.5	7.7	7.8
1999	5.3	5.4	5.5	5.6	5.6	5.7	5.9	6.0	6.0	6.0	6.2	6.5	6.5	6.8	7.0	6.8	7.0	7.0	7.2	7.3
2000	5.5	5.7	5.8	5.9	5.8	6.0	6.2	6.3	6.3	6.3	6.5	6.8	6.8	7.1	7.3	7.2	7.4	7.4	7.5	7.7
2001	5.5	5.6	5.8	5.8	5.8	5.9	6.1	6.2	6.3	6.3	6.4	6.7	6.7	7.0	7.3	7.1	7.3	7.3	7.4	7.5
2002	5.7	5.8	6.0	6.0	6.0	6.1	6.3	6.5	6.5	6.5	6.7	7.0	6.9	7.3	7.5	7.3	7.5	7.5	7.7	7.8
2003	5.6	5.7	5.9	5.9	5.9	6.0	6.3	6.4	6.4	6.4	6.6	6.8	6.8	7.1	7.4	7.2	7.4	7.4	7.5	7.6
2004	5.7	5.8	5.9	6.0	6.0	6.1	6.3	6.4	6.4	6.4	6.6	6.9	6.9	7.2	7.4	7.2	7.4	7.4	7.6	7.7
2005	5.7	5.8	6.0	6.0	6.0	6.1	6.3	6.4	6.5	6.5	6.6	6.9	6.9	7.2	7.4	7.2	7.4	7.4	7.6	7.7
2006	5.6	5.7	5.9	5.9	5.9	6.0	6.2	6.3	6.4	6.4	6.5	6.8	6.8	7.0	7.2	7.1	7.3	7.3	7.4	7.5
2007	5.7	5.8	6.0	6.0	6.0	6.1	6.3	6.4	6.4	6.4	6.6	6.8	6.8	7.1	7.3	7.2	7.3	7.3	7.5	7.6

Table C-4 (page 5 of 6)

Long-Term Government Bonds Total Returns

Rates of Return for all holding periods

Percent per annum compounded annually

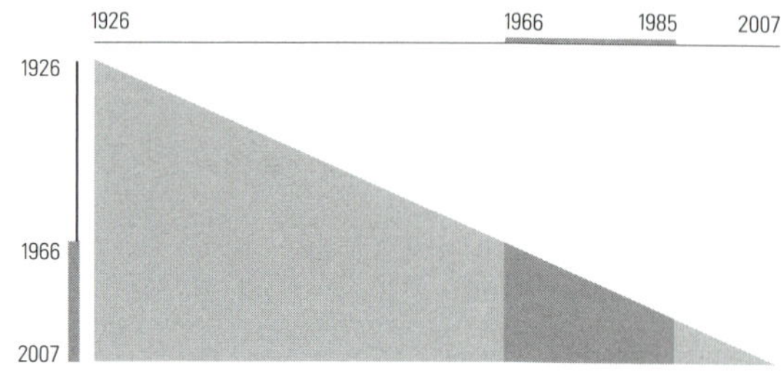

from 1926 to 2007

To the end of	From the beginning of 1966	1967	1968	1969	1970	1971	1972	1973	1974	1975	1976	1977	1978	1979	1980	1981	1982	1983	1984	1985
1966	3.7																			
1967	−3.0	−9.2																		
1968	−2.1	−4.8	−0.3																	
1969	−2.8	−4.9	−2.7	−5.1																
1970	0.0	−0.9	2.0	3.2	12.1															
1971	2.1	1.8	4.7	6.4	12.7	13.2														
1972	2.6	2.4	4.9	6.2	10.3	9.4	5.7													
1973	2.1	1.9	3.9	4.7	7.3	5.8	2.2	−1.1												
1974	2.4	2.2	3.9	4.7	6.7	5.4	2.9	1.6	4.4											
1975	3.0	3.0	4.6	5.3	7.1	6.2	4.5	4.1	6.7	9.2										
1976	4.2	4.3	5.9	6.7	8.5	7.9	6.8	7.1	10.0	12.9	16.8									
1977	3.8	3.8	5.2	5.8	7.3	6.6	5.5	5.5	7.2	8.2	7.7	−0.7								
1978	3.4	3.4	4.6	5.1	6.3	5.6	4.5	4.4	5.5	5.8	4.6	−0.9	−1.2							
1979	3.1	3.0	4.1	4.5	5.5	4.8	3.8	3.5	4.3	4.3	3.1	−1.0	−1.2	−1.2						
1980	2.6	2.5	3.5	3.8	4.6	3.9	2.9	2.6	3.1	2.9	1.7	−1.8	−2.1	−2.6	−3.9					
1981	2.5	2.5	3.3	3.6	4.4	3.7	2.8	2.5	2.9	2.7	1.7	−1.1	−1.1	−1.1	−1.1	1.9				
1982	4.4	4.5	5.5	5.9	6.8	6.4	5.8	5.8	6.6	6.8	6.5	4.9	6.0	7.9	11.2	19.6	40.4			
1983	4.2	4.3	5.2	5.5	6.3	5.9	5.3	5.3	6.0	6.1	5.8	4.3	5.1	6.4	8.4	12.9	18.9	0.7		
1984	4.8	4.9	5.7	6.1	6.9	6.6	6.1	6.1	6.8	7.0	6.8	5.6	6.5	7.9	9.8	13.5	17.7	7.8	15.5	
1985	6.0	6.1	7.0	7.5	8.3	8.0	7.7	7.8	8.6	9.0	9.0	8.2	9.3	10.9	13.1	16.8	20.9	15.0	23.0	31.0
1986	6.8	6.9	7.9	8.3	9.2	9.0	8.7	8.9	9.8	10.2	10.3	9.7	10.9	12.5	14.6	18.1	21.6	17.3	23.5	27.7
1987	6.3	6.5	7.3	7.7	8.5	8.3	8.0	8.1	8.8	9.2	9.2	8.5	9.5	10.7	12.3	14.9	17.2	13.0	16.3	16.6
1988	6.5	6.6	7.4	7.8	8.5	8.4	8.1	8.2	8.9	9.2	9.2	8.6	9.5	10.6	12.0	14.2	16.1	12.5	15.0	14.9
1989	6.9	7.1	7.9	8.3	9.0	8.8	8.6	8.8	9.4	9.8	9.8	9.3	10.2	11.3	12.6	14.6	16.3	13.2	15.5	15.5
1990	6.9	7.0	7.8	8.2	8.9	8.7	8.5	8.6	9.2	9.6	9.6	9.1	9.9	10.8	12.0	13.7	15.2	12.3	14.1	13.9
1991	7.4	7.5	8.3	8.7	9.3	9.2	9.0	9.2	9.8	10.1	10.2	9.7	10.5	11.5	12.6	14.2	15.6	13.1	14.8	14.6
1992	7.4	7.5	8.3	8.6	9.3	9.1	9.0	9.1	9.7	10.0	10.0	9.6	10.4	11.2	12.2	13.7	14.9	12.6	14.0	13.8
1993	7.8	7.9	8.6	9.0	9.6	9.5	9.4	9.5	10.1	10.4	10.5	10.1	10.8	11.7	12.7	14.1	15.1	13.1	14.4	14.3
1994	7.2	7.3	8.0	8.3	8.9	8.7	8.6	8.7	9.2	9.4	9.4	9.0	9.6	10.4	11.2	12.3	13.2	11.2	12.2	11.9
1995	7.9	8.1	8.7	9.1	9.7	9.6	9.4	9.6	10.1	10.4	10.4	10.1	10.8	11.5	12.4	13.5	14.4	12.6	13.7	13.5
1996	7.6	7.8	8.4	8.7	9.3	9.2	9.0	9.1	9.6	9.8	9.9	9.5	10.1	10.8	11.5	12.6	13.3	11.6	12.5	12.3
1997	7.9	8.0	8.6	9.0	9.5	9.4	9.2	9.4	9.9	10.1	10.1	9.8	10.4	11.0	11.8	12.8	13.5	11.9	12.7	12.5
1998	8.0	8.2	8.8	9.1	9.6	9.5	9.4	9.5	10.0	10.2	10.3	10.0	10.5	11.1	11.8	12.8	13.5	12.0	12.8	12.6
1999	7.5	7.6	8.2	8.5	8.9	8.8	8.7	8.8	9.2	9.4	9.4	9.1	9.5	10.1	10.7	11.5	12.1	10.6	11.3	11.0
2000	7.9	8.0	8.5	8.8	9.3	9.2	9.1	9.2	9.6	9.8	9.9	9.6	10.0	10.6	11.2	12.0	12.6	11.2	11.8	11.6
2001	7.7	7.9	8.4	8.7	9.1	9.0	8.9	9.0	9.4	9.6	9.6	9.3	9.8	10.3	10.8	11.6	12.1	10.8	11.4	11.1
2002	8.0	8.1	8.7	8.9	9.4	9.3	9.2	9.3	9.7	9.9	9.9	9.6	10.1	10.6	11.1	11.9	12.4	11.1	11.7	11.5
2003	7.8	7.9	8.5	8.7	9.2	9.1	8.9	9.0	9.4	9.6	9.6	9.3	9.7	10.2	10.7	11.4	11.8	10.6	11.2	10.9
2004	7.8	8.0	8.5	8.7	9.1	9.0	8.9	9.0	9.4	9.5	9.6	9.3	9.7	10.1	10.6	11.3	11.7	10.5	11.0	10.8
2005	7.8	7.9	8.4	8.7	9.1	9.0	8.9	9.0	9.3	9.5	9.5	9.2	9.6	10.0	10.5	11.1	11.5	10.4	10.9	10.7
2006	7.7	7.8	8.2	8.5	8.9	8.8	8.7	8.7	9.1	9.2	9.2	9.0	9.3	9.7	10.1	10.7	11.1	10.0	10.4	10.2
2007	7.7	7.8	8.3	8.5	8.9	8.8	8.7	8.8	9.1	9.2	9.2	9.0	9.3	9.7	10.1	10.7	11.0	10.0	10.4	10.2

Table C-4 (page 6 of 6)-a

Long-Term Government Bonds Total Returns

Rates of Return for all holding periods

Percent per annum compounded annually

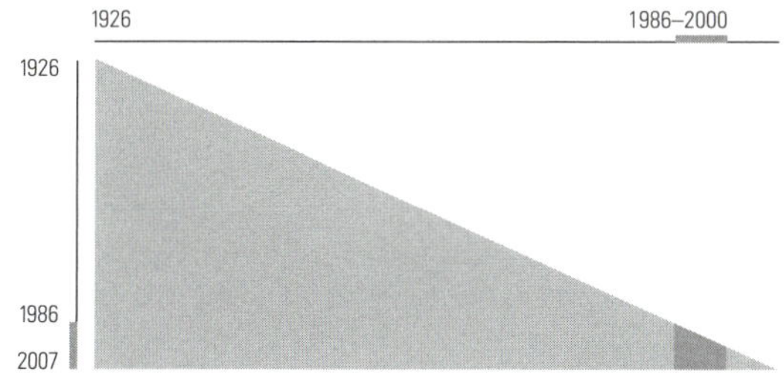

from 1926 to 2007

To the end of	From the beginning of 1986	1987	1988	1989	1990	1991	1992	1993	1994	1995	1996	1997	1998	1999	2000
1986	24.5														
1987	10.1	−2.7													
1988	9.9	3.3	9.7												
1989	11.9	8.0	13.8	18.1											
1990	10.8	7.6	11.2	12.0	6.2										
1991	12.1	9.8	13.2	14.4	12.6	19.3									
1992	11.5	9.5	12.1	12.8	11.0	13.5	8.1								
1993	12.4	10.7	13.1	13.8	12.8	15.1	13.0	18.2							
1994	9.9	8.2	9.9	9.9	8.3	8.9	5.6	4.4	−7.8						
1995	11.9	10.6	12.4	12.8	11.9	13.1	11.6	12.8	10.2	31.7					
1996	10.7	9.4	10.8	11.0	10.0	10.6	9.0	9.2	6.4	14.2	−0.9				
1997	11.1	10.0	11.3	11.5	10.7	11.4	10.1	10.5	8.7	14.8	7.1	15.9			
1998	11.3	10.2	11.5	11.7	11.0	11.6	10.5	10.9	9.5	14.3	9.1	14.4	13.1		
1999	9.7	8.6	9.6	9.6	8.8	9.1	7.9	7.8	6.2	9.2	4.3	6.0	1.5	−9.0	
2000	10.4	9.5	10.5	10.5	9.9	10.3	9.3	9.5	8.3	11.2	7.5	9.7	7.7	5.2	21.5
2001	10.0	9.1	10.0	10.0	9.4	9.6	8.7	8.8	7.7	10.1	6.8	8.5	6.7	4.7	12.2
2002	10.4	9.6	10.5	10.5	10.0	10.3	9.5	9.7	8.8	11.0	8.4	10.0	8.8	7.8	14.1
2003	9.9	9.1	9.9	9.9	9.4	9.6	8.8	8.9	8.0	9.9	7.5	8.7	7.6	6.5	10.8
2004	9.8	9.1	9.8	9.8	9.3	9.5	8.8	8.9	8.1	9.8	7.6	8.7	7.7	6.8	10.3
2005	9.7	9.0	9.7	9.7	9.2	9.4	8.7	8.8	8.0	9.6	7.6	8.6	7.7	7.0	9.9
2006	9.3	8.6	9.2	9.2	8.7	8.9	8.2	8.2	7.5	8.9	7.0	7.8	7.0	6.2	8.6
2007	9.3	8.7	9.3	9.3	8.8	8.9	8.3	8.3	7.7	8.9	7.2	8.0	7.3	6.6	8.8

Table C-4 (page 6 of 6)-b

Long-Term Government Bonds Total Returns

Rates of Return for all holding periods

Percent per annum compounded annually

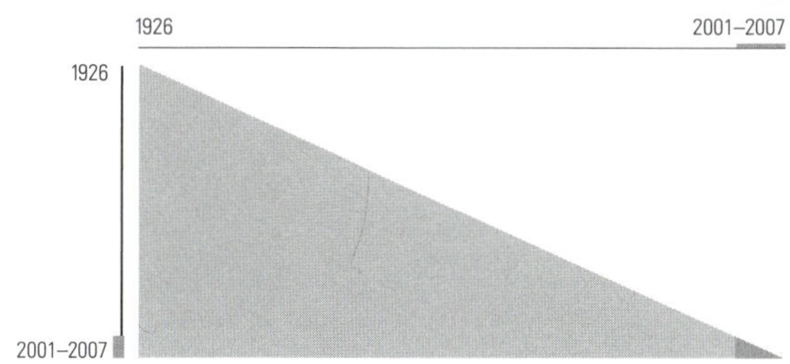

from 1926 to 2007

To the end of	From the beginning of 2001	2002	2003	2004	2005	2006	2007
2001	3.7						
2002	10.5	17.8					
2003	7.4	9.3	1.4				
2004	7.7	9.1	4.9	8.5			
2005	7.7	8.7	5.9	8.2	7.8		
2006	6.6	7.2	4.7	5.8	4.4	1.2	
2007	7.1	7.6	5.7	6.8	6.2	5.4	9.9

Table C-5 (page 1 of 6)

Intermediate-Term Government Bonds Total Returns

Rates of Return for all holding periods

Percent per annum compounded annually

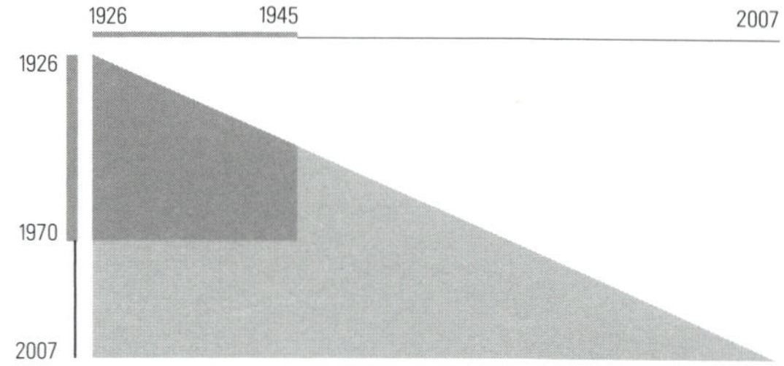

from 1926 to 2007

To the end of	From the beginning of 1926	1927	1928	1929	1930	1931	1932	1933	1934	1935	1936	1937	1938	1939	1940	1941	1942	1943	1944	1945
1926	5.4																			
1927	4.9	4.5																		
1928	3.6	2.7	0.9																	
1929	4.2	3.8	3.4	6.0																
1930	4.7	4.5	4.5	6.4	6.7															
1931	3.5	3.1	2.8	3.4	2.1	−2.3														
1932	4.2	4.0	3.9	4.7	4.3	3.1	8.8													
1933	3.9	3.7	3.6	4.1	3.7	2.7	5.3	1.8												
1934	4.5	4.4	4.3	4.9	4.7	4.2	6.5	5.4	9.0											
1935	4.7	4.7	4.7	5.2	5.1	4.8	6.6	5.9	8.0	7.0										
1936	4.6	4.5	4.5	4.9	4.8	4.5	5.9	5.2	6.3	5.0	3.1									
1937	4.3	4.2	4.2	4.6	4.4	4.1	5.2	4.4	5.1	3.8	2.3	1.6								
1938	4.5	4.4	4.4	4.7	4.6	4.3	5.3	4.7	5.3	4.4	3.6	3.9	6.2							
1939	4.5	4.4	4.4	4.7	4.6	4.3	5.2	4.7	5.2	4.5	3.8	4.1	5.4	4.5						
1940	4.4	4.3	4.3	4.6	4.4	4.2	5.0	4.5	4.9	4.2	3.7	3.8	4.6	3.7	3.0					
1941	4.1	4.0	4.0	4.2	4.1	3.9	4.5	4.0	4.3	3.7	3.1	3.1	3.5	2.6	1.7	0.5				
1942	4.0	3.9	3.9	4.1	3.9	3.7	4.3	3.8	4.1	3.4	3.0	2.9	3.2	2.5	1.8	1.2	1.9			
1943	3.9	3.8	3.8	4.0	3.9	3.6	4.1	3.7	3.9	3.4	2.9	2.9	3.1	2.5	2.0	1.7	2.4	2.8		
1944	3.8	3.7	3.7	3.9	3.7	3.5	4.0	3.6	3.7	3.2	2.8	2.8	2.9	2.4	2.0	1.8	2.2	2.3	1.8	
1945	3.7	3.6	3.6	3.8	3.6	3.4	3.8	3.5	3.6	3.1	2.7	2.7	2.9	2.4	2.0	1.8	2.2	2.3	2.0	2.2
1946	3.6	3.5	3.5	3.6	3.5	3.3	3.6	3.3	3.4	2.9	2.6	2.5	2.7	2.2	1.9	1.7	2.0	2.0	1.7	1.6
1947	3.5	3.4	3.3	3.5	3.3	3.1	3.5	3.1	3.2	2.8	2.4	2.4	2.5	2.1	1.8	1.6	1.8	1.7	1.5	1.4
1948	3.4	3.3	3.3	3.4	3.2	3.1	3.4	3.0	3.1	2.7	2.4	2.3	2.4	2.0	1.8	1.6	1.8	1.8	1.6	1.5
1949	3.4	3.3	3.2	3.3	3.2	3.0	3.3	3.0	3.1	2.7	2.4	2.3	2.4	2.1	1.8	1.7	1.9	1.8	1.7	1.7
1950	3.3	3.2	3.1	3.2	3.1	2.9	3.2	2.9	2.9	2.6	2.3	2.2	2.3	2.0	1.7	1.6	1.7	1.7	1.5	1.5
1951	3.1	3.1	3.0	3.1	3.0	2.8	3.0	2.7	2.8	2.4	2.2	2.1	2.1	1.8	1.6	1.5	1.6	1.5	1.4	1.3
1952	3.1	3.0	2.9	3.0	2.9	2.7	3.0	2.7	2.7	2.4	2.1	2.1	2.1	1.8	1.6	1.5	1.6	1.6	1.4	1.4
1953	3.1	3.0	2.9	3.0	2.9	2.7	3.0	2.7	2.8	2.4	2.2	2.1	2.2	1.9	1.7	1.6	1.7	1.7	1.6	1.6
1954	3.1	3.0	2.9	3.0	2.9	2.7	3.0	2.7	2.8	2.5	2.2	2.2	2.2	2.0	1.8	1.7	1.8	1.8	1.7	1.7
1955	2.9	2.9	2.8	2.9	2.8	2.6	2.8	2.6	2.6	2.3	2.1	2.0	2.0	1.8	1.6	1.5	1.6	1.6	1.5	1.5
1956	2.8	2.8	2.7	2.8	2.6	2.5	2.7	2.4	2.5	2.2	2.0	1.9	1.9	1.7	1.5	1.4	1.5	1.5	1.4	1.3
1957	3.0	2.9	2.9	2.9	2.8	2.7	2.9	2.6	2.7	2.4	2.2	2.2	2.2	2.0	1.9	1.8	1.9	1.9	1.8	1.8
1958	2.9	2.8	2.7	2.8	2.7	2.5	2.7	2.5	2.5	2.3	2.1	2.0	2.0	1.8	1.7	1.6	1.7	1.7	1.6	1.6
1959	2.8	2.7	2.6	2.7	2.6	2.4	2.6	2.4	2.4	2.2	2.0	1.9	1.9	1.7	1.6	1.5	1.6	1.5	1.5	1.4
1960	3.0	2.9	2.9	3.0	2.9	2.7	2.9	2.7	2.7	2.5	2.3	2.3	2.3	2.2	2.0	2.0	2.1	2.1	2.0	2.1
1961	3.0	2.9	2.9	2.9	2.8	2.7	2.9	2.7	2.7	2.5	2.3	2.3	2.3	2.1	2.0	2.0	2.1	2.1	2.0	2.0
1962	3.0	3.0	2.9	3.0	2.9	2.8	3.0	2.8	2.8	2.6	2.4	2.4	2.4	2.3	2.2	2.2	2.2	2.2	2.2	2.2
1963	3.0	2.9	2.9	3.0	2.9	2.8	2.9	2.7	2.8	2.6	2.4	2.4	2.4	2.3	2.2	2.1	2.2	2.2	2.2	2.2
1964	3.0	3.0	2.9	3.0	2.9	2.8	3.0	2.8	2.8	2.6	2.5	2.4	2.5	2.3	2.2	2.2	2.3	2.3	2.3	2.3
1965	3.0	2.9	2.9	2.9	2.9	2.7	2.9	2.7	2.7	2.6	2.4	2.4	2.4	2.3	2.2	2.2	2.2	2.2	2.2	2.2
1966	3.0	3.0	2.9	3.0	2.9	2.8	2.9	2.8	2.8	2.6	2.5	2.5	2.5	2.4	2.3	2.3	2.3	2.3	2.3	2.3
1967	3.0	2.9	2.9	2.9	2.8	2.7	2.9	2.7	2.8	2.6	2.4	2.4	2.4	2.3	2.2	2.2	2.3	2.3	2.3	2.3
1968	3.0	3.0	2.9	3.0	2.9	2.8	2.9	2.8	2.8	2.6	2.5	2.5	2.5	2.4	2.3	2.3	2.4	2.4	2.4	2.4
1969	2.9	2.9	2.8	2.9	2.8	2.7	2.8	2.7	2.7	2.5	2.4	2.4	2.4	2.3	2.2	2.2	2.2	2.3	2.2	2.3
1970	3.2	3.2	3.1	3.2	3.1	3.0	3.2	3.0	3.1	2.9	2.8	2.8	2.8	2.7	2.7	2.6	2.7	2.7	2.7	2.8

Table C-5 (page 2 of 6)

Intermediate-Term Government Bonds Total Returns

Rates of Return for all holding periods

Percent per annum compounded annually

from 1926 to 2007

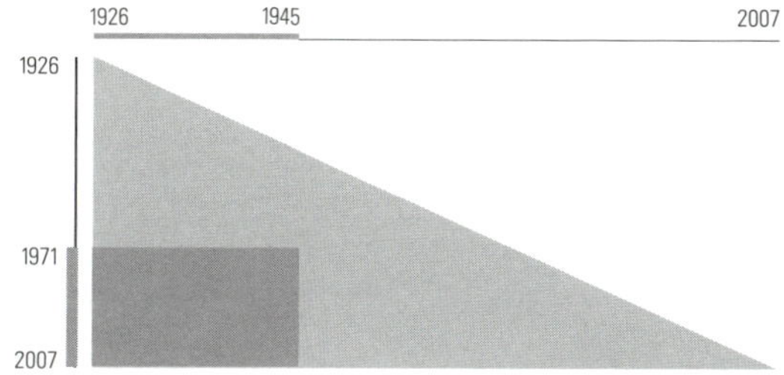

To the end of	From the beginning of 1926	1927	1928	1929	1930	1931	1932	1933	1934	1935	1936	1937	1938	1939	1940	1941	1942	1943	1944	1945
1971	3.3	3.3	3.3	3.3	3.3	3.2	3.3	3.2	3.2	3.1	2.9	2.9	3.0	2.9	2.8	2.8	2.9	2.9	3.0	3.0
1972	3.4	3.3	3.3	3.4	3.3	3.2	3.4	3.2	3.3	3.1	3.0	3.0	3.0	3.0	2.9	2.9	3.0	3.0	3.0	3.1
1973	3.4	3.4	3.3	3.4	3.3	3.2	3.4	3.3	3.3	3.1	3.0	3.0	3.1	3.0	3.0	3.0	3.0	3.1	3.1	3.1
1974	3.4	3.4	3.4	3.4	3.4	3.3	3.4	3.3	3.3	3.2	3.1	3.1	3.2	3.1	3.0	3.0	3.1	3.2	3.2	3.2
1975	3.5	3.5	3.5	3.5	3.5	3.4	3.5	3.4	3.5	3.3	3.2	3.2	3.3	3.2	3.2	3.2	3.3	3.3	3.3	3.4
1976	3.7	3.7	3.7	3.7	3.7	3.6	3.7	3.6	3.7	3.5	3.5	3.5	3.5	3.4	3.4	3.4	3.5	3.6	3.6	3.6
1977	3.7	3.6	3.6	3.7	3.6	3.6	3.7	3.6	3.6	3.5	3.4	3.4	3.5	3.4	3.4	3.4	3.5	3.5	3.5	3.6
1978	3.7	3.6	3.6	3.7	3.6	3.6	3.7	3.6	3.6	3.5	3.4	3.4	3.5	3.4	3.4	3.4	3.5	3.5	3.5	3.6
1979	3.7	3.6	3.6	3.7	3.6	3.6	3.7	3.6	3.6	3.5	3.4	3.4	3.5	3.4	3.4	3.4	3.5	3.5	3.5	3.6
1980	3.7	3.6	3.6	3.7	3.6	3.6	3.7	3.6	3.6	3.5	3.4	3.4	3.5	3.4	3.4	3.4	3.5	3.5	3.5	3.6
1981	3.8	3.7	3.7	3.8	3.7	3.7	3.8	3.7	3.7	3.6	3.6	3.6	3.6	3.6	3.5	3.6	3.6	3.7	3.7	3.7
1982	4.2	4.1	4.1	4.2	4.2	4.1	4.2	4.2	4.2	4.1	4.0	4.1	4.1	4.1	4.1	4.1	4.2	4.2	4.3	4.3
1983	4.2	4.2	4.2	4.3	4.2	4.2	4.3	4.2	4.3	4.2	4.1	4.1	4.2	4.2	4.1	4.2	4.3	4.3	4.4	4.4
1984	4.4	4.4	4.4	4.4	4.4	4.4	4.5	4.4	4.5	4.4	4.3	4.3	4.4	4.4	4.4	4.4	4.5	4.5	4.6	4.7
1985	4.6	4.6	4.6	4.7	4.7	4.6	4.8	4.7	4.7	4.7	4.6	4.6	4.7	4.7	4.7	4.7	4.8	4.9	4.9	5.0
1986	4.8	4.8	4.8	4.9	4.8	4.8	4.9	4.9	4.9	4.8	4.8	4.8	4.9	4.9	4.9	4.9	5.0	5.1	5.2	5.2
1987	4.8	4.8	4.8	4.8	4.8	4.8	4.9	4.8	4.9	4.8	4.8	4.8	4.9	4.8	4.8	4.9	5.0	5.1	5.1	5.2
1988	4.8	4.8	4.8	4.8	4.8	4.8	4.9	4.9	4.9	4.8	4.8	4.8	4.9	4.9	4.9	4.9	5.0	5.1	5.1	5.2
1989	4.9	4.9	4.9	5.0	5.0	4.9	5.1	5.0	5.1	5.0	4.9	5.0	5.0	5.0	5.0	5.1	5.2	5.2	5.3	5.4
1990	5.0	5.0	5.0	5.1	5.0	5.0	5.1	5.1	5.1	5.1	5.0	5.1	5.1	5.1	5.1	5.2	5.3	5.3	5.4	5.5
1991	5.1	5.1	5.1	5.2	5.2	5.2	5.3	5.2	5.3	5.2	5.2	5.2	5.3	5.3	5.3	5.4	5.5	5.5	5.6	5.7
1992	5.2	5.2	5.2	5.2	5.2	5.2	5.3	5.3	5.3	5.3	5.2	5.3	5.4	5.3	5.4	5.4	5.5	5.6	5.6	5.7
1993	5.3	5.3	5.3	5.3	5.3	5.3	5.4	5.4	5.4	5.4	5.3	5.4	5.5	5.4	5.5	5.5	5.6	5.7	5.7	5.8
1994	5.1	5.1	5.1	5.2	5.2	5.1	5.2	5.2	5.2	5.2	5.2	5.2	5.3	5.2	5.3	5.3	5.4	5.5	5.5	5.6
1995	5.3	5.3	5.3	5.3	5.3	5.3	5.4	5.4	5.4	5.4	5.3	5.4	5.4	5.4	5.5	5.5	5.6	5.7	5.7	5.8
1996	5.2	5.2	5.2	5.3	5.3	5.2	5.4	5.3	5.4	5.3	5.3	5.3	5.4	5.4	5.4	5.4	5.5	5.6	5.6	5.7
1997	5.3	5.3	5.3	5.3	5.3	5.3	5.4	5.4	5.4	5.4	5.3	5.4	5.4	5.4	5.4	5.5	5.6	5.6	5.7	5.8
1998	5.3	5.3	5.3	5.4	5.4	5.4	5.5	5.4	5.5	5.4	5.4	5.5	5.5	5.5	5.5	5.6	5.7	5.7	5.8	5.9
1999	5.2	5.2	5.2	5.3	5.3	5.3	5.4	5.3	5.4	5.3	5.3	5.3	5.4	5.4	5.4	5.4	5.5	5.6	5.6	5.7
2000	5.3	5.3	5.3	5.4	5.4	5.4	5.5	5.4	5.5	5.4	5.4	5.4	5.5	5.5	5.5	5.6	5.6	5.7	5.8	5.8
2001	5.3	5.3	5.4	5.4	5.4	5.4	5.5	5.5	5.5	5.5	5.4	5.5	5.5	5.5	5.5	5.6	5.7	5.7	5.8	5.9
2002	5.4	5.4	5.5	5.5	5.5	5.5	5.6	5.6	5.6	5.6	5.5	5.6	5.6	5.6	5.7	5.7	5.8	5.9	5.9	6.0
2003	5.4	5.4	5.4	5.5	5.5	5.4	5.6	5.5	5.6	5.5	5.5	5.5	5.6	5.6	5.6	5.6	5.7	5.8	5.8	5.9
2004	5.4	5.4	5.4	5.4	5.4	5.4	5.5	5.5	5.5	5.5	5.5	5.5	5.5	5.5	5.6	5.6	5.7	5.7	5.8	5.9
2005	5.3	5.3	5.3	5.4	5.4	5.3	5.5	5.4	5.5	5.4	5.4	5.4	5.5	5.5	5.5	5.5	5.6	5.7	5.7	5.8
2006	5.3	5.3	5.3	5.3	5.3	5.3	5.4	5.4	5.4	5.4	5.4	5.4	5.4	5.4	5.5	5.5	5.6	5.6	5.7	5.7
2007	5.3	5.3	5.3	5.4	5.4	5.4	5.5	5.4	5.5	5.4	5.4	5.5	5.5	5.5	5.5	5.6	5.6	5.7	5.7	5.8

Table C-5 (page 3 of 6)

Intermediate-Term Government Bonds Total Returns

Rates of Return for all holding periods
Percent per annum compounded annually

from 1926 to 2007

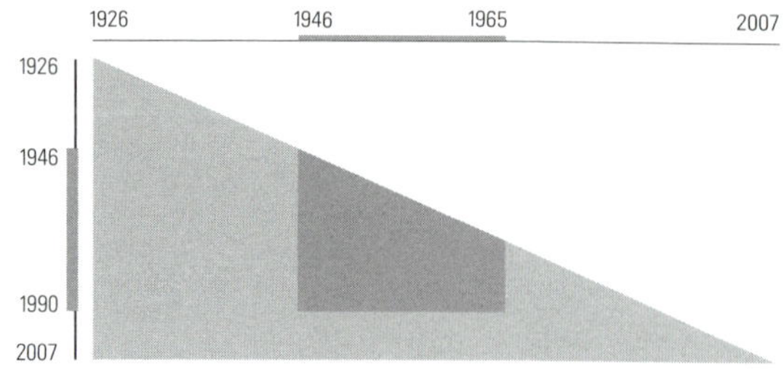

To the end of	From the beginning of 1946	1947	1948	1949	1950	1951	1952	1953	1954	1955	1956	1957	1958	1959	1960	1961	1962	1963	1964	1965
1946	1.0																			
1947	1.0	0.9																		
1948	1.3	1.4	1.8																	
1949	1.5	1.7	2.1	2.3																
1950	1.4	1.4	1.6	1.5	0.7															
1951	1.2	1.2	1.3	1.1	0.5	0.4														
1952	1.3	1.3	1.4	1.3	0.9	1.0	1.6													
1953	1.5	1.6	1.7	1.6	1.5	1.7	2.4	3.2												
1954	1.6	1.7	1.8	1.8	1.7	2.0	2.5	3.0	2.7											
1955	1.4	1.4	1.5	1.5	1.3	1.4	1.7	1.7	1.0	−0.7										
1956	1.2	1.3	1.3	1.2	1.1	1.1	1.3	1.2	0.5	−0.5	−0.4									
1957	1.8	1.8	1.9	1.9	1.9	2.1	2.3	2.5	2.3	2.2	3.6	7.8								
1958	1.5	1.6	1.6	1.6	1.5	1.6	1.8	1.9	1.6	1.3	2.0	3.2	−1.3							
1959	1.4	1.4	1.5	1.4	1.3	1.4	1.5	1.5	1.2	1.0	1.4	2.0	−0.8	−0.4						
1960	2.1	2.1	2.2	2.3	2.2	2.4	2.6	2.8	2.7	2.7	3.4	4.3	3.2	5.5	11.8					
1961	2.0	2.1	2.2	2.2	2.2	2.3	2.5	2.7	2.6	2.6	3.1	3.8	2.9	4.3	6.7	1.8				
1962	2.2	2.3	2.4	2.5	2.5	2.6	2.8	2.9	2.9	2.9	3.5	4.1	3.4	4.6	6.3	3.7	5.6			
1963	2.2	2.3	2.4	2.4	2.4	2.5	2.7	2.8	2.8	2.8	3.2	3.8	3.1	4.0	5.1	3.0	3.6	1.6		
1964	2.3	2.4	2.5	2.5	2.5	2.6	2.8	2.9	2.9	2.9	3.3	3.8	3.2	4.0	4.9	3.3	3.7	2.8	4.0	
1965	2.2	2.3	2.4	2.4	2.4	2.5	2.7	2.8	2.7	2.7	3.1	3.5	3.0	3.6	4.2	2.8	3.1	2.2	2.5	1.0
1966	2.4	2.4	2.5	2.5	2.6	2.7	2.8	2.9	2.9	2.9	3.2	3.6	3.1	3.7	4.3	3.1	3.4	2.8	3.2	2.8
1967	2.3	2.4	2.4	2.5	2.5	2.6	2.7	2.8	2.8	2.8	3.0	3.4	2.9	3.4	3.9	2.8	3.0	2.5	2.7	2.2
1968	2.4	2.5	2.5	2.6	2.6	2.7	2.8	2.9	2.9	2.9	3.2	3.5	3.1	3.5	4.0	3.0	3.2	2.8	3.0	2.8
1969	2.3	2.3	2.4	2.4	2.4	2.5	2.6	2.7	2.6	2.6	2.9	3.1	2.8	3.1	3.5	2.6	2.7	2.3	2.4	2.1
1970	2.8	2.9	3.0	3.0	3.1	3.2	3.3	3.4	3.4	3.5	3.8	4.1	3.8	4.2	4.6	3.9	4.2	4.0	4.4	4.4
1971	3.0	3.1	3.2	3.3	3.3	3.4	3.6	3.7	3.7	3.8	4.1	4.4	4.1	4.5	5.0	4.4	4.6	4.5	4.9	5.0
1972	3.1	3.2	3.3	3.3	3.4	3.5	3.7	3.8	3.8	3.9	4.1	4.4	4.2	4.6	5.0	4.4	4.7	4.6	4.9	5.0
1973	3.2	3.2	3.3	3.4	3.4	3.6	3.7	3.8	3.8	3.9	4.1	4.4	4.2	4.6	5.0	4.5	4.7	4.6	4.9	5.0
1974	3.2	3.3	3.4	3.5	3.5	3.6	3.8	3.9	3.9	4.0	4.2	4.5	4.3	4.7	5.0	4.5	4.7	4.7	5.0	5.1
1975	3.4	3.5	3.6	3.6	3.7	3.8	4.0	4.1	4.1	4.2	4.4	4.7	4.5	4.8	5.2	4.8	5.0	4.9	5.2	5.3
1976	3.7	3.8	3.9	4.0	4.0	4.1	4.3	4.4	4.5	4.5	4.8	5.1	4.9	5.3	5.6	5.2	5.5	5.5	5.8	5.9
1977	3.6	3.7	3.8	3.9	3.9	4.0	4.2	4.3	4.3	4.4	4.6	4.9	4.7	5.1	5.4	5.0	5.2	5.2	5.5	5.6
1978	3.6	3.7	3.8	3.8	3.9	4.0	4.2	4.3	4.3	4.4	4.6	4.8	4.7	5.0	5.3	4.9	5.1	5.1	5.3	5.4
1979	3.6	3.7	3.8	3.9	3.9	4.0	4.2	4.2	4.3	4.4	4.6	4.8	4.7	4.9	5.2	4.9	5.1	5.0	5.2	5.3
1980	3.6	3.7	3.8	3.9	3.9	4.0	4.1	4.2	4.3	4.3	4.5	4.8	4.6	4.9	5.2	4.8	5.0	5.0	5.2	5.2
1981	3.8	3.9	4.0	4.0	4.1	4.2	4.3	4.4	4.5	4.5	4.7	4.9	4.8	5.1	5.3	5.1	5.2	5.2	5.4	5.5
1982	4.4	4.5	4.6	4.7	4.8	4.9	5.0	5.2	5.2	5.3	5.5	5.8	5.7	6.0	6.3	6.0	6.2	6.3	6.5	6.7
1983	4.5	4.6	4.7	4.8	4.8	5.0	5.1	5.2	5.3	5.4	5.6	5.8	5.8	6.1	6.3	6.1	6.3	6.3	6.6	6.7
1984	4.7	4.8	4.9	5.0	5.1	5.2	5.4	5.5	5.6	5.7	5.9	6.1	6.1	6.3	6.6	6.4	6.6	6.7	6.9	7.1
1985	5.1	5.2	5.3	5.4	5.5	5.6	5.8	5.9	6.0	6.1	6.3	6.6	6.5	6.8	7.1	6.9	7.2	7.2	7.5	7.7
1986	5.3	5.4	5.5	5.6	5.7	5.9	6.0	6.2	6.3	6.4	6.6	6.9	6.8	7.1	7.4	7.2	7.5	7.5	7.8	8.0
1987	5.3	5.4	5.5	5.6	5.7	5.8	6.0	6.1	6.2	6.3	6.5	6.7	6.7	7.0	7.2	7.1	7.3	7.4	7.6	7.8
1988	5.3	5.4	5.5	5.6	5.7	5.8	6.0	6.1	6.2	6.3	6.5	6.7	6.7	6.9	7.2	7.0	7.2	7.3	7.5	7.7
1989	5.5	5.6	5.7	5.8	5.9	6.0	6.1	6.3	6.4	6.5	6.7	6.9	6.9	7.1	7.4	7.3	7.5	7.5	7.8	7.9
1990	5.5	5.7	5.8	5.9	5.9	6.1	6.2	6.4	6.4	6.5	6.8	7.0	7.0	7.2	7.5	7.3	7.5	7.6	7.8	8.0

Table C-5 (page 4 of 6)

Intermediate-Term Government Bonds Total Returns

Rates of Return for all holding periods
Percent per annum compounded annually

from 1926 to 2007

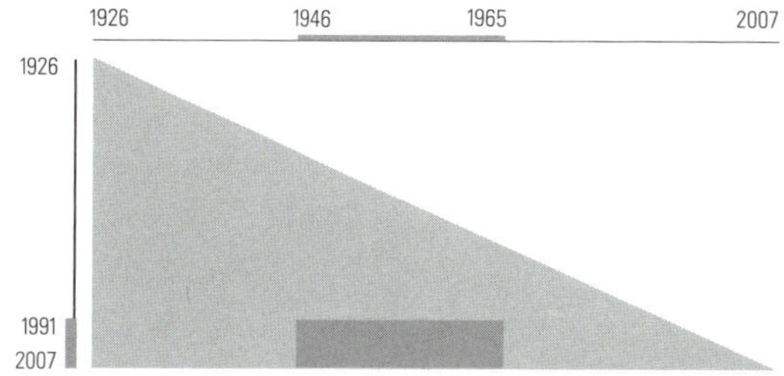

To the end of	From the beginning of 1946	1947	1948	1949	1950	1951	1952	1953	1954	1955	1956	1957	1958	1959	1960	1961	1962	1963	1964	1965
1991	5.8	5.9	6.0	6.1	6.2	6.3	6.5	6.6	6.7	6.8	7.0	7.2	7.2	7.5	7.7	7.6	7.8	7.9	8.1	8.2
1992	5.8	5.9	6.0	6.1	6.2	6.3	6.5	6.6	6.7	6.8	7.0	7.2	7.2	7.5	7.7	7.6	7.8	7.8	8.1	8.2
1993	5.9	6.0	6.1	6.2	6.3	6.4	6.6	6.7	6.8	6.9	7.1	7.3	7.3	7.6	7.8	7.7	7.9	8.0	8.2	8.3
1994	5.7	5.8	5.9	5.9	6.0	6.2	6.3	6.4	6.5	6.6	6.8	7.0	6.9	7.2	7.4	7.3	7.5	7.5	7.7	7.8
1995	5.9	6.0	6.1	6.2	6.3	6.4	6.5	6.6	6.7	6.8	7.0	7.2	7.2	7.4	7.7	7.5	7.7	7.8	8.0	8.1
1996	5.8	5.9	6.0	6.1	6.2	6.3	6.4	6.5	6.6	6.7	6.9	7.1	7.1	7.3	7.5	7.4	7.6	7.6	7.8	7.9
1997	5.8	5.9	6.0	6.1	6.2	6.3	6.5	6.6	6.7	6.7	6.9	7.1	7.1	7.3	7.5	7.4	7.6	7.6	7.8	7.9
1998	5.9	6.0	6.1	6.2	6.3	6.4	6.5	6.7	6.7	6.8	7.0	7.2	7.2	7.4	7.6	7.5	7.6	7.7	7.9	8.0
1999	5.8	5.9	6.0	6.0	6.1	6.2	6.4	6.5	6.5	6.6	6.8	7.0	6.9	7.2	7.4	7.2	7.4	7.4	7.6	7.7
2000	5.9	6.0	6.1	6.2	6.2	6.4	6.5	6.6	6.7	6.8	6.9	7.1	7.1	7.3	7.5	7.4	7.5	7.6	7.7	7.8
2001	5.9	6.0	6.1	6.2	6.3	6.4	6.5	6.6	6.7	6.8	6.9	7.1	7.1	7.3	7.5	7.4	7.5	7.6	7.7	7.8
2002	6.0	6.1	6.2	6.3	6.4	6.5	6.6	6.7	6.8	6.9	7.1	7.2	7.2	7.4	7.6	7.5	7.7	7.7	7.9	8.0
2003	6.0	6.1	6.2	6.2	6.3	6.4	6.5	6.6	6.7	6.8	7.0	7.1	7.1	7.3	7.5	7.4	7.5	7.6	7.7	7.8
2004	5.9	6.0	6.1	6.2	6.2	6.3	6.5	6.6	6.6	6.7	6.9	7.0	7.0	7.2	7.4	7.3	7.4	7.4	7.6	7.7
2005	5.8	5.9	6.0	6.1	6.2	6.3	6.4	6.5	6.5	6.6	6.7	6.9	6.9	7.1	7.2	7.1	7.3	7.3	7.4	7.5
2006	5.8	5.9	6.0	6.0	6.1	6.2	6.3	6.4	6.5	6.5	6.7	6.8	6.8	7.0	7.1	7.0	7.2	7.2	7.3	7.4
2007	5.9	5.9	6.0	6.1	6.2	6.3	6.4	6.5	6.5	6.6	6.7	6.9	6.9	7.0	7.2	7.1	7.2	7.3	7.4	7.5

Table C-5 (page 5 of 6)

Intermediate-Term Government Bonds Total Returns

Rates of Return for all holding periods

Percent per annum compounded annually

from 1926 to 2007

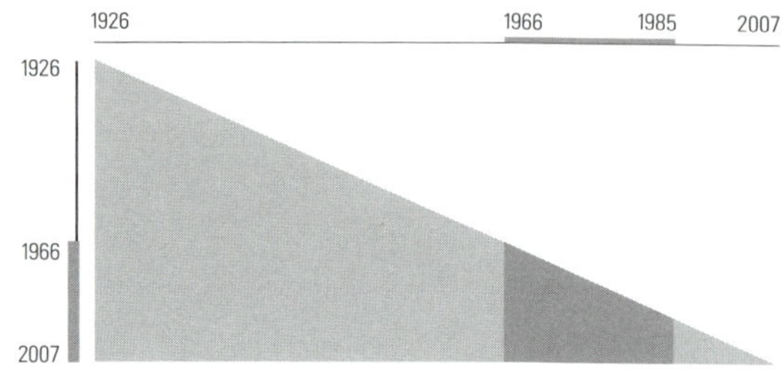

To the end of	From the beginning of 1966	1967	1968	1969	1970	1971	1972	1973	1974	1975	1976	1977	1978	1979	1980	1981	1982	1983	1984	1985
1966	4.7																			
1967	2.8	1.0																		
1968	3.4	2.8	4.5																	
1969	2.3	1.6	1.9	–0.7																
1970	5.1	5.2	6.6	7.7	16.9															
1971	5.7	5.9	7.2	8.0	12.7	8.7														
1972	5.6	5.8	6.8	7.3	10.1	6.9	5.2													
1973	5.5	5.6	6.4	6.8	8.7	6.1	4.9	4.6												
1974	5.5	5.6	6.3	6.6	8.1	6.0	5.2	5.1	5.7											
1975	5.7	5.9	6.5	6.8	8.1	6.4	5.8	6.0	6.8	7.8										
1976	6.4	6.5	7.2	7.5	8.7	7.4	7.2	7.7	8.8	10.3	12.9									
1977	5.9	6.1	6.6	6.8	7.8	6.6	6.2	6.4	6.9	7.3	7.0	1.4								
1978	5.8	5.8	6.3	6.5	7.3	6.2	5.8	5.9	6.2	6.3	5.8	2.4	3.5							
1979	5.6	5.7	6.1	6.3	7.0	5.9	5.6	5.7	5.8	5.9	5.4	3.0	3.8	4.1						
1980	5.5	5.6	5.9	6.1	6.7	5.7	5.4	5.4	5.6	5.5	5.1	3.2	3.8	4.0	3.9					
1981	5.8	5.8	6.2	6.3	6.9	6.1	5.8	5.9	6.0	6.1	5.8	4.4	5.2	5.8	6.6	9.5				
1982	7.0	7.2	7.6	7.8	8.5	7.8	7.7	8.0	8.4	8.7	8.8	8.2	9.6	11.2	13.7	18.9	29.1			
1983	7.0	7.2	7.6	7.8	8.4	7.8	7.7	7.9	8.3	8.6	8.7	8.1	9.2	10.4	12.1	14.9	17.8	7.4		
1984	7.4	7.5	7.9	8.2	8.8	8.2	8.2	8.4	8.8	9.1	9.2	8.8	9.9	11.0	12.5	14.7	16.5	10.7	14.0	
1985	8.0	8.2	8.6	8.8	9.5	9.0	9.0	9.3	9.7	10.1	10.3	10.0	11.2	12.3	13.7	15.8	17.4	13.8	17.1	20.3
1986	8.3	8.5	8.9	9.2	9.8	9.4	9.4	9.7	10.1	10.5	10.7	10.5	11.6	12.6	13.9	15.7	17.0	14.1	16.5	17.7
1987	8.1	8.2	8.6	8.8	9.4	9.0	9.0	9.2	9.6	9.9	10.1	9.8	10.7	11.5	12.5	13.8	14.5	11.8	12.9	12.5
1988	8.0	8.1	8.5	8.7	9.2	8.8	8.8	9.0	9.4	9.6	9.8	9.5	10.3	11.0	11.8	12.8	13.3	10.8	11.5	10.9
1989	8.2	8.4	8.7	8.9	9.4	9.0	9.1	9.3	9.6	9.9	10.0	9.8	10.5	11.2	11.9	12.8	13.3	11.2	11.8	11.4
1990	8.3	8.4	8.8	8.9	9.4	9.1	9.1	9.3	9.6	9.8	10.0	9.8	10.5	11.1	11.7	12.5	12.9	11.0	11.5	11.1
1991	8.5	8.7	9.0	9.2	9.7	9.4	9.4	9.6	9.9	10.2	10.3	10.2	10.8	11.4	12.0	12.8	13.1	11.5	12.0	11.7
1992	8.5	8.6	9.0	9.1	9.6	9.3	9.3	9.5	9.8	10.0	10.1	10.0	10.6	11.1	11.6	12.3	12.6	11.0	11.5	11.1
1993	8.6	8.7	9.0	9.2	9.7	9.4	9.4	9.6	9.8	10.1	10.2	10.0	10.6	11.1	11.6	12.2	12.5	11.1	11.4	11.1
1994	8.1	8.2	8.5	8.6	9.0	8.7	8.7	8.9	9.1	9.3	9.3	9.1	9.6	10.0	10.4	10.9	11.0	9.6	9.8	9.4
1995	8.4	8.5	8.8	8.9	9.3	9.0	9.0	9.2	9.4	9.6	9.7	9.5	10.0	10.4	10.8	11.3	11.4	10.1	10.4	10.1
1996	8.2	8.3	8.5	8.7	9.0	8.7	8.7	8.9	9.1	9.2	9.3	9.1	9.6	9.9	10.3	10.7	10.8	9.6	9.7	9.4
1997	8.2	8.3	8.5	8.7	9.0	8.7	8.7	8.9	9.1	9.2	9.3	9.1	9.5	9.8	10.2	10.5	10.6	9.5	9.6	9.3
1998	8.2	8.3	8.6	8.7	9.1	8.8	8.8	8.9	9.1	9.3	9.3	9.2	9.5	9.9	10.2	10.5	10.6	9.5	9.7	9.4
1999	7.9	8.0	8.2	8.4	8.7	8.4	8.4	8.5	8.7	8.8	8.8	8.7	9.0	9.3	9.5	9.8	9.9	8.8	8.9	8.6
2000	8.0	8.1	8.4	8.5	8.8	8.5	8.5	8.7	8.8	8.9	9.0	8.8	9.2	9.4	9.7	10.0	10.0	9.0	9.1	8.8
2001	8.0	8.1	8.3	8.5	8.8	8.5	8.5	8.6	8.8	8.9	8.9	8.8	9.1	9.3	9.6	9.9	9.9	9.0	9.0	8.8
2002	8.2	8.3	8.5	8.6	8.9	8.6	8.6	8.8	8.9	9.0	9.1	8.9	9.2	9.5	9.7	10.0	10.0	9.1	9.2	9.0
2003	8.0	8.1	8.3	8.4	8.7	8.5	8.4	8.6	8.7	8.8	8.8	8.7	9.0	9.2	9.4	9.7	9.7	8.8	8.9	8.6
2004	7.9	7.9	8.1	8.2	8.5	8.3	8.3	8.3	8.5	8.6	8.6	8.4	8.7	8.9	9.1	9.3	9.3	8.5	8.6	8.3
2005	7.7	7.8	7.9	8.0	8.3	8.1	8.0	8.1	8.2	8.3	8.3	8.2	8.4	8.6	8.8	9.0	9.0	8.2	8.2	8.0
2006	7.6	7.6	7.8	7.9	8.2	7.9	7.9	8.0	8.1	8.2	8.2	8.0	8.3	8.4	8.6	8.8	8.7	8.0	8.0	7.7
2007	7.6	7.7	7.9	8.0	8.2	8.0	8.0	8.0	8.1	8.2	8.2	8.1	8.3	8.5	8.6	8.8	8.8	8.1	8.1	7.8

Table C-5 (page 6 of 6)-a

Intermediate-Term Government Bonds Total Returns

Rates of Return for all holding periods
Percent per annum compounded annually

from 1926 to 2007

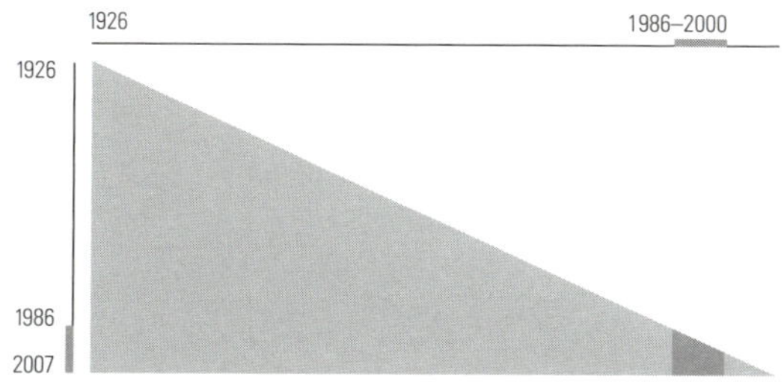

To the end of	From the beginning of 1986	1987	1988	1989	1990	1991	1992	1993	1994	1995	1996	1997	1998	1999	2000
1986	15.1														
1987	8.8	2.9													
1988	7.9	4.5	6.1												
1989	9.2	7.3	9.6	13.3											
1990	9.3	7.9	9.7	11.5	9.7										
1991	10.3	9.4	11.1	12.8	12.6	15.5									
1992	9.9	9.0	10.3	11.4	10.7	11.2	7.2								
1993	10.1	9.3	10.5	11.3	10.9	11.2	9.2	11.2							
1994	8.2	7.4	8.1	8.4	7.5	6.9	4.2	2.7	−5.1						
1995	9.1	8.4	9.1	9.6	9.0	8.8	7.2	7.2	5.3	16.8					
1996	8.4	7.8	8.3	8.6	8.0	7.7	6.2	5.9	4.2	9.2	2.1				
1997	8.4	7.8	8.3	8.6	8.0	7.8	6.5	6.4	5.2	8.9	5.2	8.4			
1998	8.6	8.0	8.5	8.7	8.3	8.1	7.1	7.0	6.2	9.2	6.8	9.3	10.2		
1999	7.8	7.2	7.6	7.7	7.2	6.9	5.9	5.7	4.8	6.9	4.6	5.5	4.0	−1.8	
2000	8.1	7.6	8.0	8.1	7.7	7.5	6.6	6.6	5.9	7.9	6.2	7.2	6.8	5.2	12.6
2001	8.1	7.6	8.0	8.1	7.7	7.5	6.7	6.7	6.1	7.8	6.4	7.3	7.0	6.0	10.1
2002	8.3	7.9	8.3	8.4	8.1	7.9	7.3	7.3	6.9	8.5	7.3	8.2	8.2	7.7	11.0
2003	8.0	7.6	7.9	8.0	7.7	7.5	6.9	6.8	6.4	7.8	6.7	7.4	7.2	6.6	8.8
2004	7.7	7.3	7.6	7.7	7.3	7.1	6.5	6.4	6.0	7.2	6.2	6.7	6.5	5.9	7.5
2005	7.4	7.0	7.2	7.3	6.9	6.7	6.1	6.0	5.6	6.7	5.7	6.1	5.8	5.2	6.4
2006	7.2	6.8	7.0	7.0	6.7	6.5	5.9	5.8	5.4	6.4	5.5	5.8	5.5	4.9	5.9
2007	7.3	6.9	7.1	7.2	6.9	6.7	6.2	6.1	5.8	6.6	5.8	6.2	6.0	5.5	6.4

Table C-5 (page 6 of 6)-b

Intermediate-Term Government Bonds Total Returns

Rates of Return for all holding periods
Percent per annum compounded annually

from 1926 to 2007

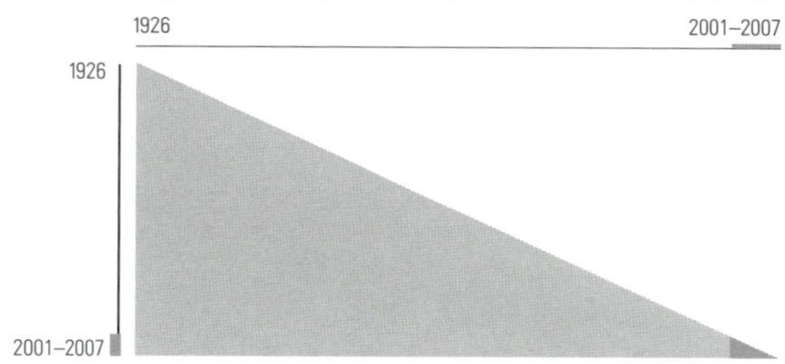

To the end of	From the beginning of 2001	2002	2003	2004	2005	2006	2007
2001	7.6						
2002	10.2	12.9					
2003	7.6	7.5	2.4				
2004	6.2	5.7	2.3	2.3			
2005	5.2	4.6	2.0	1.8	1.4		
2006	4.9	4.3	2.3	2.3	2.2	3.1	
2007	5.6	5.3	3.8	4.1	4.8	6.5	10.1

Table C-6 (page 1 of 6)

U.S. Treasury Bills Total Returns

Rates of Return for all holding periods
Percent per annum compounded annually

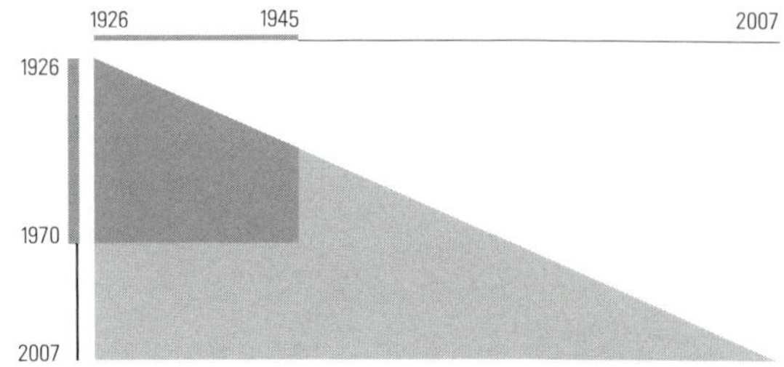

from 1926 to 2007

To the end of	From the beginning of 1926	1927	1928	1929	1930	1931	1932	1933	1934	1935	1936	1937	1938	1939	1940	1941	1942	1943	1944	1945
1926	3.3																			
1927	3.2	3.1																		
1928	3.3	3.3	3.6																	
1929	3.7	3.8	4.2	4.7																
1930	3.4	3.5	3.6	3.6	2.4															
1931	3.0	3.0	2.9	2.7	1.7	1.1														
1932	2.7	2.6	2.5	2.3	1.5	1.0	1.0													
1933	2.4	2.3	2.2	1.9	1.2	0.8	0.6	0.3												
1934	2.2	2.0	1.9	1.6	1.0	0.6	0.5	0.2	0.2											
1935	2.0	1.8	1.7	1.4	0.8	0.5	0.4	0.2	0.2	0.2										
1936	1.8	1.7	1.5	1.2	0.7	0.5	0.4	0.2	0.2	0.2	0.2									
1937	1.7	1.5	1.4	1.1	0.7	0.4	0.3	0.2	0.2	0.2	0.2	0.3								
1938	1.5	1.4	1.2	1.0	0.6	0.4	0.3	0.2	0.2	0.2	0.2	0.1	0.0							
1939	1.4	1.3	1.1	0.9	0.6	0.3	0.3	0.2	0.1	0.1	0.1	0.1	0.0	0.0						
1940	1.3	1.2	1.1	0.9	0.5	0.3	0.2	0.1	0.1	0.1	0.1	0.1	0.0	0.0	0.0					
1941	1.3	1.1	1.0	0.8	0.5	0.3	0.2	0.1	0.1	0.1	0.1	0.1	0.0	0.0	0.0	0.1				
1942	1.2	1.1	0.9	0.8	0.5	0.3	0.2	0.1	0.1	0.1	0.1	0.1	0.1	0.1	0.1	0.2	0.3			
1943	1.2	1.0	0.9	0.7	0.4	0.3	0.2	0.2	0.2	0.1	0.1	0.1	0.1	0.1	0.2	0.2	0.3	0.3		
1944	1.1	1.0	0.9	0.7	0.4	0.3	0.2	0.2	0.2	0.2	0.2	0.2	0.1	0.2	0.2	0.3	0.3	0.3	0.3	
1945	1.1	1.0	0.8	0.7	0.4	0.3	0.2	0.2	0.2	0.2	0.2	0.2	0.2	0.2	0.2	0.3	0.3	0.3	0.3	0.3
1946	1.0	0.9	0.8	0.7	0.4	0.3	0.3	0.2	0.2	0.2	0.2	0.2	0.2	0.2	0.2	0.3	0.3	0.3	0.3	0.3
1947	1.0	0.9	0.8	0.7	0.4	0.3	0.3	0.2	0.2	0.2	0.2	0.2	0.2	0.2	0.3	0.3	0.4	0.4	0.4	0.4
1948	1.0	0.9	0.8	0.7	0.4	0.3	0.3	0.3	0.3	0.3	0.3	0.3	0.3	0.3	0.3	0.4	0.4	0.4	0.5	0.5
1949	1.0	0.9	0.8	0.7	0.5	0.4	0.3	0.3	0.3	0.3	0.3	0.3	0.3	0.4	0.4	0.5	0.5	0.5	0.6	0.6
1950	1.0	0.9	0.8	0.7	0.5	0.4	0.4	0.4	0.4	0.4	0.4	0.4	0.4	0.4	0.5	0.5	0.6	0.6	0.7	0.7
1951	1.0	0.9	0.9	0.7	0.6	0.5	0.4	0.4	0.4	0.4	0.5	0.5	0.5	0.5	0.6	0.6	0.7	0.7	0.8	0.8
1952	1.1	1.0	0.9	0.8	0.6	0.5	0.5	0.5	0.5	0.5	0.5	0.5	0.6	0.6	0.6	0.7	0.8	0.8	0.9	0.9
1953	1.1	1.0	0.9	0.8	0.7	0.6	0.6	0.5	0.6	0.6	0.6	0.6	0.6	0.7	0.7	0.8	0.8	0.9	1.0	1.0
1954	1.1	1.0	0.9	0.8	0.7	0.6	0.6	0.6	0.6	0.6	0.6	0.6	0.7	0.7	0.7	0.8	0.9	0.9	0.9	1.0
1955	1.1	1.0	0.9	0.8	0.7	0.6	0.6	0.6	0.6	0.6	0.7	0.7	0.7	0.7	0.8	0.8	0.9	1.0	1.0	1.1
1956	1.1	1.1	1.0	0.9	0.8	0.7	0.7	0.7	0.7	0.7	0.7	0.8	0.8	0.8	0.9	0.9	1.0	1.1	1.1	1.2
1957	1.2	1.1	1.1	1.0	0.8	0.8	0.8	0.8	0.8	0.8	0.9	0.9	0.9	1.0	1.0	1.1	1.1	1.2	1.3	1.3
1958	1.2	1.1	1.1	1.0	0.9	0.8	0.8	0.8	0.8	0.9	0.9	0.9	0.9	1.0	1.0	1.1	1.2	1.2	1.3	1.3
1959	1.3	1.2	1.1	1.1	0.9	0.9	0.9	0.9	0.9	0.9	1.0	1.0	1.0	1.1	1.1	1.2	1.3	1.3	1.4	1.4
1960	1.3	1.2	1.2	1.1	1.0	1.0	0.9	0.9	1.0	1.0	1.0	1.1	1.1	1.2	1.2	1.3	1.3	1.4	1.5	1.5
1961	1.3	1.3	1.2	1.1	1.0	1.0	1.0	1.0	1.0	1.0	1.1	1.1	1.1	1.2	1.3	1.3	1.4	1.4	1.5	1.6
1962	1.4	1.3	1.3	1.2	1.1	1.0	1.0	1.0	1.1	1.1	1.1	1.2	1.2	1.3	1.3	1.4	1.4	1.5	1.6	1.6
1963	1.4	1.4	1.3	1.2	1.1	1.1	1.1	1.1	1.1	1.2	1.2	1.2	1.3	1.3	1.4	1.4	1.5	1.6	1.6	1.7
1964	1.5	1.4	1.4	1.3	1.2	1.2	1.2	1.2	1.2	1.2	1.3	1.3	1.4	1.4	1.5	1.5	1.6	1.7	1.7	1.8
1965	1.5	1.5	1.4	1.4	1.3	1.3	1.3	1.3	1.3	1.3	1.4	1.4	1.5	1.5	1.6	1.6	1.7	1.8	1.8	1.9
1966	1.6	1.6	1.5	1.5	1.4	1.3	1.4	1.4	1.4	1.4	1.5	1.5	1.6	1.6	1.7	1.7	1.8	1.9	1.9	2.0
1967	1.7	1.6	1.6	1.5	1.5	1.4	1.4	1.4	1.5	1.5	1.6	1.6	1.7	1.7	1.8	1.8	1.9	2.0	2.0	2.1
1968	1.7	1.7	1.7	1.6	1.5	1.5	1.5	1.6	1.6	1.6	1.7	1.7	1.8	1.8	1.9	2.0	2.0	2.1	2.2	2.2
1969	1.8	1.8	1.8	1.7	1.7	1.6	1.7	1.7	1.7	1.8	1.8	1.9	1.9	2.0	2.0	2.1	2.2	2.3	2.3	2.4
1970	2.0	1.9	1.9	1.9	1.8	1.8	1.8	1.8	1.8	1.9	1.9	2.0	2.1	2.1	2.2	2.3	2.3	2.4	2.5	2.6

Table C-6 (page 2 of 6)

U.S. Treasury Bills Total Returns

Rates of Return for all holding periods
Percent per annum compounded annually

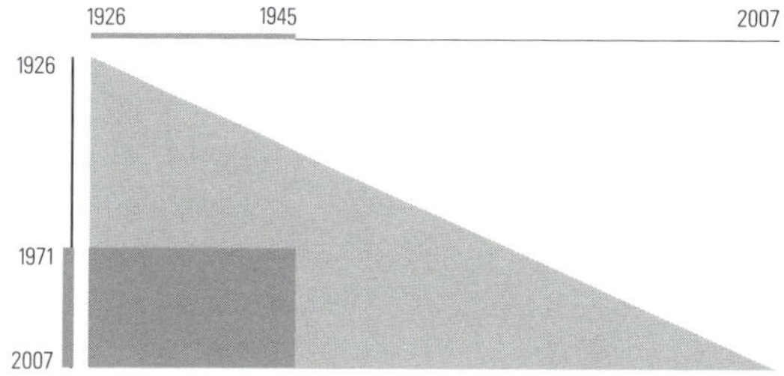

from 1926 to 2007

To the end of	From the beginning of 1926	1927	1928	1929	1930	1931	1932	1933	1934	1935	1936	1937	1938	1939	1940	1941	1942	1943	1944	1945
1971	2.0	2.0	1.9	1.9	1.8	1.8	1.9	1.9	1.9	2.0	2.0	2.1	2.1	2.2	2.3	2.3	2.4	2.5	2.6	2.6
1972	2.0	2.0	2.0	2.0	1.9	1.9	1.9	1.9	2.0	2.0	2.1	2.1	2.2	2.2	2.3	2.4	2.4	2.5	2.6	2.7
1973	2.1	2.1	2.1	2.1	2.0	2.0	2.0	2.0	2.1	2.1	2.2	2.2	2.3	2.4	2.4	2.5	2.6	2.7	2.7	2.8
1974	2.3	2.2	2.2	2.2	2.1	2.1	2.2	2.2	2.2	2.3	2.3	2.4	2.4	2.5	2.6	2.7	2.7	2.8	2.9	3.0
1975	2.3	2.3	2.3	2.3	2.2	2.2	2.2	2.3	2.3	2.4	2.4	2.5	2.5	2.6	2.7	2.8	2.8	2.9	3.0	3.1
1976	2.4	2.4	2.3	2.3	2.3	2.3	2.3	2.3	2.4	2.4	2.5	2.5	2.6	2.7	2.7	2.8	2.9	3.0	3.1	3.1
1977	2.4	2.4	2.4	2.4	2.3	2.3	2.4	2.4	2.4	2.5	2.5	2.6	2.7	2.7	2.8	2.9	3.0	3.0	3.1	3.2
1978	2.5	2.5	2.5	2.5	2.4	2.4	2.5	2.5	2.5	2.6	2.6	2.7	2.8	2.8	2.9	3.0	3.1	3.1	3.2	3.3
1979	2.7	2.6	2.6	2.6	2.6	2.6	2.6	2.7	2.7	2.8	2.8	2.9	2.9	3.0	3.1	3.2	3.3	3.3	3.4	3.5
1980	2.8	2.8	2.8	2.8	2.7	2.7	2.8	2.8	2.9	2.9	3.0	3.1	3.1	3.2	3.3	3.4	3.5	3.5	3.6	3.7
1981	3.0	3.0	3.0	3.0	3.0	3.0	3.0	3.1	3.1	3.2	3.2	3.3	3.4	3.5	3.5	3.6	3.7	3.8	3.9	4.0
1982	3.1	3.1	3.1	3.1	3.1	3.1	3.2	3.2	3.3	3.3	3.4	3.5	3.5	3.6	3.7	3.8	3.9	4.0	4.1	4.2
1983	3.2	3.2	3.2	3.2	3.2	3.2	3.3	3.3	3.4	3.4	3.5	3.6	3.6	3.7	3.8	3.9	4.0	4.1	4.2	4.3
1984	3.3	3.3	3.3	3.3	3.3	3.3	3.4	3.4	3.5	3.6	3.6	3.7	3.8	3.9	3.9	4.0	4.1	4.2	4.3	4.4
1985	3.4	3.4	3.4	3.4	3.4	3.4	3.5	3.5	3.6	3.6	3.7	3.8	3.9	3.9	4.0	4.1	4.2	4.3	4.4	4.5
1986	3.5	3.5	3.5	3.5	3.4	3.5	3.5	3.6	3.6	3.7	3.8	3.8	3.9	4.0	4.1	4.2	4.3	4.3	4.4	4.5
1987	3.5	3.5	3.5	3.5	3.5	3.5	3.5	3.6	3.7	3.7	3.8	3.9	3.9	4.0	4.1	4.2	4.3	4.4	4.5	4.6
1988	3.5	3.5	3.5	3.5	3.5	3.5	3.6	3.6	3.7	3.8	3.8	3.9	4.0	4.1	4.1	4.2	4.3	4.4	4.5	4.6
1989	3.6	3.6	3.6	3.6	3.6	3.6	3.7	3.7	3.8	3.8	3.9	4.0	4.1	4.1	4.2	4.3	4.4	4.5	4.6	4.7
1990	3.7	3.7	3.7	3.7	3.7	3.7	3.7	3.8	3.8	3.9	4.0	4.1	4.1	4.2	4.3	4.4	4.5	4.6	4.7	4.8
1991	3.7	3.7	3.7	3.7	3.7	3.7	3.8	3.8	3.9	3.9	4.0	4.1	4.2	4.2	4.3	4.4	4.5	4.6	4.7	4.8
1992	3.7	3.7	3.7	3.7	3.7	3.7	3.8	3.8	3.9	3.9	4.0	4.1	4.1	4.2	4.3	4.4	4.5	4.6	4.7	4.7
1993	3.7	3.7	3.7	3.7	3.7	3.7	3.8	3.8	3.9	3.9	4.0	4.1	4.1	4.2	4.3	4.4	4.4	4.5	4.6	4.7
1994	3.7	3.7	3.7	3.7	3.7	3.7	3.8	3.8	3.9	3.9	4.0	4.1	4.1	4.2	4.3	4.4	4.4	4.5	4.6	4.7
1995	3.7	3.7	3.7	3.7	3.7	3.7	3.8	3.8	3.9	3.9	4.0	4.1	4.1	4.2	4.3	4.4	4.5	4.5	4.6	4.7
1996	3.7	3.7	3.8	3.8	3.7	3.8	3.8	3.8	3.9	4.0	4.0	4.1	4.2	4.2	4.3	4.4	4.5	4.5	4.6	4.7
1997	3.8	3.8	3.8	3.8	3.8	3.8	3.8	3.9	3.9	4.0	4.1	4.1	4.2	4.3	4.3	4.4	4.5	4.6	4.6	4.7
1998	3.8	3.8	3.8	3.8	3.8	3.8	3.8	3.9	3.9	4.0	4.1	4.1	4.2	4.3	4.3	4.4	4.5	4.6	4.6	4.7
1999	3.8	3.8	3.8	3.8	3.8	3.8	3.9	3.9	4.0	4.0	4.1	4.1	4.2	4.3	4.3	4.4	4.5	4.6	4.6	4.7
2000	3.8	3.8	3.8	3.8	3.8	3.8	3.9	3.9	4.0	4.0	4.1	4.2	4.2	4.3	4.4	4.4	4.5	4.6	4.7	4.7
2001	3.8	3.8	3.8	3.8	3.8	3.8	3.9	3.9	4.0	4.0	4.1	4.2	4.2	4.3	4.4	4.4	4.5	4.6	4.7	4.7
2002	3.8	3.8	3.8	3.8	3.8	3.8	3.9	3.9	3.9	4.0	4.1	4.1	4.2	4.2	4.3	4.4	4.5	4.5	4.6	4.7
2003	3.7	3.8	3.8	3.8	3.8	3.8	3.8	3.9	3.9	4.0	4.0	4.1	4.1	4.2	4.3	4.3	4.4	4.5	4.5	4.6
2004	3.7	3.7	3.7	3.7	3.7	3.7	3.8	3.8	3.9	3.9	4.0	4.0	4.1	4.2	4.2	4.3	4.4	4.4	4.5	4.6
2005	3.7	3.7	3.7	3.7	3.7	3.7	3.8	3.8	3.9	3.9	4.0	4.0	4.1	4.1	4.2	4.3	4.3	4.4	4.5	4.5
2006	3.7	3.7	3.7	3.7	3.7	3.7	3.8	3.8	3.9	3.9	4.0	4.0	4.1	4.1	4.2	4.3	4.3	4.4	4.5	4.5
2007	3.7	3.7	3.7	3.7	3.7	3.8	3.8	3.8	3.9	3.9	4.0	4.0	4.1	4.2	4.2	4.3	4.3	4.4	4.5	4.5

Table C-6 (page 3 of 6)

U.S. Treasury Bills Total Returns

Rates of Return for all holding periods
Percent per annum compounded annually

from 1926 to 2007

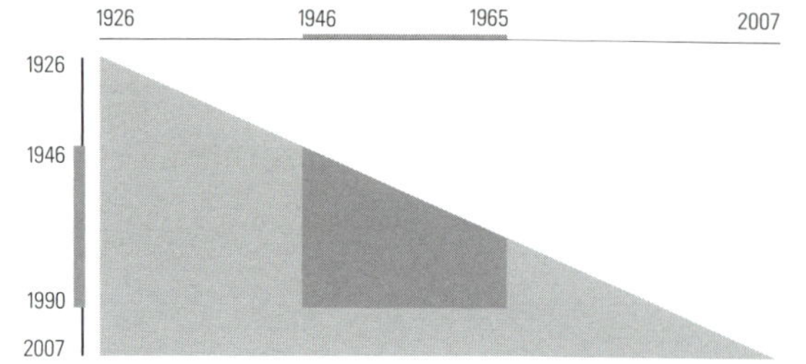

To the end of	From the beginning of 1946	1947	1948	1949	1950	1951	1952	1953	1954	1955	1956	1957	1958	1959	1960	1961	1962	1963	1964	1965
1946	0.4																			
1947	0.4	0.5																		
1948	0.6	0.7	0.8																	
1949	0.7	0.8	1.0	1.1																
1950	0.8	0.9	1.0	1.1	1.2															
1951	0.9	1.0	1.2	1.3	1.3	1.5														
1952	1.0	1.1	1.3	1.4	1.4	1.6	1.7													
1953	1.1	1.2	1.3	1.5	1.5	1.7	1.7	1.8												
1954	1.1	1.2	1.3	1.4	1.4	1.5	1.4	1.3	0.9											
1955	1.1	1.2	1.3	1.4	1.4	1.5	1.5	1.4	1.2	1.6										
1956	1.3	1.3	1.4	1.5	1.6	1.6	1.7	1.7	1.6	2.0	2.5									
1957	1.4	1.5	1.6	1.7	1.8	1.9	1.9	2.0	2.0	2.4	2.8	3.1								
1958	1.4	1.5	1.6	1.7	1.7	1.8	1.9	1.9	1.9	2.2	2.4	2.3	1.5							
1959	1.5	1.6	1.7	1.8	1.9	1.9	2.0	2.0	2.1	2.3	2.5	2.5	2.2	3.0						
1960	1.6	1.7	1.8	1.9	1.9	2.0	2.1	2.1	2.2	2.4	2.5	2.6	2.4	2.8	2.7					
1961	1.6	1.7	1.8	1.9	2.0	2.0	2.1	2.1	2.2	2.3	2.5	2.5	2.3	2.6	2.4	2.1				
1962	1.7	1.8	1.9	1.9	2.0	2.1	2.1	2.2	2.2	2.4	2.5	2.5	2.4	2.6	2.5	2.4	2.7			
1963	1.8	1.9	2.0	2.0	2.1	2.2	2.2	2.3	2.3	2.5	2.6	2.6	2.5	2.7	2.7	2.7	2.9	3.1		
1964	1.9	2.0	2.0	2.1	2.2	2.3	2.3	2.4	2.4	2.6	2.7	2.7	2.7	2.9	2.8	2.9	3.1	3.3	3.5	
1965	2.0	2.1	2.1	2.2	2.3	2.4	2.4	2.5	2.5	2.7	2.8	2.9	2.8	3.0	3.0	3.1	3.3	3.5	3.7	3.9
1966	2.1	2.2	2.3	2.4	2.4	2.5	2.6	2.7	2.7	2.9	3.0	3.0	3.0	3.2	3.3	3.4	3.6	3.8	4.1	4.3
1967	2.2	2.3	2.4	2.5	2.5	2.6	2.7	2.8	2.8	3.0	3.1	3.2	3.2	3.3	3.4	3.5	3.7	3.9	4.1	4.3
1968	2.3	2.4	2.5	2.6	2.7	2.8	2.8	2.9	3.0	3.1	3.3	3.3	3.3	3.5	3.6	3.7	3.9	4.1	4.3	4.5
1969	2.5	2.6	2.7	2.8	2.9	3.0	3.0	3.1	3.2	3.4	3.5	3.6	3.6	3.8	3.9	4.0	4.3	4.5	4.7	4.9
1970	2.7	2.8	2.9	3.0	3.0	3.1	3.2	3.3	3.4	3.6	3.7	3.8	3.8	4.0	4.1	4.3	4.5	4.7	5.0	5.2
1971	2.7	2.8	2.9	3.0	3.1	3.2	3.3	3.4	3.4	3.6	3.7	3.8	3.9	4.0	4.1	4.3	4.5	4.7	4.9	5.1
1972	2.8	2.9	3.0	3.0	3.1	3.2	3.3	3.4	3.5	3.6	3.7	3.8	3.9	4.0	4.1	4.2	4.4	4.6	4.8	4.9
1973	2.9	3.0	3.1	3.2	3.3	3.4	3.5	3.6	3.6	3.8	3.9	4.0	4.1	4.2	4.3	4.4	4.6	4.8	5.0	5.1
1974	3.1	3.2	3.3	3.4	3.5	3.6	3.7	3.8	3.8	4.0	4.1	4.2	4.3	4.5	4.6	4.7	4.9	5.1	5.3	5.4
1975	3.2	3.3	3.4	3.5	3.6	3.7	3.7	3.8	3.9	4.1	4.2	4.3	4.4	4.5	4.6	4.8	5.0	5.1	5.3	5.5
1976	3.2	3.3	3.4	3.5	3.6	3.7	3.8	3.9	4.0	4.1	4.2	4.3	4.4	4.6	4.7	4.8	5.0	5.1	5.3	5.4
1977	3.3	3.4	3.5	3.6	3.7	3.8	3.9	3.9	4.0	4.2	4.3	4.4	4.4	4.6	4.7	4.8	5.0	5.1	5.3	5.4
1978	3.4	3.5	3.6	3.7	3.8	3.9	4.0	4.1	4.2	4.3	4.4	4.5	4.6	4.7	4.8	4.9	5.1	5.3	5.4	5.5
1979	3.6	3.7	3.8	3.9	4.0	4.1	4.2	4.3	4.4	4.5	4.7	4.8	4.8	5.0	5.1	5.2	5.4	5.5	5.7	5.8
1980	3.8	3.9	4.0	4.1	4.2	4.3	4.4	4.5	4.6	4.8	4.9	5.0	5.1	5.3	5.4	5.5	5.7	5.9	6.0	6.2
1981	4.1	4.2	4.3	4.4	4.5	4.7	4.8	4.9	5.0	5.1	5.3	5.4	5.5	5.7	5.8	5.9	6.1	6.3	6.5	6.7
1982	4.3	4.4	4.5	4.6	4.7	4.8	4.9	5.1	5.2	5.3	5.5	5.6	5.7	5.9	6.0	6.1	6.3	6.5	6.7	6.9
1983	4.4	4.5	4.6	4.7	4.8	4.9	5.1	5.2	5.3	5.4	5.6	5.7	5.8	6.0	6.1	6.2	6.4	6.6	6.8	7.0
1984	4.5	4.6	4.8	4.9	5.0	5.1	5.2	5.3	5.4	5.6	5.7	5.8	5.9	6.1	6.2	6.4	6.6	6.8	6.9	7.1
1985	4.6	4.7	4.8	4.9	5.1	5.2	5.3	5.4	5.5	5.7	5.8	5.9	6.0	6.2	6.3	6.4	6.6	6.8	7.0	7.1
1986	4.6	4.8	4.9	5.0	5.1	5.2	5.3	5.4	5.5	5.7	5.8	5.9	6.0	6.2	6.3	6.4	6.6	6.8	6.9	7.1
1987	4.7	4.8	4.9	5.0	5.1	5.2	5.3	5.4	5.5	5.7	5.8	5.9	6.0	6.2	6.3	6.4	6.6	6.7	6.9	7.0
1988	4.7	4.8	4.9	5.0	5.1	5.2	5.3	5.4	5.5	5.7	5.8	5.9	6.0	6.2	6.3	6.4	6.6	6.7	6.9	7.0
1989	4.8	4.9	5.0	5.1	5.2	5.3	5.4	5.5	5.6	5.8	5.9	6.0	6.1	6.2	6.3	6.5	6.6	6.8	6.9	7.1
1990	4.9	5.0	5.1	5.2	5.3	5.4	5.5	5.6	5.7	5.8	5.9	6.0	6.1	6.3	6.4	6.5	6.7	6.8	6.9	7.1

Table C-6 (page 4 of 6)

U.S. Treasury Bills Total Returns

Rates of Return for all holding periods
Percent per annum compounded annually

from 1926 to 2007

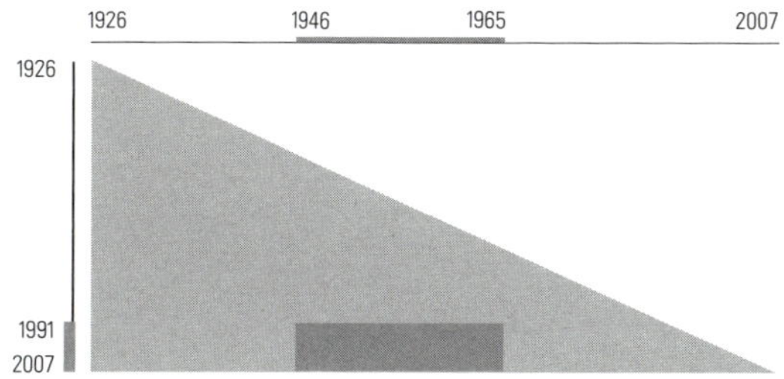

To the end of	From the beginning of 1946	1947	1948	1949	1950	1951	1952	1953	1954	1955	1956	1957	1958	1959	1960	1961	1962	1963	1964	1965
1991	4.9	5.0	5.1	5.2	5.3	5.4	5.5	5.6	5.7	5.8	5.9	6.0	6.1	6.3	6.4	6.5	6.6	6.8	6.9	7.0
1992	4.8	4.9	5.0	5.1	5.2	5.3	5.4	5.5	5.6	5.7	5.9	6.0	6.0	6.2	6.3	6.4	6.5	6.7	6.8	6.9
1993	4.8	4.9	5.0	5.1	5.2	5.3	5.4	5.5	5.5	5.7	5.8	5.9	6.0	6.1	6.2	6.3	6.4	6.5	6.7	6.8
1994	4.8	4.9	5.0	5.1	5.2	5.2	5.3	5.4	5.5	5.6	5.7	5.8	5.9	6.0	6.1	6.2	6.3	6.5	6.6	6.7
1995	4.8	4.9	5.0	5.1	5.2	5.2	5.3	5.4	5.5	5.6	5.7	5.8	5.9	6.0	6.1	6.2	6.3	6.4	6.5	6.6
1996	4.8	4.9	5.0	5.1	5.2	5.2	5.3	5.4	5.5	5.6	5.7	5.8	5.9	6.0	6.1	6.2	6.3	6.4	6.5	6.6
1997	4.8	4.9	5.0	5.1	5.2	5.2	5.3	5.4	5.5	5.6	5.7	5.8	5.9	6.0	6.0	6.1	6.3	6.4	6.5	6.5
1998	4.8	4.9	5.0	5.1	5.2	5.2	5.3	5.4	5.5	5.6	5.7	5.8	5.8	5.9	6.0	6.1	6.2	6.3	6.4	6.5
1999	4.8	4.9	5.0	5.1	5.1	5.2	5.3	5.4	5.5	5.6	5.7	5.7	5.8	5.9	6.0	6.1	6.2	6.3	6.4	6.4
2000	4.8	4.9	5.0	5.1	5.2	5.2	5.3	5.4	5.5	5.6	5.7	5.7	5.8	5.9	6.0	6.1	6.2	6.3	6.3	6.4
2001	4.8	4.9	5.0	5.1	5.1	5.2	5.3	5.4	5.4	5.5	5.6	5.7	5.8	5.9	5.9	6.0	6.1	6.2	6.3	6.4
2002	4.8	4.8	4.9	5.0	5.1	5.1	5.2	5.3	5.4	5.5	5.5	5.6	5.7	5.8	5.8	5.9	6.0	6.1	6.2	6.2
2003	4.7	4.8	4.8	4.9	5.0	5.1	5.1	5.2	5.3	5.4	5.4	5.5	5.6	5.7	5.7	5.8	5.9	6.0	6.0	6.1
2004	4.6	4.7	4.8	4.9	4.9	5.0	5.1	5.1	5.2	5.3	5.4	5.4	5.5	5.6	5.6	5.7	5.8	5.8	5.9	6.0
2005	4.6	4.7	4.7	4.8	4.9	5.0	5.0	5.1	5.1	5.2	5.3	5.4	5.4	5.5	5.6	5.6	5.7	5.8	5.8	5.9
2006	4.6	4.7	4.8	4.8	4.9	5.0	5.0	5.1	5.1	5.2	5.3	5.4	5.4	5.5	5.5	5.6	5.7	5.7	5.8	5.9
2007	4.6	4.7	4.7	4.8	4.9	4.9	5.0	5.1	5.1	5.2	5.3	5.3	5.4	5.5	5.5	5.6	5.7	5.7	5.8	5.8

Table C-6 (page 5 of 6)

U.S. Treasury Bills Total Returns

Rates of Return for all holding periods
Percent per annum compounded annually

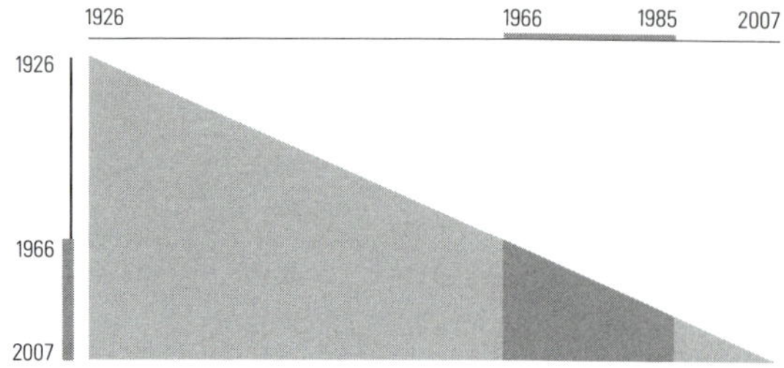

from 1926 to 2007

To the end of	From the beginning of 1966	1967	1968	1969	1970	1971	1972	1973	1974	1975	1976	1977	1978	1979	1980	1981	1982	1983	1984	1985
1966	4.8																			
1967	4.5	4.2																		
1968	4.7	4.7	5.2																	
1969	5.2	5.3	5.9	6.6																
1970	5.5	5.6	6.1	6.6	6.5															
1971	5.3	5.4	5.7	5.8	5.5	4.4														
1972	5.1	5.1	5.3	5.3	4.9	4.1	3.8													
1973	5.3	5.4	5.6	5.6	5.4	5.0	5.4	6.9												
1974	5.6	5.7	5.9	6.0	5.9	5.8	6.2	7.5	8.0											
1975	5.6	5.7	5.9	6.0	5.9	5.8	6.1	6.9	6.9	5.8										
1976	5.6	5.6	5.8	5.9	5.8	5.7	5.9	6.4	6.3	5.4	5.1									
1977	5.5	5.6	5.7	5.8	5.7	5.6	5.8	6.2	6.0	5.3	5.1	5.1								
1978	5.7	5.7	5.9	5.9	5.9	5.8	6.0	6.3	6.2	5.8	5.8	6.1	7.2							
1979	6.0	6.1	6.2	6.3	6.3	6.3	6.5	6.9	6.9	6.7	6.9	7.5	8.8	10.4						
1980	6.3	6.4	6.6	6.7	6.7	6.8	7.0	7.4	7.5	7.4	7.8	8.5	9.6	10.8	11.2					
1981	6.8	7.0	7.2	7.3	7.4	7.5	7.8	8.2	8.4	8.4	8.9	9.7	10.8	12.1	13.0	14.7				
1982	7.0	7.2	7.4	7.6	7.6	7.7	8.0	8.5	8.6	8.7	9.1	9.8	10.8	11.7	12.1	12.6	10.5			
1983	7.1	7.3	7.5	7.6	7.7	7.8	8.1	8.5	8.6	8.7	9.1	9.7	10.4	11.1	11.3	11.3	9.7	8.8		
1984	7.3	7.4	7.6	7.8	7.9	7.9	8.2	8.6	8.8	8.8	9.2	9.7	10.4	10.9	11.0	11.0	9.7	9.3	9.8	
1985	7.3	7.4	7.6	7.8	7.8	7.9	8.2	8.5	8.7	8.7	9.0	9.5	10.0	10.4	10.5	10.3	9.2	8.8	8.8	7.7
1986	7.3	7.4	7.5	7.7	7.7	7.8	8.1	8.4	8.5	8.5	8.8	9.1	9.6	9.9	9.8	9.6	8.6	8.1	7.9	6.9
1987	7.2	7.3	7.4	7.6	7.6	7.7	7.9	8.2	8.3	8.3	8.5	8.8	9.2	9.4	9.3	9.0	8.1	7.6	7.3	6.4
1988	7.1	7.2	7.4	7.5	7.6	7.6	7.8	8.1	8.1	8.1	8.3	8.6	8.9	9.1	8.9	8.7	7.8	7.4	7.1	6.4
1989	7.2	7.3	7.4	7.5	7.6	7.6	7.8	8.1	8.1	8.2	8.3	8.6	8.9	9.0	8.9	8.6	7.9	7.5	7.3	6.8
1990	7.2	7.3	7.5	7.6	7.6	7.7	7.8	8.1	8.1	8.1	8.3	8.5	8.8	8.9	8.8	8.5	7.9	7.6	7.4	7.0
1991	7.1	7.2	7.4	7.5	7.5	7.6	7.7	7.9	8.0	8.0	8.1	8.3	8.6	8.7	8.5	8.3	7.7	7.3	7.2	6.8
1992	7.0	7.1	7.2	7.3	7.3	7.4	7.5	7.7	7.7	7.7	7.8	8.0	8.2	8.3	8.1	7.9	7.3	6.9	6.7	6.4
1993	6.9	6.9	7.0	7.1	7.1	7.2	7.3	7.5	7.5	7.5	7.6	7.7	7.9	7.9	7.7	7.5	6.9	6.6	6.4	6.0
1994	6.8	6.8	6.9	7.0	7.0	7.0	7.1	7.3	7.3	7.3	7.4	7.5	7.6	7.7	7.5	7.2	6.7	6.3	6.1	5.8
1995	6.7	6.8	6.9	6.9	7.0	7.0	7.1	7.2	7.2	7.2	7.3	7.4	7.5	7.5	7.4	7.1	6.6	6.3	6.1	5.7
1996	6.7	6.7	6.8	6.9	6.9	6.9	7.0	7.1	7.2	7.1	7.2	7.3	7.4	7.4	7.2	7.0	6.5	6.2	6.0	5.7
1997	6.6	6.7	6.8	6.8	6.8	6.8	6.9	7.1	7.1	7.0	7.1	7.2	7.3	7.3	7.1	6.9	6.4	6.1	6.0	5.7
1998	6.6	6.6	6.7	6.8	6.8	6.8	6.9	7.0	7.0	6.9	7.0	7.1	7.2	7.2	7.0	6.8	6.3	6.1	5.9	5.6
1999	6.5	6.6	6.6	6.7	6.7	6.7	6.8	6.9	6.9	6.8	6.9	7.0	7.1	7.1	6.9	6.7	6.2	6.0	5.8	5.5
2000	6.5	6.5	6.6	6.7	6.7	6.7	6.8	6.9	6.9	6.8	6.9	6.9	7.0	7.0	6.8	6.6	6.2	6.0	5.8	5.6
2001	6.4	6.5	6.5	6.6	6.6	6.6	6.7	6.8	6.7	6.7	6.7	6.8	6.9	6.9	6.7	6.5	6.1	5.9	5.7	5.5
2002	6.3	6.3	6.4	6.4	6.4	6.4	6.5	6.6	6.6	6.5	6.5	6.6	6.7	6.6	6.5	6.3	5.9	5.7	5.5	5.3
2003	6.1	6.2	6.2	6.3	6.3	6.3	6.3	6.4	6.4	6.3	6.3	6.4	6.4	6.4	6.2	6.0	5.7	5.4	5.3	5.0
2004	6.0	6.1	6.1	6.1	6.1	6.1	6.2	6.2	6.2	6.1	6.2	6.2	6.2	6.2	6.0	5.8	5.5	5.2	5.1	4.8
2005	5.9	6.0	6.0	6.0	6.0	6.0	6.1	6.1	6.1	6.0	6.1	6.1	6.1	6.1	5.9	5.7	5.4	5.1	5.0	4.7
2006	5.9	5.9	6.0	6.0	6.0	6.0	6.0	6.1	6.1	6.0	6.0	6.0	6.1	6.0	5.9	5.7	5.3	5.1	5.0	4.7
2007	5.9	5.9	6.0	6.0	6.0	5.9	6.0	6.0	6.0	6.0	6.0	6.0	6.0	6.0	5.8	5.6	5.3	5.1	4.9	4.7

Table C-6 (page 6 of 6)-a

U.S. Treasury Bills Total Returns

Rates of Return for all holding periods
Percent per annum compounded annually

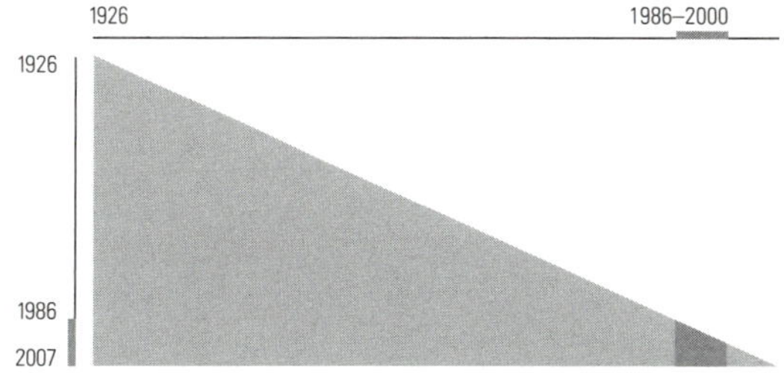

from 1926 to 2007

To the end of	From the beginning of 1986	1987	1988	1989	1990	1991	1992	1993	1994	1995	1996	1997	1998	1999	2000
1986	6.2														
1987	5.8	5.5													
1988	6.0	5.9	6.3												
1989	6.6	6.7	7.4	8.4											
1990	6.8	7.0	7.5	8.1	7.8										
1991	6.6	6.7	7.0	7.3	6.7	5.6									
1992	6.2	6.2	6.3	6.3	5.6	4.5	3.5								
1993	5.8	5.7	5.7	5.6	4.9	4.0	3.2	2.9							
1994	5.5	5.5	5.5	5.3	4.7	4.0	3.4	3.4	3.9						
1995	5.6	5.5	5.5	5.4	4.9	4.3	4.0	4.1	4.7	5.6					
1996	5.5	5.5	5.5	5.3	4.9	4.4	4.2	4.4	4.9	5.4	5.2				
1997	5.5	5.4	5.4	5.3	5.0	4.6	4.4	4.6	5.0	5.4	5.2	5.3			
1998	5.4	5.4	5.4	5.3	5.0	4.6	4.5	4.6	5.0	5.2	5.1	5.1	4.9		
1999	5.4	5.3	5.3	5.2	4.9	4.6	4.5	4.6	4.9	5.1	5.0	4.9	4.8	4.7	
2000	5.4	5.4	5.4	5.3	5.0	4.7	4.6	4.8	5.1	5.2	5.2	5.2	5.1	5.3	5.9
2001	5.3	5.3	5.3	5.2	4.9	4.7	4.6	4.7	4.9	5.0	5.0	4.9	4.8	4.8	4.9
2002	5.1	5.0	5.0	4.9	4.7	4.4	4.3	4.4	4.5	4.6	4.5	4.4	4.2	4.0	3.8
2003	4.9	4.8	4.8	4.7	4.4	4.1	4.0	4.1	4.2	4.2	4.0	3.9	3.6	3.4	3.1
2004	4.7	4.6	4.5	4.4	4.2	3.9	3.8	3.8	3.9	3.9	3.7	3.5	3.3	3.0	2.7
2005	4.6	4.5	4.5	4.3	4.1	3.9	3.7	3.8	3.8	3.8	3.6	3.5	3.2	3.0	2.7
2006	4.6	4.5	4.5	4.4	4.1	3.9	3.8	3.8	3.9	3.9	3.7	3.6	3.4	3.2	3.0
2007	4.6	4.5	4.5	4.4	4.2	4.0	3.9	3.9	4.0	4.0	3.8	3.7	3.5	3.4	3.2

Table C-6 (page 6 of 6)-b

U.S. Treasury Bills Total Returns

Rates of Return for all holding periods
Percent per annum compounded annually

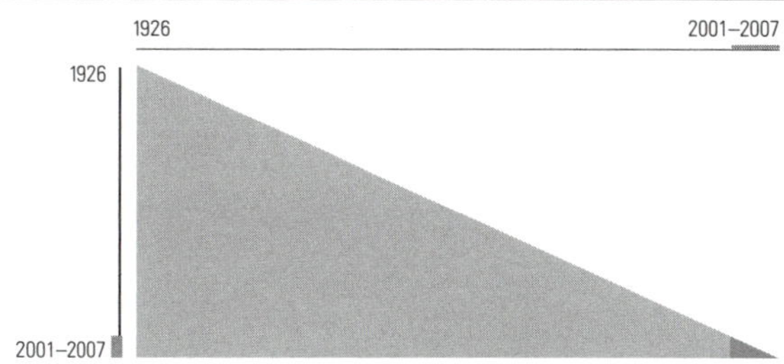

from 1926 to 2007

To the end of	From the beginning of 2001	2002	2003	2004	2005	2006	2007
2001	3.8						
2002	2.7	1.6					
2003	2.2	1.3	1.0				
2004	1.9	1.3	1.1	1.2			
2005	2.1	1.7	1.7	2.1	3.0		
2006	2.6	2.3	2.5	3.0	3.9	4.8	
2007	2.9	2.7	2.9	3.4	4.1	4.7	4.7

Table C-7 (page 1 of 6)

Inflation

Rates of Return for all holding periods
Percent per annum compounded annually

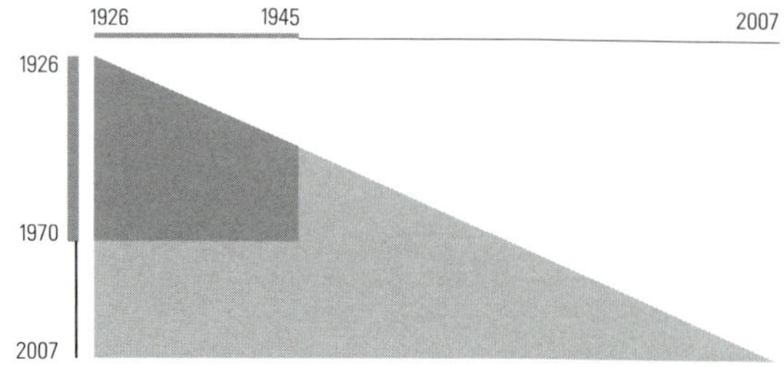

from 1926 to 2007

To the end of	From the beginning of 1926	1927	1928	1929	1930	1931	1932	1933	1934	1935	1936	1937	1938	1939	1940	1941	1942	1943	1944	1945
1926	−1.5																			
1927	−1.8	−2.1																		
1928	−1.5	−1.5	−1.0																	
1929	−1.1	−1.0	−0.4	0.2																
1930	−2.1	−2.2	−2.3	−3.0	−6.0															
1931	−3.4	−3.7	−4.2	−5.2	−7.8	−9.5														
1932	−4.4	−4.9	−5.4	−6.5	−8.6	−9.9	−10.3													
1933	−3.8	−4.1	−4.5	−5.1	−6.4	−6.6	−5.0	0.5												
1934	−3.2	−3.4	−3.6	−4.0	−4.8	−4.5	−2.7	1.3	2.0											
1935	−2.6	−2.7	−2.8	−3.0	−3.5	−3.0	−1.3	1.8	2.5	3.0										
1936	−2.2	−2.3	−2.3	−2.5	−2.9	−2.3	−0.8	1.7	2.1	2.1	1.2									
1937	−1.8	−1.8	−1.8	−1.9	−2.1	−1.6	−0.2	2.0	2.3	2.4	2.2	3.1								
1938	−1.9	−1.9	−1.9	−2.0	−2.2	−1.7	−0.6	1.2	1.3	1.1	0.5	0.1	−2.8							
1939	−1.8	−1.8	−1.8	−1.8	−2.0	−1.6	−0.6	0.9	1.0	0.8	0.2	−0.1	−1.6	−0.5						
1940	−1.6	−1.6	−1.6	−1.6	−1.8	−1.3	−0.4	0.9	1.0	0.8	0.4	0.2	−0.8	0.2	1.0					
1941	−0.9	−0.9	−0.8	−0.8	−0.9	−0.4	0.6	1.9	2.0	2.0	1.9	2.0	1.7	3.3	5.2	9.7				
1942	−0.3	−0.3	−0.2	−0.1	−0.1	0.4	1.3	2.6	2.8	2.9	2.9	3.2	3.2	4.8	6.6	9.5	9.3			
1943	−0.2	−0.1	0.0	0.1	0.1	0.6	1.5	2.6	2.9	2.9	2.9	3.2	3.2	4.4	5.7	7.3	6.2	3.2		
1944	0.0	0.0	0.2	0.2	0.2	0.7	1.5	2.6	2.8	2.9	2.8	3.1	3.0	4.1	5.0	6.0	4.8	2.6	2.1	
1945	0.1	0.2	0.3	0.4	0.4	0.8	1.6	2.6	2.7	2.8	2.8	3.0	2.9	3.8	4.5	5.2	4.2	2.5	2.2	2.3
1946	0.9	1.0	1.2	1.3	1.3	1.8	2.6	3.6	3.9	4.0	4.1	4.4	4.5	5.5	6.4	7.3	6.8	6.2	7.3	9.9
1947	1.2	1.4	1.5	1.7	1.7	2.2	3.0	4.0	4.2	4.4	4.5	4.8	5.0	5.9	6.7	7.5	7.2	6.8	7.7	9.6
1948	1.3	1.4	1.6	1.7	1.8	2.3	3.0	3.9	4.1	4.3	4.4	4.6	4.8	5.6	6.2	6.9	6.5	6.1	6.7	7.8
1949	1.2	1.3	1.4	1.5	1.6	2.0	2.7	3.5	3.7	3.8	3.9	4.1	4.2	4.9	5.4	5.9	5.5	4.9	5.2	5.8
1950	1.3	1.5	1.6	1.7	1.8	2.2	2.9	3.7	3.9	4.0	4.0	4.2	4.3	4.9	5.4	5.9	5.5	5.0	5.3	5.8
1951	1.5	1.6	1.8	1.9	2.0	2.4	3.0	3.8	4.0	4.1	4.1	4.3	4.4	5.0	5.5	5.9	5.5	5.1	5.4	5.8
1952	1.5	1.6	1.8	1.9	1.9	2.3	2.9	3.6	3.8	3.9	4.0	4.1	4.2	4.7	5.1	5.5	5.1	4.7	4.9	5.2
1953	1.5	1.6	1.7	1.8	1.9	2.2	2.8	3.5	3.6	3.7	3.8	3.9	4.0	4.4	4.8	5.1	4.7	4.3	4.4	4.7
1954	1.4	1.5	1.6	1.7	1.8	2.1	2.7	3.3	3.4	3.5	3.5	3.7	3.7	4.1	4.4	4.7	4.3	3.9	4.0	4.2
1955	1.4	1.5	1.6	1.7	1.7	2.1	2.6	3.2	3.3	3.4	3.4	3.5	3.5	3.9	4.2	4.4	4.0	3.6	3.7	3.8
1956	1.4	1.5	1.6	1.7	1.8	2.1	2.6	3.2	3.3	3.3	3.3	3.5	3.5	3.8	4.1	4.3	3.9	3.6	3.6	3.7
1957	1.5	1.5	1.7	1.8	1.8	2.1	2.6	3.2	3.3	3.3	3.3	3.4	3.5	3.8	4.0	4.2	3.9	3.5	3.6	3.7
1958	1.5	1.6	1.7	1.8	1.8	2.1	2.6	3.1	3.2	3.3	3.3	3.4	3.4	3.7	3.9	4.1	3.8	3.4	3.4	3.5
1959	1.5	1.6	1.7	1.8	1.8	2.1	2.5	3.0	3.1	3.2	3.2	3.3	3.3	3.6	3.8	3.9	3.6	3.3	3.3	3.4
1960	1.5	1.6	1.7	1.7	1.8	2.1	2.5	3.0	3.1	3.1	3.1	3.2	3.2	3.5	3.7	3.8	3.5	3.2	3.2	3.3
1961	1.4	1.5	1.6	1.7	1.8	2.0	2.4	2.9	3.0	3.0	3.0	3.1	3.1	3.4	3.5	3.7	3.4	3.1	3.1	3.1
1962	1.4	1.5	1.6	1.7	1.7	2.0	2.4	2.8	2.9	3.0	3.0	3.0	3.0	3.3	3.4	3.6	3.3	3.0	3.0	3.0
1963	1.4	1.5	1.6	1.7	1.7	2.0	2.4	2.8	2.9	2.9	2.9	3.0	3.0	3.2	3.4	3.5	3.2	2.9	2.9	2.9
1964	1.4	1.5	1.6	1.7	1.7	2.0	2.3	2.8	2.8	2.9	2.9	2.9	2.9	3.1	3.3	3.4	3.1	2.8	2.8	2.9
1965	1.4	1.5	1.6	1.7	1.7	2.0	2.3	2.7	2.8	2.8	2.8	2.9	2.9	3.1	3.2	3.3	3.1	2.8	2.8	2.8
1966	1.5	1.6	1.7	1.7	1.8	2.0	2.4	2.8	2.8	2.8	2.8	2.9	2.9	3.1	3.2	3.3	3.1	2.8	2.8	2.8
1967	1.5	1.6	1.7	1.8	1.8	2.0	2.4	2.8	2.8	2.8	2.8	2.9	2.9	3.1	3.2	3.3	3.1	2.8	2.8	2.8
1968	1.6	1.7	1.8	1.8	1.9	2.1	2.4	2.8	2.9	2.9	2.9	3.0	3.0	3.1	3.3	3.4	3.1	2.9	2.9	2.9
1969	1.7	1.8	1.9	1.9	2.0	2.2	2.5	2.9	3.0	3.0	3.0	3.0	3.0	3.2	3.4	3.5	3.2	3.0	3.0	3.0
1970	1.8	1.9	2.0	2.0	2.1	2.3	2.6	3.0	3.0	3.1	3.1	3.1	3.1	3.3	3.4	3.5	3.3	3.1	3.1	3.1

Table C-7 (page 2 of 6)

Inflation

Rates of Return for all holding periods

Percent per annum compounded annually

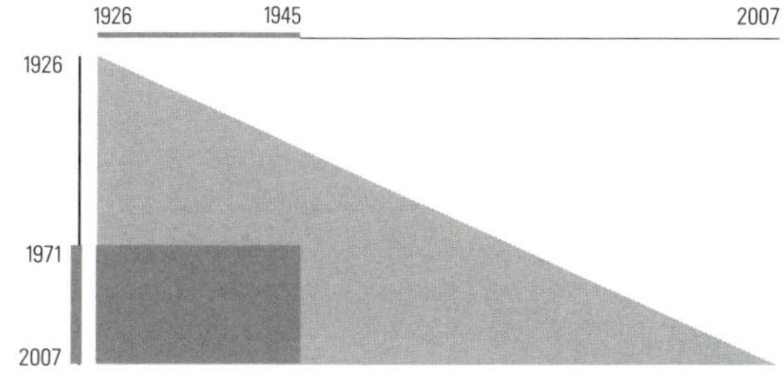

from 1926 to 2007

To the end of	From the beginning of 1926	1927	1928	1929	1930	1931	1932	1933	1934	1935	1936	1937	1938	1939	1940	1941	1942	1943	1944	1945
1971	1.8	1.9	2.0	2.1	2.1	2.3	2.6	3.0	3.0	3.1	3.1	3.1	3.1	3.3	3.4	3.5	3.3	3.1	3.1	3.1
1972	1.9	1.9	2.0	2.1	2.1	2.3	2.6	3.0	3.1	3.1	3.1	3.1	3.1	3.3	3.4	3.5	3.3	3.1	3.1	3.2
1973	2.0	2.1	2.2	2.2	2.3	2.5	2.8	3.1	3.2	3.2	3.2	3.3	3.3	3.5	3.6	3.7	3.5	3.3	3.3	3.3
1974	2.2	2.3	2.4	2.4	2.5	2.7	3.0	3.3	3.4	3.4	3.4	3.5	3.5	3.7	3.8	3.9	3.7	3.6	3.6	3.6
1975	2.3	2.4	2.5	2.5	2.6	2.8	3.1	3.4	3.5	3.5	3.5	3.6	3.6	3.8	3.9	4.0	3.8	3.7	3.7	3.7
1976	2.3	2.4	2.5	2.6	2.6	2.8	3.1	3.4	3.5	3.6	3.6	3.6	3.6	3.8	3.9	4.0	3.9	3.7	3.7	3.8
1977	2.4	2.5	2.6	2.7	2.7	2.9	3.2	3.5	3.6	3.6	3.6	3.7	3.7	3.9	4.0	4.1	3.9	3.8	3.8	3.9
1978	2.5	2.6	2.7	2.8	2.8	3.0	3.3	3.6	3.7	3.7	3.8	3.8	3.8	4.0	4.1	4.2	4.1	3.9	4.0	4.0
1979	2.7	2.8	2.9	3.0	3.0	3.2	3.5	3.8	3.9	4.0	4.0	4.0	4.1	4.2	4.4	4.4	4.3	4.2	4.2	4.3
1980	2.9	3.0	3.1	3.2	3.2	3.4	3.7	4.0	4.1	4.1	4.2	4.2	4.2	4.4	4.5	4.6	4.5	4.4	4.4	4.5
1981	3.0	3.1	3.2	3.3	3.3	3.5	3.8	4.1	4.2	4.2	4.3	4.3	4.4	4.5	4.6	4.7	4.6	4.5	4.5	4.6
1982	3.0	3.1	3.2	3.3	3.3	3.5	3.8	4.1	4.2	4.2	4.2	4.3	4.3	4.5	4.6	4.7	4.6	4.5	4.5	4.6
1983	3.0	3.1	3.2	3.3	3.3	3.5	3.8	4.1	4.2	4.2	4.2	4.3	4.3	4.5	4.6	4.7	4.6	4.5	4.5	4.6
1984	3.0	3.1	3.2	3.3	3.4	3.5	3.8	4.1	4.2	4.2	4.2	4.3	4.3	4.5	4.6	4.7	4.6	4.5	4.5	4.5
1985	3.1	3.1	3.2	3.3	3.4	3.5	3.8	4.1	4.2	4.2	4.2	4.3	4.3	4.5	4.6	4.7	4.5	4.4	4.5	4.5
1986	3.0	3.1	3.2	3.3	3.3	3.5	3.8	4.0	4.1	4.1	4.2	4.2	4.2	4.4	4.5	4.6	4.5	4.4	4.4	4.4
1987	3.0	3.1	3.2	3.3	3.3	3.5	3.8	4.0	4.1	4.1	4.2	4.2	4.2	4.4	4.5	4.6	4.5	4.4	4.4	4.4
1988	3.1	3.1	3.2	3.3	3.4	3.5	3.8	4.0	4.1	4.1	4.2	4.2	4.3	4.4	4.5	4.6	4.5	4.4	4.4	4.4
1989	3.1	3.2	3.3	3.3	3.4	3.5	3.8	4.1	4.1	4.2	4.2	4.2	4.3	4.4	4.5	4.6	4.5	4.4	4.4	4.4
1990	3.1	3.2	3.3	3.4	3.4	3.6	3.8	4.1	4.2	4.2	4.2	4.3	4.3	4.4	4.5	4.6	4.5	4.4	4.4	4.5
1991	3.1	3.2	3.3	3.4	3.4	3.6	3.8	4.1	4.1	4.2	4.2	4.2	4.3	4.4	4.5	4.6	4.5	4.4	4.4	4.5
1992	3.1	3.2	3.3	3.4	3.4	3.6	3.8	4.1	4.1	4.2	4.2	4.2	4.2	4.4	4.5	4.5	4.4	4.3	4.4	4.4
1993	3.1	3.2	3.3	3.3	3.4	3.6	3.8	4.0	4.1	4.1	4.1	4.2	4.2	4.3	4.4	4.5	4.4	4.3	4.3	4.4
1994	3.1	3.2	3.3	3.3	3.4	3.5	3.8	4.0	4.1	4.1	4.1	4.2	4.2	4.3	4.4	4.5	4.4	4.3	4.3	4.4
1995	3.1	3.2	3.3	3.3	3.4	3.5	3.7	4.0	4.0	4.1	4.1	4.1	4.2	4.3	4.4	4.4	4.3	4.3	4.3	4.3
1996	3.1	3.2	3.3	3.3	3.4	3.5	3.7	4.0	4.0	4.1	4.1	4.1	4.1	4.3	4.4	4.4	4.3	4.2	4.3	4.3
1997	3.1	3.2	3.2	3.3	3.4	3.5	3.7	3.9	4.0	4.0	4.0	4.1	4.1	4.2	4.3	4.4	4.3	4.2	4.2	4.2
1998	3.1	3.1	3.2	3.3	3.3	3.5	3.7	3.9	4.0	4.0	4.0	4.0	4.1	4.2	4.3	4.3	4.2	4.1	4.2	4.2
1999	3.1	3.1	3.2	3.3	3.3	3.5	3.7	3.9	3.9	4.0	4.0	4.0	4.0	4.2	4.2	4.3	4.2	4.1	4.1	4.2
2000	3.1	3.1	3.2	3.3	3.3	3.5	3.7	3.9	3.9	4.0	4.0	4.0	4.0	4.1	4.2	4.3	4.2	4.1	4.1	4.2
2001	3.1	3.1	3.2	3.2	3.3	3.4	3.6	3.8	3.9	3.9	3.9	4.0	4.0	4.1	4.2	4.2	4.1	4.1	4.1	4.1
2002	3.0	3.1	3.2	3.2	3.3	3.4	3.6	3.8	3.9	3.9	3.9	4.0	4.0	4.1	4.2	4.2	4.1	4.0	4.0	4.1
2003	3.0	3.1	3.2	3.2	3.3	3.4	3.6	3.8	3.8	3.9	3.9	3.9	3.9	4.0	4.1	4.2	4.1	4.0	4.0	4.0
2004	3.0	3.1	3.2	3.2	3.3	3.4	3.6	3.8	3.8	3.9	3.9	3.9	3.9	4.0	4.1	4.2	4.1	4.0	4.0	4.0
2005	3.0	3.1	3.2	3.2	3.3	3.4	3.6	3.8	3.8	3.9	3.9	3.9	3.9	4.0	4.1	4.1	4.1	4.0	4.0	4.0
2006	3.0	3.1	3.2	3.2	3.3	3.4	3.6	3.8	3.8	3.8	3.8	3.9	3.9	4.0	4.1	4.1	4.0	4.0	4.0	4.0
2007	3.0	3.1	3.2	3.2	3.3	3.4	3.6	3.8	3.8	3.8	3.9	3.9	3.9	4.0	4.1	4.1	4.0	4.0	4.0	4.0

Table C-7 (page 3 of 6)

Inflation

Rates of Return for all holding periods
Percent per annum compounded annually

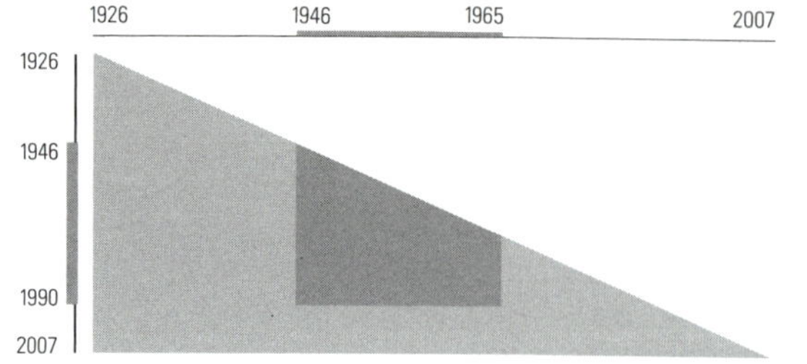

from 1926 to 2007

To the end of	From the beginning of 1946	1947	1948	1949	1950	1951	1952	1953	1954	1955	1956	1957	1958	1959	1960	1961	1962	1963	1964	1965
1946	18.2																			
1947	13.5	9.0																		
1948	9.8	5.8	2.7																	
1949	6.8	3.2	0.4	–1.8																
1950	6.6	3.8	2.2	1.9	5.8															
1951	6.5	4.3	3.1	3.2	5.8	5.9														
1952	5.6	3.7	2.6	2.6	4.2	3.3	0.9													
1953	5.0	3.2	2.3	2.2	3.3	2.4	0.8	0.6												
1954	4.4	2.8	1.9	1.8	2.5	1.7	0.3	0.1	–0.5											
1955	4.0	2.5	1.7	1.6	2.1	1.4	0.3	0.2	–0.1	0.4										
1956	3.9	2.5	1.8	1.7	2.2	1.7	0.8	0.8	0.9	1.6	2.9									
1957	3.8	2.6	2.0	1.9	2.3	1.9	1.2	1.3	1.4	2.1	2.9	3.0								
1958	3.6	2.5	1.9	1.9	2.3	1.8	1.3	1.3	1.5	2.0	2.5	2.4	1.8							
1959	3.5	2.4	1.9	1.8	2.2	1.8	1.3	1.4	1.5	1.9	2.3	2.1	1.6	1.5						
1960	3.3	2.4	1.9	1.8	2.1	1.8	1.3	1.4	1.5	1.8	2.1	1.9	1.6	1.5	1.5					
1961	3.2	2.2	1.8	1.7	2.0	1.7	1.3	1.3	1.4	1.7	1.9	1.7	1.4	1.2	1.1	0.7				
1962	3.1	2.2	1.7	1.7	1.9	1.6	1.3	1.3	1.4	1.6	1.8	1.6	1.3	1.2	1.1	0.9	1.2			
1963	3.0	2.2	1.7	1.7	1.9	1.6	1.3	1.3	1.4	1.6	1.8	1.6	1.4	1.3	1.3	1.2	1.4	1.6		
1964	2.9	2.1	1.7	1.6	1.9	1.6	1.3	1.3	1.4	1.6	1.7	1.6	1.4	1.3	1.2	1.2	1.4	1.4	1.2	
1965	2.8	2.1	1.7	1.7	1.9	1.6	1.3	1.4	1.4	1.6	1.7	1.6	1.4	1.4	1.4	1.3	1.5	1.6	1.6	1.9
1966	2.9	2.2	1.8	1.8	2.0	1.7	1.5	1.5	1.6	1.7	1.9	1.8	1.6	1.6	1.6	1.7	1.9	2.0	2.2	2.6
1967	2.9	2.2	1.9	1.8	2.0	1.8	1.6	1.6	1.7	1.8	2.0	1.9	1.8	1.8	1.8	1.9	2.1	2.2	2.4	2.8
1968	3.0	2.3	2.0	2.0	2.2	2.0	1.7	1.8	1.9	2.0	2.2	2.1	2.0	2.1	2.1	2.2	2.4	2.6	2.8	3.3
1969	3.1	2.5	2.2	2.2	2.4	2.2	2.0	2.0	2.1	2.3	2.5	2.4	2.4	2.4	2.5	2.6	2.9	3.1	3.4	3.8
1970	3.2	2.6	2.3	2.3	2.5	2.3	2.2	2.2	2.3	2.5	2.7	2.6	2.6	2.7	2.8	2.9	3.2	3.4	3.7	4.1
1971	3.2	2.6	2.4	2.4	2.5	2.4	2.2	2.3	2.4	2.6	2.7	2.7	2.7	2.7	2.8	3.0	3.2	3.4	3.6	4.0
1972	3.2	2.7	2.4	2.4	2.6	2.4	2.3	2.3	2.4	2.6	2.7	2.7	2.7	2.8	2.9	3.0	3.2	3.4	3.6	3.9
1973	3.4	2.9	2.6	2.6	2.8	2.7	2.6	2.6	2.8	2.9	3.1	3.1	3.1	3.2	3.3	3.4	3.7	3.9	4.1	4.4
1974	3.7	3.2	3.0	3.0	3.2	3.1	3.0	3.1	3.2	3.4	3.5	3.6	3.6	3.7	3.9	4.0	4.3	4.6	4.8	5.2
1975	3.8	3.3	3.1	3.1	3.3	3.2	3.1	3.2	3.4	3.5	3.7	3.7	3.8	3.9	4.1	4.2	4.5	4.7	5.0	5.4
1976	3.8	3.4	3.2	3.2	3.4	3.3	3.2	3.3	3.4	3.6	3.8	3.8	3.8	4.0	4.1	4.3	4.5	4.8	5.0	5.3
1977	3.9	3.5	3.3	3.3	3.5	3.4	3.3	3.4	3.6	3.7	3.9	3.9	4.0	4.1	4.2	4.4	4.7	4.9	5.1	5.4
1978	4.1	3.7	3.5	3.5	3.7	3.6	3.5	3.6	3.8	3.9	4.1	4.2	4.2	4.3	4.5	4.7	4.9	5.1	5.4	5.7
1979	4.3	3.9	3.8	3.8	4.0	3.9	3.9	4.0	4.1	4.3	4.5	4.5	4.6	4.8	4.9	5.1	5.4	5.6	5.9	6.2
1980	4.5	4.2	4.0	4.1	4.3	4.2	4.2	4.3	4.4	4.6	4.8	4.9	4.9	5.1	5.3	5.5	5.7	6.0	6.2	6.6
1981	4.7	4.3	4.2	4.2	4.4	4.4	4.3	4.4	4.6	4.8	4.9	5.0	5.1	5.3	5.4	5.6	5.9	6.1	6.4	6.7
1982	4.6	4.3	4.2	4.2	4.4	4.3	4.3	4.4	4.5	4.7	4.9	5.0	5.1	5.2	5.4	5.5	5.8	6.0	6.2	6.5
1983	4.6	4.3	4.2	4.2	4.4	4.3	4.3	4.4	4.5	4.7	4.9	4.9	5.0	5.1	5.3	5.5	5.7	5.9	6.1	6.4
1984	4.6	4.3	4.1	4.2	4.4	4.3	4.3	4.4	4.5	4.7	4.8	4.9	5.0	5.1	5.2	5.4	5.6	5.8	6.0	6.3
1985	4.6	4.3	4.1	4.2	4.3	4.3	4.3	4.4	4.5	4.6	4.8	4.9	4.9	5.0	5.2	5.3	5.5	5.7	5.9	6.1
1986	4.5	4.2	4.1	4.1	4.3	4.2	4.2	4.3	4.4	4.5	4.7	4.7	4.8	4.9	5.0	5.2	5.4	5.5	5.7	5.9
1987	4.5	4.2	4.1	4.1	4.3	4.2	4.2	4.3	4.4	4.5	4.7	4.7	4.8	4.9	5.0	5.1	5.3	5.5	5.6	5.8
1988	4.5	4.2	4.1	4.1	4.3	4.2	4.2	4.3	4.4	4.5	4.7	4.7	4.8	4.9	5.0	5.1	5.3	5.4	5.6	5.8
1989	4.5	4.2	4.1	4.1	4.3	4.2	4.2	4.3	4.4	4.5	4.7	4.7	4.8	4.9	5.0	5.1	5.3	5.4	5.6	5.7
1990	4.5	4.2	4.1	4.2	4.3	4.3	4.2	4.3	4.4	4.6	4.7	4.8	4.8	4.9	5.0	5.1	5.3	5.4	5.6	5.8

Table C-7 (page 4 of 6)

Inflation

Rates of Return for all holding periods
Percent per annum compounded annually

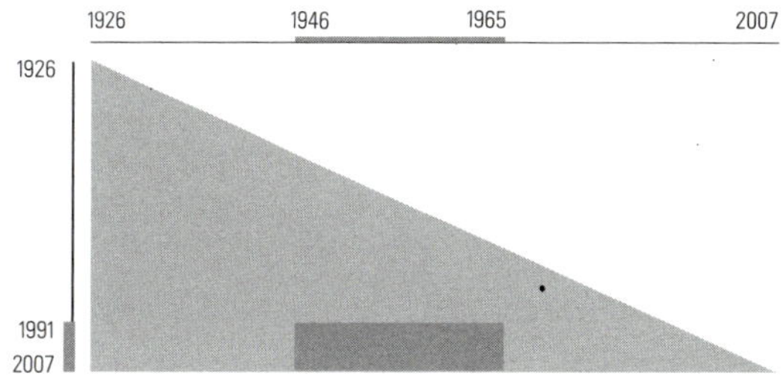

from 1926 to 2007

To the end of	From the beginning of 1946	1947	1948	1949	1950	1951	1952	1953	1954	1955	1956	1957	1958	1959	1960	1961	1962	1963	1964	1965
1991	4.5	4.2	4.1	4.1	4.3	4.3	4.2	4.3	4.4	4.5	4.7	4.7	4.8	4.8	5.0	5.1	5.2	5.4	5.5	5.7
1992	4.5	4.2	4.1	4.1	4.3	4.2	4.2	4.3	4.4	4.5	4.6	4.7	4.7	4.8	4.9	5.0	5.1	5.3	5.4	5.6
1993	4.4	4.2	4.1	4.1	4.2	4.2	4.1	4.2	4.3	4.4	4.6	4.6	4.6	4.7	4.8	4.9	5.1	5.2	5.3	5.5
1994	4.4	4.1	4.0	4.1	4.2	4.2	4.1	4.2	4.3	4.4	4.5	4.5	4.6	4.7	4.8	4.9	5.0	5.1	5.2	5.4
1995	4.4	4.1	4.0	4.0	4.2	4.1	4.1	4.2	4.2	4.4	4.5	4.5	4.5	4.6	4.7	4.8	4.9	5.0	5.1	5.3
1996	4.3	4.1	4.0	4.0	4.1	4.1	4.1	4.1	4.2	4.3	4.4	4.5	4.5	4.6	4.7	4.8	4.9	5.0	5.1	5.2
1997	4.3	4.0	3.9	4.0	4.1	4.0	4.0	4.1	4.2	4.3	4.4	4.4	4.4	4.5	4.6	4.7	4.8	4.9	5.0	5.1
1998	4.2	4.0	3.9	3.9	4.0	4.0	4.0	4.0	4.1	4.2	4.3	4.3	4.4	4.4	4.5	4.6	4.7	4.8	4.9	5.0
1999	4.2	4.0	3.9	3.9	4.0	4.0	3.9	4.0	4.1	4.2	4.3	4.3	4.3	4.4	4.5	4.5	4.6	4.7	4.8	4.9
2000	4.2	3.9	3.9	3.9	4.0	4.0	3.9	4.0	4.1	4.2	4.2	4.3	4.3	4.4	4.4	4.5	4.6	4.7	4.8	4.9
2001	4.1	3.9	3.8	3.8	3.9	3.9	3.9	3.9	4.0	4.1	4.2	4.2	4.2	4.3	4.4	4.4	4.5	4.6	4.7	4.8
2002	4.1	3.9	3.8	3.8	3.9	3.9	3.8	3.9	4.0	4.1	4.1	4.2	4.2	4.3	4.3	4.4	4.5	4.6	4.6	4.7
2003	4.1	3.8	3.8	3.8	3.9	3.8	3.8	3.9	3.9	4.0	4.1	4.1	4.1	4.2	4.3	4.3	4.4	4.5	4.6	4.7
2004	4.1	3.8	3.7	3.8	3.9	3.8	3.8	3.8	3.9	4.0	4.1	4.1	4.1	4.2	4.2	4.3	4.4	4.5	4.5	4.6
2005	4.0	3.8	3.7	3.8	3.9	3.8	3.8	3.8	3.9	4.0	4.1	4.1	4.1	4.2	4.2	4.3	4.4	4.4	4.5	4.6
2006	4.0	3.8	3.7	3.7	3.8	3.8	3.8	3.8	3.9	4.0	4.0	4.1	4.1	4.1	4.2	4.2	4.3	4.4	4.5	4.5
2007	4.0	3.8	3.7	3.7	3.8	3.8	3.8	3.8	3.9	4.0	4.0	4.1	4.1	4.1	4.2	4.2	4.3	4.4	4.5	4.5

Table C-7 (page 5 of 6)

Inflation

Rates of Return for all holding periods
Percent per annum compounded annually

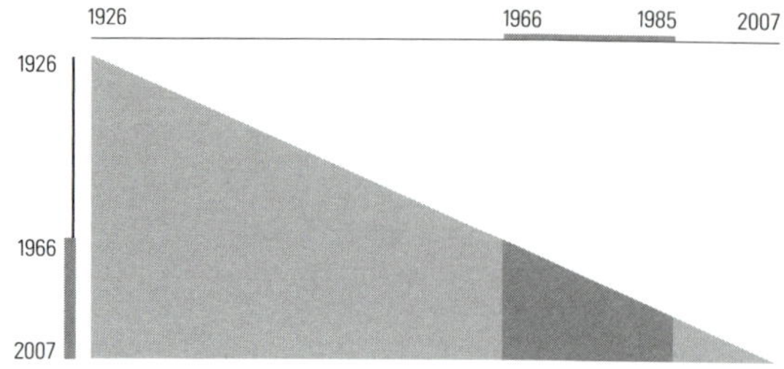

from 1926 to 2007

To the end of	From the beginning of 1966	1967	1968	1969	1970	1971	1972	1973	1974	1975	1976	1977	1978	1979	1980	1981	1982	1983	1984	1985
1966	3.4																			
1967	3.2	3.0																		
1968	3.7	3.9	4.7																	
1969	4.3	4.6	5.4	6.1																
1970	4.5	4.8	5.4	5.8	5.5															
1971	4.3	4.5	4.9	5.0	4.4	3.4														
1972	4.2	4.3	4.6	4.6	4.1	3.4	3.4													
1973	4.8	5.0	5.3	5.4	5.2	5.2	6.1	8.8												
1974	5.6	5.9	6.3	6.5	6.6	6.9	8.1	10.5	12.2											
1975	5.7	6.0	6.4	6.6	6.7	6.9	7.8	9.3	9.6	7.0										
1976	5.6	5.9	6.2	6.4	6.4	6.6	7.2	8.2	8.0	5.9	4.8									
1977	5.7	5.9	6.2	6.4	6.4	6.6	7.1	7.9	7.7	6.2	5.8	6.8								
1978	6.0	6.2	6.5	6.7	6.7	6.9	7.4	8.1	7.9	6.9	6.9	7.9	9.0							
1979	6.5	6.7	7.0	7.3	7.4	7.6	8.1	8.8	8.8	8.1	8.4	9.7	11.1	13.3						
1980	6.9	7.1	7.4	7.7	7.8	8.1	8.6	9.3	9.3	8.8	9.2	10.3	11.6	12.9	12.4					
1981	7.0	7.2	7.6	7.8	7.9	8.1	8.6	9.2	9.3	8.9	9.2	10.1	10.9	11.5	10.7	8.9				
1982	6.8	7.0	7.3	7.5	7.6	7.8	8.2	8.7	8.7	8.2	8.4	9.0	9.5	9.6	8.3	6.4	3.9			
1983	6.6	6.8	7.1	7.2	7.3	7.5	7.8	8.2	8.2	7.7	7.8	8.2	8.5	8.4	7.2	5.5	3.8	3.8		
1984	6.5	6.7	6.9	7.0	7.1	7.2	7.5	7.9	7.8	7.3	7.4	7.7	7.8	7.6	6.5	5.1	3.9	3.9	4.0	
1985	6.4	6.5	6.7	6.8	6.9	7.0	7.2	7.5	7.4	7.0	7.0	7.3	7.3	7.1	6.1	4.8	3.8	3.8	3.9	3.8
1986	6.1	6.2	6.4	6.5	6.5	6.6	6.8	7.1	6.9	6.5	6.5	6.6	6.6	6.3	5.3	4.2	3.3	3.2	2.9	2.4
1987	6.0	6.2	6.3	6.4	6.4	6.5	6.7	6.9	6.8	6.3	6.3	6.4	6.4	6.1	5.2	4.2	3.5	3.4	3.3	3.1
1988	6.0	6.1	6.2	6.3	6.3	6.4	6.5	6.7	6.6	6.2	6.1	6.3	6.2	5.9	5.1	4.3	3.6	3.6	3.5	3.4
1989	5.9	6.0	6.2	6.2	6.2	6.3	6.4	6.6	6.5	6.1	6.0	6.1	6.1	5.8	5.1	4.3	3.7	3.7	3.7	3.7
1990	5.9	6.0	6.1	6.2	6.2	6.3	6.4	6.6	6.5	6.1	6.0	6.1	6.1	5.8	5.2	4.5	4.0	4.0	4.1	4.1
1991	5.8	5.9	6.0	6.1	6.1	6.1	6.2	6.4	6.3	5.9	5.9	5.9	5.9	5.6	5.0	4.4	3.9	3.9	3.9	3.9
1992	5.7	5.8	5.9	5.9	5.9	6.0	6.1	6.2	6.1	5.7	5.7	5.7	5.7	5.4	4.8	4.2	3.8	3.8	3.8	3.8
1993	5.6	5.7	5.8	5.8	5.8	5.8	5.9	6.0	5.9	5.6	5.5	5.6	5.5	5.2	4.7	4.1	3.7	3.7	3.7	3.7
1994	5.5	5.6	5.7	5.7	5.7	5.7	5.8	5.9	5.8	5.4	5.4	5.4	5.3	5.1	4.6	4.0	3.6	3.6	3.6	3.6
1995	5.4	5.5	5.5	5.6	5.5	5.6	5.6	5.7	5.6	5.3	5.2	5.2	5.2	4.9	4.4	3.9	3.6	3.5	3.5	3.5
1996	5.3	5.4	5.5	5.5	5.5	5.5	5.6	5.6	5.5	5.2	5.1	5.1	5.1	4.8	4.4	3.9	3.6	3.5	3.5	3.5
1997	5.2	5.3	5.3	5.4	5.3	5.3	5.4	5.5	5.3	5.1	5.0	5.0	4.9	4.7	4.2	3.8	3.4	3.4	3.4	3.3
1998	5.1	5.1	5.2	5.2	5.2	5.2	5.3	5.3	5.2	4.9	4.8	4.8	4.7	4.5	4.1	3.6	3.3	3.3	3.3	3.2
1999	5.0	5.1	5.1	5.1	5.1	5.1	5.2	5.2	5.1	4.8	4.7	4.7	4.6	4.4	4.0	3.6	3.3	3.3	3.2	3.2
2000	5.0	5.0	5.1	5.1	5.1	5.0	5.1	5.2	5.0	4.8	4.7	4.7	4.6	4.4	4.0	3.6	3.3	3.3	3.2	3.2
2001	4.9	4.9	5.0	5.0	4.9	4.9	5.0	5.0	4.9	4.6	4.6	4.5	4.5	4.3	3.9	3.5	3.2	3.2	3.1	3.1
2002	4.8	4.8	4.9	4.9	4.9	4.8	4.9	4.9	4.8	4.6	4.5	4.5	4.4	4.2	3.8	3.4	3.2	3.1	3.1	3.1
2003	4.7	4.8	4.8	4.8	4.8	4.8	4.8	4.8	4.7	4.5	4.4	4.4	4.3	4.1	3.7	3.4	3.1	3.1	3.0	3.0
2004	4.7	4.7	4.8	4.8	4.7	4.7	4.8	4.8	4.7	4.4	4.3	4.3	4.2	4.1	3.7	3.4	3.1	3.1	3.0	3.0
2005	4.7	4.7	4.7	4.7	4.7	4.7	4.7	4.8	4.6	4.4	4.3	4.3	4.2	4.0	3.7	3.4	3.1	3.1	3.1	3.0
2006	4.6	4.6	4.7	4.7	4.6	4.6	4.7	4.7	4.6	4.3	4.3	4.2	4.1	4.0	3.6	3.3	3.1	3.1	3.0	3.0
2007	4.6	4.6	4.7	4.7	4.6	4.6	4.6	4.7	4.6	4.3	4.2	4.2	4.1	4.0	3.7	3.4	3.1	3.1	3.1	3.0

Table C-7 (page 6 of 6)-a

Inflation

Rates of Return for all holding periods

Percent per annum compounded annually

from 1926 to 2007

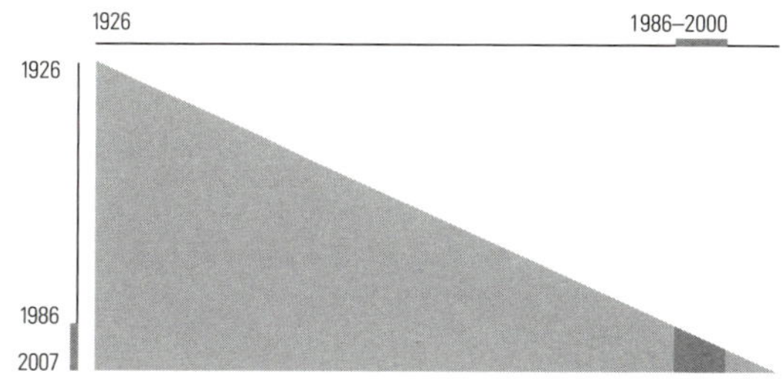

To the end of	From the beginning of 1986	1987	1988	1989	1990	1991	1992	1993	1994	1995	1996	1997	1998	1999	2000
1986	1.1														
1987	2.8	4.4													
1988	3.3	4.4	4.4												
1989	3.6	4.5	4.5	4.6											
1990	4.1	4.9	5.1	5.4	6.1										
1991	4.0	4.5	4.6	4.6	4.6	3.1									
1992	3.8	4.3	4.2	4.2	4.0	3.0	2.9								
1993	3.7	4.0	4.0	3.9	3.7	2.9	2.8	2.7							
1994	3.6	3.9	3.8	3.7	3.5	2.8	2.8	2.7	2.7						
1995	3.5	3.7	3.6	3.5	3.3	2.8	2.7	2.7	2.6	2.5					
1996	3.4	3.7	3.6	3.5	3.3	2.9	2.8	2.8	2.8	2.9	3.3				
1997	3.3	3.5	3.4	3.3	3.1	2.7	2.6	2.6	2.6	2.5	2.5	1.7			
1998	3.2	3.3	3.2	3.1	3.0	2.6	2.5	2.4	2.4	2.3	2.2	1.7	1.6		
1999	3.1	3.3	3.2	3.1	2.9	2.6	2.5	2.5	2.4	2.4	2.3	2.0	2.1	2.7	
2000	3.1	3.3	3.2	3.1	3.0	2.7	2.6	2.6	2.6	2.5	2.5	2.3	2.6	3.0	3.4
2001	3.0	3.2	3.1	3.0	2.9	2.6	2.5	2.5	2.4	2.4	2.4	2.2	2.3	2.5	2.5
2002	3.0	3.1	3.0	2.9	2.8	2.5	2.5	2.5	2.4	2.4	2.4	2.2	2.3	2.5	2.4
2003	2.9	3.1	3.0	2.9	2.7	2.5	2.4	2.4	2.4	2.3	2.3	2.2	2.2	2.4	2.3
2004	3.0	3.1	3.0	2.9	2.8	2.5	2.5	2.5	2.5	2.4	2.4	2.3	2.4	2.5	2.5
2005	3.0	3.1	3.0	2.9	2.8	2.6	2.6	2.5	2.5	2.5	2.5	2.4	2.5	2.6	2.6
2006	3.0	3.1	3.0	2.9	2.8	2.6	2.6	2.5	2.5	2.5	2.5	2.4	2.5	2.6	2.6
2007	3.0	3.1	3.0	3.0	2.9	2.7	2.7	2.6	2.6	2.6	2.6	2.6	2.7	2.8	2.8

Table C-7 (page 6 of 6)-b

Inflation

Rates of Return for all holding periods

Percent per annum compounded annually

from 1926 to 2007

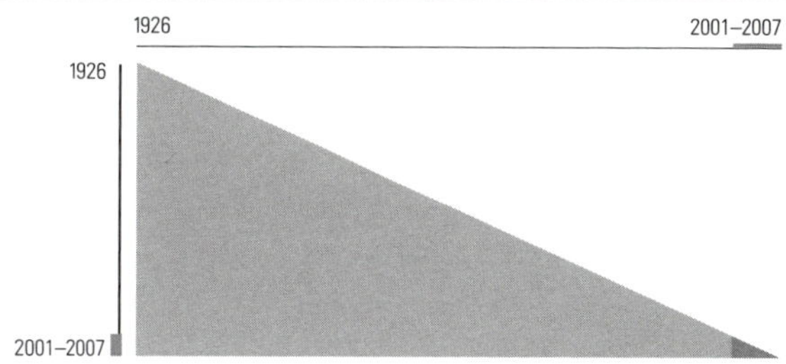

To the end of	From the beginning of 2001	2002	2003	2004	2005	2006	2007
2001	1.6						
2002	2.0	2.4					
2003	1.9	2.1	1.9				
2004	2.3	2.5	2.6	3.3			
2005	2.5	2.7	2.8	3.3	3.4		
2006	2.5	2.7	2.8	3.1	3.0	2.5	
2007	2.7	2.9	3.0	3.3	3.3	3.3	4.1

Glossary

Glossary

American Stock Exchange (AMEX)
One of the largest stock exchanges in the U.S. Securities traded on this exchange are generally of small to medium-size companies.

Arbitrage Pricing Theory (APT)
A model in which multiple betas and multiple risk premia are used to generate the expected return of a security.

Arithmetic Mean Return
A simple average of a series of returns.

Asset Allocation
The process of dividing a portfolio among major asset classes, such as stocks, bonds, or cash. Investing in a combination of investments can reduce risk and enhance returns through diversification.

Asset Class
A grouping of securities with similar characteristics and properties. As a group, these securities will tend to react in a specific way to economic factors (e.g., stocks, bonds, and real estate are all asset classes).

Balanced Mutual Fund
Fund that seeks both income and capital appreciation by investing in a generally fixed combination of stocks and bonds.

Basic Series
The seven primary time series representing Stocks, Bonds, Bills and Inflation: large company stocks, small company stocks, long-term corporate bonds, long-term government bonds, intermediate-term government bonds, U.S. Treasury bills, and inflation.

Beta
The systematic risk of a security as estimated by regressing the security's returns against the market portfolio's returns. The slope of the regression is beta.

Book-to-Market Ratio
The ratio of total book value to total market capitalization. Value companies have a high book-to-market ratio, while growth companies have a low book-to-market ratio.

Callable Bonds
Bonds that the issuer has the right to redeem (or call) prior to maturity at a specified price.

Capital Appreciation Return
The component of total return which results from the price change of an asset class over a given period.

Capital Asset Pricing Model (CAPM)
A model in which the cost of capital for any security or portfolio of securities equals the riskless rate plus a risk premium that is proportionate to the amount of systematic risk of the security or portfolio.

Convexity
The property of a bond that its price does not change in proportion to changes in its yield. A bond with positive convexity will rise in price faster than the rate at which yields decline, and will fall in price slower than the rate at which yields rise.

Correlation Coefficient
The degree of association or strength between two variables. A value of +1 indicates a perfectly positive relationship, –1 indicates a perfectly inverse relationship, and 0 indicates no relationship between the variables.

Cost of Capital
The discount rate which should be used to derive the present value of an asset's future cash flows.

Coupon
The periodic interest payment on a bond.

Currency Risk
The risk of losing money when gains and losses are exchanged from foreign currencies into U.S. dollars. Also known as exchange rate risk.

Decile
One of 10 portfolios formed by ranking a set of securities by some criteria and dividing them into 10 equally populated subsets. The New York Stock Exchange market capitalization deciles are formed by ranking the stocks traded on the Exchange by their market capitalization.

Derived Series
The components or elemental parts of the returns of the seven primary Stocks, Bonds, Bills, and Inflation asset classes. The two categories of derived series are: risk premia, or payoffs for taking various types of risk, and inflation-adjusted asset returns.

Discount Rate
The rate used to convert a series of future cash flows to a single present value.

Dow Jones Industrial Average
The oldest stock price index beginning in 1896 with 12 stocks; currently consisting of 30 representative large stocks.

Duration (Macauley Duration)
The weighted average term-to-maturity of a bond's cash flows. The weights are the present values of each cash flow as a percentage of the present value of all cash flows. Can be used to estimate price sensitivity to interest rate changes.

Economic Modeling
A type of Monte Carlo simulation that involves modeling the movements of the yield curve through time and then layering on various equity and fixed income risk premia to derive returns.

Efficient Frontier
The set of portfolios that provides the highest expected returns for their respective risk levels. The efficient frontier is calculated for a given set of assets with estimates of expected return and standard deviation for each asset, and a correlation coefficient for each pair of asset returns.

Equity REITs
Companies that own and operate income-generating real estate.

Europe Stocks
Morgan Stanley Capital International Europe Index.

FF Large Growth Stocks
A portfolio of stocks constructed by setting a book-to-market ratio cutoff at the bottom 30 percent of NYSE stocks and a market capitalization cutoff at the median of NYSE stocks and selecting all NYSE, AMEX, and NASDAQ stocks with a book-to-market ratio lower than the book-to-market cutoff and a market capitalization greater than the market capitalization cutoff. Data supplied by Eugene Fama and Ken French.

FF Large Value Stocks
A portfolio of stocks constructed by setting a book-to-market ratio cutoff at the top 30 percent of NYSE stocks and a market capitalization cutoff at the median of NYSE stocks and selecting all NYSE, AMEX, and NASDAQ stocks with a book-to-market ratio higher than the book-to-market cutoff and a market capitalization greater than the market capitalization cutoff. Data supplied by Eugene Fama and Ken French.

FF Small Growth Stocks
A portfolio of stocks constructed by setting a book-to-market ratio cutoff at the bottom 30 percent of NYSE stocks and a market capitalization cutoff at the median of NYSE stocks and selecting all NYSE, AMEX, and NASDAQ stocks with a book-to-market ratio lower than

the book-to-market cutoff and a market capitalization smaller than the market capitalization cutoff. Data supplied by Eugene Fama and Ken French.

FF Small Value Stocks
A portfolio of stocks constructed by setting a book-to-market ratio cutoff at the top 30 percent of NYSE stocks and a market capitalization cutoff at the median of NYSE stocks and selecting all NYSE, AMEX, and NASDAQ stocks with a book-to-market ratio higher than the book-to-market cutoff and a market capitalization smaller than the market capitalization cutoff. Data supplied by Eugene Fama and Ken French.

Geometric Mean Return
The compound rate of return. The geometric mean of a return series is a measure of the actual average performance of a portfolio over a given time period.

Histogram
A bar graph in which the frequency of occurrence for each class of data is represented by the relative height of the bars.

IA All Growth Stocks
A portfolio of stocks constructed using the lagged market capitalization-weighted returns of the large-, mid-, and small-cap growth series.

IA All Value Stocks
A portfolio of stocks constructed using the lagged market capitalization-weighted returns of the large-, mid-, and small-cap value series.

IA Large-cap Growth Stocks
A portfolio of stocks constructed by first selecting deciles 1-2 of the NYSE universe. Once these breakpoints are established, similar-sized AMEX and NASDAQ companies are assigned to the corresponding portfolios. The companies are then ranked by book-to-price, creating a growth portfolio (low B/P) where the total market capitalization of the growth and value indices are equal within each portfolio.

IA Large-cap Value Stocks
A portfolio of stocks constructed by first selecting deciles 1-2 of the NYSE universe. Once these breakpoints are established, similar-sized AMEX and NASDAQ companies are assigned to the corresponding portfolios. The companies are then ranked by book-to-price, creating a value portfolio (high B/P) where the total market capitalization of the growth and value indices are equal within each portfolio.

IA Mid-cap Growth Stocks
A portfolio of stocks constructed by first selecting deciles 3-5 of the NYSE universe. Once these breakpoints are established, similar-sized AMEX and NASDAQ companies are assigned to the corresponding portfolios. The companies are then ranked by book-to-price, creating a growth portfolio (low B/P) where the total market capitalization of the growth and value indices are equal within each portfolio.

IA Mid-cap Value Stocks
A portfolio of stocks constructed by first selecting deciles 3-5 of the NYSE universe. Once these breakpoints are established, similar-sized AMEX and NASDAQ companies are assigned to the corresponding portfolios. The companies are then ranked by book-to-price, creating a value portfolio (high B/P) where the total market capitalization of the growth and value indices are equal within each portfolio.

IA Small-cap Growth Stocks
A portfolio of stocks constructed by first selecting deciles 6-8 of the NYSE universe. Once these breakpoints are established, similar-sized AMEX and NASDAQ companies are assigned to the corresponding portfolios. The companies are then ranked by book-to-price, creating a growth portfolio (low B/P) where the total market capitalization of the growth and value indices are equal within each portfolio.

IA Small-cap Value Stocks
A portfolio of stocks constructed by first selecting deciles 6-8 of the NYSE universe. Once these breakpoints are

established, similar-sized AMEX and NASDAQ companies are assigned to the corresponding portfolios. The companies are then ranked by book-to-price, creating a value portfolio (high B/P) where the total market capitalization of the growth and value indices are equal within each portfolio

Income Return
The component of total return which results from a periodic cash flow, such as dividends.

Index Value
The cumulative value of returns on a dollar amount invested. It is used when measuring investment performance and computing returns over non-calendar periods.

Inflation
The rate of change in consumer prices. The Consumer Price Index for All Urban Consumers (CPI-U), not seasonally adjusted, is used to measure inflation. Prior to January 1978, the CPI (as compared with CPI-U) was used. Both inflation measures are constructed by the U.S. Department of Labor, Bureau of Labor Statistics, Washington.

Inflation-Adjusted Returns
Asset class returns in real terms. The inflation-adjusted return of an asset is calculated by geometrically subtracting inflation from the asset's nominal return.

Intermediate-Term Government Bonds
A one-bond portfolio with a maturity near 5 years.

International Stocks
Morgan Stanley Capital International EAFE® (Europe, Australasia, Far East) Index. Represents 21 developed equity markets outside of North America.

Large Company Stocks
The Standard and Poor's 500 Stock Composite Index® (S&P 500).

Liquidity Risk
The risk that an asset will be difficult to buy or sell quickly and in large volume without substantially affecting the asset's price.

Logarithmic Scale
A scale in which equal percentage changes are represented by equal distances.

Lognormal Distribution
The distribution of a random variable whose natural logarithm is normally distributed. A lognormal distribution is skewed so that a higher proportion of possible returns exceed the expected value versus falling short of the expected value. In the lognormal forecasting model, one plus the total return has a lognormal distribution.

Long-Term Corporate Bonds
Citigroup long-term, high-grade corporate bond total return index.

Long-Term Government Bonds
A one-bond portfolio with a maturity near 20 years.

Low-cap Stocks
The portfolio of stocks comprised of the 6-8th deciles of the New York Stock Exchange, including similar-sized AMEX and NASDAQ companies.

Market Capitalization
The current market price of a security determined by the most recently recorded trade multiplied by the number of issues outstanding of that security. For equities, market capitalization is computed by taking the share price of a stock times the number of shares outstanding.

Mean-Variance Optimization (MVO)
The process of identifying portfolios that have the highest possible return for a given level of risk or the lowest possible risk for a given return. The inputs for MVO are return, standard deviation, and the correlation coefficients of returns for each pair of asset classes.

Micro-cap Stocks
The portfolio of stocks comprised of the 9-10th deciles of the New York Stock Exchange, including similar-sized AMEX and NASDAQ companies.

Mid-cap Stocks
The portfolio of stocks comprised of the 3-5th deciles of the New York Stock Exchange, including similar-sized AMEX and NASDAQ companies.

Monte Carlo Simulation
A technique that starts with a set of assumptions about the estimated mean, standard deviation, and correlations for a set of asset classes or investments. These assumptions are used to randomly generate hundreds of possible future return scenarios. These returns can then be used in conjunction with a client's year-by-year cash flows, taxes, asset allocation, and financial product selections. A large number of possible "financial lives" for the client can be produced.

NAREIT
National Association of Real Estate Investment Trusts®. Membership includes U.S. REITs and publicly traded real estate companies worldwide

National Association of Securities Dealers Automated Quotation System (NASDAQ)
A computerized system showing current bid and asked prices for stocks traded on the Over-the-Counter market, as well as some New York Stock Exchange listed stocks.

New York Stock Exchange (NYSE)
The largest and oldest stock exchange in the United States, founded in 1792.

Non-Parametric
A type of Monte Carlo simulation that uses purely historical data.

Over-the-Counter Market (OTC)
A market in which assets are not traded on an organized exchange like the New York Stock Exchange, but rather through various dealers or market makers who are linked electronically.

Pacific Stocks
Morgan Stanley Capital International Pacific Index.

Parametric
A type of Monte Carlo simulation that is based on the mean, standard deviation, and correlations for the assets being forecast. These are the parameters that give this method its name. Once these parameters are set, a computer program is used to generate random samples from the bell curve that these parameters define.

Portfolio
A group of assets, such as stocks and bonds, that are held by an investor.

Price-Weighted Index
An index in which component stocks are weighted by their price. Thus, higher-priced stocks have a greater percentage impact on the index than lower-priced stocks.

Quintile
One of 5 portfolios formed by ranking a set of securities by some criteria and dividing them into 5 equally populated subsets. The micro-cap stocks are a market capitalization quintile.

R-squared
Measures the "goodness of fit" of the regression line and describes the percentage of variation in the dependent variable that is explained by the independent variable. The R-squared measure may vary from zero to one.

Real Estate Investment Trusts (REITs)
Companies that own and operate, as well as finance, income-generating real estate. To qualify as a REIT, a company is obligated to pay out at least 90 percent of its taxable profit to shareholders on an annual basis.

Return
see Total Return

Risk
The extent to which an investment is subject to uncertainty. Risk may be measured by standard deviation.

Riskless Rate of Return
The return on a riskless investment; it is the rate of return an investor can obtain without taking market risk.

Risk Premium
The reward which investors require to accept the uncertain outcomes associated with securities. The size of the risk premium will depend upon the type and extent of the risk.

Rolling Period Returns
A series of overlapping contiguous periods of returns defined by the frequency of the data under examination. In examining 5-year rolling periods of returns for annual data that starts in 1970, the first rolling period would be 1970–1974, the second rolling period would be 1971–1975, the third rolling period would be 1972–1976, etc.

Rolling Period Standard Deviation
A series of overlapping contiguous periods of standard deviations defined by the frequency of the data under examination. In examining 5-year rolling periods of standard deviation for annual data that starts in 1970, the first rolling period would be 1970–1974, the second rolling period would be 1971–1975, the third rolling period would be 1972–1976, etc.

Serial Correlation (Autocorrelation)
The degree to which the return of a given series is related from period to period. A serial correlation near +1 or -1 indicates that returns are predictable from one period to the next; a serial correlation near zero indicates returns are random or unpredictable.

Small Company Stocks
A portfolio of stocks represented by the fifth capitalization quintile of stocks on the NYSE for 1926–1981. For January 1982 to March 2001, the series is represented by the DFA U.S. 9–10 Small Company Portfolio and the DFA U.S. Micro Cap Portfolio thereafter.

S&P 500®
Stock index including 500 of the largest stocks (in terms of stock market value) in the United States representing 88 separate industries. Prior to 1957, it consisted of 90 of the largest stocks.

Standard Deviation
A measure of the dispersion of returns of an asset, or the extent to which returns vary from the arithmetic mean. It represents the volatility or risk of an asset. The greater the degree of dispersion, the greater the risk associated with the asset.

Systematic Risk
The risk that is unavoidable according to CAPM. It is the risk that is common to all risky securities and cannot be eliminated through diversification. The amount of an asset's systematic risk is measured by its beta.

Total Return
A measure of performance of an asset class over a designated time period. It is comprised of income return, reinvestment of income return and capital appreciation return components.

Treasury Bills
A one-bill portfolio containing, at the beginning of each month, the bill having the shortest maturity not less than one month.

Unsystematic Risk
The portion of total risk specific to an individual security that can be avoided through diversification.

Volatility
The extent to which an asset's returns fluctuate from period to period.

World Stocks
Morgan Stanley Capital International World Index.

Yield
The yield to maturity is the internal rate of return that equates the bond's price with the stream of cash flows promised to the bondholder. The yield on a stock is the percentage rate of return paid in dividends.

Index

Index

J

K

L

Investment Tools and Resources

2008 Ibbotson® Stocks, Bonds, Bills, and Inflation® (SBBI®) Classic Yearbook
The 2008 Ibbotson SBBI Classic Yearbook provides a comprehensive, historical view of the performance of capital markets in the United States dating back to 1926.

2008 Ibbotson® SBBI® Classic Yearbook $150

Cost of Capital Resources
global.morningstar.com/US/CofCResources
(Historical archives available online for all reports except individual company tax rates)

- **Ibbotson® Industry Cost of Capital data** is available for more than 300 industries with the same extensive analysis utilized in the Cost of Capital Yearbook, including: industry betas, multiples, cost of equity estimates, weighted average cost of capital, and much more. $100 per industry
- **Ibbotson® Individual Company Betas** are available for approximately 5,000 U.S. companies featuring the same rigorous analysis found in the Ibbotson Beta Book. $50 per company
- **Ibbotson® International Cost of Capital Report** contains up to six cost of equity estimates for 170+ countries from the perspective of U.S. investors. $250
- **Ibbotson® International Cost of Capital Perspectives Report** contains cost of equity estimates for 170+ countries from the perspective of international investors. $150
- **Ibbotson® International Equity Risk Premia Report** contains historical equity risk premia for 16 countries. $150
- **Ibbotson® Risk Premia Over Time Report** provides equity and size premia over your choice of historical time periods from 1926–2007. $130
- **Duff & Phelps, LLC Risk Premium Report** $250
- **Individual Tax Rates** are available for approximately 5,000 U.S. companies. $50 per company

New for 2008
We built a special version of the Cost of Capital Resources Center for power users of Ibbotson cost of capital and valuation data. This exciting new site features over 150,000 Ibbotson industry, valuation, company beta, and international cost of capital reports.

Users can subscribe to this new website and get unlimited access to all reports for any combination of four Ibbotson cost of capital and valuation data modules:

- **Industry Analysis**
- **SBBI Valuation Essentials**
- **Company Betas**
- **International Cost of Capital**

Visit the new site at ccrc.morningstar.com or call (888) 298-3647 for details and pricing.

2008 Ibbotson® Cost of Capital Yearbook
Providing data on more than 300 industries, the Ibbotson Cost of Capital Yearbook is a comprehensive source of market comparables. The yearbook includes:

- Five separate measures of cost of equity.
- Weighted average cost of capital.
- Detailed statistics for sales, profitability, capitalization, beta, multiples, ratios, equity returns and capital structure.

Published annually, the Ibbotson Cost of Capital Yearbook is updated with data through March 2008 (ships in June). For the most frequent data available, subscribe to quarterly Cost of Capital Updates to complement your 2008 Ibbotson Cost of Capital Yearbook. Updates ship in early August, November, and February with data through June, September, and December 2008.

2008 Ibbotson® Cost of Capital Yearbook $425
2008 Ibbotson® Cost of Capital Yearbook Quarterly Updates $650

2008 Ibbotson® Beta Book
With data on approximately 5,000 companies, The Ibbotson Beta Book provides statistics critical for calculating cost of equity with the CAPM and the Fama-French 3-factor model. Employing the most current methods, the Beta Book contains traditional 60-month levered beta calculations, unlevered betas, and betas adjusted toward peer group averages.

Published semi-annually, the First Edition provides data through December 2007 and the Second Edition provides data through June 2008.

2008 Ibbotson® Beta Book First Edition $695 (Ships in early February)
2008 Ibbotson® Beta Book Second Edition $695 (Ships in early August)
Both Editions (purchased together) $1,150

2008 Ibbotson® Stocks, Bonds, Bills, and Inflation® (SBBI®) Valuation Yearbook
The industry standard in business valuation reference materials, the Ibbotson SBBI Valuation Yearbook will help you make the most informed decisions when estimating the cost of capital. It features a comparison of the buildup method, the Capital Asset Pricing Model, the Fama-French three-factor model, and the discounted cash flow approach.

- Key Variables in Estimating the Cost of Capital table
- Nearly 500 industry risk premia
- Annual returns for decile portfolios dating back to 1926
- Discussion on estimating the cost of capital for international markets

2008 Ibbotson® SBBI® Valuation Yearbook $150

For more information or to request a product catalog, call (888) 298-3647 or visit our Web site at:
global.morningstar.com/SBBIYearbooks

NOTE: Archived editions (2007 and prior) of Ibbotson publications are available in limited quantities. Please call Product Sales at the number listed above to check availability and pricing.

Ibbotson Associates®

Ibbotson Associates is a leading authority on asset allocation with expertise in capital market expectations and portfolio implementation. Its experienced consultants and portfolio managers serve mutual fund firms, banks, broker-dealers, and insurance companies worldwide. Ibbotson Associates' methodologies and services address all investment phases, from accumulation to retirement and the transition between the two.

Visit Ibbotson.com for contact information, published research, product fact sheets and other information.

Morningstar® Indexes

Morningstar Indexes include a broad range of equity, fixed income and commodity indexes that can be used for asset allocation, benchmarking, or to serve as the basis for investment product creation and market monitoring purposes.

Visit http://indexes.morningstar.com for more information.

Morningstar® Principia®

Principia is one of the most widely used resources in the financial planning industry. With a powerful research database that includes mutual funds, stocks, variable annuities, closed-end funds, and separate accounts, advisors can conduct advanced research and analysis, monitor portfolios, and propose investment strategies.

Specialized Principia Modules include the Defined Contribution Plans module and the Asset Allocation module. The Defined Contribution module was designed to help advisors and plan sponsors build, monitor and manage 401(k), 403(b) and other types of retirement plan lineups. With the Asset Allocation module, advisors can build better portfolios for their clients by determining the asset mix most likely to achieve the highest return for a given risk level. Advanced features like efficient frontier graphing and Monte Carlo wealth forecasting help create individualized asset allocation strategies based on a client's risk tolerance, current assets, future needs, and other factors.

Morningstar Principia® Presentations and Education 2008

This library encompasses a collection of communication resources developed to assist advisors during client interactions. Specialized Microsoft® PowerPoint® presentations formerly known as Ibbotson's Asset Allocation Library introduce time-tested investment principles. Investor brochures available as PDF files address common retirement risks, while Web-based professional training explores the practical application of asset allocation methodologies. Advisors can also search and download white papers on a broad range of research. This library may be purchased separately or as part of the Principia® Suite.

For more information on Principia Presentations and Education 2008 call: 800-735-0700 or visit us online at: http://global.morningstar.com/US/PresentationMaterials

Morningstar Workstation Office Edition®

Office Edition is Morningstar's complete office system for independent advisors. This single, all-inclusive platform is designed so that advisors can use it to run their entire practice. Office Edition features the most current Morningstar research data, sophisticated planning tools, complete portfolio accounting, client management tools, e-mail and calendar functions, batch reporting, archiving, and more.

For more information on Workstation Office Edition call 1-800-886-1749 or visit us online at http://global.morningstar.com/Office

Communication and Education Resources

Designed to help advisors clearly communicate fundamental investment concepts, these materials support one-on-one client meetings, seminars, speeches, or training sessions. Use these time-saving tools to demonstrate asset allocation strategies, generate business leads, and validate portfolio recommendations. All materials are FINRA-reviewed.

In addition to the PowerPoint Presentations available through Principia Presentations and Education, we offer two convenient print packages.

Ibbotson® SBBI® Print Kit

This collection of print materials based on the popular Stocks, Bonds, Bills, and Inflation graph demonstrates both the value of asset allocation and the benefits of long-term investing.

Ibbotson® SBBI® Print Kit: $100 (includes one poster, two market charts, and three chart pads)

Market Charts

During client meetings and conversations, refer to this complete set of 15 charts to introduce time-tested investment concepts and explore different strategies.

Market Charts Kit: $235 (includes 15, 8.5" x 11" laminated prints in a portable three-ring binder)

For more information about SBBI print materials and Market Charts, please call: 866-608-9571, or visit us online at: http://global.morningstar.com/CommunicationMaterials

Morningstar® EnCorr®

Institutions worldwide use Morningstar® EnCorr® to research, create, analyze, and implement optimal asset allocation strategies within a single software. This advanced analytical software unites proven financial models, sophisticated Ibbotson methodologies, and comprehensive Morningstar investment data.

An innovative solution for conducting advanced statistical and graphical analyses, Morningstar EnCorr helps build portfolios designed to generate robust returns at varying risk levels. The software provides invaluable support to institutional investment professionals conducting in-depth portfolio research, including analysts, investment consultants, Registered Investment Advisors, and portfolio managers.

Morningstar® Direct®

Morningstar Direct is a global, multi-currency institutional research platform that provides in-depth performance and holdings analysis of investments. This web-based solution unites continuous data updates with powerful analytics to help institutions worldwide with product development, competitive analysis, marketing, investment selection, and performance evaluation.

For more information about Morningstar EnCorr or Morningstar Direct within the United States call +1 866 910 0840. Outside the United States, please contact your local office: Asia (excluding mainland China): +852 2973 4633 Australia: +61 2 9276 4445 or +61 414 819 354; Canada: +1 416 484-7818; China: +86 755 8826 3088; Europe: +44 020 3107 0020.